THE OXFORD HANDBOOK OF

LATIN AMERICAN
POLITICAL ECONOMY

THE OXFORD HANDBOOK OF

LATIN AMERICAN POLITICAL ECONOMY

Edited by

JAVIER SANTISO
AND
JEFF DAYTON-JOHNSON

OXFORD
UNIVERSITY PRESS

Oxford University Press, Inc., publishes works that further
Oxford University's objective of excellence
in research, scholarship, and education.

Oxford   New York
Auckland   Cape Town   Dar es Salaam   Hong Kong   Karachi
Kuala Lumpur   Madrid   Melbourne   Mexico City   Nairobi
New Delhi   Shanghai   Taipei   Toronto

With offices in
Argentina   Austria   Brazil   Chile   Czech Republic   France   Greece
Guatemala   Hungary   Italy   Japan   Poland   Portugal   Singapore
South Korea   Switzerland   Thailand   Turkey   Ukraine   Vietnam

Library of Congress Cataloging-in-Publication Data
The Oxford handbook of Latin American political economy /edited by Javier Santiso and Jeff Dayton-Johnson.
p.   cm.
Includes bibliographical references and index.
ISBN 978-0-19-974750-4 (cloth: alk. paper)
1. Latin America—Economic policy. 2. Latin America—Economic conditions—1982– 3. Latin America—Politics
and government—1980– I. Santiso, Javier. II. Dayton-Johnson, Jeff.
HC125.O94   2012
330.98—dc23
2011024977

CONTENTS

PART IV: POLITICAL ECONOMY OF FISCAL AND SOCIAL POLICIES

Contributors

Javier Santiso is professor of economics at the ESADE Business School and director of the ESADE Centre for Global Economy and Geopolitics.

Jeff Dayton-Johnson is associate professor of international trade and development at the Monterey Institute of International Studies.

Christopher Balding is assistant professor at the HSBC Business School of Peking University Graduate School. He has a PhD from the University of California, Irvine, in political economics.

Juan S. Blyde is currently a senior integration and trade economist at the Trade and Integration Sector of the Inter-American Development Bank.

Daniela Campello is assistant professor of politics and international affairs at Princeton University. She holds a PhD from the University of California, Los Angeles.

Fernando Henrique Cardoso is the former president of Brazil (1995–2002) and is currently president of the Instituto Fernando Henrique Cardoso (São Paulo, Brazil) and honorary president of the Brazilian Social Democracy Party.

Luis Carranza, former minister of finance in Peru, is professor of economics at the University of San Martin de Porres and director of the university's Competitiveness and Development Center.

Luciano Coutinho, PhD in Economics from Cornell University, is president of the Brazilian National Bank for Economic and Social Development (BNDES).

Christian Daude is an economist at the OECD Development Centre. He holds a PhD in economics from the University of Maryland, College Park.

Pablo Egaña is an instructor professor in the Department of Economics and researcher at the Microdata Center of the University of Chile.

Carlos Elizondo is professor of political science at the Centro de Investigación y Docencia Económicas in Mexico City. He is member of several governing boards, including Conacyt and El Colegio de México.

Marcela Eslava is associate professor of economics at Universidad de Los Andes, in Bogotá. She holds a PhD from the University of Maryland, College Park.

Antoni Estevadeordal has been manager of the Integration and Trade Sector (Vice-Presidency of Sectors and Knowledge) at the Inter-American Development Bank since July 2007.

João Carlos Ferraz is economist executive director of the Brazilian National Bank for Economic and Social Development (BNDES) and professor (on leave) of the Instituto de Economia, Universidade Federal do Rio de Janeiro, Brazil.

Kevin P. Gallagher is associate professor of international relations and on the graduate faculty of political science. He holds a BA degree from Northeastern University and an MA degree and PhD from Tufts University.

Eduardo Graeff is the head of the State of São Paulo liaison office in Brasília. He was chief congressional liaison officer and general secretary to the president of Brazil in Fernando Henrique Cardoso's administration (1995–2002).

Stephen Haber is A.A. and Jeanne Welch Milligan Professor in the School of Humanities and Sciences and Peter and Helen Bing Senior Fellow of the Hoover Institution at Stanford University.

Cecilia Martínez-Gallardo is an assistant professor of political science at the University of North Carolina at Chapel Hill. She holds a PhD from Columbia University.

Ángel Melguizo is a social insurance lead specialist in the Labor Markets and Social Security Unit of the Inter-American Development Bank.

Victor Menaldo is an assistant professor in the Political Science Department at the University of Washington.

Mauricio Mesquita Moreira is principal economist and research coordinator of the Integration and Trade Sector of the Inter-American Development Bank. He received a PhD in economics from University College London.

Alejandro Micco is an associate professor in the Department of Economics and Researcher at the Microdata Center of the University of Chile. He holds a PhD in economics from Harvard University.

André Nassif is professor of economics at the Federal Fluminense University (Universidade Federal Fluminense) and senior economist at the Brazilian National Bank for Economic and Social Development.

Rafael Oliva is an economist and was adviser to the president of the Brazilian National Bank for Economic and Social Development (BNDES) between 2007 and 2010. He holds a PhD in public administration from the Getúlio Vargas Foundation.

Sebastián Nieto Parra is an economist at the OECD Development Centre. He holds a PhD in economics from the Institut d'Études Politiques (Sciences-Po) in Paris.

Eric Parrado is professor at the Business School of Adolfo Ibáñez University and an international consultant. He is former international finance coordinator in the Ministry of Finance of Chile.

MARTÍN REDRADO is professor of international economics at the Catholic University of Buenos Aires, Argentina. He is also a partner at MR Financial Services.

CARLOS SCARTASCINI is lead economist in the Research Department of the Inter-American Development Bank. He holds a BA in economics from Universidad Nacional del Sur in Argentina and an MA degree and a PhD and in economics from George Mason University.

BEN ROSS SCHNEIDER is a professor of political science at MIT and co-director of MIT-Brazil.

PAOLO SPADONI is assistant professor in the Department of Political Science at Augusta State University in Augusta, Georgia. He holds a PhD in political science from the University of Florida.

BARBARA STALLINGS is William R. Rhodes Research Professor at the Watson Institute for International Studies, Brown University. She is also the editor of *Studies in Comparative International Development*.

ROSEMARY THORP is emeritus reader in the economics of Latin America at Oxford University and research associate at the Latin American Centre and Queen Elizabeth House.

MARIANO TOMMASI is professor of economics at Universidad de San Andrés in Argentina. He holds a PhD in economics from the University of Chicago.

ANDRÉS VELASCO was the minister of finance of Chile between March 2006 and March 2010. During his tenure he was recognized as Latin American finance minister of the year by several international publications.

LAURENCE WHITEHEAD is an official fellow in politics at Nuffield College, Oxford University, and senior fellow of the College.

THE OXFORD HANDBOOK OF

LATIN AMERICAN
POLITICAL ECONOMY

INTRODUCTION

JAVIER SANTISO AND JEFF DAYTON-JOHNSON

OBSERVERS of Latin America's economic realities have long insisted upon the close relationship between economic and political affairs in the life of the region. Economic developments have political consequences, and political phenomena and institutions in turn have economic and financial effects. In a widely cited application to Latin America, Frieden defines the methodology succinctly as follows: "Modern political economy, simply put, studies how rational self-interested actors combine within or outside existing institutional settings to affect social outcomes" (Frieden 1991, 16). Political economy has held a privileged position among social-science methodologies in studies of Latin American economies.

The exemplar of this blended economic and political analysis is Albert O. Hirschman. At the heart of Hirschman's recourse to political-economy methods is what he called "trespassing" (Hirschman 1981)—stepping over the established boundaries of academic disciplines. To understand the movement of key economic variables—income per head, wages, unemployment, the share of manufacturing in national income, poverty—economists could not restrict their attention to purely economic variables. Political phenomena—the presence or absence of democracy, the institutions of governance, the formal and informal means of resolving disputes among powerful groups—would enrich the analysis of economic outcomes. This insight was repeatedly illustrated in Hirschman's work, beginning with his assessment of the Colombian economy in the 1950s and extending through his decades of work on development policymaking (Hirschman 1958, 1968, 1985, 1987). It is our hope to inscribe this book in Hirschman's venerable tradition (on Hirschman's influence on Latin American thinkers and policy makers, see Santiso 2000).

Political economy imbues several strands of scholarship on Latin America. Modern accounts of Latin America's economic history, for example, have stressed its political dimensions (e.g., Acemoglu, Johnson, and Robinson 2001; Acemoglu and Robinson 2006; Bulmer-Thomas 2003; Thorp 1998). Meanwhile, classic political-science accounts of major political trends of the Latin American twentieth century—military dictatorships (e.g., Needler 1966) or authoritarianism (e.g., O'Donnell 1973)—likewise drew upon political-economy logic. Analyses of the economic strategies employed in the golden age of development policymaking—import-substituting industrialization, structuralism, the influential recommendations of the United Nations Economic Commission for Latin America and the Caribbean—have emphasized political-economy considerations such as the relative power of interest groups in society (Halperin Donghi 2008; Kingstone 2010; Leiva 2008).

Political-economy approaches proved particularly popular in efforts to understand the economic debacle of the 1980s: a generalized default on sovereign debts in the region, with a host of economic consequences, the stagnation of gross domestic product (GDP) per capita for well over a decade among them (Freiden 1991; Frieden, Pastor, and Tomz 2000).

The principal concern was debt, and the principal object of analysis was reform, understood in this context to mean stabilization and structural adjustment measures, later codified into the Washington Consensus (Williamson 1990; Rodrik 1996). Work on the political economy of the debt crisis broadened the scope of analysis to international factors, notably the role of international financial markets in the crisis.

Debt was one dimension of the landscape surveyed by this wave of authors; a second was democratic consolidation. Democracy has, if anything, surpassed debt as an issue for analysis, particularly with respect to the interaction of democratic politics, still imperfect in the region, and macroeconomic management—for example, the effect of elections on the timing of devaluations (Stein and Streb 2004), the relations between elections and financial markets in emerging democracies (Santiso 2012), or the effect of elections on fiscal expansion (OECD 2008, ch. 3).

The analysis of debt, democracy, and other issues of the 1980s and 1990s was accompanied by a strengthening of quantitative, frequently econometric work—not limited to Latin America—analyzing the economic effects of political variables. Much of this work was made possible by the wider availability of cross-country macroeconomic data sets such as the Penn World Tables. Thus, Alesina and Rodrik (1994), Persson and Tabellini (1994), and follow-up studies empirically explored the mechanisms linking economic inequality and growth; Easterly and Levine (1997), meanwhile, sought to isolate the effect of ethnic fragmentation on growth. The works cited here are merely the tip of an iceberg of a kind of new econometrics of political economy. In their combination of econometric work and their use of ingenious indices of social and political variables, these studies have had direct and indirect effects on research in Latin America, as in the major studies undertaken by the Inter-American Development Bank on democracy, reform, and state capacity (Stein et al. 2006; Lora 2007; Payne, Zovotto, and Mateo Díaz 2007).

Starr (2009) suggests that the work fueled by debt and democracy in Latin American political economy of the 1980s and 1990s was followed by a string of sectoral studies, and a growing consciousness of the importance of context and institutions—as opposed to blanket recommendations in the manner of the Washington Consensus. Debt and macroeconomic stabilization continue to be a focus for political-economy analysis (Centeno, James, and Londregan 2005). A new wave of political-economy studies, thus, has analyzed a new wave of economic reforms in Latin America: for example, of social-security systems (Weyland 2007), of labor markets (Cook 2007), and of innovative policies for poverty alleviation (Levy 2007).

These various strands of research and analysis have amply demonstrated the value of Hirschman's "trespassing" approach. But the essays gathered in this handbook bear witness to a new kind of trespassing: namely, flouting the border that separates policymaking and policy research. Many of the most noteworthy policy reforms undertaken in the region have been designed and led by leading economic researchers. Many of them are represented among the contributors to this book: Fernando Henrique Cardoso (former president of Brazil), Andrés Velasco (former Chilean minister of finance), Luis Carranza (former Peruvian minister of finance), Luciano Coutinho (president of Brazil's National Development Bank), and Martín Redrado (former governor of Argentina's Central Bank).

Perhaps in part as a result of this new kind of trespassing, policy choices in Latin America have changed in recent years. This is the thesis of economic possibilism identified by Santiso (2005, 2006), particularly inspired by the example of Chile, Mexico, and Brazil. Santiso argues that recent economic policymaking leaves behind a turbulent past of good revolutionaries and apostles of extreme liberalism in a region shaken by economic, structuralist, Maoist, neoliberal paradigms, models clashing—sometimes violently—with the economic and social realities of Latin America. At the end of a process that was at times painful (as in the case of Chile), some Latin American countries managed to escape from a political economy deformed by ideological prisms and to free themselves from the maximalist models supposed to resolve all the problems of underdevelopment. One by one, countries as diverse as Chile, Brazil, and Mexico moved toward pragmatic economic policies giving rise to the emergence of a possibilism in terms of economic policy.

In Brazil, for example, the economic success of the Lula years was laid by the reforms of his predecessor, Fernando Henrique Cardoso, a sociologist who adopted Hirschman's possibilism and became minister of finance and later president. In the end, one of the greatest successes of Lula has been to pursue the incremental changes pursued by Cardoso and abandon the far-left policies that he had once advocated. He helped Brazil's transition toward embracing capitalism, the irony being that this impressive transformation had been led by a leader who once denounced "neoliberalism." Lula surprised financial markets and investors, in 2002 and later, by decisively tackling inflation, reducing debt levels, and paying back bondholders while at the same time metamorphosing the country from an International Monetary Fund debtor into a creditor and pushing for social programs.

Beyond Brazil, Chile, or Mexico, other countries moved toward more pragmatic policymaking and helped recently to expand the list of possibilist countries (in particular, to include Peru, Uruguay, and Colombia). The fruits of this new pragmatic turn in policymaking can be witnessed in the region's resilient response to the global financial crisis of 2007–8 (OECD 2009, "Macroeconomic Overview" sec.). In 2010, the Latin American GDP grew by about 6 percent (IMF 2011; ECLAC 2010a), substantially higher than the Organisation for Economic Co-operation and Development (OECD) area's rate of 2.8 percent (OECD 2010a), and the debt of countries like Brazil or Peru has been awarded investment grade by ratings agencies, joining Chile in this status. In addition to macroeconomic robustness, social indicators in Latin American countries have been remarkably resilient. According to ECLAC (2010b), poverty in Latin America fell to 32 percent of the population in 2010, after rising slightly in 2009 as a result of the crisis. It is important to recall that as recently as 2002, the incidence of poverty was 44 percent. This trend is expected to continue in coming years. Luck had a lot to do with these achievements, particularly in the form of soaring prices for the commodities exported by many Latin American countries to China and other countries in Asia. But the role of public policies should not be underestimated, and the policymaking environment will be fertile ground for a new round of political-economy studies—as the contributions to this handbook illustrate.

For all these reasons, the timing is propitious for bringing together the work of the best of the new generation of Latin American political economy studies. These studies are based on the new analytical tools and insights developed in the wake of the debt crisis of the 1980s and the crisis of the 1990s; draw on varied aspects of the older strata of political-economy literature from the region; and address the new economic context of a region experiencing reasonable growth and rapid recovery from the global economic crisis that began in 2008, historic rates of poverty reduction, the addition of new Asian trading partners, and a "reprimarization" of export patterns (i.e., a growing export share of commodities, as had been the case in decades and indeed centuries past). That is the principal rationale behind this collection of essays.

The book begins by paying tribute to the new breed of trespassers mentioned earlier, those policymakers whose academic credentials would have qualified them to contribute chapters anyway , but who bring to this exercise the additional wealth of experience earned in the political arena. For this reason, we asked several current and past high-level policymakers from Latin America to provide accounts of political economy in practice in the first part of the book.[1]

The second part situates Latin American development in broader contexts: historical, geographic, and institutional. These chapters address the structural role played by wealth and income inequality in the region over centuries, as well as the important and changing consequences of global integration, including but not limited to trade liberalization. Cuba's recent economic development, so divergent from most of the region, is also detailed here. And two essays look at the growing importance of Asian economies in Latin America's development patterns today.

The chapters in the third part collect a host of political-economy phenomena of importance to Latin America, including the quality of policymaking, strains between economic and political logic in governance, and the role of cabinets in the executive branch of government; the role of financial markets and business lobbies; and the so-called natural resource curse.

The final part considers the political economy of fiscal and social policies. We emphasize fiscal policy in all its dimensions—taxes, spending, and debt—as this is arguably the most contested battlefield in economic policymaking in Latin America today. Latin American countries collect relatively little in taxes, and the structure of taxation is regressive and volatile. The results of public spending are regarded as low quality by citizens. What are the opportunities for meaningful fiscal policy reform?

The awarding of the Nobel Prize in Literature in 2010 to Peruvian novelist Mario Vargas Llosa is an indicator of continuity, perhaps; after all, fellow boom writer Gabriel García Márquez was awarded the same prize nearly a quarter century before. The upgrading of Peruvian public debt to investment grade status by the principal ratings agencies in 2009, however, is also an indicator of change in the region. The essays included in this handbook demonstrate that the Latin American economies have been transformed in many significant ways since Hirschman's pioneering studies of political economy, which coincided with the flowering of the region's literary boom. But many problems remain stubbornly persistent. Sorting out what is new and what is not, what has been achieved and what remains to be done, are critical questions. Answering them is the task the contributors to this handbook have set for themselves.

The editors express their gratitude to the contributors to this volume and to Ashley Barry, Nallely Carro Acoltzi, and Lauren Redfield for their help in preparing the manuscript for publication.

NOTE

1. These essays by new trespassers provide a useful companion piece to a similar attempt to learn from policy reform experiences in OECD countries (OECD 2010b).

REFERENCES

Acemoglu, Daron, Simon Johnson, and James A. Robinson. 2001. "The Colonial Origins of Comparative Development: An Empirical Investigation." *American Economic Review* 91(5): 1369–1401.

Acemoglu, Daron, and James A. Robinson. 2006. *Economic Origins of Dictatorship and Democracy*. New York: Cambridge University Press.

Alesina, Alberto, and Dani Rodrik. 1994. "Distributive Politics and Economic Growth." *Quarterly Journal of Economics* 109(2): 465–90.

Bulmer-Thomas, Victor. 2003. *The Economic History of Latin America since Independence*. 2nd ed. Cambridge: Cambridge University Press.

Centeno, Miguel, Harold James, and John Londregan, eds. 2005 *The Political Economy of Recurrent Debt*. Princeton, NJ: Princeton Institute for International and Regional Studies.

Cook, Maria Lorena. 2007. *The Politics of Labor Reform in Latin America: Between Flexibility and Rights*. University Park: Pennsylvania State University Press.

Easterly, William, and Ross Levine. 1997. "Africa's Growth Tragedy: Policies and Ethnic Divisions." *Quarterly Journal of Economics* 112(4): 1203–50.

ECLAC. 2010a. *Balance preliminary de las economías de América Latina y el Caribe.* Santiago: United Nations Economic Commission for Latin America and the Caribbean.

——. *Panorama social de América Latina y el Caribe.* Santiago: Nations Economic Commission for Latin America and the Caribbean.

Frieden, Jeffry A. 1991. *Debt, Development, and Democracy: Modern Political Economy and Latin America, 1965–1985.* Princeton, NJ: Princeton University Press.

Frieden, Jeffry A., Manuel Pastor, and Michael Tomz, eds. 2000. *Modern Political Economy and Latin America: Theory and Policy.* Boulder, CO: Westview Press.

Halperin Donghi, Tulio. 2008. "La Cepal en su contexto histórico." *Revista de la CEPAL* 94: 7–27.

Hirschman, Albert O. 1958. *The Strategy of Economic Development.* New Haven, CT: Yale University Press.

——. 1968. "The Political Economy of Import-Substituting Industrialization in Latin America." *Quarterly Journal of Economics* 82(1): 1–32.

——. 1981. *Essays in Trespassing: Economics to Politics and Beyond.* New York: Cambridge University Press.

——. 1985. *A Bias for Hope: Essays on Development and Latin America.* Boulder, CO: Westview Press.

——. 1987. "The Political Economy of Latin American Development: Seven Exercises in Retrospection." *Latin American Research Review* 22(3): 7–36.

IMF (International Monetary Fund). 2011. *World Economic Outlook.* Washington, DC: International Monetary Fund.

Kingstone, Peter. 2010. *The Political Economy of Latin America: Reflections on Neoliberalism and Development.* London: Routledge.

Leiva, Fernando Ignacio. 2008. *Latin American Neostructuralism: The Contradictions of Post-Neoliberal Devleopment.* Minneapolis: University of Minnesota Press.

Levy, Santiago. 2007. *Good Intentions, Bad Outcomes: Social Policy, Informality, and Economic Growth in Mexico.* Washington, DC: Brookings Institution.

Lora, Eduardo, ed. 2007. *The State of State Reform in Latin America.* Stanford, CA: Stanford University Press; Washington, DC: Inter-American Development Bank.

Needler, Martin C. 1966. "Political Development and Military Intervention in Latin America." *American Political Science Review* 60 (3): 616–26.

O'Donnell, Guillermo. 1973. *Modernization and Bureaucratic Authoritarianism.* Berkeley: University of California Press.

OECD (Organisation for Economic Co-operation and Development). 2008. *Latin American Economic Outlook 2009.* Paris: OECD Development Centre, OECD.

——. 2009. *Latin American Economic Outlook 2010.* Paris: OECD Development Centre, OECD.

——. 2010a. *Economic Outlook.* No. 88 (November), OECD, Paris.

——. 2010b. *Making Reform Happen: Lessons from OECD Countries.* Paris: OECD.

Payne, J. Mark, Daniel Zovatto, and Mercedes Mateo Díaz, eds. 2007. *Democracies in Development: Politics and Reform in Latin America.* Washington, DC: Inter-American Development Bank; Cambridge, MA: David Rockefeller Center for Latin American Studies, Harvard University.

Persson, Torsten, and Guido Tabellini. 1994. "Is Inequality Harmful for Growth?" *American Economic Review* 84(3): 600–21.

Rodrik, Dani. 1996. "Understanding Economic Policy Reform." *Journal of Economic Literature* 34(1): 9–41.

Santiso, Javier. April 2000. "Hirschman's View of Development, or the Art of Trespassing and Self-Subversion." *ECLAC Review/Revista CEPAL*: 93–111.

———. 2005. *Amérique latine: Révolutionnaire, libérale, pragmatique.* Paris: Editions Autrement.

———. 2006. *Latin America's Political Economy of the Possible: Beyond Good Revolutionaries and Free-Marketeers.* Cambridge, MA: MIT Press.

———. 2012. *Elections and Financial Markets in Emerging Democracies.* Cambridge, MA: MIT Press.

Starr, Pamela K. 2009. "The Political Economy of Reform in Latin America: Politics, Institutions, Ideas and Context." Review essay. *Latin American Research Review* 44 (3): 224–34.

Stein, Ernesto, and Jorge Streb. 2004. "Elections and the Timing of Devaluations." *Journal of International Economics* 63: 119–45.

Stein, Ernesto, Mariano Tommasi, Koldo Echebarria, Eduardo Lora, and Mark Payne. 2006. *The Politics of Policies: Economic and Social Progress in Latin America.* Cambridge, MA: Harvard University Press.

Thorp, Rosemary. 1998. *Progress, Poverty and Exclusion: An Economic History of Latin America in the 20th Century.* Washington, DC: Inter-American Development Bank.

Weyland, Kurt. 2007. *Bounded Rationality and Policy Diffusion: Social Sector Reform in Latin America.* Princeton, NJ: Princeton University Press.

Williamson, John. 1990. "What Washington Means by Policy Reform." In ed., *Latin American Adjustment: How Much Has Happened?*, edited by John Williamson. Washington, DC: International Institute of Economics

PART I

THE VIEW FROM THE INSIDE: PRACTITIONERS REFLECT ON MAKING REFORM HAPPEN

CHAPTER 1

POLITICAL LEADERSHIP AND ECONOMIC REFORM: THE BRAZILIAN EXPERIENCE IN THE CONTEXT OF LATIN AMERICA

FERNANDO HENRIQUE CARDOSO AND EDUARDO GRAEFF

BRAZIL grew 2.7 percent per year on average in the last 30 years—somewhat less than Latin America, a good deal less than the world, far less than the emerging countries of Asia in the same period, and indeed far less than Brazil itself in previous decades. If anything stands out favorably in the recent Brazilian experience, it is not growth but stabilization and the successful opening of the economy. To this we should add a political achievement: democracy, the grand cause of the people and groups who have succeeded each other in government since the departure of the military in 1985. Democracy, rather than economic stability or even development—as if one could be exchanged for the other. These three goals are not mutually exclusive, of course, although authoritarian regimes sometimes display faster gross domestic product (GDP) growth rates. For Brazil, as for other Latin American countries, *all three presented themselves as indivisible challenges* at the beginning of the 1990s.

To assume that political leaders in today's world can freely determine the pace and direction of a country's economy as they wish is as questionable as believing that an inspired military leader alone could assure victory on the battlefield. In *War and Peace* Tolstoy mocks the princes and generals who behave as if their attitudes, words, and resolutions dictated the course of history. His most acid irony is directed at the military theorists who claim to extract scientific laws from the infinite multiplicity of events. The paradox, as he sees it, is this: "The higher soldiers or statesmen are in the pyramid of authority, the farther they must be from its base, which consists of those ordinary men and women whose lives are the actual stuff of history."[1] Spy satellites, smart bombs, guided missiles, and other technological wonders may have dispelled the "fog of war" (albeit only to some extent). Advances in information technology and financial engineering, in contrast, have shown an immense capacity to increase the unpredictability of markets at certain times. Anyone who has been in charge of the foreign-exchange trading desk at the central bank of a peripheral country during a global crisis knows how hard it can be to keep calm and hold a steady course in this kind of fog on a stormy sea.

Without venturing into a philosophical discussion of the limits to free will imposed by the course of nature and history, one must acknowledge the virtual impossibility of distinguishing between what was due to the initiatives of local governments and what was imposed from outside in the economic changes experienced by Brazil and its neighbors in the region. The second oil shock (1979) and the U.S. interest-rate shock (1982) plunged almost the whole of Latin America into a decade of stagnation and inflation, while the industrialized world was recycling its economy. The search for solutions to the crisis inevitably led to the new forms of operation adopted by investors, multinational corporations, governments of central countries, and multilateral economic agencies.

This does not mean, as some market-economics theorists seem to suppose, that there are complete recipes for development that will open the doors of globalization to all countries if they are prepared to "do their homework." Nor that we Latin Americans are condemned forever to underdevelopment or merely reflex development, as used to be supposed by vulgar dependency theorists and as some people still believe. Countries experience specific historical courses, which are not limited to mechanically reproducing the global structural "model."

A historical and structural analysis of this complex reality would start with the rules according to which the global economy operates—the general, abstract determinations, in Marxist jargon—and reconstitute how they were experienced, adapted, or transformed in each relatively homogeneous group of peripheral countries. This would be the way to expose the dynamic relations between local and international social forces, and to see how adaptations and innovations in the linkages between each country or group of countries and the global economy produce different results, albeit subject to the same general conditioning factors. The framework for change is established by globalization and the information economy, but each country fits into it or fends it off in different ways. The responses can be creative; some may be more advantageous than others, and each one will depend both on circumstances such as the country's location, population, and natural resource endowment and on political decisions. National societies have different degrees of economic and cultural development, which facilitate better or worse alternatives for adapting to new circumstances.[2]

The purpose of this chapter is more modest. It is limited to setting out our particular view of recent efforts to consolidate democracy in Brazil while controlling inflation and resuming economic growth. At the same time the chapter presents, as objectively as possible, some thoughts on the limits but also the relevance of action by political leaders to set a course and circumvent obstacles to that process. Here and there, the chapter refers to the experiences of other Latin American countries, especially Argentina, Chile, and Mexico, not to offer a full-fledged comparative analysis but merely to note contrasts and similarities that may shed light on the peculiarities of the Brazilian case and suggest themes for a more wide-ranging exchange of views.[3]

1. From Inflationary Crisis to the Consolidation of Stability

1.1. Democracy in the Expectations Race

In October 2006, Luiz Inácio Lula da Silva was reelected president of Brazil, winning 60 percent of the valid votes cast in the runoff ballot, after leading the first round with 49 percent, 10 points ahead of the runner-up. Reelection was the crowning achievement for a politician with extraordinary talent as a mass communicator at the service of a democratic symbol—a migrant from the Northeast who became a union leader, the founder of a political party, and president of the republic. To voters in the least developed regions, who assured his victory, it also embodied their recognition of the policies to alleviate poverty introduced by the previous administration, which Lula extended and converted into a material anchor for his symbolic relationship with the poor. At the same time, it represented a renewal of the somewhat reticent support shown for his economic policies during his first term, when expectations of faster growth were frustrated but inflation was kept low and Brazil's integration into the global flow of trade and finance was deepened.

Brazil's situation was very far from being as comfortable at the beginning of the 1990s. Economic stagnation prevailed, a foreign debt moratorium had been declared, hyperinflation was at the gates, and the hopes and expectations awakened by democratization were giving way to widespread despondency. A consensus had formed among political scientists, economists, and observers that a combination of anachronistic ideas, defective institutions, and lack of leadership was preventing Brazil from making the changes needed to control inflation and resume economic growth. While sectors of academia, the state techno-bureaucracy, the business community, and the media were discussing reforms, the national-statism that had inspired several provisions in the "economic order" chapter of the 1988 constitution continued to exert a decisive influence on the opinions of most politicians. In the everyday scrimmage of political activity, the old practices of patronage and populism sprang back like weeds in the shade of democracy. In major decisions, the design of the nation's institutions weakened the parties and undermined support for the legislative proposals sent to Congress by the president, threatening to reproduce the pattern of executive-legislative conflict that had led to the 1964 coup. The prospect was not of a complete breakdown but of slow deterioration in democracy for lack of governability.[4]

The political literature uses the term *doble minoría* to describe the recurrent situation in Latin America where a president is brought to power by a minority of the electorate and faces difficulties in governing for lack of a majority in Congress (see Lins and Valenzuela 1994). In Brazil, the two-round system for presidential elections introduced by the 1988 constitution solved the first problem but fragmentation of the party system worsened the second. The Brazilian Democratic Movement Party (PMDB for its Portuguese abbreviation) had been the sole party of opposition to the authoritarian regime and won a large majority in the 1986 Constituent Assembly, but then split over key issues in the constitutional debate and whether to support President José Sarney or remain in opposition. Fernando Collor de Mello won the 1989 presidential election even though he formally belonged to a practically nonexistent party, evidencing the premature decay of the parties that had led the transition to democracy. In the 1990 elections the PMDB's share of the lower house fell to a fifth, representing a slim relative majority among the 19 parties with seats in the Chamber of Deputies.

Lacking a majority in Congress was not a problem for Collor in his first year as president because he was at the height of his popularity and a congressional election was looming. In his second year he realized he would have to negotiate with the main parties that had won seats in the new Congress, but by then it was too late. With his popularity rapidly eroded by the failure of his anti-inflation policy and a massive corruption scandal, the lack of a consistent majority in Congress prevented him from implementing the reforms he had promised and in December 1992 forced him out of office.

Rising inflation and falling governability seemed to have caught Brazil in a trap that was draining its energy. This inspired pessimistic prognostications about democracy's ability to win or at least tie the race with the expectations of social and economic progress that democracy itself had aroused.

1.2. The Real Plan

Peaceful mass demonstrations against Collor and compliance with due process of law in his impeachment rekindled confidence in democracy. Vice President Itamar Franco, an experienced politician, took over as president and appointed a cabinet based on a broad coalition of parties that assured him a stable majority in Congress.

The economic climate continued to deteriorate, however. The wage-price spiral accelerated, fueled by indexation, and deprived business and government of any stable value reference on which to base medium- and long-term decisions. Investors remained retrenched, although corporate rates of return and liquidity were generally positive. Inflation had reached 30 percent *per month* when President Itamar Franco appointed his fourth finance minister, in May 1993.[5]

As if this were not enough, political turbulence was back with a vengeance as Congress plunged into a rancorous investigation of a corruption scandal involving kickbacks in the distribution of budget resources that was to lead to the expulsion of several congressmen, including the majority leader.

Under these circumstances it is understandable that our promise[5] of frontally fighting the inflation scourge was received with skepticism, albeit tempered with good will, by the media, business, most congressmen, and the general public. With a president who had not been elected to that office (in Brazil, unlike the United States, the vice president is simply the running mate of the presidential candidate and is unknown to most voters) and with Congress semiparalyzed, few believed the political conditions existed to wage this battle against inflation. Time was running out, moreover: general elections were scheduled for October 1994 and a constitutional amendment had brought forward the presidential election to coincide with them. In little over a year, congressmen would leave for their constituencies to campaign and it would be impossible to pass complex legislation requiring the physical presence of a majority on the floor of the house.

What Congress, the president, and the people actually preferred was a price freeze in the style of the 1986 Cruzado Plan, which had been followed by short-lived euphoria but was still recalled with gratitude. Analysts accustomed to project the future as a rerun of the past predicted that the fiscal austerity measures included in the FHC Plan, as it was initially called, would end up like similar proposals in the Sarney and Collor administrations, gathering dust on some shelf in Congress or the Office of the President.

The success of the Real Plan, as it later became known, and the cycle of change unleashed by the plan refuted or at least relativized the diagnoses that stressed political obstacles to stabilization of the economy and the implementation of reforms in Brazil.

Even in the short time frame allowed by the electoral calendar, it proved possible to assemble at the Finance Ministry an experienced and creative technical team to furnish indispensable support for a minister who was not an economist, formulate an innovative stabilization strategy combining orthodox and heterodox measures, and win the political support to implement it—in this case the minister's experience as a member of Congress was valuable.

Fiscal policy had undermined the credibility of previous stabilization programs under Presidents Sarney and Collor. The first stage of the Real Plan comprised a series of measures designed to cover this flank: cuts in public spending, removal from earmarking of some revenues that the constitution had automatically allocated to specific expenditures, a new tax to be collected by banks on all financial transactions including the cashing of checks, and debt renegotiations with the states, several of which had been in or close to default for some years. Although they were insufficient to assure long-term fiscal equilibrium, these measures were submitted to the president, to Congress, and to the nation as a first step in tackling the structural causes of inflation. In bringing forward the proposals, the government made clear that it had no intention of repeating the discredited "shock therapy" tactics applied under previous anti-inflation programs with a heterodox core, and showed determination to dissolve the marriage between inflation and the exchequer that had become a hallmark of the Brazilian fiscal regime.[6] In passing the measures, Congress indicated that it would be possible to build a consensus around a broader reform program, giving economic agents a positive signal about the stabilization policy's chances of success. This momentum and the resulting credibility were boosted in October 1993 when Brazil ended its debt moratorium in direct negotiations with creditor banks and only informal support from the International Monetary Fund.

We believed orthodox fiscal measures were a necessary but not sufficient condition to tackle inflation at the very high levels it had reached. At some point it would be necessary to dismantle the mechanisms for wage-and-price indexation that had become generalized in the 1980s and were feeding back into inflation via inertia, making past inflation rates the floor for future inflation. The innovative, and to a certain extent audacious, aspect of this operation was the radicalization of indexation as an antidote to indexation itself, in a move that recalled homeopathy's first law, *similia similibus curantor*. A daily indexation mechanism was introduced in February 1994 (the URV, or "real value unit") as a reference for spontaneous resets to contracts and prices before the new currency began circulating on July 1 that year. This avoided litigation among private agents, or between them and the state, to "decouple" contractual rights and obligations before and after the onset of the stabilization program. Litigation arising from previous programs has resulted in a towering stack of liabilities for the National Treasury. In the case of the Real Plan only one provision has ever been invalidated by the courts, with comparatively minor consequences. Legal armor plating was a key factor in the Real Plan's credibility.

From 47 percent per month on the eve of the currency change, inflation fell to less than 3 percent per month after 30 days and has remained at a level of a single digit per year ever since.

The first batch of opinion polls on the next presidential election, released in May 1994, had shown Lula clearly in the lead at 40 percent. In October we (the Cardoso team) won the election outright in the first round with over half of all valid votes cast. This result was due mainly to the optimism aroused by the Real Plan, which also cemented the coalition of parties that backed our campaign, comprising our own party, the Brazilian Social Democracy Party (PSDB), and two center-right parties, the Liberal Front Party (PFL) and the Brazilian Labor Party (PTB), broadened in the center by the inclusion of the PMDB after the election. Although our program was by no means limited to this issue, consolidating stabilization (or "holding on tight to the real," as the popular saying put it) became the basic commitment by which our government sought support from Congress and society and would be assessed at the end of the day.

1.3. Stabilization and Structural Reform

Controlling inflation was to be not the end but the beginning of an ambitious agenda for change, as we had insisted all along. We had a clear vision of the course to steer. The overall vision as well as several specific measures on this agenda had been outlined in the original planning documents for the Real Plan.[7] But the path was made by walking, and there were many unexpected boulders and bends.

The initial impact of price stabilization on wages and incomes in general at the base of society anticipated the bonus and deferred the onus of the reforms needed to consolidate stability. A neoclassical economist would have advised us to do the opposite, anticipating the onus while fueling expectations of the bonus. Recalling Machiavelli's teachings about the risks that lie in wait for a reforming ruler, we saw this inversion of conventional economic logic as a political opportunity to sustain the support of the unorganized majority who stood ultimately to gain from the reforms and neutralize resistance from well-organized affluent minorities. We were by no means unaware of the risk of "reform fatigue." However, we were confident that relief at the sharp reduction in inflation would help Brazilian society finally see its age-old ills for what they were and fuel demands for more progress in fighting them. We would have to walk a razor's edge between these two collective sentiments: the blossoming of aspirations in response to the changes we had begun, and frustration with the pace and cost of completing the changes.

Our starting point was the conviction that the combination of hyperinflation, fiscal disequilibrium, foreign debt, and economic stagnation, which had dragged on since the 1980s, signaled the end of a development cycle in Brazil without the foundations having been laid for another cycle. The crisis had well-known proximate causes, from external oil and interest-rate shocks to mistakes and omissions by successive governments. But its underlying cause was the bankruptcy of the centralist interventionist state founded by the dictatorship of Getúlio Vargas (1937–45) and reinforced by the military regime (1964–85). Despite having enabled Brazil to enjoy 50 years of strong growth, albeit with income concentration and social marginalization, this state model had exhausted its ability to drive industrialization via state-owned enterprises, protectionist barriers, and subsidies to private enterprises.

In our view, there could be no lasting economic stability, let alone a sustained resumption of growth, if Brazil remained outside the expanding international flow of trade, investment, and technology. Despite the crisis, many Brazilian companies had managed to modernize their production and management methods, albeit less so their plant and equipment. In contrast with the public sector, private enterprise was not excessively indebted. Although business organizations had been taken by surprise by the abrupt trade liberalization promoted by the Collor admin-istration, generally speaking they displayed the capacity to face greater exposure to international competition.

To make its economy more competitive overall, however, Brazil needed a dif-ferent state model. Neither the grand protagonist of development, as in the past, nor the neoliberal minimalist state, but the "necessary state," as we preferred to call it: with more brains and muscle than bureaucratic mass to respond in a timely manner to the opportunities and turbulence of globalized capitalism. More focused on co-ordinating and regulating private enterprise than on intervening directly in the economy. And just as importantly, capable of fulfilling the promises of democracy in the social sphere without making the very beneficiaries of those promises—workers, pensioners, the poorest in general—pay for them via inflation "tax."

The 1988 constitution was not only vast, rambling, and excessively detailed; it was also highly contradictory, and still is to a large extent. It embodied major ad-vances in fundamental citizens' rights and safeguards, as well as generous provision for social rights, yet at the same time it reflected the entrenchment of vested inter-ests linked to the structures of the *varguista* state,[8] as well as privileges typical of the deep-seated patrimonialism of Brazilian culture and political institutions.

The state-owned enterprises were accommodated by inclusion in the constitu-tion of the monopoly they already held in oil and gas as well as telecommunications. In mining and shipping, there was no state monopoly, but the constitution estab-lished exclusivity for Brazilian-owned companies. In both cases the consequence was insufficient investment or none at all. The state-owned electric power utilities were also lagging behind with investments. The severe fiscal crisis meant it was necessary to eliminate or ease the constraints written into the constitution and define rules whereby the effort to foster expansion in these sectors could be shared with private enterprise, including foreign capital. Otherwise the incipient resump-tion of growth would be aborted by infrastructure bottlenecks.

For public-sector workers and civil servants the constitution guaranteed a highly privileged pension scheme, both in terms of the age, length of service, and contribution requirements and in terms of the cash values involved. Private-sector employees covered by the official scheme had far fewer advantages but nevertheless saw their benefits guaranteed or extended. Expenditure was rising faster than the capacity to generate revenue, and as a result both systems began to display growing deficits that would eventually place a huge burden on society as a whole, by forcing an increase in taxation, driving up inflation, or pressuring interest rates. Any increase in payroll taxes for the private sector as a palliative measure to contain deficit growth, on the other hand, would lead to a rise in informal economic activity: that is, an increase in the proportion of the workforce without any social security coverage at all. In sum, contrary to the promised universalization of rights, the con-stitution enshrined a social security and pension system that was highly stratified, lopsided, and unsustainable in the long term.

Public-sector workers also benefited from the extension to all civil servants, including the large number hired without competitive examinations, of life tenure and a ban on pay cuts, both of which are reserved for judges in most countries. This hindered any more ambitious effort to modernize the machinery of government, as well as making payroll expansion almost inevitable in all three tiers of government (federal, state, and municipal).

It was imperative to correct these distortions for reasons of both efficiency and equity. This is what we proposed in a series of bills to amend the constitution's provisions on state monopolies, the definition of a Brazilian-owned company, social security and pensions, and public service. The package was submitted to Congress shortly after the new government took office in January 1995. The committee stage and voting on the entire swathe of constitutional amendments lasted throughout the 1995–98 presidential term. Passage of enabling legislation took longer, with pension reform extending until the end of our second term in 2002.

1.4. Battle on Several Fronts

For the general public the debate about reform basically took the form of marches and countermarches that revolved around the constitutional amendments. These were in fact an important part but still only a part of the state reforms carried out in this eight-year period. Consolidation of stability entailed efforts on several fronts.

Financial relations, and behind them the balance of power, in the sphere of the federation were arduously renegotiated until we reached agreement on a legal framework that would limit the future indebtedness of states (as well as some medium-size and large cities), encourage them to adjust their accounts, and guarantee payment of installments on debts assumed by the federal government. In this process several state banks used by the respective governments for uncontrolled debt issuance were closed or privatized.

Private-sector banks were affected to varying degrees by the loss of the inflation revenue they were accustomed to pocketing on unremunerated deposits. One reform established a program to restructure and strengthen the banking sector, leading to changes of ownership for distressed institutions, limiting the losses to depositors, and above all averting systemic or cascading bank failure, whose effects would have been devastating. This reform also restructured and capitalized federal financial institutions.

The Collor administration had removed most nontariff barriers and reduced import tariffs. Currency stability and appreciation against the dollar made trade liberalization effective. Contrary to widespread predictions, this did not lead to the destruction of Brazilian industry. Despite difficulties here or there, industry as a whole responded positively to liberalization. It took advantage of the favorable exchange rate to import high-tech plant and inputs, benefited from expansion of the domestic market, and basically maintained the same level of complexity and integration across branches.

The state had to make its own contribution toward the reforms needed for growth to resume under the new conditions arising from economic opening. BNDES, the national development bank, increased disbursements fivefold between

1994 and 1998, to a level above R$20 billion per year (roughly $16.5 billion in 1998 U.S. dollars). The presence of such a large development bank is unique among the emerging countries and was of key importance to the restructuring of production capacity in Brazil's private sector.

Government agencies of no significance or simply nonexistent in a closed economy had to be strengthened or created in areas such as export promotion, anti-trust enforcement, agricultural defense, protection of intellectual property, and support for innovation. Structuring such agencies helped pave the way for strong export growth in both commodities and manufactures from 1999 on.

The entry of private enterprise into infrastructure sectors required a new legal framework for the granting of public service concessions and the creation of a hitherto unknown entity in the organization of the Brazilian state: regulatory bodies with the powers and political independence to protect the rights of consumers in their relations with service providers. Several such regulators were created following the passage of constitutional amendments on oil, electricity, and telecommunications.

The real was born close to parity with the dollar but not legally pegged to the dollar as the Argentine peso had been by the Cavallo Plan (1991). Rather than dollarization, we insisted on less attractive issues such as fighting the public deficit and balancing the budget. This had important implications for the consolidation of stability in Brazil. Successive attempts to realign the exchange rate in terms more favorable to Brazilian exports were aborted by external financial crises in the second half of the 1990s. Gradual devaluation of the real against the dollar until the end of 1998 lagged behind domestic inflation. Realignment eventually happened of necessity in January 1999, when the risk that our foreign-exchange reserves would be dangerously depleted by a fierce speculative attack forced the Central Bank to float the real. Widespread fears of a banking crisis and inflation acceleration proved unfounded. The structural changes already in place, albeit incomplete from our standpoint, proved sufficient to stabilize the economy without the "exchange-rate anchor."

The battle to bring states, municipalities, and the federal sphere itself into line behind the banner of fiscal sustainability intensified with the introduction of a floating exchange-rate regime and inflation targeting in 1999. To crown this normative effort, the Fiscal Responsibility Act passed in May 2000 applied strict rules to all three tiers of government regarding indebtedness and the creation of payroll and other permanent expenses.

Last but by no means least, instruments of state action had to be redesigned in order to fulfill promises of universalization of rights in the social sphere. Also via constitutional amendment, new rules were established for participation by the federal, state, and municipal governments in the financing of primary education and health care, and an Anti-Poverty Fund (Fundo de Combate à Pobreza) was created. The criteria for investment of these funds represented a major advance toward equity in public spending, since they prioritized the poorest and most vulnerable strata of the population, who had traditionally benefited least from social programs. Comprehensive changes to the design and execution of essential programs in these areas enhanced spending efficiency, especially through decentralization via the transfer of federal funds and activities to states and municipalities, partnerships with civil society, and systematic assessment of outcomes.

Not all the reforms advanced as much as we would have liked. We lack the necessary distance to judge how far they succeeded and we cannot guarantee they have reached the point of no return. However, it seems undeniable that they have now helped sustain the stability of the Brazilian economy for more than 15 years. It may be too soon to say whether they have also laid the foundations for such a significant long-term change as the creation of a new development model, as we intended.[9]

2. The Drawbacks and Force of Democratic Reformism

2.1. Plebiscitary or Consensual Democracy?

Modern formulations of the notion of political leadership emphasize institutional position and "mission." Outside this context the discussion of a leader's motivations and personal attributes falls into the banality of psychological and even biological generalization (see Petracca 2004). Our thoughts on the role of leadership in the reform process start from these two dimensions. In the case of the head of a democratic government, position is basically defined by power sharing and "mission" by the expectations of the led in their triple status as citizen-voters, voices of public opinion, and members of organized social sectors.

Let us begin with the relations with Congress and the parties, which are critical to any president's ability to lead in Brazil and other Latin American countries with presidential systems. Our reform agenda was extensive and complex, and (it bears repeating) took up most of the order of business in Congress for several years. In all, 35 constitutional amendments were passed between 1995 and 2002—36 if we include the amendment that enabled the requisite fiscal adjustment to be made in preparation for the Real Plan in 1993.[10] Each one could be passed only by three-fifths of both houses, with two readings in each house, the Chamber of Deputies and Senate. Because the rules of the lower house allowed (and, within certain limits, still allow) any party to demand that parts of a bill be voted separately, the three-fifths quorum had to be achieved for hundreds of votes. Over 500 supplementary laws, ordinary laws, and relevant provisional measures were passed in the same period.

It is most unlikely that a reform process would have entailed such a huge effort at building a consensus with the legislative branch in any other Latin American country. Did this represent a disadvantage? Considering the gap between our goals and what we actually succeeded in achieving, the answer is perhaps affirmative: the need to negotiate with Congress and the social sectors represented there every single step of the way did result to some extent in a slower pace and a narrower scope for the measures we proposed. But democracy and economic efficiency are not mutually negotiable goals in our view, as noted at the beginning of this chapter. Nor do we believe that Brazil has done worse than those of its neighbors who implemented reforms the authoritarian way.

Chile under General Augusto Pinochet (1973–90) is always cited as an example of successful reforms imposed without consulting Congress, which had been closed, or society, or at least the working class, which was silenced by vicious repression. Dictatorship is said to have been a necessary evil that enabled the Chilean economy to steer the "right course to growth" from the liberal standpoint, including deregulation, privatization, trade liberalization, and fiscal equilibrium. This view underestimates the price paid by the Chilean people, not only in lost liberties and rights but also in terms of material hardship. An orthodox shock program to tackle inflation caused a recession of more than 11 percent in 1975. The financial crisis that forced devaluation of the peso (Pinochet's "Chicago boys" also used an exchange-rate anchor) triggered another recession in 1982. Unemployment soared to nearly 20 percent and fell below 10 percent only in the late 1980s.[11] The proportion of the population living below the poverty line reached 45 percent in 1985; today it has returned to the level prevailing at the end of the 1960s, around 17 percent (Raczynski and Serrano 2005).

Nor can it be said that Concertación por la Democracia was lucky enough to receive the house in order in 1990. Inflation was 17 percent in Pinochet's last year and did not fall to single-digit levels until 1995. Although the Concertación coalition retained the principles of deregulation, privatization, and economic openness, it introduced a more rigorous fiscal policy while also restoring workers' rights and investing strongly in social policies.[12] And it did this by consensus building in Congress and with organized sectors of society despite the discretionary resources conferred on the executive by Chile's hyperpresidentialist constitution.[13] Chile's GDP grew 5.6 percent per year on average in the period 1990–2005, under Concertación-led governments, compared with only 3.1 percent in the period 1974–89 (Landerretche M. 2005).

If Chile stands out in Latin America as a successful case of integration into the global economy, it is thanks not to the legacy of the dictatorship but to what its democratic leaders have been able to achieve by leaving that legacy behind.

In Argentina the military junta that seized power in 1976 attempted liberal reforms similar to Chile's via the same authoritarian road but the results were disastrous, and the Malvinas/Falklands War made a handover to civilian rule inevitable in 1983. President Raúl Alfonsín (1983–89) received an economy that had been in deep recession for two years with inflation running at over 300 percent.

In contrast with Chile's, Argentina's democratic leaders had a difficult time establishing a lasting consensus on the direction of the economy. Alfonsín's reform proposals foundered in the face of Peronist opposition and lack of support from his own Radicals (UCR). A price freeze attempted under the Austral Plan ended in more recession and inflation of more than 600 percent in 1985, opening the gates for the Peronists to return to government with President Carlos Menem (1989–99). In 1991, as hyperinflation threatened to break out, Menem managed to wrest support from the Peronist Justicialist Party (PJ) and the opposition for the stabilization program mounted by Finance Minister Domingo Cavallo. In addition to fixing the peso by law at parity with the dollar, the plan included a fast-track privatization process. In 1992, the Olivos Pact between Peronists and Radicals laid the basis for convening a Constituent Assembly that introduced some of the reforms proposed previously by Alfonsín. But Menem's preferred instrument for implementing economic policy, including privatization, deregulation, and what little downsizing of government he undertook, was legislative delegation to the executive, which freed the president from the need to negotiate measures point by point with Congress.[14]

Without ceasing to be democratic, the road to reform in Menem's Argentina appears to have had a pronounced plebiscitary element, in which the inflationary crisis predisposed the parties and society to accept "heroic" measures and concentrated the initiative in the hands of the president. In contrast, the Chilean and Brazilian experiences fell distinctly into the camp of "consensual democracy," in which the executive must negotiate and trade concessions with the groups that have the power to veto its proposals.[15]

Argentina's short cut to stabilization may look faster at first sight but it did not go so far in terms of structural reform, and ultimately seems to have resulted in weaker rather than stronger institutions, as evidenced by the 2001–2 foreign-exchange and financial crisis. A preference for tortuous consensus building led Chile and Brazil to more solid results from the institutional standpoint. There is a significant difference between the two countries in this regard: while the agenda pursued by the Concertación can perhaps be said to have focused on rebuilding democratic social and political institutions on the scorched earth left behind by the dictatorship, the Brazilian reforms simultaneously addressed the need to build new institutions and to remove the detritus of the old *varguista* state, possibly paying a higher political price for that.

2.2. The "Political Preconditions" Fallacy

The inflationary crisis also functioned as the "midwife of history" in Brazil. With almost daily price rises averaging more than 20 percent per month, practically no sector was immune from the burden of superinflation. Everyone was affected in some way: wage workers, pensioners, and retirees, by accelerating corrosion of the purchasing power of their fixed earnings; self-employed workers and small business owners without access to the banking system, by depreciation of their limited cash assets; the upper middle class and business, by the immense difficulty of calculating, planning, and investing in a hyperinflationary environment, even with access to index-linked financial instruments. This boosted potential support for any plausible proposal to control inflation insofar as it diminished resistance to the necessary sacrifices.

Thus Brazil under the Real Plan and Argentina under the Cavallo Plan are examples of the tendency detected by Albert Hirschman in the early 1980s, when he examined what he called the social and political matrix of inflation in Latin America: "Beyond a threshold of tolerance, inflation certainly is the kind of pressing policy problem that increases the willingness of governments to take action, in spite of opposition from powerful interests, if there is firm expectation that the action will help restrain the inflation" (Hirschman 1981, 206).

To this effect of inflation was added in our case the weakening of traditional political forces for strictly political reasons. We mentioned earlier the exceptional circumstances that justified skepticism about the chances of success of a frontal attack on inflation after the impeachment of Collor: lack of direct electoral backing for his legal alternate, the corruption scandal that had all but paralyzed Congress, and pressure from the electoral calendar. Paradoxically, these very circumstances were what made the Real Plan possible. What analysts diagnosed as a lack of political preconditions turned out in fact to be a window of opportunity. In normal conditions the groups that benefited one or way or another from inflation and state disorganization, including segments of Congress, the private sector, and the state bureaucracy itself, would have mobilized more effectively to defend their interests. Only the disarray in which traditional political forces found themselves can explain why they allowed themselves to be defeated—or persuaded—by a minister and his small group of aides and sympathizers in the government, with the president's support, it is true, but with very hesitant backing from other parties apart from our own, the PSDB.

The art of politics consists of creating the conditions to achieve an objective for which the conditions are not given in advance. This is why politics is an art and not a technique. And its main weapon in a democracy is persuasion. Thanks to persuasion, to the winning over of public opinion, it eventually proved possible to build a minimum of consensus where it was presumably most difficult and certainly most necessary: inside the government, in Congress, and in the parties, that is, among the actors who make political decisions or prevent them from being made. In the midst of many doubts we had one certainty, grounded in the values of our democratic upbringing: that only a program capable of being explained and understood by ordinary people would be able to inflict a lasting defeat on inflation and set in motion the reorganization of the Brazilian state.

Credibility was a key prerequisite in a country that had suffered the consequences of the failure of successive stabilization programs in recent years. We benefited from the good will of the media, most business leaders, other organized sectors of society, and Congress itself. Despite skepticism about our chances of success they trusted the minister's seriousness of purpose and the competence of the staff. Aware of the importance of maintaining and broadening this basis of trust, we decided that there would be no surprises and no promises that could not easily be met: each step in our stabilization strategy would be announced in advance and explained to the general public, always making clear that what was involved was not unilateral action by the government but a *process* whose outcome depended on the continuing convergence of the efforts of government, Congress, private economic agents, and society as a whole.

We often came close to losing the battle for trust. As the months went by, society became more and more anxious about the acceleration of inflation, pressure built up in the government itself for decisive action, and there was increasing resistance from parties and leaders who saw the possibility of a successful stabilization program as a defeat for their own political plans. The removal of an entire currency from circulation and its replacement with a new one brought a fundamental reinforcement to this battle for trust and credibility: the *symbol* represented by the real, which synthesized the expectations of change diffused throughout society.

Even before the new currency began circulating, the parties' and politicians' radars had begun capturing the public's change of mood. The perception that this could drive a competitive presidential candidacy facilitated the task of winning support for our proposals in Congress. This is how the breakthrough was achieved: launched under the sign of a "lack of political preconditions," the Real Plan was itself to become the precondition for a realignment of political forces in favor of the reforms. Almost by saturation, the old order gave way to the new. Victory in the presidential election provided the opportunity and responsibility for anchoring this new situation in the bedrock of the nation's institutions, of moving forward with an extensive agenda of reforms necessary to "hold on tight to the real" and keep the hopes deposited in it alive.

2.3. Testing the Limits of Latin American Presidentialism

The success of the Real Plan owed much to this seizing of a window of opportunity. It took eight years of unremitting effort to consolidate stability. The continuity of the progress it was possible to achieve throughout this period depended on a political strategy with two pillars: (1) building a stable majority in Congress by sharing power in the executive with the parties in the ruling coalition and (2) leveraging the president's leadership to bring to bear both the government's forces and those of the coalition parties to push for reform, with the support of public opinion and the organized sectors of society.

Presidents can often use constitutional instruments to transform their will if not into law at least into decrees or provisional measures with the force of law,[16] and even the authority to ensure their orders are obeyed through recognition of the legitimacy of their decisions. However, to be politically effective by winning more support or smoothing the way to implementing their proposals, they do not fully exercise this virtual power but instead go about creating situations in which, although their will is not entirely patent, the policies and decisions they aim to pursue stand a greater chance of success.

It so happens that the executive branch, represented by the president and the cabinet, is only a part of the formal system of power (not to mention the domination structurally exercised by classes and segments of classes, organized in the nonformal command structure, and which bring pressure to bear on a day-to-day basis and have at their disposal power resources entrenched in a thousand ways in social practices). Congress, the parties, the courts, to cite only the other formal components of the command structure, condition the political game.

The crises that led to the resignation of President Jânio Quadros and the ouster of President João Goulart in the 1960s, and to the impeachment of Collor, left a clear lesson: the main question for the president is not *if* but *how* power should be shared. The worst mistake a president can make is to imagine having been given a mandate to govern alone. In order to keep campaign promises, Congress is needed. And to assure a majority in Congress, a president needs to build alliances, since the heterogeneity of the federation and the peculiarities of the Brazilian system of proportional representation produce party-political fragmentation in which no single party wields a majority.

With these lessons of history in mind, we set out to weld an alliance between our own party, the PSDB, and the PFL and PTB in the presidential election, and later to include the PMDB and the Brazilian Progressive Party (PPB) in the ruling coalition. A balance among the larger parties, preventing our own party from controlling Congress even when it won a majority in the lower house after the 1998 elections, proved fundamental to assuring political stability.

A respectable current of political scientists considers Latin American presidentialism a lost cause. Party fragmentation, on one hand, and the independence and rigidity of the mandates of president and Congress, on the other, are believed to lead to recurrent political impasses.[17] The PSDB, inspired by this sort of diagnosis, declared itself parliamentary in its 1988 founding manifesto. Parliamentarianism sustained a crushing defeat in a plebiscite held in 1993. Irony of history: we lost the plebiscite and a year later won the presidential election, thus having to assume the task of assuring not just the survival but the good health of the system we had considered doomed.

More recent studies underscore the idea that in Latin America instead of presidentialism it is more appropriate to speak of presidentialisms in the plural. The risk of an impasse is ever present. The means and modes of avoiding it vary according to the specificities of executive-legislative relations, party organization, and the contents of the decisions on the agenda. Only by taking these variables into account, in addition to generalizations about systems of government, would it be possible to explain the positive, albeit problematical, results achieved by democracy in some countries of the region.[18]

A peculiarity of Brazil in this regard is the arena that the coexistence between the relative weakness of the parties and the strength of Congress creates for negotiating and decision making. We are an extreme case of multiparty politics, with some 20 parties represented in the Chamber of Deputies, five or six of them relevant and none with more than 20 percent of the seats. Argentina, Chile, and Mexico, in contrast, are cases of moderately concentrated multiparty systems.

The Argentine and Chilean dictatorships closed Congress and banned parties but were unable to destroy them in practice, at least not the largest parties. The Radical Civic Union (UCR) and PJ, which had polarized Argentine politics since 1945, like Chile's Christian Democrats (PDC) and Socialists (PS), which date back to the 1920s and 1930s, survived and again assumed a leadership role after redemocratization. Their strength is due to long-standing loyalty on the part of voters and card-carrying members, as well as the discipline of backbenchers. This discipline derives from the electoral system—closed-list proportional representation in Argentina, two-member ("binominal") districts in Chile—and is reinforced by tradition. The usual penalty for congressmen who vote systematically against the party line is removal from the list at the next election or expulsion before it. Given the weight of tradition and the relative concentration of votes for the larger parties, the chances of reelection for those who leave or are expelled are slim.

We Brazilians often imagine that fewer and more united parties would facilitate negotiations between the president and Congress, and assure a faster, more consistent decision-making process. Our neighbors' experience suggests that may not always be the case. United and pugnacious parties may be a synonym for governability under parliamentarianism. Under presidentialism they sometimes serve to organize gridlock. Polarization between the PJ and UCR in Argentina, and exacerbated rivalry between right-wing, centrist, and left-wing blocs in Chile, set the stage for the collapse of democracy in both countries.

Polarization persisted in postauthoritarian Argentina; it did not reach the breaking point but severely hampered both UCR-led administrations. The intransigence of the Peronist opposition and galloping inflation led President Alfonsín to resign months before the official end of his term. President Fernando de la Rúa, who succeeded Menem, failed to complete a year in office. His government was stymied by its inability to halt or manage the crisis of confidence in the peso's parity with the dollar. In response to popular rejection of all politicians (*¡Qué se vayan todos!*), the UCR broke up and shrank while the PJ, despite electoral damage, strengthened its relative predominance, sustained by the Peronist party–union machine and its symbolic identification with the "*descamisados*" (see Torre 2004). Argentina thus appears to be shifting away from a virtual two-party system to a multiparty system with a dominant party, in which executive-legislative relations will tend to oscillate between cooperation and confrontation depending on whether the president is a Peronist.

Argentina's military junta departed the scene without leaving anyone to claim a political legacy. Pinochet's legacy, in contrast, was recognized until the end of his life by the right-wing Independent Democratic Union (UDI) and National Renewal (RN) parties, which have consistent social and electoral grass roots. This led to an alliance of the center and the Left represented by the Christian Democrats (PDC) and the Socialists (PS). The unstable triangle of the past was thus replaced by a sort of virtuous circle in which the Concertación's political consistency and economic success reinforce each other, assuring control of both the executive and Congress.

Mexico's transition to pluralist democracy is a case apart in this mosaic: somewhat of a Latin American perestroika, in which a semiauthoritarian regime opened up from the inside out and from the top down in a process led by those who were both head of government and head of the almost single party. This concentration of power enabled Presidents Miguel de la Madrid (1982–88) and Carlos Salinas de Gortari (1988–94) to overcome the deep-seated national-statism of the Institutional Revolutionary Party (PRI) and implement the economic reforms that paved the way for Mexico to join the North American Free Trade Agreement in January 1994. Successive electoral reforms since 1978 enabled the opposition to strengthen its representation in the lower house from 17 percent of seats to 48 percent in 1988 and 52 percent in 1997, leaving President Ernesto Zedillo (1994–2000) with a minority in Congress in the second half of his term. The 2000 presidential election brought the democratic routine of party alternation and made Mexico a member of the club of presidents in "*doble minoría*." National Action Party (PAN) candidate Vicente Fox was elected president (2000–2006) with 48 percent of the votes and failed to win congressional approval for his main fiscal, energy, and labor reforms.

The PRI's hegemony for more than 70 years forged a peculiar mechanism whereby the party controlled its representatives: prohibition of reelection to Congress. Without the possibility of a second consecutive term, congressmen depended on the party for access to other elective offices or political appointments. Far from questioning this legacy the PAN and Party of the Democratic Revolution (PRD), which grew in the electoral soil lost by the PRI, used it to increase the power of their national leaderships. One wonders whether this party setup will lead to negotiating and coalition practices similar to those of today's Chile or to a three-sided tug of war more like that of Chile before Pinochet.

2.4. Unique to Brazil: Strong Congress, Weak Parties

The iron law of what in Brazil has been called "coalition presidentialism" says that to maintain a stable majority in Congress, the president must share power in the executive sphere by appointing representatives of allied parties to seats in the cabinet and other positions.[19] If power sharing safeguards the president, other political actors, and the nation from the unforeseeable consequences of an impasse between president and Congress, it does not in itself guarantee the support of a majority in Congress for the legislative measures proposed by the executive. This has to be won vote by vote, bill by bill, in a Sisyphean labor for the president and the inner circle—within which the function of "political coordinator," normally performed by a minister with an office in the presidential palace, stands out as a high-turnover job.

The key problem here is that except for the so-called left-wing parties, from the variants of communist origin to the PT, Brazilian parties have little control over how their elected members vote in Congress. Although some people insist on seeing our parties through European eyes, Brazilian society is entirely different. It has less hierarchy, more mobility, far fewer stable reference points. Ideologies are too weak to define behavior. Under the dictatorship there was a straightforward alternative: some supported the regime, others fought for democracy. In a free country other choices are available. At the same time, however, there is less difference between the ideologies professed by the parties. Their platforms are very similar, and unfortunately so are their practices.

Unlike the Argentine and Chilean dictatorships, the Brazilian military kept Congress open and shut down existing parties on two occasions: in 1965, when it imposed a two-party system, and in 1979, when it abolished that system. This effectively truncated evolution of the party system. The Brazilian dictatorship itself did not leave behind an electorally competitive right-wing party or bloc, as did the Chilean, and this in turn deprived the democratic forces of a common adversary that could prevent them from dispersing. Several leaders and some of the old parties reappeared, but the political system was reorganized on a different basis: first, for a short time, it revolved around the PMDB; more recently, it has revolved around the polarization between the PT and PSDB.

Moreover, we have an electoral system that tends to push the weakness of party discipline to extremes. The existence of a large number of parties is a typical effect of proportional representation, particularly in a large heterogeneous federation like Brazil. The weak link between elected representatives and their parties is characteristic of the open-list proportional representation system adopted in Brazil, where a candidate's position on a party list depends on the number of votes he or she receives individually.

Adopted in the 1940s when Brazilian society was still predominantly rural with strongly oligarchic features, this system has long shown signs of fatigue. In a democratic mass society with whole states for electoral districts, in which hundreds of candidates contest seats in the lower house, individually competing for tens of thousands of votes, the open-list system has become a game of roulette in which the "banker"—economic power and influential corporations embedded in the state apparatus, in the private sector, or worse still in the interface between the two— always wins in the end. The rate of reelection to the Chamber of Deputies remains low at 50 percent or less, but the high turnover does not mean renewal in any measurable sense, let alone improvements in quality. Election campaigns are growing more and more expensive. Congressmen's chances of reelection depend less and less on whether they perform their duties well as a lawmaker and scrutinizer of the government's actions, and more and more on how well they cater to local or sectoral clienteles. This makes the typical congressman a representative in search of people to represent, that is, of new clienteles for whom he or she strives to cater via amendments to the budget, government favors, or legal advantages. Thus we have a representative system in which "representation," if any, is postelectoral.

In practice, this form of relationship between congressmen, parties, and the electorate, as well as the executive, makes it difficult to characterize our system of government with precision. How can one properly speak of "coalition presidentialism" when the fragmentation of interests and power foci overflow party channels? The notion is useful but needs to be contextualized. It would be greatly preferable to be able to organize stable party alliances and coalitions. In fact, the "imperial" aspect of Brazilian presidentialism derives less from the will of the president than from the effective conditions under which politics functions. Given the relative weakness of the parties and the strength of Congress, regardless of what the president wants, if one lacks strength then patronage (or "*fisiologismo*," to use the popular term for the system whereby congressmen lobby for material and political public resources) predominate over the government's capacity to define and implement an agenda of change for the nation.

Executive-legislative relations become much more volatile in the context of this type of representation. This is why attempts at building an "institutional" relationship between president and parties produce precarious results. For the same reason political negotiations, however legitimate, are seen by the public as "horse trading" and "logrolling": they are conducted almost individually or, in the case of "parliamentary fronts," by caucuses comprising members of an array of different parties, ranging for example from the PT (left-wing) to the PPB (right-wing), who join forces to pursue a specific goal, such as farm debt relief, opposition to the easing of restrictions on abortion, or advocacy of parliamentarianism.

Nevertheless, with all its delays, peculiarities, and convolutions Congress represents the interests and visions existing in society. It is up to the government (and especially the president) to understand the rules of the democratic game. The president must be balanced enough to realize that the obstructions, amendments, and feints of the legislature often create the opportunity for understandings that produce better results. Not always, of course, and in such cases it is the president's responsibility to put the foot down, insofar as the rules of the game allow. And if even then results are not forthcoming, then the participants must go back to public opinion and persistently defend decisions and points of view. This is why in a democracy the battles are incessant and the improvements, incremental.

Tension is inevitable between the president's roles as representative of the majority of the nation and organizer of a parliamentary majority. Without alliances the president cannot govern. But neither can the president govern, in the sense of carrying out the political agenda, if it is "surrendered" to Congress.

Alliances to what end? Just to stay in power or to achieve broader goals? This question must be faced right at the start of one's term, when the parties (the president's, those of the allies, or, when even with these alliances a majority cannot be assured, those of the former adversaries) sit down with a voracious appetite to discuss what shares they will each have in the spoils of power. This is the time to appoint a cabinet and leaders in Congress (to control and manage the lower and upper houses as well as lead the coalition caucus). The broader goals set limits to the concessions made to allies and the president's own party. If the president is not capable of identifying and safeguarding those parts of the executive that are essential to the implementation of the agenda, the wrong people may end up being appointed to key positions. In our case the economic area, including ministries and federal financial institutions, and the most important portfolios in the social area, starting with health and education, were not included in any power-sharing deals. Privatization of many large state-owned enterprises took out of the equation dozens of top executive positions that had traditionally been part of these negotiations. The introduction of formal procedures to choose regional and middle managers in social security, land reform, and environmental protection, among others, had the same effect. Otherwise, even in positions open to nomination by allied parties it proved possible to match political criteria, technical competence, and alignment with the government's goals.

Members of the opposition and other critics of the government accused us of subjecting Congress to a "steamroller," lubricated by handouts of jobs and budget allocations. In fact, the scope for political appointments was made narrower for the reasons given above, as was the scope for so-called parochial amendments after a scandal involving members of the budget committee in 1993. If the preferential granting of jobs and funds were the key to assuring a progovernment majority in Congress, it would be impossible to explain how we enjoyed broader support for a longer time to pass a much larger and more complex reform agenda and with far fewer resources with which to bargain than previous governments.

In our view, the key to the majority was none of the above, but the project itself: the "mission" legitimized by the ballot box and public opinion, and in whose name the government made alliances and sought backing in Congress. Common sense suggests that the more the government asks of Congress in terms of lawmaking, the higher the price it must be prepared to pay in "retail" negotiations with the parliamentarians who support it. Our experience suggests the contrary: the consistency of the government's legislative agenda, with its overarching commitment to "holding on tight to the real," did not hinder but rather facilitated the task (in itself always arduous) of keeping the extent to which specific demands from parties and allies were met within reasonable limits.

Support from the street is no substitute for support from the parties. Without stable party alliances it would have been hard for the government to overcome the 1999 foreign-exchange crisis, when the commitment to saving the real seemed momentarily endangered and the president's ratings took a plunge. A combination of tactical flexibility to negotiate and renegotiate a parliamentary majority and strategic obstinacy to pursue the key points of the reform agenda made it possible to traverse the inevitable ups and downs in presidential popularity while maintaining both the majority and the direction of the government (see Graeff 2000).

2.5. Turning the Page on National-Statism

The "mission" that legitimizes the president's actions is almost always couched by the people in generic terms, although not necessarily vague ones: controlling inflation, eradicating poverty, creating more jobs, fighting crime. The leaders must translate these diffuse expectations into a *project*, a sequence of actions that consistently lead toward the desired common good. Succeeding in this goal depends on the scope of the leaders' *vision*—the understanding of the country's past and outlook on its future—and the ability to assemble a team to formulate and implement concrete measures in accordance with this vision.

Our efforts to translate the mission of controlling inflation into a more ambitious reform project would have to surmount one major obstacle: the national-statist vision with which Brazilian culture and political institutions are imbued, and a constellation of interests linked to that vision. Politicians were not alone in the relative backwardness of their discussion of these issues in Brazil. As elsewhere, a significant number of intellectuals remained attached to a basically statist vision—self-labeled left-wing, socialist, nationalist, or progressive—even after the collapse of the Soviet Union and the acceleration of capitalist globalization had resoundingly discredited statism. Surprising alliances were seen between these fellow travelers. In discussions on fiscal adjustment, the traditional budgetary populism of those who advocate "spending now and the money will turn up later" often resorted to the pseudo-Keynesian arguments of economists venerated by the Left.

The influence sustained by national-statism in Brazil is proportional to the advances it claimed in the last century. Brazil's economy grew more than any other between 1930 and 1980. Industrialization by import substitution bequeathed an industrial base unrivaled in Latin America, vast, diversified, and, as became clear after the economic opening, reasonably competitive. Expansion of the protected domestic market sustained levels of employment at a time of explosive demographic and urban growth. The *varguista* state extended to the masses who had only recently flooded into the towns a precarious web of social protection but one that was unprecedented and far better than the insecurity to which they were exposed in the countryside.

Economic decline in the 1980s sapped the strength of the military regime but confidence in the old form of the state and its economic model remained unscathed. Most delegates to the Constituent Assembly (1987–88) assumed that democracy would be enough to put the national locomotive back on the rails of development, merely adding safeguards for individual and social rights to the pillars of the autarkic statist economy. (The same credo, by the way, was expressed by Alfonsín in his vibrant inauguration address as president of Argentina in 1983: "Con la democracia se come, se educa y se cura.")

Besides attachment to the past, alongside special interests best accommodated under the mantle of state protection, what fueled the resistance to change was a lack of clear alternatives—an ideological fog that now shrouded, now merged with the institutional obstacles to decision making. The alternatives were not self-evident, in fact. Unlike Mexico, Brazil did not have the largest capitalist economy in the world on its doorstep offering purportedly unlimited possibilities for trade and industrial integration and an exit for surplus labor. Over 10 times the size of Chile, it could not afford to confine itself to modernizing and diversifying exports of primary goods to secure jobs and incomes for its population. Exports of manufactures, in which the military regime invested with some success, took time to be recognized not as a mutually exclusive alternative but as a complement to expansion of the domestic market.

In any event, a critique of the national-statist vision matured in the five years between promulgation of the constitution and the Real Plan, driven by shock waves from the fall of the Berlin Wall and the realization that advancing information technology and the formation of regional economic blocs had opened a new stage of global capitalism. Initially waged outside the political system, the debate among specialists (mainly economists) in a few universities, centers of excellence belonging to the federal administration, and research institutions linked to trade associations gradually distilled a new vision of Brazil and its place in the world, alongside proposals for a development strategy to match the new reality. Collor embraced some of these proposals in the name of a vague "modernity." His meteoric passage shook the political world and created more room for discussion of the reforms in the media. By taking presidential intervention in politics and the economy to the ultimate level, he may actually have helped to convince public opinion of the need for a leader who without retreating into a vision of the past would be capable of restoring confidence in a less traumatic reform agenda.

When the gathering inflation crisis after Collor's impeachment crossed the threshold of society's tolerance and lowered resistance to change in Congress, a sufficiently mature agenda was ready to be offered to the nation. Our thoughts on this subject had advanced during the Constituent Assembly. The manifesto of the PSDB, founded in July 1988 by a group of dissidents who had split from the PMDB, incorporated many of the new ideas we would try to put into practice after the Real Plan was launched: less protectionism and more technological development; less corporatism and more permeability of the state to grassroots demands and participation. We criticized both the dyed-in-the-wool advocates of state monopoly and those who saw any state intervention as a threat to the market economy. Nationalization versus privatization, we warned, was a false problem when reduced to a matter of principle, without taking into account the limits and possibilities of state and private action in each sector.

It was too late to try to dissuade the Constituent Assembly from bowing to the pressure of corporatist and national-statist opinions. Later, however, when the Real Plan opened a window of opportunity, the conversation with reformist sectors of society gave us both the intellectual critical mass and the support of public opinion to move forward. The presence of a hybrid of intellectual and politician at the head of the Finance Ministry, and later as president, helped build and sustain a bridge between the government, the parties, and Congress, on one hand, and reformist groups in the universities, the techno-bureaucracy, and the business community, on the other.

Once we had defined an alternative direction and dispersed the ideological fog, resistance to change came to the fore, led by a battle-hardened minority parliamentary opposition with the PT at its core and an important segment of the labor movement, whose main constituency was among public-sector workers in the state apparatus and SOEs.

The debate about the reforms never reached the point of causing a split in society. When it became apparent that this could happen, the government preferred to limit its goals rather than fueling polarizations that might undermine democracy itself. On several occasions, however, just before difficult votes in Congress, the president appealed publicly to the sectors favorable to the government's proposals. Not in order to force Congress's hand but to counterbalance adverse pressures and legitimize the aye votes that the majority were disposed to cast—albeit without much enthusiasm, as in the case of pension reform.

The interplay of presidential leadership, Congress, and organized sectors of society would have left out the vast majority of the population and would therefore have produced limited results if it had not been for the intervention of another fundamental political instance in today's world: public opinion mediated and engendered by the mass media. Brazil is a country with relatively few readers, but with vast numbers of people who regularly watch television or listen to the radio—virtually the entire population, in fact. The supply of information from both sources, radio and television, is reasonably pluralistic and independent. The political strength of the masses informed by the electronic media made itself felt for the first time in the 1984 campaign for direct presidential elections ("Diretas Já"), which heralded the end of the military regime. All important political developments since then have evidenced the same phenomenon, from the indirect election of Tancredo Neves to the presidency to the impeachment of Collor, from the Cruzado Plan to the Real Plan, and including all the elections in between.

The presence of this diffuse actor profoundly changes the ways in which power is democratically wielded. It is not enough to be voted into office, even with tens of millions of votes, or to be vested with legal authority. Legitimation of decisions requires an unremitting effort to explain the reasons for them and convince public opinion. We made intensive use of the media to explain every step of the Real Plan and the reforms, and to sustain the support of public opinion.

Objective missteps—the abrupt floating of the exchange rate in January 1999, above all, whose inflationary impact was absorbed but which impaired society's confidence in the government—and subjective difficulties in sustaining our political agenda in the public debate cost us the 2002 presidential election. Although obviously undesired by the outgoing group, the alternation in power, planned and conducted with serenity by both the incumbent and the president-elect, proved to be an acid test not only for the consolidation of democracy but for the reform agenda itself.

Lula surprised foreign investors, the nation, and most of his own party by exchanging the rhetoric of radical opposition to the "neoliberal model" for an explicit commitment to the premises of stability and economic openness. He also maintained the fundamental premise of political stability by opting—also against the PT's hegemonistic impulses—for a broad coalition, including parties in the center and on the right in order to assure a majority in Congress.

This is not the place to emphasize the differences that persist between the poles symbolized by the PT and PSDB. The fact is that the political process has somehow reduced the intensity of those differences. No longer does anyone advocate demolishing one form of state and laying the foundations of another. In practice this issue has been decided, although it still echoes in the public debate. The dispute between "monetarists" and "developmentalists," which was a heated one inside our administration and has recently come to the fore, does not call into question concepts such as privatization, trade liberalization, or fiscal responsibility. The political cost of specific changes in these areas will tend to diminish from now on. And at least in theory this makes room on the agenda for other topics on which little progress has been made, such as tax, judicial, and electoral reforms.

3. OPPORTUNITY, PASSION, AND PERSPECTIVE

In complex societies change sometimes comes about through a "short circuit." A gesture, a strike, an emotional shock, or a galvanizing proposal can trigger a chain reaction that leads to far deeper transformations than imagined or desired at the outset. This also depends, of course, on the history of the demands, class conflicts, ideological strife, and frustrations that existed beforehand. This is what happened with the Real Plan. Tired of inflation and its negative effects, Brazilian society saw the Real Plan as a solution and backed it against the opinions of many people and many vested interests—at certain times, indeed, against a majority of *bien-pensants* and leaders who claimed to "own" the masses.

"Responsible pragmatism," however, does not explain the change. Without leaders who can present a perspective accepted as valid by the majority, significant transformations do not happen in a democratic society. And that acceptance is not blindly given. There has to be a democratic pedagogy, persuasion, an effort to "win together"; otherwise the traditional order prevails over the forces of modernization and change.

The inflationary crisis opened eyes and ears of society, including both influential organized sectors and the unorganized mass of voters, to proposals for change that in other circumstances would have been ignored or rejected. The fact that a leadership was there with the ability to take advantage of this window of opportunity was ultimately a fortunate accident. Pressing ahead with the changes required much obstinacy and some art.

Implementing policy is a collective process. We insist on the word *process*. The media, public opinion, Congress, and members of the government itself often expect and even beg for an act, for a heroic gesture, that can rapidly resolve the problems faced by the citizenry or cater to the interests of a group. The latter may perhaps be catered to by a heroic gesture, but not the interests of an entire nation. That depends on continuous action to change practices, mind-sets, and structures.

It is no accident that reform is so difficult or that anyone who genuinely desires change sometimes feels lonely. Structures resist change. Vested interests oppose them. Having a dream is part and parcel of the art of politics, whether in the older forms of ideologies, or, in modern times, inspired to a greater extent by visions than by certainties. In any event, it is always necessary to have goals and to strive to achieve them, even if they are limited to holding on to power for its own sake. And there is a permanent interplay between national and international structures (parties, churches, labor unions, companies, multilateral organizations, civil and military bureaucracies, the media), on one hand, and movements, proposals, and leaders, on the other, alongside a continuous search for ways of persuading more people and building up more strength to achieve one's goals.

If you overlook one side, whether the established order, albeit antiquated or apparently fragile, or the forces that can lead to change, with their proposals and working toward the new, albeit based on the old, you make no progress. How many times in our eagerness to pursue change are we obliged to make concessions to the other side? When the journey begins there are no certainties about who will win the wager. Political will and firmness in pursuing the goal do not assure victory. The outcome will always depend on the actions of many and the repercussions of the actions and desires of those in command.

How can a head of government, for example, promise to create a certain number of jobs if the economic variables are not utterly under control? Changes in technology, capital flows, corporate strategies, and a huge number of factors directly influence the level of employment, often dramatically reducing the number of jobs in a specific sector. The leader can, and obviously should, be committed to implementing ideas, adopting programs, and taking measures designed to improve the economic situation and increase employment, but it would be misleading to promise hard numbers.

Pragmatism with clearly defined goals involves a calculation and a wager. The calculation relates to the support required to implement the government's overall policy, even when it is detrimental to specific targets. The wager has to do with the leader's belief in the capacity of inducing (or, if necessary, forcing) allies, including the last-minute ones, to accept the goals set.

The risk of losing control of the process or of the government betraying its commitments is permanent. Reform is a dangerous adventure, because even with the best of intentions a mistaken wager can be made. Success depends on objective conditions as well as dispositions that are neither defined nor limited by the broader circle of power alone. People will be indifferent to the will and motivation of the principals, and in certain circumstances even to their successes, if the latter are not sufficiently broad and consistent enough in their vision to convince the majority.

In any event, politics is not just a continuation of war by other means, nor is it the substitution for force by submission. It is not a method for counting and separating the good from the bad. It is the art of persuading the "bad" to become "good," or at least to act as if they were, even if they do so for fear of the consequences. It is the art of transforming enemies into adversaries, adversaries possibly into allies. When cooptation occurs instead of persuasion (by different means), politics is replaced by bartering between petty interests. The drama is that the borderline between greatness and perdition is very thin indeed.

To practice this difficult art, it is not indispensable to have acquired academic training or even to spend many hours reading. Several noteworthy leaders have done neither. But a certain comprehension of history is a great help. At a time when everything is "of the world," everything is global, it is necessary to have a reasonable vision of the totality and to be capable of understanding the social conditions of one's day and age, in order to be able to exercise effective leadership, not to make a tabula rasa of what others have done but to give a better direction to what has come from the past and lay the foundations for what one wants for the future.

It also helps to have a "persuadable" temperament, to borrow a term from Jane Austen. Democracy today is a process in which the citizenry wants to participate not just by voting or even approving (in a referendum, for example) but also by deliberating. Albert Hirschman, contradicting the tradition that values vigorous and rigid political opinions, has stressed the importance of opinions being formed not before but during the process of discussion and deliberation. Open minds, spirits psychologically more inclined to convergence and compromise, who favor dialogue, among both leaders and led, would therefore be better suited to playing the democratic game on a long-term basis (see Hirschman 1995).

This shake-up in today's world has made Cicero highly relevant again, in his praise of rhetoric as a foundation for the education of the Prince. For him the noblest way of life is devotion to virtuous public service. Friendship among men, goodwill, enables good government to be grounded in the free cooperation of citizens. For these values to sustain the republic, there must be laws and people must be persuaded of their validity, which in turn requires that the statesman be capable of using reason and emotion. The interplay of these two qualities develops through what was called "rhetoric," the basis for persuasion. Obedience is obtained not through fear and coercion, but through reason and love built upon a kind of Socratic dialogue and embodying the apex of leadership.[20]

The word is the "message" in our time, and the means for its diffusion is no longer the pulpit or tribune but the electronic media. The impact of radio, and later television, could already be seen in the "mass politics" that characterized Fascist and authoritarian mobilizations in general, and that served as cement for Third World populism. Now it is democratic politics itself that appeals to these media and the Internet. Everything happens in real time regardless of physical distance, but with a difference: the Internet is essentially interactive, and little by little radio, television, and even newspapers and magazines are creating democratic spaces for the "man in the street."

Everything is made easier when there are symbols that help people visualize change. Politics deals with symbolic content, and leaders seek to exercise the modern form of what Gramsci called cultural hegemony, albeit with a different connotation. This requires an "actor's" qualities, although these cannot be dissociated from the individual's prior experience.

In the interplay between symbolism and practical achievements, leaders must be capable, through intuition or knowledge, of elaborating and transmitting a "vision" of the problems they face, a vision of society and the nation. In the case of politicians with a national following, given the framework of globalization, they must have some feeling of world affairs. Statesmanship is projecting the nation's future, seeing it in the world context, and being capable of leading it in that direction.

In a world of intercommunicating messages and increasing participation, democratic leaders, albeit conscious of class conflicts and differences, must propose values that can be shared by a majority of society. Otherwise they lose strength. Because their relationship with those they lead is not static, leaders will attempt to persuade them all the time, running the risk of losing some of the time but winning at other times. On those occasions when they win, they must strive to attract more and more people, groups, movements, and institutions to their side. When they lose, they must try to find out why, to identify the mistakes they made, and based on their convictions humbly to rebuild the widening circle of persuasion that can lead to victory.

At bottom, the capacity to symbolize and transmit messages is identical to the virtue of discerning and proposing to society a way forward that is acceptable to the led, albeit temporarily. In an interactive society this "project" cannot be conceived as an act of reason or will, but as a collective construction in which certain people—the leaders—express more completely and symbolize for a specific moment the movement of society, which is necessarily conditioned by values, by cultural models, with which and upon which they act. Leaders either point the way and blaze a trail or lose power.

But the personal attribute that is critical to the exercise of leadership, in the new politics as in the old, is still courage. Because there comes a time when it is indispensable to make decisions that upset a lot of people. It will even be necessary to make decisions almost alone, however "persuadable" one may be. A leader is someone who, once persuaded that an important decision is the right one to make, accepts only one attitude from oneself: making the decision. However hard it may be, a leader takes a road and resolves to move forward on it, even if it means swimming against the current, with persistence, because what can be seen farther ahead shows that this and not something else is what needs to be done.

Max Weber despised politicians who shrug off the consequences of their actions, blaming the pettiness of others or the world, cozily reliant on their own clear conscience and clean hands. Weber reserved his respect for the mature person (young or old) who in particular circumstances decides, "I must do this and nothing else," and takes responsibility for doing so. "That is something genuinely human and moving," he says. "In so far as this is true, an ethic of ultimate ends and an ethic of responsibility are not absolute contrasts but rather supplements, which only in unison constitute a genuine man—a man who can have the 'calling for politics'" (Weber 1958, 127).

The possibility proposed by Weber of reconciling pragmatism with ethical values and limits that transcend immediate circumstances is encouraging for a political leader in government who wonders, as we so often wondered, about the ability of implementing the necessary changes with the necessary speed by the meandering highways and byways of democracy.

Let us stay with Weber for our conclusion:

> Politics is a strong and slow boring of hard boards. It takes both passion and perspective. Certainly all historical experience confirms the truth—that man would not have attained the possible unless time and again he had reached out for the impossible. But in order to do that, a man must be a leader, and not only a leader but a hero as well, in a very sober sense of the word. And even those who are neither leaders nor heroes must arm themselves with that steadfastness of heart which can brave even the crumbling of all hopes. (1958, 128)

The experience of Brazil, like that of other important countries in Latin America, gives us reasons to keep alive our hopes for democratic reforms and renewal of the political agenda.

NOTES

1. The quotation and the points about Tolstoy are from Berlin (1979).
2. This was the approach used to analyze "dependency situations" in Latin America by Enzo Faletto and Fernando Henrique Cardoso in the 1960s. See Cardoso and Faletto (1979).
3. An earlier version of this chapter was originally developed for the Commission on Growth and Development. A more detailed account of the Brazilian experience of stabilization and economic reform can be seen in Cardoso (2006).

4. A representative sample of this view can be found in papers delivered by Brazilian and American experts at a conference organized by the University of Miami and Fundação Getúlio Vargas in late 1991. See Marks (1993).

5. One of us (Cardoso) was the fourth finance minister.

6. The implicit rationale for this marriage was that nominal revenue growth coupled with corrosion of expected expenditure in real terms guaranteed a balanced budget a posteriori, or something along these lines, allowing the government and Congress to avoid the discomfort of negotiating priorities and spending cuts a priori.

7. See the Explanatory Memoranda to the July 1993 Immediate Action Plan and the July 1994 measure that introduced the real. Both can be accessed at the Finance Ministry's website: http://www.fazenda.gov.br/portugues/real/realhist.asp.

8. In reference to Getúlio Vargas.

9. Mauricio Font speaks of "structural realignment" in referring to the balance of change in Brazil in this period. See Font (2003). For an analysis of the reforms by Brazilian scholars, some of whom participated actively in their implementation, see Giambiagi, Reis, and Urani (2004).

10. The Brazilian constitution, including all amendments, is available at http://www.planalto.gov.br/ccivil_03/Constituicao/Constitui%E7ao.htm.

11. Unless otherwise noted, all data on GDP, unemployment, and inflation in Latin American countries are from the World Bank, compiled for this chapter by Juliana Wenceslau at the Brasília office of the International Bank for Reconstruction and Development.

12. For a detailed analysis of the economic and social orientations and achievements of Concertación-led governments compared with the legacy of the dictatorship, see Raczynski and Serrano (2005).

13. On this subject, see Siavelis (2000).

14. On Argentina's experience with stabilization and reform, see Palermo (2004).

15. The distinction between majoritarian and consensual democracy is explored in Lijphart (1984).

16. The Brazilian constitution authorizes the president in cases of urgency to issue provisional measures with the force of law, which lose validity unless they are ratified by Congress in 90 days.

17. Linz and Valenzuela (1994) is representative of this type of approach.

18. For analyses that emphasize possibilities for executive-legislative cooperation, despite the conflict, see Morgenstern and Nacif (2002).

19. The Brazilian institutional system up to 1964 was first characterized as "coalition presidentialism" by Abranches (1988).

20. To understand the topicality of Cicero, see ch. 6 of the excellent book by Gerard B. Wegemer (1996).

REFERENCES

Abranches, Sérgio. 1998. "Presidencialismo de Coalizão: O Dilema Institucional Brasileiro." *Dados* 31(1): 5–33.

Alfonsín, Raúl. 1983. Inaugural Address to the Ordinary Sessions of Congress. Buenos Aires, December 1.

Berlin, Isaiah. 1979. "The Hedgehog and the Fox." In *Russian Thinkers*, by Isaiah Berlin, edited by Henry Hardy and Aileen Kelly, 22–80. London: Penguin Books.

Cardoso, Fernando Henrique. 2006. *A Arte da Política: A História que Vivi*. Rio de Janeiro: Civilização Brasileira.

Cardoso, Fernando Henrique, and Enzo Faletto. 1979. *Dependency and Development in Latin America*. Translated by Marjory Mattingly Urquidi. Berkeley: University of California Press.

Font, Maurício. 2003. *Transforming Brazil: A Reform Era in Perspective*. Lanham, MD: Rowman and Littlefield.

Giambiagi, Fábio, José Guilherme Reis, and André Urani, eds. 2004. *Reformas no Brasil: Balanço e Agenda*. Rio de Janeiro: Nova Fronteira.

Graeff, Eduardo. 2000. "The Flight of the Beetle: Party Politics and the Decision-Making Process in the Cardoso Government." Paper presented to the 5th Congress of the Brazilian Studies Association, Recife, Brazil, June 2000. Translated by Ted Goertzel. Available at http://www.crab.rutgers.edu/~goertzel/flightofbeetle.htm.

Hirschman, Albert O. 1981. "The Social and Political Matrix of Inflation: Elaborations on the Latin American Experience." In *Essays in Trespassing: Economics to Politics and Beyond*, by Albert O. Hirschman, 177–208. Cambridge: Cambridge University Press.

———. 1995. "Opinionated Opinions and Democracy." In *A Propensity to Self-Subversion*, by Albert O. Hirschman, 77–84. Cambridge, MA: Harvard University Press.

Landerretche M., Oscar. 2005. "Construyendo solvencia fiscal: El éxito macroeconómico de la Concertación." In *La paradoja aparente: Equidad y eficiencia: Resolviendo el dilema*, edited by Patricio Meller, 83–137. Santiago: Aguilar Chilena.

Lijphart, Arend. 1984. *Democracies: Patters of Majoritarian and Consensus Government in Twenty-One Countries*, 177–207. New Haven, CT: Yale University Press.

Lins, Juan, and Arturo Valenzuela, eds. 1994. *The Failure of Presidential Democracy: The Case of Latin America*. Vol. 2. Baltimore: Johns Hopkins University Press.

Marks, Siegfried. 1993. *Political Constraints on Brazil's Economic Development: Rio de Janeiro Conference Edited Proceedings and Papers*. Miami: North-South Center Press.

Morgenstern, Scott, and Benito Nacif, eds. 2002. *Legislative Politics in Latin America*. Cambridge: Cambridge University Press.

Palermo, Vicente. 2004. "Melhorar para piorar? A dinâmica política das reformas estruturais e as raízes do colapso da convertibilidade." In *Brasil e Argentina Hoje: Política e Economia*, edited by Brasílio Sallum Jr., ch. 3. Bauru, Brazil: EDUSC.

Petracca, Orazio M. 2004. "Liderança." In , *Dicionário de Política*, edited by Norberto Bobbio, Nicola Matteucci, and Gianfranco Pasquino, 713–16. São Paulo: Editora UnB; IMESP.

Raczynski, Dagmar, and Claudia Serrano. 2005. "Las políticas y estrategias de desarrollo social: Aportes de los años 90 y desafíos futuros." In *La paradoja aparente: Equidad yeficiencia: Resolviendo el dilema*, edited by Patricio Meller, 259–60. Santiago: Aguilar Chilena.

Siavelis, Peter M. 2000. *The President and Congress in Postauthoritarian Chile: Institutional Constraints to Democratic Consolidation*. University Park: Pennsylvania State University Press.

Torre, Juan Carlos. 2004. "A crise da representação partidária na Argentina." In . *Brasil e Argentina Hoje: Política e Economia*, edited by Brasílio Sallum Jr., ch. 4. Bauru, Brazil: EDUSC.

Weber, Max. 1958. "Politics as a Vocation." In *From Max Weber: Essays in Sociology*, edited by Hans Gerth and C. Wright Mills, 77–128. Oxford: Oxford University Press.

Wegemer, Gerard B. 1996. *Thomas More on Statesmanship*. Washington, DC: Catholic University of America Press.

CHAPTER 2

POLITICS OF FISCAL REFORMS IN PERU

LUIS CARRANZA

1. INTRODUCTION

Reforms in general, and fiscal reforms in particular, imply that the conditions under which agents and the state interact change. These changes affect agents' current or future flow of income, creating winners and losers, and hence different groups of interest. The implementation of reforms is a political process, where interests of every actor involved are represented directly or indirectly in the decision-making institutions. (See Stein and Tommasi 2008.)

Tax-collection actions; defining where, how, and in what ways to spend; and determining the size of fiscal imbalances are carried out considering three objectives: macroeconomic stability, the search for efficiency, and achieving as much equality as possible (see Musgrave 1961). Fiscal policies' implementation or their reforms will imply, therefore, that someone will pay more or less taxes and that someone will receive more or less transfers from the government. Moreover, frequently this conflict of interests is solved with overindebtedness, which means that the society's discount rate is very high and that society prefers to penalize future generations. (See Hiebert, Perez, and Rostagno 2002.)

Usually in a country with political instability, a fragile democracy, the lack of the rule of law, and weak institutions, political reforms are hard to implement. Moreover, if there is poverty and inequality that generate social conflicts in the country, citizens and politicians value much higher short-term benefits over long-term goals,[1] making it even harder for structural reforms to be implemented. However, the case of Peru is a clear counterexample, worthwhile to study. In spite of all those obstacles, strong fiscal and monetary institutions helped Peru overcome various crises, emerging from bankruptcy at the beginning of the 1990s to attain an economy with investment grade 20 years later. It is a clear example that political and structural reforms can be made when there is the real will to carry them out.

The next section explains the reforms implemented during the last two decades, enhancing economic and fiscal results. After that, I describe the actors and then analyze the reforms' processes. Later, I present three reform case studies: pension reform, tariffs reduction, and the Public Educational Career reform.

2. From Hyperinflation to Investment Grade

The Peruvian economy began the 1990s in a catastrophic state. During the previous decade, gross domestic product (GDP) per capita fell by 13.0 percent. Moreover, in 1990, real GDP growth was −5.1 percent and the inflation rate reached 7,649.6 percent. Fiscal collection was 10.9 percent of GDP and the fiscal deficit 8.7 percent of GDP, and there was no access to international capital markets because of the debt default during the 1980s. It was a country in bankruptcy.

After a macroeconomic stabilization process, with significant changes in fiscal, monetary, and financial policies, which also involved important structural changes in the economy, the economy stabilized and began growing (see fig. 2.1).[2] These structural changes included financial liberalization, commercial liberalization, and a privatization process, among others.

By the end of the 1990s, a succession of events in international markets provoked a contagion effect in other emerging countries. The Asian crisis during mid-1997, the Russian crisis in 1998, and the Brazilian crisis in January 1999 generated a fall in terms of trade and a restriction of capital flow, which translated into domestic credit restrictions, depreciation of the real exchange rate, and the weakening of investors' confidence. All of these elements led to a significant fall in private investment and hence in domestic demand.

This crisis made evident some structural problems in the fiscal area: (1) the market's lack of confidence in the sustainability of public finances; (2) a harmful structure to the public debt, almost entirely denominated in foreign currencies and at flexible rates, extremely dependent on credit from multilateral organizations, and without a diversified investor base; (3) a strong vulnerability of social programs; and (4) a strong dependence of fiscal income on terms of trade. As a result of these deficiencies, countercyclical policies could not be implemented to avoid the decrease in domestic demand and to provide adequate social protection to address the rise in unemployment.

The government's response focused on addressing the first issue, the lack of credibility of agents with fiscal discipline. In December 1999, it enacted the Law of

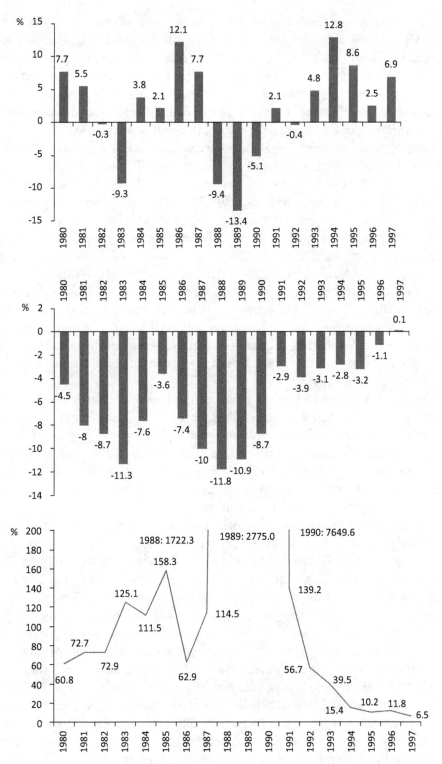

Figure 2.1 Results of structural changes in the stabilization process in Peru, 1990–97.
Note: GDP growth rate (top); fiscal deficit/surplus (middle); inflation rate (bottom).

Fiscal Prudency and Transparency (the name of which was later modified to the Law of Fiscal Responsibility), introducing fiscal rules related to balance as well as to expenditure, and created the Fiscal Stabilization Fund. The rules mandated that the fiscal deficit of the overall public sector should not be greater than 1 percent of GDP and the real annual growth rate of nonfinancial expenditure could not exceed 3 percent; there were escape clauses in case of national emergency or international crisis, with the goal of converging to the limits in a three-year period.[3]

The Peruvian economy began the 2000 decade in a deep economic depression and a severe political crisis due to the electoral process of the year 2000, the resignation of President Alberto Fujimori in November that same year, and the instauration of a transition government that would call general elections in 2001. The strength of economic institutions created during the previous decade allowed fiscal and monetary administration isolated from the political turbulence affecting the country during those years. Poor administration of public finances would have worsened the political chaos, as it would have generated inflation and overindebtedness.

According to Musgrave, the main goals of fiscal policy are linked to macroeconomic stability, efficiency, and equality. The implemented reforms targeted fixing fiscal accounts and fiscal instruments to reach those final goals. In order to do this, the government established a group of quantitative and qualitative targets that served as medium-range goals, similar to the role that inflation targeting played in stabilizing monetary policy.

In regard to stabilization, the philosophy is clearly stipulated in the second article of the Law of Fiscal Responsibility: to assure fiscal equilibrium or a surplus in the medium term. Officials implemented this philosophy through quantitative targets for deficit and expenditure growth. Another tool used to maintain stability was the active administration of public liabilities, expressed in the annual debt program, with the clear objective of reducing debt exposure to market risks and hence decreasing the vulnerability of public finances.

In order to achieve the other two goals of efficiency and equality, the government managed incomes and expenditures of the public sector and began a decentralization process in 2003. In regard to fiscal income, long-term goals were to (1) broaden the tax base and (2) change the collection structure by relying on a value-added tax (VAT) and income tax, reducing international trade taxes, and administrating selective taxes by fine-tuning them with externalities and not to the collection effect they had. As broadening the tax base through eliminating exemptions or by reducing fiscal evasion takes time, the tax restructuring process was (and is still) gradual, with a fundamental aim being maintaining the fiscal balance in a structural way. As for expenditures, the imposed goals, once expenditure growth was controlled , were to (1) improve expenditure efficiency, for capital expenditure as well as for current expenditure; (2) recompose the structure of public expenditure in order to achieve a public investment ratio of the GDP between 6 percent and 7 percent; and (3) reduce inequalities and control the government's pension expenditure.

A strong political will led the decentralization process and, despite this reform being quite important politically, in terms of achieving Musgrave's goals, there has not been much advance. Moreover, there was a partial setback, since political will did not equate to respect for basic economic principles such as economies of scale, gradualism, and accreditation processes. The next section describes the reforms implemented during the past decade.

2.1. Tax Reforms

The tax measures adopted were mostly oriented to broadening the tax base, eliminating or reducing taxes distorting economic activity, and addressing tax evasion. To broaden the tax base, in 2007 a new program dismantled tax exemptions, including indirect taxes specific to a geographical region of the country (the Amazon) and income tax exemptions for capital gains. To avoid a harsh impact on prices, tax exemptions in the Amazon region were eliminated gradually, and the program is still in progress; while the abolition of tax exemptions for capital profits was issued in 2007 but did not become enforceable until 2010. Eliminating both exemptions will lead to an estimated increase of US$360 million per annum,[4] which represents a little over 0.2 percent of GDP and about 1.7 percent greater tax revenues.[5]

Additionally, because of the high degree of income-tax evasion by businesses, the reform included a retention of 0.5 percent from businesses' net assets, serving as a tax credit against income tax. Although this change could generate a financial problem for enterprises, such retention represents between 6.5 percent and 9.7 percent of total annual income tax collection, thus helping reduce income-tax evasion.[6] Likewise, since 2002, the government has implemented special systems for collecting VAT in economic activities where informality was high and tax evasion was hard to contain.[7] These measures contributed to increase tax collection by 2.4 percentage points of GDP.[8] In 2003, in addition, the VAT rate increased by 1 percentage point, from 18 percent to 19 percent.

Another set of measures aimed at reducing economic distortions and promoting private activity. The first reform significantly reduced tariffs reductions, dropping the effective tariff rate from 5.4 percent in 2006 to 1.9 percent in 2010. Taxes on gasoline were also reduced, in a gradual modification scheme based on their impact on pollution, thereby increasing the Pigouvian efficiency of gasoline taxes on pollution abatement. Likewise, in order to avoid distortions in the labor market, in December 2004 a payroll tax called the extraordinary tax for solidarity with a rate of 1.7 percent (originally destined for a housing fund and set at 9 percent) was abolished. In addition, to eliminate the VAT anti-investment bias, in 2007 the government implemented recovering schemes for anticipated VAT funds for new investments. Although these measures had a negative impact on tax collection, gains in efficiency and the impact on economic activity clearly compensated for the initial effect on tax collection.

However, Peru still has a long way to go, as the long-term ratio of tax revenues to GDP is less than half that observed in most countries in the Organisation for Economic Co-operation and Development (OECD). In 2007, the tax share of GDP in Peru was 15.6 percent while the unweighted average rate of all OECD countries was 35.8 percent.

2.2. Expenditure Policies

Public expenditure policies are very useful tools for achieving greater efficiency and equality in the economy. One of the key elements is to assure an adequate infrastructure to improve competitiveness in the economy. This is achieved only by improving the quality and quantity of public infrastructure. The first significant reform in this area was the creation of the Public Investment National System (SNIP) in 2000. The SNIP is an administrative system with the goal of optimizing the use of public resources destined for investment; it is a "quality control" and "resource allocation" mechanism which establishes that every public investment project must follow a project cycle including preinvestment, investment, and post-investment phases.

Concerning resources for public investment, the government's final adjustment at the end of the 1990s cut public investment, and during the first half of the next decade the increased revenue was mainly used for current expenditures, maintaining a public investment–GDP ratio lower than 3 percent. With the goal of increasing public investment, the government modified the Law of Fiscal Responsibility , kept the 1 percent of GDP limit for fiscal deficit, but set a ceiling of 4 percent for real growth of government consumption,[9] allowing increased investment expenditure without direct restrictions. This way, public investment grew from 2006 to 2009 at an average annual rate of 31 percent, reaching a level equivalent to 5.3 percent of GDP in 2009, and it was expected to end 2010 at a 6.1 percent level of GDP.

To improve the efficiency of public expenditure, performance-based budgeting (PBB) was introduced in 2007. It started with social programs receiving funding of US$871 million (4.1 percent of the total budget), and currently it includes 15 social programs representing 13.2 percent of the total budget.[10]

Socially, greater public investment and focalization of public expenditure had important effects on the population's welfare. In education, the enrollment rate in primary school is now over 93 percent,[11] although only 72 percent of the population between 18 and 24 years old finishes high school. Health indicators also show improvement, in such categories as infant mortality, contagious diseases, general and specialized obstetric care, and the share of the population with access to health establishments.[12] This improvement occurred because of the conjunction of several factors: increasing urbanization, greater access to water and sewage in urban areas, and higher educational levels. Also in health-related improvement, infant chronic malnutrition declined by 4.6 percentage points, from 22.9 percent to 18.3 percent between 2005 and 2009. This improvement has been accompanied by progress in anemia prevalence in infants under 36 months and the reduction in the incidence of acute respiratory infections in the same population group.

In 2005, the government introduced a pension reform, a key element of the fiscal reform since it ended an absolutely nonequitable scheme and thereby avoided a dangerous growth in public pensions that might have destabilizing effects on public finances. The Peruvian pension system is structured by three main components: Law 19990, Law 20530,[13] and the Private Pension System. The state administers the National Pensions System according to the two laws, while private entities named Pension Fund Private Administrators manage the Private Pension System. Section 5 explains the scope and detail of this reform.

In regard to current expenditures, the budget's main component is expenditure in wages and salaries. The question confronting reformers was how to design a wage scale that provides adequate incentives to motivate public servants in their work. This question is especially important since measuring goals is hardly quantitative and powerful unions exist in the public labor structure. The case study in section 5 examines this reform.

2.3. Public Debt Administration

The crisis at the end of the 1990s got worse because of the bad structure of public liabilities. In 2001 the portion of public debt in foreign currency was 91.7 percent and the portion at flexible interest rates was 52.1 percent. Additionally, domestic debt was illiquid, as it was linked to earmarked operations (bank bailout programs, pension bonds, etc.). With the support of multilateral organizations, a significant improvement process in debt administration and market risk control began. This process professionalized and modernized the National Directorate of Public Debt, and improved the legal processes of debt management.

A financial program of market risk reduction began, converting debt in foreign currency into domestic currency through swaps and prepayments financed by issuing long-term bonds in domestic currency. As a result, in 2009, debt in domestic currency represented 34.7 percent of total debt and debt exposed to fixed interest rates increased to 75.4 percent of total debt (fig. 2.2).

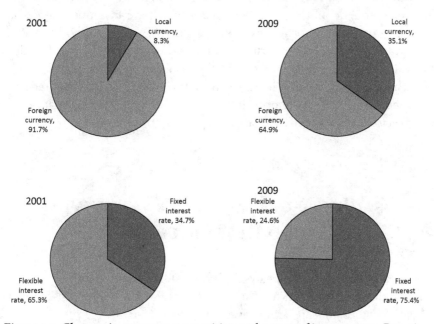

Figure 2.2 Changes in currency composition and nature of interest rates, Peruvian public debt, 2000–2009.

Public debt administration brought two positive consequences to the economy. First, it allowed the treasury to support the Central Bank in avoiding a steep appreciation in the nominal exchange rate, through its active participation in the exchange rate market by buying dollars for prepaying the external debt and for contributions to the Fiscal Stabilization Fund.[14] Second, it broadened and developed the domestic capital market. Issuing sovereign debt in domestic currency was part of a program called Market Makers, intended to build a long-term yield curve in domestic currency, thus serving as a benchmark in the capital market and hence contributing to its development, and later allowing issuance of long-term corporate bonds and mortgage loans in domestic currency.

2.4. General Fiscal Results

The implemented fiscal policies had a significant impact on public accounts and on economic performance (fig. 2.3). Public debt as a percentage of GDP fell to 26.6 percent, and there were fiscal surpluses in 2006, 2007, and 2008 of 2.1 percent, 3.1 percent, and 2.1 percent of GDP, respectively. Public investment grew significantly, giving an important impulse to economic competitiveness by reducing the infrastructure gap between Peru and other nations. The public debt reform also led to a reduction in the vulnerability of public finances to sudden cut-offs in accessibility, and, as mentioned before, to the development of the domestic capital market, giving it more depth and developing a yield curve. In fact, this reform was a fundamental element in the rapid reduction of poverty during recent years, the poverty rate dropping from 51.3 percent in 2003 to 34.8 percent in 2009.

Achievements in the fiscal and social arenas, together with the good performance of economic indicators, enabled Peru to achieve investment grade status from the three most important risk-rating agencies. In April 2008, Fitch Ratings gave a grade of BBB-, lifting Peru above the speculative debt rating. In July that same year, Standard & Poor's improved the Peruvian debt rating, and finally, in December 2009, Moody's also increased the debt rating to investment grade.

But how were all these reforms implemented? The next section examines how political actors interact with each other.

3. Political Actors: Incentives and Restrictions

Without entering into a deep analysis of political theory and political processes in Peru, I briefly describe political actors and their interaction during fiscal reforms. The main formal actors are: (1) the executive, comprising the president, the ministers, and subnational authorities, (2) the Congress, and (3) the judiciary.

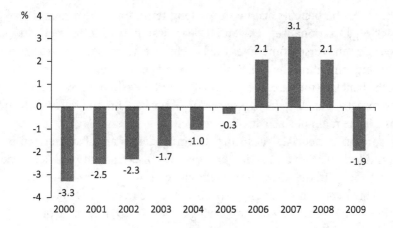

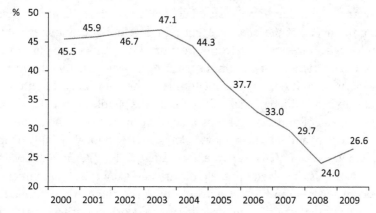

Figure 2.3 GDP growth rates (top) and public debt as a share of GDP (bottom),
Peru 2000–2009.

These formal actors have roles in the design and implementation processes of
public policies that are clearly assigned in the constitution and the nation's laws. In
a presidential system, the president is the head of state and the chief of government,
and designates the ministers of state. If there is political decentralization, subnational authorities are elected in direct elections. Besides formal actors, there are
informal actors such as social movements, business associations, labor unions, and
the media. These informal actors are affected by the reforms or have influence or
political interests in promoting or opposing certain reforms.[15]

The executive should lead the reform processes. The problem is that the goals of
the entities composing the executive are not aligned; on the contrary, sometimes
they are opposite to each other. In particular, when a change in the budget occurs,
ministers receive direct pressure from informal agents and the media, while the
president, together with the cabinet, must harmonize the opposing interests from
different sectors for the net benefit for the country, and must in doing so consider
certain restrictions or conditions.

Regarding net benefits, usually an administration or legislature pays political
costs for reforms in the short term, costs due to the pressure exerted by the affected

sectors, while the benefits accrue in the long term, for a great majority of people who lack organizational capacity and a clear awareness of future benefits (see Alesina 1994). Even worse, sometimes the benefits are perceived only after the administration implementing the policies is out of office, thus bearing the costs without seeing the benefits (they are not quantifiable, and they do not produce future votes). This asymmetry between the appropriation of the benefits and the responsibility for the costs is the main obstacle to adopting reforms.

According to neoclassical theory, laboring classes are characterized by impatience and lack of foresight, and, therefore, they discount future benefits too much (see Peart 2000). In this view, the average citizen is not always conscious of the benefits of the reforms. This lack of perspective leads to inadequate and inefficient allocation of results over time. Moreover, Irving Fisher's (1907) treatment of intertemporal consumption presumed not only that consumers lack foresight but that they are also overly impatient, and that poverty especially tends to distort the perspective by exaggerating the needs of the present. Hence, in developing economies with a high level of poverty and inequality, reforms are much more difficult to put through.

As for the restrictions or conditions affecting implementation of reforms, there are five aspects to consider: (1) the magnitude of the political cost that the government is able to bear, which partially depends on the people's approval of the executive, on the impact of protests of groups affected by the reforms, and on how citizens perceive the reform and its benefits for society; (2) the political viability of approval, in which Congress can play a key role, including the long-term viability, in which not only is Congress involved but the judiciary has a key role; (3) the financial cost of the reform—if it is too high, it may affect the sustainability of public finances, making the reform unworkable in the long run; (4) existence of a technical and legal structure capable of designing legal changes without loopholes that might generate more damage than benefits, a structure that guarantees the continuation of public services and their optimal administration under the new conditions; and (5) presence of a leader in charge of introducing the reform, defending it among formal and informal political actors, and especially, convincing the majority of the population that the reform is beneficial for the country.

As noted, a fundamental political actor is the Congress, a political entity whose representatives listen to different positions and defend certain interests, either because of ideological convictions or because they relate to the constituency they represent. Additionally, there are cases in which some congressmen can oppose the reforms because they are economically compensated to defend certain interests. These corruption cases affect the reputation of public institutions and undermine the bases of the democratic system.

In the Peruvian case, the electoral system (by allowing preferential voting for congressmen) contributes to representation of multiple parties in Congress and, even worse, to weakening the party structure inside Congress. All of this promotes "pork barrel politics," making political negotiation a very complex process, but at the same time opening space for reforms' approval, which in a biparty system is more difficult to achieve.

The judiciary is the referee when, during the implementation of any reform, the affected groups resort to it to annul the law, arguing that it violates constitutional rights or that it reduces some benefit which, in their view, is guaranteed by the law but which public institutions do not recognize because they have a different interpretation of the law.[16] In these cases, there are four major problems: (1) the suitability of the justices ruling on economic, budget, and financial matters without a clear understanding of the nature of such things; (2) the bias of the justices for political or ideological reasons, not respecting their condition of guarantors of the nation's laws; (3) the corruption that may generate unconstitutional or illegal decisions from the justices, who are the ones called to defend principles of justice (see Abed and Davoodi 2000); and (4) the inefficiency of the administration of justice, which subverts reforms' procedures and applications.

Among informal actors, labor unions and business associations stand out. For labor unions, influence depends on their political alliances and their negotiating power with the public sector. As long as political parties depend on labor support, labor legislation will tend to favor workers and promote the ability of unions to organize workplaces, thus generating strong bonds between labor and those parties. Additionally, some of their representatives are elected members of Congress. Usually pressure from labor is directed toward achieving higher salaries (for public servants unions) or greater legal protection, more social benefits, and support from the government in negotiations between unions and businesses (central syndicates). (See Haggard and Webb 1994; IADB 2005.)

As for business associations, instead of defending the principle of more competition in the economy, they end up defending greater market protection, through tariff barriers or through public acquisition legislation favoring national enterprises. Although as a number of voters this group is not significant, it exerts huge pressure through the media and the "political establishment."

In addition, social movements have had significant growth in Latin America during the last 15 years, not only in number but also in their influence in the political arena.[17] Social movements are composed of socially active individuals, established in their communities, who try to advance their interests through different channels offered by established institutions. Social manifestations may thus become an instrument of significant political pressure. Social movements can be characterized in two ways. The first concerns the relative generality or specificity of the problem generating the social movement, which determines the number of people mobilized. The second involves the degree to which the social movement intends to change public policy in a constructive way toward a certain position (i.e., being "proactive") or simply dedicates itself to vetoing government proposals or expressing dissatisfaction with government officials (i.e., being "reactive").

Another informal political actor with important leverage is the media. The media's political power depends directly on its influence on the population to take a position on a given subject. Coverage of news and themes, in terms of space and point of view, affects public opinion and has an impact on political agendas and on discussions in the executive and in Congress.

The media's influence is so important that a dynamic relationship exisits between politicians and the press. From the politicians' point of view, they can relate to the media in the following ways: (1) strategic communication, when a political goal is to be promoted or a reform explained; (2) media management to influence the interpretative frames journalists use when covering news or events; (3) introduction of a distractive element—when there is an important event that needs to remain unnoticed (and not generate debate), alternative news is released to attract public opinion and deflect attention from the first event; (4) co-optation and control, which includes propagandist use of the state media, as well as alliances with or pressure on certain journalists. The last strategy was largely used during the second half of the 1990s.

In the balance of power in a democratic system, a free and transparent media is fundamental to the system's good health. It constitutes the communication channel for the government's fiscal actions, and it serves as a brake on power abuse and political coalitions trying to take advantage of state resources.

4. THE POLITICAL PROCESS OF THE REFORMS

The process of implementing reforms has five stages. The first one is to acknowledge the problem or distortion, that is, determining what is failing in terms of economic efficiency, equality, or vulnerability of certain segments of the population to poverty or hardship. The second stage is to determine the solution to the problem. In this stage, involving drafting the reform, three requirements mentioned earlier must be met: (1) there must be a leader willing to carry out the reform, (2) a technical and legal proposal must be drafted, and (3) the reform must be financed. If the Ministry of Economy and Finance proposes the reform, the financial requirement is addressed within the ministry; if another ministry presents it, that ministry coordinates with the Treasury in regard to financing the reform. It is usually in this stage where the first problems arise, since some reforms imply budgetary costs with no substantial improvement in public services justifying that cost increase.[18] During this phase, communication is crucial, as well as the technical ability of the respective teams to conceptualize changes, in order to present a legal structure that cannot be rejected by the courts or that has loopholes, and so that the teams have a clear idea of the implementation process.

The third stage involves preparing the reform implementation strategy, which includes: (1) defining a communication strategy with the media that conveys the benefits for the country, and having information ready to rebut opposing arguments and explain the problem to be solved; (2) defining the graduality of the reform; (3) determining whether the reform is going to be announced before it is introduced or not; and (4) identifying "enhancements" so as to incorporate allies in gaining approval of the reform.

Regarding graduality, the more gradual the implementation, the slower and more incremental the achievements in efficiency or equality will be, but gradual implementation has the advantage of reducing political costs, as it delays them. In financial terms, graduality may work against the reform if taxes are created or exemptions are abolished, or in favor of it if there is an expenditure program with aligned incentives. The problem with graduality is that it does not allow consolidation of the reform's achievements, and costs of reversing it are not too high during the first years, all of which implies a redoubled effort to maintain the reform. (See *Political Challenges of Structural Reform* 2008.)

As for timing of announcing the reforms, although certain groups or sectors losing benefits can be better prepared if the government announces it before introducing it, that advance notice also gives them more time to react and begin a campaign against the reform. Sometimes the reforms require the affected sector to participate in their implementation, so announcing changes in advance is necessary in order to start preparing to implement them in systems, but the "reformer" could end up depending on the action or will of the "reformed" for their implementation.[19]

Regarding the "enhancements," a wide variety of mechanisms, direct or indirect, can seek political and social support for implementing the reforms. Among the direct "enhancements" in Peru's case, the government created transfers to "compensate" the most vulnerable groups affected by the reforms, so as to diminish social costs. Among the indirect "enhancements" were loans agreed on with multilateral organizations to finance the deficit, which required a previous program with the International Monetary Fund to guarantee sound macroeconomic policy and the implementation of several structural reforms. The need for financing served as a pressure tool used by the Ministry of Economy and Finance to convince other sectors to approve the structural reforms. In making strategic use of the conditional loans, the ministry also gained extremely valuable technical support from these institutions for designing and implementing the reforms.

The fourth stage is political approval, which will depend on the level of the law required. In the Peruvian case, tariff reforms require a supreme decree signed by the president, the Ministry of Economy and Finance, and by the ministers with responsibility for the concerned sectors. So approval discussion is held in the cabinet. On the other hand, tax reforms require laws approved by Congress. In this stage, informal actors start intervening and affect formal actors' decisions whether to approve the reform or not. To the extent that the affected interests are represented by sectoral ministers or by congressmen, a solid technical proposal should prevail among any arguments against the reform. To get approval, the first two restrictions on implementation mentioned earlier must be addressed: the absorption of the political cost and using political channels for the reform's approval in Congress or in the cabinet. The leader's job is essential to explain to members of the executive and the legislature the advantages and disadvantages of such reforms; the leader's credibility and the confidence the leader inspires are fundamental for approval of the reform. Additionally, during this phase the media's work in communicating in a nonbiased way the benefits of the reform and not overstating costs is crucial, generating a public opinion wave that is decisive in avoiding interest groups that lose income and benefits being able to impede the reform's legal approval. Although media does not always have a uniform opinion about diverse reforms, it is important to use communication channels to inform the population objectively.

Finally, the fifth stage is implementation and sustainability of the reform in the long run. A legal and technical shield is essential for people to think they are better off and for the reform not to be rejected by the judiciary, the last resort for interest groups trying not to lose their privileges.

5. IMPLEMENTATION OF FISCAL REFORMS: CASE STUDIES

This section presents three examples of fiscal reforms' implementation, enhancing the political actors' role, formal and informal, and defining the stages of the implementation process.

5.1. Pension Reform

In 2003 the Peruvian public pension system had two regimes. The first, governed by Law 19990, is a contributive pension plan, with strict contribution requirements and retirement ages, benefits determined by the government, and no indexation clauses. The other, ruled by Law 20530, dates from the nineteenth century and faced several problems. The main one was lack of equity, both within the regime (allowing exorbitant pensions not in proportion to contributions) and in comparison with the plan governed by Law 19990. The second problem was disorganization in the wage system inside the public administration, as the "leveling" benefit (the relation between wages and pensions) promoted evasive practices to increase wages easily within the state. The leveling brought not only disorder and informality but also judicial contingencies impossible to anticipate. The third problem was the strong fiscal pressure exerted by this regime, entirely unfinanced and unsustainable, given that the contributions made during the working life of the employee were not enough to finance the magnitude of the benefits he or she enjoyed. Such distortions constituted insurmountable obstacles in the process of developing a balanced, transparent, and efficient state. This identification of the problem outlined here was the first step of the reform.

The second stage began after the administration decided to implement the reform. The reform consisted of establishing increased funding for the lower pensions and a maximum pension limit; eliminating automatic leveling of active public servants' wages; closing the pension regime to new contributors; and restricting certain benefits.

Multidisciplinary working groups formed to develop a solid proposal, both in technical and legal terms, which included changing the constitution. This was necessary as it was impossible to affect any right already recognized for pensioners, as they were protected by the principle of "acquired rights" included in the first final and transitory disposition of the constitution of 1993. So changing the constitution before modifying pensions' benefits by law was essential. In confronting the restrictions, the minister of economy and finance and the deputy ministers became the leaders promoting the reform. The reform meant significant savings for the Treasury and it had a team of over 20 technicians who worked more than 15 months on the original proposal.

The third stage of strategic definition was crucial for various reasons. First, low public approval of the president, which was around one digit between September 2003 and November 2004—when the constitutional reform was approved in Congress—worked against the reform, since the margin left for the government to absorb the political cost was quite small. Second, the probability of getting Congress's approval was very low, as many pensioners were politicians or people with high political leverage, and worse, over 20 congressmen were direct beneficiaries of Law 20530 and the reform was going to affect their future pensions. Besides, the approval process of a constitutional reform requires a qualified majority (81 votes from a total of 120 congresspersons) in two successive ordinary legislatures.

The planned strategy was to work intensely with the main leaders of opinion, including media directors and editors, explaining the existing problems and the solution. Likewise, before entering the formal approval stage, both in the cabinet and in Congress, the proponents explained the reform to several ministers and some members of Congress. During this stage, they proposed some enhancements, including increases in funding the lower pensions and a gradual reduction of the higher pensions;[20] this approach reduced the impact on higher levels while winning support from the lower levels, which had a higher number of pensioners. This strategic step was crucial during the final approval stages. Although in fiscal terms it was quite expensive at the beginning, net gains in present value were still significant.

In the fourth stage of the process, the cabinet approved the constitutional reform proposal, despite the resistance of some ministers, and later sent the proposal to Congress, achieving the first favorable vote in May 2004 and the second one in November that same year. During this stage two informal social actors stood out. One was the media, which mostly carried the reform flag, informing the public about existing excessive privileges, thus leading public opinion to support the reform and therefore exerting strong pressure on the voting in Congress. Thanks to this media coverage, public opinion mostly supported the reform.[21] Among social actors, pension unions, which felt the most affected, were consulted during the drafting stage and, despite their opposition due to their losses, most of them benefited from the reform as it included an increase in funding lower pensions, defusing protests inside the union.

The last stage was not simple. In the operational part, some issues arose in how the gradual reductions were applied, which led to multiple interpretations. The most complicated step was the defense in the judiciary; the lawyers' team had to defend the reform, both in national and international courts, from people who thought their rights were affected. The last ruling—which led to reform consolidation—was on May 29, 2009, when the Inter-American Human Rights Court found in favor of the Peruvian government. Without a good legal shield, the reform would have been declared null and the financial and political costs would have been extremely high for the government.

5.2. Tariff Reform

Peru has a small economy and its only chance of achieving higher growth rates is having a development strategy based on opening its economy to the rest of world, both commercially and financially. As a small economy, it has no impact on international prices of goods and services, so the possibility of importing goods at lower prices generates a set of benefits in the economy for both consumers and producers, who use these as capital goods, intermediate goods, or inputs, gaining productive efficiency. This improvement in efficiency translates into a higher long-term growth rate.[22]

However, the process of opening the economy was limited by the slow advances in bilateral negotiations and the absence of important tariff reductions from the beginning of the 1990s due to the strong political pressure of business associations. In 2006 a tax-and-tariff reform began, aiming at higher equality and greater efficiency. To attain this efficiency, a tariff-reduction program was mandatory in order to gain competitiveness in the economy.

The Ministry of Economy and Finance decided to introduce the reform and began technical work on it with the following criteria: (1) determine reductions by blocks defined according to economic criteria, (2) reduce the average tariff and tariff dispersion, (3) reduce the number of tariff scales, (4) avoid the existence of negative effective protection (whereby Peruvian products or industries are discriminated against), and (5) apply a gradual approach to attenuate the loss in tax revenues. The technical proposal included almost every item not produced locally (basically all capital goods and some intermediate ones), and implied an effective average tariff rate of 2 percent.

As explained earlier, the legal implementation of tariff reductions is approved by a supreme decree and does not require approval in the cabinet or in Congress, so a different strategy was used from the one in the pension case. First, any communication with media and opinion leaders was postponed until after the decree was published. This meant that the reform was not announced in advance or discussed previously with the business associations, who were always against tariff reductions for protectionist reasons. In addition, the ministry decided to implement the reform in stages because of the effect on tax revenues.

Anticipating opposition from the concerned sector (represented by the Ministry of Trade, the Ministry of Production, and others), the ministry decided to present the reform program during a cabinet session and propose signing the decree during the same session. The Ministry of Trade was against the reform because it used tariffs as an instrument to negotiate free trade agreements; while the approach of the Ministry of Economy and Finance was that free trade agreements and tariff reductions were both instruments to open the economy. In the end, the cabinet approved a partial reduction that included, among other things, dropping from 4 percent to 0 percent the tariff on all items classified as capital goods.

Within the media, there was a sharp exchange of opinions between those in favor and those against the reform. One of the strongest criticisms was that tariffs on leisure boats were reduced to 0 percent, with opponents accusing the ministry of favoring the rich. The reason for this reduction was that *all* items with a 4 percent tariff were changed to a 0 percent tariff. Besides, one of the technical reasons for moving tariffs by blocks and predefined criteria was to avoid political pressure to make discretional changes in certain items. However, despite the coverage, public attention to this reform was diluted because it was published on December 28, 2006, in the middle of other important changes to the tax regime.

On February 15 and October 13, 2007, these tariff reductions were published (DS 017-2007-EF and DS 158-2007-EF respectively), replacing the previous set of tariffs. The macroeconomic context at the time included appreciation of the exchange rate and a rise in inflation, mainly because of shocks in energy and food prices. In addition to the efficiency goals, another objective was to reduce the shocks' impact on inflation through tariff reductions. It is clear that, *ceteris paribus*, a tariff reduction decreases domestic prices of imported goods and raises the demand for dollars, exerting upward pressure on the exchange rate. The October tariff reduction included 4,155 items and left three tariff scales: 0 percent, 9 percent, and 17 percent.

Between December 2006 and January 2009 (when the last tariff modification took place), almost every item tariff was reduced and the effective tariff rate decreased from 5.4 percent in 2006 to 1.9 percent in 2010 (January–April) (fig. 2.4).

This time pressure from business associations magnified. Using informal actors, such as the media, and formal actors, such as politicians, a strong campaign to reverse the tariff reductions began. One of the subjects was worthy of consideration: that there was effective negative protection—that is, discriminatory tariffs or other measures that harmed Peruvian producers—in some sectors. This led to a correction of 90 items (threads, laminated products, and wires) on October 2007 (DS 163–2007), which had tariffs reduced from 9 percent to 0 percent, but the ministry's position remained inflexible regarding the cuts already made. In March 2008 there was another important advance (DS 038-2008-EF) with 577 items, eliminating tariffs on almost all food items. One natural ally in support of the reform should be exporters, but absurdly, one of the exporters associations opposed the reform, arguing that it would generate unemployment.[23] Using this argument, different protectionist interests grouped together, led by the Lima Chamber of Commerce and the National Industrial Society. Reality proved them wrong. Peru's inflation rate during 2007 and 2008 was among the lowest in the region and growth

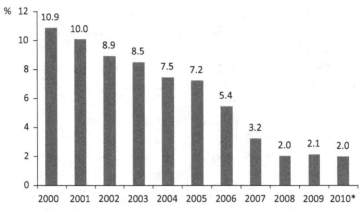

Figure 2.4 Effective tariff rates, Peru 2000–2009.

was among the highest. Moreover, employment grew 8.9 percent and 6.5 percent in 2007 and 2008, respectively.[24]

These protectionist interests did not stop at using political pressure—through ministers and congressmen—to reverse the reform; they also went to the judiciary. At the lower judiciary and administrative levels, several of these cases were rejected. However, the case of one enterprise, Cementos Lima, reached the Constitutional Court, which ruled in favor of the enterprise, forcing the collection entity to reestablish the tariff in effect before the cut, disregarding all other judiciaries' opinions in the country[25] and basing its ruling on the principle of guaranteeing profits to national enterprises. Such a principle does not exist in the Peruvian constitution, which makes the ruling a fallacy.

5.3. New Public Educational Career Law

One of the main weaknesses of the Peruvian economy is the low quality of education, evidenced in the poor performance Peru achieves in international rankings of innovation and technology. In the global competitive ranking for 2009 of the World Economic Forum, the quality of primary education in Peru ranks 131st of 134 countries; this means that compared to students in other countries, Peruvian pupils do not understand what they read and do not have mathematical or scientific abilities.[26] This meager performance in primary education explains the weakness in the knowledge chain. Likewise, in the innovation part of the same competitiveness ranking, Peru places 109th of 133 countries. This is a tremendous barrier to maintaining a high growth rate in the long run and improving income distribution.

Although this educational situation is complex and has multiple causes, a crucial factor is the poor qualification of public education teachers in the country. Teachers not only are poorly trained, badly paid, and unmotivated, but the teachers union is extremely politicized, with important mobilization power throughout the whole country. In fact, during the period 2001–6, the improvements the government tried to introduce (training, teachers' evaluation, etc.) were blocked by the

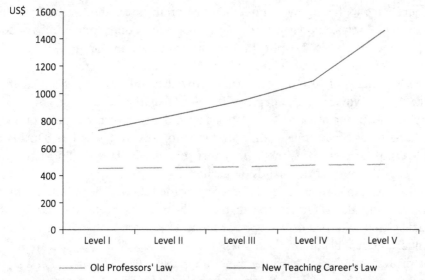

Figure 2.5 Wage increases under Peru's new Public Educational Career Law versus under the previous law.

union and, helped by low presidential approval, through national strikes the union achieved wage increases every year. This situation gave it significant political leverage, but the quality of education had not improved at all.

To address this issue, the Ministry of Education and the Ministry of Economy and Finance worked together to draft a new Public Educational Career Law with three key elements: (1) important wage improvements, (2) a provision that teachers who enter this new regime lose guaranteed employment and may be fired if they fail the mandatory evaluation exam three times, (3) teachers from the old regime can voluntarily transfer to the new one, but new appointments for teachers occur only under the new law. Additionally, the government made clear that teachers can get wage increases only through entering the new regime (fig. 2.5).

The minister of education assumed an active role as leader during the reform. The Ministry of Economy and Finance worked out the reform financing and applied a gradual scheme to make it compatible with annual budget targets and to include a certain margin of flexibility (depending on the number of job openings, which vary from year to year).

The strategy incorporated a diffusion campaign explaining the educational problem in the country, so parents would be aware of it. A trial evaluation for teachers took place despite the union's opposition, and the results were disastrous.[27] In light of this situation and media coverage, the public became conscious of the need to reform the teaching profession. Once the government won this public space and with graduality and financing determined, the ministries presented an integral program, whichincluded extensive training and a new law for careers in public education. The cabinet approved the bill and sent it to Congress for its approval.

For obvious reasons, the union strongly opposed the bill. Beginning in June 2007, the union called for a national strike, which included mobilization and violence such as taking over municipalities, train lines, and regional airports, blocking highways, and even throwing garbage and homemade bombs at some congressmen's houses. Despite the union's influence in Congress, the public opinion in favor of the law played a key role in gaining Congress's support; and at the beginning of July the bill was approved in the middle of an indefinite strike.[28] This worsened the degree of violence in the strike, but government remained firm and warned that if teachers did not return to their jobs, they would be fired. Meanwhile, classes started with substitute teachers. During the first days of January 2008, the lower courts upheld the law, and in March 2008 the first evaluation for thousands of teachers took place.

The implementation process faced a bumpy road at first. The union tried to stop teachers taking the test from entering the public teachers' profession, arguing they would be fired, and tried to gain popular support by asserting that the "privatization of education" had begun. In the first exam of March 2008, of 189,593 teachers who took the test only 151 achieved the minimum passing grade.[29] Later, after a second exam, 3,337 entered the educational profession. Currently there are 16,911 teachers in the new regime.

The implementation of the Public Educational Career Law implied a substantial change in the relationship between the government and the public teachers union. The new regime includes significant wage increases,[30] but it also requires a continuous evaluation process for teachers, and, as noted earlier, teachers can be expelled from the profession if they fail the evaluations three times. Implementation has been carried out gradually, through hiring when places are available (depending on financial resources), and passing from the old system to the new is voluntary. The impact on teaching quality has shown its first results. According to evaluation of the student census, the percentage of students with sufficient reading comprehension in primary school increased from 15.9 percent in 2007 to 23.1 percent in 2009; similarly, in math this percentage increased from 7.2 percent to 13.5 percent during the same period.

In the educational field, there were other expenditure reforms that helped the new regime pass. Programs for reparing schools were implemented under a scheme of direct funding to the school headmaster, the "One Laptop per Child" program—entirely financed with public funds—was introduced, and there were other improvements. In general figures, the budget for education between 2006 and 2009 increased 54.6 percent. The real impact of the educational career reform on pupils' performance will become apparent in the medium term; however, as mentioned before, the evaluation of 2009 shows signs of relative improvement.

Besides the implementational problems, this case also went to the judiciary. A former union leader brought an action against the Public Educational Career Law, arguing it was unconstitutional because it violated the rights to a free public education, to have a job and guaranteed employment, to be equal in the face of the law, to enjoy due process, to the nonretroactivity of the law, and to the right to be in a union and to hold a strike. The judiciary, through the Constitutional Court, fulfilled its role of interpreting the laws and declared the action unfounded in September 2009.

6. Conclusions

The results of the fiscal reform process carried out during the last decade in Peru are crucial in explaining the achievements in economic growth and poverty reduction. The problem with fiscal reforms is that implementing them implies extremely high political costs and benefits are long term, benefits that many times are not even perceived by the common citizen. In countries or regions with lower income, the discount rate for intertemporal consumption is quite high; hence, the public tends to support those measures that benefit it in the short term, no matter how harmful they can be in the long run. Moreover, if benefits are not tangible for people, they are not interested in supporting the reform. Similarly, if benefits from the reform will take time to appear and the government implementing the reform will not harvest such benefits (in popular support and future votes), it will be less eager to carry out such reform. This obstacle, which constitutes the main problem in carrying out a reform, is called appropriation of benefits and costs of the reform.

In this framework, the question arises of whether the policymaking process, and hence the carrying out of structural reforms, tends to facilitate or to limit cooperation when making economic policy. The theory of game cooperation provides a useful perspective on the characteristics of the policymaking process that will produce cooperation.

At the same time, the work done in the policymaking process is determined (up to a certain point) by the political institutions, such as the nature of the government (presidential or parliamentary), the electoral rules, the federal structure of the country, and the existence of an independent judiciary.

Particular characteristics of economic policies included in the reforms or the details of their implementation can be as important as the general policy orientation for obtaining the desired results. We can expect, as the literature demonstrates, that the effects of reform policies on social and economic conditions depend on the actions and reactions of economic and social agents, who may or may not consider their expectations about the future when deciding their answers. However, as mentioned earlier, in societies with certain characteristics, the time frame of the results is not included in the analysis, and immediate benefit is preferred; this tendency facilitates the manipulation of the masses, making the reform process vulnerable to interest groups and hence making it harder for the government to carry out the reform.

For a reform to be successful, it must meet five conditions: (1) have a leader, (2) have a good technical team to design it, shield it legally, and avoid operational problems in its application, (3) have adequate financing, (4) have backing from an administration willing to bear the political cost, and (5) have assured political viability, that is, approval of the legal instrument implementing the reform.

This is just possible if there is a good strategy behind the reform. Forming one involves obtaining allies, searching for good political timing, communicating benefits and rebutting arguments against the reform, and solving problems that may appear during the approval and implementation. In addition, to the extent possible when there is no consensus, media support is important for converting public opinion in favor of the reform. This is a key factor in defeating the legislature's resistance when proposing changes that affect political groups with important representation in that legislature.

NOTES

1. For more on impatience in political economy, see Santiso (2000).
2. For a description of the reform process, see Abusada et al. (2000).
3. The law did not implement a rule of structural fiscal balance; instead, it set a limit to the deficit and to nonfinancial expenditure growth that was slightly lower than potential GDP growth in order to achieve a process of reduction of public debt in terms of GDP. Based on historic economic cycles, government economists estimated that the recession phase would last three years on average.
4. The amount includes an estimated US$291 million for abolishing Amazon exemptions and US$70 million for abolishing those of capital profits.
5. Both percentages are calculated from 2010 GDP and tax revenues.
6. The tax on net assets has null effect on long-term collection; it just represents a temporary cash flow increase. In 2005 (April–December), net asset tax collection reached US$325 million, 9.6 percent of annual income tax collections and 3 percent of total annual tax collection.
7. This way, for example, if we have a formal buyer acquiring goods or services from small, informal, or very difficult to control sellers, the formal taxpayer keeps the VAT and pays it directly to the tax-collecting agency (as part of the retention regime). If, on the other hand, the producer sells to informal retail buyers, during the sale part of the VAT that would be received from the buyer is kept (as part of the perception regime).
8. The figures are for 2009. Collection from the special regimes targeted at informal economic activity mentioned in note 7 totaled US$3,070 million over the 2009 GDP amount of US$127,153 million.
9. This policy assumes a potential GDP growth rate of 6 percent and an inflation target of the Central Bank of 2 percent. As a result, growth in nominal expenditure was stable.
10. For 2010, strategic programs under PBB have been assigned a total amount of US$2,304 million, equivalent to 13.2 percent of the total budget. In 2009 the amount assigned was US$1,217 million, equivalent to 8.8 percent of the total budget for nine strategic programs.
11. Moreover, there are no differences between genders, geographic areas, or level of poverty, as the enrollment rate during 2007 in each case was 93 percent.
12. The indicator of improvement in contagious diseases refers to halting the spread of such diseases as tuberculosis, malaria, bartonelosis, and HIV-AIDS (ST-CIAS 2009).
13. Law 20530 has its origin in very old laws that created life pensions paid by the Treasury to a quite small group of public servants. As time went by, the application of this regime was broadened to include more beneficiaries and more benefits. It is called Living Bond (Cédula Viva), as it matches the pension to the salary received by the active worker.

14. In a flexible exchange rate regime, excessive volatility in capital flows may have a huge effect on the exchange rate. This excessive volatility may be attenuated by interventions in the exchange rate market. In the long run, the equilibrium real exchange rate will determine the nominal exchange rate, but these interventions avoid short-term volatility, so harmful to the real sector.

15. For a full description of political actors, see IADB (2006).

16. According to the IADB (2005), the judiciary may take different roles in the policymaking process. In Latin American countries these roles can be divided into four categories: (1) player with veto based on the constitution or on its preferences; (2) political player when in interpreting the laws, judges impose their preferences on the resulting policies; (3) impartial referee when judges act as an external supervisor in agreements reached by others and as a mediator between the parties; and (4) representative of society, as an alternative channel for representing marginal groups.

17. IADB (2005) ties the proliferation of this phenomenon and its powerful impact in the region to three different political system crises: weakness of the state (in maintaining the income level of those who support the system and providing adequate services for the least favored sectors), weakness of democracy, and weakness of the nation (lack of a shared national identity).

18. In 2004, the cabinet presented a proposal to make the wage system in public administration uniform, which involved major legal contingencies (the proposal implied a wage reduction for a fraction of public servants) and generated costs of around 2 percent—3 percent of GDP as an increase in current expenditure every year, without considering future pension costs. This rearrangement of public labor did not guarantee a more efficient bureaucracy or administrative improvements, as it did not introduce merit criteria for appointments and promotions and guaranteed employment remained in effect. This reform project was not approved because, although there was a leader, it did not address the other two constraints: financial and technical restrictions.

19. One of these cases occurred when the government decided to abolish the exemption for capital gains. For stock profits, the tax-holding agent would be the stock exchange, which meant the exchange had to adapt its systems. During the implementation, several problems emerged, and when the deadline for the tax to be implemented arrived, systems were not ready, which made predictable extension of the deadline. Shortly before the deadline, a bill was presented in Congress eliminating the holding agent and directing that the tax be calculated and paid according to the taxpayer's claim, which required the stock exchange to transmit all information on transactions to the tax-collecting entity. This small formal change motivated huge political pressure by the stock exchange in response, but it could not find any congressman willing to propose delaying the date for the law to be implemented.

20. The monthly limit per beneficiary was fixed at US$1,897 and a reduction rule was imposed at 18 percent per annum over the whole income until the limit was reached. In 2006 the reduction rule was modified to apply 18 percent only to the difference between the total amount and the maximum income limit.

21. In September 2004, 63 percent of the population approved the constitutional reform.

22. For more on gains from opening the economy, see Krugman (1986) and Harberger (1985), among others.

23. The exporters association president, ADEX, belonged to an economic group whose sales abroad represented a very small fraction of the group's total sales, which were mostly oriented to the domestic market. The other exporters association, COMEX, defended the measures on several occasions.

24. Figures are from the Monthly Statistic Report from the Ministry of Labor for enterprises with 10 and more workers.

25. Article 118 of the constitution determines that the president, through a supreme decree, determines the tariff structure, without any other restriction.

26. In 2003 Peru ranked last of the 41 countries participating in all evaluations of the PISA Test (an international evaluation organized by the OECD for 15-year-old students in the public and private school systems in the areas of reading comprehension, math, and science). In 2006 Peru did not participate, but it did participate in 2009. Results of these 2009 evaluations found Peru ranked last among the nine Latin American and Caribbean economies that participated in the study, and only Azerbaijan and Kyrgyzstan ranked lower than Peru among the 75 participating economies (OECD 2010).

27. The trial evaluation faced some difficulties. It was initially programmed on December 20, 2006, but the exam was stolen, so the test had to be postponed to January 8, 2007. After the evaluations, results were published: 46.8 percent of over 174,000 teachers who took the test could not perform simple arithmetic calculations and could not reproduce simple routine procedures. Only 1.3 percent achieved the maximum level in mathematical-logical reasoning. Among kindergarten and primary school teachers, the result was worse: only 0.4 percent and 0.5 percent, respectively, reached that level.

28. On July 7, 2007, Law 29062 modifying the old Teachers Law governing the public educational profession was approved.

29. The minimum passing grade was 14 of 20.

30. In the old regime, a teacher from level 5 (the highest) working 40 hours per week receives US$468, only 6.3 percent more than a teacher from level 1 (the lowest). In the new regime, the same teacher would earn US$1,390, a 197 percent raise compared to the old situation; and the teacher from level 1 would earn US$709, a 61 percent raise compared to the old regime.

REFERENCES

Abed, George T., and Hamid R. Davoodi. 2000. "Corruption, Structural Reforms, and Economic Performance in the Transition Economies." IMF Working Paper No. 132, International Monetary Fund, Fiscal Affairs Department, Washington, DC.

Abusada, Roberto, Fritz Du Bois, Eduardo Moron, and José Valderrama. 2000. *La reforma incompleta. Rescatando los noventa*. Lima: Centro de Investigación de la Universidad del Pacífico and Instituto Peruano de Economía.

Alesina, Alberto. 1994. "Political Models of Macroeconomic Policy and Fiscal Reforms." In *Voting for Reform: Democracy, Political Liberalization and Economic Adjustment*, edited by Stephan Haggard and Steven B. Webb, 37–60. New York: Oxford University Press; Washington, DC: International Bank for Reconstruction and Development, World Bank.

Fisher, Irving. 1907. *The Rate of Interest*. New York: Macmillan.

Haggard, Stephan, and Steven B. Webb. 1994. Introduction to *Voting for Reform: Democracy, Political Liberalization and Economic Adjustment*, edited by Stephan Haggard and Steven B. Webb, 1–6. New York: Oxford University Press; Washington, DC: International Bank for Reconstruction and Development, World Bank.

Harberger, Arnold. 1985. "Tax Policy in a Small, Open, Developing Economy." In *The Economics of the Caribbean Basin*, edited by Michael B Connelly and John McDermott, 1–11, New York: Praeger.

Hiebert, Paul, Javier J. Perez, and Massimo Rostagno. 2002. "Debt Reduction and Automatic Stabilisation." Working Paper No. 189, European Central Bank, Brussels.

IADB (Inter-American Development Bank). 2005. Washington, DC: Inter-American Development Bank.

———. 2006. Washington, DC: Inter-American Development Bank.

Krugman, Paul. 1986. *Strategic Trade Policy and the New International Economics*. Cambridge, MA: MIT Press.

Musgrave, Richard. 1961. "Approaches to a Fiscal Theory of Political Federalism." In *Public Finances: Needs, Sources and Utilization*, edited by James M. Buchanan, 97–134. Princeton, NJ: Princeton University Press for the National Bureau of Economic Research.

OECD (Organisation for Economic Co-operation and Development). 2010. *Pisa Results 2009*. Vol. 1: *What Students Know and Can Do: Student Performance in Reading, Mathematics and Science*. Paris: OECD.

Peart, Sandra J. 2000. "Irrationality and Intertemporal Choice in Early Neoclassical Thought." *Canadian Journal of Economics* 33(1): 175–89.

The Political Challenges of Structural Reform. 2008. APEC discussion paper (Australia) presented at the Ministerial Meeting on Structural Reform, Melbourne, Australia, August 3, available at http://aimp.apec.org/Documents/2008/MM/SRMM/08_srmm_002.doc.

Santiso, Javier. 2000. "Hirschman's View of Development, or the Art of Trespassing and Self-Subversion." *CEPAL Review* 70: 93–109.

ST-CIAS (Secretaría Técnica, Comisión Interministerial de Asuntos Sociales). 2009. *Informe Técnico de Salud*. Lima: Secretaría Técnica, Comisión Internministerial de Asuntos Sociales, Presidencia del Consejo de Ministros, Government of Peru.

Stein, Ernesto, and Mariano Tommasi, eds. 2008. *Policymaking in Latin America: How Politics Shapes Policies*. Washington, DC: Inter-American Development Bank; Cambridge, MA: David Rockefeller Center for Latin America, Harvard University.

CHAPTER 3

....

THE POLITICAL ECONOMY
OF FISCAL POLICY:
THE EXPERIENCE OF CHILE

....

ANDRÉS VELASCO AND ERIC PARRADO

1. INTRODUCTION

....

By the end of 2009, Chile was not only the newest member of the Organisation for
Economic Co-operation and Development (OECD), often described, however in-
accurately, as the rich countries´ club. On that date, Chile had arguably the best
fiscal performance in the OECD. Chile´s gross public debt was, by a large margin,
the lowest in the group. In the previous four years Chile had averaged the second
largest overall fiscal surplus in the OECD, second only to oil-producing Norway´s.

Things were not always that way. In 1982 Chile had suffered simultaneous and
massive currency and banking crises. Foreign debt, both public and private, had to
be rescheduled. The cost of the bailout was to weigh heavily on public finance in
years to come. Chile´s economy grew fast in the second half of the 1980s and this
helped turn around fiscal accounts. But even then, when the military dictatorship
ended and the country returned to democracy in 1990, gross public debt stood at a
substantial 45 percent of the gross domestic product (GDP). And to that one had to
add another 33 percentage points of GDP in the debt issued to future pensioners as
part of the transition to a private social security system.

How did Chile make the transition, in just two decades, from a fiscally weak to
a fiscally strong economy? Sure enough, fast economic growth (especially until the
late 1990s) and high copper prices (especially after 2004) helped. But history is
replete with countries that squandered the fiscal benefits of growth. And in Latin
America, commodity booms almost always have triggered booms in government
spending, with governments spending not only the additional commodity revenue
but also the additional credit that high commodity prices typically triggered.

Unsurprisingly, those booms almost always ended in disaster—including, of course, fiscal disasters. Chile did something different. And in the *what*, the *how*, and the *why* of that experience there may be useful lessons for other nations.

Chile's fiscal discipline was not born overnight. Already in the reform period of the 1970s and in the growth period of the second half of the 1980s important policies were applied—privatization of money-losing enterprises was one, simplification and modernization of the tax code was another—that helped strengthen public accounts. With democracy's return, and in contrast with many pessimistic prognostications, the administrations of Patricio Aylwin (1990–94) and Eduardo Frei (1994–2000) showed a deep-seated commitment to fiscal prudence, which they upheld even when it clashed with the expectations and demands of public sector unions and of some of the more populist members of the ruling left-of-center Concertación.

In the new century Chile's prudent fiscal policy entered a stage of institutionalization and consolidation. The administration of Ricardo Lagos (2000–2006) introduced the key practice—in force still today—of constructing budgets on a cyclically adjusted basis and of setting explicit targets for the cyclically adjusted (or "structural") budget balance. In turn, the administration of Michelle Bachelet (2006–10) crafted and passed the 2006 Fiscal Responsibility Law, which formalized the "structural" approach to fiscal policy and set up two sovereign wealth funds to hold and invest the resulting fiscal savings.

This chapter discusses first, in some detail, what these policies entailed and how they were applied. Much thinking and design went into this approach—some of it local, some of it adapted from successful experiences such as that of Norway. The chapter also examines the economic results of the shift in fiscal policy. The effects on fiscal variables were large: as we documented at the outset, a sharp drop in public debt and record fiscal surpluses in years of high copper prices. This fiscal prudence also mattered for some key macro variables, among them the real exchange rate and the volatility of output growth. The basic message is simple: shifting from a procyclical to a mildly countercyclical fiscal stance has helped stabilize both relative prices and economic activity.

Last but certainly not least, the chapter focuses on the political economy of the problem. What political failures existed and how did the rule help alleviate them? We tackle these questions with the help of a simple model, which we use to organize and motivate the discussion of Chile's budget politics.

2. POLITICS AND FISCAL POLICY: A LITTLE THEORY

A first question is: why would a country need a fiscal rule? What is the policymaking failure that requires fiscal behavior to be constrained by such a rule? In this section we outline a model of such a policymaking failure. We then explore its implications in later sections.

2.1. The Basic Setup

The essence of the story is a decentralized mechanism for deciding on spending. There are n symmetric groups, indexed by i, so that $i =1,2 \ldots n$. Each can be thought of as a particular constituency or recipient of government resources. Public expenditure on group i can be interpreted as subsidies to its members or spending on a public good that benefits only those in group i, such expenditure can be financed out of a constant stream of government income τ. We suppose there is a shock ϵ_t to government income, which is *i.i.d.* with mean zero and finite variance.

Any excess of expenditure over revenues can be financed by borrowing in the world capital market at a constant gross real rate $1 + r$, which is exogenous (the economy is small and open). Accumulated debts are a joint liability of all n groups, as would be the case with the national debt in any country. The government budget constraint therefore is:

$$b_t = (1+r)b_{t-1} + \tau + \varepsilon_t \cdots \sum\nolimits_{i=1}^{n} g_{it},$$ (1)

where b_t is the stock of the internationally traded bond held by the government at time t, earning the interest rate $1+ r$. We also impose the solvency condition:

$$\lim_{t\to\infty} b_t (1+r)^{-t} \geq 0.$$ (2)

Each group i has the objective utility function:[1]

$$U = \sum\nolimits_{s=t}^{\infty} \log(g_{it})(1+r)^{-(s-t)}.$$ (3)

2.1.1. *Planner's Solution*

If a planner solves the problem on behalf of the n groups, treating each of them symmetrically, the optimal spending rule is

$$g_{it} = \frac{1}{n}\left(rb_{t-1} + \tau + \frac{r}{1+r}\varepsilon_t \right).$$ (4)

Each group spends a share $1/n$ of permanent income $rb_{t-1} + \tau$ and of a portion of the transitory shock ϵ_t. Then, aggregate spending is given by

$$g_t = ng_{it} = rb_{t-1} + \tau + \frac{r}{1+r}\varepsilon_t.$$ (5)

Using this rule in budget constraint (1) we have

$$b_t - b_{t-1} = \frac{\varepsilon_t}{1+r}.$$ (6)

There is a budget surplus and government assets are accumulated whenever the shock ϵ_t to fiscal income is positive, and vice versa. That is, the government saves (dissaves) whenever it experiences a positive (adverse) income transitory income shock. This is in accordance with the smoothing theory of Barro (1980).

2.1.2. *Political Equilibrium*

Now suppose each of the n fiscal groups acts independently, each setting the path $\{g_{it}\}_{t=0}^{\infty}$ through lobbying or another political mechanism. Notice that all interest groups still share the same budget constraint, enjoying "common access" to government resources.

This policymaking regime can be interpreted in one of several ways, all of which have counterparts in countries' recent experience. First, spending pressures may arise from sectoral ministers or parliamentary committees with special interests (see von Hagen 1993; von Hagen and Harden 1995; Alesina, Hausmann, et al. 1999). Second, spending may be set by decentralized fiscal authorities representing particular geographical areas. The cases of Argentina and Brazil are instructive. Third, transfers may be determined by money-losing state enterprises facing soft budget constraints.

2.1.3. *Solving the Game among the n Groups*

Focus on a simple class of Markovian strategies in which spending is a function of the state variable only. In this log-linear setting one can postulate a linear policy rule for each player:

$$g_{it} = \phi\left(b_{t-1} + \frac{\tau}{r} + \frac{\varepsilon_t}{1+r}\right), \tag{7}$$

where ϕ is a parameter to be endogenously determined.

Now suppose that group i expects that all other groups will employ rule (7). Then, assets evolve according to:

$$b_t = [(1+r) - (n-1)\phi]\left(b_{t-1} + \frac{\tau}{r} + \frac{\varepsilon_t}{1+r}\right) - g_{it}. \tag{8}$$

Group i's best response is therefore the solution to the problem

$$V(b_{t-1}) = \max_{g_{it}} E_t\{\log(g_{it}) + (1+r)^{-t} V(b_t)\}, \tag{9}$$

subject to (8). The Euler equation that corresponds to this problem is:

$$E_t g_{it+1} = [1 - (n-1)\phi]g_{it}. \tag{10}$$

Combining (8) and (10) and imposing symmetry one obtains:

$$g_{it} = \left(\frac{1+r}{1+nr}\right)\left(rb_{t-1} + \tau + \frac{r}{1+r}\varepsilon_t\right). \tag{11}$$

Hence, each group spends a share $\dfrac{1+r}{1+nr} > \dfrac{1}{n}$ of permanent income $rb_{t-1} + \tau$ and a portion $\dfrac{r}{1+r}$ of the transitory shock ε_t.

Therefore, aggregate spending is

$$ng_{it} = g_t = \left(\frac{n+nr}{1+nr}\right)\left(rb_{t-1} + \tau + \frac{r}{1+r}\varepsilon_t\right). \tag{12}$$

And the equilibrum budget surplus or deficit is:

$$b_t - b_{t-1} = \frac{\varepsilon t}{1+nr} - \frac{n-1}{(1+nr)}(rb_{t-1} + \tau). \tag{13}$$

2.1.4. *Overspending and Inefficient Asset Dynamics*

How do the planner's solution and the political outcome differ? First, contrast the dynamics of spending. Under the political equilibrium, aggregate spending is larger ($\dfrac{n+nr}{1+nr} > 1$, since $n>1$). The share spent of permanent income $rb_t + \tau$ is larger. That is, too much (relative to the optimum) is spent out of permanent income.

The portion that is spent out of the transitory income shock ε_t is also larger than in the planner's solution. Or put differently, under the political equilibrium a smaller share of the income shock ε_t is saved via a budget surplus: $\dfrac{1}{1+r}$ under the planner, $\dfrac{1}{1+nr}$ under the political equilibrium. And when ε_t is negative, the dissaving is too small. Fiscal policy is not as countercyclical as it ought to be. This is a violation of optimal smoothing.

What about the evolution of government assets? Under the planner's solution, experiencing no shock ($\varepsilon_t = 0$) implies a balanced budget (recall equation (6) above). Under the political equilibrium, on the other hand, $\varepsilon_t = 0$ does not imply the budget is balanced. On the contrary, there is a trend deficit of size $\dfrac{n-1}{1+nr}(rb_{t-1} + \tau)$.

To summarize, relative to the planner's solution the decentralized political equilibrium implies (1) overspending; (2) an inadequate reaction to shocks; and (3) inefficient budget deficits and asset decumulation. What is the intuition behind these results? Very simple: property rights are not defined over government assets. A portion of government wealth not spent by one group will be spent by another.

This creates an incentive to raise spending above the collectively efficient rate. Another way to see this has to do with the return to saving. The return on government wealth accruing to each group is $(1 + r) - (n - 1)\phi$. Since this return is below the rate of time discounting $(1 + r)$, each group has incentives to draw down government assets.

Where does a fiscal rule come in? We think of the rule as a way of overcoming the inefficiencies associated with the decentralized political equilibrium. For the rule to play this role, it has to include mechanisms for dealing with the tendency toward overspending and deficits, as well as with the insufficient saving displayed in response to temporary positive income shocks.

3. THE CASE OF CHILE: INITIAL CONDITIONS

3.1. Fiscal Performance before 2000

Some countries have introduced fiscal rules as a last-ditch attempt to turn around a difficult fiscal situation. This was not the case of Chile. On the contrary, Chile applied the new system from a position of relative fiscal strength. That may have contributed to its viability and success.

Between 1990 and 1999 Chile ran fiscal surpluses in nine of those 10 years (see fig. 3.1). In that period the country achieved an average fiscal surplus of 1.5 percent of GDP and reduced the public debt from 44.8 percent of GDP in 1990 to 13.9 percent in 1999. This amounted to a strong fiscal performance, not just by Latin American standards but by the standards of any nation, rich or poor.

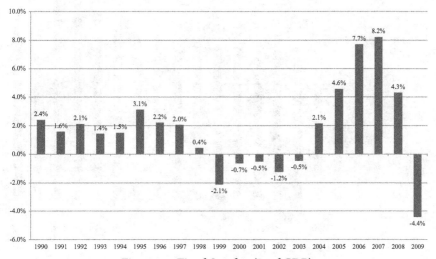

Figure 3.1 Fiscal Surplus (% of GDP).

Source: Budget Office and Central Bank of Chile.

3.2. Fiscal Institutions

A fiscal rule is an example of fiscal institutions at work. The stronger the institutional setup, the more likely a fiscal rule will be established and maintained. Chile had a strong starting point, enjoying sound fiscal accounts and reasonably robust budget institutions at the outset. The first thing to note is that Chile, in contrast to other Latin American countries such as Mexico, Colombia, Argentina, and Brazil, is fiscally very centralized. All taxes are levied by the central government. Local governments get a transfer equal to the value of property taxes paid; all other tax revenue accrues to the central authorities. Local governments also get transfers from the center according to preset formulas. Even though local governments have important spending responsibilities (including schools and local clinics), they are legally unable to borrow.

Public enterprises have considerable autonomy in their day-to-day operations, but their annual budgets must be approved by the central government. Like local governments, they cannot borrow without the approval of the Finance Ministry. The action, therefore, is in the fiscal stance of the central government. What institutions and procedures determine that stance, and how good are those procedures?

Alesina, Ardagna, et al. (1999) compiled an index of fiscal institutions for Latin America. The index includes measures of how hierarchical or collegial and how transparent or opaque budget procedures are, with more hierarchical and transparent mechanisms associated with better fiscal performance. Chile leads the pack along with Mexico and Jamaica (see fig. 3.2). This measure of "strength" of fiscal institutions correlates well with one measure of fiscal performance, the average fiscal surplus in 1990–2000 (see fig. 3.3).

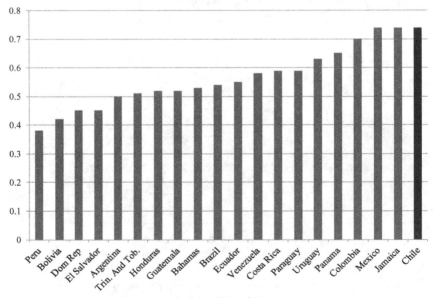

Figure 3.2 Index of Fiscal Institutions.

Source: Alesina et al (1999).

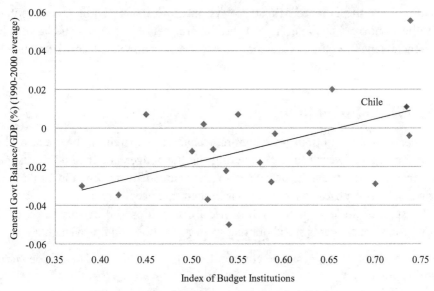

Figure 3.3 Fiscal Balance and Budget Institutions.
Source: Alesina et al (1999).

Chile´s budget-making rules are unusual in the relative power they give the executive vis-à-vis the legislature. Several legal features, some of them dating back to the 1920s, stand out:

- Only the executive can "initiate" bills involving changes in expenditure or taxation. If a member of Congress wishes to submit such a bill, he or she needs the sponsorship of the executive.
- The budget process has very stringent deadlines: the executive must submit the budget to Congress by September 30 and Congress must have approved the budget (with the amendments it has introduced) by November 30. Otherwise, the budget bill initially submitted by the executive becomes the law of the land.
- Congress can cut but cannot increase expenditure (on any one item or overall) in the course of budget approval.

The effect of such rules is to focus congressional discussions largely on the microeconomics of the budget—parliamentarians endeavor to ensure their preferred items are indeed funded, either by reassigning funds from other spending items or from the special reserve known as the Tesoro Público—but the overall spending ceiling is typically not at stake. However, on occasion congressional coalitions can threaten to withdraw support from programs dear to the government as a way of forcing the executive to sponsor spending increases on certain items, but this is seldom done on a scale large enough to alter the overall macro limits.

The overall spending ceiling is set not in the course of congressional discussions but in the previous stage: when intraexecutive negotiations set priorities and decide spending on nonentitlement, expensive items: typically public investment projects or new subsidy or transfer programs. This is a lengthy process, lasting several months. Here the Finance Ministry plays an important role (all spending items must be authorized by the ministry) and the president has the first and last say, but nonetheless meaningful discussions and negotiations do take place. The manner in which these negotiations take place, therefore, is crucial.

3.3. Why a Fiscal Rule?

If Chilean fiscal institutions were hierarchical and transparent, if the executive had important legal power to control spending and the budget, and if Chile´s fiscal performance over the previous decade was more than adequate, why did Chile in the early 1990s need a fiscal rule? What was broken that needed fixing?

In spite of the overall strength of fiscal institutions and performance, in the early 2000s five elements stood out that were susceptible to improvement:[2]

- Fiscal policy was designed and applied with little reference to a longer-term framework.
- Nor did the design of fiscal policy explicitly separate cycle from trend. For instance, the impact of higher copper prices on allowable expenditures is obviously different if the price increase is expected to be permanent or transitory.
- Intraexecutive budget negotiations were not guided by an explicit procedure or framework. Pursuit of sound fiscal policies was largely dependent on the commitment and determination of the president and the finance minister. That commitment was present in the 1990s, but could not be assumed to exist automatically under all circumstances.
- While explicit government liabilities were quite limited (in January 2000 public debt stood under 15 percent of GDP), other contingent liabilities needed to be quantified and eventually reduced. Among them were government guarantees to pensioners in the private social security system and to private operators of concessional public works (roads and tunnels).
- Local governments (municipalities), prevented from issuing debt, occasionally did it de facto simply by running up unpaid bills to contractors and suppliers. Public hospitals operating within the central government displayed a similar habit.

As we will see below, the introduction of a fiscal rule helped correct the first four of these five problems.

4. THE FISCAL RULE IN ACTION

4.1. What Did the Rule Do?

A fiscal policy based on a structural balance rule, used for some time by a few industrialized economies (see IMF 2009), was a significant innovation in Chile.

During the 1990s Chile's fiscal policy was distinguished by its prudence, but public spending remained very sensitive to the revenue cycle, itself dependent on the economic cycle. And there was no explicit rule or framework to guide behavior and expectations concerning fiscal performance.

In 2001, a self-imposed fiscal rule (not a legally binding requirement) was introduced for the central government budget. Under the rule, annual fiscal expenditure is equal (except for a target surplus—see below) to the central government's structural income. Therefore, expenditure is independent of short-term fluctuations in revenues caused by cyclical swings in economic activity, the price of copper, and other variables that determine effective fiscal income. The fiscal rule aims to smooth government expenditure over both cycles, spending only permanent income (structural revenues). The government saves during upswings and dissaves during downturns. In this way it can avoid two problems that have long plagued Latin American fiscal policies: surges in spending when commodity prices rise and the economy picks up and drastic tightenings of fiscal spending when commodity prices drop and the economy slows. Hence, the growth of public expenditure becomes much more stable over time.

The Chilean structural surplus rule is based on three long-term variables: the price of copper, the price of molybdenum, and the trend growth of GDP. Income of the Chilean government stems from two main sources: copper-related revenue and tax revenues, with the latter heavily influenced by economic activity. To avoid biases in the estimation of these values, since the 2002 and 2003 Budget Laws, the estimation of the long-term price of copper and the GDP trend, respectively, has been entrusted to independent committees of experts. In the case of the price of copper, each committee member submits estimates of the average price of copper (per pound in the London Metal Exchange) for the next 10 years. Then the Budget Office calculates the average estimate for the next 10 years for each expert. The experts' estimates are averaged, excluding the minimum and maximum.

Similarly, to determine the value of the GDP trend, each committee member submits estimates of gross fixed capital formation, the labor force, and total factor productivity for the next five years. For each of the three variables, the trimmed mean is calculated for each year, eliminating the minimum and maximum. Using these variables, the Budget Office constructs series of capital stock hours worked (adjusted for education). The filtered series of hours worked, adjusted for education and total factor productivity, plus the unfiltered series of capital stock, are used as inputs in a Cobb-Douglas production function, whose parameters are estimated by the Finance Ministry based on information from the national accounts and the National Statistics Bureau. With this production function and the inputs above, the Budget Office calculates the GDP trend for the period.

The system began operating with the 2001 budget bill, sent to Congress in September 2000. From the start the rule involved a structural surplus target set at 1 percent of GDP. This meant that the actual surplus should average 1 percent of GDP over the cycle. Why was this necessary? The authorities at the time pointed to three reasons. First, the fisc was still a net debtor in an amount equal to 11 percent of GDP. Second, there existed a potentially large stock of contingent liabilities—associated with minimum pension guarantees and public works concessions—as well as external vulnerabilities associated with currency mismatches and potential borrowing constraints. Third, Central Bank's financial position, weakened by the 1982–83 bank bailout, remained delicate, with the bank showing in the late 1990s an operating deficit of around 1 percent of GDP. Larger public savings could provide the resources to tackle all these issues.

These original conditions have evolved favorably in recent years. Largely thanks to the implementation of the fiscal structural balance rule, the fisc accumulated net assets and eventually became a net creditor. The government reduced the risks associated with currency mismatches and identified and quantified the contingent liabilities of the Treasury.[3] Finally, the financial situation of the Central Bank of Chile improved. These developments would eventually allow the government to reduce the structural balance target to 0.5 percent of GDP, starting with the 2008 Budget Law.

4.2. Fiscal Results

What did the application of the rule achieve? A few results follow.

4.2.1. *Consolidated Central Government Balance*

The consolidated central government balance, defined as the difference between total revenue and total expenditure of the consolidated central government, is traditionally used to analyze the financial sustainability of the Treasury. The current European credit crisis has reminded us that Treasury financial insolvencies have disastrous economic and social consequences for the population, from which it may take years to recover.

Application of the rule in a context of high average copper prices meant a large increase in the effective budget surplus, which began rising in 2005 and reached 8.2 percent of GDP in 2007. Since 2006 fiscal surpluses have reached historical levels, with a cumulative tax savings equivalent to 17.3 percent of GDP (see fig. 3.4 and table 3.1).

4.2.2. *Total Central Government Debt*

The level of government debt is also an important indicator of financial sustainability. It is not feasible to maintain a high level of debt relative to GDP over a long period without falling into insolvency. Keeping public debt at low levels increases the credibility of the Treasury as a debt issuer. It also improves access to external financing and reduces the cost of borrowing for companies issuing international debt, as the sovereign debt acts as a benchmark.

Since 1990, the Chilean government has never had debt levels as low as in the period 2006–9 (see fig. 3.5). On average for that period, the gross debt was equivalent

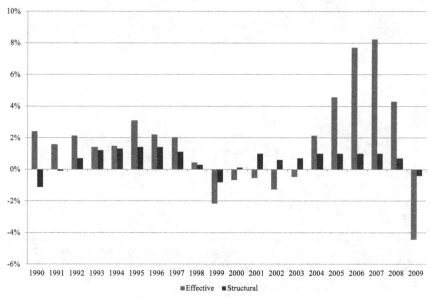

Figure 3.4 Effective and Structural Fiscal Balance (% of GDP).
Source: Budget Office and Central Bank.

Table 3.1. Fiscal Balance (% of GDP)

Period	Average Effective Balance
1990–93	1.9
1994–99	1.2
2000–2005	0.6
1990–2005	1.2
2006–9	4.3
1990–2009	1.8

Source: Budget Office and Central Bank of Chile.

to 5.2 percent of GDP, in contrast to the period 1990–2005, which reached 19.8 percent of GDP (see table 3.2), and especially in 1990, when gross debt climbed to almost
45 percent of GDP. While in 2008 and 2009 there was a slight increase in gross debt,
partly to fund the Fiscal Stimulus Plan of 2009, the trend indicates that debt will
remain at historically low levels.

Chile's public debt is also one of the lowest in the world. OECD estimates indicate
that in 2009 its members had an average public debt equivalent to 90 percent of GDP.

4.2.3. *Financial Assets Held by the Treasury*

As a counterpart to debt, the level of the central government's financial assets is
a signal of financial strength, which is especially relevant in periods of financial
crisis. In the context of the structural balance policy, the high incomes of the

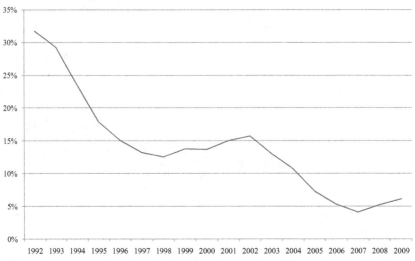

Figure 3.5 Public Debt (% of GDP).
Source: Budget Office and Central Bank of Chile.

Table 3.2. Public Debt (% of GDP)

Period	Total Debt
1990–93	36.1
1994–99	16.1
2000–2005	12.6
1990–2005	19.8
2006–9	5.2
1990–2009	16.9

Source: Budget Office and Central Bank of Chile.

Treasury in 2006–9 resulted in a record increase of financial assets since 1990 (see fig. 3.6), reaching 11.9 percent of GDP on average in the period, compared with 4.0 percent of GDP on average over the period 1990–2005 (see table 3.3). This accumulation of financial assets helped to finance the Fiscal Stimulus Plan of 2009. In spite of the crisis, at the end of 2009 Chile had gross assets equivalent to 9.3 percent of GDP, implying that the next administration (which took over in 2010) inherited financial assets like no other before in the history of Chile.

4.2.4. *Net Debtor or Creditor Position*

The net debt position of the central government is perhaps the most revealing indicator of its financial solvency. In the period 2006–9, for the first time in its history the government of Chile reached a net creditor position, equivalent to an average of 6.6 percent of GDP in 2006–9, which contrasts with a net debtor position for the period 1990–2005 that averaged 15.8 percent of GDP (see table 3.4).

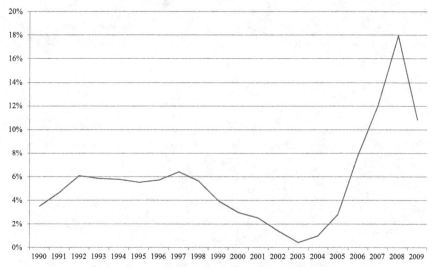

Figure 3.6 Fiscal Financial Assets (% of GDP).

Source: Budget Office and Central Bank.

Table 3.3. Fiscal Financial Assets (% of GDP)

Period	Total Debt
1990–93	5.0
1994–99	5.5
2000–2005	1.9
1990–2005	4.0
2006–9	11.9
1990–2009	5.6

Source: Budget Office and Central Bank of Chile.

Table 3.4. Net Government Position (Assets Minus Liabilities as % of GDP)

Period	Total Debt
1990–93	-31.1
1994–99	-10.5
2000–2005	-10.7
1990–2005	-15.8
2006–9	6.6
1990–2009	-11.3

Source: Budget Office and Central Bank of Chile.

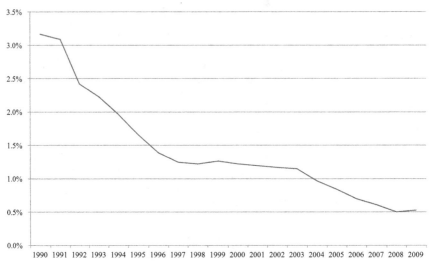

Figure 3.7 Average Interest Payments (% of GDP).
Source: Budget Office and Central Bank.

4.2.5. *Interest Expenditure*

High levels of consolidated central government debt not only indicate a weak financial position, they also increase the costs of financing and make raising new debt for the government and local companies difficult. Since debt has dropped to historically low levels, average interest expenditure has also been reduced to record low levels (see fig. 3.7). Interest expenses have been minimized to 0.6 percent of GDP and 2.9 percent of average consolidated spending, in contrast with 1.6 percent of GDP and 8 percent of spending in the 1990–2005 period (see table 3.5). The importance of paying lower interest is that instead of having to pay financial obligations to close out past commitments, these resources can be used for current public policy priorities, namely either investment or social spending, which directly benefit the country's population.

4.2.6. *Country Risk*

The perception that foreign investors have of Chile is reflected in measures of country risk. Fiscal management is one factor that strongly affects foreign investors' confidence. Therefore, proper management is reflected in lower country risk, improving access to and the cost of external financing for both the government and domestic firms. Chile's country risk has been lower than that of the reference countries. This relationship continued even when the global economic crisis hit the markets. Chile's country risk increased, but to a lesser extent than that of the reference countries. This situation is particularly striking when it is compared with the current situation of some European countries (see fig. 3.8).

4.3. The Chilean Rule in Practice: Asset Dynamics

How did the rule operate in practice and what kind of dynamics did it imply for government assets and liabilities?

Table 3.5. Interest Payments

Period	% of GDP	% Total Expenditure
1990–93	2.7	13.3
1994–99	7.3	7.3
2000–2005	5.1	5.1
1990–2005	1.6	8.0
2006–9	0.6	2.9
1990–2009	1.4	7.0

Source: Budget Office and Central Bank of Chile.

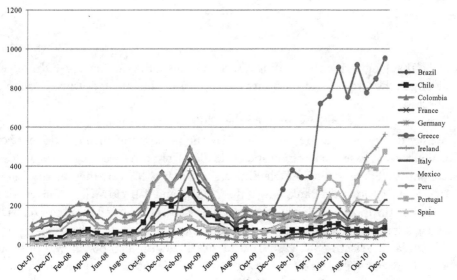

Figure 3.8 Country Risk (Basis Points).
Source: Bloomberg.

If the surplus target is s_t, the rule mandates that spending follow:

$$g_t = E_{t-1}(rb_{t-1} + \tau + \varepsilon_t - s_t) = rb_{t-1} + \tau - s. \tag{14}$$

The law of motion for assets is

$$b_t = (1+r)b_{t-1} + \tau + \varepsilon_t - g_{t-1}. \tag{15}$$

Combining the two we have

$$b_t - b_{t-1} = s_t + \varepsilon_t, \tag{16}$$

so that asset accumulation fluctuates with the realized shock. Expressing this as shares of income we have

$$b'_t - b'_{t-1} = s' - \left(\frac{\gamma}{1+\gamma}\right)b'_{t-1} + \varepsilon'_t, \tag{17}$$

where $x'_t = x_t/y_t$, y_t is GDP, γ is the rate of growth of GDP, and where the surplus target is assumed to be fixed as a share of GDP. The intuition behind this equation is simple: the government accumulates assets as a result of the surplus target (since s' > 0) and if and when the random shock is beneficial (ϵ > 0). Thus, in the absence of a sequence of bad shocks, net assets should grow with time (or net debt should fall, the same thing). This is exactly what happened throughout the decade beginning in 2000.

In steady state our last equation becomes

$$b' = \left(\frac{\gamma}{1+\gamma}\right)s', \tag{18}$$

so that long-term asset holdings are a multiple of the surplus target: the larger the target, the larger the stock of net assets toward which the government should expect to converge.

Given these conditions, in 2007 the Chilean government began considering whether the target equal to 1 percent of GDP should be maintained indefinitely. For that purpose it requested a study and evaluation from three well-regarded Chilean economists: Eduardo Engel (Yale University), Mario Marcel (then at the Inter-American Development Bank, now at the OECD), and Patricio Meller (Universidad de Chile). The three argue in a paper that the 1 percent rule could lead to excessive asset accumulation (see Engel, Marcel, and Meller 2007).

Similarly, Velasco et al. (2007), using fiscal data up to 2006, show a possible path for government net assets. The authors conclude that the Chilean government would be a net creditor to the tune of 17 percent of GDP by 2010. Based on this reasoning, the Chilean Finance Ministry announced in 2007 that the 2008 budget would be designed with a lower surplus target of 0.5 percent of GDP.[4]

5. MACRO EFFECTS OF THE STRUCTURAL APPROACH TO FISCAL POLICY

While the fiscal policy has become countercyclical since the implementation of the structural balance rule, GDP has become less volatile. The obvious question is whether these good things happened because of the change in fiscal policy or because of some event (e.g., exogenous shocks became less volatile) or some other economic policy.

In this context, Franken, Le Fort, and Parrado (2006) show that economic policy conditions registered the largest reduction in volatility, even larger than the

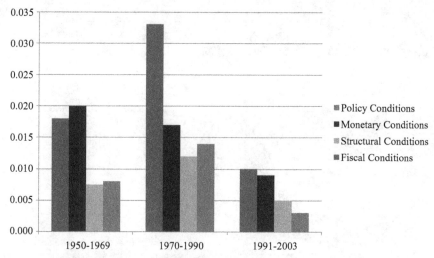

Figure 3.9 Volatility of Gap Components: Policy Conditions.
Source: Franken et al. (2006).

output gap itself. This suggests that demand management and structural policies have made an economically significant contribution toward moderating business cycle fluctuations—in terms of both magnitude and amplitude. This outcome reflects the strengthening of the macroeconomic policy framework and an ongoing process of institutional building. On disaggregating this trend, the authors find that the volatilities associated with structural and monetary policies fell to about half their previous values, while the volatility of fiscal policy fell much more markedly (see fig. 3.9).

Resilience is commonly defined as the capacity to withstand shocks. It can thus be understood as the economy's capacity to limit the volatility of the output gap when confronting exogenous shocks. To measure resilience after external shocks— the most important type of exogenous shocks faced by the Chilean economy— Franken et al. (2006) computed the ratio of the volatility of external shocks to the volatility of the output gap. Resilience from external shocks deteriorated markedly in the 1970s and 1980s and then improved sharply in the 1990s, to a slightly higher level than in the 1950s and 1960s.

The evidence gathered suggests that the Chilean economy has become more resilient to external shocks. An interpretation that helps reconcile these facts is that policy actions can play a role as shock absorbers. Improved resilience to external shocks may result from policy actions that more effectively stabilize output, which would be manifested, for example, in a shift in the policy component from procyclical (positive correlation with the output gap) to countercyclical (negative correlation).

Overall, the strengthening of the policy framework in the last period of the sample (including the floating of the exchange rate, the adoption of the fiscal rule, and the refinement of the inflation-targeting framework) seems to have played a significant role in the observed increase in the economy's resilience. This bodes well for

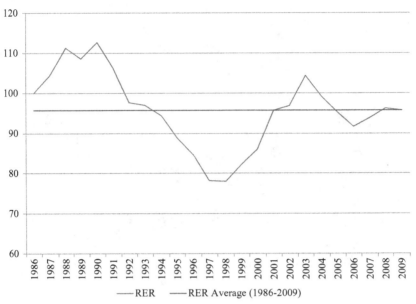

Figure 3.10 Real Exchange Rate (1986 = 100).
Source: Central Bank of Chile.

these positive developments to be sustainable in the future. In addition, in a small open economy—where the external sector plays a key role—the stabilizing action of a prudent fiscal policy has been central to the external competitiveness of the economy. Indeed, the competitiveness of the Chilean economy has remained stable, largely because of the implementation of a fiscal policy framed in the context of the structural balance rule and the implementation of an investment policy that keeps these savings abroad. In recent years, with high average copper prices, the application of the fiscal rule has reduced the effect on the real exchange rate. Despite the significant increase in the terms of trade in recent years, the real exchange rate is currently slightly below the average real exchange rate between 1990 and 2009 (see fig. 3.10).

6. The Political Economy of the Rule

Our discussion above suggests that there were two potential commons problems in the elaboration and approval of the Chilean budget: one among spending ministers who do not fully internalize the social costs of additional expenditure and one among parliamentarians who, representing individual districts, fully value the local benefits of additional spending but do not fully internalize the costs either. The introduction of the fiscal rule helped ameliorate both problems.

Begin with the interaction among ministers in the early phase of budget preparation and negotiation within the executive. It matters a great deal how this process is structured. One alternative is to channel individual spending requests first and then let the spending ceiling emerge from the simple aggregation of those demands. An alternative is for a ceiling to be preset and then within that ceiling spending ministers bargain over their spending shares.

The latter system is clearly preferable, for it induces individual players to internalize the aggregate budget constraint. But the question arises: how is the spending ceiling to be determined? The fiscal rule provided the answer. Government could only spend its long-term, cyclically adjusted income (or slightly less, if the target implied a surplus); windfalls had to be saved. Such a ceiling had several advantages: it was objectively determined; it was simple and easy to explain; it was intuitive (government was doing what any household would do: saving windfalls for a rainy day).

As a result, much of the debate and media speculation centered on what parameters the independent committees would issue and what they would imply for the spending ceiling (typically expressed, in Chilean practice, as the percentage real increase in spending over the previous year). Once the ceiling was set it was seldom questioned. Debate centered on how individual spending demands could be accommodated within the preset framework.

The operation of the rule also eased the relationship between executive and legislature in the process of amendment and approval of the budget. We saw above that Congress did not (and does not) have the power autonomously to increase spending on any given item. But negotiations did take place—sometimes fairly tense and charged negotiations—with blocks of parliamentarians withholding support for some items in an attempt to get other items funded. Having a preset and objectively chosen ceiling gave these discussions a measure of discipline, with individual players understanding that additional spending demands could not be too large, since they had to be funded by cuts elsewhere. The existence of a publicly acknowledged system also helped individual congressmen or senators explain to their constituencies why a particular spending item may not receive as much funding as the constituency might have desired.

It is important to underscore that the surplus target (at whatever level it was set)—and hence the spending ceiling—was a self-imposed discipline, not a legally mandated requirement. Recall that until the 2006 approval of the Fiscal Responsibility Law, the whole system rested on the power of decree of the executive, which could be changed at a moment's notice by another decree. And after passage, the law forced the government to prepare its budget on a cyclically adjusted basis (it also mandated that the government allocate the resulting savings into the two sovereign wealth funds), but the actual level of the surplus target continued to be a free-choice variable for the executive.

Why then, one might ask, was it a useful and credible disciplining device for the discussions both within the government and between the executive and the legislature? One answer is that the ceiling provided by the rule served as a natural coordinating device or focal point. That is, agents may have understood that, in the absence of such a coordinating device, spending demands would mount and eventually the costs would be paid by all. No agent would want to be the first unilaterally to reduce its spending claims. But if others are expected to do it because of the existence of an externally imposed spending ceiling, then each agent individually may wish to do so as well.[5]

Notice that for the rule to play this role, what is essential is that it generate a ceiling in an objective, predictable, and comprehensible way. It is not essential that the ceiling be based on a cyclical adjustment or on any other particular criterion. This is not to say that the cyclically adjusted or structural approach did not play a key role in improving fiscal performance; it did. The point, rather, is that the Chilean rule played a dual role: that of improving the political economy and thus the overall orientation of fiscal policy (by virtue of disciplining bargaining interactions both within and outside the executive) and that of improving the macro properties of fiscal policy (by eliminating procyclicality and introducing some mild countercyclicality).

Finally, note that the rule, by incorporating a positive surplus target in its early years, helped alleviate one more potential problem of the pre-2000 fiscal policy stance: that associated with contingent fiscal liabilities. At a general level, lowering public debt and accumulating assets provides a cushion against the materialization of those claims. More specifically, the Pension Reform of 2008 made explicit some of the pension liabilities that until then had (partially) been implicit and contingent. To match that, the Pension Reserve Fund (PRF) created in 2006 began accumulating to the tune of a minimum of 0.2 percent and a maximum of 0.5 percent of GDP annually. An external actuarial review conducted by Stella and Guerra (2010) found that the PRF is on course to having sufficient resources to meet pension-related eventualities.

7. FROM THE BUDGET RULE TO THE SOVEREIGN WEALTH FUNDS

Application of the fiscal rule led, as we have seen above, to a substantial accumulation of government financial assets. Those assets had to be invested and managed. The institutional setup for doing that was provided by the 2006 Fiscal Responsibility Law. The law created two sovereign wealth funds (SWFs) as vehicles for managing those assets. The PRF was designed to help fulfill fiscal obligations in the areas of pensions and social security. Specifically, the fund is earmarked as backing for the government's guarantee of basic old-age and disability solidarity pensions and solidarity pension contributions for low-income pensioners.

The Economic and Social Stabilization Fund (ESSF) was created to finance fiscal deficits that may occur during periods of weak growth or low copper prices; it can also be used to pay down public debt and finance the PRF. In this way, it helps to reduce cyclical variations in fiscal spending, ensuring long-term financing for social programs.

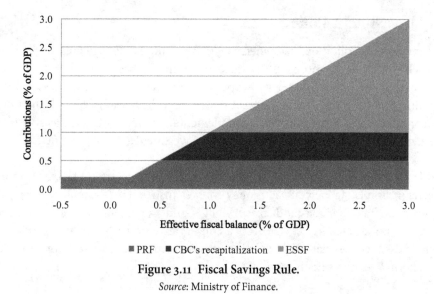

Figure 3.11 Fiscal Savings Rule.
Source: Ministry of Finance.

7.1. Capital Contributions

The minimum annual amount paid into the PRF is equivalent to 0.2 percent of the previous year's GDP, although if the effective fiscal surplus exceeds this amount, the contribution can rise to a maximum of 0.5 percent of the previous year's GDP. The transfer of resources must be made during the first half of the year. Under the Fiscal Responsibility Law, the government was authorized to capitalize the Central Bank of Chile (CBC) during five years beginning in 2006 by an annual amount of up to the difference between the government's contributions to the PRF and the effective fiscal surplus, with an upper limit of 0.5 percent of GDP. In 2006, 2007, and 2008, this capitalization was equivalent to 0.5 percent of GDP.

The remainder of the effective surplus, after payment into the PRF and capitalization of the CBC, must be paid into the ESSF. Repayments of public debt and advanced payments into the ESSF during the previous year can, however, be subtracted from this contribution (see fig. 3.11).

7.2. Institutional Framework

Investment of the assets of the PRF and the ESSF calls for a clear and transparent institutional framework that provides the necessary structure for making and implementing decisions, monitoring risk, and controlling investment policy. The basis for this framework was established in the Fiscal Responsibility Law. In addition, in 2006 the Finance Ministry appointed the CBC—subject to the approval of its governing board—as the fiscal agent for the management of both funds and established the general framework for their administration. The Finance Ministry also created the Financial Committee in 2007 to advise the finance minister on the investment of the assets of the ESSF and the PRF (see fig. 3.12).

7.3. Investment Policy

The investment policy, defined when the PRF and the ESSF were created, involved asset classes similar to those used by the CBC for international reserves. This choice was based mainly on the CBC's vast experience managing these asset classes. In the first quarter of 2008, a new investment policy more closely aligned with the funds' characteristics was drawn up, but its implementation was postponed as a result of the global financial crisis, and the original investment policy remained in force throughout 2008–10.

Under the original policy, 66.5 percent of the funds' assets are held as nominal sovereign bonds, 30 percent as money market instruments—such as short-term highly rated bank deposits and treasury bills—and 3.5 percent as inflation-indexed sovereign bonds (see fig. 3.13). This is a conservative policy, given that it does not include asset classes with higher levels of risk, such as equities, corporate bonds, and alternative investments.

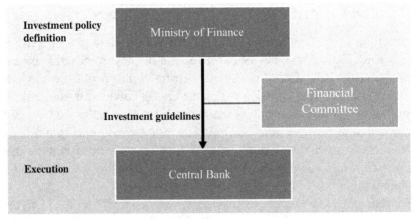

Figure 3.12 Institutional Framework.
Source: Ministry of Finance.

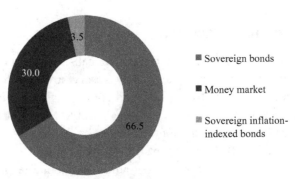

Figure 3.13 Investment Policy.
Source: Ministry of Finance.

In addition, a reference allocation by currency has been established, specifying 50 percent in U.S. dollars, 40 percent in euros, and 10 percent in yen, with a restriction of a variation of up to five percentage points on these values. These guidelines also allow investments in instruments in other currencies but require exchange-rate coverage tied to one of the three other currencies. Notice that this investment strategy involves investing all of the funds' assets in foreign currency and outside the country. This may seem surprising, given that the bulk of the government's spending commitments are denominated in pesos. There are three reasons for this choice.

First, an investment policy based only on foreign currency is a natural hedge that generates a countercyclical influence on government income. Given the negative correlation between the nominal exchange rate and the price of copper, the government tends to accumulate resources when copper is high and the peso strong, and to dis-save whenever the opposite occurs. Put differently, the countercyclical effect provided by the movements of the exchange rate in response to the most likely medium term path of the copper price may be sufficient to replace a potentially costly hedging strategy. Second, saving the resources abroad helps stabilize the real exchange rate. The potential conversion of copper revenues (which the government receives in U.S. dollars) into local currency may generate a significant appreciation of the exchange rate, generating the so-called Dutch Disease despite the application of the structural balance rule. This is avoided by keeping the savings in foreign currency. Third, the magnitude of sovereign asset accumulation relative to local financial market size could create a bubble with the associated negative consequences. To reduce this risk the government of Chile decided to invest both funds entirely in foreign currency and outside the country.

The investment policy adopted by Chile's two SWFs was very conservative, but this conservatism would serve the country well when the financial crisis hit. Despite the financial turbulence, the Chilean SWFs had among the highest returns of all the world's SWFs with data available in 2008. In 2009, international markets displayed a boom in riskier asset prices, so many SWFs enjoyed strong recoveries in their market values; meanwhile, Chile stayed with the same prudent portfolio with consequent lower returns in the year. On average, the rates of return of the Chilean funds in the 2007–9 period were still higher than those of their peers.

7.4. Transparency

The Chilean government's commitment to developing and improving all aspects of the funds' management includes the transparency of their decisions and access to relevant information. To this end, it systematically prepares and publishes reports about the SWFs' positions, provides information about the main issues discussed in each meeting of the Financial Committee and about its recommendations, and discloses all significant decisions about the SWFs' management adopted by the Finance Ministry.

To guarantee public access to all relevant information about the ESSF and the PRF, the Finance Ministry has created special websites in Spanish and English containing all monthly, quarterly, and annual reports about the funds; the recommendations of the Financial Committee and its annual report; the legal and institutional framework for the funds; and news releases and other information. This commitment to effective and opportune access to information was particularly important in 2008 when the global financial crisis and the liquidity problems experienced by different financial institutions around the world meant increased demand for information about the position of the institutions in which the funds' assets were deposited as well as about the intermediaries and custody services used. This led to a decision to publish quarterly reports about these institutions, rather than the annual report issued through September 2008.

As part of Chile's commitment to best SWF practices, the government decided to participate actively in initiatives launched by several international organizations in a bid to establish an operating framework for SWFs and promote their transparency. Both the Finance Ministry and the CBC have taken an active role in the International Working Group of Sovereign Wealth Funds (IWG). The IWG concluded its discussions with a broad agreement on best principles and practices of SWFs. This agreement is known internationally as the "Santiago Principles." Chile's active role in this meeting reflects its government's commitment to promoting transparency in the management of resources that belong to all Chileans and to the creation of a permanent forum for the exchange of views and information among different SWFs and the countries in which they invest.

Chile's efforts to improve transparency have been internationally recognized. In a ranking published by the Peterson Institute for International Economics in April 2008 the ESSF was awarded 82 points out of 100 for transparency and accountability, taking sixth place out of 34 SWFs. In the overall ranking, which also included other aspects, such as fund structure, objectives, fiscal treatment, organization, corporate governance, and use of derivatives, the ESSF ranked eighth. Similarly, in 2009, Chile obtained a perfect score in the Sovereign Wealth Fund Institute's global ranking of transparency and good administration of the world's 45 major sovereign funds.

8. Impact of the Global Financial Crisis

When the global financial crisis hit, Chile's economy was in an excellent position to mitigate its effects. The country's preparedness was, to a great extent, the result of lessons learned from previous crises. After a 1982 banking crisis, Chile began to implement prudent and modern financial regulations with high standards of supervision. This allowed Chile to face the recent global credit crunch with a solid and well-capitalized financial system.

The 2007–9 global financial crisis was the first crisis Chile had confronted with a flexible exchange rate. That policy helped it avoid building up currency exchange imbalances and facilitated the application of countercyclical policies. The inflation-targeting framework implemented by the CBC led naturally to an easing of monetary policy in the context of plummeting inflationary expectations resulting from the softening of the business cycle and the collapse of oil prices. The flexible exchange rate provided a natural cushion to accommodate fluctuations in external conditions. The CBC also accumulated a prudent quantity of international reserves that, together with treasury assets, helped Chile face the liquidity restrictions that began to arise in the latter months of 2008.

Last but certainly not least, Chile could face the financial crisis. Public debt was negligible and the Treasury was a net creditor for the first time in its history. This combination of factors endowed Chile with a "fiscal space" to engage in countercyclical fiscal policy that many other nations in the world—many of them in Europe—were sorely lacking. When the crisis hit, the first priority was to avoid a liquidity crunch in the domestic financial system. In October 2008, the Finance Ministry and the CBC implemented a number of measures to ensure the economy's liquidity in both national and foreign currencies. The CBC stopped buying U.S. dollars to accumulate reserves; opened a window for US$500 million auctions of 28-day currency swaps, which it later expanded to 180 days; eased collateral requirements for repurchase agreements (repo operations); and temporarily loosened bank reserve rules. At the same time, the government auctioned off US$1.05 billion of Treasury assets in U.S. dollars to be deposited in the local banking system.

Next came the fiscal response. Chile's government put in place opportune, substantial, and temporary fiscal measures. In January 2009, Chile became one of the first countries to react to the global crisis by announcing an extraordinary fiscal stimulus plan. Close to US$4 billion, equivalent to 2.8 percent of GDP, was assigned to this package from the ESSF. At the time it was announced, this 2009 fiscal plan was the world's second largest as measured by resources committed relative to the economy's size.

To implement this expansionary fiscal policy, Chile opted for a diversified strategy, combining increases in public investment with transfers, employment subsidies, credit subsidies and stimuli, capitalization of state enterprises, and tax discounts. Special emphasis was placed on transitory measures, giving economic agents greater incentives to increase their short-term demand to take advantage of these stimuli.

The logic behind this design was as follows: in a situation of extraordinary uncertainty, with most components of private demand falling sharply, previous estimates of fiscal multipliers become unreliable, since it is nearly impossible to guess how private spending will react to the fiscal expansion. Given this uncertainty, it is prudent to act on many fronts simultaneously, maximizing the chances that at least a subset of fiscal stimuli will have the desired effect (see Blanchard et al. 2008).

These measures were proportional to the shock the country was facing. The 2009 fiscal stimulus (drop in tax collection plus increased spending) was similar in magnitude to the estimated decline in nonmining exports. Thus, the fiscal impulse could hope to stabilize available private income. The fiscal plan was enhanced in

March 2009 with 20 additional measures to stimulate the credit market—known as the Pro-Credit Initiative—and one month later with an unprecedented proemployment agreement among government, workers, and businesses.

The sharp drop in aggregate demand hit fiscal revenues very hard. In addition, over the course of 2009 Chile experienced deflation, with the consumer price index falling by 1.4 percent. Since expenditure is fixed in the budget in nominal terms, this meant a higher-than-anticipated real increase in expenditure. The combination of sharply lower revenues and higher outlays meant that by the end of the year the fiscal deficit was higher than it had been estimated at the time of the launching of the fiscal stimulus. In the end the actual total deficit reached 4.5 percent of GDP and the structural deficit 1.3 percent of GDP, substantially higher than the structural balance that had been forecasted earlier in the year.[6]

The gap was financed by drawing down from the ESSF. Implementation of the stimulus and the drop in tax collection led the government to use the ESSF again in June 2009, drawing down US$4 billion on top of what had already been withdrawn in the first half of the year. Given the objectives of the funds, countercyclical fiscal policy triggered disbursements from the ESSF and not from the PRF (see figs. 3.14 and 3.15).

Expansive countercyclical policies were aided by an aggressive reduction in the CBC's monetary policy rate, taking advantage of lower inflationary perspectives and a widening output gap. The rate decrease of 775 basis points over the course of 2009 brought the CBC's interest rate to a historic low of 0.5 percent.

To enhance the monetary policy stimulus, in mid-2009 the CBC adopted unconventional monetary policy measures, mostly by establishing a term lending facility for the banking system at the current monetary policy rate. The CBC announced that monetary policy would remain at that level until at least the second quarter of 2010. There was a deliberate effort to coordinate the government's fiscal and monetary policies. Chile stood out as the country with the most aggressive countercyclical policies, which substantially eased credit conditions and injected a large fiscal stimulus (see fig. 3.16).

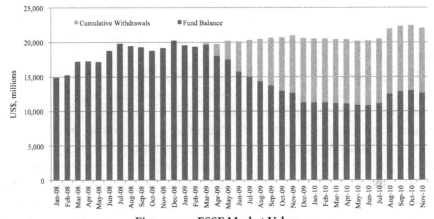

Figure 3.14 ESSF Market Value.
Source: Ministry of Finance.

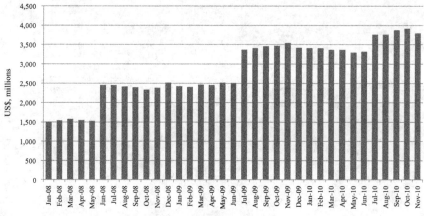

Figure 3.15 PRF Market Value.

Source: Ministry of Finance.

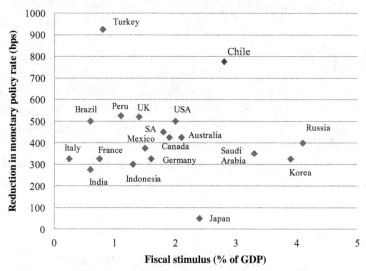

Figure 3.16 Fiscal and Monetary Policy Stimuli.

Source: International Monetary Fund and Bloomberg.

These policies paid off. Given the magnitude of the shock, the contraction in output was relatively small and short-lived. Figure 3.17 shows one proxy for the exogenous shock—the size in the drop of export values as a share of GDP—plotted against the fall in output from precrisis peak to trough. The figure shows that in a large sample of countries, both emerging and developed, only two (Norway and Canada) clearly outperformed Chile in the sense of having experienced both a larger export drop and a smaller output contraction.

In the end, real GDP fell by 1.5 percent in 2009, with the recovery in demand and output visible already beginning in the third quarter of 2009. A tremendous earthquake hit Chile in February 2010, causing substantial loss of life, destruction of the capital stock put at around US$8 billion, and long-lasting production dislocations in

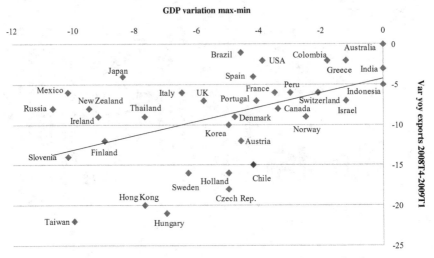

Figure 3.17 Output Contraction and Negative Export Shocks.
Source: International Monetary Fund and World Bank. "yoy" = year on year.

the south-central portion of the country. But all this damage could not hold back the recovery: Chile's economy grew 5.3 percent in 2010, with investment rising sharply both for cyclical reasons and to meet the needs of reconstruction. As of the time of writing, the country stands poised to have another strong year in 2011, with consensus forecasts putting growth in the vicinity of 6 percent, the highest in Latin America. This all suggests that the countercyclical fiscal and monetary policies were extremely effective: by limiting the size and the collateral damage of the 2009 demand collapse, they created the conditions for a strong and healthy recovery.

9. CONCLUSIONS

Over the past quarter century, Chile has proven that the unthinkable is possible: a middle-income emerging nation can have a fiscal policy that is sounder and more sustainable than the fiscal policies of most nations, rich or poor. The mantra of this policy has been very simple: act responsibly, design policy for the long run, and accumulate enough fiscal space so that fiscal policy can play a stabilizing role in the short run. This orientation also implies a decidedly countercyclical approach during both phases of the cycle: saving during the period of high copper prices and using those accumulated resources during the global economic crisis.

This new approach to fiscal policy also improved the political dynamics of budget design and approval. Structural income (minus the targeted surplus) provided a spending ceiling that helped discipline competing claims by spending ministers and parliamentarians. Chile's budget-making arrangements, at the outset stronger than those of many emerging markets, were improved even further.

Chile's fiscal policy underwent two demanding tests. In the early years of the copper boom, the key was to show that the copper windfall could be saved, in spite of mounting political pressures to the contrary. During the financial crisis, the key was to demonstrate that accumulated fiscal resources could be used aggressively to cushion the impact on economic activity and employment. Chile's fiscal policy passed both tests, and with good marks.

But success should not breed complacency. Not everything is taken care of in Chile's public finances. There are several challenges ahead. The first challenge that must be met is to gradually withdraw the fiscal stimulus that began in 2009. As the economy recovers sharply, the unusual fiscal stimulus is no longer necessary. On the contrary, a tighter fiscal policy leaves more room for the necessary monetary tightening to be more gradual, thus limiting incentives for capital inflows and helping prevent an excessively sharp appreciation of the Chilean peso. The macroeconomics of the situation is clear, but the political challenges are nonetheless there: the inertia of maintaining transitory spending programs that were created to confront a specific situation should be avoided.

The second challenge has to do with the institutional structure of fiscal policy. Using external and independent committees to fix the long-term price of copper and the growth trend has proven very successful. There is room to build on this success and provide more institutional structure for other aspects of that approach's application: for instance, in determining what changes need to be made to the methodology for calculating structural or long-term fiscal income. This methodology needs to be continuously improved to reflect underlying structural change in the economy. A balance must be struck between precision and simplicity: only a rule that is simple enough can be understood by the population and will remain legitimate and politically acceptable. At the same time, an effort must be made continuously to provide additional degrees of transparency and accountability. In this context, the current government formed an Advisory Committee that issued its final report in 2011 (Comité Asesor para el Diseño 2011).[7] This is an opportunity to take further steps to improve further the successful Chilean approach to fiscal policy.

The third challenge is permanent: how to improve continuously the quality of public spending. It is not enough to merely ensure the availability of fiscal resources and the sustainability of programs and benefits provided to the population. These benefits need to be high quality and must be provided efficiently.

NOTES

1. Note that the rate of time discounting is assumed to be equal to the world rate of interest. This eliminates standard reasons for running fiscal deficits or surpluses.

2. As IMF (2009) pointed out, fiscal rules have typically been introduced when countries have already made at least some initial progress toward fiscal consolidation and macroeconomic stability.

3. The main contingent liabilities of the Treasury in Chile are pensions, so the Pension Reserve Fund was created to meet these pension obligations.

4. The target was later driven to zero at the outset of the world financial crisis.

5. Formally, such a coordinating device would be enough to ensure such a "good equilibrium" if the underlying game among the many players displayed multiple equilibria, so what the device would do is simply coordinate expectations and actions on one give outcome—in this case, one without overspending. But notice, that was not the case in the model presented above, which displayed only one equilibrium for the set of strategies considered. However, if the model were extended to include "history-dependent strategies," in which actions depend on histories and not only on the current state, then the game would display many equilibria, and a rule such as this one could serve to provide coordination around a welfare-preferred outcome. See Benhabib, Rustichini, and Velasco (2001) for a discussion of history-dependent strategies in a related model.

6. That is the structural balance calculated employing the methodology that was in use in 2009. In mid-2010 the new administration, following a preliminary report by the Advisory Committee (see below), introduced some methodological changes that, if applied retroactively, would have enlarged the 2009 structural deficit. The bulk of the difference has to do with the treatment of temporary tax cuts, which, in the 2009 methodology, were not considered to alter structural or "permanent" income.

7. The Advisory Committee, in a preliminary report, issued some technical recommendations regarding changes to the existing methodology for calculating structural fiscal income. In particular, it proposed that all temporary tax changes should be treated as if they were permanent. It also recommended eliminating the cyclical adjustment to interest income. We do not agree with these recommendations, which move the methodology away from the spirit of trying to approximate the "permanent income" of the fisc.

REFERENCES

Alesina, Alberto, Silvia Ardagna, Roberto Perotti, and Fabio Schiantarelli. 1999. "Fiscal Policy, Profits and Investment." NBER Working Paper 7207, National Bureau of Economic Research, Washington, DC.

Alesina, Alberto, Ricardo Hausmann, Rudolf Hommes, and Ernesto Stein. 1999. "Budget Institutions and Fiscal Performance in Latin America." *Journal of Development Economics* 59(2): 253–73.

Barro, Robert. 1980. "A Capital Market in an Equilibrium Business Cycle Model." *Econometrica* 48(6): 1393–417.

Benhabib, Jess, Aldo Rustichini, and Andres Velasco. 2001. "Public Capital and Optimal Taxes without Commitment." *Review of Economic Design* 6(3–4): 371–97.

Blanchard, Olivier, Carlo Cottarelli, Antonio Spilimbergo, and Steven Symansky. 2008. "Fiscal Policy for the Crisis." IMF staff position note, International Monetary Fund, Washington, DC.

Comité Asesor para el Diseño de una Política Fiscal de Balance Estructural de Segunda Generación para Chile. 2011. *Propuestas para Perfeccionar la Regla Fiscal: Informe Final.* Report prepared for the Government of Chile, Santiago. Available at www.dipres.gob.cl.

Engel, Eduardo, Mario Marcel, and Patricio Meller. 2007. "Meta de Superávit Estructural: Elementos para su análisis." Report prepared for the Ministry of Finance, Government of Chile, Santiago. Available at www.dipres.gob.cl.

Franken, Helmut, Guillermo Le Fort, and Eric Parrado. 2006. "Business Cycle Responses and the Resilience of the Chilean Economy." In *External Vulnerability and Preventive Policies*, edited by Ricardo Caballero, César Calderón, and Luis Felipe Céspedes. Santiago: Central Bank of Chile.

IMF (International Monetary Fund). 2009. "Fiscal Rules—Anchoring Expectations for Sustainable Public Finances." IMF staff paper, December, International Monetary Fund, Washington, DC.

Stella, Peter, and María Lucía Guerra. 2010. *Estudio Económico-Financiero de Evaluación del Impacto de los Aportes de Capital del Fisco en el Balance Proyectado del Banco Central de Chile*. Study prepared for the Budget Office, Government of Chile, Santiago. Available at www.dipres.gob.cl.

Velasco, Andrés, Alberto Arenas, Luis Felipe Céspedes, and Jorge Rodríguez. 2007. "Compromisos Fiscales y la Meta de Superávit Estructural." Estudios de Finanzas Públicas, Ministerio de Hacienda, Dirección de Presupuestos, May, Santiago.

von Hagen, Jürgen. 1993. "Monetary Union, Money Demand, and Money Supply: A Review of the German Monetary Union." *European Economic Review* 37(4): 803–27.

von Hagen, Jürgen, and Ian Harden. 1995. "Budget Processes and Commitment to Fiscal Discipline." *European Economic Review* 39(3–4): 771–79

CHAPTER 4

INDUSTRIAL POLICY AND ECONOMIC TRANSFORMATION

LUCIANO COUTINHO,
JOÃO CARLOS FERRAZ,
ANDRÉ NASSIF, AND RAFAEL OLIVA

1. THE RELEVANCE OF INDUSTRIAL POLICIES FOR ECONOMIC DEVELOPMENT

From the Smithian classic tradition and the 1950s seminal work on growth (Solow 1956) to recent endogenous growth contributions (Romer 1986), from the forefathers of development economics (Rosenstein-Rodan 1943; Prebisch 1949; Hirschman 1958) to Schumpeter and his evolutionist followers (Freeman 1987, Nelson and Winter 1982), a consensus exists on the determining factors of economic development. The development of a country is related to economic transformation deriving from technological change and from increasing the knowledge content of economic activities that induce as well as sustain productivity gains (Lin and Monga 2010, Krugman 1990).

But how is such a machine of growth put into motion? Do Schumpeterian entrepreneurs and the market suffice? Gerschenkron (1962) has shown that there cases of countries managing to successfully overcome economic backwardness in the absence of an active state are rare. Along the same lines, Chang (2003, 2) argues that "developed countries did not get where they are now through the policies and the institutions that they recommend to developing countries today. Most of them actively used 'bad' trade and industrial policies, such as infant industry protection and export subsidies." Amsden (2001, 185) also asserts that "as a catch-up strategy, free trade appears to have been limited to Switzerland and Hong Kong." Evans (2008, 1) is even sharper: "history and development theory support the proposition: 'no developmental state, no development.'"

In this chapter, we define industrial policies as an articulated set of policy instruments, of a horizontal and sectoral nature, aimed at specific economic activities or agents, with the aim of: (1) strengthening competences (fixed investment, skills, innovation, and technological capabilities), (2) inducing productivity (labor and capital), and (3) strengthening the market position of firms (exports, internationalization of firms, small and medium enterprises (SMEs) and clusters of SMEs, attracting foreign direct investment). Higher levels of competences, productivity, and market share should, in turn, contribute to a country's economic transformation and development. As industrial policies are aimed at structural change, inevitably, they must be considered within a long-term perspective, and they surpass the time span of government administrations that usually last from four to six years. As pointed out by CEPAL (2007, 8), "production development policies imply an effect on problems whose resolution requires continuity over a period measured in decades and not in years."

The literature on industrial policies is, to say the least, very passionate: pro and con arguments are usually constructed based on previous propositions on what roles the state and the market in economic development should have. The evidence put forward, however, is based on examples that could go either way: they are functional, or they are harmful to development.[1] Still, recently and in the context of the international financial crisis, which may even be a cognitive crisis, policymakers, academics, and opinion makers are becoming more receptive to policies that, until very recently, were ostracized: industrial policy is gaining space in the public policy agenda.

After a period in which the prevailing view saw fiscal austerity and inflation control as top priorities along with a regulatory role for the state, the recent crisis required immediate and unprecedented state activism, around the world, to prevent a generalized economic meltdown. Such activism brought back, with increasing force, the debate on its role in economic development. Although it is evident that, in coming years, the state will be an important player in managing crises and sustaining economic growth, the contours of its presence, as well as the extent and depth of its intervention, are still to be defined. The elaboration of the upcoming economic reasoning for different modes of intervention—there will be differences as countries differ!—will come in the economic literature, and, most certainly, a consensus will not be reached.

Nevertheless, practitioners are actively designing and starting to implement industrial policies everywhere. Very few countries have *not* placed a high priority on these policies; nations such as South Korea and China give them very high priority. Others are transforming the relationship between the state and the private sector, for example, Japan and Russia. Even the United States is bringing to the policy arena unexpected activism (Office of the President 2010). These are all examples of a new generation of industrial policies aimed at strengthening abilities of firms in each country to face upcoming competitive challenges.

In this chapter, we do not intend to criticize ideas of those against or in favor of industrial policies. We have learned from history that intervention is place- and time-specific and, more importantly, it can be successful, or it can fail. Our approach is first, to outline the normative debate of those authors who do see a scope for state intervention (section 2); second, to propose a policy framework (section 3); and third, to examine the Brazilian Industrial Policy, the Política de Desenvolvimento Produtivo, or PDP (MDIC 2008, 2009), launched in 2008 (sections 4, 5, and 6).

The Brazilian case is relevant because not only is it a different policy experiment from the typical one, but it may also provide lessons for other experiments being performed in different regions of the world. The PDP is a new institutional arrangement deviating from conventional sectorally biased industrial policies: it is comprehensive in sectoral terms; it is aimed at specific targets, mobilizing significant public resources; its design for governance is responsibility oriented; and it is intensive in fostering public-private cooperation.

Our analysis of the Brazilian PDP focuses on two main issues. First, we analyze, in detail, the PDP's aims, reach, and instruments. This is relevant, as history, economic structure, and development constraints, prospects, and aspirations define, for every country, singular institutions. These, in turn, mold singular industrial policies. As Cimoli, Ferraz, and Primi (2005, 37) propose, "Policy goals, instruments and capabilities must be tailored to country specific context and time requirements." Thus, we examine whether Brazil's PDP is grounded on the needs and challenges of existing economic structure. Second, a much-debated issue on industrial policies is related to "government failure." The quest for efficiency in public efforts is especially relevant—the subject matter is the use of scarce and public funds.[2] To a large extent, in the past, this matter was not handled as it should have been, as Latin Americans have proved to be excellent at diagnosis, quite apt at proposing policies, inefficient in policy implementation, and negligent in carrying out policy evaluation.[3] Thus, the chapter examines the PDP's effectiveness, that is, the extent to which and how policy propositions were implemented in Brazil.

In short, the purposes of this chapter are, first, to discuss the relevant role of industrial policies in economic development; and second, taking Brazil as a case study, to analyze the implementation process of an industrial policy, in particular, issues associated with institutional coordination and policy management. The chapter culminates with an evaluation of whether the Brazilian PDP is starting to contribute to the economic transformation of the country.

One last word: in its empirical section, this chapter does not attempt to assess the results of the Brazilian Industrial Policy. This is an embryonic policy—it was launched in 2008—and one should bear in mind that industrial policies should be assessed from a long-term perspective, since boosting competitiveness and fostering structural transformation are ongoing processes.

2. The Normative Debate (among Those Favoring Industrial Policies)

From the vast literature dating back to List ([1841]1909) and Prebisch (1949) and, more recently, Brander (1986), Rodrik (2004), and Greenwald and Stiglitz (2006), two economic phenomena favor the adoption of industrial policies:[4] (1) learning processes associated with an embryonic industrial stage of development and (2) the creation of positive spillovers or externalities that benefit third parties, frequently a characteristic of increasing returns from economic activities. From a theoretical perspective, Greenwald and Stiglitz (2006)[5] demonstrate how developing countries, with a fragile industrial base, are not able to disseminate technological spillovers within and among sectors, thus impeding long-term and sustained increases in productivity. The argument that follows is that, unless governments implement industrial policies that promote new industries, growth in developing economies will tend to stagnate in the long term. Hausmann and Rodrik (2003) develop the argument that governments must play a significant role in fostering industrial growth and change.

Within the realm of development economics, arguments in favor of industrial policies are not so controversial. The debate is not whether there are economic reasons for the practice of industrial policies, but rather how to engage in such practices without experiencing "government failures" that would hinder the achievement of their purposes in the long run—to reduce competence and technology gaps, as well as the disparity in per capita income between developing and developed countries.

In order to organize this debate, we have provocatively and schematically divided authors into two fields: the "modern-liberal" field and the "activist-evolutionist" field. The modern-liberal field includes those favoring state intervention with instruments that are predominantly "horizontal," for correcting market failures; the activist-evolutionists defend the use of "horizontal" or "vertical" instruments for inducing structural change, or, as pointed out by Peres and Primi (2009, 6), "(i) the position which places trusts in the market's adjustment mechanisms, leaving minimal leeway for the state to act to correct market failures; and (ii) an approach that synthesizes Schumpeterian, evolutionist and structuralist (schools)."

The modern-liberal approach places emphasis on leveling of playing fields. Its advocates recognize the economic relevance of increasing returns as well as externalities, and that markets do not operate, fully and always, at the frontier of economic efficiency. Yet as they deem the natural result of a capitalist development process imperfect competition (as Schumpeterian supporters do), arguments in favor of industrial policy are based on the concept of "market failures." Market failures are limited in scope and relatively shallow. The main normative implication of this conceptual option is that public intervention must aim preferably at correcting failures and at inducing externalities, preferably those associated with the innovation process.

The use of policy instruments earmarked for correcting market failures is only justified if such failures do not surpass risks inherent to government failures. When arguing that the public sector is, typically, much more misinformed than the market, thus running high risks of "failing" when making choices, the modern-liberal supporters recommend horizontal public policies such as education, infrastructure, and support for research and development (Lerner 2010). Selective support for the industrial sector is, in general, shunned and, if not, only justified to stimulate specific activities, such as exports. However, the available empirical evidence, based on descriptive or econometric statistics, is not conclusive. For example, reviewing empirical literature on trade policies—an option typically recommended by authors of the modern-liberal approach—Rodríguez and Rodrik (2001) did not find strong evidence that trade policies—especially open trade policies—necessarily lead to economic growth.

As emphasized by Haque (2007, 3), "the market failure approach has tended to restrict policy discussion to a narrow range of situations, and government's role in industrial promotion is cast more or less as a residual activity, to be undertaken reluctantly and cautiously." Also, there may be an interesting consequence of horizontal policies that is largely overlooked by most analysts: most policies of this kind, when effectively implemented, can have differentiated impacts among economic agents. As capabilities and competences are singular, those with higher capabilities can be better positioned to place bids for nonsectorally biased innovation grants, for instance. Another example: experienced exporters can obtain access to tax benefits more easily than newcomers. Thus, while formally providing similar opportunities to all, if the government does not take preventive actions, horizontal instruments may reinforce initial conditions. This is even more pronounced in a context where inequality and heterogeneity in capabilities prevail among economic agents.

The standpoint of the activist-evolutionist approach is that firms differ. They not only are intrinsically singular in terms of the direction of decisions they make, the capabilities they accumulate, and the performance they achieve but also, and to a great extent, they differ according to the sector in which they operate. Sector paradigms define minimum efficient levels of economies of scope and economies of scale. Activist-evolutionists take for granted that innovations—in production processes, products, opening of markets, and exploring new types and sources of inputs, as well as organizational change, in keeping with the classic conception of Schumpeter (1942)—are the determining factors of economic development. For Dosi, Pavitt, and Soete (1990), firms and countries have absolute differentials ("gaps") in technological capabilities and innovative potential. Such differentials produce effects on the competitive position of firms, as well as on the specialization pattern and long-term growth potential of countries. Even though they recognize that static comparative advantages influence the short-term specialization pattern, these authors emphasize that innovation predominantly influences changes in trade specialization and the potential for economic growth in the long term. In addition to this, given the existence of increasing returns that surface, simultaneously, as both the cause and effect of innovation and of technological progress, the absolute gaps between firms and countries outline courses of development with strong path-dependent and locked-in features (Arthur 1989).[6]

Therefore, a country with a production structure that is mainly "technology inten-sive" tends to remain on a course of development that benefits from the fruits of tech-nical progress, reinforcing, cumulatively, its position in relation to others, while a country with economic activities that are mainly intensive in natural resources, or labor, would also remain on such a development path, in the absence of structural change. As a result, differences between the two groups would remain and even grow stronger over time if productivity levels increase faster in the former group than the latter.

From a normative perspective, the activist-evolutionist approach brings together

> a diverse group of economists and thinkers on development whose common denominator is their recognition of: (i) the intrinsic, qualitative and quantitative differences between sectors and among production activities; (ii) the specificities of knowledge and technology, and their catalyzing role in development processes; (iii) the absence of automatic adjustment mechanisms; and (iv) the role of institutions in shaping the transition to higher levels of development associated with the transfer of human and financial resources to activities with increasing returns. (Peres and Primi 2009, 6)

For these economists, policies to transfer resources under the guidance of a laissez-faire approach, or aimed solely at correcting market failures, may improve efficiency in static terms. Yet in spite of contributing to reinforcing the pattern of specialization and the comparative advantages of a country, they tend to reduce the growth potential of the economy in the long term. Dosi et al. (1990) conclude that it would be possible to increase the level of Ricardian (i.e., static) efficiency, but at the cost of reducing Schumpeterian (i.e., dynamic) efficiency.

Activist-evolutionists see an important and strategic role for the state: to foster structural change. For this, they favor comprehensive industrial policies incorporating not only horizontal mechanisms but also selective intervention in sectors that are strate-gically relevant to economic development. The most important candidates are economic activities that are bound to have, potentially, three features: significant increases in pro-ductivity, products with high income elasticity, and economic activities that generate technological progress and disseminate it to others.

3. A Framework for Industrial Policy: Drivers, Effectiveness, and Coordination

3.1. Policy Drivers: Interaction between Policy Pull and Demand Push

Cimoli, Ferraz, and Primi (2005) propose the existence, in Latin America and the Caribbean, of two policy models: one in which policies pushed supply conditions, the other in which policy actions were pulled by demand.[7] The supply model was adopted in the region throughout the import-substitution period (1950s to 1970s). The demand model was employed during the period of economic liberalization (1980s to 1990s). Yet both have serious design flaws: they were conceptually designed as linear models in the sense that they presupposed that automatic benefits would follow once emphasis was placed either on supply or demand conditions.

In the linear supply model, the state plays a prominent role in identifying priority sectors to receive incentives and in acting as a direct agent in production through state-owned companies. The linear supply model placed emphasis on expanding investment in and upgrading technology of what were then mature industries (mostly commodity based) and of technology-intensive industries, such as information and communication technology. The model embodied a hierarchical dirigisme system in which investment decisions, especially by state-owned companies, provided guidance for private (national or foreign) resource allocation.

Even though such a strategy has contributed to the diversification of economic activities, especially in large economies such as Argentina, Brazil, and Mexico, its main weakness was the assumption that knowledge and innovation flows would run linearly and efficiently among and through economic agents, bringing about efficiency and competitiveness to an entire set of related economic activities. As assessed by Cimoli, Ferraz, and Primi (2005, 16), "knowledge was supposed to naturally flow and circulate among economic agents once it had been slotted in the economic system by public institutions." However, as the model also implemented high levels of effective protection, the dynamic effects of the supply model were very limited since economic agents were not facing competitive pressures internally or from potential entrants.

In the linear demand model, the underlying hypothesis is that, responding to signals from changes in relative prices, the market is better placed than the state to correctly identify those economic activities with lower opportunity costs to engage in technological upgrading. Such a model is diametrically opposite to the supply model: it is not a system centralized on few agents, nor is it hierarchic or sector differentiated. This is a model in which the private sector places its demands—in a context of economic liberalization, where economies are increasingly exposed to competition from imported goods and services—and the public sector proposes incentives for specific but nonsectorally biased targets: exports, innovation, quality, and productivity. For these, generic incentives are made available, in the form of indiscriminate tax-relief schemes or credit programs.

However, the most relevant problem is the linear approach to demand. That is, the model presupposes that, to attend to the needs of private demand, policy instruments, once activated, operate automatically and efficiently. Such a linear process does not necessarily happen: first, because private sector demands tend to concentrate on efforts required to overcome short-term challenges with no concern for developing strategic and long-term advantages; second, because firms differ, some agents may be better placed than others to benefit from incentives made available. Existing innovative companies, or larger enterprises, have higher probability of gaining access to horizontal benefits than the noninnovative ones, or those of a smaller size with less capacity to mobilize resources needed to take advantage of incentive schemes.

In short, Latin America and the Caribbean developed and implemented diametrically opposite policy modes of intervention—the supply and the demand models—each prevailing in a different moment of the region's recent economic history: import substitution and economic liberalization, respectively. However, both have similar structural problems: the embedded linear approach. Economists believed that once the model was triggered, automatic results would follow. Being linear, both models could not respond to the challenges imposed by the dynamic nature of relationships among economic agents. To a great extent, the linear approach—automatic response either to supply or demand signals—impeded the access to or the development of "a network of formal and informal threads, embodied in what is called the National Innovation System" (Cimoli, Ferraz, and Primi 2005, 7). Thus, because of their design, the supply and the demand models of industrial policies were bound to fail.

The distinction between policies driven by public supply *versus* policies driven by market signals is also erroneous. Even if the leading role in production and innovation activities is taken up by the private sector, relations between suppliers and clients (of goods, services, and knowledge) imply a wide array of institutions, including those of public ownership. Every policy goal, be it investment, innovation, or exports, involves a large number of institutions—public and private. For each policy objective, the myriad public institutions involved with incentives (tax rebates, credit programs), regulation (on behalf of consumers, the environment, competition, intellectual property), and technical assistance (support for exports, standardization and certification) are numerous. This is also the case of private sector institutions (business associations, technical support and research centers, training centers). To have private and public institutions agreeing on actions and converging to a proposed policy target requires not only the active involvement of all but also the grueling task of coordination, a role to be played by public agencies. Therefore, to overcome the dichotomy between supply-push and demand-pull models, Cimoli, Ferraz, and Primi (2005, 34) propose that "a more suitable and pragmatic technology policy model should promote coordination and articulation between the two, fostering the design and the implementation of a coordinated set of horizontal, vertical, selective and competition policies." These would be more effective if organized by sectors or industrial clusters and value chains.

3.2. Development Levels and Institutional Capabilities as Conditioning Factors for the Effectiveness of Industrial Policies

How can structural change be promoted, that is, the evolution of economic activities directed toward higher levels of competence? Industrial policies may or may not aim at attainable targets, depending on how the answer to this question is posed. The answer must address, simultaneously, two related issues: the level of development of policymaking (and implementing) capabilities and the level of development of economic activities.

The level of policymaking capability at a given moment defines the potential scope of an effective industrial policy. It does not seem reasonable to suppose that relevant institutions for the success of industrial policies are always the same, everywhere, all the time. Two main reasons can be cited. First, each policy strategy requires institutions of a very specific nature and magnitude. Strategies focused on correcting market failures, for example, need institutional capacities to provide public goods and to regulate infrastructure sectors, among other requirements. Strategies inspired by the activist-evolutionist model are coordination intensive. This means that the level of institutional development of the state is a critical issue. Second, the level of development of policymaking capabilities that any given country possesses is always conditioned by its own historical, cultural, social, and economical development levels.

The level of development of economic activities defines the scope for further advance. Evolution must be embedded in a policy design, but policy goals must aim at a feasible evolution process. To a great extent, existing production capabilities at any given moment, in any country and sector, define evolution and transformation possibilities. Leapfrogging is always possible, but within the restrictions imposed by existing and potential competences to be explored. As Lin and Monga (2010, 23) clearly described, "industrial policies . . . usually fall into one of two broad categories: (i) they attempt to facilitate the development of new industries that are too advanced . . .; or (ii) they try to facilitate the development of new industries that are consistent with the latent comparative advantage of the economy. Only the latter type of industrial policy is likely to succeed." Nevertheless, it is necessary to take into consideration that, in many cases, history shows that competitive advantages leading to structural change can be fostered. Thus, while the second approach is obviously more feasible, the first path to development cannot be completely discarded.

In this sense, it may be necessary, in order to promote structural change and economic development in the long run, to incorporate the proposition of Hausmann and Rodrik (2003): to prioritize investments in activities of higher knowledge density, but in direct relation to or close to existing levels. This proposition finds support in the framework developed by Hidalgo and Hausmann (2009, 10570), in which they show that "the level of complexity of a country's economy predicts the types of products that countries will be able to develop in the future."

Different tools can be devised to further identify potential activities to be fostered. Hausmann, Rodrik, and Velasco (2008) propose the Growth Diagnostics Framework, an approach based on the decision-tree methodology that identifies the most relevant constraints on low growth for a given country and how to isolate and make them the focus of policy actions. Lin and Monga (2010) point out that the concern of their model is largely of a macroeconomic nature and propose a step-by-step guide for microlevel policymaking. As shown in figure 4.1, depending on the complexity of policy objectives, larger or smaller requirements for institutional capabilities will be required.

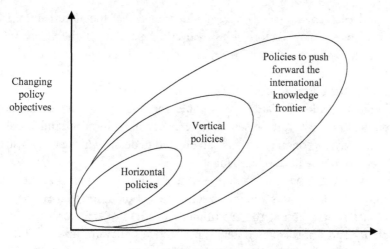

The evolution of institutional capacity in time

Figure 4.1 The relationship between policy objectives and policy capabilities
Source: Adapted from Peres and Primi 2009:17.

The arsenal of industrial policy comprises a set of six policy instruments: financing, taxation, trade-related measures, public procurement, technical and informational assistance, and regulation. These are conditioned by two strategic macroeconomic variables: the real interest rate and the exchange rate. Depending on the direction they take and the stability they achieve in the short and long term, the interest rate and the exchange regimes may play a benign or a malign influence on the arsenal of industrial policy.

Financing conditions—interest rates, loan duration, the availability of equity and venture capital funds, and so on—determine the cost of capital; the structure of a tax system defines incentives for firms to run a business; trade-related measures—tariffs, nontariff measures—define conditions for more or less competition from imports in a given economy; procurement from public authorities may or may not induce the development of local competences; technical support may provide informational means for firms to define a business plan in a given direction; regulations affecting competition, consumers, the environment, intellectual property, and the operation of utilities define the rules of the game on a given playing field. Each policy instrument is, per se, a powerful tool to induce a developmental path for firms, or, if the private sector gains control of (or "captures") an industrial policy, to generate significant and undesirable rents for a group of agents to the detriment of a wider constituency.

The traditional debate on industrial policy has, in fact, concentrated on dilemmas of this sort: which instruments are relevant and how the state can avoid being exploited (captured).[8] This chapter takes a different stance based on a pragmatic and analytical viewpoint. From a pragmatic perspective, it seems unnecessary to circumscribe, a priori, the arsenal of an industrial policy to a limited set of instruments if all or some of them can be effective means to attaining a policy goal. To define which are relevant, it is necessary to emphasize an analytical perspective deriving from the literature on competition and industrial organization. Coutinho and Ferraz (1994) and Ferraz,

Kupfer, and Haguenauer (1996) have demonstrated that the aforementioned set of policy instruments may be more or less relevant, depending on the nature of the economic activity under consideration, and on what level of development the firms in a given sector, in a given country, and at a given moment are at. For example, patents are crucial in the pharmaceutical industry and relatively less so in mining. Environmental regulations for the latter are essential and less so for software development. The argument here is that the essential features of competition and industrial organization of any given economic activity can be used to define which policy instruments are relevant to induce its development.

Still, even if it is possible to define which policy instruments are relevant, the most important question is whether a state can put them to effective use. If industrial policies should aim at the evolution of productive structures toward higher productivity and knowledge content, an effective policy framework should, first, design objectives starting with the assets a given country possesses at a given moment and, second, ensure close correspondence between policy objectives and institutional capabilities. If the institutional capacity needed to diagnose, propose, implement, and assess policies for a given policy objective is lacking, policymakers must undertake considerable and explicit efforts to overcome existing weaknesses. Institutions are, at the same time, the cause and the effect of development processes. Development arises not only from the evolution of innovation capabilities but also from changes in policy-related institutions. From such a perspective, policy effectiveness is partly determined by the extent to which policy objectives are, at a given moment, within the reach of existing policymaking (and implementing) capabilities. Concurrently, a policy design should incorporate the means to tackle existing institutional shortcomings and advance toward more ambitious goals. This is of fundamental importance for policy effectiveness.

Stiglitz (1998) proposes a "policy prescription" to be considered by policymakers: (1) recognize that "development" presupposes feasible and attainable targets; (2) make explicit the existing restrictions related to available resources and policymaking—or policy-implementing—capabilities; (3) design policies within the reach of initial constraints, but establish priority targets to gradually overcome institutional bottlenecks; and (4) even if existing limitations must be taken as a reference for elaborating feasible policies at a given moment, institutional shortcomings must not serve as an a priori argument for the lack of initiatives aimed at building up capabilities required for more complex policy objectives.

3.3. The Public and Private Relationship: Avoid Capture, Foster Coordination

So far, the discussion on the development of a policy framework has remained within the realm of public institutions. This is insufficient, as industrial policies, by definition, are aimed at the business sector. Thus, the nature of the relationship between the public and private sectors must be duly considered.

As is well known, one of the most relevant criticisms made of public policies—which industrial policies are part of—is the private initiative's potential capture of the state. Dangers involved are so great that those concerned with the issue find in it substance enough to disparage every attempt at promoting industrial policies in Latin America and elsewhere, at any time. The easy way out—drawing from past eastern Asian experiences—is to defend the possibility of an insulated bureaucracy in the state to run industrial policies. Insulated bureaucracies have three main assets: good knowledge of which competitive and technological challenges are relevant, access to relevant instruments and the capacity to use them effectively, and "untouchability"—not falling prey to attempts made by business sectors to attain results favorable, financially or otherwise, to themselves.

However, the very notion of "insulation" is nonapplicable to democratic and open societies—like most countries in the world in the twenty-first century. The very notion that industrial policy targets and the mobilization of instruments can be established without consultation is very undemocratic. It is also naïve to believe that the business sector will not try to defend and lobby for its interests. How can such a dilemma be dealt with? Four requirements may help to mitigate capture processes.

First, in each stage of a policy process—from diagnosis to design, implementation, and assessment—the role of public and private agents must be made explicit. Second, every policy action must state previous benefits and obligations to those involved, making it clear what implications each one will be subjected to once policy implementation takes place. Third, mechanisms of oversight should be in place in order to improve the transparency of and accountability for public actions. In most countries there are institutions playing such a role, and they should be fostered. Finally, an active media, operating in an ambiance of institutionalized freedom of the press, is a most valuable defense mechanism against the process of capture of the state by petty, private interests.

The business sector is well placed to state competitive challenges it faces. This does not mean that businesses have accurate and necessary knowledge, as information failure is one of the shortcomings a segment in the private sector may face, at a given place and time. The business sector also has a legitimate role to play in the design stage, in proposing what businesses believe are the policy instruments needed to overcome competitive challenges. Naturally, as recipients of policy benefits or constraints, they will be relevant actors in the implementation phase. In addition, being the object of policies, they can be of great importance at the assessment stage.

Any government administration has the mandate—bestowed by citizens' votes—to define priorities and to operate policy instruments, within a given set of resource constraints. State bureaucracy must bring together, organize, and filter demands, assessing and defining the best use of scarce resources. It should also state, negotiate, and implement obligations associated with any benefits conveyed to the business sector.

Are these considerations sufficient to eliminate the dangers of regulatory capture? Certainly not, as the implementation of industrial policies involves political processes in which vested interests may win the upper hand. Mitigation of capture, though, is possible, can be effective, and must be pursued. In this vein, Evans (1995), Stiglitz (1998), and Devlin and Moguillansky (2009) have emphasized that partnerships and public-private alliances—that is, consultation and coordination between public and private institutions focusing on concrete objectives—are necessary mechanisms for avoiding capture and putting policies on an effective course.

4. Winds of Change: The Return of Industrial Policy in Brazil

Starting in the early 1990s, a process of economic liberalization was put into motion in Brazil. Trade barriers were removed and privatization enforced. Policies of this nature changed the competitive landscape in the country as pressure for competition increased in most sectors. Until then, they had been relatively insulated from imports. From then onward, the nature of industrial policies closely resembled the linear demand-pull model.

The government expanded export financing at the BNDES, the Brazilian Development Bank, and placed emphasis on fostering quality and productivity at the FINEP, the innovation agency of the Ministry of Science and Technology. In addition, it attempted to expand the sources and amount of funding for science, technology, and innovation through the creation of 14 sectoral funds, financed from levies placed on recently privatized economic activities, and aimed at scientific infrastructure (Almeida et al. 2008). While the former type of actions addressed the ongoing needs of the private sector, the latter was laying the grounds for more substantial changes. These sectoral funds provided extra sources of financing to upgrade research infrastructure in the country—of merit in itself—while contractual rules imposed the need for research institutes to partner with the business sector when bidding for funds. Firms emphasizing innovation saw this as an opportunity to expand their activities while sharing costs with the public sector. Petrobras, for example, was able to expand its innovation efforts by developing, through financing for the oil and gas fund, an extensive network of research institutes.

The Lula administration (2003–10), however, brought about significant changes to the policy landscape. During the first administration (2003–6), it placed policy emphasis on instituting, developing, and strengthening political and economic credibility by means of stressing and implementing a macroeconomic policy based on fiscal responsibility, a floating exchange rate, and an inflation target regime.

The return of an explicit industrial policy came in 2004 with the enactment of the Industrial, Technological, and Foreign Trade Policy (PITCE), whose main objectives were to strengthen efficiency, expand exports, and, above all, increase innovation capabilities of Brazilian firms. The innovation part of the policy focused on specific economic activities, most of them involving high technology. It made sectoral choices—capital goods, software, semiconductors, pharmaceuticals—and emphasized generic technologies, such as biotechnology and nanotechnology. The administration gave particular attention to revamping policy instruments and strengthening the financing and legal apparatus.[9]

The policy created two agencies to support industrial development and exports: the Brazilian Agency for Industrial Development and the Brazilian Agency for Promoting Exports and Investments. These agencies have a private legal status, which provides them with a higher degree of operational freedom, making it possible to engage in supporting studies, policy formulation, and export promotion with greater agility than traditional public institutions. Following policy guidelines, the BNDES expanded existing sectoral programs, like Prosoft, for information and communication technology industries, or proposed new ones, like Profarma, for pharmaceutical businessses, which were, programmatically, organizational innovations for the bank. Prosoft and Profarma were designed based on a fine diagnosis of Brazilian and international industries and aimed at segments in which Brazilian firms could have competitive opportunities. These programs had a specific budget and more favorable credit conditions than traditional lines of credit for investment.

The PITCE was the first attempt to implement an explicit industrial policy—including sectoral choices—after the country experimented with supply-push and demand-pull models of policy at different times. It was proposed when the Lula administration was implementing a macroeconomic policy—aimed at cooling down inflationary and exchange-speculative pressures—that was soon praised in Brazilian and international markets for its solidity. The PITCE can be read as a first experiment in bringing together different agencies from the Ministry of Finance, the Ministry of Industry and Trade, and the Ministry of Science and Technology to organize a proactive policy for industrial development. Suzigan and Furtado (2006) argue that the PITCE was an advance because it placed emphasis on innovation, it set clear goals, and it promoted institutional changes. Nevertheless, they assert, it also had important weaknesses: a lack of interaction with the government's economic policy, ineffectiveness in the use of some of the policy instruments, and a lack of intrastate coordination. They see the most important problem, however, as the choice of sectors—software, semiconductors, pharmaceuticals, and capital goods—which were too limited in size and scope, with the exception of capital goods, to induce development in industry and the economy as a whole.

Nevertheless, the PITCE laid the grounds for a more ambitious policy, the 2008 PDP. The administration took note of the PITCE's major shortcomings, as we will show, and, unlike in past experiments, designed the PDP not only for an open economy but for a benign context, with increasingly positive growth prospects. The PDP equipped the Brazilian state with the minimum tools for more proactive action for industrial development.

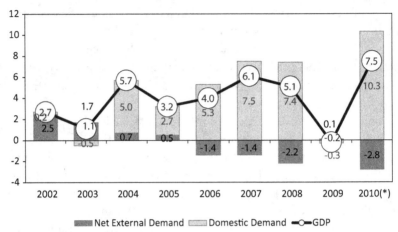

Figure 4.2 The evolution of Brazilian GDP: 2002–10 (%).

Source: IBGE. 2010: Forecast by BNDES

5. THE PRODUCTION DEVELOPMENT POLICY: FRAMEWORK AND GOVERNANCE

5.1. Industrial Policy to Sustain Growth

As figure 4.2 shows, from 2004 onward the Brazilian economy entered a path of sustained growth, largely led by internal demand. An expanding middle class boosted consumption, and investment has grown ahead of the gross domestic product (GDP) since mid-2005.

During Lula's second term, the aim of economic policy changed, favoring growth and investment. This strategic change led to the proposition and implementation of four major development-oriented policies:

> MF (2007): Growth Acceleration Program, aimed at expanding Brazil's infrastructure with investments amounting to US$332 billion in the first phase (up to 2010), and US$480 billion for the 2011–14 period;
> ME (2007): Educational Development Program, aimed at expanding and improving the quality of education at all levels;
> MST (2007): Science, Technology, and Innovation Plan of Action, aimed at increasing GDP expenditures in science, technology, and innovation from 1.02 percent to 1.5 percent, with investments of US$22 billion between 2007 and 2010;
> MDIC 2008: Production Development Policy, aimed at fostering investment, strengthening innovation capabilities, expanding exports, and supporting micro-, small-, and medium-sized enterprises with a budget of approximately US$115 billion in credit and US$12 billion in tax deductions.

In May 2008, the PDP was launched under the motto "innovate and invest to sustain long-term growth" in Brazil. The PDP differs from the PITCE—and most industrial policy initiatives elsewhere—in four aspects: sectoral reach, goal-oriented approach, organizational format, and the nature of relations with the business sector.

5.2. The Sectoral Approach

First, the PDP is very comprehensive in sectoral terms. As the country possesses a complex production base, the PDP did not opt for a selective sectoral approach. Rather, it took a comprehensive and evolutionary approach to (1) identify the stage of development of various segments, (2) define corresponding competitive challenges, and (3) propose an appropriate course of action, with adequate policy instruments for each one. It organized policy instruments and agencies into six categories: credit, tax incentives, technical assistance, public procurement, trade policies, and regulation. The government engaged and implemented these tools horizontally or vertically, whichever was appropriate.

Thus, acceleration of capital depreciation and improvements in credit conditions for investment were not sectorally biased, benefiting all those willing to expand capacity. But sectoral actions were also implemented. Two examples may help make clear the process of defining targets and actions for specific purposes: pharmaceuticals and software. In regard to pharmaceuticals, the Ministry of Health defined a specific set of drugs and medicines that would be a priority in public procurement for distribution in hospitals and clinics around the country. Targeting them, the BNDES renewed and expanded its program for pharmaceutical development, proposing special and low-cost credit conditions. In regard to software, analysis carried out by the Ministry of Finance, Trade, and Industry, the Ministry of Science and Technology, the Brazilian Agency for Industrial Development, and the BNDES pointed out that the potential to expand software exports was being hindered by the structure of the taxation system, in this case, taxes on the payroll. Thus, the PDP proposed a special tax deduction on the pay roll supporting software exports.

Figure 4.3 illustrates the PDP's sectoral coverage, including 34 programs that were organized in accordance with three competitive challenges:

Consolidate and expand leadership for those on the competitive edge. The focus was placed on supporting business sector initiatives in mergers and acquisitions as well as internationalization, in addition to strengthening governance structures of firms.

Strengthen competitiveness. The focus was on sectors with positive export prospects and the potential to expand in the local market, inducing externalities along production chains of clients and suppliers. These sectors require instruments associated with supporting investment and technical assistance.

Build up technological capabilities. The focus was on activities that can generate and disseminate technical progress in the economy, requiring instruments that are adequate to promote innovation and build the capacity of human resources.

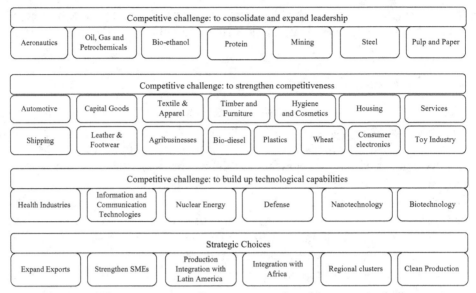

Figure 4.3 The organization of PDP programs based on strategic challenges.

Source: MDIC 2008

There was a fourth set of programs—strategic choices—that were previous choices not oriented to specific economic activities, but rather to issues that cross-cut most sectors, thus contributing to aggregate sustainability: SMEs, exports, integration with Latin America and Africa, clean production.

There are four reasons for choosing nonsectoral selectivity: (1) a cognitive limitation: it is a hard task to select priority sectors at a time of intense technological change; (2) pragmatics: a favorable fiscal situation and availability of credit for investment at the Brazilian Development Bank did not impose an a priori resource constraint—it was more important to develop substantive and cohesive plans of actions for each sector; (3) the emphasis given to preserving and valuing the diversity of the Brazilian industrial structure; and, finally, (4) the conception of the PDP as a "policy of varied geometry," according to which an economic activity could be included in the PDP, or removed from it, if an adequate "agenda for action"—the equivalent of a "business plan" for a firm—could be designed, proposed, negotiated between the state and the business sector, and then implemented.

5.3. Policy Orientation

The second differentiating aspect of the PDP is its goal-oriented nature. The PDP embodies a set of specific, measurable, objective targets for 2010, aimed at providing a clear orientation and direction focused on development, thus inducing and coordinating expectations and establishing references for policy monitoring. Two types of targets were put forward: "macrotargets" and "program targets."

There were four macrotargets to be reached by 2010, reflecting the main driving force of the policy: (1) increasing the investment rate from 17.6 percent to 21 percent

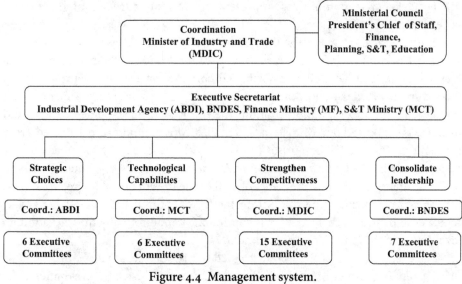

Figure 4.4 Management system.
Source: MDIC (2008)

of GDP; (2) boosting private research and development from 0.51 percent to 0.65 percent of GDP; (3) expanding the share in world exports from 1.18 percent to 1.25 percent; and (4) increasing the number of micro- and small-sized export companies by 10 percent. For targets specific to each program, the policymakers carefully diagnosed the competitive challenges and opportunities pursuant to each system before defining those targets. In several cases, the assessment of competitiveness benefited from previous dialogue with the business sector.

5.4. Policy Governance

The third differentiating aspect of the PDP is the explicit definition of instruments, resources, and responsibilities for the various tasks involved in the policy. The PDP design influenced the structuring of a sophisticated management system, inspired by three aims: (1) to define performance responsibilities to assure the efficient implementation of the policy; (2) to promote the articulation of the PDP along with other development policies and to the business sector; and (3) to induce the coordinated use of policy instruments.

Figure 4.4 presents the PDP's governance system, identifying roles and responsible institutions. The first aspect to be observed is the PDP's hierarchical design. The allocation of responsibilities and the effective engagement of different agencies is a great challenge for any public policy, and the Brazilian initiative is no exception. This is even more pronounced given the PDP's targets, the attempt to mobilize relevant policy instruments, the diversity of the Brazilian industrial structure, and the wide variety of competitive challenges facing different industries. Thus, the PDP required the involvement of a large number of public officials and agencies. By September 2010, around 400 public servants were part of different executive committees, representing over 60 agencies of the federal government.

The general coordination of the policy is carried out by the Ministry of Development, Industry, and Trade, which reports to the National Council of Industrial Development. This council is a forum comprising government representatives, businessmen, workers, and academics, and it is chaired by the president of the republic. In the federal administration, the minister of development, trade, and industry is supported by a Ministerial Council, to whom reports are delivered every six months. The council comprises ministers with responsibility for areas directly related to the PDP—finance, planning, science and technology, and education—and it is coordinated by the minister chief of staff of the presidency of the republic. This minister has a coordinating role within the federal administration. Such a governance design ensures that the PDP is continuously monitored by the relevant high level authorities of the federal government.

The executive role of the PDP is carried out by an Executive Secretariat comprising representatives of the Brazilian Agency for Industrial Development, the Ministry of Finance, the Ministry of Science and Technology, and the BNDES. These institutions have the mandate, the instruments, and the resources to provide most of the means necessary to implement a Brazilian industrial policy.

The implementation of the PDP's programs requires two different levels of coordination: coordination by program groups, carried out by institutions with a seat on the Executive Secretariat, and executive committees, which are the basic units in charge of managing implementation of the policy. Program group coordination mainly involves establishing guidelines for the programs and monitoring activities developed by executive committees. The executive committees pool representatives of agencies relevant to each industrial segment. Their main tasks are to define policy challenges, to interact with the business sector, and to propose and implement an agenda for action that includes the proposition of goals and the establishment of needs in terms of relevant policy instruments. Because it is expected that many of these would be common to all—tax incentives for investments, for example—policy needs are channeled to Group Coordination, which conducts a first applicable screening, and then to the Executive Secretariat, which brings together demands, assesses them, and, consequently, turns them down, puts them on a waiting list, or implements them, depending on availability of resources.

Pooling different federal agencies led to the identification of actions that were common to the PDP and other development policies, especially the Science, Technology, and Innovation Plan. In promoting the integration of the PDP with the innovation policy, the administration implemented two mechanisms: one to define common policy targets (e.g., in research and development) and one to induce agencies to cross-reference their specific actions to both policies. For example, the FINEP, which, as noted earlier, is part of the Ministry of Science and Technology, defines priorities—in terms of sectors and credit conditions in its different programs—in keeping with PDP.

5.5. Public-Private Coordination

The fourth innovative aspect of the PDP is the implementation of institutional "spaces" for public-private interaction and coordination. Since the 1990s, sectoral public-private chambers or forums have been in place. Initially, during the Collor government (1989–91), sectoral chambers (câmaras setoriais) were set up to negotiate prices and wages in a country with high inflation. At that time, competitiveness was not their first priority. Representation at sectoral chambers was at a very high level (ministerial, from the government's side). Once participants reached agreements, implementation followed. Later, when the government proposed an industrial policy, the Collor administration tried to use the chambers for competitiveness purposes, but the attempt was short-lived as the government came to an abrupt end with Collor's impeachment. During the Itamar administration (1991–93), officials attempted to revive the space for dialogue between public and private sectors, but the only chamber to function was the Automobile Chamber, used to negotiate tax incentives for local production in return for a commitment from the private sector to maintain employment at agreed levels.

During the Fernando Henrique Cardoso years (1994–2002), the approach and objectives associated with sectoral chambers changed, and the focus was on competitive issues, but there was no reference to an explicit industrial policy. The administration fostered a demand-pull policy model, and these chambers were functional in identifying private sector needs. It is interesting to note that, during these years, similar experiences were being promoted elsewhere. In Colombia, Foros de Competitividad, initiated by the private sector but then taken over by the government, were extensively promoted, apparently leading to cases of success, such as upgrading the coffee industry (Sistema Nacional de Competitividad/Colombia 2008).

In Brazil, the mechanism served various purposes. At a basic level, these chambers were used merely as mechanisms to allow voices of discontent in the private sector "let off steam" or present demands from that could hardly be implemented when instability and volatility prevailed in the Brazilian economy. Still, even if no practical purposes were served, at this basic level, the chambers did serve the purpose of bringing demands that were mostly voiced in closed government offices in Brasília to the public domain. Usually, the business sector would express the difficulties it was going through, and present a long list of demands—mostly related to tax, tariff, and credit conditions. Meeting such demands would resolve the difficulties the industry was going through. Very little was said in terms of the compromises an industry would accept if its proposals were accepted by public authorities. These, in turn, given the economic difficulties they were going through, would take the list of demands and promise they would be duly considered—which was not the case, most of the time.

On very few occasions were the sectoral chambers an effective mechanism for policy negotiation and compromises from both parties. The one outstanding case is the automobile industry, as mentioned earlier, in which a tax incentive was given in exchange for not laying off the work force for a certain period. This case is noteworthy not only for the negotiation of government incentives in return for business commitments but also for illustrating two phenomena: first, that these chambers could be effective if a business sector had political leverage; second, that these measures could be implemented without being referred to a higher-level industrial policy.

In short, with very few exceptions, until recently, the "space" of public-private interaction did exist, but it consisted of a coordination mechanism with limited effectiveness, as the private sector would produce "shopping lists" that were relatively easy for the government to turn down because of resource constraint.

The PDP faced the challenge of changing the status quo of sectoral chambers. To do so, the government recognized that public-private interaction was necessary (1) to coordinate information when any given industry and its competitive challenges are developing; (2) to negotiate measures: from the government's side, to disclose policy intentions and from the private sector, to compile policy demands; and (3) to monitor the progress of policies and to raise issues that should be further considered.

As noted above, the PDP coordinates the results of public-private negotiations so as to make demands from different sectors compatible and assess their importance given available resources. Therefore, by explicitly valuing public-private interaction, the PDP intends to minimize the possibility of the private sector capturing the public sector—a recurring issue raised in the literature on industrial policies.

6. IMPLEMENTING THE POLÍTICA DE DESENVOLVIMENTO PRODUTIVO

In this section we discuss the effectiveness of the PDP. First, we analyze achievements reached in light of the PDP's explicitly proposed 2010 targets. Secondwe assess the effectiveness of the implementation process. Third, we comment on the extent to which intrastate and public-private interaction have improved and whether the "productive agenda" has gained priority in the public debate.[10]

6.1. Achievements

Several years have gone by since the PDP was launched in May 2008. At that time, the Brazilian GDP was growing (quarter to quarter) at around 7 percent, and investment (fixed capital formation to GDP), at 17 percent (see fig. 4.5). Then the international crisis came in full force—triggered by the default of Lehman Brothers. By the second quarter of 2009, investment had plunged to −16 percent, compared to the first quarter. However, by the second quarter of 2010, the economy was growing at 8.8 percent, and investment, at 26.5 percent (compared to the first quarter of 2010). Such a drastic recovery in investment rates was partially influenced by the PDP. As we show later, having an effective policy framework in place helped Brazilian authorities deal with the international financial crisis.

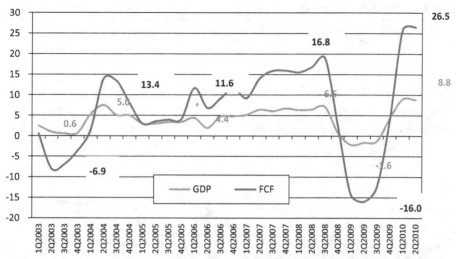

Figure 4.5. The evolution of GDP and Growth of Fixed Capital Formation: quarterly growth in percentage: 2003–10

Source: IBGE

However, the crisis did have an impact on the targets set in May 2008. As table 4.1 shows, of the four main targets (related to investment, research and development, exports, and SME development), the only one to be reached will be the one related to exports (target 1.25 percent of world exports; expected result, 1.30 percent). The reason for this is more related to the severe slump in world trade due to the international crisis than to the vitality of Brazilian exports: by the end of the first quarter of 2009, Brazilian exports had fallen 17 points, when compared to export levels in September, 2008. By June 2010, it was still four points below that level.

Private research and development will increase from 0.51 percent (research and development to GDP) to 0.60 percent, but that mark is still short of the expected target of 0.65 percent; the number of exporting SMEs, instead of increasing by 10 percent from the 2007 baseline, will increase only 6.7 percent. Meanwhile, investment to GDP, the main concern of the Brazilian Industrial Policy, which was expected to grow from 17.6 percent to 21 percent by the end of 2010, is expected to remain at 19 percent.

Do these results indicate failure, since targets were not reached, or success, because of the little variation observed, given the size and complexity of the international financial crisis? Given the short span of time and the intervening force of external factors, an adequate assessment of the policy should probably not consider whether targets were reached, but rather whether the evolution of indicators is on a positive or negative path. In this sense, while it is true that targets proposed for the Brazilian Industrial Policy were negatively affected by external events, the expected results indicate, for most targets, that the direction of evolution is positive.

In this sense, the PDP provided the framework and the policy instruments to induce firms to move toward more investment, innovation, and exports, and added

Table 4.1 PDP Targets and Results

	Position 2008	PDP Target by 2010	Expected Situation 2010
Investment/GDP (%)	17.6	21.0	19.0
Business sector R&D[a]/GDP (%)	0.51	0.65	0.60
Exports (share in world exports, %)	1.18	1.25	1.30
Number of exporting SME increased by 10%		+ 10	+ 6.7

[a] Research and development
Source: PDP Executive Secretariat.

incentives for SMEs. More importantly, such a framework was most useful in enabling Brazil to face the crisis: the government was mobilized for industrial development, and when the crisis came, significant efforts were made to mitigate its negative impact through the behavior of firms.

The policy gave particular attention to investment. In March 2009, investment levels were 21 points below the level registered in September 2008. However, by June 2010, investments had recovered, reaching a level that was three points above 2008's. It is widely perceived in Brazil that, to a great extent, such dramatic recovery in investment rates was due to proactive actions taken under the framework of the PDP, by the BNDES and the Ministry of Finance. Two measures can be considered of strategic importance.

First, in December 2008, the Ministry of Finance provided a substantial low-cost, long-term loan of around US$55 billion to the BNDES. The strategic reason and the message behind such a loan were simple, yet very powerful: there would not be a credit crunch in Brazil for good and sound investment projects. Second, in June 2009, another powerful joint action by the Ministry of Finance and the BNDES was announced: to drastically reduce the cost of investment by means of a temporary interest rate equalization program for acquiring capital goods. The Investment Maintenance Program (PSI) was planned in May 2009, when signs of economic stabilization were becoming apparent thanks not only to efforts from the Central Bank, which provided extra liquidity to banks, but also to temporary tax relief for acquiring durable goods, which kept household consumption patterns intact after September 2008. At that time, the government decided that providing significant incentives for investment could lead to investment decisions, bringing back growth in capital, which had been strongly affected by the international crisis.

The PSI made it possible to reduce the final interest rates (from 10.5 to 4.5 percent for most capital goods). As figure 4.6 shows, the reaction of firms was quite immediate and significant. The chart shows the BNDES's disbursements for the acquisition of machinery through its second-tier operations, involving most commercial banks in the country. The movement is clear: at the beginning of the international crisis, in September 2008, the daily average reached a record—R$149.6 million. From that point, the level plummeted, reaching its lowest level in July 2009, when

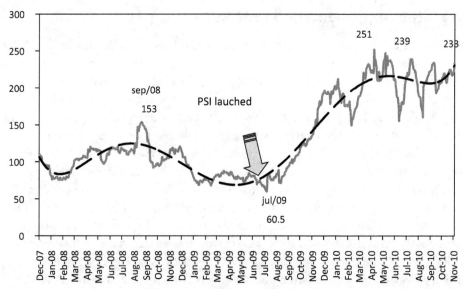

Figure 4.6 Daily disbursements of BNDES to finance capital goods acquisition through financial institutions US$ million.

Source: BNDES

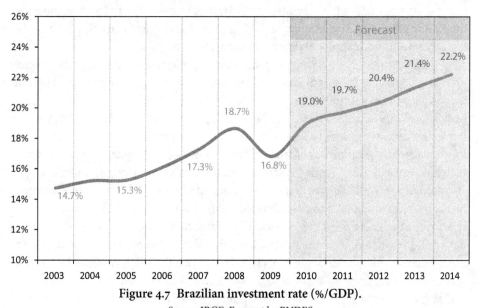

Figure 4.7 Brazilian investment rate (%/GDP).

Source: IBGE. Forecast by BNDES

the daily average reached R$60 million. This was precisely the moment the PSI was launched. When the program became operational, the trend reversed, and disbursements started to grow. By June 2010, daily disbursements were at R$240 million. As mentioned above, it is widely believed that these policies played an important role in the recovery of the investment trend in the Brazilian economy, as figure 4.7 shows.

6.2. The Implementation Process

By September 2010, some 420 policy measures had been proposed under the PDP's framework: 29 percent were related to financing, 31 percent to technical assistance and information, 26 percent to tax measures, 8 percent to regulation, and 6 percent to trade disputes. Practically all of them (99 percent) were fully operational: 41 percent were related to the investment target, 29 percent to exports, 20 percent to innovation, and 10 percent to SME development. These breakdowns provide valuable information on the nature of the Brazilian Industrial Policy in terms of effectiveness and the orientation of the policy.

First, the Brazilian Industrial Policy can be considered rather effective, as potential beneficiaries can gain access to most measures. Making measures operational is not an easy task. Two examples illustrate the potential difficulties and how the PDP dealt with them. First, if a proposed measure—for example, spread or loan duration—is under the responsibility of a specific agency, such an agency must be closely aligned with the applicants under and managers of the policy. That is, priorities in such an agency must reflect an industrial policy's targets. This is the case at the BNDES for long-term financing and FINEP—which also serves as a specialized innovation bank. Because the BNDES and the Ministry of Science and Technology each have a seat on the PDP's Executive Secretariat, such coordination is easier. Second, if a measure involves changes in legislation, the administration must not only coordinate the actions of different ministries—Industry and Trade, Finance, Chief of Staff of the Presidency—but also involve members of the Congress and the Senate to support it so that it will have a smooth approval process in the legislature.

To a great extent, the PDP's effectiveness can be explained, first, through the political priority given to the Industrial Policy by the Lula administration; second, the commitment to it by relevant ministries, in particular Trade and Industry, Science and Technology, and Finance; and, third, the information system put in place to manage the implementation process for its measures. This system, developed by the Brazilian Agency for Industrial Development, ensured online information at the development stage of each measure and each agenda for action of all the PDP's executive committees.

Second, the PDP's orientation is quite straightforward: investment-related measures predominated. From accelerated depreciation of capital to tax relief and interest rate cuts, these were measures with a significant impact on the cost of capital before and, especially, after the international financial crisis, as mentioned above. The economic reasoning behind it is very clear. First, when the PDP was launched, investment was already growing ahead of GDP, but, even so, levels were very low: by 2007, it was at 17.6 percent of GDP. Embedded in the PDP is the need to strengthen the momentum of growth and to induce long-term sustainability brought about by expanding production capacity: mitigation of supply bottlenecks, price stability, and job creation.

6.3. Intragovernment and Public-Private Interactions

As previously pointed out, enhancing institutional coordination within the state, among different agencies and between the public and private sectors, is a common challenge for the success of industrial policies in any country. Naturally, the construction of the coordination framework tends to take on different outlines in each nation, reflecting the possibilities and limitations brought on by preexisting conditions, as well as by the underlying options for policies chosen in each case.

Industrial policy strategies that do not take into account preexisting practices, or those that favor horizontal mechanisms and the strengthening of the existing production specialization pattern of an economy, tend to be less intensive in coordination when compared to strategies that try to change established policy practices, or those aiming at promoting shifts in the production structure. Strategies of this latter type imply mobilizing government and economic agents to promote practices and targets that are less familiar. Such strategies may require identifying and developing new government instruments and processes, and consequentially for a new policy model, which, to be effective, calls for all parties involved to make considerable efforts to learn new ways.

The Brazilian PDP draws from the experience of the industrial policy—the PITCE—implemented in Lula's first administration (2003–6). This policy was fundamental in the administration's breaking away from the practices of the Fernando Henrique Cardoso administration, when priorities were placed on macroeconomic stabilization and economic liberalization, especially of trade, and privatization. As an explicit industrial policy that proposed sectoral choices, the PITCE reintroduced the state to the need to coordinate and mobilize agencies and instruments toward specific goals: to promote high-technology sectors, such as pharmaceuticals and capital goods. Nevertheless, no attempt was made then to propose explicit policy targets to be achieved in a given period. Therefore, the PITCE provided the training grounds on which a new generation of industrial policy could develop further.

In addition, broader strategies involving a larger number of sectors, aims, and targets tend to impose more critical coordination needs, especially within the state, putting pressure on existing institutional resources and requiring new forms of interaction. From this perspective, coordination challenges are exacerbated depending on how broad the scope of the industrial policy is and how strict the terms related to reaching established targets are—or what the desired "speed" of the policy is.

In any event, regardless of the strategy adopted, in general, the question of the appropriateness of the coordination frameworks of industrial policy draws attention to at least two dimensions associated with policy *management*: the development of institutional spaces to promote dialogue, in organized bases, between different levels of government and between such levels and the private sector; and the establishment of routines that, using the policy's aims as a reference, structure the efforts of public and private agents.

Regarding the first aspect, we have already highlighted the importance of spaces for dialogue as a precondition for effectively creating public-private alliances— which, as also mentioned, are increasingly understood as a necessary ingredient for the success of industrial policies. No less important, however, is the development of levels of dialogue between different governmental institutions, especially in strategies of more complexity and broader scope, when an effective combination of different policy instruments is required. In these cases, which demand cooperative dynamics between agencies and organizations that do not have a hierarchical relationship, the existence of organized spaces for the shared assessment of propositions, as well as for negotiation, mediation, and the solution of conflicts, may be decisive in making the policy effective. To achieve this goal, a dimension that requires special attention is the establishment of routines that structure the efforts of public and private agents, in and outside institutional spaces for public-private and public-public dialogue.

It would not be productive here to try to come up with a list of specific routines that are relevant to efficiently operating spaces for public-public and public-private dialogue. Still, it is possible to establish some general application principles that were tried in the Brazilian Industrial Policy: public disclosure of the calendar for meetings with announced agendas; persistence in attaining efficient and balanced political and technical representation; and the will to show effectiveness, the costs and benefits of measures to be argued and proposed, and, especially, establishing standards for benefits that should be reflected in commitments and obligations. Of special relevance for inducing learning processes within the state was the emphasis that the Executive Secretariat gave to ensuring that every sectoral committee should develop and propose an agenda for action.

Putting together and negotiating an agenda—based on a common blueprint for all—was an effective exercise in learning by designing and learning by implementing which involved (1) efforts toward reaching a common diagnosis of competitive challenges, (2) the identification of relevant policy instruments that should be triggered, (3) the negotiation of consensus with the private sector as to which measures should be put in place, and (4) negotiation with agents that had a mandate over them to actually put them in place. Establishing and consolidating these routines demanded great coordination and mobilization efforts by the members of the Executive Secretariat.

The minister of development, trade, and industry and the minister of finance played a strategic role. Both had a very clear outline of the strategic role the Brazilian Industrial Policy was playing in the stage of development the country was going through. Their common ground was the priority given to facilitating and inducing investment by the private sector. Even if tax-relief measures and subsidies provided by the PSI program were relevant to the fiscal balance of the country, the minister of finance had a clear vision that, in the long run, expanding capacity would mean more economic activities and, with them, more social, economic, and fiscal benefits for the country.

It also became clear that instruments and procedures for accountability of policymaking should be stimulated and strengthened. These accounts cover activities developed by both the public sector and the private sector, enabling appropriate monitoring. In this sense, besides the government's across-the-board provision of information that enabled assessment of the PDP's progress and results—in periodic reports, seminars, dedicated sites—it became increasingly important that the private sector commit to giving attention to public efforts and their outcomes. The National Confederation of Industry Brazil and the Federation of Industries of the State of São Paulo both played particularly relevant roles in this sphere by bringing together PDP managers to discuss its development in their periodic meetings with sectoral associations as well as by gathering information on the effectiveness of policy measures among their constituencies.

In summary, what has Brazil achieved after a number of years of the PITCE and the PDP? At the current development stage of industry and of the Brazilian PDP, two achievements deserve a brief comment. First, there has been a process of "refreshing," updating, and upgrading public debate on "where is Brazilian industry headed?" The discussion over what industrial setup the country should have has gained space in the media, as well as with opinion makers and public and private strategists. This is even more pronounced in the face of emerging activism on the part of other countries, the prospects of fierce competition in world markets, and the attractiveness of the Brazilian economy for the years ahead. In relation to that, a second achievement should be pointed out: the agenda of competitiveness, innovation, and quality job creation has gained space in the public debate over the development of Brazil.

7. Industrial Policy for Economic Transformation: The Way Ahead

The progress of nations is directly associated to the competitive capacity of their corporations, which, in its turn, is related to growing returns in scale, increases in productivity, and, especially, the capability for innovating. Considering the existing differences in production, innovation, and competitive competences and practices among countries, in absolute and relative terms, public policies that make effective and efficient use of horizontal, selective, and nonselective policy instruments may contribute to overcoming these existing disparities. This viewpoint is partially shared by modern liberals and more emphatically defended by activist-evolutionists. However, in this chapter we have traced how the normative implications of the two schools of thought do not take into account, fully, the challenges and the realities faced by policy practitioners in a context of open economies and a world in crisis.

The first factor that separates scholars from practitioners has to do with the generic nature of their prescriptions and the extensive use of historic examples as paths to be followed. The Brazilian case clearly shows that industrial policies are unique and are, in keeping with history, affected by the structure of each economy, the stage of its development, and the aspirations of each society. In addition, industrial policies suffer restrictions of an economic and institutional nature, and these define ambitions as well as limitations in each country.

Even if recognizing, identifying, and considering existing restrictions is essential, this chapter reveals the potential that exists in every country to advance its development process through active government policies for the business sector. Most countries have instruments that are widely accepted in multilateral treaties and could be implemented more or less intensely with potential gains. Just to mention one, if governmental procurement policies were not only intensified but also linked to the purpose of promoting well-accepted goals—such as the universalization of elementary schooling—and the use of computers and the Internet in schools, they could contribute, simultaneously, to the improvement of human capacity building and to adding incentives for economic activities in the area.

However, it is also true that most countries have established policy systems—incentives and regulations—that must be enhanced in order to ensure the efficiency of policies implemented. This chapter has taken a clear stance: existing obstacles must not be taken as absolute and impassable restrictions, which lead to only limited and defensive industrial policies being adopted or none at all. Such limitations must be considered as a starting point for designing and implementing possible industrial policies with a vision to incorporate, in time, more ambitious policy strategies, as countries manage to climb to more advanced levels of institutional modernization. Quite correlated to this evolutionary process of policymaking is the need to take an evolutionary perspective on policy goals and ambitions. Policymaking capabilities allowing, an industrial policy should be able to discern different competitive challenges of different economic sectors and move on from there, aiming at the stage of development they are in, but with a vision as to which direction they could evolve in. The scope of the policy, the extent of "horizontality" or "verticality" of a policy, the instruments that should be put to use, the sophistication of the institutional apparatus, the setup and the ambitions of a policy should evolve in light of the sophistication of the economic structure and the stage of development the country is in. This is why an industrial policy is singular to every nation. Experiences such as the Brazilian one depicted in this chapter should be taken as "food for thought," not as role models to be followed.

Even so, from a practical perspective, there are a few generic lessons that can be drawn from the Brazilian Industrial Policy. First, in the absence of political priority at the highest level, an attempt to implement an industrial policy may be ineffective, as scarce resources will be the source of constant dispute with other public policies. Second, without the active involvement and commitment of the government's financial ministry, there is no industrial policy. This does not mean, necessarily, that staff from that ministry have the accumulated and sufficient knowledge as to where an industrial policy should be aimed. Full cooperation among various ministries and agencies with the mandate along with the relevant instruments is a must for an effective industrial policy. Third, the "management" dimension of an industrial policy should not be understated. Well-defined responsibilities and hierarchies, explicit efforts in mobilizing different agencies, the proposition and implementation of clear road-map follow-up, and monitoring mechanisms for public servants are also necessary ingredients for the implementation of an industrial policy. Finally, without setting up, practicing, and expanding interaction with the business sector, the government may not reach objectives of industrial policies. Coordination and information challenges should draw a lot of attention from policymakers.

It is important to emphasize that rising above the shortcomings that are inherent to institutional management has never been, at any time or place, an easy and immediately achievable task for any country that has managed to promote catching up. As it is not, this means that improving industrial policies should be understood as a process in which obstacles, once identified, tend to be eliminated as instruments required for such elimination are introduced. Besides this, mechanisms may entice social agents—companies, governments, workers, and others—to incorporate industrial policy as a key strategic asset in promoting a structural change, and, ipso facto, economic and social development. To be an effective instrument of economic transformation, an industrial policy should be a permanent state policy.

NOTES

This work is dedicated to Chris Freeman for his role in fostering a renewed research agenda on economic development based on classics, such as Schumpeter and Kontratieff. An earlier version of this text was discussed at the InnovaLatino Experts Meeting: Innovation and Development in Latin America, held by the OECD Development Center (Oct. 1, 2009, Buenos Aires).
We thank Mario Cimoli and Wilson Peres, who kindly read preliminary drafts of this chapter. When this chapter was written, we all worked at the BNDES, the Brazilian Development Bank, Luciano Coutinho as the president, João Carlos Ferraz as vice president, and André Nassif and Rafael Oliva as economists.

1. There is at least one benefit from a heated debate: in most articles, each author's political and ideological preferences surface clearly.

2. See, for example, Rodrik (2004), Amsden (1989, 2001), Gilpin (2001), and Evans (1995, 2008).

3. Thanks to Wilson Peres for the insight. As pointed out by CEPAL (2007, 8), "Of the [relevant] issues [constantly appearing] is the need for systematic processes to evaluate the impact of policies, and the persistent failures when implementing them."

4. We make no attempt in this chapter to compile and review the literature biased against industrial policies.

5. They use a model with two countries, two sectors (industrial and agricultural), and one production factor (work).

6. According to Arthur (1989), a process of technological change is path dependent in the sense that past events ("history") exercise strong influence over innovations, learning and technological progress, and become locked in when historical events submit the economy to the monopoly of a given technology (considered superior or decadent, depending on the case).

7. Their focus was on science and technology policies in Latin America and the Caribbean, but the argument suits well the discussion on the direction and drivers of industrial policies.

8. Rent-seeking behavior must be avoided at all costs—the matter under consideration is the use of scarce public resources—and the next section will consider the issue in more detail.

9. PITCE is available at http://www2.desenvolvimento.gov.br/sitio/ascom/ascom/ polindteccomexterior.php. The revamping and strengthening came especially through Law 10,973/2004 (Lei de Inovação), aimed at fostering integration between scientific and technological institutes and innovative firms, and Law 11,196/2005 (Lei do Bem), aimed at fomenting private spending in research and development through tax incentives.

10. A word of caution: the aims of this section are modest and do not include an assessment of the impact of the PDP. A policy aimed at investment, innovation, and exports and thus, at industrial transformation should not and maybe cannot be properly and fully appreciated or assessed after only a few years.

REFERENCES

Almeida, Francisco Alberto Severo, Isak Kruglianskas, Marcelo Foresti de Matheus Cota, Roberto Sbragia, and Antonio Teodoro Ribeiro Guimarães. 2008. "Política de Inovação Tecnológica no Brasil: Uma Análise da Gestão Orçamentária e Financeira dos Fundos Setoriais." *Revista de Informação Contábil* 2(4): 102–16.

Amsden, Alice. 1989. *Asia's Next Giant: South Korea and Late Industrialization*. Oxford: Oxford University Press.

———. 2001. *The Rise of the "Rest": Challenges to the West from Late-Industrializing Economies*. New York: Oxford University Press.

Arthur, Brian W. 1989. "Competing Technologies, Increasing Returns, and Lock-in by Historical Events." *Economic Journal* 99: 116–31.

Brander, James A. 1986. "Rationales for Strategic Trade and Industrial Policy." In *Strategic Trade Policy and the New International Economics*, edited by Paul R. Krugman, 23–46. Cambridge, MA: MIT Press.

CEPAL (Economic Commission for Latin America and the Caribbean). 2007 *Cinco Piezas de Políticas de Desarrollo Productivo*. Serie Desarrollo Productivo No. 176. Santiago: CEPAL

Chang, Ha-Joon. 2003. *Kicking Away the Ladder: Development Strategy in Historical Perspective*. London: Anthem Press.

Cimoli, Mario, João Carlos Ferraz, and Annalisa Primi. 2005. *Science and Technology Policies in Open Eeconomies: The Case of Latin America and the Caribbean*. Serie Desarrollo Productivo No. 165. Santiago: CEPAL.

Coutinho, Luciano, and João Carlos Ferraz. 1994. *Estudo da Competitividade da Indústria Brasileira*. Campinas: Papirus.

Devlin, Robert, and Graciela Moguillansky. 2009. "Alianzas Público-privadas como estrategias nacionales de desarrollo a largo plazo." *Revista de la Cepal* 97: 97–116.

Dosi, Giovanni, Keith Pavitt, and Luc Soete. 1990. *The Economics of Technical Change and International Trade*. Pisa: Laboratory of Economics and Management (LEM), Sant'Anna School of Advanced Studies.

Evans, Peter. 1995. *Embedded Autonomy: States and Industrial Transformation*. Princeton, NJ: Princeton University Press.

———. 2008. "Constructing the 21st Century Developmental State: Potentialities and Pitfalls." Paper presented at the Conference "Potentials for and Challenges of Constructing a Democratic Developmental State in South Africa" Conference, Magaliesburg, South Africa, June 4.

Ferraz, João Carlos, David Kupfer, and Lia Haguenauer. 1996. *Made in Brazil: Desafios competitivos para a indústria brasileira*. Rio de Janeiro: Campus.

Freeman, Christopher. 1987. *Technology Policy and Economic Performance: Lessons from Japan.* London: Pinter.

Gerschenkron, Alexander. 1962, *Economic Backwardness in Historical Perspective: A Book of Essays.* Cambridge, MA: Belknap Press of Harvard University Press.

Gilpin, Robert. 2001. *Global Political Economy: Understanding the International Economic Order.* Princeton, NJ: Princeton University Press.

Greenwald, Bruce, and Joseph Stiglitz. 2006. "Helping Infant Economies Grow: Foundations of Trade Policies for Developing Countries." *American Economic Association Papers and Proceedings* 96(2): 141–46.

Haque, Irfan ul. 2007. "Rethinking Industrial Policy." UNCTAD Discussion Paper No. 183, United Nations Conference for Trade and Development (UNCTAD), April Geneva. Available at www.unctad.org.

Hausmann, Ricardo, and Dani Rodrik. 2003. "Economic Development as Self-discovery." *Journal of Development Economics* 72(2): 603–33.

Hausmann, Ricardo, Dani Rodrik, and Andrés Velasco. 2008. "Growth Diagnostics." In *The Washington Consensus Reconsidered: Towards a New Global Governance*, edited by N. Serra and Jospeh E. Stiglitz, 324–54. New York, Oxford University Press.

Hidalgo, César, and Ricardo Hausmann. 2009 "The Building Blocks of Economic Complexity." *Proceedings of the National Academy of Sciences* 106(26): 10570–75.

Hirschman, Albert O. 1958. *The Strategy of Economic Development.* New Haven, CT: Yale University Press.

Krugman, Paul R. 1990. *The Age of Diminished Expectations.* Cambridge, MA: MIT Press.

Lerner, Josh. 2010. *The Boulevard of Broken Dreams: Why Public Efforts to Boost Entrepreunership and Venture Capital Have Failed—and What to Do about It.* Princeton, NJ: Princeton University Press.

Lin, Justin Yifu, and Celestin Monga. 2010. "Growth Identification and Facilitation: The Role of the State in the Dynamics of Structural Change." Policy Research Working Paper No. 5313, World Bank, Washington, DC.

List, Friedrich. [1841]1909. *Das Nationale System der Politischen Ökonomie.* Translated by Sampson S. Lloyd as *National System of Political Economy*, London: Longmans, Green.

MDIC (Ministry of Development, Industry and Commerce). 2008. *Inovar e Investir para Sustentar o Crescimento. Oportunidade para uma Política de Desenvolvimento Produtivo.* Brasília: Ministry of Development, Industry, and Commerce. Available at http://www.desenvolvimento.gov.br/pdp/index.php/sitio/inicial.

———. 2009. *Relatório de Macrometas: Política de Desenvolvimento Produtivo—Maio/2008–Junho/2009.* Brasília: Ministry of Development, Industry, and Commerce.

ME (Ministry of Education). 2007. *Plano de Desenvolvimento da Educação.* Brasilia: Ministry of Education, Available at http://portal.mec.gov.br.

MF (Ministry of Finance). 2007. *Programa de Aceleração do Crescimento.* Brasilia: Ministry of Finance, Available at http://www.fazenda.gov.br.

MST (Ministry of Science and Technology). 2007. *Ciência, Tecnologia e Inovação para o Desenvolvimento Nacional: Plano de Ação 2007–2010.* Brasilia: Ministry of Science and Technology.

Nelson, Richard, and Sidney G. Winter. 1982. *An Evolutionary Theory of Economic Change.* Cambridge, MA: Harvard University Press.

Office of the President, 2010. "The Recovery Act: Transforming the American Economy through Innovation." United States Government.

Peres, Wilson, and Annalisa Primi. 2009. *Theory and Practice of Industrial Policy: Evidence from the Latin American Experience.* Serie Desarrollo Productivo No. 187. Santiago: CEPAL.

Prebisch, Raúl. 1949. "O Desenvolvimento Econômico da América Latina e seus Principais Problemas." *Revista Brasileira de Economia* 3(3): 47–111.

Rodríguez, Francisco, and Dani Rodrik. 2001. "Trade Policies and Economic Growth: A Skeptic's Guide to the Cross-national Evidence." In *Macroeconomics Annual 2000*, edited by Ben Bernanke and Kenneth Rogoff. Cambridge, MA: MIT Press for National Bureau of Economic Research.

Rodrik, Dani. 2004. "Industrial Policy for the Twenty-first Century." Unpublished report for United Nations Industrial Development Organization. Available at http://rodrik. typepad.com.

Romer, Paul M. 1986. "Increasing Returns and Long-Run Growth." *Journal of Political Economy* 94: 1001–37.

Rosenstein-Rodan, Paul N. 1943. "Problems of Industrialization of Eastern and South-Eastern Europe." *Economic Journal* 53: 202–11.

Schumpeter, Joseph. 1942. *Capitalismo, Socialismo e Democracia*. Rio de Janeiro: Zahar.

Sistema Nacional de Competitividad/Colombia 2008. *Mejora en el Clima de Inversión: El rol de las alianzas público-privadas para la competitividad*. Bogotá: Presidencia de la República, Alta Consejería para la Competitividad y Productividad.

Solow, Robert M. 1956. "A Contribution to the Theory of Economic Growth." *Quarterly Journal of Economics* 70: 65–94.

Stiglitz, Joseph. 1998. "Towards a New Paradigm of Development." 9th Prebisch Lecture at UNCTAD, United Nations Conference on Trade and Development, October 19, 1998, Geneva.

Suzigan, Wilson, and João Furtado. 2006. "Política Industrial y Desarrollo." *Revista de la CEPAL* 89: 75–91.

CHAPTER 5

MONETARY POLICY UNDER UNCERTAINTY

MARTÍN REDRADO

1. INTRODUCTION

The intrinsic complexity of economic relations, that is, the interconnection among the relevant variables, the changing behavior of the economic structure, and the interpretation of the different phenomena by the economic agents, forces monetary policy to be developed in a highly uncertain world. The analogy of the car driver is appropriate to describe the monetary policy process. In this analogy, the economy is represented by the car, the monetary authority is the driver, and policy actions are taps on either the brake or the accelerator. Accordingly, if the economy is running too slowly, then policymakers cut the interest rate (pressure on the accelerator), thereby stimulating aggregate demand. On the contrary, if the objective is to reduce the level of output, then the Central Bank switches to the brake by raising the interest rate.

However, monetary policymaking is far from simple, which renders the previous analogy misleading. First, policymakers deal with informational constraints that are far more severe than those faced by real-world drivers. The second problem with this analogy arises from the central role of private-sector expectations in determining the impact of monetary policy actions. Therefore, if making monetary policy is like driving a car, then the car is one that has an unreliable speedometer, a foggy windshield, and a tendency to respond unpredictably and with a delay in the working of the accelerator or the brake (Bernanke 2004).

We live and, therefore, have to pursue monetary policy in a highly uncertain world. Alan Greenspan (2003) defined this phenomenon in his own words: "uncertainty is not just an important feature of the monetary policy landscape; it is the defining characteristic." This statement may seem evident, almost redundant, especially to those of us who have had to weather crises, either as economic policymakers or in the private sector under changing financial conditions.

Financial crisis demonstrates that being a central banker is not an easy task. And being a governor of an emerging market economy with a fragile institutional framework could be even more complex. Trust me: a year at the Central Bank of Argentina could be like a whole tenure at the Fed! A vivid example of this unstable macroeconomic environment and its impact on monetary policy is provided by the volatility of central banks' institutional framework.

Emerging market economies and Latin American countries, in particular, have a history of higher turnover of the central bank governor than that in developed economies. Between 1995 and 2004, the average term for a central bank governor of an advanced economy was 5.2 years, compared to 4.8 years for a central bank governor of a developing country (Crowe and Meade 2007). In the case of Argentina, the systematic removal of the head of the central bank is even on another scale. The Central Bank of Argentina has had 55 different governors since its foundation in May 31, 1935, which yields an average tenure below a year and a half (i.e., 1.4 years, or a turnover rate of 0.73). On the other hand, the Federal Reserve shows an average tenure of 6.4 years between its creation in 1914 and 2010 (i.e., a turnover of 0.15). Figure 5.1 shows clearly the differences in turnover between the two countries. However, it is interesting to point out that even in the United States, where financial stability has been the exception rather than the rule, the volatility increased during times of stress: during the Great Depression, the United States had three central bank governors in a period of seven years.

The purpose of this chapter is to describe how the presence of uncertainty limits the effectiveness of monetary policy and, as a result, its implementation. Monetary and financial policy in developed economies during the so called great moderation period tended to focus on price stability, with little regard to developments in asset

Number of Central Bank Governors

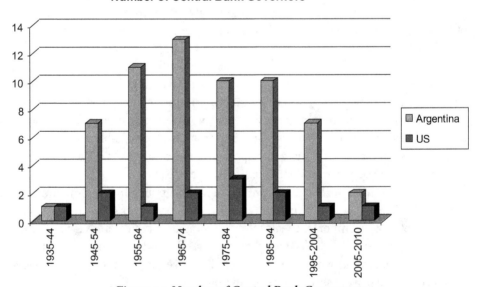

Figure 5.1 Number of Central Bank Governors.

and credit markets. Financial stability was left in the background, perhaps in the belief that it would follow from price stability and that risks could be properly limited by banks' self-assessment mechanisms. In contrast, developing countries have long (and painfully) learned the lesson of the importance of financial stability for macroeconomic performance—as evidence by recurring crises in the 1980s, 1990s, and 2000s, in different circumstances, but all featuring the substantial role of some sort of financial imbalance. Thus, if only a short time ago monetary policy could be adequately described by a simple "Taylor rule," nowadays a more complex central bank "reaction function" is called for. This entails a rebalancing of monetary policy objectives, putting the proper functioning of the financial system on par with macroeconomic stability. Thus, newer approaches such as quantitative easing, enhanced regulation, and supervision techniques have taken the stage. In the developing world, we have seen in recent years policy strategies that include foreign reserve accumulation as a form of self-insurance, active foreign exchange operations to mitigate excessive volatility, and the use of alternative mechanisms to provide liquidity when needed, recognizing the impact that the dynamics of financial conditions could have on macroeconomic stability.

In emerging markets, we have to conduct monetary policy under deep uncertainty. Despite the considerable progress in many countries of the emerging world, it is undeniable that our macroeconomic behavior substantially differs from that of countries with higher relative development. Not only are shock-absorption mechanisms in developed economies (such as financial depth) absent, but that absence also works as an amplifying force, deepening the effects of shocks. All in all, the same external disturbance that might cause temporary internal imbalances in a developed country might lead in our economies to diverging paths in key variables, and this would imply a costly return back to equilibrium.

This chapter enters this unchartered territory. Section 2 reviews the recent contributions to the literature so as to identify the influence of uncertainty on monetary policy. Section 3 analyzes how uncertainty affects policymaking, particularly in emerging economies, while section 4 examines the implications of uncertainty for monetary policymaking.

2. Monetary Policy and Uncertainty

Until recently, the notion of uncertainty was not systematically embedded into the theoretical body of monetary policy. The "world," as defined by a given model, was considered to be perfectly known by decision makers. Economists gave consideration, at the most, to the notion of risk which, unlike uncertainty, entails knowing the probability distribution function of an event. However, thanks to the contributions made by Walsh (2004), research on the conditions under which monetary policy develops has underlined uncertainty as a core issue.

Some time ago, research revealed a consensus that implicitly assumed that central bankers knew the true economic operating model. It assumed they were able to correctly follow all relevant variables and could accurately determine the different impulses affecting the economic system. Under this perspective, the only remaining "uncertainty" was, in fact, the actual realized value of these random disturbances.

However, monetary policy decisions are affected by different uncertainty sources. For instance, information problems hinder the determination of the different phases of the economic cycle. In addition, policymakers ignore the exact nature of economic relations and of the equilibrium values of the relevant variables. In turn, economic agents play a critical role when they build their expectations, thus impacting the effectiveness of policy decisions. Besides, this last factor is compounded by structural conditions under which both policymakers and private agents must address a learning process about the new environment and modify their behavior accordingly.

The different uncertainty sources are reflected in the specific problems that central banks face when designing and implementing the monetary policy. Even more, they restrain the way information is processed and the procedures to determine the most adequate intervention and operation rules. However, most of these developments are applicable to advanced economies, relatively less prone to a crisis (or, at least, to frequent crises) and characterized by a high degree of macroeconomic stability. Despite the remarkable advances of many Latin American countries in recent times, it is irrefutable that the macroeconomic behavior of the region is considerably different from that of countries with higher relative development. The recurrent shocks have disruptive effects on output evolution. Particularly, more volatile economies exhibit lower growth rates.

Because, as noted, the shock-absorption mechanisms operating in developed economies operate as amplification mechanisms in the less developed countries, making the impact of the shock more severe and meaning returning to balance tends to generate high costs, it is not a coincidence that in developing countries consumption is more volatile than output, exactly the opposite of what happens in an advanced economy. As pointed out by Sargent (1993), uncertainty can be especially intense in transition economies. In these countries, the "right" model, the value of structural parameters, the transmission mechanisms, and the nature of shocks are not accurately known. Under such circumstances, the lessons agents draw can sharply increase uncertainty, translating into adaptive responses that alter the economic structure on a permanent basis.

Various manifestations of the uncertainty concept inherent to every economy feed one other in the emerging world. Thus, the idea that the uncertainty of the environment is crucial when analyzing monetary policy options does not come exclusively from methodological or epistemological considerations. It also stems from the concrete difficulties faced by policymakers under changing scenarios, which frequently occur, unfortunately, in Latin American countries.

Uncertainty about how the economy really works (about how monetary policy transmission mechanisms operate) leads governments, on many occasions, to implement a monetary policy more conservatively than if they know the structure of the economy in depth. Emerging countries' uncertainty aversion is evident to some extent in what some authors have called "fear of floating," in relation to the allegedly excessive exchange rate stability (several additional reasons account for this phenomenon of relative stability in the exchange rate, such as the scarce development of hedging instruments), while the same phenomenon in industrialized countries is known as interest rate smoothing. An element referred to the central bank's credibility (not to appear erratic in the reading of the cycle and, thus, in the modification of the rates) may be behind the interest rate smoothing cycles of rate increase and decrease.

Recent studies show that economic agents go through a "learning period," where their behavior is not necessarily compatible, in the limit, with that of agents with rational expectations. In other words, economic players are forced to learn while interacting, thereby adding more complex behaviors that standard models do not always capture. In exploring the policymakers' task, several articles (such as Levin, Wieland, and Williams 2003) have shown the significant challenges posed by the analysis under uncertainty. Thus, the authors have emphasized that optimal policies in some countries may perform poorly under different conditions.

This has led to the notion of "robustness": it is highly desirable that monetary policy rules sustain themselves against changes in the economy's behavior. For example, a given policy may be considered optimal by policymakers and simultaneously have very negative consequences if the *true* model governing the behavior of the variables differs from the model assumed by the policymakers. An alternative policy, meanwhile, could be somewhat less effective in the case where the true economic model coincides with the model underlying the policy, but it could be less harmful if the operating conditions go against those initially assumed. Against this backdrop, this second best option—though not necessarily optimal under all potential circumstances—could be considered more robust than the first alternative.

Given the incomplete knowledge about some key structural aspects of the economy and the asymmetric distribution of the costs and benefits of specific outcomes, Greenspan has advocated a "risk-management" approach for monetary policy definition (Blinder and Reis 2005). Under such circumstances, the risk-management approach proposes a forecast-based policy, whose purpose is to combine economic models with the opinion of the experts to project scenarios. It is singular because it focuses on the analysis of the probability distribution of economic outcomes. Therefore, low-probability—but potentially harmful—events are included in the analysis. Under this approach, what matters is the distribution of them, and not just the average or most likely outcome, a fact used to decide monetary policy actions (Greenspan 2004). Consequently, the outcome of a low-probability event with severe adverse consequences may then be considered riskier than the costs of having insured against a contingency that does not occur.

Simple instrumental rules may have a good performance similar to that of much more complex "optimal" reaction functions. There is consensus on the fact that pursuing such rules may provide an adequate reference framework for decision making by monetary authorities. Unusual—and sometimes usual—circumstances require giving a preeminent role to the analysis and judgment of monetary policymakers, in line with the principles of the risk-management approach. Model-based rules should thus be an important supplement to the judgment based on the careful analysis of empirical evidence and data, but they cannot replace it.

When designing and implementing monetary policy, it is necessary to take these considerations into account, as well as the characteristics of the local and international macroeconomic environments. Otherwise, the monetary policy will not only be inconsistent but will also become an additional source of uncertainty, as occurred in Argentina.

Recurrent macroeconomic instability episodes have been one of the most distinctive features of the aggregate operating dynamics of this country. It is not a coincidence that, in the last 25 years, the Argentine economy has been off the dynamic economic stability path (defined as the range between two standard deviations from the long-term trend) one-third of the time, against 18 percent for Australia or 25 percent for Brazil. These countries are comparable in terms of resources and position in the world; therefore, Argentina is expected to be somewhat symmetrical regarding the impact of external shocks. These phenomena have been severely harmful for long-term performance and not for free in terms of welfare: excessive volatility is likely to be the main factor behind Argentina's economic stagnation in the last decades of the past century. (See fig. 5.2.)

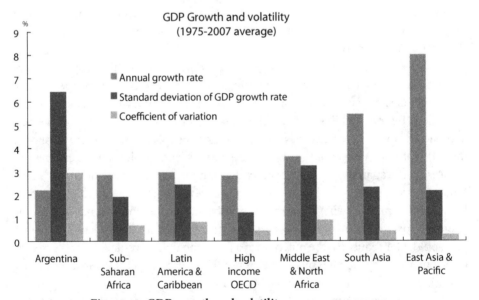

Figure 5.2 GDP growth and volatility, 1975–2007, average.

3. UNCERTAINTY AND MONETARY POLICY IMPLEMENTATION

The last 25 years have been prolific in terms of the lessons learned from crises of different origin and consequences for the monetary and financial system. The channels through which excessive volatility affects economic performance are different. Argentina has undergone two types of crises:

- Crises arising from ex ante nominal volatility, characterized by a highly persistent variation in the nominal signals received by agents (high inflation), leading to a shortening of the horizon, conservative behavior, financial anemia, and money functions' loss of value.
- Crises arising from nominal stability established by law (such as convertibility), which encourages bold behavior by agents and "shortcuts" to financial depth but in the end cause mass defaults if the rule is not accompanied by consistent macroeconomic policies in the real economy.

In those economies where society has developed an aversion to high risk and the need to prevent the next crisis becomes a priority objective, the demand for macroeconomic policy coordination is more critical. If there are doubts about the intertemporal solvency of any policy set, the monetary policy's conventional room for maneuver can be limited. Likewise, the effectiveness of the traditional tools is affected. For example, Argentina's credit channel is shallow, as the last 25 years have shown (see fig. 5.3).

Credit to Private Sector / GDP (1980-2007 average)

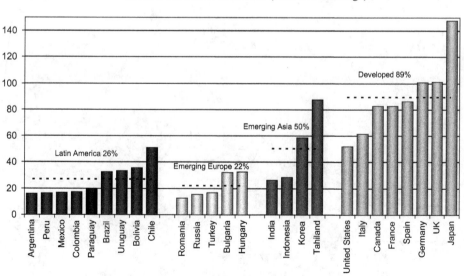

Figure 5.3 Credit to Private Sector / GDP (1980–2007 average)
Source: Prepared by the author based on World Bank information.

When designing the monetary policy, it is relevant to consider the fiscal, financial, and external conditions of the economy. An autistic monetary regime that ignores these issues, and thus risks becoming an additional source of uncertainty, would be useless. In Sargent's words (2008), there is no robust monetary regime for an inconsistent fiscal policy. Argentine history is revealing, particularly underlining the close link between the lack of fiscal solvency and inflation. In recent years the threat has eased because of budgetary surplus, but the literature on fiscal dominance is not limited to the current period. In this context, it is well known that the tax-revenue structure depends on the current relative price structure, hence the need to address the issue under a general equilibrium approach. Similarly, any doubt about the financial system's solvency or the external sustainability may restrain monetary policy's room for maneuver.

Regarding external solvency, it would be inconsistent to tailor exchange rate policy to temporary trends: the pressure in favor of the appreciation of currencies was partly related to commodity prices (through the current account; see fig. 5.4) and the investors' risk appetite (through the capital account), which may clearly be temporary rather than permanent forces.

Rajan and Subramanian (2011) have highlighted the difference in treatment according to whether the trend is due to permanent or temporary factors. In a financial world characterized by capital flow volatility, a massive amount of capital may lead to some kind of "Dutch disease," with unsustainable paths and high volatility of real variables. These kinds of problems may be more frequent in small economies, where the financial market is usually negligible compared to international

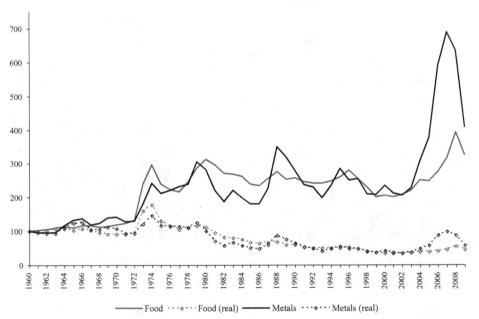

Figure 5.4 **Commodity price trends, nominal and inflation-adjusted (real).**
Source: Based on IMF information.

flows and where it is difficult to know the equilibrium level of real variables. Thus, temporary forces operating from the same side of the market may lead to nominal exchange rate overshooting (whether up or down). Far from leading to adjustment toward the long-term equilibrium level, this may cause an excessive volatility and distort relative price signals for savings and consumption.

Ultimately, it is evident that the uncertainty faced by an economy such as Argentina's is not limited to the notion of risk. While in the case of risk, the stochastic process to generate data is known, in the conditions of uncertainty discussed here the true model ruling macroeconomic function is unknown. A frequency distribution bar chart of the Argentine gross domestic product in the last 25 years would show that it is equally likely to grow or fall at a 10 percent rate; therefore, there are empirical problems in projecting the trend of fundamental variables. For instance, the 1998 national budget expected a 4.7 percent growth rate the following year and, in fact, in 1999 the decline exceeded 3 percent. This is an eloquent illustration of the problem in hand. Similar references could be mentioned with respect to the long-term equilibrium exchange rate or the consumption path.

Against an uncertain backdrop, it is appropriate to avoid euphoria and adopt robust, gradual, and coordinated policies to lead the economic convergence process toward its "cruising speed." In this sense, making decisions but simultaneously keeping open options to explore alternative paths is highly valuable. However, in a context of high nominal uncertainty, such as a widespread breach of contracts, there will be a demand on monetary authorities to provide clear and stable rules since the economic agents will relate these facts to excessive past discretion.

In this framework, the classical dilemma of rules versus discretion cannot be addressed with a "corner solution." Extreme strategies, such as rigid rules and lock-in rules, would be useless and they would not even meet the initial objective of building fast credibility if agents do not perceive their consistency with the remaining policies. On the other extreme, pure discretionary strategies cannot be pursued either. The demand for flexibility would be the perfect "excuse" for "not having a plan" and would validate the persistent trends in nominal variable imbalances. Between both ends, the pillars of the domestic economy must be built progressively and patiently around a path that adequately combines the appropriate doses of flexibility and credibility.

This approach is not an isolated case in the world. A study by Levy Yeyati and Sturzenegger (2005) indicates that only 50 percent of the countries that adopted the inflation-targeting model—where there is theoretically no intervention by the central bank in the exchange rate market—are effectively pursuing a free-floating regime policy. Moreover, after the Lehman Brothers collapse almost all emerging markets with inflation targeting had to intervene in the foreign exchange market to avoid excessive volatility. In fact, the international financial community both at the national and supranational levels is in a process of revisiting not only central bank goals and instruments but also the whole macroeconomic policy set. For instance, the International Monetary Fund has just published a report that discusses the problems of the policy interest rate as a single monetary policy instrument among many (Blanchard, Dell'Arriccia, and Mauro 2010). As regards the monetary policy, this revisiting resulted initially in the recovery of money-basic functions, normalizing the financial system, and then in the rebuilding of the transmission channels of traditional policy tools so as to use them adequately when the economy is close to its steady state.

In general, five transmission channels can be identified: interest rate, credit, exchange rate, asset prices, and expectations. Naturally enough, it is only meaningful to speak of monetary policy transmission mechanisms when there are nominal rigidities, both in goods and assets markets, that hinder an immediate accommodation of price levels. In a world characterized by flexible prices, all transmission mechanisms are alike and the question about the channels that might help the most to explain monetary policy transmission to the activity level becomes irrelevant.

In an economy in transition toward a steady state, not only the precise links among fundamental variables are unknown but also, and even more importantly, many policy tools that are typical of the steady state are unavailable. Many decades of fixed-exchange-rate regimes—including a currency board that lasted more than 10 years—followed by high devaluations and a hyperinflation processes make a difference between Argentina and neighboring countries in terms of absorbing significant swings in the exchange rate without threatening financial and monetary stability. The exchange rate cannot fully work as a shock absorber, as swings in the foreign-exchange market boost both uncertainty and market participants' substitution toward foreign currencies—channeling funds outside the financial system.

This peculiar economic history and idiosyncrasy not only affects the power of the instrument of the different branches of economic policy but also influences the way economic agents react to incentives and policies in a context where the precise connections among fundamental variables are unknown. Since the crisis, people markedly favor liquid forms of money to the detriment of wider monetary aggregates.

Therefore, in an economy like ours with precedents such as confiscation of deposits (1989, 2001), hyperinflation (1989, 1990), megadevaluations (1989, 1990, 1991, 2002), and a default on the public debt (2001), the monetary system cannot set itself an exclusive goal and ignore the economy's health and vulnerabilities. In these types of economies, where society has developed a high aversion to risk, the need to prevent a crisis becomes a priority. The past "haunts us" and leads us to adopt a prudent and asymmetrical strategy in response to exogenous forces: until enough evidence proves otherwise, we are forced to dramatically "shift the burden of proof" and assume that every negative shock is permanent and that, a priori, positive forces are temporary. The buildup of liquidity buffers in good times now allows us to weather the storms in an unprecedented way for our history.

In the specific case of emerging countries that are very prone to financial and fiscal crises (such as Argentina), where dollarization levels are high, we need to design a monetary regime that is sufficiently robust to weather the challenges that we face in the transition phase toward a long-term equilibrium. And to have a sizable amount of foreign reserves is of the essence. In the absence of an international lender of last resort, there is no substitute for a sound, strong domestic liquidity policy. Many emerging market economies have been accumulating large stocks of foreign reserves, which allow them to be better prepared to face the global crisis. International reserves have reached a degree of coverage that was previously unseen in Argentina and they proved to be very useful in preserving monetary and financial stability by providing dollars to the market and in strengthening the demand for local currency in times of turbulence.

In particular, the four-pillar risk-management strategy of the Central Bank during my tenure (the convergence between money supply and demand through yearly targets, a managed floating exchange rate regime, a countercyclical policy and liquidity networks in local and foreign currency, and adequate banking regulation and supervision) allow us to overcome every stress episode and minimize the impact on the real economy. It also prevents inconsistencies that could weaken that economy's sustainability over time.

In recent times, the Argentine economy has undergone periods of remarkable tensions in the local market and the Central Bank's policies responded as expected. The fact that four episodes in recent years (July–October 2007, April–June 2008, September–November 2008, and March 2009) could be successfully addressed shows in a conclusive manner the soundness of the approach adopted by the Central Bank. In each episode, the first action was to provide the means required to normalize the demand for money and stabilize the exchange-rate market. Then, with simple tools, the injection of liquidity to guarantee systemic stability was ensured.

The bank took some measures to neutralize the impact of a higher demand for foreign currency on money supply through liquidity injection, mainly redemption of the Central Bank's bonds and notes in the secondary market and partial renewals. This prevented an excessive pressure on interest rates and simultaneously ensured the fulfillment of monetary targets. Also, the Central Bank offered swaps between fixed and variable interest rate instruments so as to create a reference for the temporary structure of nominal interest rates in longer periods than those currently traded in the market. In addition, and with the objective of preventing excessively cautious behavior by banks and fostering the use of their foreign currency excess resources to finance the business sector, the Central Bank made available a new option to gain access to rediscounts in foreign currency.

The Central Bank also applied a nonflexible exchange rate and monetary regime, on the basis of a managed float approach and a strict follow-up of the relevant monetary aggregates. This regime has ensured stability and at the same time built a healthy financial system (without currency mismatches or an excessive exposure to the public sector) that has progressively resumed its role as households' savings intermediator (see fig. 5.5).

The managed floating-exchange-rate regime does not offer an "exchange rate guarantee" favoring short-term capital inflows and is intended to prevent high volatility from distorting consumption, saving, and investment decisions. The objective is not to inhibit the convergence of variables to their long-term values but to

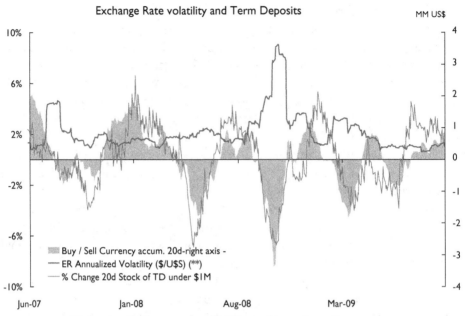

Figure 5.5 Exchange rate volatility and term deposits, 2007–9.

avoid an excess volatility likely to cause unnecessary disturbances in economic decision making. The prudential reserves accumulation by the Central Bank during the upswing of the international financial cycle enabled the orderly evolution of the exchange-rate market in those episodes (see fig. 5.6). By definition, any countercyclical policy must begin during a boom, and thinking that this favorable scenario could last forever would have been a short-sighted reading of recent Argentine history.

The Central Bank of Argentina's respect for the special characteristics of the Argentine economy, which has suffered several financial crises in recent decades, frames the bank's monetary and financial policy options of within the context of a thorough review of the balance among the different policy objectives by central banks. The bank gives special consideration to the role and weight of price stability, output stability, and financial stability.

4. CONCLUSIONS

Monetary policy is managed under a high degree of uncertainty about the real economic structure and the way in which specific policy actions affect price evolution and the output level. This is particularly marked in emerging economies. Against a backdrop of high uncertainty, in countries still in transition toward a steady state and trying to overcome decades of a sharp decline, the monetary authority must

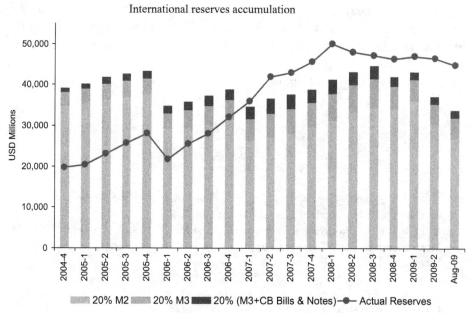

Figure 5.6 International reserves accumulation.

Source: Based on IMF information.

provide and ensure monetary and financial stability. In the case of Argentina, uncertainty is compounded by a long tradition of macroeconomic instability. Monetary regimes have unsuccessfully gone from one extreme to the other. The periods of relative stability have been short-lived, due to inconsistencies in the approaches that should have ensured macroeconomic solvency.

In these cases, the monetary regime cannot address an objective in isolation and ignore the condition of the economy and its vulnerabilities. Therefore, in order to reach long-term stability, a central bank must take into account this historical evolution, particularly its effects on the behavioral pattern of economic agents, in addition to the uncertainty factors inherent in monetary policy management. In this context, it is crucial to combine the use of models with the judgment of the experts to facilitate a thorough interpretation of economic phenomena. In turn, simple rules may provide valuable information to enable central banks to compare results and determine different policy options.

To this end, the robust strategy added to the theoretical consistency shown in this chapter has proved to be the best approach for the current stage of the Argentine economy. Its effectiveness was evident in recent quarters, when the bank provided a quick response to preserve monetary and financial stability in the face of a new international context. Undoubtedly, this scheme reinforces the need for permanent and comprehensive work to reconcile tools and objectives. This is also the challenge faced in building institutions and simultaneously contributing to growth with stability and social inclusion, which is, after all, the ultimate goal of every economic authority with a strategic vision.

Otherwise, all efforts will be in vain and there will be another fall in the classical Argentine pendulum, going endlessly from one extreme of likely policies to the other. In fact, there is a twofold challenge ahead, which is synchronic rather than sequential: making progress in the fulfillment of policymakers' objectives and simultaneously building institutions for the benefit of future generations.

REFERENCES

Bernanke, Ben. S. 2004. "The Logic of Monetary Policy." Speech to the National Economists Club, December 2, 2004, Washington, DC.

Blanchard, Olivier J., Giovanni Dell'Ariccia, and Paolo Mauro. 2010. "Rethinking Macroeconomic Policy." IMF staff position note SPN/10/03, February 12, 2010, Washington, DC.

Blinder, Alan S., and Ricardo Reis. 2005. "Understanding the Greenspan Standard." Paper presented at "The Greenspan Era: Lessons for the Future" Conference of the Federal Reserve Bank of Kansas City, Jackson Hole, WY, August 25, 2005

Crowe, Christopher, and Ellen Meade. 2007. "Evolution of Central Bank Governance around the World." *Journal of Economic Perspectives* 21: 69–90.

Greenspan, Alan. 2003. Speech at "Monetary Policy under Uncertainty" Symposium of the Federal Reserve Bank of Kansas City, August 29, 2003, Jackson Hole, WY.

———. 2004. "Risk and Uncertainty in Monetary Policy." Speech at the Meetings of the American Economic Association, San Diego, January 3.

Levin, Andrew T., Volker Wieland, and John Williams. 2003. "The Performance of Forecast-Based Monetary Policy Rules under Model Uncertainty." *American Economic Review* 93: 622–45.

Levy Yeyati, Eduardo, and Federico Sturzenegger. 2005. "Classifying Exchange Rate Regimes: Deeds vs. Words." *European Economic Review* 49: 1603–35.

Rajan, Raghuram G., and Arvind Subramanian. 2011. "Aid, Dutch Disease, and Manufacturing Growth." *Journal of Development Economics* 94(1):106–18

Sargent, Thomas J. 1993. *Bounded Rationality in Macroeconomics.* Oxford: Clarendon Press.

———. 2008. "Evolution and Intelligent Design." *American Economic Review*, 98(1): 5–37.

Walsh, Carl E. 2004. "Implications of a Changing Economic Structure for the Strategy of Monetary Policy." UC Santa Cruz SCCIE Working Paper No. 03-18, University of California, Santa Cruz.

PART II

THE POLITICS
OF ECONOMICS:
HISTORICAL,
GEOGRAPHICAL,
INSTITUTIONAL
APPROACHES

....

CHAPTER 6

A HISTORICAL PERSPECTIVE ON THE POLITICAL ECONOMY OF INEQUALITY IN LATIN AMERICA

....

ROSEMARY THORP

THE object of this essay is to explore the historical evolution of the political economy of inequality, with a view to what we might learn for the future. "Political economy" here refers to the *interaction* of politics and economics: I evaluate how and why inequality appears so deeply embedded and so extreme in the Latin American case. The chapter concerns inequality within countries, and finds that a significant part of the story, though by no means all, turns on inequality between Latin America and the international economy. I do not reflect—for reasons of space and competence—on a third aspect, the topic of inequality over time but between Latin American countries—for example, the implications of the growing strength of Brazil in the region, or the political economy of the various trading arrangements and their impact on the balance of interests and power.

The essay seeks to make three points. First, what we find as we observe the different historical periods is that inequality is often functional for growth—supportive of the particular growth path, even constructed at times to facilitate the growth path. This gives us insight into the embeddedness of inequality. Second, I argue that a balanced analysis has to explore fully both the "initial conditions" beloved of recent institutional economics[1] and the process: the interactions over time between domestic and international forces, and within the elements of the domestic economy and polity itself. The insights of the dependency analysis still have their place.[2]

Third, I argue that it is crucial to look beyond income inequality, to all aspects of inequality—social, political, ethnic, racial, gender—as well as economic. In some instances, geography also plays a key part in the interactions, as the chapter shows. This complexity is important not only for human development, but because the core interactions of the political economy over time lie in these meeting places.

The essay first provides a preliminary discussion of data. Section 2 considers the colony, section 3 the export economy boom period, and section 4 the period of state-led industrialization. Section 5 takes a brief look at recent events.

1. A Preliminary Note on Data

The construction of data on inequality is at a point of fascinating innovation and fresh ideas in regard to the dimension of income—all of which is good news except for the comfort of a handbook author, since it is not a good moment to tell a simple and authoritative story. And the systematic collection of data on the distributional side of social, political, ethnic, and gender dimensions has barely begun. The important aspect of inequality between groups of people, as well as between individuals, has been firmly established as important in the work of Stewart (2008) and the CRISE team[3] but historical data do not yet exist except in piecemeal form.

Until the last 15 years, household survey data were the only serious source, and they began in the 1970s with very few earlier points (Argentina, Chile, Colombia, and Mexico). Table 6.1 gives the authoritative data set of Altimir, after he had made a careful review of comparability. It shows a very high degree of inequality, and how certain countries—the Southern Cone but not Brazil, and Costa Rica—were convincingly less unequal than the average around the 1960s but converged with the rest of the region subsequently.[4] In the last 15 years, creative and enterprising work has been carried out using wages, land prices, and the improving estimates of gross domestic product, to show the way the booming export economy from the 1870s to the 1920s was associated with distinctly worsening equality.[5] This work is still tentative, particularly in regard to comparisons of absolute levels, as the authors themselves are the first to point out,[6] but the trend to increasing inequality in this early export boom is now well established.[7] Coatsworth (2005) has suggested that the literature exaggerates the importance of the colony in creating inequality, but as shown below, it was the creation of institutions shaping and embedding inequality for future generations that matters for this analysis.

The middle of the twentieth century remains the least well-documented period. Recent work on this period has focused on income shares, not comparable with later work using household surveys and difficult to interpret without detail on numbers and distribution within the share. New work by Frankema (2009) shows the labor share of national income peaking in the middle decades of the century for Argentina, Brazil, and Mexico, confirming Prados de la Escosura (2005); Fitzgerald (2008) is consistent with this using a different methodology.

Table 6.1. Gini Coefficients; Distribution of Households according to Total Household Income

	Argentina	Brazil	Chile	Colombia	Colombia	Costa Rica	Mexico	Uruguay	Venezuela
	Urban	National	Santiago	National	Urban	National	National	Montevideo	National
1938				0.45					
Early 1950s	0.37		0.44	0.51			0.59		
Early 1960s	0.41	0.57	0.46	0.54	0.57		0.61		
Early 1970s	0.42	0.63	0.47	0.52	0.57	0.44		0.33	0.49
Early 1980s	0.46	0.62	0.52	0.46	0.54	0.40	0.48	0.43	0.39
Early 1990s	0.52	0.63	0.52	0.53	0.56	0.42	0.53	0.40	0.40
1990	N.a.	0.63	0.55			0.44	0.54 (1989)	N.a.	0.47
Average last three years of data[a]	0.53	0.60	0.55	0.58		0.43	0.52	0.45	0.43

[a] For Argentina, 2004–6; for Brazil, 2006–8; for Chile, 2000, 2003, 2006; for Colombia, 2002, 2004, 2005; for Mexico, 2005, 2006, 2008; for Peru, 2003, 2007, 2008; for Uruguay, 2007, 2008; for Venezuela, 2006–8.

Source: For 1938 to early 1990s, Thorp (1998, 352), using figures prepared by Oscar Altimir, to include only those estimates that can be considered as reasonably comparable. For the exact years of the figures given, see Thorp (1998, 352). For 1990 to the present, see ECLAC (2009).

In the 1970s, trends were divergent, and some countries improved though others worsened in terms of income distribution. The worsening of recent decades is accepted fact and well documented, above all in the disastrous 1980s, as is the contribution of the very rich to this inequality (Palma 2003; Reygadas 2010). The clear exception of Cuba is also accepted (Mesa Lago 2000). Also well documented, though insufficiently tested, are the signs of improvement in distribution in some countries since the 1990s (Cornia and Martorano 2011; Gasparini and Lustig forthcoming). However, as I comment below, the improvement, even if genuine, does no more than restore the distribution of 1980.

2. THE COLONIAL PERIOD

The colonization of Latin America began at the end of the fifteenth century and lasted for four centuries. The Spanish colonized the Andes and much of Central America in pursuit of precious metals. The Portuguese colonized what would be Brazil, and the British, French, and Dutch, various countries of the Caribbean. The legacy did vary with the colonizer, though less than some writers have concluded. Independence came at different points mostly in the first four decades of the nineteenth century, though some tiny Caribbean states waited till very recent times to secure their independence, and a few are still protectorates. The discussion that follows refers only to the major colonization projects of Spain and Portugal.

In all of Latin America, huge land grants from the Crown, plus the need of the local elite for cash as well as labor, created the strong patterns in factor markets made famous in extensive literature, though with many variations in the themes.[8] In some places local populations were effectively wiped out, so in macabre manner allowing a somewhat less unequal path after independence (e.g., in parts of what became Chile, Argentina, and Paraguay). In some places local power structures maintained an element of community autonomy and legitimacy of Indian leadership (e.g., in what would become Bolivia), whereas in others the leadership was killed and the renewed differentiation produced the phenomenon of middlemen seeking absorption into criollo/mestizo culture at the expense of indigenous identity (e.g., Peru) A place like Guatemala had very little in the way of resources, which at least meant that the indigenous populations were allowed to conserve relative autonomy in the isolation of the highlands. But the variations were not enough to invalidate the general story. In the most extreme cases, indigenous peoples were physically resettled in new groupings to make it easier to administer a head tax and impose labor requirements. Repression was meted out when rebellion occurred, leading to the wholesale killing of indigenous leaders and the subsequent exclusion of the indigenous elite from education.

Such behavior was facilitated by a value system that saw Indians as inferior, since they were not Christian. The values of the time also saw nothing wrong in slavery, which was widespread, with importation of slaves from Africa, above all to Brazil and the Caribbean; slaves were the most deprived and abused sector of the population.

The colony thus created a powerful institutional legacy. Four aspects are key for the political economy of subsequent inequality:

The colony created and embedded the overlap between class and ethnicity that is perhaps the outstanding characteristic of twentieth-century inequality in Latin America. (The overlap with gender inequality is also tight, but the political economy implications of having gender in the equation are not clear: an important research theme.)

Over four centuries, it embedded Latin America in the international economy as a supplier of raw materials. Imperial trading rules carefully limited the growth of industry.

It created institutions around labor supply, especially what North (1990) calls "informal" institutions, including customs, attitudes, and prejudices, and a web of obligations that would persist through Independence.

Finally, it instituted the extreme inequality in land ownership that is still observable in the twenty-first century. Coatsworth (2005) rightly observes that land only became economically valuable later on, as demand for its products rose, but what concerns us here is the institutional shaping, the embedding of values, and the control of and unequal access to labor and water as well as land.

3. THE POSTINDEPENDENCE EXPORT ECONOMY GROWTH PHASE

The early years of independence were uniformly years of political instability and complexity, but gradually the whole of the continent was sucked into the massive expansion of world trade, propelled by falling transport costs and rising demand in Europe. Some countries grew early (the sugar economies, Argentina with hides and beef, Peru with guano, Chile with copper, Brazil with coffee); the integration of others was delayed because of internal chaos (Colombia, where the coffee boom could only get going once civil war ended at the beginning of the twentieth century). Some ended their growth spurt early—for Ecuador, cocoa collapsed at the beginning of the 1920s, as did nitrates demand in Chile. But the general pattern of strong export growth from somewhere around 1870 to the Great Depression is a valid generalization.

So also is the key feature for my analysis of inequality: the shortage of mobile labor, man- or womanpower that could effectively be mobilized for the expanding sector. In a static model such a feature would suggest improvement in the labor share of national income: in fact all countries moved to resolve the labor crisis by means that would ensure a relative decline in labor's share. However, this came about in different ways. We can divide the continent into three parts for this purpose.[9]

For countries with an open frontier and demand for agriculture, and lacking an indigenous population or a tradition of slavery, immigration was the answer. Thus Argentina, Chile, and Uruguay—and Costa Rica as the Central American exception—did all they could to attract European immigrants into agriculture. The early notion, that immigrants might become smallholding settlers as in North America, proved wrong: the huge numbers of immigrants who came from southern and eastern Europe were less educated and less prepared for farming than their counterparts in North America. They came as somewhat reluctant tenants or often seasonal workers. Some returned, others eventually moved to the city, often seeking education for their children. Others settled in Buenos Aires but migrated seasonally to work in agriculture.[10] The result was dramatic: the price of land rose over 10 times in Argentina between 1870 and 1913 (Bértola forthcoming, table 3.12), and the relative price shift of land versus labor was the core of the worsening income distribution.

A second group of countries also drew heavily on immigration as a solution, but to replace the slaves that had provided over centuries the solution to the problem of labor supply. These were particularly the sugar economies of Brazil and Cuba and other Caribbean countries. The immigrants that came in great quantities toward the end of the nineteenth century were typically poorer and less educated than those arriving farther south, and were absorbed into an ex-slave culture. Labor relations were appalling, and Brazil even introduced legislation to prevent immigrants from owning land. Conditions were so bad that at one point the Italian consul forbade more immigration to Brazil. Import of coolie labor continued after the end of slavery. The import of laborers was into production of sugar and cotton in Peru, sugar in Cuba, and henequen in Mexico, with indentured labor from Korea and elsewhere (Bulmer-Thomas 1994, 87). Panama and some smaller Caribbean countries also used this system.[11]

In sugar, inequality was further entrenched by the technological changes coinciding with the end of slavery. With a significant increase in capital intensity in the "central", the sugar processing plant, a divide was created between the poor and marginal colonos—settlers in search of work—and the small industrial labor force. The settlers were at the mercy of the seasonality of cane cutting, with unemployment for eight months of the year. "In the 1880s," notes Fraginals (1986, 203), "the owners of the new centrales were able to set up an efficient flow of migrant workers who would arrive at the beginning of January and leave at the end of April." These workers came from the Canary Islands and poor provinces of Spain and other Caribbean countries where living standards were extremely low and there was overpopulation and high unemployment. The inequality of sugar economies such as Brazil and Cuba was deeply embedded through this process.[12]

Other countries—less attractive to European immigrants and possessing large indigenous populations—focused their efforts on deepening the institutions that kept an indigenous population subservient and available. Indigenous communities continued to lose their land, and many forms of forced labor remained and were extended. In the Andean countries and in Guatemala, forced labor for public works continued, as did many forms of exploitation through debt bondage and company stores. "Enganche" or "hooking" was common: the initial loan would "hook" a person into migrating, with a debt impossible to pay back when most pay took the form of tokens to be used in the company store. Violence was frequent, to enforce debt bondage or to quell rebellion. Again there were variations—Bolivia continued to show more indigenous autonomy—but the generalization is well founded.

The variation in forms and degrees of exploitation sometimes had to do with the way geography interacted with social, political, and economic forces. Since the survival of indigenous populations was related in part to isolation and mountainous terrain, geography sometimes reinforced the exclusionary forces of the export economy, especially if the capital was lowland and the indigenous population in the highlands.

The direct investment driving much of the export growth did not challenge the landowning monopoly of the elite, nor thereby its local power base. With crops that did not experience economies of scale, with some exceptions, foreigners did not want to hold land, which brought with it unwished-for involvement in complex labor arrangements and social relations. When because of debt they were forced to, it was an unhappy experience to be ended as soon as possible (Duncan Fox in Peruvian cotton is an example—see Thorp and Bertram 1978). Some export crops required ownership to secure land concentration, economies of scale, and control of labor—for example, the banana plantations—and the labor regimes were correspondingly oppressive.

Violence was thus a common part of labor relations and of the enforcement of land ownership the degree and type of violence varied with the commodity and the geography. Capital markets took the form of international borrowing and direct investment, and direct foreign investment particularly in rural contexts reinforced unequal labor relations, with notorious and well-documented situations of extreme behavior, such as the United Fruit Company in Central America and the mining camps of the Andes.

Tension and instability of course required expenditure on the military and police at the expense of social expenditure, threats of invasion and armed insurrection even more so. Mexico was a prime example of this, suffering foreign invasion, regional revolts, and peasant insurrections (Coatsworth 1988). Such pressures meant that the immediate imperative of fund-raising was such that taxes had to be raised in the most effective way possible—on foreign trade, at the cost of developing internal institutions. Coatsworth and Williamson (2004, 217) have shown compellingly how Latin America turned to taxes on trade following independence, sometimes as a response to a protectionist lobby but generally under the imperative of revenue necessity: "Weak governments, under attack from within and without, *remember now the Japanese collected tax on a few mines, Taiwanese, important!*

abandoned internal taxes that required an extensive and loyal bureaucracy and concentrated tax collection efforts instead on a few ports and mines. This was an "institutional deforming" that would embed inequality by making any more redistributive growth path through taxation quite beyond the bounds in later decades.

The heart of the political economy in the long half century from the 1870s to the Great Depression is thus that growth, and elite interests, benefited from mechanisms that increased labor supply and inequality. Far from being a restraint, inequality was functional for growth, just as it was in the colonial period. But it was growth based on primary product exports, continuing the legacy of the colony but more importantly continually shaped by the relation with the international economy, where through those years relative prices gave no scope to a different route. Further, the economic path reinforced and further embedded the social, political, and ethnic inequality of the colonial period. Indigenous populations continued to be perceived as inferior; liberal reforms of the newly independent countries were meant to change the face of such inequalities, but were notable for form, not substance.

The major difference with the immediate postindependence period was that once the worst episodes of political instability or external threat were passed, there now began to be investment in capabilities—especially primary education. There were differences in timing: countries suffering periods of turbulence, such as Mexico and Colombia, were hardly in a position to invest in education. The investment in education was most notable in our first group of countries, responding to pressure from urban and largely immigrant populations. This had an impact on literacy; literacy rates typically improved in a 30–40 year period, starting some 10–15 years after the beginning of the serious expansion of primary education, and this period typically occurred around the end of the nineteenth century for our first group of countries (table 6.2). The expansion of literacy reinforced the impact on political equality of the expansion of suffrage, which also occurred earlier in this group of countries than on the rest of the continent.[13]

more literacy, earlier suffrage

Countries characterized by grave political instability or deep social and ethnic inequality invested only later in education and with less impact on literacy. This forms an important part of the analysis of inequality: Peru can be cited as an emblematic case, where elites anxious to restrain the political threat of Indian masses did put export revenue into education—but as table 6.3 shows, literacy rates in the Peruvian Sierra, the heartland of the indigenous population, had hardly improved by 1940. This was a consequence of the failure to tackle either the power structure or the related culture of discrimination and prejudice.[14]

Health expenditure, though not extensive, was more egalitarian at this early period: elites, and perhaps especially foreign companies, did not relish malaria or other such threats, and their safety required mass campaigns of public health (the later decades of the twentieth century would be less egalitarian in this regard). Summarizing the political economy of the years of export-led boom, we can say that the increase in inequality was universal, and was so because it was functional to the type of growth driven by the international market. Some countries—the temperate

Table 6.2. Timing of Literacy Improvement, 1870–1995

Period	Countries Achieving Their Significant[a] Improvement in This Period	Ranking according to Literacy in 1995
18??–1908	Uruguay[b]	1
1870–1920	Argentina	2
1890–1930	Chile	4
	Cuba[c]	3
1900–1940	Costa Rica	5
1910–	—	
1920–	—	
1930–80	Mexico	11
	El Salvador	16
	Panama	10
1940–80	Peru	12
	Dominican Republic	15
	Venezuela	10
1950–80/90	Brazil	13
	Colombia	9
	Ecuador	10
	Bolivia	14
1960–	Honduras	17
	Guatemala	19
	Nicaragua	18
1970–	Haiti	20

[a] The definition of *significant* is a change of more than seven points. Paraguay has been excluded since no data were available.
[b] First data are for 1908, showing that the improvement had already occurred.
[c] Data from 1900.
Source: Thorp (1998), using data prepared by Shane Hunt.

Table 6.3 Peru: Illiteracy Rates by Region (Percentage of Adult Population)

Year	Lima	Other Coast	North and Central Sierra	Southern Sierra	Selva
1876	45.4	74.0	85.8	91.8	85.8
1940	10.6	40.6	66.2	79.8	51.0
1961	10.5	28.3	50.8	61.8	39.3
1972	10.3	23.0	43.8	49.6	34.4

Notes: Illiteracy rates: I_{1876} = do not read or write / total population; I_{1940} and I_{1961} = do not read or write and older than six / population older than six; I_{1972} = do not read or write and older than five / population older than five. (b) See Thorp and Paredes 2010 for the definition used for region.
Source: Thorp and Paredes 2010, using data from the national censuses.

zones with open frontiers mainly—benefited from some softening of inequality in the form of education and possibly suffrage, but even there strong inequality in land ownership and in political power underpinned both a worsening in and a considerable degree of inequality.

4. Inequality in the Middle Years of the Twentieth Century

As is well known, for the larger Latin American countries, these are the peak years of an industrial process looking to the domestic market, once the international market crashed in 1929, with World War II providing a renewed stimulus to some primary products, but not all, and in addition cutting off vital supplies. The immediate postwar years saw the United States refusing to provide Marshall Plan aid to Latin America and a consequent renewed stimulus to look to the domestic market.

It might be thought, therefore, that the political economy of inequality might have centered on the clear new need of a buoyant and sizable internal market, generating a public policy interest in redistribution. However, this would be a false conclusion. First, many countries—particularly the small economies of Central America but equally several Andean countries—saw a rapid renewal of growth led by the export of primary products. Second, industrialization in the larger economies did begin to hit market limits by the 1960s, but the leading sectors were by that date consumer durables, and notably automobiles—hardly to be rescued by redistribution. Rather, the preexisting inequality in all its dimensions, economic and political, shaped and framed industrial growth and was then in its turn reinforced, since the heart of the new industrial expansion was notably capital intensive, based on imported and capital-intensive technology. Direct foreign investment played a large role, with tariff hopping its key strategy for surviving and evading protection. There were many good elements in the process, notably a large investment in building the institutions of a modern economy—public revenue, finance, and banking above all, and serious investments in social policy. Also, notably in the Southern Cone, industrialization supported and stimulated the emergence of an organized labor movement, important in promoting more equality. Growth was strong, and the countries with the most coherent political economies[15] (Brazil, Chile, and Colombia) were beginning to find their way through to a renewed stimulus to industrial exports and modern "openness," when the debt crisis put an end to the whole experiment (politics having turned the situation around earlier in Chile).

Meantime, the failure to provide adequate urban employment combined with the rapid rise in population growth and migration to cities was leading to the new key characteristic of the postwar political economy of inequality—informal urban employment. Country experience varied depending on the economic structure and

Table 6.4 Latin America: Estimates of the Informal Sector, 1980 (Percentage)

Country	Economically Active Population Not Covered by Social Security	Underemployed[a] within the Economically Active Population
Argentina	30.9	25.7
Bolivia	81.5	74.1
Brazil	13.0[b]	44.5
Chile	32.7	28.9
Colombia	80.3	41.0
Costa Rica	51.6	27.2
Dominican Republic	88.7[c]	40.6
Ecuador	78.7	63.3
El Salvador	88.4	49.0
Guatemala	66.9	50.9
Honduras	85.6	49.7
Mexico	59.5	40.4
Nicaragua	81.1	52.1
Panama	47.7	45.5
Peru	62.6	55.8
Uruguay	34.2[d]	27.1
Venezuela	55.8	31.5
Latin American average	56.3[e]	42.2

[a] Defined by PREALC as the sum of self-employed workers minus professionals, unremunerated family workers, domestic servants, and "traditional" rural workers.
[b] Coverage in 1980 is based on selected assistance programs according to universalistic criteria rather than tied to employment.
[c] 1985 figure.
[d] Based on a probability survey of Montevideo's working-class population in 1985. Official figures report near-universal coverage based on selected programs extended to all citizens.
[e] Weighted average.
Source: Portes and Schauffler (1993, 53).

the dynamism of the modern sector (García and Tokman 1984). But the common experience was a clear rise in urban underemployment from 1950 to 1980. In the latter year, as table 6.4 shows, some 40 percent of the economically active population on average might be considered underemployed. This in the short term allowed income in the poorest sector to be a little higher than it might have been—but must surely have negative longer run implications.

A topic not fully researched yet is the political economy of "informality." While the sector bridges many levels of income and types of activity and income generation, without doubt a major role is as a residual for those who must survive. Presumably, it tends to divert organizational skill to survival and to significantly reduce time for political activity. At a minimum, it does not further political equality and may well aggravate it, by feeding systems of patronage and dependency. For countries with significant ethnic group inequalities, these would also tend to be reinforced.

A further consequence was that welfare measures in regard to the labor force—paid vacations, sickness benefits, and so on—were steadily undermined in their impact on inequality, since they were designed to affect formal labor, which over time meant the labor elite only. The continued large role of direct foreign investment also meant pressures "not to rock the boat." The limited reach of social policy in regard to inequality was also a product of its urban bias. This was particularly true in health. Once the logic of control of epidemics was no longer the main driver of health expenditure, money now tended to be spent on large hospitals in major urban centers, not on primary health care at the local level.

The exception was Cuba, which following the revolution gradually made health and education a top priority. As mentioned earlier, Cuba is the only country to achieve a substantial improvement in income distribution, in the process creating an exportable capacity in health care (Mesa Lago et al. 2000). Two increasingly important public policy areas in Latin America in the 1950s to the 1970s were agrarian reform and tax reform. Both were promoted by outside forces, in particular the Alliance for Progress, a foreign-policy initiative of the United States, reacting to the threat posed by the success of the Cuban Revolution.

Land reform had varying degrees of internal backing, and some significant measures achieved, most of all in Chile. But generally, it proved far too easy for political inequality to undermine even well-designed measures of agrarian reform. Hirschman's *Journeys toward Progress* (1968), despite its title, remains the classic study of how reform can be made nonreform. He describes the water of the Brazilian dams in the northeast glistening in the moonlight while the terrain below goes unirrigated for lack of effective expropriation measures (1968, 47).

Land reform also did not touch gender inequality: women were typically ignored in reform legislation. In the prevailing culture, rules such as one household member as the named beneficiary discriminated against women. They were not part of the decision-making bodies in the various corporate forms of organization being created (Deere 1985).

Tax reform could equally be nullified by evasion (see Hirschman 1968 again on Colombia), but also could be simply dismissed, as external availability of money proved adequate in the short term and politically less threatening. Dependence on external inflows compounded the politics of "not rocking the boat." In such a spirit, social pressures, which were real, were increasingly answered by repression, with military dictatorships or with conservative, if formally elected, regimes. Labor organization was significantly weakened and social movements had great trouble achieving coherence in the face of repression.

Thus despite tentative data, we can conclude that while income distribution did not worsen, it did not radically improve either. And politically the underlying positive forces of population growth, wide suffrage, and investment in capabilities were softened in their impact on inequalities. Income distribution was no longer "functional" in the larger economies but shaped and was in turn shaped by industrialization, in a reinforcing process. The negative significance for growth was not readily perceived in the short term.

5. THE DEBT CRISIS AND BEYOND

The political economy of the debt crisis and inequality has been well analyzed. Borrowing that had seemed rational with export growth and negative real interest rates suddenly became unsustainable, and by 1981 abrupt stabilization and adjustment were forced on the continent. The political economy analysis of the adjustment highlights the extent to which it was convenient for bankers (and for elements of domestic elites), given the widespread view that the previous period had fostered excessive state intervention and fiscal imprudence. The domestic measures took no account of the need for well-functioning institutions to support a return to a market focus, and policymakers were encouraged to deceive themselves into thinking that recovery would "solve" poverty and inequality. Compensation funds became a popular measure to soften the short-term social cost. "Institutional" reforms, insofar as there were any, harmed equity, with a focus on removing imperfections, above all in labor and land markets; political developments weakened if not destroyed the elements of labor organization in the formal sector, while military dictatorships and the narrowing of the formal labor market had already significantly weakened the union movement. The combined effect of all these factors on income distribution was extreme.

Within the decade it was becoming clearer to many analysts that compensation funds were not adequate and that an altogether different approach was needed, focused on capabilities, both in the state and in the labor force, and productive employment, if growth and equity were to go together. However, the depth of the implicit challenge in that shift was not recognized: the need to change attitudes, ways of making decisions, if a bureaucracy accustomed to a different world was now to support healthy, detailed supply-side policies.

Meanwhile, and very interestingly, little by little some democratic surprises were happening. By 2007, eight countries could be described as having governments seriously committed to challenging the status quo in the interest of the have-nots (Cornia and Martorano 2011). Many countries by now had elections at the level of municipal governments. Several countries now experienced the first clear reversal of worsening inequality we have records of. Thus in 14 of the 18 countries studied by Cornia and Martorano (2011), between 2003 and 2007, distribution improved. The causes were partly from the conjuncture of rapid growth responding to international prices and partly several strands of social policy maturing and starting to affect both poverty and inequality (Gasparini and Lustig forthcoming; Cornia and Martorano 2011; on social policy, see Ferreira and Robalino forthcoming; Uthoff Botka 2011).

It is far too early to review these trends in "handbook" style, and inappropriate for a "historical perspective". Recent very interesting analyses suggest the statistical and political economy connection between increased democracy, policies of challenge, and impact in inequality data (Huber et al. 2006; Cornia and Martorano 2011). However, scholars cannot pronounce authoritatively on the sustainability of the political economy analysis, particularly because in several cases growth is being driven by extractives, notorious products for an unhealthy political economy. Even today, policymakers do not fully grasp the depth of the political economy problem generated by the overlap between social policies targeting redistribution and the unpleasant realities of decentralization or its failure. Even policies that are well intentioned, supported and articulated at the national level, fail when they have to be executed in local contexts where incompetence and lack of political will combine to frustrate intentions. Further, there are a significant number of countries where the weakening of political parties over many years leaves a gap of institutions, leading to maverick elections of outsiders without parties who frequently disappoint. And recent political violence or its threat makes it easy to make the case for repressive policies.

For all these reasons, one can only signal a combination of hope, curiosity, and concern for the fragility of the positive phenomena.

6. CONCLUSION

This essay has focused on the political economy of inequality within countries, and the way that has been shaped over time in part by unequal relations with the more developed world. It has stressed the importance of understanding inequality as going beyond income, as needing to be analyzed as political, social, gender, ethnic, and racial forms, to name the most central aspects of a vast topic. I have argued this both as a matter of a full concept of human development and as intrinsic to the political economy. The interaction of different aspects of inequality—above all the social, political, economic, and ethnic ones—is fundamental, I argue, to the political economy of the dynamics of the embedding of inequality over decades. For some countries, geographical inequality becomes a further crucial element.

Thus in the colonial period, the institutions shaped by the needs of colonial exploitation and by the values of the colonizing actors embedded a culture of exploitation based on prejudice and discrimination, a culture of domination, which served well the labor needs of the colony and were not easily disbanded with independence. The colony firmly embedded Latin America as a supplier of primary products, again a key legacy and integrally related to the dynamics of the persistence of inequality. After a period of chaos and instability, the surge of international demand for Latin American resources (with differences of timing) meant again acute labor needs. I have shown how the different responses of different types of country—immigration, domestic labor arrangements—though with variations, produced the same result: a worsening of income inequality. Even where "liberal" regimes were supposed to be reducing restrictions on indigenous peoples, the inter-actions of political inequality with the demands of the market consolidated exploi-tation, with communities losing land and labor, and land concentration increasing. The harmony between now-domestic elites and foreign capital consolidated a growth path that kept labor cheap and docile—in fact cheapened labor. The South-ern Cone countries (and Costa Rica) with large immigrant labor forces, without traditions either of slave labor or Indian exploitation, and still with open frontiers saw a worsening but one accompanied by progress in education and (probably) less severe inequality than in other countries of the region.

The middle of the twentieth century saw a different growth path of the large and medium economies, as the external market collapsed and the early industry of the nineteenth century began to thrive with protection, by the 1940s and '50s deliberate protection allied with new surges of foreign investment. The inequality of the pre-vious periods now framed this phase, interacting with aspects of the growth path to create a further reinforcement in inequality, though typically not a further wors-ening and in the short term in some countries, some improvement. Lack of markets did appear to be an obstacle that more equality would have helped—but by the 1960s the lines facing narrow markets were consumer durables—hardly likely to boom in a redistributing strategy. This middle period was important for modern-izing institutional developments, now not aimed at cheapening labor since demo-graphic trends had by now created a surplus of available labor. The institutions of a modern economy now came into place—but so also did an industrial sector that failed to provide jobs. The growth in informality undermined the provision of wel-fare. And in countries with significant indigenous populations, the failure to chal-lenge the local power structures and the depth of discrimination and prejudice led to even significant rates of expenditure on education doing relatively little for equality.

The collapse of growth with the debt crisis and the necessity of strong adjust-ment policies produced a severe worsening of equity, with even the outliers—the Southern Cone—converging now to a remarkable collection of Ginis in the .57–62 range. The initial naïve application of the neoliberal model helped this pattern. But in a number of significant countries, at long last political inequality was beginning to shift—at least allowing the possibility that democracy combined with genuine increases in education and political capabilities might be producing shifts in income distribution, in part rooted in innovative social policies. But we need to end on a glass half full–half empty query: one lesson of history is not the determining role of the economy, but the strength of economic forces, and the new paths needed to establish opportunities for productive labor and competitive strength in the world market for such jobs. I have emphasized repeatedly the functional role of inequality in growth. Further reflection is required on how the positive dimensions of the re-lation between growth and equity can be augmented and a political base for growth with equity be firmly built, despite the legacy of heterogeneous economic structures.

This constructive work will be particularly hard in those countries where the world boom in extractives, the continuing role of China, and the insistent adverse political economy of extractives and equity provide particularly tough challenges.

NOTES

José Antonio Ocampo and Luis Bértola generously shared the draft of their forthcoming book and commented in detail on my first draft. I owe many insights and improvements to them. Pablo Astorga, Jeff Dayton-Johnson, José Carlos Orihuela, and Diego Sánchez Ancochoa also provided helpful comments.

1. Coatsworth (2005) provides an excellent review of recent writing, moving the discussion in a nice political economy direction. As he says, the two "streams" in new institutional economic history have been moving closer together. Both emphasize the importance of institutions, but one puts more emphasis on natural endowments influencing institutions (e.g., Engerman and Sokoloff 1997), and the other on the political economy of colonial rule (e.g., Acemoglu, Johnson, and Robinson 2001, 2005). Coatsworth situates these contributions in the broader context of core new recent texts on the economic history of Latin America; his list is Haber (1997); Coatsworth and Taylor (1998); Cárdenas, Ocampo, and Thorp (2000); and Bulmer-Thomas, Coatsworth, and Cortés Conde (2006).

2. Bértola (forthcoming) provides an excellent essay on the evolution of institutions: he makes very well the point that in the new institutional economics, the emphasis on the significance of the colonial period ignores the early Latin American writing that develops this theme, and in particular the insightful book by Cardoso and Pérez Brignoli (1979).

3. CRISE is the acronym for Centre for Research on Inequality, Ethnicity and Human Security, a research centre funded by the U.K. Department of International Development (DFID) and based at the University of Oxford. See the website at www.crise.ox.ac.uk.

4. Venezuelan data are something of a surprise, and need further investigation: it seems curious that a significant oil economy comes toward the lower end of the comparative Latin American picture. A recent revision by a leading Venezuelan scholar (Baptista 2006) moves the whole series to a range comparable with the most severely unequal Latin American countries.

5. See Williamson (1999); Bértola et al. (2010); Frankema (2009a); Prados de la Escosura (2005); and various articles in the *Revista de Historia Económica—Journal of Iberian and Latin American Economic History* in 2010. Fitzgerald (2008) uses productivity data by sector to experiment with a sectoral distribution, but his data begin only in 1900.

6. See the editors' introduction to the special issue of the *Revista de Historia Económica—Journal of Iberian and Latin American Economic History* in 2010.

7. At another level of generality, Williamson (2010) boldly covers five centuries, analyzing relative price data rather than institutions. He concludes that Latin America prior to the colonization by Europe was no more or less unequal than any other preindustrial area. He agrees with the authors cited above, arguing that inequality was constructed during the colony but more particularly during the export economy boom after independence.

8. See Gibson (1984) for a full account of such variations.

9. The classification parallels that of Cardoso and Pérez Brignoli (1979).

10. Adelman (1961) compares Argentina and Canada, to make these points by contrast.

11. In Peru the importing of laborers continued until guano declined in the 1870s. In the Caribbean the system continued until past the turn of the twentieth century.

12. See Fraginals (1986) for the different dimensions of this inequality in Cuba: the position of wage-earning slaves, or that of the *jornalero*, and the veterans of the Cuban Army of Liberation. See also Stolcke (1974) for a historical perspective on Cuban inequality.

13. Engerman and Sokoloff (1997) argue that it was done to attract immigrants; it seems more likely to have been a consequence.

14. Frankema (2009b) in a creative exercise shows how Latin American countries in general were more prone than other parts of the world to experience relatively high rates of dropouts and low rates of completion in primary education. His data are for 1950 on, but we can reasonably assume that the same phenomenon was present in earlier years.

15. The thesis of Thorp (1998) is that "coherence" of the political economy, residing above all in a well-functioning public-private relationship, implied nothing about income redistribution, and usually meant interest in preserving the status quo. The export economy histories of Brazil and Colombia above all yielded unusual coherence in the public-private relationship and the consequent ability to manage public policy, especially the macro, while income distribution worsened but was not the concern of elites.

16. Hirschman cites the preamble of one of the numerous irrigation bills.

REFERENCES

Acemoglu, Daron, Simon Johnson, and James A. Robinson. 2001. "The Colonial Origins of Comparative Development: An Empirical Investigation." *American Economic Review* 91(5): 1369–1401.

———. 2005. "The Rise of Europe: Atlantic Trade, Institutional Change and Growth." *American Economic Review* 95: 546–79.

Adelman, Irma. 1961. *Theories of Economic Growth and Development*. Stanford, CA: Stanford University Press.

Baptista, Asdrúbal. 2006. *Bases cuantitativas de la economía venezolana, 1830–2002*. Caracas: Fundación Polar.

Bértola, Luis. Forthcoming, "Institutions and the Historical Roots of Latin American Divergence." In Ocampo and Ros forthcoming.

Bértola, Luis, Cecilia Castelnovo, Javier Rodríguez Weber, and Henry Willebald. 2010. "Between the Colonial Heritage and the First Globalization Boom: On Income Inequality in the Southern Cone." *Journal of Iberian and Latin American History–Revista de Historia Económica* 28(2): 307–41.

Bulmer-Thomas, Victor. 1994. *The Economic History of Latin America since Independence*. Cambridge: Cambridge University Press.

Bulmer-Thomas, Victor, John Coatsworth, and Roberto Cortés Conde, eds. 2006. *The Cambridge Economic History of Latin America*. Cambridge: Cambridge University Press.

Cárdenas, Enrique, José Antonio Ocampo, and Rosemary Thorp, eds. 2000. *An Economic History of Twentieth Century Latin America*. 3 vols. London: Palgrave.

Cardoso, Ciro F. S., and Héctor Pérez Brignoli. 1979. *Historia Económica de América Latina, IBII*. Barcelona.

Coatsworth, John H. 1988. "Patterns of Rural Rebellion in Latin America: Mexico in Comparative Perspective." In *Riot, Rebellion, and Revolution: Rural Social Conflict in Mexico*, edited by Friedrich Katz, 21–62. Princeton, NJ: Princeton University Press.

———. 2005. "Structures, Endowments, and Institutions in the Economic History of Latin America." *Latin America Research Review* 40(3): 126–44.

Coatsworth, John and Alan M. Taylor. 1998. *Latin America and the World Economy since 1800*. Cambridge, MA: Harvard University Press.

Coatsworth, John H., and Jeffrey G. Williamson. 2004. "Always Protectionist? Latin American Tariffs from Independence to Great Depression." *Journal of Latin American Studies* 36(2): 205–32.

Cornia, Giovanni Andrea, and Bruno Martorano. 2011."External Shocks, Policy Changes, and Income Distribution: Latin America during the Last Decade." In *Overcoming Inequality and Poverty*, edited by Volpy Fitzgerald, Judith Heyer, and Rosemary Thorp, 172–201. London: Palgrave.

Deere, Carmen Diana. 1985. "Rural Women and State Policy: The Latin American Agrarian Reform Experience." *World Development* 13(9): 1037–53.

ECLAC (Economic Commission for Latin America and the Caribbean). 2009. *Panorama Social*. Santiago: ECLAC.

Engerman, Stanley L., and Kenneth L. Sokoloff. 1997. "Factor Endowments, Institutions and Differential Paths of Growth among New World Economies: A View from Economic Historians of the United States." In Haber 1997, 260–305.

Ferreira, Francisco, and David Robalino. Forthcoming. "Social Protection in Latin America: Achievements and Limitations." In Ocampo and Ros. forthcoming.

Fitzgerald, Volpy. 2008. "Economic Development and Fluctuations in Earnings Inequality in the Very Long Run: The Evidence from Latin America, 1900–2000." *Journal of International Development* 20: 1028–48.

Fraginals, M. M. 1986. "Plantation Economies and Societies in the Spanish Caribbean, 1860–1930." In *Cambridge History of Latin America*, edited by Leslie Bethell, 4. Cambridge: Cambridge University Press.

Frankema, Ewout. 2009a. *Has Latin America Always Been Unequal? A Comparative Analysis of Asset and Income Inequality in the Long Twentieth Century*. Leiden: Brill.

———. 2009b. "The Expansion of Mass Education in Twentieth Century Latin America: A Global Comparative Perspective." *Revista de Historia Económica–Journal of Latin American Economic History* 27(3): 359–95.

García, Norberto, and Víctor Tokman. 1984. "Changes in Employment and the Crisis." *CEPAL Review* 24: 103–15.

Gibson, Charles. 1984. "Indian Societies under Spanish Rule." In *The Cambridge History of Latin America*, vol. 2, *Colonial Latin America*, edited by Leslie Bethell, 381–419, Cambridge: Cambridge University Press.

Gasparini, Leonardo C., and Nora Lustig. Forthcoming. "The Rise and Fall of Income Inequality in Latin America." in Ocampo and Ros. forthcoming.

Haber, Stephen, ed. 1997. *How Latin America Fell Behind: Essays on the Economic History of Brazil and México, 1800–1914*. Stanford, CA: Stanford University Press.

Hirschman, Albert O. 1968. *Journeys toward Progress: Studies of Economic Policy-making in Latin America*. New York: Greenwood Press.

Huber, Evelyne, François Nielsen, Jenny Pribble, and John D. Stephens. 2006. "Politics and Inequality in Latin America and the Caribbean." *American Sociological Review* 71: 943–63.

Mesa-Lago, Carmelo, Alberto Arenas de Mesa, Ivan Brenes, Verónica Montecinos, and Mark Samara 2000. *Market, Socialist and Mixed Economies: Comparative Policy and Performance in Chile, Cuba and Costa Rica*. Baltimore: Johns Hopkins University Press.

North, Douglass. 1990. *Institutions, Institutional Change, and Economic Performance*. Cambridge: Cambridge University Press.

Ocampo, José Antonio, and Jaime Ros, eds. Forthcoming. *Handbook of Latin American Economics*. New York: Oxford University Press.

Palma, José Gabriel. 2003. "National Inequality in the Era of Globalization: What Do Recent Data Tell Us?" In *The Handbook of Globalisation*, edited by Jonathan Michie. Cheltenham: Edward Elgar.

Portes, Alejandro, and Richard Schauffler. 1993. "Competing Perspectives on the Latin American Informal Sector." *Population and Development Review* 19(1): 33–60.

Prados de la Escosura, Leandro. 2009. "Lost Decades? Economic Performance in Post-Independence Latin America." *Journal of Latin American Studies* 41: 279–307.

Reygadas, Luis. 2010. "The Construction of Latin American Inequality." In P., ed., (2010), *Indelible Inequalities in Latin America: Insights from History, Politics, and Culture*, edited by P Gootenberg, 23–51. Durham, NC: Duke University Press.

Stewart, Frances, ed. 2008. *Horizontal Inequalities and Conflict: Understanding Group Violence in Multiethnic Societies*. Basingstoke: Palgrave Macmillan.

Stolcke, Verena. 1974. *Marriage, Class, and Colour in Nineteenth-Century Cuba: A Study of Racial Attitudes and Sexual Values in a Slave Society*. Cambridge: Cambridge University Press.

Thorp, Rosemary. 1998. *Progress, Poverty and Exclusion: An Economic History of Latin America in the Twentieth Century*. Washington, DC: Inter-American Development Bank.

Thorp, Rosemary, and Geoffrey Bertram. 1978. *Peru, 1890–1977: Growth and Policy in an Open Economy*. New York: Columbia University Press.

Thorp, Rosemary, and Maritza Paredes. 2010. *Ethnicity and the Persistence of Inequality: The Case of Peru*. Basingstoke: Palgrave Macmillan.

Uthoff Botka, A. 2011. "Social Security Reforms in Latin America." In Ocampo and Ros forthcoming.

Williamson, J. 1999. "Real Wages Inequality and Globalization in Latin America before 1940." Spec. issue of *Revista de Historia Económica–Journal of Iberian and Latin American Economic History* 17: 101–42.

———. 2010. "Five Centuries of Latin American Inequality." *Revista de Historia Económica–Journal of Iberian and Latin American Economic History* 28(2): 227–52.

CHAPTER 7

CUBAN ECONOMIC POLICIES, 1990–2010: ACHIEVEMENTS AND SHORTCOMINGS

PAOLO SPADONI

1. INTRODUCTION

The Cuban Revolution of 1959 profoundly transformed the political landscape, economic organization, class structure, and foreign relations of Cuba. Through a major process of agrarian reform, nationalization of private property (including all U.S.-owned assets on the island) and elimination of foreign investment, expansion of employment, and income redistribution, Cuba virtually eradicated capitalism in favor of a socialist economic system emphasizing inclusive development (Pérez-Stable 1999, 84). Efforts to elicit a new popular consciousness based on moral incentives and social obligations also took center stage. In order to reduce economic dependency on the United States and mitigate the pressure of a comprehensive U.S. embargo, Fidel Castro proclaimed himself to be a Marxist-Leninist and signed favorable trade agreements with the Soviet Union under which Cuban sugar was exchanged for Soviet oil, machinery, technology, and credits. In short, Cuba embraced a development path that was quite different from that of any other Latin American country.

Cuba's most distinguished feats under socialism cannot be overlooked, among them substantial improvements in health-care indicators, the formation of a highly educated and skilled labor force providing a considerable resource in human capital, low levels of unemployment, an egalitarian access to basic social services, and, at least until the late 1980s, a rather equitable distribution of wealth. The socialist model remains in place today, but its organizational policies have changed several times over the past 50 years. Between 1959 and 1989, Cuban economic policies oscillated from idealistic antimarket moves that often pursued improbable targets to pragmatic concessions to the market, with the latter being introduced essentially to address the shortcomings of the former and thus avoid potential threats to the stability of the regime and that of its economic system. While spurring inequality and unemployment, moves toward the market generally resulted in improved macroeconomic performance and living standards, strengthening the regime to the point it felt safe to initiate a new idealistic cycle (Mesa-Lago 2004).

Cuba's offensive against capitalism in the immediate aftermath of the revolution was accompanied by the pursuit of unlikely goals like self-sufficiency in food and rapid industrialization through an import-substitution approach. These objectives were replaced in the mid-1960s by a greater focus on sugar production and exports, showing the difficulties in overcoming the country's traditional monoculture dependency. In the second half of the 1960s, the Castro regime further radicalized its policies with a push for more centralized decision making, the nationalization of all small private businesses, the expansion of rationing and free social services, and a greater use of moral stimulation. It was only in 1971 that Cuba launched a new system of planning characterized by modest decentralization, increasing attention to enterprise efficiency and market mechanisms, and emphasis on material rather than moral incentives. In 1986, however, Havana's authorities embarked on a "rectification process" that abandoned the timid market-oriented measures of the previous decade and a half.

A number of policy shifts have also occurred in Cuba in the post–Cold War period, most notably a structural adjustment program in the wake of the Soviet demise that resulted in the enactment of limited capitalist-style reforms, a subsequent retrenchment during an economic boom, and the latest round of market-based reforms by Raúl Castro in the midst of a global economic crisis and domestic financial problems. But some key differences from the past should be underscored. First, although political considerations have continued to determine the nature and scope of economic policymaking, the latter's main objective moved from "the defense of socialism" to "the defense of the achievements of socialism" after the constitutional reform of 1992 replaced Marxism-Leninism with nationalism as the guiding principle of the revolution (Rojas 2006). Second, the antimarket cycle of the mid-2000s increased state control over the economy and tried to breathe new life into the egalitarian precepts of the Cuban model, yet it lacked the idealistic character of the cycles of the 1960s and 1980s given that socialism's failings had already saturated popular consciousness. Finally, Raúl Castro's initiatives represent a clear and much-needed departure from previous ways of managing the Cuban economy, suggesting that his reforms, albeit insufficient, are meant to stay and perhaps will be deepened in the future.

This study provides an analysis and assessment of Cuban economic policies in the post–Cold War era, with an emphasis on recent developments. When its former benefactor, the Soviet Union, collapsed in the early 1990s, the Cuban economy took a nosedive. With the loss of the external support that had sustained its economy in the form of favorable trade terms, subsidies, and aid,[1] Cuba's real gross domestic product (GDP) plummeted by a cumulative 34.8 percent between 1990 and 1993. Cuban exports and imports also fell dramatically during this period. Thus, owing to the disappearance of the economic and financial system in which it had been situated during the Cold War era, Cuba suffered debilitating blows and was forced to devise new and effective strategies to reinsert itself into the global market economy.

The implementation in September 1990 of an austerity program called "the special period in time of peace" stimulated a more pragmatic stance toward economic policy. The program consisted of a series of measures intended to conserve energy and raw materials, stimulate food production, expand markets for exports and imports, and accelerate the development of international tourism. Between the second half of 1993 and 1994, other measures were adopted: the legalization of the possession and circulation of U.S. dollars, with important implications for remittances from Cubans living abroad and state-owned dollar stores and exchange houses open to the public; authorization of self-employment and the breakup of the state monopoly on land to set up agricultural cooperatives; reorganization of the central administration of the state and reduction of bureaucracy with the establishment of a new structure of ministries and institutes for both horizontal and vertical functions; creation of free farmers' markets; and the active promotion of foreign direct investment (FDI) (Jatar-Hausmann 1999, 61–62). On the whole, these reforms were crucial in keeping the Cuban economy afloat during the 1990s and laying the foundations for future growth.

Between 2003 and 2006, the government of Fidel Castro reversed some of the liberalizing reforms it had implemented a decade earlier to secure the survival of a system then on the verge of collapse (Pérez-Stable 2007, 17). Among various moves, it reduced the number of Cuban agencies responsible for imports, reasserted central control over the tourism industry, eliminated the commercial circulation of the U.S. dollar in Cuba, and ordered state enterprises to deposit all the hard currency they obtained through business activities into a single account at the Cuban Central Bank, then request bank permission to use the money. A process of economic recentralization, which took place amid strong growth and coincided with the emergence of Venezuela as a critical source of support for the Cuban economy, lasted until Fidel Castro fell ill and temporarily relinquished power to his younger brother Raúl in late July 2006. Since then, and particularly following his appointment as president in February 2008, Raúl Castro has introduced a number of small but significant reforms primarily intended to improve living standards on the island, boost domestic production and efficiency, and overcome deteriorating economic conditions. At present, the list of problems that negatively affect the Cuban economy and pose key challenges for the future includes sizable fiscal and trade deficits, a massive foreign debt in hard currency, low productivity and low efficiency, depressed real wages, a dual currency system that distorts prices, incomes, and incentives, declining revenues from tourism activities and nickel exports, the precarious conditions of public transportation and housing, an undercapitalized national industry, and a liquidity crunch (CEPAL 2010; Ritter 2010; Mesa-Lago 2009).

2. MACROECONOMIC PERFORMANCE

During the profound recession that started in 1990 and reached its lowest point in 1993, Cuba's GDP shrank by an annual average rate of about 10 percent. Since then, as shown in figure 7.1, economic growth has been positive even though the rate fluctuated considerably from year to year. The Cuban economy witnessed a remarkable expansion between 2005 and 2007 but suffered a deceleration in 2008 and especially in 2009, according to official figures (ONE 2010). While extensive damage from three major hurricanes and the world economic crisis were important causes of economic deterioration, a GDP slowdown was projected by local economists even before the hurricanes hit the island in late 2008. It should be noted that in 2005 the Castro government adopted a new formula for the calculation of its gross domestic product and revised upward previously reported figures. Cuba's new "sustainable social" GDP formula, which substantially inflates the size of the economy, recognizes the value added of subsidized social services (health care, education, sports) provided by the Cuban state to its population and to citizens from other countries, primarily to Venezuelans. Although there is little doubt that the Cuban economy improved markedly in 2005–7,[2] the reliability of Cuba's GDP figures and the magnitude of its announced economic growth have been met with skepticism by several analysts (Pérez-López and Mesa-Lago 2009; Mesa-Lago 2008; Pérez-López 2006).

Cuba's recent economic expansion (see table 7.1), at least until 2008, was mainly fueled by the dynamism of internal demand due to increased public investment and private consumption, and above all by growing exports of goods and services. As for

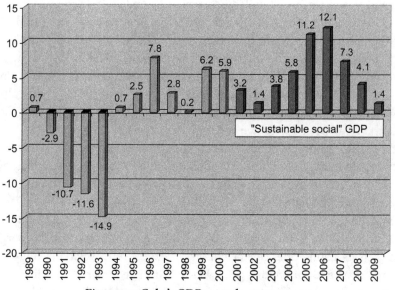

Figure 7.1 Cuba's GDP growth, 1989–2009.
Sources: ONE (2010) and previous years; CEPAL (2010).

Table 7.1. Real GDP by Expenditure, 2004–9 (Millions of Pesos at Constant 1997 Prices)

	2004	2005	2006	2007	2008	2009
Private consumption	19,380	19,453	23,093	23,443	23,029	23,234
Government consumption	9,245	10,206	11,012	12,164	12,475	12,691
Gross fixed investment	3,484	4,633	5,837	5,976	7,287	5,547
Exports of goods and services	6,017	8,876	8,993	10,234	11,418	11,891
Imports of goods and services	5,297	6,661	8,023	7,934	8,519	7,011
Total GDP	32,830	36,507	40,912	43,883	45,690	46,352

Source: ONE (2010).

the latter, thriving exports of professional services under an oil-for-doctors barter agreement with Venezuela and, to a smaller degree, substantial revenues from nickel exports and international tourism were key stimulating factors. Mounting imports of goods, meanwhile, reduced the overall growth rate. In 2009, despite reduced imports, the GDP slowed primarily as a result of lower levels of government investment in connection with a severe liquidity shortage and nearly stagnant private consumption.

External sector statistics exhibited in table 7.2 indicate that Cuba's exports of goods and services nearly doubled between 2004 and 2007, increasing from about $6.1 billion to $11.9 billion. Growing receipts from exports of services, in particular, offset the traditional goods trade deficit and produced a widening surplus in the overall trade balance during this period. They also stimulated a surplus in the current account of Cuba's balance of payments in 2007 and an expansion of its international reserves. Yet it is worth emphasizing that imports of goods also rose dramatically, peaking at an unprecedented $14.2 billion in 2008. That year, Cuba ran its first trade balance deficit since 2003 and the largest in many years. In a clear sign of deteriorating economic conditions, the country's current account balance turned negative again in 2008. Total exports of goods and services decreased in 2009 but a much larger drop in imports of goods helped produce a surplus in both the trade and current account balances.

Regarding the merchandise trade, nickel is currently the biggest hard currency earner among Cuba's export goods. By relying on one product of this sort, Cuba shares with its Latin American neighbors an exposure to volatile swings in commodity demand and commodity prices, and accordingly suffered the fall in both with much of the rest of the region during the global economic crisis of 2008–9. Earnings from nickel exports are particularly sensitive to prices of the metal in the international

Table 7.2. **Cuban External Sector, 2004–0 (US$ Million)**

	2004	2005	2006	2007	2008	2009
Exports of goods	2,332	2,159	2,925	3,686	3,664	2,879
Nickel	1,068	994	1,347	2,081	1,434	841
Pharmaceuticals	165	240	306	288	296	520
Sugar	268	150	216	194	223	216
Tobacco products	217	225	246	236	234	212
Imports of goods	5,615	7,604	9,498	10,079	14,234	8,909
Fuel/lubricants	1,310	1,945	2,287	2,383	4,562	2,649
Machinery/equipment	1,214	1,819	3,097	3,006	3,155	1,785
Foodstuffs	1,121	1,435	1,329	1,647	2,421	1,607
Manufactured goods	693	894	1,060	1,102	1,549	1,050
Exports of goods and services	6,121	8,963	9,870	11,918	12,506	11,171
Imports of goods and services	5,841	7,822	9,744	10,333	14,806	9,284
Trade balance (goods and services)	280	1,141	126	1,585	-2,300	1,887
Net current transfers	974	-367	278	-212	505	476
Current account balance	120	140	-215	489	-2,000	730

Sources: ONE (2010) and previous years; EIU (2010); data of Centro de Estudios de la Economía Cubana (CEEC), Havana.

market given that the island's three active ore-processing plants (the largest one is 50 percent owned by the Canadian company Sherritt International) in the eastern province of Holguín are now operating close to full capacity and production has therefore remained at similar levels in recent years. Skyrocketing prices caused nickel revenues to grow from nearly $1.1 billion in 2004 to a record $2.1 billion in 2007. Two years later, as prices plummeted, revenues were less than half of that amount. Cuban vice president José Ramón Machado Ventura warned in April 2009 that such a negative trend may run the risk of making the country's nickel industry unprofitable.[3]

Other important export products for Cuba are pharmaceuticals, sugar, tobacco, and fuels. Exports of generic medicines, vaccines, and other pharmaceutical goods have benefited from the promotion of partnerships and the formation of joint ventures with companies from East Asia (China, Malaysia, and India), the Middle East (Iran), and Africa (Namibia and Algeria) to tap developing and emerging market countries where barriers to entry are relatively low and Cuban products face less severe licensing and registration hurdles (Spadoni 2004, 129). The once-mighty sugar industry saw a steady decline in the post–Cold War era and by 2009 accounted for less than 8 percent of Cuba's total exports of goods, roughly the same as the tobacco industry. Although fuel exports are not included in the external sector data of Cuba's Office of National Statistics, a Cuban scholar reported that in 2008 they were the second largest source of foreign exchange income after nickel, generating about 22 percent (worth nearly $800 million) of Cuba's total revenues from exports of goods (Pérez Villanueva 2009). The reopening in December 2007 of the Cienfuegos oil refinery, a joint venture between the Venezuelan state-run firm Petróleos de Venezuela S.A. and Cuba Petróleo, made a key contribution. Even so, it has been claimed that the Castro government resells on the open market a substantial portion of the oil it acquires from Venezuela on preferential terms (Corrales 2006).

Booming revenues from exports of professional services and new credit lines from Venezuela and China triggered unprecedented levels of merchandise imports before serious economic problems that began around mid-2008 took a toll on Cuba's finances and forced it to reduce its purchases from abroad. Cuba has been in the past, and remains today, heavily dependent on imported fuels and foodstuffs. Between 2004 and 2008, imports of fuels and lubricants more than tripled and those of foodstuffs more than doubled, to a great extent because of soaring prices. Along with manufactured goods, Cuba's principal imports include various types of machinery and equipment that have been used in recent years to upgrade the poor conditions of the island's main infrastructures.

Given that Havana's authorities tend to favor trade relations with countries providing government-backed credits with generous repayment terms, it is not surprising that Venezuela and China are today, in that order, Cuba's top merchandise trading partners. Trade with Venezuela is centered on Cuban purchases of oil and, to a much lower extent, food, construction material, and other products. China is a major importer of Cuban nickel and sugar and has been supplying the island with buses, locomotives, farm equipment, and domestic appliances. Spain, Canada, Brazil, and the United States have also substantial trade dealings with Cuba (ONE 2010). The United States, in particular, has ranked first among the island's sources of imported food since 2002, following historic U.S. legislation in October 2000 allowing this kind of trade for the first time in nearly 40 years. In 2009, however, Cuba purchased less food from abroad and slashed many other imports as the Castro government implemented austerity measures to cope with financial shortages and significantly curtailed its investment plans in key sectors such as energy, transportation, and housing. Put simply, the economic pie is now smaller for all of Cuba's trading partners and will remain so until the Cuban economy shows concrete signs of improvement. Furthermore, a drastic reduction of Cuban imports from Venezuela in 2009 that coincided with a difficult economic situation in the oil-producing South American country and flattening Cuban exports of medical and other professional services suggest that the Castro regime's special relationship with the Venezuelan government of Hugo Chávez might be unsustainable in the long run.

The only official data on the flow of foreign direct investment into Cuba are those reported in the country's balance of payments, but they have not been updated since 2001. Cuban statistics indicate that accumulated FDI was little more than $2 billion between 1993 and 2001, with large fluctuations from year to year. This is significantly lower than in many other Latin American countries. Yet we should remember that the Castro government resorted to foreign investment in the early 1990s out of necessity, and essentially against its will. Cuban authorities have always made clear that government policy is not intended to create a market economy and develop a large private sector but rather to favor a state economy that regulates foreign capital so that the benefits of investment go to the entire society. Moreover, Cuba's business environment and its economic system are very different from those of its neighbors. Therefore, quantitative cross-country comparisons based on delivered FDI have a limited value. In any case, the stock of FDI has continued to grow since 2002 even if the number of joint ventures with overseas partners has diminished (Morris 2008, 790). Canada and European countries like Spain and Italy currently account for about half of total active joint ventures in Cuba, but the vast majority of all new mixed enterprises authorized since 2005 have been formed with state firms from Venezuela.

3. SOURCES OF GROWTH

During the 1990s, the Cuban economy experienced a crucial transformation from an economy centered on agriculture and especially sugar production to one based on services such as international tourism. It witnessed yet a new dramatic change in the post-2004 period principally as a result of Venezuela's financial largesse and its booming ties with Cuba (Sánchez Egozcue and Triana Cordoví 2008). Whereas in 1989 exports of goods represented more than 90 percent of the country's total exports, by 2009 they accounted for just 26 percent. In 2009, services accounted for over three quarters of Cuba's GDP, generated the vast majority of foreign exchange revenues, and received the biggest share of all investments.

Table 7.3 highlights the aforementioned changes by presenting data on the main sources of growth of the Cuban economy at different times over the past two decades. In 1990, when the Soviet Union was about to disintegrate, Cuba's sugar industry brought in $4.3 billion worth of exports representing 73 percent of the island's total hard currency revenues. Nickel exports and an incipient tourism industry made a modest contribution. In the post–Cold War era, Cuba emerged again as one of the Caribbean's most popular holiday destinations. International tourism expanded dramatically and produced growing earnings throughout the 1990s to become, as local officials often described it, the "engine" of the Cuban economy (Cerviño and Cubillo 2005; Peters 2002). Gross revenues from tourism activities represented 42.6 percent of Cuba's total exports of goods and services in 2004 according to official

Table 7.3. Cuba's Total Exports of Goods and Services by Sector, 1990–2007 (%)

	1990		2004		2007	
Sugar	73.0	Tourism	42.6	Professional services	44.0
Nickel	6.7	Nickel	19.4	Tourism	21.2
Tourism	4.1	Transportation	6.3	Nickel	17.6
Agropecuary products	3.1	Sugar	5.0	Telecom services	3.6
Tobacco	1.9	Tobacco	4.0	Pharmaceuticals	2.4
Fishing	1.7	Fishing	1.6	Tobacco	2
Other goods	4.7	Other goods	12.5	Sugar	1.7
Other services	4.8	Other services	8.6	Others	7.5

Sources: Calculations of the author from ONE and CEEC data; BCC (2005).

data of the Cuban Central Bank. That year, nickel exports accounted for nearly 20 percent of total earnings while the share of sugar was just 5 percent.

As far as Cuba's economic growth is concerned, foreign direct investment and remittances deserve a special mention. It cannot be denied that FDI has produced a number of positive effects on the Cuban economy. Foreign investment raised the competitiveness of Cuban goods both domestically and internationally, helped Cuba find new markets for its main exports, and stimulated import substitution. Overseas firms have a major influence over the production of nickel and fuels and play a significant role in the marketing of pharmaceutical products, cigars, and sugar. More in general, foreign participation is particularly strong in all the industries that have experienced the biggest expansion in the past 20 years, namely oil, mining, electricity generation, tourism, and telecommunications. Also notable are joint ventures with foreign partners that boosted domestic supplies to the tourism industry and to the increasingly important internal market in hard currency (Spadoni 2010, 86–94).

Family remittances from abroad are captured by the Castro government mainly through sales in state-owned hard currency stores. Annual remittances to Cuba, primarily sent by Cuban Americans to relatives left behind, were estimated to be $537 million in 1995, $700–900 million between 1997 and 2002, and over $1 billion between 2003 and 2007 (Spadoni 2010, 148; Nova González 2006). Some scholars contended that money sent from overseas was actually the single most important factor in reactivating the Cuban economy in the second half of the 1990s (Monreal 1999, 50). In effect, if we take into account the high economic costs incurred by the Cuban state in tourism and other sectors, remittances were in net terms the biggest source of foreign exchange for the country at least until 2004.

But almost everything has changed since then due to the Venezuelan factor. Since 2000, Cuba has been receiving 98,000 barrels of high-quality Venezuelan oil per day and paid for it with medical and educational services. By 2008, there were approximately 37,000 Cuban doctors, nurses, and other health-care personnel staffed in clinics and various social programs abroad, mostly in Venezuela.[4]

Furthermore, Cuba has greatly benefited from the launch, in late 2004, of the program Operation Miracle, financed by Hugo Chávez, under which Cuban doctors are providing free eye surgery to patients from several Latin American and African countries.

In 2007, foreign exchange income from exports of professional services accounted for 44 percent of Cuba's total exports of goods and services. Revenues from international tourism dropped to 21.2 percent of the total, about half their level of 2004. The relative contribution of nearly every other sector of the Cuban economy (including nickel and sugar) underwent a similar downward trend. Cuba's earnings from the sale of professional services could have been as high as $5.2 billion in 2007, even higher than earnings produced by exports of sugar in 1990. The current role of Venezuela as Cuba's main economic lifeline and engine of growth is beyond question.

4. ECONOMIC CHALLENGES

The macroeconomic bonanza that Cuba enjoyed between 2005 and 2007 produced some concrete benefits for the island's population. In addition to sizable oil supplies from Venezuela, during this period Havana's authorities contracted for large stocks of rice cookers, television sets, refrigerators, and other consumer products from China that were made available to Cuban families at subsidized prices. Growing imports of foodstuffs also helped boost the supply of goods through the rationing system. Even more important, the Castro government stepped up investment in housing and urban development, electricity, roads, waterworks, transportation, and other infrastructures. Most notably, it launched a new housing construction program, purchased thousands of container-sized diesel generators from Spain, Germany, and South Korea for the country's aging energy grid, and acquired locomotives and a fleet of new buses from China, Russia, and Belarus for interprovincial and urban routes. As a result, many new homes were built, daily electricity blackouts that had plagued Cuba for years virtually disappeared, and chronic transportation problems eased a little.

Despite such improvements, several problems of the Cuban economy remain unresolved and constitute crucial challenges for the future. First, Cuban salaries are largely insufficient to satisfy all necessities, and in many cases even the most essential living requirements. As described in table 7.4, while the nominal average salary on the island rose from 188 pesos in 1989 to 429 pesos in 2009, the real average salary (adjusted for inflation) was in 2009 almost four times lower than 20 years before (Vidal Alejandro 2010a). Similarly, during this period the nominal average pension grew from 56 to 241 pesos, but in 2009 the real average pension was still less than half of its value in 1989 (Mesa-Lago 2010). To make things worse, Cuban citizens receive their wages and pensions in regular Cuban pesos (CUPs) yet, due to

Table 7.4. Evolution of Average Salary and Pension, 1989–2009

Year	Inflation (%)	Consumer Price Index (1989 = 1)	Nominal Average Salary (Pesos)	Real Average Salary (Pesos 1989)	Nominal Average Pension (Pesos)	Real Average Pension (Pesos 1989)
1989	—	1.00	188	188	56	56
1990	2.6	1.03	187	182	57	55
1991	91.5	1.96	185	94	85	43
1992	76.0	3.46	182	53	91	26
1993	183.0	9.78	182	19	92	9
1994	-8.5	8.95	185	21	93	10
1995	-11.5	7.92	194	24	95	13
1996	-4.9	7.54	202	27	96	13
1997	1.9	7.68	206	27	97	13
1998	2.9	7.90	207	26	98	12
1999	-2.9	7.67	222	29	103	13
2000	-2.3	7.50	238	32	105	14
2001	-1.4	7.39	252	34	107	14
2002	7.3	7.93	261	33	113	14
2003	-3.8	7.63	273	36	119	16
2004	2.9	7.85	284	36	121	15
2005	3.7	8.14	330	41	179	22
2006	5.7	8.61	387	45	192	22
2007	2.8	8.85	408	46	194	22
2008	-0.1	8.84	415	47	236	26
2009	-0.1	8.83	429	48	241	27[a]

[a] Calculation of the author.

Sources: Vidal Alejandro (2010a); Mesa-Lago (2010); ONE (2010).

generalized shortages of goods available, they are compelled to buy convertible pesos or CUCs at the current unofficial exchange rate of 24 CUPs per 1 CUC in order to purchase the products they need in expensive stores dealing only with the latter currency. The convertible peso was introduced in 1994 and its value has been pegged at US$1.08 since April 2005. The U.S. currency was taken out of circulation in November 2004 but its possession remains legal. Although they enjoy rent-free housing, heavily subsidized utility services, and free health care and education, most Cubans must rely on remittances from abroad, tourism-related tips, incentive payments in hard currency, and services such as house rental, restaurants, and taxis, among others, to supplement their meager peso salaries and pensions and meet basic needs. The existing monetary duality in Cuba is the cause of growing income inequalities, inefficiencies, and corruption.

Many Cubans have great difficulty in acquiring food and other items they need not only because of the limited purchasing power of their salary in regular pesos but

Table 7.5. Agricultural Production, 2004–9 (Thousand Tons)

	2004	2005	2006	2007	2008	2009	Change 2004–9
Roots and tubers	1,946.4	1,801.8	1,330.2	1,378.6	1,392.5	1,565.6	-19.6%
Plantains	1,215.6	773.5	871.8	990.9	758.2	670.4	-44.8%
Vegetables	4,095.9	3,203.5	2,672.1	2,603.0	2,439.3	2,548.8	-37.8%
Rice	244.4	184.3	217.1	196.2	207.5	281.8	+15.3%
Corn	398.7	362.5	305.4	368.8	325.7	304.8	-23.5%
Beans	132.9	106.2	70.6	97.2	97.2	110.8	-16.6%
Citrus	801.7	554.6	373.0	469.0	391.8	418.0	-47.9%
Other fruits	908.0	819.0	746.5	783.8	738.5	748.0	-17.6%
Total	9,743.6	7,805.4	6,586.7	6,887.5	6,350.7	6,648.2	-31.8%

Source: ONE (2010).

also because of scarce domestic production, especially in the agricultural sector. The latter suffered a massive decapitalization in the first half of the 2000s and reforms came to a halt. Between 2004 and 2006 (table 7.5), the production of virtually all staple crops witnessed a steep decline, which was mirrored by a reduction in sales and pressure on prices in free farmers' markets. The output of certain crops like roots and tubers, rice, and beans has began to recover since then, but in 2009 Cuba's total agricultural production was still 31.8 percent below its level of 2004. While Havana's authorities have attributed the recent poor agricultural performance to the damage caused by hurricanes and drought, it is clear that the overall situation underscores major problems in the organization of Cuban agriculture and is particularly worrisome if we consider that imports of foodstuffs were slashed by more than $800 million in 2009. Albeit with different views on the nature and extent of necessary changes, Cuban economists in and outside Cuba agree that the island's agricultural sector needs a reduced state role in production, distribution, and other areas, fewer hurdles that prevent the development of productive forces, and a greater presence of foreign investment (Nova González 2009; Alvarez 2004).

Critical issues in the tourism sector have also emerged in recent years. Gross revenues from tourism activities (figure 7.2) expanded from $243 million in 1990 to $2.34 billion in 2008, but plunged by more than 10 percent in 2009 despite a slight increase in arrivals. In terms of tourist expenditures, annual gross revenues per tourist increased from $715 in 1990 to $1,475 in 1995. Since then, they have decreased steadily to just $867 in 2009, about 41 percent below the level of 1995. This suggests that the future contribution of tourism to economic growth could diminish greatly once the sector reaches its maturity. Some scholars argued that Cuba's ability to attract tourists from new markets as a way to compensate for a very low rate of repeat tourism might have run its course. The low rate of return is apparently motivated by the poor quality of Cuban food and services (Espino 2008, 136). Another shortcoming of the island's leisure industry is exemplified by its elevated operational costs. In May 2003, a high-ranking

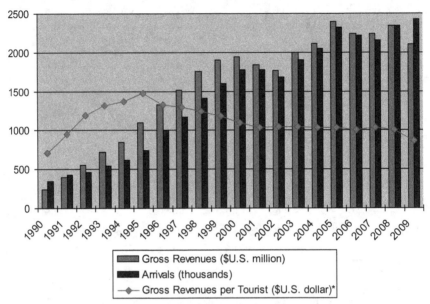

Figure 7.2 International tourism in Cuba, 1990–2009.

Source: ONE (2010). *Calculations of the author.

Cuban official estimated the cost per dollar of gross income from tourism activities at $0.80, which would mean for the country a net result of just $0.20 for every dollar captured in the sector (Spadoni 2010, 141). The declining trend in the average spending per tourist, excessive costs, and probably a loss of competitiveness due to rising prices represent key challenges for Cuba's tourism industry that cannot be overlooked.

Large inefficiencies in government-run businesses are one of the greatest weaknesses of a socialist economy like that of Cuba that remains almost entirely controlled by the state. The limited market-friendly reforms of the 1990s, albeit beneficial, clearly failed to tackle this problem. The economic performance of most state firms in Cuba is adversely affected by overcentralization, particularly in the form of currency controls, red tape, mismanagement, and widespread illegalities. The latter, of course, raise the question of whether the rules in place are bad for economic performance or simply poorly enforced. Illegalities are more a consequence of the system than a cause of its failings, given that it is extremely difficult for many Cubans to satisfy their basic needs without engaging in some unlawful activities. In a modest sign of decentralization, Cuba's new banking rules enacted in July 2009 eliminated the requirement for state enterprises to obtain Central Bank approval for hard currency expenditures in excess of $10,000 and turned over management of such transactions to government ministries. However, the Cuban Central Bank still maintains a single account for hard currency deposits of state firms and exercises full control over the allotment of those resources. Multiple exchange rates also introduce a number of hidden subsidies, hinder the proper working of the market, and result in a distorted accounting system that makes it nearly impossible to gauge the true profitability of enterprises (Domínguez 2004, 31).

The deplorable conditions of the island's main infrastructures constitute another major challenge. Along with low salaries and scarce food availability, persistent transportation problems, a huge housing shortage, and the continuing deterioration of homes and buildings top the list of Cubans' complaints. The transportation sector in Cuba was one of the slowest to recover from the acute economic crisis of the early 1990s. Owing to a shrinking fleet of public buses and taxis, the total number of Cuban passengers transported each year declined six-fold between 1989 and 1998, with only a modest recovery since then. The volume of passengers has increased markedly since 2007 as many newly purchased vehicles hit the road, but in 2009 it was still about the same as in 1971, when the Cuban population stood at just 8.7 million, roughly 2.5 million less than its current size. As for housing, Havana's authorities estimated in 2005 that 500,000 new homes were needed across the country and that 43 percent of the existing stock was either in mediocre or poor shape. In order to reduce the housing deficit, the Castro government embarked on an ambitious investment program in 2006 that resulted in the construction and renovation of 111,373 homes that year, of which more than two-thirds were self-built by Cuban citizens with the state providing material and expertise. Since 2007, though, Cuba has regularly failed to meet annual targets due to slow construction execution, disorganization, lack of necessary resources, and excessive bureaucratic hurdles (Pérez Villanueva 2008a). Chronic deficiencies in transportation, housing, and other basic facilities and services will require substantial new investments in the future.

Cuba began to experience serious liquidity problems in late 2008 mainly caused by a combination of low nickel prices, unprecedented food imports, and an estimated $10 billion worth of damage from hurricanes. But the island's financial system also suffered because of an excess emission of convertible pesos used for international transactions that were not backed by adequate levels of foreign exchange reserves (Vidal Alejandro 2010b). On the issue of cash shortages, it must emphasized that the government-backed credits Cuba receives from China and other countries and its revenues from the export of professional services to Venezuela are funds committed to the purchase of products from these countries. The Castro government must rely primarily on nickel exports, tourism, and remittances to build foreign exchange liquidity and reserves. Moreover, because it is considered an extremely high credit risk, Cuba has virtually no access to medium- and long-term financing from banks and international institutions and must seek short-term loans at high interest rates. Between August and December 2008, Havana informed the governments of France, Germany, and Japan that it was unable to respect its debt payments as scheduled and that official debts needed to be renegotiated.[5] Around the end of that year, it froze hundreds of millions of dollars in the Cuban bank accounts of foreign businesses on the island. The crisis was further exacerbated in 2009 by the global economic recession and plummeting earnings from nickel sales and tourism activities.

The exposure of foreign banks in Cuba (table 7.6) sheds some light on the country's financial troubles. According to the Bank for International Settlements, claims

Table 7.6. Claims of Foreign Banks on Cuba by Nationality of Reporting Banks, 2003–9 (Year-end in US$ Millions)

Country	2003	2004	2005	2006	2007	June 2008	2008	June 2009	2009
France	574	455	466	521	670	674	566	478	726
Spain	313	321	314	391	413	448	444	419	421
Germany	189	207	184	230	306	276	237	191	196
Italy	134	125	92	66	63	103	117	92	113
Netherlands	312	298	237	201	134	112	96	93	90
Austria	71	72	67	57	93	93	34	28	24
Japan	35	68	98	65	111	110	30	26	39
Belgium	3	17	13	8	24	34	28	27	26
Sweden	21	26	18	14	20	35	28	26	21
United Kingdom	30	33	31	27	20	12	9	12	11
Switzerland	69[a]	3	1	3	40	2	1	—	—
Canada	—	75	—	—	—		—	—	—
European Banks	1,555[b]	1,557	1,429	1,524	1,802	1,808	1,585	1,388	1,648
Total Foreign Claims[c]	2,216	2,245	2,211	2,266	2,648	2,310	2,034	1,819	2,158

[a] September 2003.
[b] March 2004.
[c] Claims refer to financial assets such as short-term loans, debt securities, and equities.
Source: Bank for International Settlements (www.bis.org).

of foreign banks on Cuba, which refer to financial assets such as short-term loans, debt securities, and equities, rose by almost 20 percent between 2003 and 2007. They continued to increase until March 2008 and began to fall considerably only in the second half of 2008 when the Cuban crisis began. The biggest drops in banking exposure were indeed those of financial entities from France, Germany, and Japan. Foreign credit reached its lowest point in June 2009 and started to grow again (especially French loans) in the second half of that year as Cuba began to release some funds in frozen bank accounts by offering overseas companies monthly payments over the next five years at a 2 percent interest rate, albeit with no established penalty for missed payments.[6] While some foreign firms accepted the offer given that their funds would no longer be linked to a nonperforming asset, several bank accounts were still frozen by mid-2010 and Cuban payments to various business partners kept being delayed.

It is still too early to determine whether Cuba's liquidity troubles and worsening economic conditions will lead to another full-blown crisis. But if we move beyond conjunctural factors to identify the broader reasons for the economic malaise, it is safe to argue that Cuba suffers more from low productivity, high inefficiency, little export diversification, and other shortcomings of its market-averse policies than anything else.

Above all, the distortions caused by multiple exchange rates, excessive bureaucratic intervention, an overly centralized decision-making process, and foreign exchange controls are largely responsible for the inefficiency of Cuban state enterprises. Furthermore, depressed real salaries and the dual currency system hamper workers' motivation and productivity. Medical services exported to Venezuela triggered macroeconomic growth and helped secure steady oil supplies, but they have very little multiplying effects in the Cuban economy. Even nickel is somehow concentrated within itself because it is extracted on the island but refined abroad (Sánchez Egozcue and Triana Cordoví 2008). What the nickel situation demonstrates is that Cuba is not immune to certain vulnerabilities of "dependent" capitalist development. Cuba not only is battered by international swings in commodity prices and demand like the liberal, market-oriented economies of Latin America but also does not generate significant value-added goods in its primary production, as is true of too many commodity-dependent economies in the region. The sugar and tourism industries have significant ripple effects, yet the former is facing an inexorable decline and the latter has lost steam in recent years. Foreign investment remains relatively low even though it has made an important contribution to the economic performance of Cuba's key export sectors and other industries geared toward the domestic market. A more substantial presence of foreign investment in agricultural production might help revert declining outputs and improve food availability. The deplorable conditions of housing and public transportation are also among the most pressing challenges. It goes without saying that Cuba needs profound economic reforms to properly address these problems.

5. Reforms under Raúl Castro

In a keynote speech on July 26, 2007, Raúl Castro maintained that "structural and conceptual changes" were needed to foster development and blasted key problems that anger many Cubans such as high food prices, low state wages, heavy regulation, and chronic infrastructure deficiencies. Regarding living standards, he pointed out that "any increase in wages or decrease in prices, to be real, can only stem from a greater and more efficient production and services offer, which will increase the country's incomes."[7] Most Cubans interpreted Raúl's words as a call for deep changes to the existing economic system, not just cosmetic ones. Popular expectations for reforms were fueled by a government-sponsored national debate in the second half of 2007 during which ordinary people at workplaces and in neighborhoods across the island proposed fixes to the inadequacies of the socialist system.

More attentive to practical concerns than his brother Fidel, Raúl Castro has taken up the very difficult tasks of expanding the country's productive base, increasing the efficiency of state enterprises, and creating more jobs with higher salaries. In his first speech as Cuba's new president on February 24, 2008, Raúl vowed to strengthen agricultural and livestock production and improve their marketing, encourage a gradual and prudent revaluation of the Cuban peso, reduce unsustainable state subsidies, and do away with excessive restrictions in Cuban society and its state-run economy. Yet he made no mention of structural changes and warned: "Some things need time for they should be thoroughly studied since a mistake brought about by improvisation, superficiality or haste could have substantial negative consequences. Good planning is most important for we cannot spend more than we have."[8] In essence, the younger Castro laid out a clear set of priorities and expressed his readiness to enact economic reforms, but he hinted that the overall process was bound to move slowly and apparently with a rather narrow scope. This is indeed what has happened so far. Initially centered on decentralizing measures in agriculture, Raúl's initiatives were broadened to tackle problems in several other areas of the Cuban economy. But government plans to expand self-employment that have yet to be fully implemented and a major land reform with a few other measures in the agricultural sector have been, respectively, the only structural and "near-structural" changes to date. A wide gap remains between Raúl's actual reforms and those urged by Cubans in the aforementioned national debate.

Not surprisingly, Raúl Castro has put agriculture at the top of his agenda. Domestic production is largely insufficient, many plots of land across the island are falling into disuse, and high prices of imported products severely affect the finances of a country like Cuba that imports an astounding 70 percent of its consumed food. In September 2008, the Cuban government announced a major expansion of an ongoing program (which began in late 2007) offering underused and fallow state land in usufruct to residents to plow as part of a sweeping effort to bolster local production and replace food imports. By the end of 2009, some 100,000 Cuban applicants had already received 2.3 million acres representing approximately 52 percent of all fallow state land in Cuba.[9] Additional measures were introduced. Havana's authorities increased what the state pays for farm goods, granted private farmers and cooperatives the right to purchase their own supplies directly at municipal markets rather than relying on supplies being assigned by the central government, allowed some producers to sell a small part of their output directly to consumers at fixed prices, and deepened decentralization in agriculture by establishing the subordination of productive units to newly formed municipal organizations.

Higher levels of agricultural production would push down the prices of food staples in farmers' markets, thus boosting real wages in Cuba and enhancing living standards. Furthermore, a greater supply of domestically produced agricultural goods, along with similar results in other industrial sectors geared toward the local market, would stimulate the reevaluation of the Cuban peso vis-à-vis the convertible peso and help the government achieve its long-standing goal of closing the gap between the two currencies. It is indicative of Cuba's production problems that the unofficial CUP/CUC exchange rate has remained unchanged since March 2005 despite strong GDP growth. Even the distribution of millions of Chinese electric stoves at subsidized prices and higher peso wages and pensions have done little to adjust the purchasing power of the Cuban population. Considering Cuba's recent financial difficulties, the Central Bank could formally devalue the CUC against the U.S. dollar and other foreign currencies. This would benefit the external sector of the Cuban economy by promoting exports and import substitution and raising the competitiveness of the tourism industry (Vidal Alejandro 2009). However, there is no doubt that an eventual CUP/CUC unification and a much-needed increase of real salaries require wide-ranging reforms that address problems in the productive sphere and guarantee an adequate functioning of the economy (Peters 2009; Pérez Villanueva 2008b).

In search of more efficiency and productivity, Raúl Castro has revamped the state wage system by removing salary caps for Cuban public employees, rolled back their retirement by five years, and significantly expanded the process of business management known as *perfeccionamiento empresarial* (perfecting the state company system). State workers can now earn without limit and their salary ceiling is more closely tied to performance. They can also hold more than one job at the same time as established by a new labor law in June 2009. With a rapidly aging population, the retirement age for men is being gradually moved (the process is set to conclude in 2015) from 60 to 65 and for women from 55 to 60. Regarding perfeccionamiento, it was first adopted by the Cuban armed forces in 1988 and later exported to civilian enterprises. This business model has no exact analogy either in capitalist economies or in socialist ones. It is based on the adoption of modern management and accounting practices, the promotion of greater decision-making autonomy for local managers, and the payment of wages linked to productivity (Peters 2001). It should be noted that the armed forces have a significant presence in Cuba's key economic areas including tourism, civil aviation, agriculture and cattle, import-export services, hard currency retail activities, real estate, and construction (Mora 2004).[10]

In line with his stated pledge to make life easier for ordinary citizens, Raúl Castro ended restrictions on Cubans buying computers, DVD players, and cellular phones, and allowed them to stay at hotels once reserved for foreign tourists and rent cars at state agencies. Other reforms included a new housing decree clarifying the property rights of long-term public employees, the lifting in December 2008 of a nine-year ban on new licenses for private taxi drivers, and streamlining changes in the administration and day-to-day operations of construction projects. Meanwhile, the Cuban government stepped up its efforts to curb social expenditures and lessen the paternalistic role of the state in the economy in favor of higher wages and targeted welfare. Besides cutting spending on education and health care, the two pillars of the Cuban Revolution, it replaced subsidized meals at many workplace canteens in Havana with an extra daily monetary allotment to workers as part of a plan to save money and create a new market in lunchtime catering for private and state-run outlets. A number of state gratuities and subsidized goods and services are being reconsidered even though free health care, education, and social security will continue to be guaranteed.

On August 1, 2010, Raúl Castro's administration announced that its government would allow more Cubans to work for themselves and set up small businesses in various areas as a way to create jobs for 1 million excess workers who will be laid off over the next five years. The idea is to rationalize the bloated state sector, ease the payroll burden on public finances, and generate revenues for the government through taxation. In the first phase of the program, set to be completed in October 2011, Cuban authorities will issue 250,000 new licenses for self-employment in 178 job categories (mainly low-skilled jobs). Self-employed Cubans in 83 lines of work will be able for the first time to hire employees and thus operate as microenterprises. They will be allowed to sell goods and services to the state and even to rent their place of business from other Cubans.[11]

Taken as a whole, Raúl Castro's reforms are positive—but too limited in scope. Even so, heightened popular expectations for major economic changes were largely unmet and numerous problems remain. Four of them, in particular, should be priority targets for Cuba. First, productive forces in agriculture (and in other sectors) are far from realizing their potential. Despite land redistribution and other measures, key property-related issues such as the right of farmers to decide how to use the land, what crops to plant, to whom to sell products, and at what price have yet to be adequately addressed. Progress in these areas, along with timely and sufficient inputs and greater recognition of the role of the market, would foster better conditions for a successful production cycle (Nova González 2010). Second, the much-touted wage reform introduced a different scheme of rewards for state workers, but a substantial growth of real salaries will come about only through an increase in the supply of domestic products made available to Cubans in the same currency in which they are paid or through a revaluation of that currency, which also depends on production levels (Pérez Villanueva 2010). Third, multiple exchange rates create segmented markets and distort relative prices, thus preventing an accurate measure of economic results and affecting the ability of local authorities to devise appropriate economic policies. Although they were common to many Latin American economies in the 1980s, with noxious consequences for efficiency, multiple exchange rate regimes in the region were drastically reduced as part of the liberalizing reforms of the 1990s. Fourth, crucial obstacles will continue to stifle private initiative in Cuba even if the island's authorities are serious about expanding the nonstate sector. Along with fair and not too burdensome taxation rates, the success of the process will depend on the availability of substantial microloans for the new contingent of self-employed Cubans to help them set up businesses and the creation of a wholesale domestic market to meet their demand for equipment and supplies. Because of the present unfavorable economic conditions, the Cuban government can do neither. And above all, self-entrepreneurs need an internal demand for their goods and services that current economic policies are unable to stimulate (Vidal Alejandro and Pérez Villanueva 2010).

Last, it is clear now that Raúl Castro is not contemplating sweeping liberalizing changes in Cuba and will likely opt for the implementation of gradual and limited economic reforms within the existing socialist framework. Raúl Castro presented the measures on self-employment as a "structural and conceptual change," adopting the same expression he had used in 2007.[12] But he reiterated his commitment to keep "perfecting" socialism and failed to recognize the root causes of Cuba's economic problems, which inevitably lie at the systemic level. A prominent Cuban scholar explained these problems better than anyone else. He wrote that the Cuban economy is like "a plot of land that instead of the labors of a gardener requires the strength of a bulldozer." In his opinion, Cuba needs complex structural changes that modify the organization and working of the economy. Yet these changes must be accompanied, if not preceded, by a reform of the overall economic system that redefines certain basic premises on property relations, the stimulation to work, and the calculation of economic results (Monreal 2008). This is precisely where Raúl Castro's approach is falling short.

6. CONCLUSION

Over the past two decades, the Cuban economy has witnessed a number of important changes. During the 1990s, international tourism and remittances replaced the once-thriving sugar industry as the top sources of hard currency for the cash-strapped Castro government. More recently, a productive partnership with Venezuela converted exports of Cuban professional services into the island's main engine of growth and triggered strong macroeconomic performance in 2005–7 before a major liquidity crunch and other problems ushered in a recession. As for economic policies, timid but significant market-style emergency measures in the first half of the 1990s helped Cuba weather the devastating impact on its economy of the fall of the Soviet Union and spur a revival. Between 2003 and 2006, Fidel Castro intensified recentralizing efforts and reversed some of these measures amid improved economic conditions. Since officially taking over as president in early 2008, Raúl Castro has implemented several reforms to cope with mounting economic difficulties and supposedly improve the functioning of Cuban socialism. What has not changed throughout this whole period, however, is that Cuba continues to suffer from all the inefficiencies, red tape, and distortions of a state-dominated economy. Albeit significant, Raúl Castro's reforms have yet to address, let alone fix, the fundamental shortcomings of Cuba's socialist system.

While rejecting the notion that Cuba's economic policies are based on capitalist recipes and making clear that no large-scale market reforms are in the pipeline, Raúl Castro has loosened the government's grip on the economy somewhat with the launch of decentralizing schemes in agriculture, the elimination of salary limits for state workers, and the elimination of various state subsidies. He also began to promote small private businesses in apparent recognition that many services in Cuba may be provided more efficiently by private entities than by the state. Raúl Castro's intent is to enhance efficiency and productivity, raise salaries, boost food availability, and reduce costly imports. Yet the ability of his reform process to provide a cure for Cuba's main economic problems is hindered by an insufficient systemic focus. Apart from the fact that deeper and more structural changes should be introduced, Havana's authorities seem to be more committed to saving socialism from its notorious deficiencies than making it truly better by reconsidering some of its overarching principles. Although certain key aspects of Cuban socialism are commendable and should be preserved, the current economic system on the island can serve neither as an effective tool to unleash productive forces nor as a model to foster actual development.

NOTES

I wish to thank Carmelo Mesa-Lago and Susan Eckstein for their comments and suggestions on an earlier version of this study.

1. In addition to "coordinated supply plans" and exports, Hernández-Catá (2001) estimated that Soviet subsidies and aid to Cuba averaged $4.3 billion a year between 1986 and 1990.

2. Even the Central Intelligence Agency and the Economist Intelligence Unit, most likely relying on the traditional GDP formula, put Cuba's growth, respectively, at 9.5 percent in 2006 and 6.5 percent in 2007 (CIA 2007; EIU 2008).

3. Reuters, "Cuba Says All Nickel Plants Remain Open," April 20, 2009.

4. *Granma International*, "Cuba Is to Extend Services Provided by Its Medical Personnel to 81 Countries during the Year," April 3, 2008.

5. Marc Frank, "Global Crisis, Storms Hit Cuba Finances," Reuters, December 17, 2008.

6. Marc Frank, "Cuba Offers Payback Plan for Frozen Bank Accounts," Reuters, March 2, 2010.

7. Raúl Castro's speech of July 26, 2007, delivered in the city of Camagüey, is available at http://www.granma.cubaweb.cu/secciones/raul26/02.html.

8. Raúl Castro's inaugural address of February 24, 2008, delivered before the National Assembly, is available at http://www.juventudrebelde.co.cu/cuba/2008-02-24/key-address-by-comrade-raul-castro-ruz-president-of-the-state-council-and-the-council-of-ministers/.

9. Patricia Grogg, "What about the Changes?," Inter Press Service, March 31, 2010.

10. For more on the Cuban armed forces' growing role in the economy in the post-1990 period, see Klepak (2005, 75–102).

11. Leticia Martínez Hernández, "Mucho Más Que un Alternativa," *Granma*, September 24, 2010.

12. Raúl Castro's speech of August 1, 2010, delivered before the National Assembly, is available at http://www.cuba.cu/gobierno/rauldiscursos/2010/esp/r010810e.html.

REFERENCES

Alvarez, José. 2004. *Cuba's Agricultural Sector*. Gainesville: University Press of Florida.

BCC (Banco Central de Cuba). 2005. *Economic Report 2004*. Havana: BCC.

CEPAL (Comisión Económica para America Latina y el Caribe). 2010. *Estudio Económico de America Latina y el Caribe 2009–2010*. New York: United Nations.

Cerviño, Julio, and José María Cubillo. 2005. "Hotel and Tourism Development in Cuba: Opportunities, Management Challenges, and Future Trends." *Cornell Hotel and Restaurant Administration Quarterly* 46(2): 223–46.

CIA (Central Intelligence Agency). 2007. *The World Factbook*. Washington, DC: CIA.

Corrales, Javier. 2006. "Cuba's New Daddy." *Hemisphere: A Magazine of the Americas* 17: 24–29.

Domínguez, Jorge I. 2004. "Cuba's Economic Transition: Successes, Deficiencies, and Challenges." In *The Cuban Economy at the Start of the Twenty-First Century*, edited by Jorge I. Dominguez, Omar Everleny Pérez Villanueva, and Lorena Barberia, 17–47. Cambridge, MA: Harvard University Press.

EIU (Economist Intelligence Unit). 2008. *Country Profile Cuba*. London: EIU

———. 2010. *Country Report: Cuba*. London: EIU

Espino, María Dolores. 2008. "International Tourism in Cuba: An Update." In *Cuba in Transition*, vol. 18, 130–37. Washington, DC: Association for the Study of the Cuban Economy.

Hernández-Catá, Ernesto. 2001. "The Fall and Recovery of the Cuban Economy in the 1990s: Mirage or Reality?" Working Paper WP/01/48, International Monetary Fund, Washington, DC.

Jatar-Hausmann, Ana Julia. 1999. *The Cuban Way: Capitalism, Communism and Confrontation*. West Hartford, CT: Kumarian Press.

Klepak, Hal P. 2005. *Cuba's Military, 1990–2005: Revolutionary Soldiers during Counter-Revolutionary Times*. New York: Palgrave Macmillan.

Mesa-Lago, Carmelo. 2004. "Economic and Ideological Cycles in Cuba: Policy and Performance, 1959–2002." In *The Cuban Economy*, edited by Archibald R. M. Ritter, 25–42. Pittsburgh: University of Pittsburgh Press.

———. 2008. "The Cuban Economy at the Crossroads: Fidel Castro's Legacy, Debate over Change and Raul Castro's Options." Working Paper 19/2008, Real Instituto Elcano, Madrid.

———. 2009. "La Economía de Cuba Hoy: Retos Internos y Externos." *Desarrollo Económico* 5: 421–50.

———. 2010. "Estructura Demográfica y Envejecimiento Poblacional: Implicaciones Sociales y Económicas para el Sistema de Seguridad Social en Cuba." Paper presented at 10th Semana Social Católica, Consejo Arquidiocesano de Laicos de La Habana, Havana, June 16–20.

Monreal, Pedro. 1999. "Las Remesas Familiares en la Economía Cubana." *Encuentro de la Cultura Cubana* 14: 49–62.

———. 2008. "El Problema Económico de Cuba." *Espacio Laical* 4(14): 33–35.

Mora, Frank O. 2004. "The FAR and Its Economic Role: From Civic to Technocrat-Soldiers." Occasional Paper Series, Institute for Cuban and Cuban-American Studies, Miami.

Morris, Emily. 2008. "Cuba's New Relationship with Foreign Capital: Economic Policy-Making Since 1990." *Journal of Latin American Studies* 40(4): 769–92.

Nova González, Armando. 2006. *Cuba: Sector Externo*. Havana: Centro de Estudios de la Economia Cubana.

———. 2009. "La Agricultura en Cuba: Actualidad y Transformaciones Necesarias." Paper presented at the International Conference on "Cuba Today and the Road Ahead," San José, Costa Rica, February 3–4.

———. 2010. *La Agricultura Cubana: Medidas Implementadas para Lograr Incrementos en la Producción de Alimentos, Análisis y Valoración*. Havana: Centro de Estudios de la Economia Cubana.

ONE (Oficina Nacional de Estadísticas). 2010. *Anuario Estadístico de Cuba 2009*. Havana: ONE.

Pérez-López, Jorge F. 2006. "The Cuban Economy in 2005–2006: The End of the Special Period?" In *Cuba in Transition*, vol. 16, 1–13. Washington DC: Association for the Study of the Cuban Economy.

Pérez-López, Jorge F., and Carmelo Mesa-Lago. 2009. "Cuba's GDP Statistics under the Special Period: Discontinuities, Obfuscation, and Puzzles." In *Cuba in Transition*, vol. 19, 153–67. Washington DC: Association for the Study of the Cuban Economy.

Pérez-Stable, Marifeli. 1999. *The Cuban Revolution: Origins, Course, and Legacy.* New York: Oxford University Press.

———. 2007. "Looking Forward: Democracy in Cuba?" In *Looking Forward: Comparative Perspectives on Cuba's Transition*, edited by Marifeli Pérez-Stable, 17–46. Notre Dame, IN: University of Notre Dame Press.

Pérez Villanueva, Omar Everleny. 2008a. *Apuntes sobre la Vivienda en Cuba.* Havana: Centro de Estudios de la Economía Cubana.

———. 2008b. *La Economía en Cuba: Un Balance Actual y Propuestas Necesarias.* Havana: Centro de Estudios de la Economía Cubana.

———. 2009. *Cuba: Evolución Económica Reciente.* Havana: Centro de Estudios de la Economía Cubana.

———. 2010. "Notas Recientes sobre la Economía en Cuba." Paper presented at 10th Semana Social Católica, Consejo Arquidiocesano de Laicos de La Habana, Havana, June 16–20.

Peters, Philip. 2001. *State Enterprise Reform in Cuba: An Early Snapshot.* Arlington, VA: Lexington Institute.

———. 2002. *International Tourism: The New Engine of the Cuban Economy.* Arlington, VA: Lexington Institute.

———. 2009. *Raulonomics: Tough Diagnosis and Partial Prescriptions in Raul Castro's Economic Policies.* Arlington, VA: Lexington Institute.

Ritter, Archibald R. 2010. "Cuba in the 2010s: Creative Reforms or Geriatric Paralysis?" *Focal Point* 9(3): 12–13.

Rojas, Rafael. 2006. "L'idéologie du postcommunisme cubaine." *Problèmes d'Amérique latine* 61–62: 87–103.

Sánchez Egozcue, Jorge Mario, and Juan Triana Cordoví. 2008. "An Overview of the Cuban Economy, the Transformations Underway and the Prospective Challenges It Faces." Working Paper 31/2008, Real Instituto Elcano, Madrid.

Spadoni, Paolo. 2004. "The Current Situation of Foreign Investment in Cuba." In *Cuba in Transition*, vol. 14, 116–38. Washington, DC: Association for the Study of the Cuban Economy.

———. 2010. *Failed Sanctions: Why the U.S. Embargo against Cuba Could Never Work.* Gainesville: University Press of Florida.

Vidal Alejandro, Pavel. 2009. *La Política Monetaria y la Macroeconomía en Cuba: 2008–2009.* Havana: Centro de Estudios de la Economía Cubana.

———. 2010a. *Estabilidad y Política Monetaria en Cuba.* Havana: Centro de Estudios de la Economía Cubana.

———. 2010b. "La Crisis Bancaria Cubana Actual." Paper presented at 10th Semana Social Católica, Consejo Arquidiocesano de Laicos de La Habana, Havana, June 16–20.

Vidal Alejandro, Pavel, and Omar Everleny Pérez Villanueva. 2010. "Entre el Ajuste Fiscal y los Cambios Estructurales: Se Extiende el Cuentapropismo en Cuba." *Espacio Laical*, digital supplement 112, October.

CHAPTER 8

GLOBAL AND REGIONAL INTEGRATION IN LATIN AMERICA AND THE CARIBBEAN, 1990–2010

JUAN BLYDE, ANTONI ESTEVADEORDAL, AND MAURICIO MESQUITA MOREIRA

1. INTRODUCTION

Global integration and regional integration are strategic platforms countries can use to maximize the growth and welfare benefits of trade, investment, and cooperation. Today, most of the countries in Latin America and the Caribbean (LAC) recognize this guiding principle and are actively pursuing policies to foster their insertion into the regional and global economies.

This hard-won consensus, though, was slow to come. LAC's long and self-inflicted absence from the world markets during the era of import substitution cost it dearly in foregone growth opportunities. The region fell badly behind other developing economies, particularly East Asia, which was much quicker to see the growth benefits of trade integration (fig. 8.1). It was only in the late 1980s and early '90s that LAC made a concerted effort to reintegrate itself in the world economy, pursuing an aggressive multipolar integration strategy, which included unilateral, regional, and multilateral liberalizations.

It took longer than expected for the growth benefits of this strategy to emerge, but they have become unmistakable in the last decade. Since 2003, the region's gross

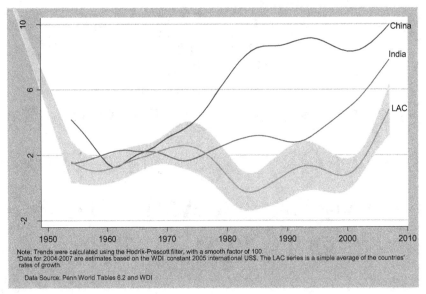

Figure 8.1 GDP Per Capita Annual Growth: China, India, Korea, and L. America
1954–2007. Hodrick-Prescott filter, 2000 Constant Prices.

domestic product (GDP) has been growing at an annual average rate of 5 percent, driven by a 17 percent annual growth of its exports and record influx of foreign investment, which topped US$128 billion in 2008. The 2008–9 crisis has hit the region hard, with sharp drops in exports (−22%) and GDP (−1.7%), but unlike past experiences, recovery has been swift and most countries in the region resumed growth in 2010.

Despite the unmistakable progress, it would be unwarranted to conclude that the LAC has a comfortable position in the world economy or that its trade-led growth has reached a sustainable path. In fact, judging by three of the main characteristics of its recent trade performance, it can be argued that LAC has yet to reap the full growth benefits of trade and integration. To begin with, LAC's trade volumes are still relatively small. For instance, the region has a lot of ground to cover before it matches its share of the world markets in the early 1960s (fig. 8.2), which predates the full impact of the import substitution policies.

Second, LAC still has its exports concentrated in a relatively small number of goods and services, particularly price-volatile, basic natural resources. As figure 8.3 shows, with a few notable exceptions such as Brazil and Mexico, most countries in the region have levels of export concentration that are well above the "norm" for their levels of per capita income. The intense competition in manufacturing and the high demand for commodities coming from countries such as China and India suggests that, ceteris paribus, this vulnerability is likely to increase.

Finally, the growth benefits of trade and integration have normally been concentrated in a few regions, either well endowed with natural resources or benefiting from proximity to the major markets, increasing regional disparities and undermining

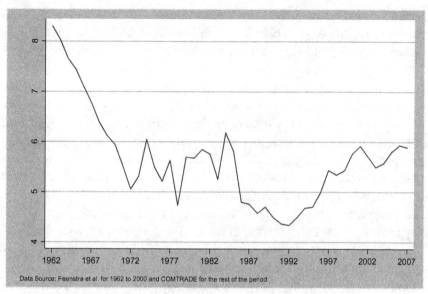

Figure 8.2 LAC's Share of the World Exports 1962–2007.

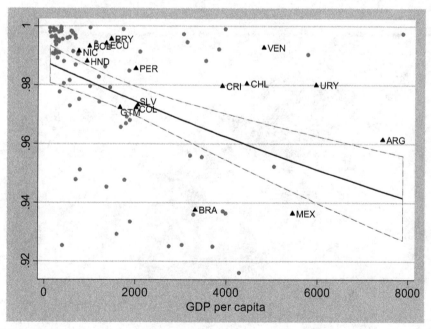

Figure 8.3 Predicted and actual export concentration index (Gini) as a function of per capita income.

Source: Volpe (2010)

support for trade and integration (fig. 8.4). A similar problem has been observed in terms of the distribution of benefits across the member states of trade agreements.

These characteristics suggest that LAC has still a sizable "trade and integration gap" to fill before it can rely on these drivers to meet its elusive ambitions of fast and sustainable growth. Perfecting integration within the region and increasing its exposure to worldwide trade would go a long way toward achieving these ambitions, for various reasons. Regional integration helps countries overcome some of the disadvantages of small size. In a world economy where economies of scale are rife, by getting together, countries could offer their firms, in effect, an enlarged domestic market, helping them compete against their considerably larger counterparts in the developed and developing world (e.g., China and India). A larger domestic market would help not only by increasing local firms' production runs but also by allowing them to learn faster and therefore develop new products.

Perfecting regional integration could also provide continuous progress in opening new opportunities for businesses, investments, and cooperation, especially when multilateral negotiations advance at a slower pace. The current difficulties of the Doha Round only underscore this point. Regional integration would also be a move with lower adjustment costs (i.e., factory closures and unemployment) since a smaller number of countries are involved, and would avoid unilateral liberalization's typical costs of asymmetrical market access.

A more integrated Latin American and Caribbean region also increase these countries' bargaining power in international negotiations and their ability to

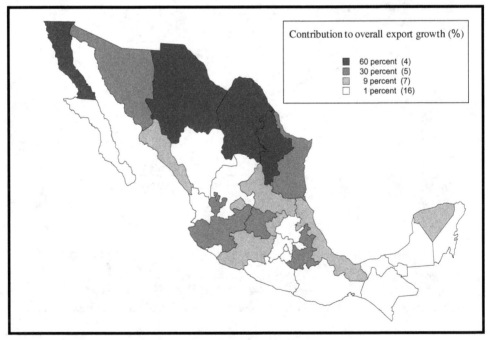

Figure 8.4 Mexico: Contribution to export growth, by state 1993–2003.
Source: Ernesto Lopez Córdova for the Integration and Trade Sector.

cooperate and develop regional public goods. Finally, increasing the exposure of the region to worldwide trade would reduce the potential detrimental effects of regional integration, like those that could arise from trade diversion.

But while these are strong arguments for continuing in the pursuit of more regional and global integration, moving ahead could be difficult because of the lack of resources, political will, or institutional weaknesses, among many other things. And even if progress can be achieved, the potential gains can hardly be taken for granted. Their feasibility and impact hinge very much on how the policies, incentives, and institutions are designed and how effectively traditional (e.g., tariffs and nontariff barriers) and nontraditional trade costs (transport costs and those of trade facilitation) are minimized. If incentives and institutions are badly misjudged and if trade costs remain high, the chances of regional integration being a drag on economic development are considerable.

It is against this background that this chapter takes a close look at the policy challenges related to closing LAC's integration gap, with a focus on regional integration. The next section presents a brief summary of the region's integration steps, including the various integration strategies that have been followed over time as well as their rationale. Section 3 provides a general diagnostic of the state of integration of LAC, highlighting the most salient problems. Based on this diagnosis, section 4 presents a summary of the main policies' actions, discussing some of the initiatives that are currently in place and underscoring the main challenges and opportunities ahead.

2. TAKING STOCK OF LAC's INTEGRATION EFFORTS

The integration efforts in the region were pioneered by Central America in the early 1960s with the establishment of the Central American Common Market. Those efforts were later followed by the Andean Group (a common market project that evolved into the Andean Community), the Caribbean Free Trade Association (later CARICOM), and more ambitious initiatives such as the Latin America Free Trade Association (South America plus Mexico), which evolved into the Latin America Integration Association.

Yet the nature of LAC integration has fundamentally changed since those pioneering efforts of the so-called old regionalism (IADB 2002). The turning point came in the early 1990s. Until then, LAC's integration landscape was characterized by partial free trade agreements, usually behind high tariff barriers against the rest of the world. The debt crisis of the 1980s and the ensuing market-oriented reforms of the 1990s radically changed this landscape, promoting a different brand of regionalism—the open or new regionalism—with deeper, more compressive, and more open integration initiatives at home and abroad, which led to the consolidation of five subregional trade blocs in the hemisphere—Andean Community, Central American Common Market, CARICOM, Mercado Comun del Sur (MERCOSUR), and North American Free Trade Agreement (NAFTA).

With the emergence of the new regionalism, LAC countries began pursuing what can be called a dynamic, multipolar economic integration strategy, which operates on different levels: cutting tariffs unilaterally, signing comprehensive regional trade agreements (RTAs), within and outside the region, and supporting multilateral trade liberalization initiatives. This strategy has led to a set of institutional networks that integrates LAC countries regionally and globally (see Estevadeordal and Suominen 2009). In the last several years, for example, the region has been pursuing bilateral intraregional free trade agreements (FTAs) such as the MERCOSUR–Andean Community FTAs of 2004 and the U.S.–Central America–Dominican Republic FTA of 2005. More recently, with the entry into force in the past two years of free trade agreements between Panama and Honduras, Guatemala, and Nicaragua as well as the agreement between Colombia and the Northern Triangle countries of El Salvador, Guatemala, and Honduras, the trading nexus between Central and South America has developed further, in addition to the existing agreements between several Central American countries and Chile. The year 2009 marked the coming into force of revamped and modernized agreements Chile reached with Colombia and Peru. Peru has agreements in force with both Canada and the United States, and Colombia has signed FTAs with both countries.

Those intraregional FTAs have also been complemented by transcontinentalism. For instance, to name a few cases, Mexico has an FTA in force with Japan, while Chile has agreements in place with China, Korea, and Japan. More recently, Peru is contributing to transpacific integration with the commencement of agreements with Singapore in August 2009 and more recently with China in March 2010, on top of an agreement with Thailand signed in 2006. Peru also signed agreements with South Korea and Japan in 2011. Similarly, Costa Rica signed FTAs with Singapore and China in April 2010. Chile's agreement with Australia became effective in March 2009. Meanwhile, Colombia is advancing in negotiations with Korea. The deepening web of agreements between economies in Latin America and East Asia is at the same time creating a framework for a future transpacific accumulation zone. The Trans-Pacific Economic Partnership agreement between Chile, Brunei Darussalam, New Zealand, and Singapore, in place since 2006, is now forming the nucleus of talks including the United States, Australia, Vietnam, and Peru to form a Trans-Pacific Partnership that would join these Asia-Pacific Economic Cooperation members, many of which have existing FTAs between them, into a much larger single free trade space.

Countries of Latin America have also been reaching across the Atlantic for agreements with the European Union (EU). Mexico launched an FTA with the EU in 2000, as did Chile in 2003. The EU–Caribbean Forum agreement was signed in late 2008. Additionally, Colombia and Peru concluded negotiations in 2010 with the European Union and the European Free Trade Association. Similarly an agreement between the EU and Central America was concluded in 2010. In addition to the transpacific and transatlantic fronts, MERCOSUR has concluded an agreement with India and South Africa.

3. The State of LAC's Integration Today

These various levels of trade relationships have allowed LAC to enjoy the gains of trade and integration faster than would have been possible through more complex multilateral trade negotiations, such as the latest Doha Round, whose benefits are more promising, but whose conclusion remains elusive. However, this rapid and sometimes disorderly expansion of the trade frontier has not come without costs and challenges, among which at least five are worth mentioning: (1) to perfect the existing agreements, (2) to promote convergence among them, (3) to bring down nontraditional trade costs, (4) to further expose the region's RTAs to the world trade, and (5) to address the unequal distribution of the gains from trade within the region.

3.1. Imperfect Trade Agreements

LAC's proliferation of RTAs since the early 1990s, while impressive, has been accompanied by an array of imperfections that has often originated at the drawing board and has sometimes developed over time. Many of these imperfections not only hold back regional integration but are also, in many cases, detrimental to the welfare and growth of the very members of the agreements. Providing a detailed list of the issues for every RTA in LAC is clearly beyond the scope of this chapter, but a few examples from one of the more advanced agreements in the region, MERCO-SUR, clearly illustrates the point.[1]

MERCOSUR was created in 1991 with the signing of the Treaty of Asunción. The agreement was established under the following four core objectives: (1) the free movements of goods, services, and factors of production among countries, (2) the establishment of a common external tariff and the adoption of a common commercial policy, (3) the coordination of macroeconomic and sectoral policies between the parties, and (4) the harmonization of laws in order to strengthen the integration process.

We do not have to dig deep to find shortcomings in the accomplishment of some of these objectives. Take for instance the issue of free movements of goods, services, and factors within the bloc. Almost two decades after the agreement was signed, the notion of free movement of goods, for example, has only been partially accomplished, essentially with respect to tariffs. But the movement of goods across member states has been limited by many other obstacles. The list is long and varied: from quantitative restrictions to technical barriers, the member states have employed a range of instruments that also include antidumping duties, the discriminatory use of domestic taxes, difficulties in obtaining import licenses, and even blockages. These imperfections have been introduced and removed over time, often on an ad hoc basis, sometimes as a response to animosities generated from macroeconomic and financial difficulties and sometimes as a response to the pressure of interest groups. It is important to note that this type of action tends to hurt more the smaller members of the agreement, which are usually more dependent on the trade flows within the bloc.

The above example shows clearly that if the very first principle of a FTA cannot be fully guaranteed at all times, expecting success in the more demanding set of objectives, like forming a customs unions or harmonizing policies and legislations, would be a tall order for many of the agreements in the region. Examples of imperfections in the trade agreements, like those just referred to, can be found in most of the region's agreements. This is a pervasive feature of the state of integration in LAC. In the next section, we highlight some key considerations, which should be part of a policy agenda to move LAC integration forward.

3.2. The Challenge of Convergence

The second challenge is also related to the web of trade agreements that have proliferated over time, forging a veritable "spaghetti bowl" of multiple and often overlapping agreements (see fig. 8.5) that entail a number of risks (Estevadeordal et al. 2009). First, the multiplicity of agreements can "balkanize" the regional and global trading systems. If the various agreements carry widely distinct features, they can impose undue transaction costs for traders, investors, and governments operating

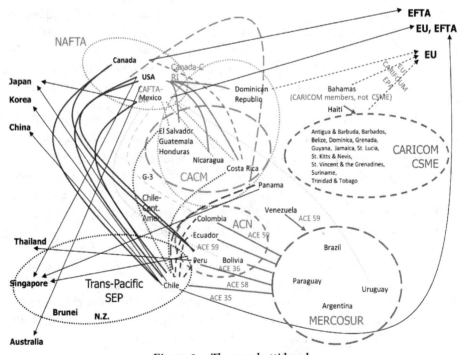

Figure 8.5 The spaghetti bowl.

Source: IADB, Integration and Trade Sector

in several RTA markets simultaneously. The spread of RTAs also risks the rise of hub-and-spoke systems centered on a few hub countries, where the potential cost savings from the accumulation of production among the spokes remain untapped. Furthermore, the broad proliferation of RTAs means that while any given country will likely be an insider to a number of RTAs, it will also be an outsider to dozens of others. As outsiders, even the most prolific integrator countries can end up facing some degree of discrimination and preference erosion around the world.

The most feasible option for the countries in LAC to deal with the problems posed by the spaghetti bowl is to build bridges among the existing RTAs—strive for some form of convergence by gradually harmonizing the various RTAs in the Americas, and implementing accumulation of production among them. The starting point and initial focus of such an effort could be market access and rules-of-origin provisions.

The good news is that there seem to be some favorable conditions for such a convergence to take place. For instance, the liberalization programs in most of the RTAs in LAC work in a relatively similar fashion. Most of them deliver deep liberalization by the 10th year into the RTA, and most RTAs afford prolonged protection to the same or similar sectors—agriculture, in particular. Today, tariff elimination— the first precondition for accumulation—is advanced in the region: not only do many RTA members belong to many RTAs in the region, serving as key nodes between agreements, but most RTA members have already liberalized at least some four-fifths of their tariff lines to each other, and nearly all of them will have freed trade on more than 90 percent of their products within the next decade, or by 2016. There are also some "RTA families," such as those formed by MERCOSUR and by the NAFTA members, respectively, within which the differences across regimes are not very large. Similarly, there are a number of sectors, such as arms, wood products, and precision instruments, where the differences in rules of origin across the entire hemisphere are marginal and, in some cases, nonexistent.

But going from potential to actual convergence is easier said than done, as the process is plagued with several challenges. We will highlight those challenges and present some key considerations to move forward in the next section.

3.3. Nontraditional Trade Costs

The third challenge is related to bringing down nontraditional trade costs, particularly transport costs. The combination of decades of trade liberalization and damaging neglect of the transport infrastructure has led transport costs in the region to become the most important barrier to trade. This point is evident in figure 8.6, which gives a broad picture of trade costs for both LAC's intra- and extraregional trade. For both imports (left graph) and exports (right graph), most of the countries are on the left of the diagonal, that is, transport costs are higher than tariffs by a large margin.

Figure 8.7 shows that transport costs in the region are not only higher than tariffs but also considerably higher than those incurred by the developed or emerging world. Most LAC countries, for example, face higher freight rates in their exports to the United States than countries in the Far East and in Europe. This is particularly striking for countries such as those in the Caribbean, which are very close to the United States. Most countries in the Southern Cone, as expected, lie at the higher end of the spectrum, but these countries, as well as some countries from Central America that are near the United States, like Guatemala and Panama, face freight rates that are even higher than China's or Oceania's. These results are confirmed even after controlling for differences in the composition of the trade (see Mesquita Moreira, Volpe, and Blyde 2008).

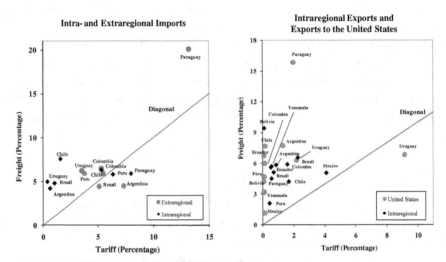

Source: Author's calculations based on ALADI dataset and U.S. Census Bureau
Note: Freight is the ratio of freight expenditures to imports. Tariff is the ratio of tariff revenue to imports. Import data for Paraguay and Colombia are for 2000 and 2003, respectively. Intraregional exports include Argentina, Brazil, Chile, Peru and Uruguay

Figure 8.6 Ad valorem tariffs and freights in LAC, 2006.

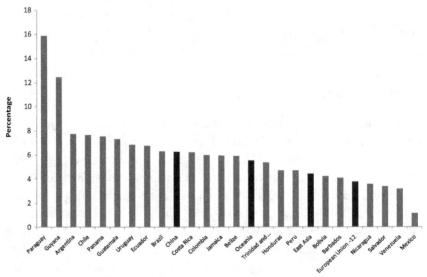

Figure 8.7 Freight expenditures as a share of exports to the United States, 2006.

Source: IADB, Integration and Trade Sector

The question then is what drives these high transport costs in LAC. Unlike tariffs, transport costs are not fixed by fiat, but respond to variables such as trade flows, the quality of the countries' infrastructure, and the degree of competition in the transport industry. Bringing transport costs down, therefore, goes well beyond the political economy of protection and requires a more complex set of policy actions than those involved in the typical trade liberalization. It is then important to know what lies underneath these costs.

Mesquita Moreira, Volpe, and Blyde (2008) perform a series of econometric exercises to analyze their determinants, and they find that trade composition accounts for most of the difference between LAC's transport costs and those of the United States or Europe. The goods that the region imports or exports, particularly the latter, are considerably "heavier." It does not take too much effort to understand why. Grains, minerals, and commodities in general are very "heavy" products to the extent that they have very high weight-to-value ratios. Since freight costs have been shown to be directly proportional to weight-to-value ratios (Hummels 2001), natural resources exporters pay relatively more to transport their goods. Therefore, poor and costly transport infrastructure can severely undercut the rents that countries can extract from their natural resources, transferring income from producers to monopolistic and inefficient freight-forwarders or private operators of ports, roads, and airports. Thus, for a region heavily dependent on the export of natural resources, transport infrastructure is of strategic importance.

If we leave composition aside, the (in)efficiency of the transport infrastructure arises as the main determinant of the region's higher transport costs. For example, port and airport efficiency generally explain about 40 percent of the differences in shipping costs between LAC and the United States and Europe (Mesquita Moreira, Volpe, and Blyde 2008). A third factor contributing to the higher freight rates in LAC—although to a lesser extent than transport efficiency—is the weak competition among shipping companies.

3.4. Low Exposure to Worldwide Trade

Despite substantial progress made in the last decades in bringing external tariffs down, the reality is that most subregional agreements still have unduly high tariffs in many sectors, particularly in South America and in the Caribbean. Figure 8.8, for example, shows the current most-favored-nation tariffs imposed by Argentina and Brazil. It is striking to see that still today there are so many Harmonized Commodity Description and Coding System chapters with tariff rates in the 20–30 percent range.

Even though it can be argued that higher protection leads to higher preferences and scale gains, this relationship is far from linear. Low levels of preferences can lead to scale gains, but as preferences reach a certain point, a perverse dynamics sets in, inverting this relationship. High preferences discourage restructuring, learning, and exports. They also impose heavy losses on the smaller partners of the agreement through trade diversion. Apart from these negative effects, high tariffs also undermine the objective of a unified market, making the task of creating custom unions virtually impossible as members that import the high-tariff goods apply for exemptions.

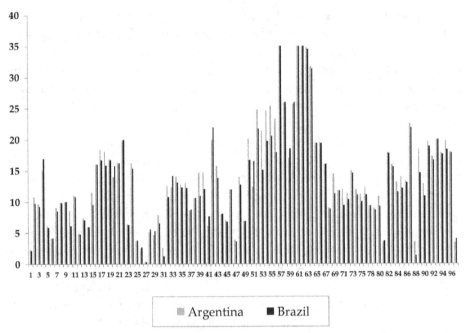

Figure 8.8 Most-favored-nation tariffs, average by Harmonized Commodity Description and Coding System chapter, 2010.

Source: IADB, Integration and Trade Sector

MERCOSUR is again a good case in point. Central to this agreement was the approval of a common external tariff that is the cornerstone of the bloc's common trade policy. Particularly problematic was the issue of protecting capital goods as well as computing and telecommunications products. The smaller countries wanted their tariffs on such goods to be kept as low as possible to keep investment costs low and to preserve their access to foreign technology, while Brazil wanted to raise tariffs as high as possible to protect local production of these goods. A compromise was made with use of exceptions, but they make the task of completing the custom unions an elusive goal. Additionally, the relatively high levels of protection that were set by the agreement not only created the problems raised above but also presented a major stumbling block for initiatives to bring new partners into the agreement, like Chile, as they would have to adjust upward their much lower most-favored-nation tariffs.

There should be no doubt that LAC's various integration agreements still have some room to cover in lowering their protection levels in order to maximize the impact of international trade.

3.5. Unequal Distribution of the Net Benefits of Integration

Another challenge to LAC's integration prospects is the distribution of the gains from trade among members of a RTA or within the regions of a particular country. Take for instance the case of a typical RTA. On the one hand, smaller economies within an RTA are the ones that tend to benefit disproportionately from a trade agreement that ensures preferential access to large regional markets. On the other hand, the small countries are more vulnerable to the RTA imperfections owing precisely to their increased exposure to regional trade. As we mentioned earlier, imperfections are plentiful among the region's RTAs, particularly with respect to the free flow of goods, fueling resentment and discontent among the smaller member states.

The situation is aggravated by the South-South nature of these agreements, with countries sharing similar factor endowments and technology. These conditions imply that the countries' comparative advantages tend to overlap, suggesting that a great deal of their trade is bound to come from outside the region. This, in turn, increases the risk that a misguided move toward regional integration will generate trade diversion (e.g., the replacement of efficient, extraregional suppliers by inefficient, regional ones) and the agglomeration of economic activity in the large regional countries (since the advantages of size are not balanced by significant differences in the prices of capital and labor) (Venables 2003).

A related concern is the issue of an uneven distribution of trade gains within a particular country. Trade and economic geography theory indicates that opening to trade typically reduces the incentives to locate near the large metropolis of the country because firms start selling to the world market and get some of their inputs from that market as well. But when trade barriers fall, another issue starts to become very relevant for the firms: the transport costs of selling to the world market. High domestic transport costs within the country might create powerful incentives for the firms to move close to the main ports or borders of the country to minimize such costs. Therefore, even though trade liberalization might reduce concentration away from the large city, high transport cost within the country may lead to another type of agglomeration, in this case close to the main ports or the borders of the country. The example of Mexico, in which the opening to trade led to a migration of economic activity from the center to the northern states—close to the U.S. market—without any effect in the southern states, is consistent with this story (see fig. 8.4).

4. AN INTEGRATION AGENDA
MOVING FORWARD

The diagnosis presented in the previous section points to a policy agenda with five key components that complement each other, moving toward the ultimate goal of a unified regional market, but that have different degrees of political, institutional, and technical difficulties: (1) perfecting and (2) harmonizing the existing agreements, (3) addressing nontraditional trade costs, (4) maximizing the region's exposure to worldwide trade, and (5) ensuring an equitable distribution of costs and benefits among countries and regions.

The agenda for perfecting the existing trade agreements is well known and would involve in most cases measures such as:

- Removal of intrazone tariffs and nontariff measures;
- Establishment of a custom union;
- Harmonization of customs procedures, rules of origin, sanitary measures, and technical standards;
- Harmonization and full implementation of antitrust legislation;
- Establishment of a well-functioning and institutionalized dispute-settlement mechanism.

After a promising beginning, where important steps were taken toward the formation of a single market in each of the subregional agreements, the reality is that progress has stalled or even suffered setbacks in the last decade, as was the case of the agreements in South America. The real challenge here is not so much to find resources or technical solutions, but to build a political consensus toward addressing the economic fundamentals of these agreements.

The agenda for harmonizing and bridging the existing agreements, whose gains can be substantial (Estevadeordal et al. 2009), is bound to be complex, particularly considering the several regional RTAs and the vast range of RTA provisions in the hemispheric agreements that would have to be reconciled. The first step in such a process might thus be to launch a regional mechanism—perhaps a technical group of experts—that monitors and catalogues RTA tariffs and disciplines, reports to the members on the existing rules, solicits views from the stakeholders about the functioning and pitfalls of the status quo spaghetti bowl of agreements, and puts forth technical proposals for reforms to RTAs that would make them more effective.

Several issues need to be resolved before moving forward. Take for instance the topic of coverage for a convergent regime. Answering this question can be aided by a diagnosis of the extent and degree of overlap of tariff liberalization in the various RTAs and of the extent to which the various RTAs are compatible with each other. There are perhaps three main options.

One alternative is an "all disciplines–all RTAs" approach: harmonizing all rules (including those regulating services, investment, competition policy, and so on) among all RTAs in the region. This approach would be a backhanded approach to creating a single regional RTA zone.

A second and seemingly more feasible alternative would be a "selected RTAs–selected disciplines" approach. This measure would at first instance have to entail knitting subsets of the existing RTAs together. The initial focus of such a convergence could be market access provisions and rules of origin. The convergence packet could be gradually expanded to incorporate further disciplines or countries (i.e., move toward an all countries–all disciplines model), perhaps with some form of ratcheting up of variable geometry.

The third option, or a sequel to the second one, would be some combination of the two—for instance an "all disciplines–selected RTAs" or "selected disciplines–all RTAs" approach. While the likelihood of the first one taking place is higher, the latter could be quite feasible in selected disciplines, such as investment frameworks or trade facilitation protocols. Indeed, the selected disciplines–all RTAs approach would involve all countries of the region, and allow them to focus on the most crucial elements in RTAs for facilitating trade and investment in the Americas.

Some important considerations for any convergence process are worth stressing. One is the inclusion of the private sector in the process. While the role of government is to form and redefine international agreements, moving toward convergence should incorporate actors in the private sector, particularly because they are the end users of RTAs and thus hold the best information about the operation of RTAs and the problems posed by the RTA spaghetti bowl. A second consideration is to ensure that the convergence processes neither jeopardize the existing degree of liberalization in the region nor contravene global liberalization. Indeed, a primary goal of the convergence process in the region should also be to promote more liberal trade globally. This would give insider producers access to supplies outside the expanded accumulation zone and reduce the prospects for trade diversion.

So far the region's best hope for addressing this challenge has emerged in the context of initiatives such as the Arco Initiative, which involves Mexico, Central America, Panama, Peru, Ecuador, Colombia, and Chile. These are clearly welcome news and an indication that this advance has developed some traction. Ideally, political conditions permitting, such an initiative should be later extended to incorporate the other countries in the region.

The nontraditional trade costs have been typically left at the margins of integration initiatives, despite the combination of relatively simple technical solutions and high returns. There have been advances in the more traditional, trade-facilitation issues such as custom procedures and sanitary and phytosanitary measures, but there is still much to be done bilaterally and across and within the subregional agreements to minimize these "frictions."

The transport-costs agenda is arguably in the worst shape, as it has been barely addressed by subregional and bilateral agreements. Even at the level of the individual country, progress has been sometimes slow and dispersed. For instance, in regard to ocean transportation, some countries have eliminated cargo reserves for state-owned shipping companies, privatized national flag carriers, and given concessions to several port operations. However, not everybody has moved at the same pace. Many ports in Central America, for example, have yet to learn from the experience of countries such as Colombia in which concessions to private terminal operators brought modern port operating practices, resulting in significant reductions in ship waiting and turnaround time and increases in berth productivity.

Concerning air transportation, the regulation aspect of the region seems to be particularly dysfunctional (Ricover and Negre 2004). Based on old bilateral agreements with stringent limitations on market access, the regulation of air transport services in LAC has failed to move in tandem with the liberalization efforts observed in other parts of the world, which have been mostly undertaken through "open skies" agreements. These agreements have contributed to significantly reducing the costs of air transportation. Micco and Serebrisky (2006), for example, show that the open skies agreements signed by the United States have generated, on average, a reduction of 8 percent in air transport costs.

While some countries in LAC have signed bilateral open skies agreements with the United States, very few of these agreements exist within the region (WTO 2005). Pursuing similar bilateral agreements between countries in the region could be a significant way of reducing the substantial government intervention that is currently present in LAC. A bolder liberalization approach, however, would be a multilateral open skies agreement for LAC with the objective of creating a truly regional integrated market.

In regard to land transportation, besides the obvious problems related to several decades of underinvestment in the road networks of most of the countries, lack of modal competition is many times an additional factor that can contribute to the problem. Here, progress has been made mostly on an individual basis without a concerted effort to envision how a region that is physically integrated should look. The exceptions are two regional initiatives, the Initiative for the Integration of South American Regional Infrastructure in the South and Plan Mesoamérica in Central America, which target the regional transport infrastructure, alongside energy and communication. These initiatives were created outside the realm of regional trade agreements, but they have been helpful in disseminating information and in coordinating national policies. They would clearly gain in effectiveness from (1) being integrated into the mainstream of trade initiatives and agreements, (2) combining efforts to achieve region wide coverage, and (3) incorporating better financial incentives to promote regional projects.

As for exposure to worldwide trade, keeping protection low against the rest the world, with tariffs around the Organisation for Economic Co-operation and Development's average of 5 to 6 percent, is crucial for the success of any regional integration initiative in LAC. As mentioned in the previous section, despite substantial progress made in recent decades in bringing external tariffs down, most subregional agreements still have high levels of protection in many sectors, particularly in South America and in the Caribbean.

As argued before, low tariffs at home should be complemented by low-cost access to the world's main markets. Again, the region's record is this area is spotty. Countries such as Chile, Mexico, and Peru are leading the way in terms of signing free trade agreements with the most important markets in the world, whereas the other countries and their subregional agreements clearly lag behind. The slow progress in the Doha Round makes it clear that a market-access strategy based only on multilateral negotiations is not enough. Agreements with other countries and regions have to be part of the menu if governments want to reap the benefits of regional integration sooner rather than later.

The objective of equitable distribution of costs and benefits is, perhaps, among the suggested objectives of the regional integration strategy, the one that brings the most daunting political and technical challenges. There is a legitimate and growing demand for the costs and benefits of integration to be distributed fairly among member countries, and to ignore this demand is to put the whole initiative in peril (see, e.g., Blyde, Fernández-Arias, and Giordano 2008). It is important, though, to focus on the integration policies that are directly affecting the outcomes, instead of falling into a much more complex debate on how to eliminate economic and social asymmetries among member countries, a goal that would require actions that go well beyond trade and integration.

As argued before, high external tariffs can bias the distribution of cost and benefits against the smaller, poorer countries as they are likely to pay the costs of trade diversion and have none of the benefits. Bringing down protection against the rest of the world is then a simple way of ensuring that integration does not aggravate any preexisting asymmetries and works to lift the incomes of all countries in the region. Likewise, creating the conditions for a fully unified market would disproportionately benefit the smaller, poorer countries as they gain access to their partners' larger markets.

There are other sources of biases that are not related to trade policy, but that can have powerful indirect effects, such as asymmetries in the macro- (e.g., exchange-rate regimes) and microeconomic policies (e.g., subsidies and fiscal incentives), as attested by LAC's own recent history. There has been no shortage of initiatives in the region to address these issues of "macroeconomic coordination" and "regulation of industrial policies," but they have all fallen short of having a significant impact. They invariably face the formidable obstacle of the countries' unwillingness (or lack of incentives) to forgo their sovereignty rights to define their own domestic policies.

Despite these difficulties, macroeconomic coordination and regulation of industrial policies should remain a strategic goal for LAC's regional integration, but should be seen as a long-term proposition, conditional on more credible signs of political will. The goals related to external protection and market unification should take precedence, not only because of their feasibility and high returns. The worst effects of exchange rate misalignments have been mitigated by the region's convergence (with a few exceptions) toward sound fiscal and monetary policies, and, on industrial policies, countries can always resort to World Trade Organization measures to reduce asymmetries.

The focus on policies that directly affect the distribution of the costs and benefits of integration does not preclude measures to address economic and social asymmetries, along the lines of Europe's cohesion policy. In fact, agreements such as MERCOSUR and CARICOM have already taken steps in this direction with the establishment of funds geared to investment projects in the smaller and poorer members.

These policies can help mitigate the adjustment costs of integration and build political goodwill. However, they should not be seen in any circumstances as a substitute for direct action on external protection and market unification. They do not address the root causes of the problem, and the level of income and the fiscal constraints of the larger and richer countries of the region do not allow for a substantial, European-style transfer of resources.

5. CONCLUDING REMARKS

LAC has come a long way from the days of inward orientation and closed regionalism. Since the early 1990s, it has embraced trade and integration as a strategic platform for growth and development and the results are there for anyone to see. After a difficult transitional period, in which the region had to come to terms with the legacy of a long period of fiscal indiscipline, growth has resumed, led, to a great extent, by greater openness and integration at home and abroad.

Despite the progress, LAC still arguably has a sizable "trade and integration gap" to fill. Its share of the world trade remains small—even by its own early-twentieth-century standards—its exports too concentrated in a limited number of products and the benefits of trade unevenly distributed across the region, even within the countries. The policy agenda to fill this gap asks for greater regional and global integration to expand and consolidate the growth and welfare gains from trade.

In this chapter, we concentrate on developing a diagnosis and set of actions that would leverage the contribution of regional integration to attain this objective. The diagnosis pinpoints too many imperfect RTAs, with little convergence of rules among them; high nontraditional trade costs, particularly those related to transportation; lingering high tariffs on extraregional trade; and, partially as a result, a much skewed distribution of trade gains among RTA partners, particularly biased against the smaller countries.

The agenda for actions described includes a series of complementary measures, which command more political than technical skills. They include actions to perfect RTAs and promote convergence among them, as well as measures to bring extraregional tariffs down and to compensate the countries and subregions that have yet to see the benefits of greater trade and integration. If implemented, these measures could ensure that the scale and allocation benefits of regional integration are maximized and better distributed throughout the region. This, in turn, would give LAC a better base to expand and diversify its presence in the world markets.

NOTE

1. For a detailed description of the challenges faced by MERCOSUR today, see IADB-INTAL (2010).

REFERENCES

Blyde, Juan S., Eduardo Fernández-Arias, and Paolo Giordano, eds. 2008. *Deepening Integration in MERCOSUR: Dealing with Disparities*. Washington, DC: Inter-American Development Bank.

Estevadeordal, Antoni, Kati Suominen, Jeremy T. Harris, and Matthew Shearer. 2009. *Bridging Regional Trade Agreements in the Americas*. Washington, DC: Inter-American Development Bank.

Hummels, David. 2001. "Toward a Geography of Trade Costs." Unpublished manuscript, Purdue University.

IADB (Inter-American Development Bank). 2002. *Beyond Borders: The New Regionalism in Latin America*. Baltimore: Johns Hopkins University Press for the Inter-American Development Bank.

IADB-INTAL (Inter-American Development Bank—Institue for the Integration of Latin America and the Caribbean)–. 2010. Mercosur Report No. 14, 2008 Second Semester–2009 First Semester, Buenos Aires.

Mesquita Moreira, Mauricio, Christian Volpe, and Juan Blyde. 2008. *Unclogging the Arteries: The Impact of Transport Costs on Latin American and Caribbean Trade*. Special Report on Integration and Trade, Inter-American Development Bank, Washington, DC, and David Rockefeller Center for Latin American Studies, Harvard University.

Micco, Alejandro, and Tomás Serebrisky. 2006. "Competition Regimes and Air Transport Costs: The Effects of Open Skies Agreements." *Journal of International Economics* 70:.

Ricover, Andrés, and Eugenio Negre. 2004. "Estudio de Integración del Transporte Aéreo en Sudamérica," Inter-American Development Bank, Washington, DC.

Venables, Anthony J. 2003. "Regionalism and Economic Development" In *Bridges for Development: Policies and Institutions for Trade and Integration*, edited by Robert Devlin and Antoni Estevadeordal, 51–74. Washington, DC: Inter-American Development Bank.

WTO (World Trade Organization). 2005. *World Trade Report, 2005: Exploring the Links between Trade, Standards and the WTO*. Geneva: World Trade Organization.

....

CHAPTER 9

DOES ASIA MATTER? THE POLITICAL ECONOMY OF LATIN AMERICA'S INTERNATIONAL RELATIONS

BARBARA STALLINGS

....

THE Monroe Doctrine has formed the basic context for Latin America's international relations for nearly two centuries. Established by the U.S. government in 1823 to limit Europe's presence in the hemisphere, it did not prevent substantial European trade and investment in the nineteenth and twentieth centuries, especially in South America. Indeed, Britain had to enforce the doctrine for a number of years. From time to time in the post–World War II period, a new rival, the Soviet Union, intruded directly or indirectly in the region. John F. Kennedy invoked the doctrine to justify confronting Moscow over the missiles in Cuba, and it was also used as an excuse for overthrowing several governments considered to be communist threats. A third challenge came from the Far East with Japanese trade and investment that peaked in the 1980s and more recently China's new activism in a number of Latin American countries. Despite periodic declarations by prominent authors that the Monroe Doctrine is dead (Smith 1994; Castañeda 2009), all of these rivals have recognized a U.S. sphere of influence in the hemisphere.

In this chapter, I focus on the most recent of the outside challenges, studying the political economy of East Asia in Latin America. I examine what some consider the current Chinese threat in light of the Japanese experience in Latin America two decades earlier. I argue that China, like Japan, has economic interests in the region, but that both have limited their activities for two main reasons. First, their bilateral relationships with the United States are far more important to them than their links with Latin America. Second, Latin America is a less significant partner than other developing regions. As a consequence, for better or worse, the United States remains the dominant power in the region even if the main U.S. actors—both the government and the private sector—have neglected their southern neighbors in recent times.

The first section of the chapter analyzes Japanese political-economic relations with Latin America, focusing on the 1970s and 1980s. The second section turns to China's more recent experience in comparison with that of Japan. The third section identifies winners and losers from the East Asian countries' activities in the region.

1. Japan and Latin America

Japan's relationships with Latin America differ substantially from its interactions with East Asia. East Asian neighbors have been incorporated into industrial production networks through investment and intraindustry trade, which resulted in rapid export-led growth. In Latin America, by contrast, both Japan and the United States have engaged in a combination of investments in natural resources and production for the local market. Where trade has been involved, it has usually been of an interindustry type.[1] Japan's differs from the U.S. approach to Latin America in the tight relationship between the Japanese government and its private sector and its focus on economic relations while eschewing attempts at political influence at the local level. In part, its political aim has been to avoid antagonizing the United States.[2]

The modern history of Japan and Latin America began with immigration. In two periods when the Japanese government felt itself in a very weak position—the early twentieth century and after World War II—it organized state-sponsored emigration to relieve social and economic pressures. Seeking new sources of cheap labor, a number of Latin American countries agreed to accept the Japanese immigrants, which initiated the notion of complementarities between Japan and Latin America (Kunimoto 1993; Masterson and Funada-Classen 2003; Endoh 2009).[3] Brazil was the major destination and now has the largest Japanese population outside of Japan itself. An estimated 1.5 million people of Japanese descent are currently living in Brazil (Japanese Ministry of Foreign Affairs 2010). Other important receiving countries included Peru, Mexico, and Argentina.

The two emigration waves meant that when Japan began to take an interest in trading with and investing in Latin America, it had a ready-made reception committee that could function as a bridge to local governments and business communities. Japanese trade with Latin America followed what some have called a colonial pattern. That is, for the most part Japan exports industrial goods and imports raw materials. In addition to this inequality, the relative importance of the two sets of partners is also unequal. While Latin America was never very significant as a trade partner for Japan, its importance declined over the postwar period. In the 1950s to 1970s, around 7 percent of Japan's total trade was with Latin America; since then the average has been only 4 percent—although there was some resurgence in the past decade. From the Latin American perspective, the importance of trade with Japan has varied substantially by country. In the heyday of trade with Japan, in the late 1980s and early 1990s, Japan was among the most important partners for a number of countries. For Brazil, Mexico, and Peru, it was second behind the United States in most years; in Chile, it was sometimes the most important partner. Overall for the region, Japan represented about 6 percent of Latin America's trade in 1990. In general, and especially recently, the trade balance has been in Japan's favor (calculated from IMF 1991).[4]

Japanese trade with Latin America—as elsewhere—has been tightly linked with foreign direct investment (FDI). Not surprisingly, given Brazil's large size, vast natural resources, and the immigrant population, Japan's earliest investments were in that country. They began in the mid-1950s, when Japan was still struggling to recover from World War II, and coincided with the push toward import-substitution industrialization in Latin America and the need for foreign resources. Usiminas, the biggest steel complex in Latin America, was one of the four largest Japanese foreign ventures worldwide in that decade. Ishibras, the biggest shipyard in the region, was another Japanese undertaking in this period, as was the initial Toyota operation in Brazil (Hollerman 1988; Torres 1993).

The most important Japanese investments in the region took place in the 1970s and 1980s, particularly after the first oil crisis in 1973. The oil shock worried the Japanese greatly in terms of access to natural resources in general, not just petroleum, and Latin America was seen as an area that could provide them. In the 1970s, then, a number of so-called national projects were launched. These were joint public-private ventures to produce goods that would be exported to Japan. They usually involved one of Japan's trading companies, one or more industrial firms, and a government agency. Although the government did not put in much money, its contribution signaled official support. Most projects involved raw materials, such as iron ore (Brazil), nonferrous metals (Peru and Chile), grains (Brazil and Argentina), wood (Chile), and salt deposits (Mexico).

As host countries began to demand greater local processing, this coincided with environmental concerns and rising energy costs in Japan itself, and resulted in an increase in semiprocessing of raw materials before export to Japan. Such processing was often carried out as joint ventures with local state-owned firms; typical products included iron ore, pulp and wood chips, aluminum, and semifinished steel (Horisaka 1993). The official figure for the total stock of Japanese investment in Latin America, as of 1994, was US$55 billion. Of this, US$19 billion was in tax havens and US$22 billion was in Panama as the counterpart of the flag-of-convenience trade referred to above. This left US$14 billion in onshore investment in the region, of which the vast majority was in Brazil (60 percent) and Mexico (20 percent) (calculated from JETRO 2010 data).[5]

In the late 1970s and early 1980s, Japanese banks followed the lead of their industrial counterparts and the trading companies, moving into Latin America in a large-scale way. They employed two modes of operation. On the one hand, they participated in some national projects, such as a Peruvian oil pipeline, Mexican port and pipeline facilities, a steel complex in western Mexico, an agricultural complex in central Brazil, and a large-scale multipurpose project in the Amazon. On the other hand, they took part in the large syndicated loans that were the main form of lending in that period.

Lacking international experience in general and knowledge of Latin America in particular, the banks tended to follow the U.S. lead in the syndicated loans. These were generally arranged by U.S. or European financial institutions for sovereign borrowers in Latin America and elsewhere. The timing was important in that the Japanese banks got in at the end of a decade of sovereign lending. As U.S. banks began to realize the dangers of a looming debt crisis and withdrew, Japanese financial institutions took their place in managing loan syndicates as well as buying shares of loans. Thus, by 1982, when the Latin American debt crisis broke, U.S. banks held 31 percent of Latin American debt and Japanese banks held 16 percent. As a share of total international loans, Latin American debt constituted 38 percent of Japanese bank loans outstanding compared to 36 percent for the United States (Stallings 1990).

As was the case with other parts of the Japanese private sector, the banks coordinated their activities closely with the Japanese government. The latter, in turn, initially followed the U.S. lead in dealing with the debt crisis. The process typically involved forming creditor committees for individual countries and providing new loans so that debtors could continue to make interest payments and thus save U.S. banks from having to declare the loans in arrears. With the encouragement of the Japanese government, Japanese banks participated in these exercises until the mid-1980s. Then they devised an initiative to take their loans off their books to free up capital for new lending, while the Japanese government took the lead in proposing a new strategy to cut Latin America's debt payments and so promote long-term development rather than simply avoiding interest arrears. Known as the Miyazawa Plan, the Japanese ideas were incorporated into the U.S.-sponsored Brady Plan, which eventually led to a resolution of the debt crisis (Stallings 1990).

It appeared in the 1980s that Japan would take a more active role on the international stage. The government increased its stake in the international financial institutions, sought a bigger role at the United Nations, and occasionally took the lead in new international initiatives. In Latin America, Japan stepped up its activities at the Inter-American Development Bank, provided assistance during the debt crisis, and helped with reconstruction in Central America. As it turned out, however, the new activism did not last, because of the bursting of an asset bubble in Japan itself. The government's delayed response led to a decade of deflation and stagnation that still lingers to some extent today. As a result, Japanese trade and investment in Latin America fell off substantially.

The most notable recent activities have been in the trade area, where Japanese corporations pushed their government to join the worldwide rush to negotiate free trade agreements (FTAs). The second FTA that Japan signed was with Mexico. It was promoted by firms with investments in Mexico that relied heavily on the import of components from Japan. These firms feared that the North American Free Trade Agreement (NAFTA), which went into effect in 1994, would undermine their ability to compete in the U.S. market and in Mexico itself due to higher Mexican tariffs and other discriminatory policies against non-FTA countries. The Mexican FTA went into effect in 2005; it was followed shortly afterward by an FTA with Chile, and one has been signed with Peru (Solís 2009).

While economic relations with Latin America lag far behind those with Asia and the industrial countries, Japan has begun to take a new look at the region in the last half decade. A prominent Japanese academic and former government official says this is due to greater stability and growth in Latin America, but he also hints that competition with China is partially responsible. Trade has picked up, and new investment is emerging, especially in the mining sector. Government surveys also show that Japanese firms are viewing Brazil and Mexico as sites for production for local markets in electronics and technology (Tsunekawa 2010; ECLAC 2010, ch. 5). In the meantime, however, China has entered the region in a very significant way.

2. CHINA AND LATIN AMERICA

Although the People's Republic of China (PRC) and Japan have often conflictive relations as they compete for hegemony in East Asia, they nonetheless share many characteristics, including their approach to Latin America. Like Japan's, China's interactions with the region began with immigration flows. Much later they were followed by economic relations focusing on interindustry trade and FDI, under the oversight of the Chinese government. Like Japan, China also stresses economic over political relations in Latin America and takes care not to antagonize the United States in its sphere of influence.

Chinese emigration to Latin America, which has not been as well studied as the Japanese process, began in the sixteenth and seventeenth centuries as an offshoot of the Manila-Acapulco trade connection (Slack 2010). The main immigration flow, however, was the so-called coolie trade in the nineteenth century, whereby unskilled manual laborers from southern China left to seek economic opportunities in Cuba and Peru, but also in Mexico, Argentina, and Central America (Look Lai 2010). Finally Chinese immigrants arrived in the twentieth century as a result of the communist victory on the mainland, the PRC takeover of Hong Kong and Macao, and several instances of anti-Chinese violence, such as that in Indonesia in the late 1990s. There are Chinatowns in a number of Latin American countries, but little systematic information exists on them. One of the reasons they do not form as cohesive a community as the Japanese immigrants is that many are from Taiwan, Hong Kong, and Macao in addition to those from the PRC. They have also inter-mingled with the Latin population more than the Japanese have.

Given the dispersed nature of the Chinese population in Latin America and their frequent lack of allegiance to the current Chinese regime, Chinese economic initiatives have not been able to take advantage of the overseas Chinese in Latin America as they have in Asia and elsewhere. Rather, trade and investment have been mainly organized from Beijing on a government-to-government basis. High-profile visits by Chinese leaders have played an important part in the process. Most prominently, President Hu Jintao made three multicountry trips to Latin America in the last decade—in 2004, 2008, and 2010. Other top-ranking leaders also visited various countries in the region. New initiatives tended to be announced in connec-tion with these trips.

China's trade with the rest of the world increased dramatically after it joined the World Trade Organization (WTO) in 2001. In current dollars, its total trade (exports plus imports) increased by almost four and a half times between 2000 and 2008, rising from US$474 billion to US$2,560 billion. Trade with Latin America acceler-ated much faster, increasing more than tenfold in the same period—from around US$12 billion to US$140 billion—from a very low base. The combined figures meant that Latin American trade increased as a share of overall Chinese trade, from 2.8 percent in 2000 to 5.5 percent in 2008.

Looking at trade relations from the other perspective, they are more important for Latin America than for China itself. Between 2000 and 2008, exports to plus imports from China rose from 1.5 percent to 7.7 percent of Latin America's total trade. For some countries, China has become a dominant partner. In 2008, it was the number one export destination for Chile, number two for Argentina, Brazil, and Peru, and number three for Venezuela.[6] While China has a large trade surplus with the world as a whole, from the point of view of Chinese data, its trade with Latin America is relatively balanced. Latin American statistics, by contrast, indicate the region has a large deficit with China. This is an area that requires more study.[7]

Like Japan, China exports industrial goods and imports raw materials. This af-fects Latin American countries differentially, depending on their production and trade structures. In particular, South American commodity exporters—especially Brazil, Argentina, Chile, and Peru—have been able to increase their exports to China by large amounts, taking advantage both of higher demand in China and higher international prices because of the increased demand. These countries have trade surpluses with China. Mexico and Central America, which mainly export in-dustrial goods, sell minimal amounts to China despite a large volume of imports, resulting in large trade deficits.

Several institutional changes have been implemented to promote trade between China and Latin America. First, China has signed FTAs with Chile, Peru, and re-cently Costa Rica. Second, China has convinced many governments in the region to recognize it as a market economy within the WTO framework, which makes it more difficult for partner countries to charge China with dumping. Third, China has joined Japan as an external member of the Inter-American Development Bank (IDB) and as a permanent observer at the Organization of American States (OAS).

Like Japan's, China's trade is closely tied to financial relations—although the details vary in the two cases. Statistics on Chinese outward FDI show Latin America as a very important destination, accounting for about one sixth of the total, but the vast majority of this money goes to the Cayman and Virgin Islands. For example, in 2008, of the US$3.7 billion of Chinese FDI flows to Latin America, US$3.6 billion went to these two locations. From there it is invested around the world, but little goes to Latin America itself. Excluding the tax havens, official data indicate that the stock of Chinese FDI in Latin America in 2008 was approximately US$1.4 billion. The largest destinations were Brazil, Peru, Argentina, Mexico, and Venezuela— ranging from US$156 million and US$217 million each (Chinese [PRC] Ministry of Commerce 2008). Very recent trends, however, may substantially change this picture. Reports indicate that Chinese investment surged in Latin America, especially through mergers and acquisitions that reached over $10 billion in 2010 (ECLAC 2011).

Little systematic information is available on the sectoral composition of the investments. The U.N. Economic Commission for Latin America and the Caribbean (ECLAC) has published some data, based on information from Chinese consulates in the region, which confirms the general assumption that the main sectoral destination is petroleum and gas. Smaller investments are found in mining, fisheries, telecommunications, and some light industry. These investments are generally carried out by large government-controlled firms. The most active are the major oil companies. Others include Minmetals, Baosteel, Huawei Technologies, Lenovo (which bought IBM's laptop computer operations), and companies producing motorcycles and electronics (ECLAC 2008, 63).

In addition to FDI, Chinese institutions have begun making large loans to Latin American governments since the 2008–9 financial crisis. The main lender is the China Development Bank (CDB), but the Export-Import Bank has also been involved. Both are policy banks designed to support Chinese government priorities. Most of the loans are to support the extraction of petroleum and are secured by revenue from its sale to China's national oil companies. Of the $69 billion of energy-backed loans since 2008, Latin American countries have received $40 billion—Venezuela $29 billion, Brazil $10 billion, and Ecuador $1 billion (Downs 2011). Argentina received a further $10 billion from the CDB, but this was to facilitate the purchase of Chinese industrial goods.

Like Japan, China has generally avoided political involvements in Latin America— despite efforts by Hugo Chávez to incorporate China into his anti-American alliance. Nonetheless there is one important exception. About half of the countries in the world that still recognize Taiwan rather than the PRC are located in Latin America and the Caribbean. Since eliminating Taiwan's diplomatic ties is a major goal of Chinese foreign policy, it has been trying to win over these countries. A major victory was achieved in 2007 when Costa Rica switched its diplomatic relations. China has been rewarding it heavily with investment and an FTA in hopes of enticing other countries to follow suit (Wilson 2009).

As I discuss below, China has displaced Japan as the major Asian trading partner for Latin America. While data on investment are more difficult to find and
interpret, China probably still lags behind Japan—although anecdotal information
suggests that important Chinese projects may be under way. Whether the benefits
of relations with this new partner exceed the costs is a controversial issue to which
I now turn.

3. Winners and Losers in Asia-Latin American Relations

This section focuses on two categories of winners and losers—international (the
United States versus Asia) and intraregional (within the Latin American region).
The main question of interest internationally is whether China threatens U.S. interests in Latin America. Although we already know the denouement with respect to
Japan, I also review what things looked like at the peak of Japan's international
power in the late 1980s. At the intraregional level, I examine the relative costs and
benefits to Latin America as a region and to individual countries of the growing role
of China and the still important presence of Japan.

3.1. International Winners and Losers

Before I compare the Asian countries with the United States, it is interesting to see
how they relate to each other in the Latin American context. Figure 9.1 shows
exports to and imports from Latin America for Japan and China between 1990 and
2008. It indicates that 2002 was the turning point when the two Asian countries
switched positions. Until then, Japan had dominated Latin America's trade with
Asia. Afterward, even though Japan's trade accelerated, China's rose much faster. By
2008, China's trade (at around US$70 billion each for exports and imports) was
more than twice as large as that of Japan (less than US$30 billion for each trade
component). Indeed, it is this very rapid increase in China's trade with Latin America that is the basis for most of the interest in the new role of China in the region.

Where does this rapid increase in trade leave China in comparison to the
United States? Table 9.1 provides data on the value of exports and imports, the share
of total exports and imports, and the value and share of FDI for the United States,
China, and Japan in Latin America in 2000 and 2008. The data displayed—the most
recent that are available for all three countries—provide a crucial starting point for
analyzing international influence in Latin America. A number of important conclusions can be drawn from the table about static and dynamic relationships.

The United States continues to be far and away the most important of the three
in terms of the absolute value of economic relations with the region. Focusing on

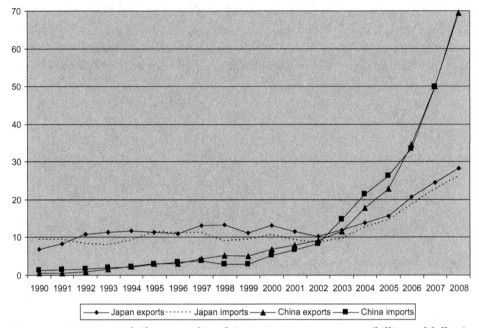

Figure 9.1 Japanese and Chinese trade with Latin America, 1990–2008 (billions of dollars).
Source: IMF (various years).
Note: Japanese exports exclude Panama.

Table 9.1. U.S., Chinese, and Japanese Trade with and Investment in Latin America, 2000 and 2008

	United States		China		Japan	
	2000	2008	2000	2008	2000	2008
Export value ($ billion)	167.5	288.0	6.9	69.7	13.1[a]	28.3[a]
Export share (%)	21.7	22.2	2.8	4.9	2.7	3.6
Import value ($ billion)	210.8	385.3	5.3	70.3	10.7	26.1
Import share (%)	17.0	17.8	2.4	6.2	2.8	3.4
FDI stock ($ billion)[b]	154.5	204.5	0.4[c]	1.4	8.3	22.3
FDI share (%)[b]	11.9	6.4	1.2	0.8	3.0	3.0

[a] Excludes Panama.
[b] Excludes tax havens.
[c] 2003.
Sources: IMF (2007, 2009); U.S. Department of Commerce (2010); Chinese (PRC) Ministry of Commerce (2008); JETRO (2010).

the 2008 data, U.S. exports to Latin America are four times those of China and ten times those of Japan. The differences with respect to imports are larger. The U.S. domination in FDI stock is even greater, although the stock figures are of course affected by the longer period of U.S. investment in the region. The same conclusions are found when we inspect the data on the relative importance of these relationships to the three countries. Latin America is far more important to the United States than to Japan or China as a share of exports, imports, and investments. In static terms, then, the United States continues to dominate economically.

A dynamic comparison changes these conclusions somewhat. Both China and Japan have increased their exports to and imports from Latin America at a faster pace than has the United States. For example, while U.S. exports to Latin America rose by 72 percent in current dollars between 2000 and 2008, Japan's exports more than doubled and China's increased tenfold. In part, this is a statistical artifact since it is easier to increase from a low base, but the differences are nonetheless important. Although much lower than China's, Japan's increase is interesting since it represents a resurgence after two decades of declining presence in Latin America. Not surprisingly, the share of U.S. trade with Latin America has changed little, while both Japan's and especially China's has risen. FDI presents a somewhat different picture. U.S. FDI stock in Latin America rose in absolute terms by about one-third in this period, but the share fell by half from 12 to 6 percent as other regions proved more attractive. China's share fell by 50 percent although the absolute amount increased rapidly—again from a very low base. The amount of Japan's investment grew substantially, but the share remained the same.

Despite the fact that China's economic presence in Latin America is so much smaller than that of the United States, some political actors have argued that China poses a threat to the United States in its sphere of influence. Interestingly, very similar comments were heard about Japan in the 1970s and 1980s. For example, a State Department analyst said:

> There is a good reason to believe that an increasing share of Japan's raw material imports will come from Latin America. Japan is thus moving into an area long regarded as our back yard, while the United States becomes more dependent on its traditional Latin American sources of raw materials and its relations in the area are bedeviled by nationalism and economic conflicts of interest. In this context there would seem to exist a serious possibility of conflict with Japan over access to raw materials, which significantly affects the overall United States security-political-economic relationship. (qtd. in Muñoz 1981, 84–85)

Along the same lines, a key member of the Western Hemisphere Subcommittee of the House International Relations Committee said in 2008:

> I am very concerned with the rise of influence China is pursuing in our Hemisphere and I believe it is important that the United States grasps the economic, social, and national security implications of a Latin America under the thumb of China. Once China is able to move in and expand control, it will be difficult to turn the tide. (qtd. in Jenkins 2010, 829)

Although there are significant differences between Japan and China, in neither case is there evidence of an attempt to challenge the United States in Latin America—despite the type of concerns expressed above. Relations with the United States are too important to place them in jeopardy through conflicts in Latin America. Japan was eminently cautious about provoking U.S. antagonism anywhere in the world, since it had elected a strategy after World War II of pursuing economic development while placing its security needs in U.S. hands. Moreover the United States was its chief trade partner, buying over one-third of Japan's exports in the 1980s, and conflicts over their bilateral trade were such that Japan certainly did not want additional friction in Latin America. Whenever Japan appeared to be getting out ahead of the United States in diplomatic issues in the region, consultations were quickly arranged to tamp down the disagreement, and opportunities for cooperation were sought whenever possible (Matsushita 1993).[8] By the early 1990s, the situation had changed significantly. Japan's economic crisis led it to turn inward; its slower growth (and its technological advances) meant that its need for natural resources declined; and it grew closer to Asia. For all of these reasons, the notion of conflict with the United States in Latin America virtually disappeared.

Of course China today differs from Japan in the 1980s in many ways. One of the most important is that China is still a developing country, as it frequently reminds the world. Consequently, China's rapid growth is likely to continue for longer, and its need for resources will not fall off as rapidly. In addition, China's huge size means that the volume of its resource needs exceeds that of Japan. China's level of development also means that it is more dependent on FDI with its access to technology and markets than Japan ever was, and U.S. firms are a major source. Finally, despite the fact that the United States is a key trade and investment partner for China, the security situation between the two is much different than the U.S.-Japan relationship. Rather than the United States providing a security umbrella, security policy between the two countries is competitive. Nonetheless, there is no evidence that China wants to challenge the United States or join an anti-U.S. alliance as some Latin American governments have proposed.

Two Latin American experts in China have recently spoken to this issue. A semiofficial academic says: "China understands the sensitive character of its deepening ties with Latin America, a region traditionally perceived as the backyard of the United States, and in no way should China's growing presence be interpreted as a challenge to U.S. hegemony in the hemisphere" (Jiang 2008, 28). An independent academic signals the same line: "Clearly, the current regime's main concern in the Western Hemisphere is to avoid any geopolitical consequences resulting from its expansion into Latin America" (Xiang 2008, 52).

In addition to Japan and China not wanting to challenge the United States because of their reliance on the U.S. economy (and, in Japan's case, on U.S. security assistance), both also have interests in other developing regions that are more important to them than Latin America. Asia is far and away the most important region for both—including mutual trade and investment with each other. Most of their trade and FDI are carried out in the Asian region, including the new division of labor in Asia whereby Japan, Korea, and Taiwan export capital goods and inputs to China where they are assembled. A portion of the final goods is exported back to the more developed Asian countries, but more frequently they are sold in U.S. and European markets.

Both Japan and China are also very active in Africa. China's foreign aid, investment, and trade in Africa are well known and documented in many recent publications (e.g., Alden 2007; Rotberg 2008; Brautigam 2010). A large share of its oil comes from sub-Saharan Africa, as do many of its other minerals. Africa has also become a significant market for light consumer goods. Both China and Japan sponsor large-scale forums every several years, where African leaders travel to Beijing and Tokyo and receive promises of more aid, investment, and trade. Japan's interest in Africa, in part a response to China's presence there, is not as well documented but is increasing. It also sees the African continent as an important source of natural resources and expanding markets (Lehman 2010; Lumumba-Kasongo 2010).

Finally, we must take into account Latin America's own interests. As I discuss below, most Latin American countries want diversification of economic and political relations. While Europe has been the dominant source of diversification away from U.S. domination in trade and investment, Asia is also attractive from this perspective. Brazil has long been involved in complementary relations with Japan. Even Mexico, with its especially close ties with the United States, wanted to attract Japanese trade and investment as a counterweight to the NAFTA treaty (Székely 1993). But neither Mexico nor other Latin American countries ever saw Japan as replacing the United States. The same is true with China. Latin Americans are interested in the China market and hope for Chinese investment, but China faces an additional problem that Japan does not have. For most—though perhaps not all— Latin American countries, China's authoritarian political system limits the desire to have more than economic ties or to be occasional allies in international negotiations (Stallings 2009).

3.2. Intraregional Winners and Losers

The Latin American region as a whole appears to have benefited substantially from the growing presence of China in recent years, just as it seemed to benefit from Japan's activities in the 1970s and 1980s. In both cases, profitable new trade relations were established, FDI and loans were provided, and opportunities for economic and political diversification were enhanced. Nonetheless, two important caveats must be added to this apparently positive picture. On the one hand, certain countries and sectors have benefited far more than others. On the other hand, even those who seem to be benefiting most have doubts about the Asian ties. These doubts are more salient with respect to China today than they were with Japan earlier on, but similar problems are perceived. Moreover, as will be seen, Asian economic relations have yet to contribute as much to diversification as might have been anticipated.

As discussed, figure 9.1 shows how overall regional trade with Japan and China increased in the last two decades. Looking from the Latin American perspective, table 9.2 disaggregates these trade flows to show the differences across countries for Japan in its heyday in 1990 and for both Japan and China in 2008. As is apparent, certain South American commodity exporters were the principal beneficiaries of the Asia trade. The leading copper exporters, Chile and Peru, headed the list in terms of their access to East Asian markets, both in 1990 and the present; Brazil, as a major iron ore and grain producer, followed in third place. For China, Argentina and Uruguay, as agricultural exporters, were among the leading trade partners, together with Costa Rica. The latter became an important partner only in 2006 in

Table 9.2. Latin American Exports to Japan and China by Country, 1990 and 2008

Country	Amount ($ Million)			Share (%)[a]		
	Japan (1990)	Japan (2008)	China[b] (2008)	Japan (1990)	Japan (2008)	China[b] (2008)
Argentina	395	505	3,014	3.2	0.7	9.1
Bolivia	10	236	140	0.8	4.1	2.4
Brazil	2,671	6,115	18,214	8.3	3.0	9.0
Chile	1,248	7,253	10,882	14.6	10.3	15.5
Colombia	261	372	443	3.9	1.0	1.2
Costa Rica	15	312	2,064	1.1	2.0	15.3
Dominican Republic	35	42	112	3.9	0.6	1.6
Ecuador	70	102	385	2.5	0.6	2.1
El Salvador	6	19	7	1.1	0.4	0.2
Guatemala	28	113	32	2.0	1.5	0.4
Honduras	78	32	16	8.2	0.5	0.3
Mexico	1,610	2,046	2,045	5.4	0.7	0.7
Panama	2	5	46	0.6	0.4	4.0
Paraguay	3	82	23	0.3	1.6	0.4
Peru	430	1,942	4,251	12.9	6.9	15.3
Uruguay	21	120	618	1.2	1.8	9.2
Venezuela	550	158	5,573	3.4	0.1	4.7
Total	7,433	19,454	47,865	5.9	2.2	5.7

[a] Share of each Latin American country's total trade with Japan or China and regional totals. Regional totals are IMF's "Western Hemisphere" category.
[b] Includes Hong Kong and Macao when relevant.
Source: IMF (1991, 2009).

connection with the switch in diplomatic recognition mentioned above. For Japan in 1990, the other important beneficiary was Mexico, which has been one of the main losers with respect to China's entry into the region; Mexico's links with Japan have also contracted over the last two decades.

Table 9.3 shows complementary data on FDI stock for Japan and China. For China, the year is 2008. For Japan, the latest country disaggregation is for 2004; the table also shows data for 1994, when Japan was more active in the region. Again there are substantial inequalities for both, but Japan clearly has had much greater concentration in its investments—with Brazil accounting for nearly two-thirds in both 1994 and 2004.[9] Mexico, in turn, was the recipient of around 20 percent of Japanese investment in both years. Argentina, Chile, Peru, and Venezuela had much smaller amounts, and other countries had virtually none. China's investment concentrated on basically the same countries, but the distribution among them was more even.

Table 9.3. Latin American Recipients of Japanese and Chinese FDI Stock, 1994, 2004, 2008

Country	Amount ($ Million)			Share (%)[a]		
	Japan (1994)	Japan (2004)	China (2008)	Japan (1994)	Japan (2004)	China (2008)
Argentina	545	1,139	173	3.8	4.4	15.6
Bolivia	0	0	27	0	0.0	2.4
Brazil	8,849	16,095	217	62.3	62.0	19.6
Chile	430	778	58	3	3.0	5.2
Colombia	154	242	14	1.1	1.0	1.3
Costa Rica	75	79	0	0.5	0.3	0.0
Dominican Republic	3	3	0	0	0.0	0.0
Ecuador	17	17	87	0.1	0.1	7.9
El Salvador	36	52	0	0.3	0.2	0.0
Guatemala	9	9	0	0.1	0.0	0.0
Honduras	31	32	0	0.2	0.1	0.0
Mexico	2,793	5,818	173	19.7	22.4	15.6
Panama	21,784	33,787	67	na	na	na
Paraguay	36	84	5	0.3	0.3	0.5
Peru	701	785	194	4.9	3.0	17.5
Uruguay	31	37	2	0.2	0.1	0.2
Venezuela	494	770	156	3.5	3.0	14.1
Total	35,988	59,727	1,173			
Total without Panama	14,204	25,940	1,106	100.0	100.0	100.0

[a] Share of Japan or China's FDI to Latin America.
Sources: JETRO (2010); Chinese (PRC) Ministry of Commerce (2008).

A third way of comparing the costs and benefits of the Asia relationships is to look at the types of goods that Latin America exports to Japan and China. (Unfortunately no similar breakdown is available for FDI.) Table 9.4 shows that exports to Japan are somewhat more sophisticated than those to China. Around 70 percent of Latin America's exports to China are primary goods (agricultural products, minerals, or energy-related products), while only 50 percent of exports to Japan are so classified. This means that only 30 percent of goods going to China are industrial products, with processed natural resources accounting for two-thirds of the industrial category. Industrial exports to Japan are about evenly divided between natural-resource-intensive goods and low-technology items such as food, beverages, tobacco, textiles, apparel, shoes, and furniture. Durable consumer and capital goods are not a large component of exports to either country.

These data make clear that the heart of the economic relationship between Latin America and East Asia—both Japan and China—is the search for natural resources.[10] This is the main reason that certain countries have been the beneficiaries of growing

Table 9.4. Latin American Exports to Japan and China by Type of Good, 2008

Exports	Amount ($ Million)		Share (%)[a]	
	Japan	China	Japan	China
Primary goods	5,807	21,294	49.4	69.2
Agricultural products	1,537	9,723	13.1	31.6
Minerals	4,136	8,642	35.2	28.1
Oil, gas, and coal	136	2,929	1.1	9.5
Industrial goods	5,849	9,261	49.7	30.1
Traditional products	2,590	2,037	22.0	6.6
Food, drink, tobacco	2,212	1,055	18.8	3.4
Other traditional products	378	982	3.2	3.2
Natural-resource-intensive goods	2,434	5,437	20.7	17.7
Durable consumer goods, vehicles	299	218	2.5	0.7
Capital goods	526	1,569	4.5	5.1
Other goods	109	233	0.9	0.8
Total	11,765	30,787	100.0	100.0

[a] Share of Latin America's total exports to Japan and China.
Source: ECLAC (2009, annex table II.1.B).

trade ties. They are the ones that can provide the desired products, while the industrial exporters have been left behind. Mexico, in particular, has suffered from the China relationship since it exports minuscule amounts to China, while facing stiff competition from China in its own market and in the United States. Moreover, a number of assembly plants have moved from Mexico to Asia (Dussel Peters 2007; Gallagher and Porzecanski 2010, ch. 4). Central American countries have suffered from similar competition.

While China and Japan have similar trade and investment profiles, it is noteworthy that Japan has a greater concentration in the industrial sectors. This can be seen in both trade and investment. For example, more of Japan's investment is in Mexico, which is mainly an exporter of industrial goods. While systematic data on sectoral composition of investment are not available, we know that Japanese investment in Mexico is mostly in electronics and autos. Likewise, Japan has a more diversified set of economic relations with other countries. It has industrial investments in Brazil as well as investments in natural resources. Diversification is also found in other countries, both in terms of processing natural resources instead of sending raw materials and in importing light consumer goods.

As mentioned earlier, Latin American countries have two types of concerns with respect to the growing Asian ties. First is the more obvious one of unequal access. This relates both to countries that are left out, but also to sectors and even firms that are excluded from benefits. In this sense, it is not just Mexico and Central

America but also the industrial sector in commodity-exporting countries. Brazil's main industrial association (FIESP) has complained about the government's recognition of China as a market economy, which makes it harder to press dumping charges in the WTO. Industrialists in Chile and Argentina have lodged similar complaints as Chinese goods enter their markets in greater amounts. Unlike the situation with respect to Japan, Latin America is also concerned that it is losing FDI to China. The evidence is mixed (Devlin, Estevadeordal, and Rodríguez-Clare 2006, ch. 3; Lederman, Olarreaga, and Perry 2009, ch. 4).

The second preoccupation centers on natural resources and the implications for development in South America. The problems with commodity exports are well known—greater price volatility and (perhaps) a long-term deterioration in the terms of trade. At the same time, exchange rate movements and other aspects of the Dutch disease make it more difficult to build strong industries, which are considered preferable because of greater chances for employment and increased productivity.[11] Latin America fears returning to its nineteenth-century trade specialization—exporting raw materials and importing industrial goods.

It is interesting to contrast Latin America's trade with Asia and other regions. The pattern with Europe is similar to that with Asia—Latin America exports natural resources and imports industrial goods. Trade with the United States and the region itself is more concentrated on industrial goods. Over two-thirds of exports to the United States are industrial products, while three-quarters of exports to the rest of Latin America and the Caribbean are so classified. Of these, nearly 25 percent of exports to the United States are high-technology goods. These figures can be misleading, however, because of the role of Mexico. Mexico is the largest exporter in Latin America and sells the vast majority of its goods to the United States. Many of these goods are involved in U.S. production networks, including autos. When Mexico is excluded from the data, only 40 percent of Latin American exports to the United States are industrial goods—about the same share as for Japan, although more are of a medium or high-technology type (calculated from ECLAC 2009, annex tables II.1.B and II.2.B).

Finally, the issue of diversification needs to be mentioned. Less reliance on the United States has long been a goal of Latin America, even of Mexico. While it might be thought that Asian trade has played a positive role in this regard, the data indicate otherwise. Imports from Asia have certainly increased as a share of total Latin American imports, but this is not the difficult part of diversification. Export trends show that Asia has not helped. Indeed, the U.S. export share increased between 1990 and 2008, from 39 to 44 percent, while the European share dropped substantially, from 25 to only 13 percent. In the meantime, the share of exports going to Asia actually fell slightly—from 10.7 to 9.6 percent—because Japan's share was larger in 1990 than China's share is today (calculated from ECLAC 2009, annex table II.1.B).[12]

Foreign direct investment provides a somewhat different picture. The U.S. share of Latin America's total FDI has been declining steadily over the last two decades. It fell from 45 percent of the total in 1990 to 36 percent in 2000 to 21 percent in 2008.[13] Unfortunately, it is not easy to determine which countries were filling the gap. Best estimates are that Europe has increased its share; in particular, Spain was a major investor in the region in the 1990s and continued to invest in the 2000s. In addition, large Latin American ("trans-Latin") firms have become active investors, and most of their resources have been invested in neighboring countries.[14] Asian investment, by contrast, has not been an important force in the diversification away from the United States. Japanese FDI did not increase much in the 1990s—although it has picked up a bit recently. As we saw, official data on Chinese FDI show a very small amount in Latin America outside the tax havens, but recent investments and announcements of future plans suggest substantial increases. Although experience tells us that not all announcements materialize in concrete projects, China—and perhaps Japan—could become more important players in coming years.

4. CONCLUSIONS

Japan in the 1980s was very much like China today. It was an Asian power that was becoming a central global player. It was challenging the United States and Europe in their own markets and beginning to trade with and invest in developing regions with traditional ties to them. One of these areas was Latin America, which the United States has long considered an area of particular interest.

This chapter compares Japan and China in two ways. First, it explains the similar ways that each engaged with Latin America during the twentieth century and into the present. Second, it analyzes how they affected the United States and Latin America, asking who are the winners and losers at the international and regional level. This final section summarizes the main points made and finishes with a brief look forward to ask whether Asia will be an important part of Latin America's future.

Japan and China themselves are major international success stories, rising from humble recent beginnings—though boasting proud histories—to attain major economic and social achievements. In both cases the state played a powerful role in their rise, including the search for natural resources to feed their surging production systems. It was in this search that both came to Latin America. In both cases, it was the Asian countries that took the lead in their forays into the region.

Both Japan and China initially encountered Latin America through immigration, followed by trade and then investment. Until the early 2000s, Japanese trade was significantly larger than that of China, but in 2002 China took the lead and now accounts for more than double the exports and imports of Japan. Both, however, are dwarfed by the U.S. and European trade with the region. The characteristics of the trade relations are quite similar—both Japan and China mainly export industrial products and import raw materials. At the margin Japan imports more industrial goods than China does, which is important for Latin America.

Both countries have traditionally combined trade and foreign investment. This characteristic can be seen in the Asian region itself, and it has been repeated in Latin

America. Japan took this combination furthest in the 1970s with its "national projects" in areas such as iron ore and grain in Brazil, copper in Chile and Peru, and oil and salt in Mexico, but it also invested in the industrial sector—ships and steel in Brazil, electronics and autos in Mexico. China has yet to replicate these investments, relying instead on long-term contracts sometimes backed by loans. Nonetheless, China has recently announced investment projects involving natural resources and other sectors.

Some observers fear that the Asian entrée into Latin America could threaten U.S. interests in the region. There is no evidence thus far that this is the case. Indeed, it could be argued that both have helped by stabilizing Latin American economies in time of trouble when the United States could not—or would not—come to the rescue. Examples are the Japanese role in resolving the 1980s debt crisis and China's role in lifting Latin America out of recession in the late 1990s and early 2000s and in 2008–9. As mentioned, the United States remains the biggest trader and investor in Latin America as a whole and in most individual countries. European countries are the other major outside players, while Asia occupies a minor position thus far.

One of the main characteristics of both Japanese and Chinese trade and investment is that it has focused on a small group of commodity exporters. Japan also has strong relations with Mexico, which China lacks. Latin American countries are hesitant about the Chinese activities in the region—more so than they were about Japan in its heyday in the 1970s and 1980s—for two main reasons. One is that only a limited number of countries, sectors, and firms have benefited from China's trade and investment while others have suffered severe losses. The other is the fear of being returned to their nineteenth-century specialization of exporting raw materials and importing industrial goods, which they see as detrimental to their development prospects.

What is the future likely to hold with respect to East Asia's role in Latin America? In the case of Japan, its long-running economic crisis led it to withdraw from many of its Latin American activities in the 1990s. Its trade share fell and investment tailed off. In the last few years, however, it has become more active again—perhaps in light of the growing presence of its archrival, China. China, by contrast, engaged Latin America in a big way only in the 2000s, with its trade increasing more than tenfold in that decade and investment beginning to follow. Both countries are members of the IDB and hold permanent observer status at the OAS. Despite their economic interests in the region, however, both countries have been careful to avoid antagonizing the United States. Their bilateral U.S. relations are far more important to them than their relations with Latin America, and both economies are centered in the rapidly expanding Asian region. The most likely scenario is that this pattern will continue in the foreseeable future. Indeed, it is possible that the activism of the two Asian powers will renew U.S. interest in the region.

A central question is how Latin America will behave. Until now it has rarely taken the lead in seeking out Japan or China—with the exception of Hugo Chávez, who would like to form a political alliance with Beijing. There is little evidence that China is interested. What would be more beneficial for Latin American countries, as a number of observers have argued, is to develop a strategy to improve the quality of their economic relations with Asia—looking for ways to raise the value added in their trade and to induce the Asian countries to invest in sectors other than raw materials extraction. Whether this comes about will be an important determinant of the future development path of the region and its relations with Asia.

5. Further Reading

A number of general overviews of Latin America's relations with Japan and China provide extensive data and discussion of topics covered in this chapter. Country studies and individual articles are too numerous to include here, but some have been collected in the volumes mentioned below. With respect to Japan, there are only a few works since interest in that country never rose to the level that characterizes current hopes and fears about China. The leading examples are Moneta (1991), Purcell and Immerman (1992), and Stallings and Székely (1993). China has stimulated a far larger volume of studies. Jenkins (2010) provides an excellent review of many of them, classifying them into approaches that are positive, negative, and neutral about the impact of China's role in Latin America. Overviews include Funakashi and Loser (2005); Devlin, Estevadeordal, and Rodríguez-Clare (2006); Arnson, Mohr, and Roett (2007); Santiso (2007); ECLAC (2008); Roett and Paz (2008); Jenkins and Dussel Peters (2009); Lederman, Olarreaga, and Perry (2009); Gallagher and Porzecanski (2010); and ECLAC (2011).

NOTES

1. A colorful depiction of the difference between the two regions is Mortimore's notion of Asia's flying geese versus Latin America's sitting ducks (Mortimore 1993). Only in Mexico and, to a lesser extent, Central America has the United States incorporated its neighbors in a way similar to the pattern in East Asia.

2. The main instance in which Japan intervened politically in Latin America was when it felt its reputation was at stake and with the blessing of the United States. In 1992, Peruvian president Alberto Fujimori dissolved the Congress, and Japan took diplomatic steps to convince him to restore democratic rule (De la Flor 1993). Ten years later, Fujimori took refuge in Japan to avoid legal charges in Peru and was acknowledged as a Japanese citizen.

3. Endoh (2009) has a different interpretation, which views the Japanese emigrants as part of an informal empire.

4. The data on Japanese exports to Latin America are inflated by flag-of-convenience operations in Panama. This involves the sale of ships to Japanese companies based there, financed by investment that also inflates the FDI figures. To give an idea of the magnitude, 30 percent of Japanese exports to Latin America in 1990 went to Panama, while imports from Panama were only 1.2 percent (calculated from IMF 1991).

5. Even this figure may be inflated. The only way to get country-by-country data on Japanese FDI is the sum of reported intentions to invest. Thus the figure includes investment that did not materialize and excludes withdrawals, but it also excludes reinvested earnings.

6. During the U.S. slump in 2009, China became Brazil's largest export market.

7. Based on the International Monetary Fund's *Direction of Trade Statistics Yearbook* (2010), the total value of exports plus imports between China and Latin America in 2008 was about the same from both partners' perspectives, roughly US$150 billion. China's statistics indicate that both exports and imports were about $70 billion each, as shown in figure 9.1. Latin America's data, by contrast, show about US$50 billion of exports to China and US$100 billion of imports. Large discrepancies are also found at the individual country level. This is not unusual; for example, similar discrepancies are found in U.S.-China trade. Some portion of the difference is attributable to China's use of Hong Kong (and occasionally Macao) as an intermediary for some of its trade, but this is insufficient to resolve the discrepancy.

8. This does not mean that the United States and Japan agreed on everything, including development policy, but these disagreements were not allowed to get out of hand. See Stallings (1993) for case studies on U.S.-Japan relations in several issue areas with respect to the developing world.

9. I eliminate Panama for reasons mentioned in n. 4.

10. In Latin America, unlike Africa, the focus has been on minerals and agricultural products. Oil has not been a major product going to China or Japan. This is mainly because of transport costs and the fact that Venezuela's oil is a heavy variety that requires special kinds of refineries; see Palacios (2008) for more details.

11. Some of these fears about natural resource exports are overblown, or perhaps even wrong, but the perception remains that they are not good for the economy.

12. Intraregional exports increased from 16 to 19 percent, and those to "other" countries rose from 11 to 14 percent.

13. I calculated these shares by dividing U.S. FDI stock in Latin America (U.S. Department of Commerce 2010) by total Latin American FDI stock (UNCTAD 1990–2010) for the relevant years.

14. See ECLAC (2005) and subsequent issues of this publication for data and discussion of trans-Latin firms.

REFERENCES

Alden, Chris. 2007. *China in Africa*. London: Zed Books.

Arnson, Cynthia, Mark Mohr, and Riordan Roett. 2007. *Enter the Dragon? China's Presence in Latin America*. Washington, DC: Woodrow Wilson Center for Scholars.

Brautigam, Deborah. 2009. *The Dragon's Gift: The Real Story of China in Africa*. New York: Oxford University Press.

Castañeda, Jorge G. 2009. "Adios, Monroe Doctrine: When the Yanquis Go Home." *New Republic*, December 28. Available at http://www.tnr.com/print/article/world/adios-monroe-doctrine (accessed July 15, 2010).

Chinese (PRC) Ministry of Commerce. 2008. *Statistical Bulletin of China's Outward Foreign Direct Investment*, Available at http://hzs2.mofcom.gov.cn (accessed July 20, 2010).

De la Flor, Pablo. 1993. "Peruvian-Japanese Relations: The Frustration of Resource Diplomacy." In Stallings and Székely 1993, 171–90.

Devlin, Robert, Antoni Estevadeordal, and Andrés Rodríguez-Clare, eds. 2006. *The Emergence of China: Opportunities and Challenges for Latin America and the Caribbean.* Cambridge, MA: Harvard University Press for the David Rockefeller Center for Latin American Studies.

Downs, Erica. 2011. *Inside China, Inc: China Development Bank's Cross-Border Energy Deals.* Washington, DC: John L. Thornton China Center, Brookings Institution.

Dussel Peters, Enrique, ed. 2007. *Oportunidades en la relación económica y comercial entre China y México.* Mexico City: UNAM.

ECLAC (Economic Commission for Latin America and the Caribbean). 2005. *Foreign Investment in Latin America and the Caribbean.* Santiago: ECLAC.

———. 2008. *Economic and Trade Relations between Latin America and Asia-Pacific: The Link with China.* Santiago: ECLAC.

———. 2009. *Latin America and the Caribbean in the World Economy 2008–2009.* Santiago: ECLAC.

———. 2010. *Latin America and the Caribbean in the World Economy 2009–2010.* Santiago: ECLAC.

———. 2011. *People's Republic of China and Latin America and the Caribbean: Ushering in a New Era in the Economic and Trade Relationship.* Santiago: ECLAC.

Endoh, Toake. 2009. *Exporting Japan: Politics of Emigration toward Latin America.* Urbana: University of Illinois Press.

Funakashi, Tomoe, and Claudio Loser. 2005. *China's Rising Economic Presence in Latin America.* Washington, DC: Inter-American Dialogue.

Gallagher, Kevin P., and Roberto Porzecanski. 2010. *The Dragon in the Room: China and the Future of Latin American Industrialization.* Stanford, CA: Stanford University Press.

Hollerman, Leon. 1988. *Japan's Economic Strategy in Brazil: Challenge for the United States.* Lexington, MA: Lexington Books.

Horisaka, Kotaro. 1993. "Japan's Economic Relations with Latin America." In Stallings and Székely 1993, 49–76.

IMF (International Monetary Fund). 1990–2010. *Direction of Trade Statistics Yearbook.* Washington, DC: IMF.

Japanese Ministry of Foreign Affairs. 2010. *Japan-Brazil Relations.* Available at http://www.mofa.go.jp/region/latin/brazil/index.html (accessed August 11, 2010).

Jenkins, Rhys. 2010. China's Global Expansion and Latin America. *Journal of Latin American Studies* 42(4): 809–37.

Jenkins, Rhys, and Enrique Dussel Peters, eds. 2009. *China and Latin America: Economic Relations in the Twenty-first Century.* Bonn: Deutsches Institut für Entwicklungspolitik.

JETRO (Japan External Trade Relations Organization). 2010. *Japan's Outward FDI.* Available at http://www.jetro.go.jp/en/reports/statistics/data/rnfdi_01_e.xls (accessed July 12, 2010).

Jiang, Shixue. 2008. "The Chinese Foreign Policy Perspective." In Roett and Paz 2008, 27–43.

Kunimoto, Iyo. 1993. "Japanese Migration to Latin America." In Stallings and Székely 1993, 99–121.

Lederman, Daniel, Marcelo Olarreaga, and Guillermo E. Perry, eds. 2009. *China's and India's Challenge to Latin America: Opportunity or Threat?* Washington, DC: World Bank.

Lehman, Howard, ed. 2010. *Japan and Africa: Globalization and Foreign Aid in the 21st Century*. London: Routledge.

Look Lai, Walton. 2010. Asian Diasporas and Tropical Migration in the Age of Empire: A Comparative Overview. In *The Chinese in Latin America and the Caribbean*, edited by Walton Look Lai and Chee-Beng Tan, 35–63. Leiden: Koninklijke Brill NV.

Lumumba-Kasongo, Tukumbi. 2010. *Japan-Africa Relations*. Basingstoke: Palgrave Macmillan.

Masterson, Daniel M., with Sayaka Funada-Classen. 2003. *The Japanese in Latin America*. Urbana: University of Illinois Press.

Matsushita, Hiroshi. 1993. "Japanese Diplomacy toward Latin America after World War II." In Stallings and Székely 1993, 77–90.

Moneta, Carlos. 1991. *Japón y América Latina en los años noventa*. Buenos Aires: Planeta.

Mortimore, Michael. 1993. "Flying Geese or Sitting Ducks? Transnationals and Industry in Developing Countries." *CEPAL Review* 51: 15–34.

Muñoz, Heraldo. 1981. "The Strategic Dependency of the Centers and the Economic Importance of the Latin American Periphery." In *From Dependency to Development: Strategies to Overcome Underdevelopment and Inequality*, edited by Heraldo Muñoz, 59–92. Boulder, CO: Westview Press.

Palacios, Luisa. 2008. "Latin America as China's Energy Supplier." In Roett and Paz 2008, 170–89.

Purcell, Susan Kaufman, and Robert M. Immerman, eds. 1992. *Japan and Latin America in the New Global Order*. Boulder, CO: Lynne Rienner.

Roett, Riordan, and Guadalupe Paz, eds. 2008. *China's Expansion into the Western Hemisphere*. Washington, DC: Brookings Institution Press.

Rotberg, Robert I., ed. 2008. *China into Africa: Trade, Aid, and Influence*. Washington, DC: Brookings Institution Press.

Santiso, Javier, ed. 2007. *The Visible Hand of China in Latin America*. Paris: OECD Development Centre.

Slack, Edward R., Jr. 2010. "Sinifying New Spain: Cathay's Influence on Colonial Mexico." In *The Chinese in Latin America and the Caribbean*, edited by Walton Look Lai and Chee-Beng Tan, 7–31. Leiden: Koninklijke Brill NV.

Smith, Gaddis. 1994. *The Last Years of the Monroe Doctrine, 1945–1993*. New York: Hill and Wang.

Solís, Mireya. 2009. "Japan's Competitive FTA Strategy: Commercial Opportunity versus Political Rivalry." In *Competitive Regionalism: FTA Diffusion in the Pacific Rim*, edited by Mireya Solís, Barbara Stallings, and Saori N. Katada, 198–215. Basingstoke: Palgrave Macmillan.

Stallings, Barbara. 1990. "The Reluctant Giant: Japan and the Latin American Debt Crisis." *Journal of Latin American Studies* 22(1): 1–30.

———, ed. 1993. *Common Vision, Different Paths: The United States and Japan in the Developing World*. Washington, DC: Overseas Development Council.

———. 2009. "Latin America's View of China: Interest, but Scepticism." In *Development Models in Muslim Contexts: Chinese, 'Islamic' and Neo-liberal Alternatives*, edited by Robert Springborg, 26–46. Edinburgh: Edinburgh University Press.

Stallings, Barbara, and Gabriel Székely, eds. 1993. *Japan, the United States, and Latin America: Toward a Trilateral Relationship in the Western Hemisphere*. Baltimore: Johns Hopkins University Press.

Székely, Gabriel. 1993. "Mexico's International Strategy: Looking East and North." In Stallings and Székely 1993, 149–70.

Torres, Ernani. 1993. "Brazil-Japan Relations: From Fever to Chill." In Stallings and Székely 1993, 125–48.

Tsunekawa, Keiichi. 2010. "Japan Facing a New Latin America." *AJISS Commentary*, July 27. Available at http://www.worldsecuritynetwork.com/printArticle3.cfm?article_id=18358 (accessed August 11, 2011).

UNCTAD (United Nations Commission on Trade and Development). 1990–2010. *World Investment Report*. Geneva: UNCTAD.

U.S. Department of Commerce, Bureau of Economic Analysis. 2010. Balance of payments and direct investment position data, available at http://www.bea.gov/international/ii_web/timeseries2.cfm?econtypeid=1&dirlevel1id=1&Entitytypeid=1&stepnum=1 (accessed July 5, 2010).

Wilson, Maya. 2009. "China Courts Costa Rica; Expands Its Presence in Washington's Backyard." Council on Hemispheric Affairs, Washington, DC. Available at http://www.coha.org/china-courts-costa-rica-expands-its-presence-in-washington%E2%80%99s-backyard/(accessed July 20, 2010).

Xiang, Lanxin. 2008. "An Alternative Chinese view." In Roett and Paz 2008, 44–58.

CHAPTER 10

A CATALYST FOR HOPE: CHINA'S OPPORTUNITY FOR LATIN AMERICA

KEVIN P. GALLAGHER

1. Introduction

Although both China and Latin America and the Caribbean (LAC) have sought to reform their inward-looking economies and move toward integration into world markets for the last 30 years, the political economy of the two approaches is strikingly different. LAC nations to varying degrees deployed the infamous "Washington Consensus" that emphasizes the rapid liberalization of trade and investment regimes and the general reduction of the state in economic affairs. China has taken a more gradual and managed approach to globalization. To draw on the work of Albert Hirschman (1958, 1970a), the Chinese targeted "induced investments" into strategic areas that would not only help the nation export but also build domestic production capabilities.

In 1980, approximately when China and LAC began their reforms (1978 for China, 1982 for LAC), LAC's economic output was seven times that of China's and 14 times that of China in per capita terms. As table 10.1 shows, China's gross domestic product (GDP) has now surpassed LAC's, thanks to an impressive growth rate of 8 percent per annum, compared to 3.8 for LAC. Per capita income has grown 1.8 percent per annum on the LAC side—and has been very volatile and spotted with crises at that. In contrast, China has experienced a fairly steady increase in per capita income to the tune of 6.6 percent each year.

Table 10.1. Growth in China and LAC, 1980 to 2008

	LAC	China
GDP in 2008 (2000 US$, trillions)	2.6	2.7
GDP growth (%, 1980–2008)	3.8	8.1
GDP per capita in 2008 (PPP $2005)	9,758	5.515
Per capita growth (%, 1980–2008)	1.8	6.6

Source: World Bank 2010

China's impressive success in many ways has been good news for LAC, for it has provided a boost to primary commodities exports in Latin America and the Caribbean that has played a role in boosting economic growth in LAC both before and in the aftermath of the global financial crisis. At the same time, however, there have been signs that China's increasing ability to outcompete LAC in home and world markets in terms of manufactured goods may erode the level of diversity in the LAC export basket and threaten the region's growth prospects in the longer-run.

The rest of the chapter is divided into five sections. The second section discusses the positive impact of China's economic expansion on the commodity-driven boom in LAC. The third section examines the impact that China is having on the ability of LAC manufacturers to penetrate world manufacturing markets. Section 4 presents a brief overview of the different approaches to economic reform deployed in LAC and China. Section 5 begins a discussion regarding how all these factors may converge to affect the political economy of LAC's policies in years to come.

2. CHINA AND THE LATIN AMERICAN COMMODITIES BOOM

China's miraculous growth and development has benefited LAC. Especially since China's entry into the World Trade Organization in 2001, LAC has seen its exports in a handful of primary commodities sectors surge to China. China's demand for those commodities has also played a role in increasing the global prices of such commodities and has thus triggered a double boost to LAC exports that has not significantly declined in the wake of the global financial crisis.[1]

Before the crisis, Latin American growth was being fueled by a commodities export boom. On average, GDP growth in LAC increased by more than 3.4 percent per annum for a total of 21 percent in real terms between 2000 and 2008. Exports grew almost 12 percent each year and total export growth during the period was over 90 percent. Between 2000 and 2008 LAC exports to China grew by almost 400 percent, dwarfing the overall LAC export growth of 65 percent during the period. Between 2006 and 2008 alone, LAC exports to China continued to grow. Indeed, during that period they grew by 40 percent and reached US$72 billion dollars in 2008, close to 5 percent of LAC's total exports.

China's unprecedented economic growth and its entry into the World Trade Organization (WTO) in 2001 have had direct and indirect effects on LAC's export and growth performance. Direct effects result from bilateral LAC-China trade. Indirect effects result from China's overall demand for LAC's top products and the extent to which that demand drove up prices for those products. I address each in turn.

There is no doubt that China had a positive effect on LAC export growth during the boom. In terms of bilateral trade, however, the fanfare should be tempered. The large increase in LAC exports to China barely held ground in terms of total Chinese import shares, and trade to China represented a relatively small amount of total LAC exports. In addition, as we shall now see, only a handful of countries and sectors accounted for almost all of the LAC export surge to China.

The benefits of LAC-China trade were highly concentrated in a few countries and sectors. Previous calculations I have done showed that in 2006 just 10 sectors in six countries accounted for 74 percent of all LAC exports to China and 91 percent of all commodities exports to China. Indeed, products in the top five sectors—ores and concentrates of base metals (largely copper ores), soybeans, iron, crude petroleum, and copper alloys—constituted 60 percent of all exports to China and 75 percent of commodities exports to China (Gallagher and Porzecanski 2010). As table 10.2 shows, these trends intensified through 2008. By 2008, these 10 sectors produced 95 percent of all primary commodities exports to China, and 86 percent of all exports to China.

The third column shows the percentage of total LAC exports to China in a particular commodity from a particular country—for 2008. Looking at the first line then, for soybeans, Brazil (59%) and Argentina (40%) account for 99 percent of all LAC soybean exports to China. In 2006, a mere handful of countries accounted for LAC exports to China in these 10 commodities. By 2008, as table 10.2 shows, these trends only intensified. Not surprisingly, as these countries are among the largest in LAC, this table reveals that just six nations dominated the majority of LAC exports to China: Argentina, Brazil, Chile, Colombia, Mexico, and Peru. Four of the countries, Argentina, Brazil, Chile, and Peru, showed up as the most dominant exporters to China. Mexico and Colombia accounted for the majority of exports of nonferrous metal waste and scrap metal to China, but did not make a significant contribution to exports to China in any other sector. Other research has compared the exports of various LAC countries with the import potential of China and found that for countries and sectors other than those on this list, the potential to trade with China in the future is very low (Blázquez-Lidoy, Rodríguez, and Santiso 2006).

Table 10.2. Five Countries, Ten Sectors, Dominate LAC Trade to China

Sector	Share of Total LAC Exports to China (%)	Country (2008) (Country Share of LAC Exports to China in Sector, %)
Soybeans and other seeds	22.0	Brazil (59), Argentina (40)
Ores and concentrates of base metals	14.7	Chile (49), Peru (38)
Iron ore and concentrates	13.8	Brazil (87), Peru (5)
Copper alloys	12.8	Chile (96)
Crude petroleum	7.2	Brazil (58), Argentina (25)
Soybean oil and other oils	5.8	Argentina (62), Brazil (35)
Pulp and waste paper	3.6	Chile (51), Brazil (47)
Feedstuff	2.5	Peru (72), Chile (24)
Nonferrous base metal waste and scrap	2.1	Mexico (43), Chile (33)
Tobacco unmanufactured; tobacco refuse	1.0	Brazil (92), Argentina (8)
Total	85.6	

Finally, for the four major countries and sectors in table 10.3, I calculate the ratio of exports to China in a sector to a country's total exports in that sector for 2008. For some sectors exports to China were a very large part of a country's total exports in a sector and a large percentage of total LAC exports in that sector.

What stands out most is that 75 percent of all soybeans exported from Argentina were destined for China and that 48 percent of all soybeans exported from Brazil went to China as well. Of Brazil's iron exports, 30 percent went to China.

Indirectly, during the boom, increases in Chinese demand tightened supplies and raised global prices for many commodities, leading to a rise in exports. This drove up prices and increased overall demand for LAC goods (International Monetary Fund 2008; World Bank 2009). Gallagher and Porzecanski (2010) calculate the share of Chinese import growth as a percentage of world export growth in LAC's top 17 commodities sectors. For instance, Chinese imports accounted for 5.5 percent of the growth in crude petroleum exports between 2000 and 2006. In many sectors Chinese demand accounted for well over 10 percent of total world export growth during the period and on average it accounted for 17 percent of the rise in demand for LAC's top exports. As discussed earlier, base metals, copper, iron ore, soy, and pulp and paper are the core LAC exports to China. Chinese demand for global exports in these products was quite high, with 54 percent of the increase in world iron ore exports going to China, 57.8 percent of all soy, and more than 118.9 percent of pulp and paper.[2] In other words, indirectly through demand and subsequent

Table 10.3. Share of China Exports in Selected Countries and Sectors, 2008

Country, Sector	Exports to China in Sector (2005 US$)	% Total Country Exports in Sector
Argentina		
Crude petroleum	656,569,941	43
Soybeans and other seeds	3,275,256,691	75
Soybean oil and other oils	1,333,737,904	22
Brazil		
Soybeans and other seeds	4,831,263,424	48
Iron ore and concentrates	4,433,865,636	30
Crude petroleum	1,544,880,273	12
Pulp and waste paper	626,789,897	18
Tobacco unmanufactured; tobacco refuse	333,316,952	14
Chile		
Ores and concentrates of base metals	2,668,990,686	19
Copper alloys	4,477,391,748	21
Pulp and waste paper	674,451,270	28
Non-ferrous base metal waste and scrap	260,112,161	44
Peru		
Ores and concentrates of base metals	2,093,555,535	29
Feedstuff	672,012,544	49

price increases, China was indirectly responsible for much of Latin America's commodity export boom.

China's foreign direct investment (FDI) in the region mirrors the trends in trade. Given that China is demanding primary products on the import side, it should come as no surprise that FDI, with a few exceptions, tends to be drawn toward the same sectors in which China imports. Estimates of Chinese FDI into Latin America vary, but it has been at least US$10 billion between 2005 and 2010. Table 10.4 lists some of the major Chinese FDI projects in LAC during that period (the total exceeds $10 billion because many of the projects are multiyear and all the pledged funds have not been expended). As the table shows, the majority of FDI is in the copper, oil, and iron sectors.

One exception is the auto sector, where there are Chinese investments in both Uruguay and Mexico. In both these cases, Chinese auto firms are "market seeking" or "efficiency seeking." Chinese auto companies are in these two countries to serve the markets in these nations but also to serve as export platforms for their larger market neighbors.

Table 10.4. Large Project FDI in Latin America, 2005–10

Year	Month	Investor	Quantity (US$, Millions)	Share Size (%)	Partner/Target	Sector	Subsector	Country
2005	May	Minmetals				Metals		Cuba
2005	June	Minmetals	550		Codelco	Metals	Copper	Chile
2005	September	CNPC and Sinopec	1,400		Canada-based EnCana	Energy	Oil	Ecuador
2006	September	Sinopec	420		ONGC, Omimex of USA	Energy	Oil	Columbia
2007	February	Zijin Mining	186		Monterrico Metals	Metals	Copper	Peru
2007	June	Chalco	790		Canada-based Peru Copper	Metals	Copper	Peru
2007	June	Chery Auto	100			Transport	Autos	Uruguay
2007	December	Minmetals and Jiangxi Copper	450		Canada's Northern Peru Copper Metals		Copper	Peru
2008	May	Chinalco	2,150			Metals	Copper	Peru
2009	February	Shougang Group	1,000			Metals	Iron	Peru
2009	September	State Construction Engineering	100	2.75	Baha Mar Resort	Real estate	Tourism	Bahamas
2009	November	Wuhan Iron and Steel	400	22	MMX Mineracao	Metals	Iron	Brazil
2009	December	Shunde Rixin	1,900	70		Metals	Iron	Chile
2009	December	Hebei Zhongxin	400			Transport	Autos	Mexico
2010	March	State Grid	1,050		Quadra Mining	Metals	Copper	Chile
2010	March	East China Minerals (Jiangsu)	1,200		Itaminas	Metals	Iron	Brazil
2010	March	CNOOC	3,100	50	Bridas	Energy		Argentina

2010	April		CNPC	900		Energy	Oil	Venezuela
2010	Peru		China Sci-Tech	255		Chariot Resources	Metals	Copper	Peru
2010	May		State Grid	1,720		Cobra, Elecnor, and Isolux	Power		Brazil
2010	May		Sinochem	3,070	40	Peregrino Field	Energy	Oil	Brazil
2010	August		Chery Auto	700	100		Transport	Autos	Brazil
2010	September		Chongching Co	300			Real estate	Soy land	Brazil
2010	September		Sany Heavy Industry	100			Manufacturing	Metalworking	Brazil
	Total			$22,241					

Source: Scissors 2010; Sinolatin 2010; Ellis 2009; author interviews and newspaper research

3. Taking Away the Ladder? China and the Competitiveness of Latin American Manufacturing

As China creates new markets for LAC commodities, it is also putting strain on the ability of LAC manufacturers to compete with their Chinese counterparts in world markets. Based on measures of export similarity and market share, only a handful of countries presently compete with China: Argentina, Brazil, Chile, Colombia, Costa Rica, and Mexico. Of LAC's manufactures in these countries, 94 percent are threatened by China, representing 40 percent of all LAC exports. LAC manufactures are still growing, but at a slower pace and in sectors where China is rapidly increasing its global market share.

Over the past 25 years there has been significant growth in the world economy and that growth has been propelled by a surge in global manufacturing exports. The experiences of China and LAC did not deviate from that trend. Indeed they manifest it, and China's growth has been nothing short of extraordinary. The numbers on the right vertical axis of figure 10.1 depict the steep increase in world manufacturing exports from 1985 to 2006. The numbers of the left vertical axis juxtapose the experiences of China and LAC.

While in 1985 the size of the global manufacturing export market was approximately US$952 billion, in 2006 the market grew to more than $7 trillion—a 674 percent increase. Within that growing market, both Chinese and Latin American manufacturing exports also grew significantly, albeit in a completely different order of magnitude. In terms of volume, Chinese manufacturing exports grew even faster than world manufactures exports, by a factor of 24, between 1985 and 2006. LAC

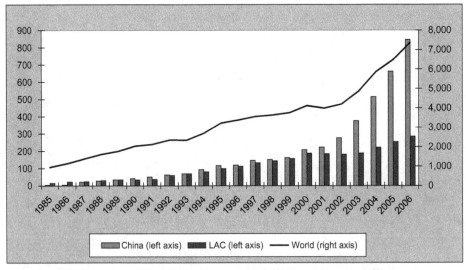

Figure 10.1. Manufacturing exports, billions of current dollars

exports also bucked the global trend by increasing by a factor of 13. Part of this difference, of course, is explained by the fact that in 1985 Latin American manufacturing exports were significantly higher than Chinese exports. In 1985 Latin America exported more than US$22 billion, but China exported only around $3.5 billion. However, that is only part of the picture.

3.1. Potential Impact: Comparisons of Export Structures

Most of the studies in the early part of the decade compared the export structures of China and LAC. The majority of these studies took a rather optimistic view about the relative competitiveness of China and LAC in manufacturing, with the exception of Mexico and some Central American countries. The nations of South America, in this view, exported a significantly different basket of goods to the world relative to China. Therefore the exports of China and LAC could be seen as complimentary rather than rival. However, more recent studies that use this approach have come to different conclusions.

The comparison of export structures entails examining "the statistical correlation between the export structures of China and LAC (higher correlation indicates greater potential for competition and rising correlations over time suggest that the potential is growing)" (Lall and Weiss 2005, 169). Lall and Weiss compare the export structures of countries in LAC with that of China. The only two countries whose export structure significantly correlates with China's are Mexico and Costa Rica (correlations are, respectively, 0.470 and 0.274.) All other countries' correlations are 0.068 or less (Lall and Weiss 2005, 187).

Again, comparisons of export structure are based on the assumption that similar export structures will suggest highest potential for competition. An earlier study depicts the consensus then on this issue:

> In general terms, the results suggest that there is no trade competition between China and Latin America. . . . [Moreover] this trade competition is even decreasing rather than increasing over the recent period of time. Not surprisingly, countries that export mainly commodities face lower competition (. . .) Paraguay, Venezuela, Bolivia, and Panama are those that exhibit the lowest figures among 34 selected economies, i.e. those are the countries that suffer less from Chinese trade competition. Brazil could be considered as an intermediate case between Mexico and Venezuela. (Blázquez-Lidoy, Rodríguez, and Santiso 2006, 22)

However, a more recent Inter-American Development Bank (IADB) study was the first to predict that the export structures of China and LAC may run into each other at some point. The IADB study found that over time the two areas' export profiles were beginning to converge and therefore fierce competition could ensue in the future: "As China and Latin America—and Mexico in particular—have converged toward increasingly similar export baskets, especially in manufacturing industries, direct competition has intensified" (Devlin, Estevadeordal, and Rodríguez -Clare 2006, 123). Very recent work compiled by the World Bank suggests that the IADB's predictions have come true, at least for some countries. Gordon Hanson and coauthor Raymond Robertson (2009) find that in Argentina, Brazil, Chile, and Mexico (LAC's main manufactures exporters), export capabilities were strong where China's were also strong. This suggests that the majority of LAC manufactures exports could potentially be under threat from China in both world and home markets. In summary, as the decade after China's accession to the WTO went on, and empirical research followed, China's potential threat seemed to be coming a real one.

Most importantly, however, the approach of comparing the export profiles of China and LAC has significant limitations, recent research has shown. Comparing export structure has been recently criticized in the peer-reviewed literature. Rhys Jenkins has a comprehensive analysis of such methodologies in the journal *World Economy* (2008). First, most analyses that compare export structures do not focus much on the period following China's accession to the WTO in 2001 nor the entrance into force of the WTO's Agreement on Textiles and Clothing in 2005. Second, indexes that look at export structure normally only do so at one time and therefore overlook changes in the competitive threat of a nation over time. Third, export structure indexes are weighted measures of the significance of the fit between two countries' exports—and thus they will underestimate the structure of a larger nation with a more diversified export base compared with smaller countries. For a more accurate picture, ample data are now available to examine actual levels of export penetration among China and LAC.

3.2. Competition in World Markets

In just over a quarter century, China went from insignificance to becoming the most competitive manufactures exporter in the world. At the same time most LAC nations stayed insignificant and those that gained some ground have struggled to maintain it. Only Mexico seems to be (somewhat) holding on.

Table 10.5 ranks the most competitive manufactures nations as measured by their share of total world manufactures exports from 1980 to 2006. In terms of relative competitiveness, a quick look at the evolution of China's competitive position in comparative perspective highlights how dramatic China's gains in manufacturing competitiveness have been (Gallagher and Porzecanski 2010). Chinese growth has driven China to the second position in terms of manufacturing exports (table 10.5 also shows the evolution of manufacturing exports for the United States and Germany, the other major players in the manufacturing export market). If Hong Kong is counted (and China certainly counts it!), China has leapfrogged to become the most competitive manufacturer in the world.

Since 1980, China has steadily captured an ever increasing share of world manufacturing exports. While in 1986 China's manufacturing exports represented only 0.4 percent of world manufacturing exports, by 2006, China had become second

Table 10.5. China: Taking Away the (Manufacturing) Ladder? (Percentage of World Manufacturing Exports)

1980	1985	1990	1995	2000	2006
17.0% Federal Republic of Germany	17.2% Japan	15.6% Federal Republic of Germany	15.6% USA	12.8% USA	14.5% Germany / 11.8%
15.4% USA	14.8% Federal Republic of Germany	13.0% USA	13.0% Japan	12.4% Japan	10.4% China / 11.5%
13.8% Japan	14.2% USA	12.8% Japan	12.8% Germany	12.2% Germany	10.2% USA / 10.2%
8.4% France	6.6% France	6.9% France	6.9% France	6.1% France	5.3% Japan / 7.5%
8.0% United Kingdom	6.4% Italy	6.6% Italy	6.6% Italy	5.8% China	5.0% France / 4.7%
7.0% Italy	6.1% United Kingdom	6.2% United Kingdom	6.2% United Kingdom	5.2% Italy	4.7% Italy / 4.4%
4.2% Belgium-Luxembourg	4.5% Canada	3.6% Belgium-Luxembourg	3.6% China, Hong Kong SAR	4.8% United Kingdom	4.6% United Kingdom / 4.1%
3.6% Netherlands	3.6% Belgium-Luxembourg	3.5% China, Hong Kong SAR	3.5% China	3.6% China, Hong Kong SAR	4.5% China, Hong Kong SAR / 4.0%
2.8% Canada	3.0% Netherlands	3.2% Netherlands	3.2% Republic of Korea	3.4% Canada	3.7% Republic of Korea / 3.7%
2.5% Switzerland	2.8% Republic of Korea	3.0% Canada	3.0% Belgium-Luxembourg	3.2% Republic of Korea	3.6% Belgium / 3.2%
2.4% Sweden	2.4% China, Hong Kong SAR	2.8% Republic of Korea	2.8% Canada	3.1% Mexico	3.3% Netherlands / 2.9%
2.0% China, Hong Kong SAR	2.2% Switzerland	2.3% Switzerland	2.3% Netherlands	3.0% Belgium	2.8% Singapore / 2.7%
1.8% Republic of Korea	2.1% Sweden	2.1% China	2.0% Singapore	2.9% Singapore	2.7% Canada / 2.5%

(continued)

Table 10.5. *(continued)*

1980		1985		1990		1995		2000		2006	
Austria	1.5%	1.5%	Spain	1.9%	Sweden	1.9%	Switzerland	2.0%	Netherlands	2.7%	Mexico	2.5%
Spain	1.5%	1.5%	Austria	1.8%	Spain	1.8%	Spain	1.9%	Spain	1.9%	Spain	1.9%
Poland	1.2%	1.2%	Singapore	1.7%	Singapore	1.7%	Mexico	1.8%	Malaysia	1.8%	Switzerland	1.6%
Denmark	1.0%	1.0%	Brazil	1.6%	Austria	1.6%	Malaysia	1.6%	Switzerland	1.5%	Malaysia	1.5%
Singapore	0.9%	0.9%	Denmark	0.9%	Denmark	0.9%	Sweden	1.6%	Sweden	1.4%	Sweden	1.4%
Finland	0.7%	0.7%	Finland	0.7%	Malaysia	0.7%	Austria	1.3%	Thailand	1.2%	Austria	1.3%
Norway	0.6%	0.6%	Czechoslovakia	0.7%	Brazil	0.7%	Thailand	1.2%	Ireland	1.1%	Thailand	1.2%
Ireland	0.4%	0.4%	Poland	0.6%	Finland	0.7%	Denmark	1.0%	Austria	1.0%	Czech Republic	1.0%
India	0.4%	0.4%	Ireland	0.6%	Ireland	0.7%	Ireland	0.8%	Philippines	0.8%	Poland	1.0%
Australia	0.4%	0.4%	Norway	0.5%	Thailand	0.6%	Finland	0.7%	Denmark	0.7%	Turkey	0.9%
Portugal	0.3%	0.3%	Turkey	0.5%	Portugal	0.6%	Brazil	0.6%	Indonesia	0.7%	Ireland	0.9%
South African Customs Union	0.3%	0.3%	Malaysia	0.4%	Czechoslovakia	0.5%	Portugal	0.5%	Finland	0.7%	India	0.8%
Malaysia	0.3%	0.3%	Portugal	0.4%	Mexico	0.5%	Indonesia	0.5%	Brazil	0.7%	Brazil	0.8%
Greece	0.2%	0.2%	India	0.4%	Yugoslavia	0.5%	India	0.5%	India	0.6%	Hungary	0.8%
Argentina	0.2%	0.2%	China	0.4%	India	0.4%	Czech Republic	0.5%	Hungary	0.6%	Denmark	0.7%
Thailand	0.2%	0.2%	Israel	0.3%	Norway	0.4%	Turkey	0.5%	Czech Republic	0.6%	Finland	0.7%
Philippines	0.1%	0.1%	Australia	0.3%	Turkey	0.4%	Poland	0.4%	Poland	0.5%	Russian Federation	0.6%
New Zealand	0.1%	0.1%	Thailand	0.2%	Poland	0.3%	Australia	0.4%	Turkey	0.5%	Philippines	0.5%
Hungary	0.1%	0.1%	Greece	0.2%	Australia	0.3%	Israel	0.3%	Russian Federation	0.5%	Indonesia	0.5%
Saudi Arabia	0.1%	0.1%	Pakistan	0.2%	Israel	0.3%	Norway	0.3%	Israel	0.4%	Slovakia	0.4%

Tunisia	0.1%	Argentina	0.2%	Indonesia	0.3%	South African Customs Union	0.3%	Portugal	0.4%	Portugal
China, Macao SAR	0.1%	Venezuela	0.1%	Pakistan	0.2%	Hungary	0.2%	Australia	0.3%	Ukraine
Colombia	0.1%	Philippines	0.1%	Romania	0.2%	Philippines	0.2%	South Africa	0.3%	Romania
Bangladesh	0.1%	Saudi Arabia	0.1%	Greece	0.2%	Pakistan	0.2%	Norway	0.2%	South Africa
Peru	0.1%	Indonesia	0.1%	Argentina	0.1%	Slovenia	0.2%	Slovakia	0.2%	Israel
Indonesia	0.0%	New Zealand	0.1%	Philippines	0.1%	Argentina	0.2%	Ukraine	0.2%	United Arab Emirates
Morocco	0.0%	China, Macao SAR	0.1%	Saudi Arabia	0.1%	Slovakia	0.2%	Pakistan	0.2%	Australia
Cyprus	0.0%	United Arab Emirates	0.1%	United Arab Emirates	0.1%	Romania	0.2%	Argentina	0.2%	Vietnam
New Caledonia	0.0%	Hungary	0.1%	Tunisia	0.1%	Greece	0.1%	Romania	0.2%	Norway
Kenya	0.0%	Bangladesh	0.1%	Morocco	0.1%	Saudi Arabia	0.1%	Slovenia	0.2%	Saudi Arabia
Sri Lanka	0.0%	Tunisia	0.1%	New Zealand	0.1%	Tunisia	0.1%	United Arab Emirates	0.1%	Slovenia
Syria	0.0%	Morocco	0.1%	China, Macao SAR	0.1%	Croatia	0.1%	Vietnam	0.1%	Pakistan
Mauritius	0.0%	Colombia	0.0%	Venezuela	0.1%	New Zealand	0.1%	Luxembourg	0.2%	Argentina
Trinidad and Tobago	0.0%	Uruguay	0.0%	Syria	0.1%	Colombia	0.1%	Greece	0.1%	Bangladesh
Iceland	0.0%	Mauritius	0.0%	Colombia	0.1%	Venezuela	0.1%	Belarus	0.1%	Greece
Jamaica	0.0%	Jordan	0.0%	Bangladesh	0.1%	Dominican Republic	0.1%	Morocco	0.1%	Luxembourg

(continued)

Table 10.5. (*continued*)

1980		1985		1990		1995		2000		2006	
Senegal	0.0%	Peru	0.0%	Egypt	0.1%	China, Macao SAR	0.1%	Tunisia	0.1%	Belarus	0.1%
Ecuador	0.0%	Zimbabwe	0.0%	Malta	0.0%	Morocco	0.1%	Saudi Arabia	0.1%	Tunisia	0.1%
Algeria	0.0%	Cyprus	0.0%	Sri Lanka	0.0%	Malta	0.1%	Colombia	0.1%	Colombia	0.1%
Malawi	0.0%	Trinidad and Tobago	0.0%	Mauritius	0.0%	Kazakhstan	0.0%	Costa Rica	0.1%	Lithuania	0.1%
Cameroon	0.0%	Oman	0.0%	Uruguay	0.0%	Lithuania	0.0%	New Zealand	0.1%	Bulgaria	0.1%
Bolivia	0.0%	Cote d'Ivoire	0.0%	Peru	0.0%	Egypt	0.0%	Croatia	0.1%	Morocco	0.1%
Fiji	0.0%	Syria	0.0%	Qatar	0.0%	Chile	0.0%	Bulgaria	0.1%	Croatia	0.1%
Madagascar	0.0%	Barbados	0.0%	Cyprus	0.0%	Mauritius	0.0%	China, Macao SAR	0.1%	Estonia	0.1%
French Polynesia	0.0%	Egypt	0.0%	Chile	0.0%	Estonia	0.0%	Estonia	0.1%	New Zealand	0.1%
Faeroe Islands	0.0%	Libya	0.0%	Jordan	0.0%	Uruguay	0.0%	Malta	0.1%	Iran	0.1%
Togo	0.0%	Chile	0.0%	Zimbabwe	0.0%	Jordan	0.0%	Venezuela	0.1%	Costa Rica	0.1%
Martinique	0.0%	Jamaica	0.0%	Trinidad and Tobago	0.0%	Oman	0.0%	Lithuania	0.1%	Kazakhstan	0.1%
Niger	0.0%	Kenya	0.0%	Kuwait	0.0%	Syria	0.0%	Chile	0.0%	Chile	0.1%
Liberia	0.0%	Iceland	0.0%	Costa Rica	0.0%	TFYR of Macedonia	0.0%	Iran	0.0%	Serbia	0.0%
Yemen	0.0%	Nepal	0.0%	Oman	0.0%	Latvia	0.0%	Egypt	0.0%	Syria	0.0%
Guadeloupe	0.0%	Algeria	0.0%	Kenya	0.0%	Peru	0.0%	Kazakhstan	0.0%	Jordan	0.0%
Reunion	0.0%	Madagascar	0.0%	Algeria	0.0%	Zimbabwe	0.0%	Oman	0.0%	Latvia	0.0%
Burkina Faso	0.0%	Fiji	0.0%	Guatemala	0.0%	Qatar	0.0%	Mauritius	0.0%	Venezuela	0.0%
French Guiana	0.0%	Martinique	0.0%	Libya	0.0%	Costa Rica	0.0%	Kuwait	0.0%	Qatar	0.0%

Congo	0.0%	Congo	0.0%	Jamaica	0.0%	Bahrain	0.0%	Cambodia	0.0%	Malta	0.0%
Greenland	0.0%	Saint Lucia	0.0%	El Salvador	0.0%	Cyprus	0.0%	Peru	0.0%	Egypt	0.0%
Mali	0.0%	Malawi	0.0%	Nepal	0.0%	Kuwait	0.0%	Uruguay	0.0%	Peru	0.0%
Angola	0.0%	Ecuador	0.0%	Haiti	0.0%	Guatemala	0.0%	TFYR of Macedonia	0.0%	China, Macao SAR	0.0%
Ethiopia	0.0%	Guadeloupe	0.0%	Fiji	0.0%	Cote d'Ivoire	0.0%	Serbia and Montenegro	0.0%	Trinidad and Tobago	0.0%
Samoa	0.0%	Papua New Guinea	0.0%	Iceland	0.0%	Kenya	0.0%	Qatar	0.0%	Bosnia Herzegovina	0.0%
Seychelles	0.0%	Dominica	0.0%	Cameroon	0.0%	El Salvador	0.0%	Jordan	0.0%	TFYR of Macedonia	0.0%
Cape Verde	0.0%	Reunion	0.0%	Senegal	0.0%	Trinidad and Tobago	0.0%	Trinidad and Tobago	0.0%	Mauritius	0.0%
Cayman Islands	0.0%	Faeroe Islands	0.0%	Papua New Guinea	0.0%	Nepal	0.0%	Latvia	0.0%	Cote d'Ivoire	0.0%
Central African Republic	0.0%	Paraguay	0.0%	Barbados	0.0%	Ecuador	0.0%	Guatemala	0.0%	Oman	0.0%
Vanuatu	0.0%	French Guiana	0.0%	Paraguay	0.0%	Jamaica	0.0%	El Salvador	0.0%	Zimbabwe	0.0%
		Greenland	0.0%	Panama	0.0%	Iceland	0.0%	Bahrain	0.0%	Uruguay	0.0%
		Bolivia	0.0%	Martinique	0.0%	Algeria	0.0%	Zimbabwe	0.0%	Kenya	0.0%
		Seychelles	0.0%	Brunei Darussalam	0.0%	Bolivia	0.0%	Nepal	0.0%	Guatemala	0.0%
		Ethiopia	0.0%	Ecuador	0.0%	Republic of Moldova	0.0%	Madagascar	0.0%	Ecuador	0.0%

(continued)

Table 10.5. (continued)

1980	1985	1990	1995	2000	2006
	Grenada 0.0%	Saint Lucia 0.0%	Kyrgyzstan 0.0%	Cote d'Ivoire 0.0%	Nigeria 0.0%
	Kiribati 0.0%	Madagascar 0.0%	Senegal 0.0%	New Caledonia 0.0%	Cyprus 0.0%
	Niue 0.0%	Honduras 0.0%	Paraguay 0.0%	Cyprus 0.0%	Bahrain 0.0%
		Bolivia 0	Barbados 0	Bolivia 0.0%	El Salvador 0.0%
		Faeroe Islands 0	Panama 0	Syria 0.0%	New Caledonia 0.0%
		Reunion 0	Nicaragua 0	Lebanon 0.0%	Cuba 0.0%
		Malawi 0	French Guiana 0	Ecuador 0.0%	Iceland 0.0%
		Guadeloupe 0	Cameroon 0	Lesotho 0.0%	Albania 0.0%
		French Guiana 0	Guadeloupe 0	Swaziland 0.0%	Honduras 0.0%
		Nicaragua 0	Bahamas 0	Bahamas 0.0%	Republic of Moldova 0.0%
		Dominica 0	Zambia 0	Kenya 0.0%	Swaziland 0.0%
		Togo 0	Togo 0	Iceland 0.0%	Ghana 0.0%
		Seychelles 0	Ethiopia 0	Jamaica 0.0%	Georgia 0.0%
		Ethiopia 0	Honduras 0	Albania 0.0%	Bolivia 0.0%
		Grenada 0	Martinique 0	Fiji 0.0%	Madagascar 0.0%
		Mali 0	Saint Lucia 0	Botswana 0.0%	Azerbaijan 0.0%
		Greenland 0	Sudan 0	Algeria 0.0%	Namibia 0.0%
		Suriname 0	Reunion 0	Turkmenistan 0.0%	Zambia 0.0%
		Djibouti 0	Niger 0	Republic of Moldova 0.0%	Armenia 0.0%
		Vanuatu 0	Malawi 0	Zambia 0.0%	Senegal 0.0%
		Samoa 0	Andorra 0	Paraguay 0.0%	Botswana 0.0%
			Yemen 0	Honduras 0.0%	Algeria 0.0%

Madagascar	0.0%	Cuba	0.0%	Paraguay	0.0%
Belize	0.0%	Sudan	0.0%	Brunei Darussalam	0.0%
Uganda	0.0%	Mongolia	0.0%	Bahamas	0.0%
Dominica	0.0%	Barbados	0.0%	United Republic of Tanzania	0.0%
Benin	0.0%	Senegal	0.0%	Yemen	0.0%
Haiti	0.0%	Panama	0.0%	Kyrgyzstan	0.0%
Cape Verde	0.0%	Azerbaijan	0.0%	Barbados	0.0%
Mozambique	0.0%	Georgia	0.0%	Occupied Palestinian Territories	0.0%
Guinea	0.0%	Niger	0.0%	Uganda	0.0%
Burkina Faso	0.0%	Namibia	0.0%	Mongolia	0.0%
Central African Republic	0.0%	Ghana	0.0%	Fiji	0.0%
Maldives	0.0%	Tajikistan	0.0%	Jamaica	0.0%
Congo	0.0%	Kyrgyzstan	0.0%	Gabon	0.0%
Saint Vincent and the Grenadines	0.0%	Armenia	0.0%	Mozambique	0.0%
Saint Kitts and Nevis	0.0%	Papua New Guinea	0.0%	Burundi	0.0%
Mauritania	0.0%	Nigeria	0.0%	Panama	0.0%
Suriname	0.0%	Grenada	0.0%	Andorra	0.0%

(continued)

Table 10.5. *(continued)*

1980	1985	1990	1995	2000	2006
			Gambia 0.0%	French Polynesia 0.0%	Malawi 0.0%
			Aruba 0.0%	Ethiopia 0.0%	Sudan 0.0%
			Grenada 0.0%	United Republic of Tanzania 0.0%	Ethiopia 0.0%
			Seychelles 0.0%	Nicaragua 0.0%	Nicaragua 0.0%
			Burundi 0.0%	Maldives 0.0%	Aruba 0.0%
			Greenland 0.0%	Malawi 0.0%	
			Guinea-Bissau 0.0%	Andorra 0.0%	
			Comoros 0.0%	Yemen 0.0%	
			Kiribati 0.0%	Guyana 0.0%	
				Cameroon 0.0%	
				Dominica 0.0%	
				Burkina Faso 0.0%	
				Togo 0.0%	
				Aruba 0.0%	
				Belize 0.0%	
				Saint Kitts and Nevis 0.0%	
				Mozambique 0.0%	
				Cape Verde 0.0%	
				Gabon 0.0%	
				Mali 0.0%	
				Uganda 0.0%	

Country	Percentage
Antigua and Barbuda	0.0%
Suriname	0.0%
Saint Lucia	0.0%
Saint Vincent and the Grenadines	0.0%
Benin	0.0%
Guinea	0.0%
Turks and Caicos Islands	0.0%
Greenland	0.0%
Eritrea	0.0%
Central African Republic	0.0%
Anguilla	0.0%
Gambia	0.0%
Vanuatu	0.0%
Montserrat	0.0%
Tonga	0.0%
Cook Islands	0.0%
Comoros	0.0%
Burundi	0.0%
Sao Tome and Principe	0.0%

Table 10.6. Exports to the World, Percentage Threatened

	Direct Threat (%)	Partial Threat (%)	Total (%)
Argentina			
As % of manufacturing exports in 2006	37	59	96
As % of all exports in 2006	10	16	27
Brazil			
As % of manufacturing exports in 2006	20	70	91
As % of all exports in 2006	9	30	39
Chile			
As % of manufacturing exports in 2006	29	53	82
As % of all exports in 2006	2	4	5
Colombia			
As % of manufacturing exports in 2006	15	66	81
As % of all exports in 2006	5	20	25
Costa Rica			
As % of manufacturing exports in 2006	36	60	96
As % of all exports in 2006	22	36	58
Mexico			
As % of manufacturing exports in 2006	70	28	99
As % of all exports in 2006	52	21	72
LAC			
As % of manufacturing exports in 2006	62	31	94
As % of all exports in 2006	27	14	40

only to Germany as an exporter of manufactures, with 11.5 percent of world manufacturing exports. Argentina and Brazil have somewhat maintained a small share of world manufacturing exports (around 1 percent for Brazil, 0.2 percent for Argentina) but have fallen down the export ladder as other countries have gained market share. Mexico, on the other hand, succeeded in increasing its share and climbing up the export ladder (going from 0.5 percent of world manufacturing exports in 1990 to 3.3 percent in 2000). Since 2000, however, Mexico's share and position as a manufacturing exporter have begun to erode again (reaching 2.5 percent of world manufacturing exports in 2006.)

How have Latin American countries fared in term of China's threat in the world, when unprotected by proximity and a web of preferential trade agreements? Not that well. Table 10.6 shows calculations of the percentage of all world exports under threat from China by country. For LAC as a whole, we find that 62 percent of manufacturing exports fall under Lall's definition of a direct threat, and over 31 percent fall under a partial threat. Thus, those manufacturing exports under threat represent 94 percent of all LAC's manufacturing exports and *40 percent of all LAC exports in 2006*, and add up to more than US$260 billion.

For the largest manufacturers in the region, the threat level in world markets is significantly higher than the threat level in LAC markets, which I look at in detail in the next section. Consistent with the literature on the subject, the situation for Mexico is the most grave (and thus discussed in depth in the next section). In fact, 99 percent of Mexico's manufacturing exports are under threat from China, representing 72 percent of Mexico's entire exports. In addition, 96 percent of Costa Rica's exports are under threat, or 58 percent of all Costa Rica's exports. Brazil and Argentina also see over 90 percent of their manufactures exports under threat, but those exports under threat represent less than the LAC average with 39 and 27 percent respectively.

How has Latin America fared after the crisis? One region that has received relatively little attention is Central America. For years these countries have been working to hook their economies to the U.S. market, with a particular emphasis on clothing and apparel exports. Beginning in the 1980s, most Central American nations set up export processing zones that export textiles and clothing to the United States. By 2001, 87 percent of all El Salvadoran exports to the United States were from such zones. For Honduras, the figure was78 percent, and Guatemala and Nicaragua each export 63 percent of their exports to the United States were from export processing zones.

The capstone of such efforts was the Central American Free Trade Agreement between the United States, Central American nations (excluding Panama), and the Dominican Republic (CAFTA, for short). CAFTA, by lowering tariffs and locking in access to the U.S. economy, was supposed to solidify Central America as a clothing hub. Then China crashed the party.

In 2001, both China and Central America sold approximately US$6.5 billion worth of clothing exports to the United States, with each holding approximately 12 percent of the U.S. market for clothing. In 2004, the year before CAFTA went into effect and after China's WTO entry was in full swing, Central American exports to the United States reached $7.5 billion and China's were still in the same order of magnitude at $10.7 billion.

Yet as figure 10.2 shows, since CAFTA went into effect, Central American exports of clothing to the United States have fallen by 25 percent. How could this happen? Clothing exports to the United States from Central America in 2009 were down from US$7.5 billion in 2004 to $5.6 billion but China's were up to $24.3 billion—a 127 percent increase for China since 2004. The Central American share of U.S. clothing imports has declined to 8.7 percent. China now holds 38 percent of the U.S. import market for clothing.

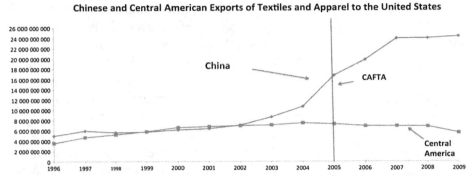

Figure 10.2 Chinese and Central American Exports of Textiles and Apparel to the United states.

4. TWO GLOBALIZATIONS

Like LAC, China embarked on a process of economic reform over a quarter of a century ago. Like LAC, it has sought to shift away from a focus on domestic markets to an embrace of the world economy. Nevertheless, China's industrial development is very different from LAC's in two important ways. The LAC reforms are discussed at length in other parts of this volume, but to varying degrees have been infamously described as following a "Washington Consensus" that focuses on a rapid liberalization of trade and investment regimes and a general reduction of the role of the state in economic affairs (Williamson 1990). First, in contrast to LAC, China has taken a more gradual and experimental approach to integration. Second, alongside reforms, China continued a parallel set of targeted government policies to support and nurture industrial development.

In a somewhat similar fashion to LAC, China underwent a period of state-led industrialization from the late 1940s until 1978. This period has been referred to as the period of "Big Push Industrialization." Similar to the period of import-substituting industrialization in LAC, during the Big Push China's goal was to move toward rapid industrialization through import substitution. The basic strategy was to invest in the strategic industries identified by government decision makers. Integration with the global economy was extraordinarily low (Naughton 2007).

Of the targeted industries, 80 percent were "heavy" industries, such as steel, which were linked with coal, iron ore, machinery, and other sectors. A number of other industries such as chemical fertilizers, motor vehicles, and electric generating equipment were also among those created by the government. Almost all of these industries became dominated by state-owned enterprise (SOEs) and the planners assigned them production targets and prices. The government also allocated the labor force to industrial firms. Viewed through one lens, this effort was successful, as it created the industrial base of the country. From 1952 to 1978, industrial output grew at an annual rate of 11.5 percent and the share of industrial sector in GDP increased from 14 to 44 percent while the share of agriculture fell from 51 to 28 percent (Naughton 2007).

These policies also involved some shortcomings. First and foremost, the focus on industrialization neglected the growth of household consumption and the development of the countryside. Whereas capital formation grew at more than 10 percent per year from 1952 to 1978, private consumption grew only 4.3 percent annually. Employment generation was also low, given the capital-intensive nature of the main targeted industries. Perhaps the gravest shortcoming was the lack of technological capabilities of the targeted firms. Further, human capital formation did not expand enough for these sectors to become efficient and competitive internationally (Naughton 2007).

Whereas LAC roughly started its reform period following the oil crisis in 1982, Chinese economic reforms started in 1978, two years after the death of Mao Zedong. In this year, China embarked on a program of economic reform aiming at strategic integration into the world economy by following a "dual track" policy. The policy consisted of liberalizing FDI and inflow of imported inputs to selected industries while buttressing those sectors to the point of maturity and nurturing other sectors until they were ready to face competition with imports. From a theoretical perspective, such an approach is quite analogous to the work of Albert O. Hirschman, who stressed the need to find "induced investments," defined as those that trigger net beneficiaries of external economies: backward and forward linkages (Hirschman 1958). Since then, according to the literature, China's industrial strategy has been three-pronged. First, government policy aimed at creating endogenous productive capacity, in the form of targeting specific industries through state ownership (i.e., SOEs) or government support, paying increasing attention to science and technology policy, and linking the SOEs with the private sector and research institutes. Second, and a very important factor, Chinese support for domestic industry has always had an eye on markets outside China. China has also gradually and strategically integrated into world markets in order to gain access to technology, finance, and world markets.

Third, in undertaking economic reform, China's new leaders followed an experimental approach. Free trade and a market-based economy could be seen as an end in itself in the case of LAC; it was taken for granted that such a transition by itself would enhance learning through trade and lead to the deepening of industrialization and promotion of growth. By contrast, Chinese policy was based on using the market and trade as a means to development. Hence, in the eyes of Chinese policy-makers, market and government policies were to supplement each other while the weight of each would change as the economy would develop.

> It was never conceivable to Chinese policy-makers that their economy would postpone economic development until after an interlude of system transformation. It was always assumed that system transformation would have to take place concurrently with economic development, and indeed that the process of economic development would drive market transition forward and guarantee its eventual success. Individual reform policies were frequently judged on the basis of their contribution to economic growth (rather than to transition as such). In the beginning the approach was followed because reformers literally did not know where they were going: they were reforming "without a blueprint" and

merely seeking ways to ameliorate the obvious serious problems of the planned economy. But even after the goal of a market economy gradually gained ascendance in the minds of reformers, it was not anticipated that market transition would be completed until the economy reached at least middle-income status. And in fact, that is exactly what eventually happened. (Naughton 2007, 86)

China's gradual and experimental approach to reform allowed for the development of domestic firms and industries before liberalizing fully. More importantly, it also created an environment so that the potential "losers" from liberalization would be less numerous (Naughton 2007).

Deng Xiaoping referred to this strategy characterized as gradual and dual track as "*mozhe shitou guo he* (crossing the river by feeling the stones)" (Sweetman and Zhang 2009, 45). Until 1984, LAC's industrial policy was geared to intervene strongly in specific sectors. Since then, the policy has been to let markets largely determine the profile of manufacturing and exports. As Mesquita Moreira puts it:

> from LAC manufacturer's point of view, the omnipresence and generosity of the Chinese state has a very practical and immediate implication, that is to heavily tilt the playing field in favor of their Chinese competitors, either local or foreign affiliates, in a scenario where they already face endowment, productivity and scale disadvantages. (Mesquita Moreira 2007, 365)

Again, LAC reform is discussed in far greater detail elsewhere in this volume and can only receive limited attention here. All that can be noted here is that is that LAC manufacturing during the reform period has been hindered by at least three factors: the past, market failure, and policy space.

In terms of the past, during the import-substituting industrialization period in LAC, the region had built and supported numerous manufacturing industries. Many of the firms within those industries were extremely inefficient by global standards. What is more, the process of industrial policy was (and is) a costly one. The crises in the region when reforms originated made it virtually impossible to secure financing for the industrial policies that were in place. Taken together, the combination of the fairly weak performance of industrial policy and the lack of funds to support it made thinking about industrialization much less in fashion during the reform period.

From an "ideas" or even ideological perspective, the new focus of the LAC policymaker was naturally (given the previous emphasis on the state) that markets rule and dismantling the state's role in economic affairs was of paramount importance. However, the liberalization period was rife with market failure that did not work in LAC's favor.

As Hirschman (1970b, 2) argued "there are the well-known, large realms of monopoly, oligopoly, and monopolistic competition: deterioration in performance of firms operating in that part of the economy could result in more or less permanent pockets of inefficiency and neglect." In places such as Mexico, scholars have shown how trade and investment liberalization in the presence of global oligopolies crowded out domestic investment and productive capabilities, leading to what Hirschman (1958) referred to as "enclave export industries." Before liberalization,

Mexico was seen as having what Hirschman called the "minimum economic size" necessary to be a beneficiary, defined as securing profit and competing with foreign firms (Hirschman 1958; Wilson 1992). Unfortunately, domestic industries have largely been wiped out in key manufacturing export sectors, leaving behind "enclave economies" (Gallagher and Zarsky 2007).

Third, even if LAC nations were able to overcome the stigma of the past and have the necessary institutions to deal with market failure, most LAC nations have signed trade and investment agreements that run much deeper than the commitments under the WTO. Whereas under the WTO, nations have the "policy space" to, for instance, require joint ventures between foreign and domestic firms in order to transfer technology and foster technological learning, most of the free trade agreements and bilateral investment treaties signed by LAC governments do not permit such policy space (Thrasher and Gallagher 2010).

Even more fiercely debated than the role of industrial policy is the role of Chinese macroeconomic policy in increasing competitiveness. China has infamously adopted a managed approach to monetary and exchange policies where the yuan is pegged to the dollar and coupled with capital controls to grant the country independent monetary policies. Chinese economists have shown that China's capital controls have not only been effective in maintaining financial stability before and during the global financial crisis, but they will also be essential to help China loosen its hold on the exchange rate over time (Yu 2008; Yongzhong 2010).

Mexico has been able to tame inflation in the past decade, yet that success has come at the cost of exchange rate appreciation relative to China. Before the crisis hit, China's yuan was pegged at a low rate to the dollar but Mexico's exchange rate has been persistently overvalued against the dollar and therefore the yuan. This further accentuates the tendency to import inputs but also hampers Mexico's competitiveness with China (Gallagher and Zarsky 2007; World Bank 2010). In the aftermath of the financial crisis, Mexico suffered a collapse of the peso and the competitive pressure with the yuan was put on temporary hold. However, massive inflows of capital to countries like Brazil, for example, led to 30 percent appreciation of the real versus the yuan in 2009–10. In June 2010 the Chinese went back to a gradual appreciation of the exchange rate that is analogous to its appreciation from 2005 to 2008 (roughly 3 percent per year) so it remains to be seen how relative exchange rates will affect competitiveness in years to come.

6. Conclusions

This chapter has provided a brief overview of the positive impact of China's rise on LAC and of some areas of concern. Further research on the extent to which exchange rate policy, industrial policy, tariff liberalization, and other policies have improved China's competitiveness vis-a-vis LAC is needed. At this point, however, it is clear that China seems to be driving up demand for primary products from LAC on the one hand, and eroding LAC's ability to compete for manufacturing in world markets on the other. In the longer run, these twin trends could put LAC back to the conditions of the nineteenth century.

LAC will have to overcome some significant political economy issues as future relations unfold. First, the region will have to balance the new "winners and losers" of trade with China. China's demand accentuates the rising power of commodities exporters in LAC and also accentuates the struggles of domestic manufacturing producers as well. Given that economy-wide effects of commodities exporting are smaller than manufacturing, such trends could heighten political tensions. Take soybeans in Brazil, for instance. As shown earlier in the chapter, China's demand accounts for over half of all Brazil's soybean production. Between 1995 and 2009 Brazil's soy production increased by a factor of four while employment decreased by 75 percent as the sector became highly mechanized. Moreover, increased demand since 1995 has caused 528,000 square kilometers of deforestation in the Brazilian Amazon. Such trends have given voice to and sparked labor organizations and national and global environmental organizations to mobilize around the social consequences of expanded production (Pérez, Schlesinger, and Wise 2009; Wise 2009).

On the manufacturing end, increased pressure from China in home and world markets has already begun to be felt. Bowing to local political pressure, in 2010 Argentina placed temporary restrictions on Chinese light manufacturing imports. China quickly retaliated by halting soybean imports from Argentina (citing other reasons). As shown earlier in the chapter, exports of soy to China represent over 75 percent of all Argentina's soy exports. The Chinese counterrestrictions not only have caused economic harm but have pitted manufacturing against agricultural interests.

In a nutshell, China's rise has brought significant benefit to LAC, but has posed new risks as well. It remains to be seen whether the region can harness some of the benefits to mitigate some of the costs of these dramatic changes in the LAC-China relationship. Rather than scapegoating China, the region would do well to learn from China's rather different model of globalization. To draw a last analogy to Hirschman, China can be a "catalyst for hope" in LAC.

NOTES

1. For the majority of the calculations in this chapter, I use trade data from the United Nations Statistics Division's "Commodity Trade Statistics Database," or COMTRADE (United Nations Statistics Division 2009). I download data at the three-digit level (SITC Rev. 2) and classify it using Sanjaya Lall's "Technological Classification of Exports" developed in Lall (2000).

2. The reason why the percentage of pulp and paper can exceed 100 is that my analysis actually divides the *change* in Chinese import demand by the *change* in world exports. Even though Chinese imports could never exceed world exports, in some cases

the growth in Chinese imports exceeds the growth in world exports, as a result of a reduction of imports in other markets.

REFERENCES

Blázquez-Lidoy, Jorge, Javier Rodríguez, and Javier Santiso. 2006. "Angel or Demon? China's Trade Impact on Latin American Countries." *CEPAL Review* 90: 15–41.

Devlin, Robert, Antoni Estevadeordal, and Andrés Rodríguez-Clare, eds. 2006. *The Emergence of China: Opportunities and Challenges for Latin America and the Caribbean.* Washington, DC: Inter-American Development Bank; David Rockefeller Center for Latin American Studies, Harvard University.

Gallagher, Kevin P., and Lyuba Zarsky. 2007. *The Enclave Economy: Foreign Investment and Sustainable Development in Mexico's Silicon Valley.* Cambridge, MA: MIT Press.

Gallagher, Kevin P., and Roberto Porzecanski. 2010. *The Dragon in the Room: China and the Future of Latin American Industrialization.* Stanford, CA: Stanford University Press.

Hanson, Gordon H., and Raymond Robertson. 2009. "China and the Recent Evolution of Latin America's Manufacturing Exports." In *China's and India's Challenge to Latin America: Opportunity or Threat?,* edited by Daniel Lederman, Marcelo Olarreaga, and Guillermo Perry. Washington, DC: World Bank.

Hirschman, Albert O. 1958. *The Strategy of Economic Development.* New Haven, CT: Yale University Press.

———. 1970a. *A Bias for Hope: Essays on Development in Latin America.* Boulder, CO: Westview Press.

———. 1970b. *Exit, Voice, and Loyalty.* Cambridge, MA: Harvard University Press.

International Monetary Fund. 2008. *World Economic Outlook.* Washington, DC: IMF.

Jenkins, Rhys. 2008. "Measuring the Competitive Threat from China for Other Southern Exporters." *World Economy* 31(10): 1351–60.

Lall, Sanjaya. 2000. "The Technological Structure and Performance of Developing Country Manufactured Exports, 1985–98." *Oxford Development Studies* 28(3): 337–69.

Lall, Sanjaya, and Josh Weiss. 2005. "People's Republic of China's Competitive Threat to Latin America: An Analysis for 1990–2002." *Oxford Development Studies* 33(2): 163–94.

Mesquita Moreira, Mauricio. 2007. "Fear of China: Is There a Future for Manufacturing in Latin America?" *World Development* 35(3): 355–76.

Naughton, Barry. 2007. *The Chinese Economy: Transitions and Growth.* Cambridge, MA: MIT Press.

Pérez, Mamerto, Sergio Schlesinger, and Timothy A. Wise. 2009. *The Promise and Perils of Agricultural Trade Liberalization: Lessons from Latin America.* Medford, MA: Tufts University Global Development and Environment Institute.

Sweetman, Arthur, and Jun Zhang. 2009. *Economic Transitions with Chinese Characteristics: Thirty Years of Reform and Opening Up.* Kingston, ON: Queen's University Press.

Thrasher, Rachel Denae, and Kevin P. Gallagher. 2010. "21st Century Trade Agreements: Implications for Development Sovereignty." *Denver Journal of International Law and Policy* 38(2): 313–50.

United Nations Statistics Division. 2009. United Nations Commodity Trade Statistics Database (COMTRADE). New York: United Nations Statistics Division.

Williamson, John, ed. 1990. *Latin American Adjustment: How Much Has Happened?* Washington, DC: Institute of International Economics.

Wilson, Patricia. 1992. *Exports and Local Development: Mexico's New Maquiladoras.* Austin: University of Texas Press.

Wise, Timothy. 2009. "Promise or Pitfall? The Limited Gains from Agricultural Trade Liberalisation for Developing Countries." *Journal of Peasant Studies* 36(4): 855–70.

World Bank. 2009. *Global Economic Prospects 2009: Commodities at the Crossroads.* Washington, DC: World Bank.

———. 2010. *World Development Indicators.* Washington DC: World Bank.

Yongzhong, Wang. 2010. "Effectiveness of Capital Controls and Sterilizations in China." *China and the World Economy* 18(3): 106–24.

Yu, Yongding. 2008. "Managing Capital Flows: The Case of the People's Republic of China." ADB Institute Discussion Paper No. 96, Asian Development Bank, Manila.

PART III

THE POLITICS OF ECONOMICS AND THE ECONOMICS OF POLITICS

CHAPTER 11

HOW (NOT) TO PRODUCE
EFFECTIVE POLICIES?
INSTITUTIONS AND
POLICYMAKING IN LATIN
AMERICA

MARIANO TOMMASI
AND CARLOS SCARTASCINI

ANALYSTS and practitioners have always searched for policy recipes to solve the economic and social problems of developing countries. The last "universal recipe" recommended and adopted throughout Latin America was the market-oriented reform package of the 1990s. The varied and less-than-stellar performance that ensued has redirected intellectual attention. The so-called Washington Consensus has lost its intellectual appeal and has been replaced by a number of initiatives, none of which has completely gained center stage. Perhaps one of the most respected lines of reasoning is the one pioneered by Dani Rodrik and others, which calls for "homemade" as opposed to universal solutions: identify the most binding constraints to development in your country, experiment with policy or institutional innovations to see what works for you, and adjust accordingly (see, e.g., Hausmann, Rodrik, and Velasco 2005).

Both the old-style policy recipes and the new more eclectic approach place a heavy burden of responsibility on the countries' capacity to develop and implement complex public policies. But what determines the ability of different polities to pro-duce effective public policies? This chapter reports on one line of inquiry, which argues that the relevant economic and social outcomes depend not so much on the titles of those recipes (whether the pension system is "public pay-as-you-go" or "pri-vate defined contribution") but on a number of characteristics of the actual imple-mentation of those policies, such as their stability, their capacity for adjusting to changing circumstances, their enforcement, and so on. Countries able to generate policies with such attributes reap the benefits of specific initiatives more than others. If the policies adopted do not have such attributes—no matter how good they look on paper—they are unlikely to achieve good development outcomes.

These characteristics, in turn, derive from the process by which policies are discussed, decided, implemented, evaluated, and modified; that is, from the *policy-making process* (PMP) of each country. Policymaking is a continuous process. Aspects of that very process affect the economic and social impact of the policies. Perhaps that is more easily seen from the perspective of one characteristic of pol-icies that has received a lot of attention in modern economic theory: credibility. The effects of policies on the final economic and social outcomes of interest depend on the actions and reactions of economic and social agents, who take into account their expectations about the future of the policies in question before deciding on their responses. As Rodrik (1989, 2) explains in reference to trade reform,

> it is not trade liberalization per se, but *credible* trade liberalization that is the
> source of efficiency benefits. The predictability of the incentives created by a trade
> regime, or lack thereof, is generally of much greater importance than the *structure*
> of these incentives. In other words, a distorted, but *stable* set of incentives does
> much less damage to economic performance than an uncertain and unstable set
> of incentives generated by a process of trade reform lacking credibility.[1]

Credibility, which is related to what in our framework we call stability, is part of the set of characteristics of policies that influence their effect on development outcomes.

Before starting to look into that process, the policymaking process, let us pro-vide one example of a "market-oriented" reform undertaken in many Latin Ameri-can countries, which in some cases has been a resounding failure for the reasons emphasized in this chapter. We will use the example of the so-called privatization of the pension system in Argentina. Pension policy is an issue with transaction char-acteristics that make it particularly prone to trouble. The underlying economic transaction consists of taking money from people currently working (in the formal sector), in exchange for returning that money 30 years from now, when the worker reaches retirement age.[2] There are so many things that could go wrong during those 30 years that it is no wonder that pension systems are such a hot political problem in almost any country.

Argentina has had its fair share of problems with the pension system. It was created by President Juan Perón as a pay-as-you-go (PAYG) system. At that time, most of the population was uninsured against impoverishment in old age, so the program was very popular. Regrettably, the system was running large deficits within a few years of its creation. Pension funds were managed discretionally (and as a tool of patronage politics) by the executive, to finance a wide range of social programs and other activities. Also, the underlying demographic and economic assumptions of the system were totally unrealistic, particularly for those groups that received special treatment (such as public employees). Minor reforms were implemented during the 1970s and 1980s, but none of them solved the problem. The large deficit of the social security system was one of the causes of the late 1980s hyperinflation crisis. Among the many problems of the system, the low rate of contribution was salient, with a large fraction of people avoiding contributing to the system.

In a nutshell, the main problems of the public system were low compliance of individuals and opportunistic political manipulation by the government, which often translated into "stealing people's pensions." In 1993 the public PAYG system was replaced by a multipillar system, based on private individual contributory worker accounts, complemented by a public redistributive fund. The individual accounts were managed by private fund administrators (AFJP), regulated by a newly created agency, Superintendence of AFJPs. The government characterized the reform as a "privatization," and it claimed that the new system was invulnerable to political discretion. It also expected that the new system of individual accounts would increase contributions, given that in the new regime workers had a clear property right to their individual savings.

Unfortunately, none of those expectations was fulfilled. It seems that people (rightly) anticipated that the "privatization" of the funds was not enough of a guarantee against expropriation, because compliance even declined. And those pessimistic expectations were dutifully fulfilled by the government of the day during the crisis of the early 2000s, by forcing the AFJPs to hold government paper, on which the government later defaulted, and even more blatantly by the administration of Cristina Fernández de Kirchner that again nationalized the system. In November 2008, after 14 years of operation of private individual accounts, the government nationalized the entire system and pension policy shifted back to a public pay-as-you-go model. Individual pension fund accumulation, however, no longer mattered for the calculation of benefit entitlements, which started to follow a defined-benefit formula based on earnings and years of contributions only. The resources accumulated in individual accounts over 14 years (worth about 9.5 percent of the gross domestic product [GDP] in December 2008) was transferred to ANSES and put under public administration (Arza 2009). The management of these funds has been the source of great debate, but the consensus view of most independent observers is that it has been used to cover short-term government financial needs as well as to increase spending for various electoral and patronage purposes.[3] What is beyond debate is that the Kirchner reform did not do anything to solve the fundamental problems of the system.[4]

This example illustrates the fact that public policies are more than their "titles" and that what really matters for policies to induce good performance and outcomes are some fundamental state capabilities, such as the ability to commit not to expropriate, or the ability to enforce compliance. The example suggests that Argentina has always lacked those capabilities, in the old days of the public PAYG pension system, during the time of the private system of individual accounts, and certainly in the current time of the newly nationalized system. As we explore in more detail below, these weaknesses of Argentine policies and policymaking are much more general than in just the example of pensions.

Discovering how policies influence behavior and hence aggregate outcomes, exploring the conditions under which some reforms are most likely to give good fruits, and identifying effective ways to improve development outcomes requires an understanding of the processes within which countries develop instrument policies, that is, policymaking processes.

The analytical prism we are reporting on uses an eclectic approach drawing from (institutional) economics and political science. It views the PMP as a political process that involves various actors (politicians, interest groups, citizens) who interact in a variety of arenas (such as Congress, back rooms of the presidential palace, or the street) which can be more or less transparent, and more or less adequate for achieving reasonable bargaining outcomes. We view the PMP as a series of bargains and exchanges among political actors whose behavior depends on their interests, incentives, and constraints, and on their expectations about the behavior of other actors. These incentives, in turn, are shaped by the workings of political institutions (the legislature, executive-legislative relations, political parties, the judiciary, and public administration) in each country.

A number of recent studies have investigated the workings of political institutions, policymaking processes, and the resulting policy outcomes in Latin America, via various case studies as well as cross-country empirical analysis within Latin America and more broadly (see, e.g., IDB 2005; Stein and Tommasi 2007; Stein et al. 2008; and Scartascini, Stein, and Tommasi 2008, 2009, and 2010). Space constraints preclude us from describing those studies in any detail, but we give here a succinct summary of the conclusions of some of those studies. We start by defining the dependent variables, which are the characteristics of public policies that we believe are important to grasp so as to understand the performance of the countries in Latin America.

1. THE QUALITIES OF PUBLIC POLICIES

Several characteristics of policies condition whether they deliver the expected welfare impacts. These characteristics include:

Policy stability: the capacity to sustain policies over time (especially across changes in administration).
Policy adaptability: the capacity to adapt policies to changing economic conditions or to change policies when they are clearly failing.
Policy implementation and enforcement: the ability to implement and enforce public policies.

Policy coordination and coherence: the degree to which different policies
operating over the same realities are well articulated.

Efficiency: the extent to which policies reflect an allocation of scarce resources
that ensures high returns.

Public regardedness: the extent to which policies promote the general welfare as
opposed to funneling private benefits to certain individuals, factions or regions.

In a number of studies, we have tried to come up with empirical proxies for these
policy characteristics for Latin American countries (for instance, IDB 2005; Stein and
Tommasi 2007), and for broader (but shallower) international samples (for instance,
Berkman et al. 2008). Figure 11.1 places the Latin American countries in a comparative worldwide perspective, using an aggregate index of the qualities of policies.[5]

The studies have shown that better policy characteristics are associated with better
development outcomes, as summarized in table 11.1, which presents basic and partial correlations (controlling for GDP per capita in 1990) between the six public policy variables
and the policy index with two measures of development, growth of GDP and change in
the Human Development Index. (See Scartascini, Stein, and Tommasi 2008 for details.)

We have also found preliminary evidence that the quality of policies seems to
matter for the effectiveness of public expenditures (Scartascini, Stein, and Tommasi
2008).[6] As summarized in figure 11.2 for the case of public spending on health, (1) if
a country's policy environment is not good, spending more on health has no clear
effect on improving life expectancy, and (2) as countries develop a better policy
environment, they tend to benefit more from a given amount spent.

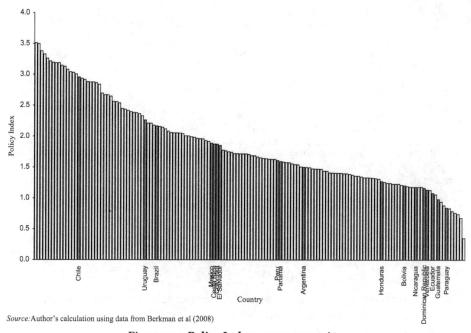

*Source:*Author's calculation using data from Berkman et al (2008)

Figure 11.1 Policy Index across countries.

Source: Authors' calculations using data from Berkman et al. (2008)

THE POLITICS OF ECONOMICS AND THE ECONOMICS OF POLITICS

Table 11.1. Features of Public Policies and Economic Development

	Stability	Adaptability	Coordination and Coherence	Implementation and Enforcement	Public Regardedness	Efficiency	Obs
Latin American countries							
GDP per capita growth 1990–2007	0.443*	0.46**	0.465*	0.536*	0.695***	0.537**	18
	0.257	0.307	0.345	0.400	0.555**	0.404*	18
Human Development Index (change) 1990–2005	0.581***	0.684***	0.71***	0.607***	0.594***	0.748***	18
	0.532**	0.5912***	0.678***	0.546**	0.544**	0.708***	18
Developing countries							
GDP per capita growth 1990–2007	0.392***	0.304***	0.328***	0.173*	0.197**	0.238***	113
	0.296***	0.333***	0.341***	0.199**	0.243***	0.248***	107
Human Development Index (change) 1990–2005	0.379***	0.401***	0.458***	0.312***	0.418***	0.446***	97
	0.192*	0.291***	0.301***	0.11	0.217**	0.253***	97

Note: Simple correlations between policy qualities and political variables are shown in the first row of each subgroup.
Partial-out correlations (controlling for GDP per capita of 1990) are shown in a second row of each subgroup.
* $p < .10$; ** $p < .05$; *** $p < .001$.
Source: Authors' calculations using data from World Development Indicators and Berkman et al. (2008)

2. What Explains the Quality of Policies?

The policymaking process in modern-day democracies can be understood as a process of bargains and exchanges among various political and socioeconomic actors.[7] Some of these exchanges are consummated instantly ("spot transactions"), while in many other cases current actions or resources are exchanged for promises

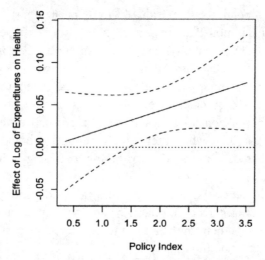

Figure 11.2 **Effects of Policy Index and health expenditures on changes in life expectancy (dotted lines represent 95 percent confidence interval).**

of future actions or resources ("intertemporal transactions"). Issues of credibility and the capacity to enforce political and policy agreements are crucial for political actors to be able to engage in intertemporal transactions.[8]

A number of features characterize the political transactions surrounding public policies: (1) politics and policymaking take place over time, (2) the relative political power of various actors changes over time, (3) there are elements of both conflict and commonality of interests in almost any relevant policy issue, (4) the socioeconomic reality in which policies operate changes over time, (5) most policies could be characterized by two decision frequencies: moments of major institutional definition and regular policymaking under those rules, and (6) many of the changing realities in (4) are such that it would be impossible for political or policy agreements to cover every feasible future circumstance.

Scholars have developed models capturing those features, using the logic of repeated games, to analyze policymaking (Spiller and Tommasi 2007, ch. 2). As a result of such analysis, it is possible to explain the characteristics of policies and ultimately certain patterns of development. The ability of a polity to cooperate determines whether certain characteristics of policies are attainable. For example, in less cooperative policymaking environments, policies might be too volatile or too rigid, poorly coordinated, and in general of low quality due to insufficient investment (Spiller and Tommasi 2007, 41–42).

A number of characteristics of policymaking processes and political institutions have been found to matter to promote more cooperative policymaking and hence policies of high quality (IDB 2005; Stein and Tommasi 2007; Scartascini, Stein, and Tommasi 2009). These include:

Well-institutionalized political parties (especially parties that have national, programmatic orientations). Institutionalized programmatic parties tend to be consistent long-term players. A political system with a relatively small number of institutionalized parties (or coalitions) is more likely to generate intertemporal cooperation, and to lead to the emergence of consensual sustained policy stances on crucial issues (i.e., *políticas de estado*—policies of the state rather than merely of the government in office).

A legislature with strong policymaking capabilities. Legislatures are the ideal arenas for the striking of efficient political bargains. Policies tend to be better when legislatures develop policymaking capacities and constructively engage in national policymaking, rather than when they simply adopt a subservient role, rubber-stamping the wishes of the executive (or blindly opposing in a nonconstructive manner)

An independent judiciary. A well-functioning and independent judiciary can be a facilitator of exchanges, fostering bargains among political actors by providing enforcement that binds them to their commitments, and by ensuring that none of the players oversteps its boundaries.

A well-developed civil service. A strong and technically competent civil service can contribute to the quality of public policies by making policies more stable, by enhancing the overall quality of implementation, and by preventing special interests from capturing the benefits of public policy.

In previous work we have constructed indicators of several of these institutional capabilities for a number of Latin American countries (IDB 2005; Stein and Tommasi 2007) and also shallower indicators for a larger number of countries from international data sources (Scartascini, Stein, and Tommasi 2008, 2009).[9] Figure

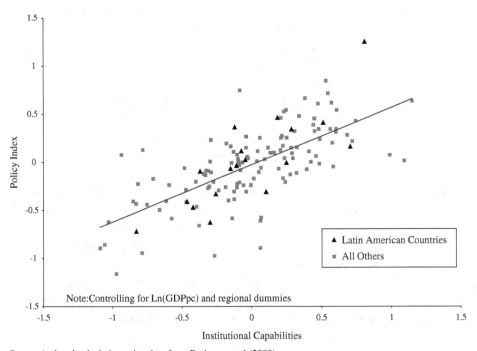

Source: Authors' calculation using data from Berkman et al (2008)

Figure 11.3 Quality of Public Policies and Institutional Capabilities.

11.3 summarizes some of that empirical work by plotting an index of the quality of public policies against an aggregate indicator of those institutional capabilities.

Table 11.2 provides some summary information for a number of Latin American countries, which indicates that stronger institutional capabilities are connected to better policy qualities.

The table visually summarizes the main findings, where dark gray represents high values of variables; light gray, intermediate values; and white, low values. Countries with high (low) values on the policy index tend to have high (low) values for many of the institutional variables. The table clearly shows that many of these institutional characteristics are interrelated. The high concentration of dark cells in the upper part of the table suggests that the variables are not independent.

Table 11.2. Political Institutions and the Qualities of Policies

Country (by Policy Index Level)	Congress Capabilities Index	Judicial Independence	Party System Institutionalization	Party System Nationalization[a,b]	Programmatic Parties[b]	Bureaucracy Index
Chile	1.77	2.82	1.87	0.90	8.00	2.69
Uruguay	1.39	3.29	2.61	0.89	7.00	1.14
Brazil	1.11	2.07	1.66	0.64	2.00	2.02
Mexico	0.99	1.80	2.05	0.78	2.00	1.67
Costa Rica	0.88	2.94	2.04	0.85	1.00	2.89
Colombia	0.99	1.79	1.86	—	0.00	1.89
El Salvador	0.99	1.71	1.56	0.83	7.00	0.63
Peru	0.70	1.21	1.69	0.50	0.00	1.46
Panama	0.77	1.21	1.81	0.78	0.00	0.87
Argentina	0.65	1.26	1.74	0.59	2.00	1.52
Honduras	1.26	1.08	1.97	0.91	2.00	1.06
Bolivia	0.61	1.19	1.51	0.71	0.00	0.64
Nicaragua	0.58	0.65	1.57	0.88	8.00	1.09
Dominican Republic	0.77	1.77	1.79	0.84	0.00	1.28
Venezuela	0.62	0.62	1.48	0.61	0.00	0.93
Ecuador	0.32	0.77	1.55	0.74	1.00	1.44
Guatemala	0.58	1.23	1.29	0.76	0.00	0.58
Paraguay	0.67	0.88	1.76	0.73	1.00	0.77

Note: Countries are classified according to their policy index values. The values for each country on each variable are shaded such that dark gray represents "high" values, light gray represents "medium" values, and white represents "low" values.
—Indicates data not available.
[a] Adequate data for party system nationalization are not available for Colombia for 2002. For the case of Ecuador, party system nationalization data correspond to 1998.
[b] Data from Jones (2008).
Source: Authors' calculation using data from Berkman et al. (2008).

That is not surprising from our perspective. Several of the "institutional" variables, such as having a strong congress heavily involved in policymaking, or an independent supreme court, are the reflection of the equilibrium behavior of a number of relevant political actors. If a supreme court is able to maintain or develop its independence over time, it is because it is in the best interest of other actors (such as the president) not to meddle with the supreme court in pursuit of short-term political benefits. Strong congresses and independent judiciaries are not built overnight, but are the outcome of processes of investing in the quality and credibility of such institutions, and such processes are interrelated.

These processes in some cases can lead to equilibria characterized by virtuous dynamics. Executives will not tinker with the composition of the supreme court, and this will help increase the court's independence and reputation. Strong and independent judiciaries will tend to adequately enforce the domain and prerogatives of other institutional arenas such as congress, which will then enhance the incentives for legislators to invest in their individual and collective capabilities, and so forth. But these processes can also result in vicious institutional dynamics, where the opposite will tend to happen. Executives will be inclined to meddle with the judiciary and to overstep in the domains of congress, lowering the incentives to invest in important legislative careers and the institutionalization and strengthening of congress.

Coincidentally, the actions of citizens and pressure groups will tend to reinforce the strength or weakness of these institutional actors and arenas. When congress and the political party system are effective conduits of preference aggregation and political bargaining, various relevant actors place their bets (investments) in those institutions, and most citizens believe that those are the spaces where relevant decisions are made, and this whole logic reinforces and become self-fulfilling. On the contrary, if such institutional arenas are not taken seriously and everybody knows that the way of getting something out of the political system is to blockade a road or to bribe the president, those investments in the institutionalization of congress or parties are not undertaken and the weakness of formal institutions is reinforced. Polities might be stuck with higher or lower levels of institutionalization (Scartascini and Tommasi 2009).

This discussion suggests that the incentives of presidents, the strength of congress, and the independence of the supreme court are likely to be co-determined in equilibrium, and all these things are likely to have an effect on the quality of policies. This suggests the presence of multiplicity of equilibria, in technical language. If for any reason a particular political system enters into a virtuous circle, it is likely to build up its strength over time. The opposite will tend to happen when such virtuous circles do not have time to build or are broken (Mailath, Morris, and Postlewaite 2001). This suggests that particular historical events or critical political junctures, including personalities and leadership qualities, will matter—inducing *path dependence*. The next section explores such interdependencies in one particular country case that illustrates the workings of institutions, policymaking, and the resulting policy characteristics, in general equilibrium. For brevity we focus here on the case of Argentina; a comparative collection of country case studies is presented in Stein et al. (2008).

The reason for focusing on countries one at a time relates to another important aspect of our diagnostic. Contrary to a simplistic interpretation of the political economy literature relating political institutions to policy outcomes, the average "partial equilibrium" connection between one specific institutional trait (say, one characteristic of the electoral system) and the qualities of resulting policies identified in cross-national empirical data cannot be extrapolated to a universal recommendation in favor of that particular institutional trait.[10] Countries are characterized by a vector of institutional traits that interact to determine equilibrium behavior, and the county studies we are relying on (Stein et al. 2008) have suggested that often "secondary" institutional rules such as budget procedures (see Alston et al. 2008 on Brazil) or federal fiscal arrangements (as we will argue below for the case of Argentina) turn out to be crucial determinants of policymaking. In order to think about reforms of political institutions, one needs a country-based approach conveying detailed knowledge of institutional context and historical background, allowing an understanding of the interactions among factors that affect the incentives of the makers of policy (Spiller, Stein, and Tommasi 2003.)[11]

3. PUBLIC POLICIES AND THE POLICYMAKING PROCESS IN ARGENTINA

Argentina is a country of consistent economic and social underperformance.[12] Various authors have identified its policy volatility and, more generally, the low quality of its public policies as one important factor in explaining such underperformance (Hopenhayn and Neumeyer 2005; Mody and Schindler 2006; Prados de la Escosura and Sanz-Villarroya 2009).

The most noticeable characteristic of Argentine policies is their instability. This can be seen quite clearly in the wide swings in overall economic policy orientation. Spiller and Tommasi (2008) present an index of economic policy volatility; Argentina ranks as the fourth most volatile country in a sample of 106 countries. The contrast between the pro-market reforms of the Menem administrations (1989–1999) and the statist stance of Nestor and Cristina Fernández de Kirchners' administrations since 2003 show that "lack of direction" in a dramatic manner. This policy volatility occurs also at a more micro level. Social programs, for instance, are frequently reshuffled when new ministers or secretaries take office, a frequent event in Argentina. Often this reshuffling involves substantial tinkering with the geographic distribution of funds. Argentina also shows great volatility in policies as crucial as trade policy and fiscal policy (Spiller and Tommasi 2007; Mody and Schindler 2006), and this volatility has been identified as one of the key factors in the poor growth performance of the country (Hopenhayn and Neumeyer 2005).

Argentina not only suffers from policy volatility, but it is also a weak enforcer of its policies, near or at the bottom of the international list in its ability to enforce tax collection, social security contributions, and payment of minimum wages (Spiller and Tommasi 2008).

Bouzas and Pagnotta (2003, 90–92) describe the policymaking process in relation to international trade negotiations (a crucial policy area for a country with the size, economic structure, and location of Argentina) in the following terms: deficient coordination and wasteful competition among multiple offices; diffuse assignment of responsibilities (which has a negative impact on efficiency and effectiveness of policies); lack of an adequate arena or institutionalized procedure for deliberation, consensus creation, or the definition of general direction of policy; no formal coordination mechanisms; sporadic and haphazard congressional intervention; interbureaucratic struggles; unstable bureaucratic structures; high rotation of top-level civil servants; use of temporary top personnel, which prevents the accumulation of institutional experience, precisely in an area were knowledge is so strategic; low level of institutional learning; and lack of effective coordination across units in the federal structure.

All these characteristics are also present in the making of policy in various other areas reported in Spiller and Tommasi (2007), including social policies, pension policy, fiscal federalism, and public utilities. The characteristics of the policy-making process include deficiencies of the budget process, which gives excessive discretion to some executive actors; insufficient involvement by Congress; instability of the bureaucratic structures in charge of implementation; instability of top bureaucratic personnel; noncooperation in the interactions between national authorities and provincial authorities; noncooperation in interactions among and within national ministries; involvement of provincial governors as relevant actors in national policy; and making of promises that are not fulfilled.

4. POLITICAL INSTITUTIONS AND POLICYMAKING IN ARGENTINA

Why does Argentina, historically a country of relatively high human capital and high levels of human development, have such a dysfunctional way of making public policies? At least part of the explanation seems to lie with the institutional factors identified earlier. As the comparison in table 11.2 shows, and as Spiller and Tommasi (2007) abundantly document, Argentina presents very low values in all institutional domains identified as conducive to good long-term policymaking, especially if one adjusts for the country's level of human development.[13] It has a very weak national Congress, it lacks a party system that is programmatically institutionalized, the judiciary is highly politicized and does not provide for the adequate enforcement of intertemporal agreements, and its public bureaucracy has consistently declined in professionalism in relative terms for many decades.

The reasons behind those very weak institutional capabilities are complex. Certainly there is no one explanation as in the simplistic early institutionalist literature; it is not because it is presidential rather than parliamentary (look at Chile); nor is it because it has "proportional representation" in its electoral system. It is the combined outcome of a number of institutional features, in particular those organizing the federal political and fiscal structure of the country, coupled with some historical legacies and the reinforcing dynamics generated by the behavior of various actors toward these institutions in the current Argentine equilibrium.

More broadly and more specifically than the institutional indicators used in cross-country comparisons, Spiller and Tommasi (2007 and 2008) characterize the Argentine policymaking process in a number of propositions about the behavior of some of the main actors and characteristics of the main institutional arenas:

1. Congress is not an important policymaking arena.
2. The executive has often substantial leeway to take unilateral policy action.
3. Provincial political powers (especially provincial governors) are very important in national policymaking.
4. There is a symbiotic interaction between national and provincial policy-making that operates through political and federal fiscal channels.
5. Fiscal federalism considerations are a factor in almost every policy issue, adding transaction difficulties and rigidities to policymaking.
6. Given the incentives of the executive of the day, of legislators, and of provincial governors, there is little investment in policymaking capacities in several spheres.
7. The bureaucracy is not an effective corps to which to delegate the technical implementation of policy bargains.
8. The judiciary does not provide much intertemporal "glue" to political or policy agreements.
9. Nongovernmental actors in the policy process (such as business groups and unions), lacking a well-institutionalized environment for political exchange, usually follow strategies that attempt to maximize short-term benefits.

In a nutshell, the national policymaking arena of Argentina is populated by actors who have little incentive and few instruments to engage in intertemporal policy agreements. This policymaking environment is one that generates policies that change with every administration (if not faster), and that leads to lack of coordination, poor enforcement, and low-quality implementation. The reasons behind this peculiar policymaking environment leading to poor-quality policies and hence poor economic and social outcomes are a mix of historical legacies from the many democratic interruptions of the twentieth century, some particularities of political and fiscal institutions in the country, and the reinforcing effects of the behavior of political actors over time.

As noted, this is in part the carryover outcome of decades of political instability from 1930 to 1983. Political instability has left an imprint through path-dependent behavior in Congress, the courts, the bureaucracy, and the federal fiscal system, as well as through the actions and expectations of nongovernmental actors.[14]

Political instability, however, is not the only factor contributing to short-sighted behavior and lack of capabilities for the development of "politicas de estado." Other reasons, of more weight almost three decades after the return to democracy, stem from the incentives generated by current electoral rules and partisan practices, and by the federal fiscal system of Argentina. These variables arrange in a way so that the most important policy initiatives undertaken in Argentina originate in the executive branch, which then attempts to get its favored polices through a Congress with few capabilities for serious discussion and analysis of the effects of alternative policies, and where the necessary votes for the passage of the executive's initiatives are obtained via exchanges with provincial leaders, who are much more interested in fiscal favors to run their local political machineries than in the specific contents of policies.

The weaknesses of the national legislature, and the main focus of the powerful governors on fiscal favors, leaves the national policymaking arena of Argentina inhabited by short-sighted executives, transient by nature, who try to maximize political advantages in the short term. The two most successful presidents of the post-democratization period, Carlos Menem and Nestor Kirchner, undertook important changes in national policies of completely opposed political philosophy, but utilizing the same political logic of exchanges with their fellow provincial patrons. This mode of policymaking is one of the explanations for Argentina's infamous policy volatility, which in turn relates to the lack of credibility of policy, and hence to the failure to achieve desirable economic and social outcomes.[15]

In what follows we summarize some of the building blocks of the picture above: the weakness of Congress, the (provincial) electoral connection, politics in the provinces, fiscal federalism, and the reinforcing dynamics among these factors.

As table 11.2 shows, Argentina ranks quite low within the Latin American sample in the index of policymaking capabilities of Congress (the value of the index is almost one-third of Chile's). Argentine legislators do not invest in developing strong congressional institutions, do not specialize in technical committees, and tend to have quite brief legislative careers (Saiegh 2010; Jones et al. 2002). Their reelection rates are 17 percent, a number that is quite low when compared with the 43 percent of Brazil or the 59 percent of Chile, let alone the 83 percent of the United States. Looking at the determinants of high turnover, one discovers that it is not the result of voters' rejection. Most legislators simply do not appear on the provincial party list for the next election. Those who do have a two-thirds probability of being reelected. That conditional reelection rate is lower than the 94 percent in the United States, but comparable to that of many other countries that have, nonetheless, much higher unconditional reelection rates. The short tenure of Argentine legislators arises from the fact that those in charge of compiling the list of candidates (the "selectorate") simply do not reappoint them. Given that electoral districts coincide with provinces, and given the mechanisms of internal candidate selection, this selectorate is constituted by provincial party elites (De Luca, Jones, and Tula 2002; Jones 2008).

These *amateur* legislators are, however, *professional* politicians. After serving a term in Congress, they are shifted to other political activities in the party, the province, or the federal government (Jones et al. 2002; Jones 2008). Argentine legislators, by and large, are responsive not to any particular group of citizens, but to the leaders of their party in the province,[16] especially when those leaders coincide with the provincial executive. In order to better understand the main exchanges of Argentine politics, then, it is necessary to understand the incentives of those subnational players. To do that, we "scale down" and look into the politics of Argentine provinces.[17]

Even though there is an important degree of interprovincial heterogeneity, most Argentine provinces are polities with restricted political competition and a high concentration of power in the hands of the governor, in which the main political linkages with the citizenry are patronage-based rather than programmatic. Those features, especially the weak division of powers, have been reinforced over time since the return to democracy in 1983 through changes in provincial constitutions and electoral laws, as well as through judicial manipulation introduced by powerful governors in favorable political circumstances. The political domination that many governors exercise over their province is largely based on the (exclusive political access to) financial resources provided by the peculiar federal fiscal arrangements of Argentina.

Provincial governments undertake a large share of total spending in Argentina, yet they collect only a small fraction of taxes. That means that provincial politicians enjoy a large share of the political benefit of spending, yet pay only a small fraction of the political cost of taxation. On average, provinces finance only 35 percent of provincial spending with their own revenues. This fiscal imbalance is uneven across provinces and extremely large for some of them. In a large number of less populous provinces, the transfers received constitute over 80 percent of provincial revenue. The difference between spending and revenues, the vertical fiscal imbalance, is financed from a common pool of resources, under the country's Federal Tax-Sharing Agreement. Even though the Argentine tax-sharing agreement appears on paper to be fairly automatic, in practice there has been over the years a number of channels by which the national government has had discretion at the margin in the allocation of funds to the provinces. The methods by which these channels have been modified are multiple, and their relative use and importance has varied over time, depending on various economic and political circumstances, but the underlying political logic has always been the same (Ardanaz, Leiras, and Tommasi 2010; Wibbels 2003).

In this logic, most provincial governments are resource-hungry political units eager to extract fiscal favors from the national government. In turn, the federal government needs votes in Congress to implement nationwide economic policies. This situation creates potential gains from trades between presidents and governors while Congress merely serves as the "ratifier" of agreements that are struck in other more informal arenas.

Since the president in practice has exclusive policy initiative, and the powerful institutional actors with whom he or she has to negotiate care only about fiscal exchanges, there is very little institutional room for the representation of substantive socioeconomic interests[18] or for programmatic discussion. Faced with this institutional playing field, socioeconomic actors and societal interests tend to take whatever short-term road is available to them in order to obtain favorable policies. In the case of large business interests, the most effective mode of influence is often attempting to bribe the executive (Schneider 2010). In the case of actors in a lower niche of the socioeconomic scale but with the capacity for physical mobilization, the strategy and venue of choice has been to blockade the streets and roads of the country, pressuring governments and imposing costs in those arenas as a way of having their voice heard (Scartascini and Tommasi 2009).[19]

This behavior on the part of socioeconomic actors has reinforcing effects on the quality of institutions. The fact that socioeconomic actors take such short-cut actions outside institutionalized political arenas like parties or the legislature reinforces the weaknesses of those arenas and hence becomes a self-fulfilling prophecy. These equilibrium mechanisms are the ones leading to the strong correlation of strength across institutional domains in the Latin American sample summarized in table 11.2.

5. CONCLUSIONS

If we return to the opening issues, one insight coming out of the agenda the chapter reports on is that there does not seem to be a "magic bullet" in terms of political reforms that will produce good policymaking under all circumstances. Understanding the overall workings of the political process and of the policymaking process in each country, with its specific historical trajectory, is a crucial prerequisite for developing appropriate reform proposals not only in terms of policies but also in terms of political institutions.

During the market-oriented reform era, many economists in developing circles were enthusiastic about the potential effects of those reforms in countries like Argentina. As emphasized in this chapter, changing those "grand titles" of policies might not be the way of improving outcomes, if some more fundamental characteristics of policies remain deficient. That suggests that policy reforms should be undertaken with a good diagnostic of the politico-institutional environment in which they will operate.

When focusing at a higher level on attempting to modify basic institutions,[20] caution and good diagnostics are also recommended. There are instances in which institutional reforms that seem a good idea when considered in isolation ("in partial equilibrium") could have unexpected negative consequences when filtered through the political system of specific countries. For instance, international organizations and other actors have been pushing for the decentralization of the public sector in Latin America. Decentralization is supposed to bring about a more accountable and responsive public sector, closer to the people. Decentralization has indeed brought some democratization and efficiency enhancement in some cases, but it has also fragmented policymaking and weakened the national policymaking arena with deleterious consequences in some other cases.[21] For instance in Argentina, decentralization seems to have reinforced subnational political machineries, increasing the subnational drag to national policymaking, one of the key problems of the Argentine case.

We close the chapter by repeating a point we have made in earlier work (Tommasi 2006). In his Ely Lecture to the American Economic Association, Arnold Harberger argued that there are enough people out there pleading for special interests, and that we economists should plead for the general interest, interpreted as economic efficiency. In his words, "If we are silent about the efficiency costs or benefits of policies, who else is going to represent them?" (Harberger 1993, 5). We want to conclude on a somewhat similar note. Our food for thought for economists (and others) in the business of recommending and analyzing economic policies is that institutions and processes might be more important than policies. We have to think twice before forcing our favorite policy onto a polity at the expense of violating principles such as a reasonable degree of societal consensus, congressional debate, or judicial independence.

NOTES

1. For models formalizing the effects of policies of uncertain duration in several economic contexts, see Calvo (1996, sec. 5) and Calvo and Drazen (1998).

2. Clearly, pension systems serve other purposes, such as redistribution and insurance "against" a longer-than-expected life.

3. The lack of complete agreement over the current use of pension funds is in part due to the lack of transparency with which the current Argentine government maintains the relevant information (Urbiztondo et al. 2009).

4. See, for instance, Arza (2009). Rofman, Fajnzylber, and Herrera (2008, 1) provide an interesting contrast between pension policymaking in Argentina and Chile. They argue that "in recent years authorities in both countries coincided on identifying insufficient coverage among the elderly and adequacy of benefits as the most critical problems. As a result of differences in political economy and institutional constraints, responses were different. In Chile, a long and participatory process resulted in a large reform that focuses on impacts on the medium term, through a carefully calibrated adjustment. In Argentina, instead, reforms were adopted through a large number of successive normative corrections, with little public debate about their implications, and immediate impacts on coverage and fiscal demands."

5. See Scartascini, Stein and Tommasi (2008) for details on the construction of each of the variables as well as for the construction of the aggregate index.

6. This result comes from running a simple ordinary least squares specification explaining a country's change in the health index between 1995 and 2005 based on our policy index, and expenditures on health and education (measured as the log of average expenditures between 1998 and 2005), and an interaction effect between the two independent variables.

7. See Spiller, Stein, and Tommasi (2003) and Spiller and Tommasi (2007) for a more detailed account and formalization of this framework.

8. In addition to the key *time* dimension, there is a *spatial* element to these bargains, as these can take place in arenas with varying levels of "institutionalization": while on one extreme, formal institutions such as congress and parties are the central locus of demands by socioeconomic actors, at the other end of the spectrum, the "street" can provide the space for interest groups to deploy alternative political technologies (e.g., road blockades) to influence economic policy (Scartascini and Tommasi 2009).

9. For instance, for the international index of congressional capabilities, we used the average of two data sources: the effectiveness of lawmaking bodies (from the *Global Competitiveness Report* [World Economic Forum 2004]) and the population's confidence in its parliament or legislature (based on responses from the World Values Survey). In the more detailed construction of the variable for the Latin American subsample, we additionally include measures of legislators' characteristics (average experience, education) and organizational and political characteristics of the legislatures (specialization in committees, strength of committees, whether they are the place to build political careers, whether they are endowed with technical expertise). The correlations between the variables available at the international level and the more detailed variables for the Latin American sample are quite high (IDB 2005; Saiegh 2010, and references there). The index attempts to capture characteristics of legislators and legislatures that impinge upon the capacity of a congress to participate constructively in the making of policy.

10. Some of the founding fathers of that literature are well aware of that, as reflected in Alesina, Persson, and Tabellini (2006, 206), when they say that they "are skeptical of unequivocal claims about the superiority of one set of institutions over all others. . . . In a given situation, a set of institutions may be clearly preferable to others. But a normative judgment requires detailed knowledge of the concrete situation and its specific social and historical ramifications. Knowing the average effects of institutions is unlikely to be enough."

11. Similarly, authors such as Rodden (2009) have recently shown the importance of relying more on analytical narratives than cross-country regressions for understanding institutions across the world.

12. This and the next sections of the chapter are based largely on Tommasi (2008) and Spiller and Tommasi (2003, 2007, and 2008), and references therein.

13. A more detailed contrast between Argentina and Chile, a country of a similar level of development and cultural background but profound policymaking differences, is provided in Tommasi (2008) and references there.

14. The frequent switches back and forth between democratically elected governments and military dictatorships led to the frequent replacement of all Supreme Court justices, which limited the independence of the Court and weakened its role in the consideration of citizens and other actors. Similarly, the absence of legislative power during military dictatorships taught interest groups to work directly with the executive.

15. For brevity we are describing the Argentine policymaking game in its "president on top" stage. The Argentine policymaking game switches between that stage and a stage in which the president cannot do anything and the country is virtually paralyzed, often followed by dramatic economic crises such as the hyperinflation of the late 1980s or the downfall of the convertibility regime in the early 2000s. The switch between stages responds to the political alignment of governors for or against the president, which in turns depends on whether the fiscal situation allows the executive to buy enough support (Tommasi 2008).

16. Leiras (2006) provides a cogent argument of why, unlike the case in other federations, national political parties reproduce this geographical political fragmentation and hence do not act as general aggregators of substantive national economic interests either.

17. The next paragraphs draw from Ardanaz, Leiras, and Tommasi (2010) and references therein.

18. This is related to the fact that the Argentine political system strongly underrepresents middle class, ideological, programmatic, urban voters (Torre 2003)—the type of voter who tends to demand higher standards of accountability (Stokes 2006).

19. This logic applies not only to the unemployed in the by-now-famous *piquetes*, but it applies to any case in which the de jure power of a relevant set of political actors tends to underrepresent them in comparison to their ability to put collective action together and threaten economic disruption. The very visible 2008–9 demonstrations of rural producers in Argentina against large increases in export taxes by the Cristina Fernández de Kirchner administration are a case in point. Those demonstrators were not the dispossessed, but an economic sector underrepresented in the Argentine political system.

20. See Tommasi (2004) for a scheme of multiple institutional levels, in which political institutions are more fundamental than policies.

21. Monaldi (2010) describes some of the impacts of decentralization on policymaking in Latin America in the last couple of decades.

REFERENCES

Alesina, Alberto, Torsten Persson, and Guido Tabellini. 2006. "Reply to Blankart and Koester's Political Economics versus Public Choice: Two Views of Political Economy in Competition." *KYKLOS* 59(2): 201–8.

Alston, Lee, Marcos Melo, Bernardo Mueller, and Carlos Pereira. 2008. "The Choices Governors Make: The Roles of Checks and Balances and Political Competition." Unpublished manuscript, University of Colorado.

Ardanaz, Martín, Marcelo Leiras, and Mariano Tommasi. 2010. "The Politics of Federalism in Argentina and Its Effects on Governance and Accountability." Unpublished manuscript, Universidad de San Andrés.

Arza, Camila. 2009. "Back to the State: Pension Fund Nationalization in Argentina." Working Paper No. 72, December, Centro Interdisciplinario para el Estudio de Políticas Públicas, Buenos Aires.

Berkman, Heather, Carlos Scartascini, Ernesto Stein, and Mariano Tommasi. 2008. "Policies, State Capabilities, and Political Institutions: An International Dataset." Unpublished manuscript, Inter-American Development Bank, Washington, DC.

Bouzas, Roberto, and Emiliano Pagnotta. 2003. *Dilemas de la Política Comercial Externa Argentina*. Buenos Aires: Fundación OSDE and Universidad de San Andrés.

Calvo, Guillermo A. 1996. *Money, Exchange Rates, and Output*. Cambridge, MA: MIT Press.

Calvo, Guillermo A., and Allan Drazen. 1998. "Uncertain Duration of Reform: Dynamic Implications." *Macroeconomic Dynamics* 2(4): 443–55.

De Luca, Miguel, Mark P. Jones, and María Inés Tula. 2002. "Back Rooms or Ballot Boxes? Candidate Nomination in Argentina." *Comparative Political Studies* 35(4): 413–36.

Harberger, Arnold. 1993. "The Search for Relevance in Economics." *American Economic Review* 83(2): 1–16.

Hausmann, Ricardo, Dani Rodrik, and Andrés Velasco. 2005. "Growth Diagnostics." John F. Kennedy School of Government, Harvard University, March.

Hopenhayn, Hugo A., and Pablo A. Neumeyer. 2005. "The Argentine Great Depression, 1975–1990." In *Sources of Growth in Latin America. What Is Missing?*, edited by Eduardo Fernández-Arias, Manuelli, and Juan Blyde, 119–56. Washington, DC: Inter-American Development Bank.

IADB (Inter-American Development Bank). 2005. *The Politics of Policies: Economic and Social Progress in Latin America and the Caribbean 2006 Report*. Washington, DC: Inter-American Development Bank.

Jones, Mark P. 2008. "The Recruitment and Selection of Legislative Candidates in Argentina." In *Pathways to Power. Political Recruitment and Candidate Selection in Latin America*, edited by Peter M. Siavelis and Scott Morgenstern, 41–75. University Park: Pennsylvania State University Press.

Jones, Mark P., Sebastián Saiegh, Pablo T. Spiller, and Mariano Tommasi. 2002. "Amateur Legislators, Professional Politicians: The Consequences of Party-Centered Electoral Rules in Federal Systems." *American Journal of Political Science* 46(3): 656–69.

Leiras, Marcelo. 2006. "Parties, Provinces and Electoral Coordination: A Study on the Determinants of Party and Party System Aggregation in Argentina, 1983–2005." PhD diss., University of Notre Dame.

Mailath, George, Stephen Morris, and Andrew Postlewaite. 2001. "Laws and Authority." Unpublished manuscript, Yale University.

Mody, Ashoka, and Martin A. Schindler. 2006. "Argentina's Growth: A Puzzle?" Unpublished manuscript, International Monetary Fund, Washington, DC.

Monaldi, Francisco. 2010. "Decentralizing Power in Latin America: The Role of Governors in National Policymaking." In Scartascini, Stein, and Tommasi 2010, 177–216.

Prados de la Escosura, Leandro, and Isabel Sanz-Villarroya. 2009. "Contract Enforcement, Capital Accumulation, and Argentina's Long-Run Decline." *Cliometrica* 3(1): 1–26.

Rodden, Jonathan. 2009. "Back to the Future: Endogenous Institutions and Comparative Politics." In *Comparative Politics*, edited by Mark Lichbach and Alan Zuckerman, 333–57. Cambridge: Cambridge University Press.

Rodrik, Dani. 1989. "Credibility of Trade Reform—A Policy Maker's Guide." *World Economy* 12(1): 1–16.

Rofman, Rafael, Eduardo Fajnzylber, and Germán Herrera. 2008. "Reforming the Pension Reforms: The Recent Initiatives and Actions on Pensions in Argentina and Chile." SP Discussion Paper No. 831, World Bank, Washington, DC.

Saiegh, Sebastián M. 2010. "Active Players or Rubber-Stamps? An Evaluation of the Policymaking Role of Latin American Legislatures." In Scartascini, Stein, and Tommasi 2010, 47–76.

Scartascini, Carlos, and Mariano Tommasi. 2009. "The Making of Policy: Institutionalized or Not." Working Paper No. 108, Inter-American Development Bank, Washington, DC, November.

Scartascini, Carlos, Ernesto Stein, and Mariano Tommasi. 2008. "Political Institutions, State Capabilities, and Public Policy: International Evidence." Research Department Working Paper No. 661, Inter-American Development Bank, Washington, DC, December.

———. 2009. "Political Institutions, Intertemporal Cooperation, and the Quality of Policies." Working Paper No. 676, Research Department, Inter-American Development Bank, Washington, DC.

———. 2010. *How Democracy Works: Political Institutions, Actors and Arenas in Latin American Policymaking*. Washington, DC: Inter-American Development Bank; David Rockefeller Center for Latin American Studies, Harvard University.

Schneider, Ben Ross. 2010. "Business Politics and Policy Making in Contemporary Latin America." In Scartascini, Stein, and Tommasi 2010, 217–46.

Spiller, Pablo T., Ernesto Stein, and Mariano Tommasi. 2003. "Political Institutions, Policy-making Processes and Policy Outcomes: An Intertemporal Transactions Framework." Unpublished manuscript, Inter-American Development Bank, Washington, DC.

Spiller, Pablo T., and Mariano Tommasi. 2003. "The Institutional Foundations of Public Policy: A Transactions Approach with Application to Argentina." *Journal of Law, Economics, and Organization* 19(2): 281–306.

———. 2007. *The Institutional Foundations of Public Policy in Argentina*. Cambridge: Cambridge University Press.

———. 2008. "Political Institutions, Policymaking Processes, and Policy Outcomes in Argentina." In Stein et al. 2008, 69–110.

Stein, Ernesto, and Mariano Tommasi. 2007. "The Institutional Determinants of State Capabilities in Latin America." In *Annual World Bank Conference on Regional Development Economics: Beyond Transition*, edited by François Bourguignon and Boris Pleskovic, 193–226. Washington, DC: World Bank.

Stein, Ernesto, Mariano Tommassi, Pablo T. Spiller, and Carlos Scartascini, eds,. 2008. *Policymaking in Latin America: How Politics Shapes Policies*. Cambridge, MA: David Rockefeller Center for Latin American Studies, Harvard University.

Stokes, Susan C. 2006. "Do Informal Rules Make Democracy Work? Accounting for Accountability in Argentina." In *Informal Institutions and Democracy. Lessons from Latin America*, edited by G. Helmke and S. Levistky, 125–40. Baltimore: Johns Hopkins University Press.

Tommasi, Mariano. 2004. "Crisis, Political Institutions and Economic Reforms: The Good, the Bad, and the Ugly." In *Toward Pro-Poor Policies: Aid, Institutions and Globalization*, edited by Bertil Tungodden, Nicholas Stern, and Ivar Kolstad, 135–64. Proceedings of the Annual World Bank Conference on Development Economics, Europe. Washington, DC: World Bank; New York: Oxford University Press.

———. 2006. "Presidential Address: The Institutional Foundations of Public Policy." *Economia* 6(2): 1–36.

———. 2008. "Un país sin rumbo: Política, Políticas Públicas y Desarrollo en Argentina (con una leve comparación al caso chileno)." Unpublished manuscript, Universidad de San Andrés.

Torre, Juan Carlos. 2003. "Los huérfanos de la política de partidos: Sobre los alcances y la naturaleza de la crisis de representación política." *Desarollo Economico* 42 (168): 647–65.

Urbiztondo, Santiago, Marcela Cristini, Cynthia Moskovits, and Sebastián Saiegh. 2009. "The Political Economy of Productivity in Argentina: Interpretation and Illustration." IADB Working Paper No. 102, Inter-American Development Bank,Washington, DC.

Wibbels, Erik. 2003. "Bailout, Budget Constraints and Leviathan: Comparative Federalism and Lessons from the U.S." *Comparative Political Studies* 36(5): 475–508.

World Economic Forum. 2004. *Global Competitiveness Report*. Executive Opinion Survey. Available at http://www.weforum.org/.

Zuvanic, Laura, and Mercedes Iacoviello. 2005. "El rol de la burocracia en el PMP en América Latina." Unpublished manuscript, Inter-American Development Bank, Washington.

CHAPTER 12

THE POLITICS OF GLOBAL FINANCIAL MARKETS IN LATIN AMERICA

DANIELA CAMPELLO

1. INTRODUCTION

The 1990s witnessed a major change in the markets for Latin American sovereign debt. After the prevalence of private bank loans in the 1970s and 1980s, the securitization of Latin American debt prompted an expansive market for sovereign bonds (Gooptu 1993; Kahler 1998; Stallings 2006; Griffith-Jones 2000). The deregulation of countries' capital accounts facilitated the entry of broader classes of investors and encouraged the growing integration of Latin American capital markets that has occurred since then (fig. 12.1).

These developments have drastically altered the relations between governments and investors in the region. The phenomenon has not gone unnoticed in the international political economy literature, and a new research agenda has been developing in an attempt to understand the new terms of this relationship (Santiso and Martínez 2003; Santiso 2003; Block, Vaaler, and Schrage 2005, 2006; Jensen and Schmith 2005; Renno and Spanakos 2009; Campello 2010). Scholars interested in the politics of finance have been particularly devoted to understanding changes in the way creditors' political preferences are manifested in the new scenario, as well as the conditions under which these preferences influence policymaking.

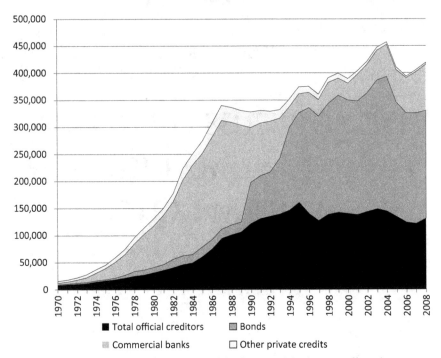

Figure 12.1 Latin American public foreign debt (US$, millions).

Compared to previous decades, when bankers and multilateral institutions used direct leverage to shape governments' policy agenda (Thorp 1987; Stallings 1992), investor influence is now exerted through a more elusive mechanism, which takes place in the context of what has been referred to as a "confidence game" (Bresser-Pereira 2001; Santiso 2003). In this game, "exit" is the most likely response of uncoordinated investors to prospects of unfavorable government policies (Hirschman 1977).[1] A sudden reversal in market confidence, as frequently evidenced in recent Latin American history, can carry severe economic and political consequences. Hence, governments of these countries, in which low domestic savings create a high dependence on international capital, have become increasingly aware of, and responsive to, the signals that reveal market sentiments.

On their part, governments also send signals designed to foster or maintain investors' confidence. These signals can include the adoption of a specific policy or the appointment of a finance minister or central banker who is well regarded in the investment community, and their goal is often to reinstate governments' commitment to a pro-investor agenda. On other occasions, however, presidents may reveal their disregard for investors' confidence by suggesting, as did a newly elected Rafael Correa in Ecuador in 2006, that "nervous investors should take a Valium."[2] The factors that account for governments' varied responses to investors' preferences in Latin American countries are still little explored by the political economy literature.

The mechanisms that underlie the confidence game between government and markets in a scenario of increased capital mobility are the main object of this essay. The following section puts the recent changes in Latin American financial markets into historical perspective. Section 3 reviews theories about the political consequences of the internationalization of domestic financial markets and discusses how these theories can illuminate the experience of emerging economies in the region. Next, I survey major empirical findings on the consequences of financial integration in the particular case of Latin American countries. The subsequent section moves from macroconsequences of capital mobility to its microfoundations; I examine what recent work tells us about how financial markets "vote" in Latin American elections and explore the conditions under which this vote influences policymaking. The last section proposes potential venues for future research.

2. Background

From the aftermath of the Great Depression and the massive defaults of the 1930s until the late 1960s, foreign financial investment was mainly absent from Latin America (Edwards 1998). After the first oil price shock of 1973; however, the efforts to recycle petrodollars, coupled with strong pressures on oil importers' capital accounts, paved the return of private lending to the region. Contrary to the "dance of millions" that occurred in the 1920s, when banks served as intermediaries that sold Latin American government bonds to individual investors, in this lending boom banks were the direct financiers of governments' debt (Drake 1989; Sachs 1989; Dornbusch 1989).

Between 1971 and 1981, net loans to Latin America amounted to US$61.3 billion, compared to US$7.3 billion between 1961 and 1970. The oversupply of international credit made financing unusually inexpensive, with interest rates sometimes reaching negative levels (Thorp 1998). As a result of the fierce competition among creditors, loans were offered with little oversight and no strings attached, leaving governments with plenty of room to use capital at their own discretion. From all loans made to Latin America in the decade, 83 percent were channeled to the public sector, 36 percent of those directly to governments (Stallings 1987).

Following the sharp rise in American interest rates in 1979 and the widespread panic caused by the Mexican default in 1982; capital flows to Latin America reversed dramatically. Average real interest rates went from negative 6 percent in 1981 to 14.6 percent in 1982. Net transfers of resources dropped from about 30 percent in 1977 to negative 40 percent of the region's exports in 1987 (Thorp 1998).

In contrast to the credit boom of the 1970s, when political leaders had the autonomy to decide the destination of borrowed money, in the 1980s there was a dramatic deterioration of governments' policy space.[3] In their efforts to roll current debt and raise new money from lenders of last resort, such as the International Monetary Fund (IMF) and the World Bank, Latin American governments were subject to stringent conditions, starting with a focus on macroeconomic adjustment in the early 1980s and evolving to include massive structural reforms from 1985 on (Stallings 1992). Despite some debate about the effectiveness of conditionality in the 1980s (Kahler 1992), there is little doubt that the region has experienced profound economic adjustment since then (fig. 12.2).

In this period, a creditors', cartel, composed of a few large banks and with the support of creditor governments and the IMF, faced a group of debtor countries that proved incapable of coordinating. The resulting power asymmetry left the latter with little room to maneuver in policymaking (O'Donnell 1985; Drake 1989). The pervasive implementation of painful structural reforms and the limited number of sovereign defaults, particularly staggering when compared to countries' responses to the 1930s crisis, evidence creditors' capacity to influence governments' agendas during the 1980s (Drake 1989; Lindert and Morton 1989).

It took Latin American countries close to a decade, after the 1982 collapse, to return to the international financial markets. This return finally happened with the securitization of countries' loans into bonds, which was advanced by the Brady Plan from 1989 on. This process, which facilitated the selling of assets on the part of banks and enabled debtor countries to start borrowing and issuing bonds again,

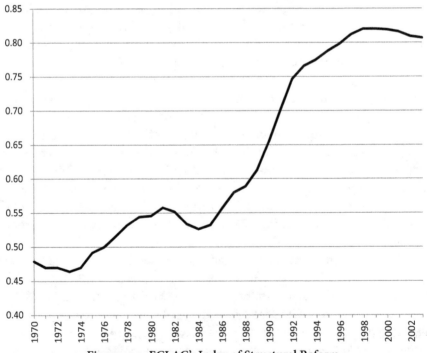

Figure 12.2 ECLAC's Index of Structural Reform.
Source: Escaith and Paunovic (2004).

created the conditions for the development of a market for Latin America's sovereign debts.

The impact of the Brady Plan was dramatic; in 1997 US$305 billion of loans and US$2;403 billion of Brady bonds were traded, compared with the US$70 billion face value of loans traded in secondary markets in 1989. The securitization of loans allowed banks to sell distressed debt off their balance sheets and free up capital for more productive uses (Buckley 2008). The creation of a market for Latin American sovereign debt, and the widespread liberalization of countries' capital accounts that followed in the region (Brooks 2004s), thus created the conditions for the new wave of fresh capital inflows to Latin American economies that materialized in the early 1990s.

Financial liberalization, coupled with the new structure of financial markets, had important economic consequences for Latin American economies. Among them was a significant rise in the volatility of capital inflows to the region, and economies' increased susceptibility to financial crises.[4] As a result, the attempt to cushion the severe consequences of sudden capital flight prompted governments to accumulate unprecedented levels of international reserves (Obstfeld, Shambaugh, and Taylor 2008) (fig. 12.3).

Increased atomization and mobility also changed the mechanisms through which investors' preferences affect policymaking in Latin America, a topic explored in the next section.

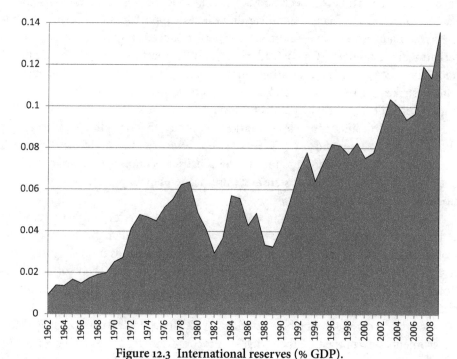

Figure 12.3 International reserves (% GDP).
Source: Total reserves minus gold and gross domestic product in current US$ (millions) for Latin American emerging economies, World Databank.

3. CONSEQUENCES OF THE INTERNATIONALIZATION OF DOMESTIC FINANCIAL MARKETS

The political consequences of economic integration are a central theme of the international political economy literature. Over the past decades, most of this debate has centered on the accuracy of "efficiency" and "compensation" hypotheses to describe patterns of governments' response to integration.[5]

The efficiency hypothesis contends that the easier it is for asset holders to move their capital out of a given country, the stronger become the incentives for governments to implement policies that increase domestic rates of return on investment (Strange 1986; Cerny 1995; Garrett 1991; Dryzek 1996; Drezner 2001). In the particular case of financial integration, scholars argue that policies likely to diminish the expected return of portfolio investment should be subject to the "disciplining effects" of capital markets. Whenever investors anticipate the implementation of such policies, they should respond by "exiting" domestic economies. Depending on the magnitude of this exit, governments can experience results ranging from a rise in the cost of capital to severe pressures in the balance of payments, among other deleterious economic effects.

As established by the literature on economic voting (Fiorina 1981; Lewis-Beck 1988; Remmer 1993; Lewis-Beck and Stegmeier 2000; Stokes 2001; Samuels 2004), bad economic performance significantly reduces support for incumbent governments. In Latin American economies, this performance is highly dependent on international capital flows (Calvo, Leiderman, and Reinhart 1996; Izquierdo, Romero, and Talvo 2008) and, hence, on investors' confidence; for this reason the effect of capital strikes on the economy should be a concern for all policyholders in the region, regardless of their ideological leaning.[6]

As capital mobility increases, markets' capacity to "discipline" governments should also increase, and for this reason supporters of the efficiency hypothesis expect financial liberalization to foster a consensus in economic policies toward the neoliberal model of a minimal state and minimal deregulation preferred by international financial players.

Compensation theorists, on the contrary, argue that investors' higher leverage to influence policymaking should be offset by voters' stronger demands for protection from the disruptions typical of an open economy. These demands should create incentives for politicians to further welfare policies in order to maintain their country's economic and social stability (Rodrik 1998; Garrett 1998; Boix 2000). Since these incentives should mostly affect left-wing parties, which typically retain stronger support from poorer citizens, compensation theorists do not predict ideological convergence. Leftist governments, in contrast to their right-wing counterparts, are expected to accept paying higher costs of capital, and possibly even slowing rates of economic growth, in order to maintain the network of social protection that their constituencies demand.

Compensation theory proponents have found considerable empirical support in the literature on developed countries. Scholars have shown that, in many cases, the size of the state has grown with globalization (Quinn 1997; Rodrik 1998), and that divergence in welfare regimes remains in developed economies (Kitschelt et al. 1999). With respect to parties within a country, some authors observe macroeconomic convergence but also that parties pursue distinct strategies in supply-side policies (Garrett 1998). Others contend that not even macroeconomic policies converge when properly controlled for exchange-rate regime (Oatley 1999). Nevertheless, it is important to note that in many analyses, policy variation between and within countries seemed to decrease in the 1990s (Oatley 1999; Boix 2000), suggesting that convergence may still potentially occur.

Most studies implicitly rest on the assumption that governments' adoption of efficiency or compensation strategies depends on a balance between citizens' capacity to mobilize around economic interests and hold governments accountable and investors' ability to impose "market discipline." If this is correct, there are many reasons to expect that the compensation hypothesis does not apply to the Latin American reality.

On one side, the lack of strong, encompassing labor unions, low levels of mobilization, and cliental practices suggest little citizen capacity for influencing the policy agenda (Kurtz 2004; Weyland 2004). On the part of investors, low domestic savings and, therefore, high dependence on international finance potentially increase financiers' leverage to influence policymaking, compared to developed economies. Not surprisingly, scholars observe that rising insecurity and increasing dislocation resulting from economic openness are likely to reduce Latin American citizens' capacity for demanding, let alone obtaining, compensation (Kurtz and Brooks 2008).

It is also worth noting that capital mobility has been associated with an increase in the volatility of capital inflows to Latin America (Griffith-Jones 2000), and that these flows are generally pro-cyclical in less developed countries (Reinhart and Rogoff 2009). Based on this evidence, scholars have also suggested that a higher frequency of financial distress, on top of these countries' limited access to international financial markets in bad times, is another mechanism through which globalization hinders welfare (Wibbels 2006).

Empirical work on the political impact of capital openness in Latin America is modest compared to the literature on that impact in developed nations and is also more inclined to support efficiency claims. Most cross-national studies that investigate the impact of measures of globalization and the size of the state find a negative association, frequently captured by trade exposure (Kaufman and Segura-Ubiergo 2001; Rudra 2002), and find that partisanship is irrelevant (Huber, Mustillo, and Stephens 2008).

With respect to finance, measures of capital account openness are negatively related to welfare expenditures and tax burdens on business. Overall, however, the effects observed are either weak or null (Kaufman and Segura-Ubiergo 2001; Wibbels and Arce 2003; Avelino, Brown, and Hunter 2005).

Arguably, poor measures of financial integration and the lack of reliable data especially in the case of less developed countries have exhausted the type of large *N* studies on the political impact of capital openness. In response, recent research has been moving away from macroanalyses and toward a search for the microfoundations of investors' political clout in a scenario of increased capital mobility. The following section examines this literature.

4. The Microfoundations of Investors' and Governments' Confidence Game

After initial efforts to capture the broad patterns that associate capital mobility and policy choices, recent research has been moving toward identifying mechanisms that translate portfolio investors' increased exit capacity into effective political influence. Mosley (2003) was a pioneer in arguing that learning investors' policy preferences is a necessary starting point for studying how these preferences influence governments' agendas. Toward this end, the author conducted interviews with institutional investors and concluded that they consider distinct sets of policies when making allocation decisions in developed and emerging economies. In the former, investors' concerns are restricted to macroeconomic policies; in the latter, supply-side policies also matter.[7]

These different criteria arise from the fact that emerging economies are subject not only to exchange rate and inflationary risks but also to default risk. This creates incentives for portfolio managers to assess not only governments' capacity but also their willingness to serve debt. In estimating governments' capacity to pay, investors take supply-side policies, such as the objects of governments' expenditures or the structure of tax systems, into consideration. In order to evaluate willingness to pay, which is not assumed a priori in emerging economies, political information, such as electoral results, parties' ideology, and technocrats' background, turns out to be relevant.

In addition, Mosley observes that "market participants view the range of possible policy outcomes as relatively wide in emerging markets: some governments pursue capital-friendly policies, but others may advocate policies hostile to international investors" (Mosley 2003, 129). This wide range of policies increases uncertainty about returns, as well as the need to scrutinize every possible signal to anticipate the program a government will likely advance in office and its effects on investment returns.

In the particular case of Latin America, a number of factors contribute to explaining these perceptions and justifying investors' attention to politics. Low domestic savings and trade concentration in commodity products severely increase countries' exposure to exogenous shocks, creating cycles of booms and crises that have only accelerated with the liberalization of capital flows (Gavin, Hausmann, and Leiderman 1995; Calvo, Leiderman, and Reinhart 1996; Eichengreen and Mody 1998; Izquierdo, Romero, and Talvo 2008). These cycles not only raise uncertainties

about economic performance but also affect countries' reliance on portfolio investment and, therefore, markets' influence on policymaking.

During booms, governments, particularly those on the left, have strong
incentives to advance redistributive policies; high income inequality increases the
electoral payoff of such policies (Campello 2010). When experiencing crises, conversely, governments of all ideological leanings tend to adopt pro-cyclical adjustments and stringent orthodox economic measures (Wibbels 2006), arguably in an
attempt to attract international finance. The concentration of political power in the
hands of presidents only worsens policy volatility, and these factors altogether help
explain the wide range of policies investors perceive in the region.

The expectation that investors respond to politics in less developed countries
finds consistent empirical support in the literature. An increasing number of studies
have focused on elections in an attempt to explore investors' policy preferences
based on their actual behavior rather than declared preferences. If partisanship theories are correct in contending that political parties promote policies consistent
with the preferences of their core constituencies (Hibbs 1977; Alesina 1987), the anticipation of these policies should be observable in the behavior of market players
during elections. Investors should, therefore, "exit" economies where unfavorable
governments are likely to win, and this behavior should be observable in a variety
of market indexes.

In the case of stock markets, price movements reflect changes in expectations
about the future performance of firms. Events anticipated to affect companies'
results in the future are likely to change the present value of their shares and, as investors buy or sell them accordingly, stock prices tend to adjust. Expectations that a
new government will increase taxes or regulation should resonate in stock prices.
Stock market indexes, a weighted or unweighted group of individual firms' stocks,
also reflect these prospects and are, therefore, a good proxy for investors' appraisals
of future governments' policies. Additionally, political events that affect investors'
risk perception of a given country end up also affecting the value of firms that operate in that country, whose risk perceptions incorporate the country risk.[8] This relationship is even clearer in sovereign bond markets, where governments' measures
directly affect their capacity to pay debt.

Partisanship theories often assume that conservative governments favor economic growth over income equality and advance "investor-friendly" policies
(Santiso 2003; Block, Vaaler, and Schrage 2006) such as lower taxation and public
expenditures (Wibbels and Arce 2003), deregulation of labor markets (Lopez de
Silaneset al. 2004), and monetary and fiscal conservatism (Oatley 1999). These policies raise business profitability in the short term and should make capital holders
better off.[9]

Conversely, progressive governments are expected to accept higher levels of inflation and to expand the public sector to lower unemployment. They are also less
prone to balance budgets and more inclined to increase social expenditures and
taxes to fund them (Garrett 1998; Leblang and Bernhard 2006; Hays, Stix, and
Freeman 2000; Bartels 2008) and to default on public debt. If assumptions about

partisanship hold, investors should expect returns to decrease when the Left is in office, and mobile capital should exit economies when elections are expected to bring about a left turn in office.

Scholars have documented investors' reaction to ideology and "punishment" of left-wing incumbents in case studies of Latin American countries. The Brazilian 2002 presidential election stands out as a typical example of this phenomenon (Santiso, and Martínez 2003; Jensen and Schmith 2005; Renno and Spanakos 2006). Six months before the election, expectations that the leftist Workers Party would displace the center-right government led to a drop of more than 50 percent in the country's stock market, provoked capital flight that precipitated a 40 percent devaluation of the real, and doubled the country's risk assessment (Santiso and Martínez 2003; Jensen and Schmith 2005; Renno and Spanakos 2006). Even though the Workers Party's candidate Lula da Silva won the election, the party altered the composition of its policymakers and policy in order to respond to market imperatives (Campello 2010).

Figure 12.4 compares stock markets' behavior during the election of a center-right and a center-left candidate, Fernando Henrique Cardoso in 1994 (fig. 12.4a) and Lula in 2002 (Fig. 12.4b), respectively. It shows that the Brazilian stock market index closely tracks the emerging markets' stock market index for two years, but there is a decoupling in the months that precede each election. Arguably, the sharp rise in Brazilian indexes reveals markets' positive response to the prospects of Cardoso's victory in 1994, the opposite occurring in the case of Lula in 2002.

A similar dynamic occurred in the election in Argentina of Carlos Menem, whose program called for state ownership of heavy industries, a social pact to deal with inflation, and the suspension of the country's debt service (Stokes 2001). Stock market indexes, which collapsed in the months before the election, resumed an upward trajectory only as Menem announced an unexpectedly conservative cabinet and launched a tough austerity program explicitly rejected during the campaign. Ecuador and Venezuela also experienced investors' negative reactions to the election of leftist leaders, which reversed when the presidents moderated their policies after inauguration (Campello 2010).

Such experiences are not unique to these countries. Scholars have found consistent and differentiated market responses to governments' ideology in the region as a whole. Block, Vaaler, and Schrage (2006) show that rating agencies are more likely to downgrade less developed countries' sovereign bonds during elections when the Right is expected to lose, and bondholders seem to perceive higher investment risk in developing countries when a left-leaning candidate is expected to win an election (Block, Vaaler, and Schrage 2005; Moser 2007; Campello 2006).

With respect to the impact of capital flight on governments' agendas, Campello (2010) examines Latin American presidential elections since re-democratization and finds that (1) leftist candidates inaugurated in the midst of a currency crisis tend to switch to an investor-friendly agenda after inauguration in an attempt to build confidence among investors and attract financial capital to the economy, and (2) that currency crises are more likely to occur when the Left is elected in the region,

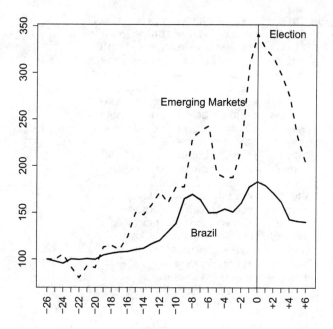

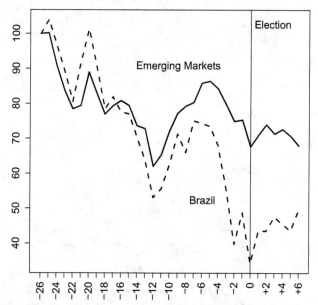

Figure 12.4 Stock markets' "vote" in two Brazilian elections.
Source: Stock market indexes for Brazil (S&P) and emerging markets (International
Financial Corporation and Data Stream Stock Market Index for 1994
and 2002, respectively).

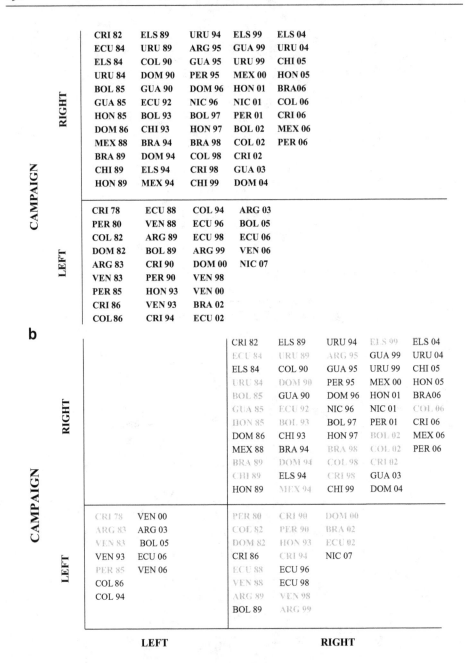

GOVERNMENT

Figure 12.5 Policy switches in Latin America.

Figure 12.5a (top) represents Latin American presidential elections, classified into Left and Right according to the campaign rhetoric of the winning candidate.

Figure 12.5b (bottom) represents Latin American presidential elections, classified into Left and Right according both to the campaign rhetoric of the winning candidate (*y* axis) and to the policies launched in that president's first year in office (*x* axis). Elections marked in gray were held under a currency crisis (extreme currency depreciation or loss of international reserves).

which is consistent with previous findings in broader samples of less developed countries (Leblang 2002).

Figure 12.5 illustrates this evidence, and displays a pattern typical of Latin American economies, in which candidates who campaign on a left-wing agenda switch to a neoliberal program immediately after inauguration (Drake 1991; Roberts 1996; Stokes 2001). Elections marked in gray in figure 12.5b are those held under severe currency pressures.

All this evidence points to a puzzle worth discussing. If there is a direct association between policies that investors care about and their influence over these policies (Mosley 2003), the anticipation of markets' punishment should be enough to prevent governments from significantly deviating from investors' preferences. The latter, knowing that a policy switch will follow, would have no reason to react to partisanship. Put simply, neither investors' negative reactions to the Left nor policy switches should persist under the possession of complete information, and much less so over a period of three decades (Drake 1991; Roberts 1996; Stokes 2001; Campello 2010). Arguably, an explanation for these peculiar patterns observed in Latin American political economies has to admit some level of uncertainty about how investors' reactions influence governments' agenda in the region.

I propose that this uncertainty has two major components. One results from recent liberalization of financial markets and from the fact that investors and governments are still "learning" about how to interact in this scenario. Studies on developed countries show that financial crises are common after financial liberalization, and countries such as France (Helleiner 1994), Australia, and New Zealand (Quiggin 1998) illustrate how elections can contribute to such crises. The other component is associated with Latin American countries' high exposure to exogenous shocks. These shocks alter countries' economic prospects, affecting both market participants' willingness to invest and countries' reliance on portfolio investment. The next section explores this argument.

5. EXOGENOUS SHOCKS AND MARKET DISCIPLINE IN LATIN AMERICA

Economists have long debated the relative importance of international ("push") and domestic ("pull") factors in determining capital flows to less developed countries (Eichengreen and Mody 1998). In the particular case of Latin America, Calvo, Leiderman, and Reinhart's (1996) influential work demonstrated that 50 percent of inflows can be attributed to exogenous causes, confirming previous studies on the topic (Gavin, Hausmann, and Leiderman 1995). A decade later, Izquierdo, Romero, and Talvo (2008) tested these findings in an updated sample and confirmed that

both capital flows and economic growth in the region are fundamentally determined by changes in the international costs of capital and variations in commodity
prices. Latin American economies, at varied levels, become more attractive to
capital when international interest rates are low and when commodity prices are
booming.

Empirical analyses show that falling interest rates in the developed world
encourage investors to seek better investment opportunities in less developed
countries, which tend to offer higher returns to capital. The credit booms of the
1970s and early 1990s are examples of this process (Edwards 1998). Conversely,
when international interest rates are high, investors tend to "fly to quality,"
moving capital to the developed world in search of safer investment opportunities. This phenomenon was observed in the early 1980s, and also in the mid- to
late 1990s.

A boom in commodity prices, as occurred between 2004 and 2008; is another
major determinant of investment flows and economic performance in Latin American
countries in which exports are mostly concentrated in primary products (fig. 12.6).
Booming export prices accelerate economic growth and have a trickling-down effect
on the domestic economy as a whole. A sudden drop in these prices, conversely,
depresses export revenues and growth rates.

These exogenously driven cycles of boom and bust contribute to an explanation
of why market discipline has not, so far, led to ideological convergence in Latin

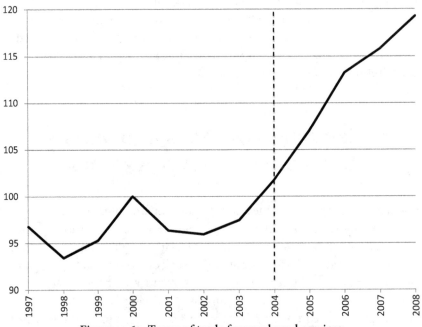

Figure 12.6a Terms of trade for goods and services.
Source: ECLAC

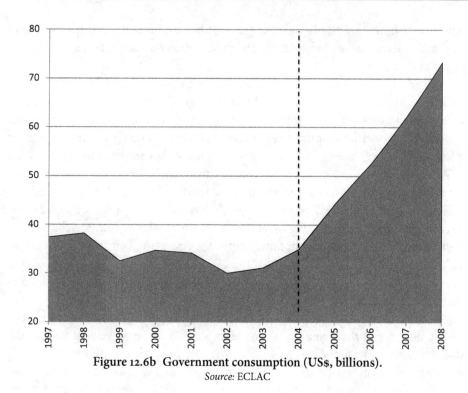

Figure 12.6b Government consumption (US$, billions).
Source: ECLAC

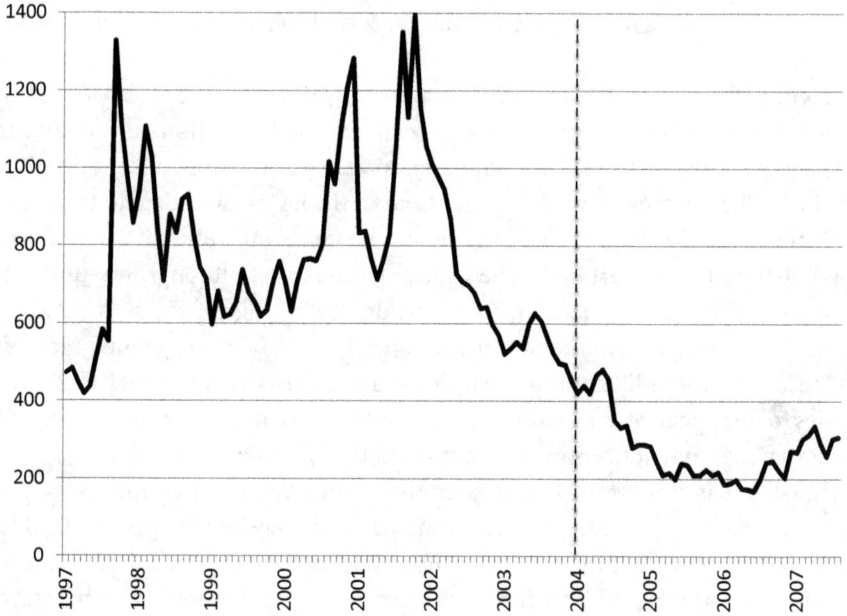

Figure 12.6c Sovereign risk, Latin America.
Source: EMBILT, Bond Spreads, Global Financial Data

America. In other words, they unravel the logic behind investors' reactions to ideology during elections, and also why leftist governments display a persistent pattern of policy switches.

My argument is simple. Capital flows tend to be pro-cyclical in Latin American countries. Therefore, during booms, investors not only become more complacent with governments' policies (Mosley 2003), but governments also become less dependent on portfolio capital. Even if investors react negatively to the prospects of a left turn in government, in booming times presidents can tell markets to "take a Valium." Given the strong payoff for redistributive policies, there is a clear incentive for leftist governments to use this room to maneuver to advance income redistribution, regardless of markets' reactions. Negative reactions are, themselves, also less likely to occur during booming times, since investors tend to be more complacent in these periods. In this context, for example, the rise of the Left in Latin American policies, which has attracted much of analysts' attention since the early 2000s, cannot be dissociated from the increased policy space provided by an unprecedented commodity price boom.

During currency crises, the opposite should happen. Governments experiencing pressure in their balance of payments become more dependent on international finance. In order to prevent sharp currency devaluations in floating exchange-rate regimes or losses of international reserves under fixed exchange rates, leaders have incentives to signal to markets their intention to advance a pro-investor agenda and in this way reattract capital to the economy. Likewise, investors' willingness to divert capital to Latin American countries also diminishes during these crises, increasing the importance of governments' efforts toward confidence building. In this context, Santiso (2003, 27) observes that "Latin America's reform fever of 1990s must be seen in the context of the urgent need for new capital inflows."

Hence, the fact that leftist governments are sometimes capable of advancing their announced agendas explains why their revealed intentions to do so during campaigns may sometimes be credible to voters and investors alike. Speculations about whether Andrés Manuel López Obrador, the leftist candidate in the Mexican 2006 presidential election, was of Lula's or Venezuelan president Hugo Chávez's type illustrate this uncertainty. The crucial issue is that although the uncertainty associated with recent financial liberalization should disappear as investors and governments repeatedly interact, uncertainties caused by exogenous factors are structural and more likely to persist. There are no reasons to expect these uncertainties to disappear, at least while Latin American economies remain dependent on foreign savings and concentrated in commodity exports.[10]

Finally, it is important to consider that Latin American countries vary with respect to their exposure to exogenous shocks, and therefore the prospects of ideological convergence in response to financial markets' "discipline" should also vary. In countries less exposed, in which uncertainties in governments' and markets' relations mainly result from recent liberalization, ideological convergence is more

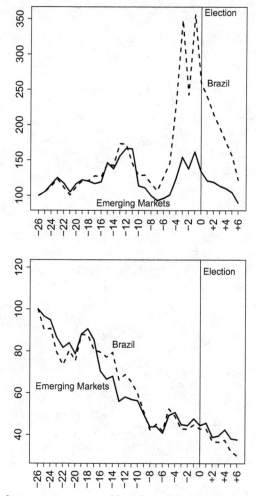

Figure 12.7 Policy convergence and bond markets' reactions, 2002 and 2006.

likely to occur over time. Contrarily, in countries in which exposure to exogenous shocks is high, governments' capacity to deviate from investors' agenda should vary markedly with time. Leftist governments in these countries are more likely to follow a pattern of radical redistribution in "good times" and policy switches in "bad times."

Brazil and Ecuador provide good examples of these two types. After the crisis triggered by the Brazilian 2002 elections, and the government's policy switch, in the 2006 election the political discourses of Left and Right mostly converged around market-friendly policies, and markets reacted with indifference (Campello 2010), as figure 12.7 shows.

In Ecuador, where negative reactions and a policy switch also occurred in 2002,[11] convergence did not follow in the 2006 elections (fig. 12.8), held in the midst

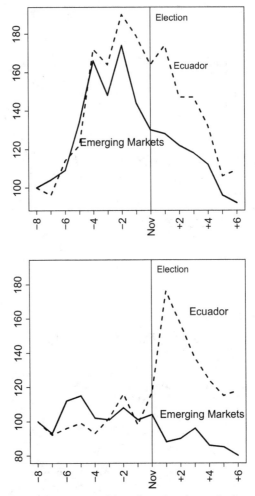

Figure 12.8 Policy divergence and bond markets' reactions, 2002 and 2006.

of a commodities boom. On the contrary, Correa won after a leftist campaign, and advanced the leftist program once in office. Markets reacted negatively but the government met this reaction with indifference.

The difference between the two cases is that, although both countries experienced "good times" in 2006; the effect of the boom was far more relevant to the latter. The Ecuadorean economy, with its dependence on oil exports, is significantly more vulnerable to cycles of booms and busts than Brazil, which is less reliant on commodity exports and on international trade itself. The fact that conditions changed so much in Ecuador between 2002 and 2006 explains how Correa was able to advance his leftist agenda while Lucio Gutiérrez was severely constrained from doing so.[12] Although this proposition attempts to explain the variation observed in these and other cases with respect to potential convergence, a systematic evaluation is still needed.

6. CONCLUSION

My goal in analyzing the politics of financial markets in Latin American emerging economies is not to compare the capacity of current financial investors for influencing policymaking with that attained by private banks and multilateral institutions during the 1970s and 1980s. Rather, I have attempted to uncover potentially new mechanisms through which market participants exert influence over governments' agendas, in a scenario of increased capital mobility and where financial markets rely on the decisions of individual, nonorganized players.

I suggest that this new structure requires understanding, since it establishes the context in which investor-government relations occur. Authors have shown that markets reveal ideological preferences with respect to Latin American governments; portfolio investors' reactions during elections are consistent and partisan, favoring right-leaning governments and punishing left-leaning ones. The "disciplining" or "constraining" effects of these reactions, however, vary quite significantly in the region, as do patterns of ideological convergence between parties in domestic political systems. I have argued that these variations can be explained only by relaxing equilibrium assumptions in the interactions between investors and governments. Investors' reactions to partisanship, as well as long-standing patterns of policy switches, indicate that this "equilibrium" has not been reached as theorists would expect under possession of complete information. I argue that an explanation for this puzzle demands a study of the sources of uncertainty that prevent equilibrium from occurring.

I, then, contend that these uncertainties are of two types, one that tends to disappear as governments and investors repeatedly interact in a scenario of increased capital mobility, and another that is structural and should be expected to persist. The latter is associated with a reliance on commodity exports and foreign funding that exposes countries to exogenously driven cycles of booms and busts, where both governments' reliance on international finance and investors' willingness to divert capital to Latin America vary substantially. In booming times, thus, governments become less dependent on finance, and investors are at the same time more attracted to the region. In these periods, leftist governments face incentives to promote as much redistribution as possible, and to openly confront investors' preferred agenda. During crises, conversely, governments' reliance on foreign finance is at its highest, but financiers' willingness to invest is low. These are the periods when the Left switches policies and converges to a more conservative agenda, likely to boost countries' attractiveness to capital inflows.

Considering the reasonable variation in countries' exposure to exogenous cycles of booms and busts, I predict that ideological convergence is more likely to occur in countries where this exposure is low. In these cases, the uncertainties due to recent liberalization should diminish with time, and those associated with exogenous factors should not be sufficient to release governments from market discipline. In the most exposed countries, conversely, even if uncertainties of investors and governments about each other's behavior diminish as financial integration evolves, dramatic cycles of booms and busts and substantial variation in governments' reliance on finance should sustain a pattern of policy switches in bad times and radical redistribution in good times.

If this rationale is correct, then, two different concerns arise with respect to the long-term political consequences of capital mobility in Latin America. In countries highly exposed to exogenous cycles of booms and busts, political volatility and lack of consistency between governments can become problematic, while electoral betrayals could potentially undermine parties' legitimacy and even provoke a collapse of these parties in the aftermath of crises, where performance is punished more harshly after party brands are diluted (Lupu 2011).

In cases where market discipline effective leads to political convergence, though, risks are of another sort. If capital mobility fosters political convergence between Left and Right, but income inequality still persists, it is possible that demands for redistribution cease to be channeled through the political system, increasing the risk of apathy or political ruptures (Kurtz 2004; Weyland 2004).

NOTES

1. See Santiso (2003) for an encompassing discussion of markets' alternative use of "voice" to express policy preferences.

2. The entire quotes goes: "If the country-risk goes up because of speculators worrying over our ability to pay the debt, I don't care. The country-risk I care about is children suffering. If they're nervous, let them take a Valium. What else can I do? " (Hayes 2006.)

3. I define policy space as a subspace of the universe of policy options available to a country in an ideal world without policy constraints.

4. Griffith-Jones (2000) shows that although the average value of inflows remained stable, the standard deviation of such flows doubled between 1975–81 and 1991–98.

5. See Cohen (1996) and Mosley (2003) for an extensive review of this literature.

6. See Lindblom (1982) and Przeworski (1988) for early discussions of the so-called structural power of business in the context of closed economies.

7. See Cohen (1996) for a review of arguments about the different kinds of impact globalization should have on macroeconomic and supply-side policies.

8. It is worth noting that although the literature provides strong theoretical support for the claim that government ideology affects financial markets in a distinguishable way, it does not necessarily imply that all sectors of the economy experience such effects in the same manner. For example, see Den Hartog and Monroe (2008) for a study of how a change from Republicans' to Democrats' control of the U.S. senate produced differentiated effects on oil and gas stocks' returns, even considering a general downward trend in the market resulting from the same event.

9. It is worth noting that the long-term effect of such policies is disputable. Endogenous-growth theorists, for instance, might claim that social expenditures in health and education are likely to increase business profitability in the long run.

10. This concentration increased after trade liberalization occurred in the 1990s.

11. Investors' strong reactions to the election in Ecuador are certainly part of a wider movement away from Latin America and emerging markets more broadly in a period of increased risk aversion, but this does not invalidate the logic. The currency pressures experienced by Gutiérrez increased the need for an IMF agreement, which itself demanded a policy switch.

12. There are other political and institutional factors that certainly contribute to explaining why Lula did not reverse his policy switch after conditions eased, but there is not space to discuss the topic in detail here. It is important to note, though, that reelection of the same leader is hardly one of them, since Chávez switched in 1998 and adopted his original agenda as soon as he had policy space to do so. See Campello (2010) for a detailed discussion of these cases.

REFERENCES

Alesina, Alberto. 1987. "Macroeconomic Policy in a Two-Party System as a Repeated Game." *Quarterly Journal of Economics* 102(3): 651–78.

Avelino, George, David S. Brown, and Wendy Hunter. 2005. "The Effects of Capital Mobility, Trade Openness, and Democracy on Social Spending in Latin America, 1980–1999." *American Journal of Political Science* 49(3): 625–41.

Bartels, Larry M. 2008. *Unequal Democracy: The Political Economy of the New Gilded Age.* Princeton, NJ: Princeton University Press.

Block, Steven, Paul M. Vaaler, and Burkhard N. Schrage. 2005. "Counting the Investor Vote: Political Business Cycles Effects on Sovereign Bonds Spreads in Developing Countries." *Journal of International Business Studies* 36: 62–88.

Block, Steven, Paul M. 2006. "Elections, Opportunism, Partisanship and Sovereign Ratings in Developing Countries." *Review of Development Economics* 10(1): 154–70.

Boix, Carles. 2000. "Partisan Governments, the International Economy, and Macroeconomic Policies in Advanced Nations, 1960–93." *World Politics* 53(1): 38–73.

Bresser-Pereira, Luiz Carlos. 2001. "Incompetência e Confidence Building por trás de 20 Anos de Quase-Estagnação da América Latina." *Revista de Economia Política* 21(1): 141–66.

Brooks, Sarah M. 2004. "Explaining Capital Account Liberalization in Latin America: A Transitional Cost Approach." *World Politics* 56(3): 389–431.

Buckley, Ross P. 2008. *The International Financial System: Policy and Regulation.* New York: Wolters Kluwer.

Calvo, Guillermo, Leonardo Leiderman, and Carmen M. Reinhart. 1996. "Inflows of Capital to Developing Countries in the 1990s." *Journal of Economic Perspectives* 10(2): 123–39.

Campello, Daniela. 2006. "External Sources of Domestic Politics: Portfolio Investors and the Election of the Left." Paper presented at the 2006 Annual Meeting of the Midwestern Political Science Association, Chicago, April 6–9.

Campello, Daniela. 2010. "Do Markets Vote? Financial Integration and Democracy in Developing Countries." Unpublished manuscript, Princeton University.

Cerny, Philip. 1995. "The Dynamics of Financial Globalization: Technology, Market Structure, and Policy Response." *Policy Sciences* 27: 319–42.

Cohen, Benjamin. 1996. "Phoenix Risen: The Resurrection of Global Finance." *World Politics* 48(2): 268–96.

Den Hartog, Chris, and Nathan W. Monroe. 2008. "The Value of Majority Status: The Effect of Jeffordsís Switch on Asset Prices of Republican and Democratic Firms." *Legislative Studies Quarterly* 33(1): 61–84.

Dornbusch, Rudiger. 1989. "The Latin American Debt Problem: Anatomy and Solutions." In *Debt and Democracy in Latin America*, edited by Barbara Stallings and Robert Kaufman, 7–22. Boulder, CO: Westview Press.

Drake, Paul. 1989. Debt and Democracy in Latin America, 1920s-1980s. In *Debt and Democracy in Latin America*, edited by Barbara Stallings and Robert Kaufman, 39–58. Boulder, CO: Westview Press.

———.1991. "Comment: The Political Economy of Latin American Populism." In *The Macroeconomics of Populism in Latin America*, edited by Rudiger Dornbusch and Sebastian Edwards, 35–40. Chicago: University of Chicago Press.

Drezner, Daniel W. 2001. "Globalization and Policy Convergence." *International Studies Review* 3(1): 53–78.

Dryzek, John S. 1996. *Democracy in Capitalist Times*. Oxford: Oxford University Press.

Edwards, Sebastian. 1998. "Capital Inflows to Latin America: A Stop-Go Story?" NBER Working Paper Series No. 6441, National Bureau of Economic Research, Washington, DC.

Eichengreen, Barry, and Ashoka Mody. 1998. "What Explains Changing Spreads on Emerging-Market Debt." NBER Working Paper No. 6408, National Bureau of Economic Research, Cambridge, MA.

Escaith, Hubert, and Igor Paunovic.2004. "Structural Reforms in Latin America and the Caribbean, 1970-2000: Indexes and Methodological Notes." Available at SSRN, http://ssrn.com/abstract=1158491.

Fiorina, Morris. 1981. *Retrospective Voting in American National Elections*. New Haven, CT: Yale University Press.

Garrett, Geoffrey. 1991. "Political Responses to Interdependence: What's 'Left' for the Left?" *International Organization* 45(4): 539–64.

———. 1998. "Global Markets and National Politics: Collision Course or Virtuous Circle?" *International Organization* 52(4): 787–824.

Gavin, Michael, Ricardo Hausmann, and Leonardo Leiderman. 1995. "Macroeconomics of Capital Flows to Latin America: Experience and Policy Issues." *RES Working Papers* No. 4012, Inter-American Development Bank, Washington, DC.

Gooptu, Sudarshan. 1993. "Portfolio Investment Flows to Emerging Markets." Working Paper No. 1117, Debt and International Finance, International Economics Department, World Bank, Washington, DC.

Griffith-Jones, Stephany. 2000. "International Capital Flows to Latin America." Serie Reformas Economicas No. 55, Growth, Employment and Equity: Latin America in the 1990s, presented at Conference on Globalization and Democracy, University of Minnesota, May 26–27.

Hayes, Monte. 2006. "Ecuador Leader Eyes Wealth Distribution." Associated Press, December 2.

Hays, Jude, Helmut Stix, and John R. Freeman. 2000. "The Electoral Information Hypothesis Revisited." Unpublished manuscript. Earlier versions presented at the l999 Meeting of the Midwest Political Science Association and at the Conference on Globalization and Democracy, University of Minnesota, May 26–27.

Helleiner, Eric. 1994. *States and the Reemergence of Global Finance*. Ithaca, NY: Cornell University Press.

Hibbs, Douglas. 1977. "Political Parties and Macroeconomic Policies." *American Political Science Review* 71(4): 1467–87.

Hirschman, Albert O. 1977. "Exit, Voice and the State." *World Politics* 31(1): 90–107.

Huber, Evelyne, Thomas Mustillo, and John D. Stephens. 2008. "Politics and Social Spending in Latin America." *Journal of Politics* 70(2): 420–36.

Izquierdo, Alejandro, Randall Romero, and Ernesto Talvi. 2008. "Booms and Busts in Latin America: The Role of External Factors." IADB Working Paper No. 631, Inter-American Development Bank, Washington, DC.

Jensen, Nathan, and Scott Schmith. 2005. "Market Responses to Politics: The Rise of Lula and the Decline of the Brazilian Stock Market." *Comparative Political Studies* 38: 1245–70.

Kahler, Miles. 1992. "External Influence, Conditionality, and the Politics of Adjustment." In *The Politics of Economic Adjustment*, edited by Stephan Haggard and Robert R. Kaufman, 89–138. Princeton, NJ: Princeton University Press.

Kahler, Miles.1998. "Capital Flows and Financial Crises in the 1990s." Introduction to *Capital Flows and Financial Crises*, edited by Miles Kahler, 69–92. Ithaca, NY: Cornell University Press.

Kaufman, Robert R., and Alex Segura-Ubiergo. 2001. "Globalization, Domestic Politics, and Social Spending in Latin America: A Time-Series Cross-Section Analysis, 1973–97." *Quarterly Journal of Economics* 53(4): 553–87.

Kitschelt, Herbert, Peter Lange, Gary Marks, and John D. Stephens. 1999. *Continuity and Change in Contemporary Capitalism*. Cambridge: Cambridge University Press.

Kurtz, Marcus. 2004. "The Dilemmas of Democracy in the Open Economy: Lessons from Latin America." *World Politics* 56: 262–302.

Kurtz, Marcus J., and Sarah M. Brooks. 2008. "Embedding Neoliberal Reform in Latin America." *World Politics* 60: 231–80.

Leblang, David A. 2002. "The Political Economy of Speculative Attacks in the Developing World." *International Studies Quarterly* 46: 69–91.

Leblang, David, and William Bernhard. 2006. *Democratic Processes and Financial Markets*. Cambridge: Cambridge University Press.

Lewis-Beck, Michael. 1988. *Economics and Elections: The Major Western Democracies*. Ann Arbor: University of Michigan Press.

Lewis-Beck, Michael, and Mary Stegmeier. 2000. "Economic Determinants of Electoral Outcomes." *Annual Review of Political Science* 3(2): 183–219.

Lindblom, Charles. 1982. "The Market as Prison." *Journal of Politics* 44(2): 324–36.

Lindert, Peter H., and Peter J. Morton. 1989. "How Sovereign Debt Has Worked." In *Developing Country Debt and the World Economy*, edited by Jeffrey D. Sachs, 225–36. Chicago: University of Chicago Press.

Lopez de Silanes, Florencio, Juan Carlos Botero Simeon Djankov, and Rafael La Porta. 2004. "The Regulation of Labor." *Quarterly Journal of Economics* 19(4): 1339–82.

Lupu, Noam. 2011. *Party Brands in Crisis: Partisanship, Brand Dilution, and the Breakdown of Political Parties in Latin America*, Ph.D. dissertation, Princeton University.

Moser, Christopher. 2007. "The Impact of Political Risk on Sovereign Bond Spreads— Evidence from Latin America." Unpublished manuscript, University of Mainz.

Mosley, Lana. 2003. *Global Capital and National Governments*. Cambridge: Cambridge University Press.

Nieto Parra, Sebastian and Javier Santiso. 2008. "Wall Street and Elections in Latin American Emerging Democracies." Working Paper No. 272, OECD Development Centre, Paris.

Oatley, Thomas. 1999. "How Constraining Is Capital Mobility? The Partisan Hypothesis in an Open Economy." *American Journal of Political Science* 43(4): 1003–27.

Obstfeld, Maurice, Jay C. Shambaugh, and Alan M. Taylor. 2008. "Financial Stability, the Trilemma, and International Reserves." NBER Working Paper No. 14217, National Bureau of Economic Research, Cambridge, MA.

O'Donnell, Guillermo. 1985. "External Debt: Why Don't Our Countries do the Obvious?" *CEPAL Review* 27:.

Przeworski, Adam. 1988. "Structural Dependence of the State on Capital." *American Political Science Review* 82(1): 11–29.

Quiggin, John. 1998. "Social Democracy and Market Reform in Australia and New Zealand." *Oxford Review of Economic Policy* 14(1): 76–95.

Quinn, Dennis. 1997. "The Correlates of Change in International Financial Regulation." *American Political Science Review* 91.

Reinhart, Carmen, and Kenneth Rogoff. 2009. *This Time Is Different: Eight Centuries of Financial Folly*. Princeton, NJ: Princeton University Press.

Remmer, Karen. 1993. "Economic Determinants of Electoral Outcomes." *American Political Science Review* 87(2): 393–407.

Renno, Lucio, and Anthony Spanakos. 2006. "Economic Fundamentals, Financial Markets, and Voting Preferences: The 1994, 1998, and 2002 Brazilian Presidential Elections." *Dados* 49(1): 11–40.

Renno, Lucio, and Anthony Spanakos. 2009. "Speak Clearly and Carry a Big Stock of Dollar Reserves: Sovereign Risk, Ideology, and Presidential Elections in Argentina, Brazil, Mexico, and Venezuela." *Comparative Political Studies* 42: 1292–1316.

Roberts, Kenneth. 1996. "Economic Crisis and the Demise of the Legal Left in Peru." *Comparative Politics* 29(1): 69–92.

Rodrik, Dani. 1998. "Why Do More Open Economies Have Bigger Governments?" *Journal of Political Economy* 106(5): 997–1032.

Rudra, Nita. 2002. "Globalization and the Decline of the Welfare State in Less-Developed Countries." *International Organization* 56(2): 7411–45.

Sachs, Jeffrey D. 1989. Introduction to *Developing Country Debt and the World Economy*, edited by Jeffrey D. Sachs, 1–36. Chicago: University of Chicago Press.

Samuels, David. 2004. "Presidentialism and Accountability for the Economy in Comparative Perspective." *American Political Science Review* 98(3): 425–36.

Santiso, Javier. 2003. *The Political Economy of Emerging Markets—Actors, Institutions and Financial Crises in Latin America*. New York: Palgrave McMillan.

Santiso, Javier, and Juan Martínez. 2003. "Financial Markets and Politics: The Confidence Game in Latin American Emerging Markets." *International Political Science Review* 24(3): 363–95.

Stallings, Barbara. 1987. *Banker to the Third World*. Berkeley: University of California Press.

———. 1992. "International Influence on Economic Policy: Debt, Stabilization, and Structural Reform." In *The Politics of Economic Adjustment*, edited by Stephan Haggard, and Robert R. Kaufman, 41–88. Princeton, NJ: Princeton University Press.

———. 2006. *Finance for Development*. Washington, DC: Brookings Institution Press.

Stokes, Susan. 2001. *Mandates and Democracy: Neoliberalism by Surprise in Latin America*. Cambridge: Cambridge University Press.

Strange, Susan. 1986. *Casino Capitalism*. New York: Basil Blackwell.

Thorp, Rosemary. 1998. *Progresso, Pobreza e Exclusão: Uma História Económica da América Latina no Século XX*. Washington, DC: Inter-American Development Bank.

Thorp, Rosemary, and Laurence Whitehead. 1987. *Latin American Debt and Adjustment Crisis*. Pittsburgh: University of Pittsburgh Press.

Weyland, Kurt. 2004. "Neoliberalism and Democracy in Latin America: A Mixed Record." *Latin American Politics and Society* 46(1): 135–57.

Wibbels, Erik. 2006. "Dependency Revisited: International Markets, Business Cycles, and Social Spending in the Developing World." *International Organization* 60: 433–68.

Wibbels, Erik, and Moises Arce. 2003. "Globalization, Taxation, and Burden-Shifting in Latin America." *International Organization* 57: 111–36.

CHAPTER 13

CABINET STABILITY AND POLICYMAKING IN LATIN AMERICA

CECILIA MARTÍNEZ-GALLARDO

1. INTRODUCTION

Changes to the composition of Latin American cabinets usually get wide coverage in the media—the vast powers of presidents and their cabinet ministers are legendary in most Latin American countries and cabinet changes are often considered an indication of the health of the government and the direction of its policies. Rapid turnover is typically associated with governments that face strong pressure to change policy, with governments that are ineffective and cannot get policies implemented, or with weak governments that use cabinet posts in exchange for support from the legislature or influential political groups. Further, the capacity of government ministers for implementing policy is a recurring theme in evaluating policymaking, and cabinet changes are often seen as hampering ministers' ability to develop the expertise necessary to design more effective policies. The implication is that presidents delegate a great deal of policymaking powers to ministers and that they in turn exert a good deal of influence on the process through which policy directives at the cabinet level become policy outcomes.

In the academic literature, the perception that changes in the composition of the government have consequences for the government's performance is also prevalent. Frequent turnover is associated with less specialization and with problems between ministers and the bureaucracies they head. Scholars commonly argue that ineffective policymaking results when ministers are changed frequently and thus cannot develop a more specialized background (for example, see Stepan and Skach 1993). Further, this turnover creates "leadership vacuums," leaving inexperienced newcomers with little or no authority with the bureaucracy in charge of the ministry (Chang, Lewis, and McCarty 2001, 3; see also Blondel 1985; Mackenzie 1987; Stepan and Skach 1993; Linz 1994; Heclo 1988). The relationship between domestic political institutions and policymaking has been studied most carefully in the economic area, where frequent turnover is associated with shorter time horizons for politicians, which hamper the long-term transactions that are essential for stable and coherent public policy.

How cabinets are formed and why they change is not only important for the day-to-day political capacity of the government. There are good reasons to believe that cabinet politics also play an important role in the durability of the political regime.[1] In the literature, scholars have argued that cabinet appointments can be used as "safety valves" to avoid the escalation of interbranch conflict (Mainwaring and Shugart 1997; Sanders 1981) or as a device to build support in the legislature (Stepan and Skach 1993; Amorim Neto 2006; Martínez-Gallardo 2008). If this is the case, understanding patterns of government formation seems especially important in the presidential regimes of Latin America where constitutional crises have been common and the record of democratic survival has been particularly poor (Przeworski et al. 2000). Although full-blown democratic breakdowns have become rarer in the region since the 1980s, other types of political instability have increased, in particular the type of interinstitutional conflict that we would expect to be associated with patterns of cabinet instability.[2]

However, despite the widespread perception that cabinet formation is of central importance in the politics of presidential systems, we still have surprisingly little systematic information about how presidential cabinets are formed and why they change, and about the consequences of patterns of cabinet stability for the politics and policies of these regimes. In the context of Latin American political systems, an important body of work has develop in recent years that explores patterns of cabinet formation and change (Cheibub, Przeworski, and Saiegh 2004; Amorim Neto 2006; Martínez-Gallardo 2009) and that tries to understand the causes of institutional crises (Pérez-Liñán 2007; Negretto 2006), but work on the effect of cabinet politics on the policymaking and governing strategies of presidents remains limited, especially outside the economic area.

In this chapter I use data on the composition of cabinets in the presidential systems of Latin America to show variation in patterns of cabinet stability across the region. First I review the existing literature on different ways to measure political stability, in particular the stability of cabinets, the causes of cabinet instability, and the link between cabinet stability and policymaking. The last two sections provide data on patterns of cabinet stability in Latin America and on its relationship with different aspects of policymaking in the region.

2. Measuring Political Stability in Presidential Systems

Traditionally, work on the stability of Latin American political systems focused mainly on *regime* stability. At least partly driven by the number of democratic breakdowns in the region, comparative work on presidentialism concentrated mostly on the relationship between presidential constitutional frameworks and democratic stability. Scholars invested much work in trying to understand how differences in presidential and parliamentary institutions affect the likelihood that countries will remain democratic or suffer a transition to an autocratic regime.[3] A related strand of the literature has studied the stability of *governments*. While a regime breakdown involves a wholesale change in the constitutional structure of a country, government changes usually take place within the existing constitution and involve a transfer of power from one set of political actors to another. In parliamentary regimes, a very sophisticated research agenda has evolved that studies the political and institutional factors that lead to more or less stable governments. This literature has produced theoretical and empirical models to explain the dynamics that lead parliamentary governments to end through an election, a change of prime minister, or a change in the partisan composition of the government.

Presidential systems, however, have fixed terms, and so work on the stability of governments was traditionally limited to studying why some presidents finish their mandates before the end of their constitutional term.[4] This research agenda studies a subset of presidential regimes where "normal politics" fails, but it does not address the issue of how presidential governments are formed and how presidential systems vary in their ability to provide stable and effective government. More recently work has extended research on the political stability of presidential systems to study changes in the partisan makeup of cabinets and patterns of coalition building (see Aleman and Tsebelis 2008; Martínez-Gallardo 2009; Kellam 2007; Altman 2000). The main question that motivates this work is what determines whether parties join or leave the government and resulting patterns of coalition stability?

Another way of understanding political stability, however, is by looking at the stability of the actors who conduct the everyday business of governing and shape government policy. Indeed, work on both regime and government stability suggests that there are good reasons to narrow our focus further and study the stability of cabinets. First, the accumulated knowledge we have suggests that cabinet changes sometimes underlie these broader types of instability. The main mechanisms that the regime stability literature turns on rely on the relative capacity of chief executives for using appointments as political resources to deal with policy and political crises and on their capacity to use appointments to secure cooperative relationships with the legislature in order to mitigate problems that arise from the dual legitimacy inherent in separation-of-powers systems. By narrowing the focus from studying the effect of constitutional arrangements on democratic stability to studying the relationship between institutional choice and cabinet stability, we can learn more about the mechanisms that link institutions and change within presidential systems.

An additional reason to narrow the focus and study cabinet stability is that much of the literature suggests that turnover of individual ministers is linked to the ability of governments to implement policy effectively. If cabinet members have an important degree of influence over policymaking—if they provide the leadership needed to manage large bureaucratic agencies, if they provide the knowledge and expertise necessary to design and implement policy, if they provide the political skills required to help the policy process along—differences in the stability of the cabinet's membership should affect the performance of the government. In the next section I explore the relationship between the stability of cabinets and policymaking in Latin America.

3. CABINET POLITICS AND POLICYMAKING

Patterns of cabinet formation and stability are crucial in shaping policymaking in presidential regimes. Through cabinet formation, presidents determine the number and nature of the veto players who will participate in decision making and, consequently, the ease with which agreements over policy will be reached. The structure of the cabinet itself, in particular the number of ministries and the division of labor among them, is crucial in shaping relations of cooperation and accountability among members of the government. Finally, the stability of cabinets once they are formed allows the accumulation of experience and allows the types of intertemporal agreements that are so crucial in designing and implementing good policies.

3.1. Cabinet Formation and the Number of Cabinet Positions

In presidential systems, cabinet formation is dominated by the president, who can determine largely at will the composition of the cabinet. In contrast to parliamentary regimes, presidents do not need the approval of a parliamentary majority to name the cabinet and so presidents whose party does not obtain majority representation in congress do not need to include in their cabinet other parties in order to obtain such a majority. However, presidents still need legislative approval to get their policy agenda through congress and so coalitions are formed frequently, especially by presidents whose party does not have majority representation in congress. Table 13.1 shows the incidence of coalition government in 12 Latin American countries. Single-party governments are most common in Costa Rica and Mexico, where presidents tend to have majority representation in the legislature. By contrast, in Brazil and Chile, no president after 1990 has obtained a majority of seats in the legislature and every president has sought the support of other parties through coalition building. Overall, coalitions are the most common form of government in the presidential regimes of Latin America.

The most obvious way in which coalition building affects policymaking is by providing presidents with the necessary support to pass legislation and implement their policy agenda. In presidential systems in particular, coalition building is one way in which presidents face the challenge of assuring a smooth passage of their political agenda through a legislature in which they do not hold a majority (Martínez-Gallardo 2009; Amorim Neto 2006; Cheibub, Przeworski, and Saiegh 2004), as well as move future policy closer to their own preferences (Cheibub and Limongi 2002).

However, dividing political authority among parties with potentially divergent interests might also increase the cost of agreement and make policymaking less efficient (Spiller, Stein, and Tommasi 2003). Distributing power among more veto players is typically seen in the literature as an obstacle to policy change, especially economic reform (Haggard and Kaufman 1992 Haggard and McCubbins 2001; but see Gehlbach and Malesky 2010), and it is seen as contributing to adverse economic conditions either through the uncertainty attached to bargaining over coalition formation (Laver and Shepsle 1996; see Moore and Mukherjee 2006 for a different perspective) or by increasing the number of veto players (Kastner and Rector 2003). In the literature on political economy in particular, coalition governments have been linked empirically to higher public spending (Bawn and Rosenbluth 2006; Mukherjee 2003; Roubini 1991; Roubini

Table 13.1. Coalition Building in Latin America, 1982–2006

Country	Years	Coalition[a]	Majority President[b]	Average Number Government Parties
Brazil	1989–2006	1.00	0.00	5.25
Chile	1989–2006	1.00	0.00	4.78
Paraguay	1989–2003	0.31	0.66	1.37
Peru	1985–2006	0.90	0.60	2.34
Uruguay	1985–2005	0.84	0.00	2.22
Venezuela	1984–2006	0.52	0.50	1.52
Ecuador	1984–2002	0.60	0.00	2.34
Argentina	1983–2003	0.16	0.42	1.21
Colombia	1982–2006	0.83	0.67	2.26
Mexico	1982–2006	0.00	0.62	1.00
Bolivia	1982–2003	0.81	0.00	2.74
Costa Rica	1982–2003	0.00	0.50	1.00

[a] Proportion of cabinets in which ministers of more than one party were represented.
[b] Proportion of cabinets where the president's party had a majority of seats in the legislature.
Source: Based on Martínez-Gallardo (2009).

and Sachs 1989; Grilli, Masciandaro, and Tabellini 1991), higher inflation (Edwards and Tabellini 1991), and the volatility of financial markets (Bernhard and Leblang 2006).[5]

Whether coalition governments will find it more difficult to coordinate policy, however, will vary across countries depending on the extent of the president's authority as well as variations in the degree to which agreement is made harder by ideological divisions or the number of parties involved in decision making. Amorim Neto and Borsani (2004), for example, argue that the size of the president's party and the extent to which presidents have strong authority to reign in their own party have an important effect on the president's ability to coordinate with coalition partners over government spending. The degree of ideological convergence within the governing coalition should also have an effect on the ability of the president to reach agreements on policy (de Swann 1973; Axelrod 1970). Transaction costs should be lower in ideologically connected cabinets than in cabinets where ideological divisions make greater compromises necessary.[6] These costs should also be lower when fewer parties are involved in decision making. Table 13.1 shows that in Latin America not only are coalitions formed frequently but the number of parties included in those coalitions varies widely, from 2.22 in Uruguay to Chile and Brazil, where the average number of parties was above 4.5. Empirically, as I will discuss below, coalitions are associated with higher levels of ministerial turnover (Martínez-Gallardo 2008), and larger coalitions are associated with more defections from the government and shorter-lived cabinets (Martínez-Gallardo 2009).[7]

The ability to coordinate and reach agreements over policy should depend not only on the number of political veto players but also on the number of political units with authority over a policy area. The number of portfolios, in particular, is important in determining how decisions are made, and the efficiency and coherence with which policy is designed and implemented. Where decision making is divided among too many political units, decisions will tend to be less efficient, coordination more difficult, and oversight more complicated. In Latin American presidential systems, the number of cabinet positions varies from a high of around 25–27 positions in Brazil and Venezuela to a low of 12 in Uruguay. As figure 13.1 shows, these numbers tend to vary over time as well, as different politicians adjust their cabinet to reflect changing political circumstances. Whether the number of cabinet positions is an obstacle to coherent policymaking will depend on how clearly jurisdictions are defined and how functions are divided among agencies (see, for example, Oszlak 2002 on Argentina).

3.2. Cabinet Stability

Even where the number of cabinet positions is low, the frequency with which individual ministers are changed is also central to policymaking. Patterns of cabinet turnover are closely related to the ability of political actors to reach cooperative outcomes and to acquire the expertise necessary to make good policy. The relationship between political stability and policy outcomes has been studied most carefully

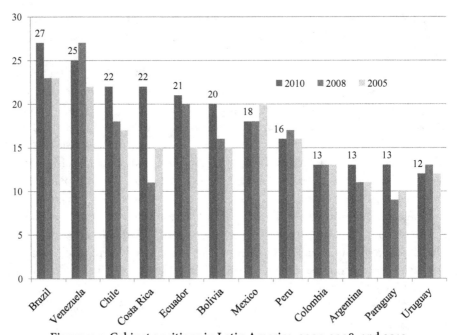

Figure 13.1 Cabinet positions in Latin America, 2005, 2008, and 2010.

Sources: CIA World Leaders (https://www.cia.gov/library/publications/world-leaders-1/index.html) and country-specific government Web pages.

in the area of economic policymaking. This literature has related economic performance to different types of political instability, including the stability of cabinet membership. The central argument is that political instability produces uncertainty about whether politicians will be in office in the next period, and this uncertainty means they have no incentives to fully internalize the costs associated with their policy choices (Persson and Tabellini 2000) or to commit credibly to intertemporal arrangements (Spiller, Stein, and Tommasi 2003). Political instability can also lead to constant changes in policy and volatility that might affect the economic performance of the government (Aisen and Veiga 2010).

The stability of the cabinet in particular is necessary to promote long-term policies and, importantly, to see the implementation of programs and policies through to completion. Frequent turnover in the cabinet makes coordination more difficult and induces politicians to pursue policies that deliver short-term, not long-term, benefits (Simmons 1994; Ozler and Tabellini 1991). Empirically, researchers have shown that this type of myopic behavior increases public debt and reduces public investment and growth (Amorim Neto and Borsani 2004; Alesina et al. 1992; Cukierman, Edwards, and Tabellini 1992; Ozler and Tabellini 1991; Roubini 1991; Roubini and Sachs 1989). To differing degrees, the same is true in other policy areas where intertemporal bargains are crucial to cooperative outcomes. Huber (1998), for example, tests the effect of cabinet stability on the ability of parliamentary governments to contain health-care costs. Unfortunately, there is very little empirical work connecting turnover in the cabinet to policy performance outside the economic arena.

Cabinet instability can also hamper relationships of accountability between politicians and bureaucrats (Huber 1998; Blondel 1985). Managing large bureaucratic agencies demands that different actors with often divergent interests work together, and turnover makes coordination among different levels of the bureaucracy difficult. Further, leadership vacuums produced by rapid turnover will tend to leave room for inefficiency and even corruption in executive agencies (Chang, Lewis, and McCarty 2001). Additionally, longer tenures should promote more stable and coherent policy outcomes by allowing politicians to follow the policies they put in place to completion. In contrast, policy switches or bureaucratic inaction should be expected where ministers are changed frequently. Abuelafia et al. (2009), for example, explore the effect of turnover on the ability of bureaucrats to execute the budget.

Stable tenures also contribute to the accumulation of policy expertise and experience that are central to policymaking (Blondel 1985; Stepan and Skach 1993). Continuity allows cabinet ministers to develop expertise specific to the policy area in which they work and to develop skills (political and managerial) that are likely to improve the quality of their performance (Huber and Martínez-Gallardo 2008). The accumulation of knowledge and the creation of institutional memory are impeded when there is high turnover, as priorities tend to shift and learning has to start anew. Corrales (1999, 2004), for example, argues that high turnover in the ministries in charge of education policy is one of the obstacles to adoption of education reform. Further, the lack of incentives to gain information tends to heighten the informational asymmetry between politicians and permanent bureaucrats and this asymmetry is likely to lead to bureaucratic drift (Huber and Shipan 2002).[8]

In the next section I use data on the composition of cabinets in Latin America to analyze patterns of turnover of individual ministers in the region. As I will show, there is wide variation in the degree of cabinet stability across these presidential systems, variation that we would expect to have important consequences for the ability of governments to make policy. In subsequent sections I relate these patterns of cabinet stability to aspects of policymaking like the ability of ministers to coordinate and their capacity for accumulating knowledge and integrating it into policymaking.

4. PATTERNS OF CABINET STABILITY IN LATIN AMERICA

As I described before, there has been much empirical work done on the democratic stability of presidential and parliamentary regimes. The last decade has seen a huge effort to measure the probability that countries with certain institutional, political, economic, or cultural characteristics will remain democratic (see, e.g., Stepan and

Skach 1993; Pzreworski et al. 2000; Cheibub 2002). The parliamentary literature includes a substantial stock of empirical knowledge about when and how governments form, how cabinets look, how portfolios are distributed, and, more recently, when and why ministers are appointed and reshuffled. Different measures of ministerial stability in these regimes have been used to link turnover to different institutional and political variables and to link stability to policy outcomes: Simmons (1994), for example, measures cabinet stability as the number of times each year in which at least 50 percent of the cabinet changed or the prime minister was replaced and relates this measure to economic policy during the interwar years.[9] Huber (1998) uses more disaggregated measures to associate turnover with the ability to contain costs in health care. Dewan and Dowding (2005 also use such measures, to relate resignations in the British cabinet to popular support for the government, as do Huber and Martínez-Gallardo (2004, 2008) to study the determinants of changes in both the choice of individual ministers and the party composition of the cabinet.

This effort, however, has not been paralleled in the literature on presidential systems. There is very limited empirical work on the stability of presidential governments that takes individual ministers as the unit of analysis and that studies the role of cabinet changes in the political process.[10] In this section I use data on individual ministerial tenures across 12 Latin American countries to explore patterns of cabinet stability in the presidential countries of the region. The data set observes the cabinet of each country and records, within the limits imposed by the availability of data, every time there is change in a portfolio.[11] The countries included in the data set are Argentina, Bolivia, Brazil, Chile, Colombia, Costa Rica, Ecuador, Mexico, Paraguay, Peru, Uruguay, and Venezuela.[12] The data extends over nearly three decades (1980s, 1990s, and part of the 2000s) but exact years included for each country vary depending on data availability (see table 13.1 for exact years included for each country). The data set includes information for 1,959 different individual politicians (58 are presidents), throughout 64 presidential administrations.

Table 13.2 shows a first way to think about the stability of ministers, which is by counting the number of individual ministers included in the data set per country (excluding the president). This number varies from 71 for Paraguay to 272 for Peru. Since the period for which I have data is different for each country, the final column in table 13.2 provides the ratio of ministers per month of data; by this measure, Paraguay is still the country with the lowest turnover of ministers and Bolivia, Venezuela, and Peru are the countries with the most ministers per month of data. A high number of ministers can be due to at least two different things, a large cabinet or a high level of turnover (or both, obviously), but these figures give a first approximation of the differences in the stability of the countries in the data set. As I have discussed, both large cabinets and high turnover have been associated with higher obstacles to policymaking.

A second way to measure the stability of individual cabinets is through the time they remain in their positions. Although the data set includes 1,959 individuals, many of these occupied more than one portfolio or occupied a position in different

Table 13.2. Ministers per month of data

Country	Months	Ministers	Ministers/Month
Peru	318	272	0.86
Venezuela	324	240	0.74
Bolivia	286	211	0.74
Colombia	319	210	0.66
Ecuador	276	190	0.69
Brazil	324	188	0.58
Mexico	323	144	0.45
Costa Rica	268	132	0.49
Argentina	280	105	0.38
Uruguay	302	100	0.33
Chile	314	96	0.31
Paraguay	283	71	0.25
All countries	3618	1959	0.54

Source: Based on Martínez-Gallardo (2008).

cabinets or in the same government but at different times. Although time served in the government surely allows politicians to gather certain types of expertise like negotiating with other political actors and becoming familiar with the political process, most of the arguments described above are based on the idea that time in a *particular* policy area is central to policymaking—it allows politicians to accumulate knowledge and build relationships with the bureaucrats in their agency but it also provides other political actors a signal that the government's policy agenda will be followed through to completion. Taking into account time served in a single portfolio, cabinet stability is generally low in Latin America. In the time covered by these data, about 18 percent of all ministers in South America, Mexico, and Costa Rica remained six months or less in the same portfolio. In fact, nearly 70 percent of all the observations in the data set had tenures of less than two years (with presidential terms that vary between four and six years), with a mean duration of 22.22 months.[13]

But portfolio stability for specific countries varies widely. Table 13.3 shows the average time that ministers stayed in a specific portfolio by country, and this average as a proportion of the president's fixed term. Again, Peru, Bolivia, and Venezuela are the countries with the lowest average tenure length; ministers in these countries (as well as in Colombia) tend to stay in office for less than a third of the length of the president's term. By contrast, in Costa Rica and Mexico ministers stay in their posts over half of the length of the president's term on average.

The importance of accumulating knowledge and specialization, however, is not uniform across policy areas, and looking at average stability might hide variation in patterns of stability across portfolios. Some policy areas are usually thought of as requiring more specialization, more expertise—finance being one more or less obvious example—while others are thought of as more "political." In more

Table 13.3. Mean Duration in a Portfolio

Country	Duration	SD	Duration/Term	SD	N
Argentina	19.83	19.71	0.35	0.37	163
Bolivia	14.10	10.89	0.29	0.23	267
Brazil	18.56	17.47	0.38	0.36	224
Chile	30.36	18.34	0.48	0.31	134
Colombia	16.53	11.02	0.34	0.23	289
Costa Rica	30.55	14.91	0.64	0.31	182
Ecuador	17.16	13.28	0.36	0.28	223
Mexico	37.22	23.99	0.52	0.33	211
Paraguay	22.61	17.58	0.38	0.29	82
Peru	13.76	10.90	0.23	0.18	360
Uruguay	26.80	21.93	0.45	0.37	169
Venezuela	19.15	15.43	0.30	0.25	349
All countries	22.22	16.29	0.39	0.29	2653

Note: Duration is measured as the average number of months in office of all the ministers in the country. If the same individual occupied more than one portfolio or was part of the government at different times, each stint in the cabinet is counted as a different observation. Duration/Term is the average duration for all ministers in a country, as a proportion of the presidential term. For both measures, the standard deviation (SD; also in months) indicates how much individual durations within the country varied.
Source: Based on Martínez-Gallardo (2008).

"technical" areas, we would expect to see fewer reshuffles—fewer changes from one portfolio to another—because it should be harder to replace someone who has a specific set of skills. By contrast, it should be relatively easier to find political appointees with political experience, with relevant political connections, with useful relationships with political parties or interest groups. Moreover, some portfolios might be used specifically by presidents as bargaining chips that they can use to negotiate with the legislature or with other political actors over policy. In consequence, we would expect to see more reshuffles in these "political" portfolios. Araujo et al. (2004), for example, argue that in Ecuador there is a clear division between "political" ministries (Agriculture, Communications, Defense, Education, etc.) and "technical" ministries (mostly economic), in which the president uses the former to reward political allies and build policy coalitions in Congress, and explicitly shields the latter from political pressures.

Recent literature finds empirical support for the idea that presidents across the region use certain portfolios to bargain with congress (Martínez-Gallardo 2008; Amorim Neto 2006), although it is not entirely clear that there is one (or more) ministries that are shielded from this dynamic across the region. In terms of the stability of tenures, Martínez-Gallardo (2008) finds that tenure rates are not any different between finance ministers and other ministers and this finding is supported by Escobar-Lemmon and Taylor-Robinson (2010). Foreign affairs ministers, however, do have significantly longer tenures than ministers in other areas.

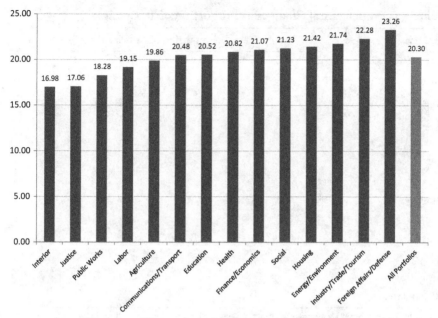

Figure 13.2 Average portfolio stability by policy area.
Average duration (measured in months) for ministers occupying portfolios in each policy
area. Data cover years between 1982 and 2006; see table 13.1 for exact years included for
each country. Based on Martínez-Gallardo (2008).

Figure 13.2 shows some evidence for this sort of pattern. Among the policy areas
where we observe the longest average tenure are energy, industry, defense, and
foreign affairs, all of which are typically considered more specialized policy areas.[14]
By contrast, evidently political ministries like justice, interior, labor, and public
works all have short average tenures. But the distinction is not always clear-cut.
Even the most "technical" portfolios can be used by the president as a concession
to the opposition (or some other political group) in exchange for votes or political
support. Ministers in social portfolios (including social security and social development, as well as housing and education), for example, have tenures that are well
above the average, and that are no different from ministers in the economic area.

Reaching broad, cross-country, conclusions about patterns of stability in
specific policy areas is difficult given that there is wide variation within policy
areas, across countries. The tenure of finance ministers across the region provides a good example. Measured as a proportion of a presidential term, the lon-
gest-lasting finance ministers are found in Uruguay and Chile, where they last
around 65 percent of the presidential term on average.[15] Next are finance ministers
in Mexico, who last around 59 percent of a term on average, followed by ministers
in Costa Rica and Colombia, who are in their positions around 44 percent of a term.
The most unstable finance ministers are found in Ecuador and Peru (20 percent)
and Venezuela and Bolivia (26 percent). These differences ought to be related to the
government's ability to coordinate over, and commit to, long-term economic policies and ultimately to better policy outcomes. Differences in other policy areas are

Table 13.4. Nonelectoral Changes as Proportion of all Changes

Country	Proportion of Nonelectoral Changes
Peru	0.75
Colombia	0.62
Argentina	0.58
Brazil	0.58
Venezuela	0.57
Bolivia	0.56
Ecuador	0.50
Paraguay	0.50
Uruguay	0.49
Chile	0.48
Mexico	0.47
Costa Rica	0.27
All countries	**0.53**

Note: Number of cabinet changes that happen between elections (i.e., excluding the government appointed by a new president after his or her election) as a proportion of the total number of appointments made by a president throughout a term.
Source: Based on Martínez-Gallardo (2008).

even more marked; the average duration of ministers in the social policy area varies from a low of 22 percent of a term in Peru to a high of over 80 percent in Paraguay and Costa Rica.

An important issue in talking about the length of ministerial tenures in presidential systems is that, unlike their counterparts in parliamentary democracies, ministers in presidential countries typically exit the cabinet when the president who appointed them leaves at the end or his or her term. This means that some ministers who could have potentially stayed longer in the cabinet are forced to step down by a constitutionally mandated election (see Martínez-Gallardo and Schleiter 2010). Table 13.4 shows the number of changes that happen between presidential elections in the presidential countries of Latin America as a proportion of all changes to the cabinet. This variable is highly correlated with the length of ministerial tenures; Peru has the highest number of changes between elections and also has the ministers with the shortest tenures and Costa Rica has the smallest number of changes and the longest tenures. Two notable outliers are Argentina and Ecuador. In Argentina nearly 60 percent of changes to the cabinet happen between elections; however, the duration of ministers is only slightly under the mean for all countries. By contrast, tenure length in Ecuador is practically the same as in Brazil but less than half of all changes to the cabinet happen between elections. This is due at least in part to the fact that Ecuador had six different presidents between 1995 and 2005.

Finally, figure 13.3 explores the temporal dimension of cabinet stability. There is the possibility that patterns of cabinet stability vary over time, as the contextual and

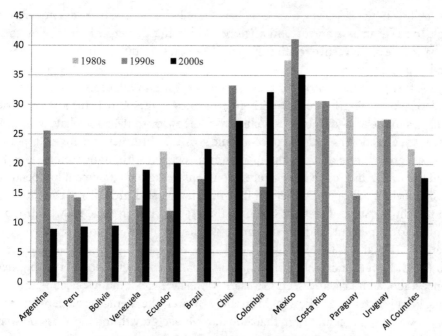

Figure 13.3 **Average portfolio stability by decade.**
For each decade, bars represent the average duration in months for administrations that
started at any point during the decade. For the 2000s, only complete administrations
were included (e.g., Lula's first term is included but not his second). Data after 2000 are
incomplete, see table 13.1 for details on years included for each country. Based on
Martinez-Gallardo (2008).

structural factors that give rise to them change. As we will see in the next section,
changes in economic conditions, in the identity of political actors, and in the
distribution of political power among them should affect ministerial tenure lengths
in a country, over time. The obvious difficulty in comparing ministerial duration
across the last three decades, however, is that the data set has only partial coverage of
the years since 2000 and there is the risk of underestimating the stability of cabinets
formed in these years. As a partial solution, figure 13.3 includes only complete administrations and divides them in three groups according to the year the president took
office: administrations that took office between 1980 and 1989, those that started
between 1990 and 1999, and those that started after 2000. This still means that the
data for the last decade are partial since only 12 complete administrations started after
2000, compared with 24 that started in the 1980s and 30 that started in the 1990s.

Taking into account the limitations of the data, figure 13.3 shows that the average duration of cabinet ministers across the region has decreased steadily in the
last three decades, from an average of 22.6 months for cabinets that took office in
the 1980s to 17.7 months for those that started after 2000. In fact, ministerial tenures
have increased in Brazil and Colombia with regard to the previous two decades and
in Venezuela and Ecuador with regard to the last decade only. In Argentina, Peru,
Bolivia, Chile, and Mexico the trend in ministerial tenures has been toward more

instability. In the cases of Costa Rica, Paraguay, and Uruguay, there are not enough data to make an assessment. Although no clear pattern emerges at first sight, there are a couple of suggestive relationships between these numbers and some economic and political indicators.

A first potential reason for these patterns is variation in economic conditions. Indeed, comparing figure 13.4 with growth rates suggests that in most countries changes in the level of cabinet stability from the 1990s to the 2000s have moved in the same direction as patterns of economic growth.[16] In Argentina, for example, an average growth rate of 5.3 in the 1990s was associated with higher tenure lengths, and a decrease in growth rates after 2000 to an average of 3.4 percent has been accompanied by a drop in cabinet stability. In Ecuador, also, growth and stability have moved in the same direction: down in the 1990s, when average growth dropped from 3 to 1.7 percent, and up after 2000 when they increased to an average of 5.2 percent. The same is true in Bolivia and Chile, where average growth rates declined and so did levels of cabinet stability. Venezuela, Brazil, and Colombia have grown since 2000, and have also seen increases in the average duration of cabinet ministers. Peru is a clear exception to this trend, however; the average growth rate for the 1990s was 4.17 percent, lower than the 4.8 average growth for the years between 2000 and 2006 and yet stability has increased.

Of course, politics matters too, but it is not clear from figure 13.3 in which way it matters. Increases in cabinet stability are compatible with sharp declines in indexes of political constraints (as in Colombia, Ecuador, or Venezuela) as well as continuing stability in constitutional limits, like Brazil.[17] Perhaps the common trait among countries where we see increased stability is a strong, popular president. Despite the differences in these leaders' governing strategies and relationship with other institutions, we see increased stability in Brazil and Venezuela, where Presidents Luiz Inácio Lula da Silva and Hugo Chavez have had average approval rates over 50 percent, much higher than their immediate predecessors, or in Colombia and Ecuador, where approval rates for Presidents Alvaro Uribe and Rafael Correa averaged around 75 percent. Instability, in contrast, seems to have grown in countries like Mexico or Bolivia, where social conflict grew significantly in the years after 2000, despite relatively popular presidents.[18] In the next section I explore how these and other factors shape patterns of cabinet stability.

5. What Explains Patterns of Cabinet Stability?

As I have mentioned, there is very limited work that connects patterns of stability like the ones illustrated above to institutional and contextual factors and that uses data on individual ministerial appointments to systematically test arguments about these connections. This is especially true with regard to presidential political systems. In the next paragraphs I review the main arguments offered by the existing literature about the factors that explain variation in ministerial tenures, and examine some of the existing empirical evidence that has been brought to bear on them.

Two views of turnover are most prevalent in the existing literature on patterns of cabinet stability. A first way of thinking about ministerial turnover is as part of the process through which party leaders or presidents search for the people best suited for particular posts. Chang, Lewis, and McCarty (2001) and Gordon, Anderson, and Tomlinson (2001), for example, assess the impact of different personal and institutional factors on the likelihood that an appointee gets promoted within the government or leaves the government altogether. In the parliamentary context, Huber and Martínez-Gallardo (2008) also propose a view of ministerial changes in parliamentary democracies as tools that party leaders use to sift through the pool of available candidates and find the best fit for each job. In this view, the extent to which reshuffles will be used depends on the uncertainty that party leaders face regarding the qualifications of candidates for positions, the amount of trust between the parties involved in cabinet formation, the degree to which positions give their occupants policymaking authority, and the constraints that party leaders face when trying to make changes.

A related way to think of cabinet turnover is as responses by the prime minister to crises that produce a dip in the government's support. Dewan and Dowding (2005 argue that in parliamentary systems, reshuffles have a "corrective effect": in the face of a scandal or crisis, the prime minister is rewarded for getting rid of a minister who is perceived to be responsible. This view of reshuffles combines the notion that cabinet reshuffles are means of changing policy in a direct way, with a more political view of appointments as resources that the chief executive can use to shore up support.

In line with the idea that appointments are political resources as much as they are policy tools, a second view of reshuffles grows from the literature on cabinet duration and conceives of ministerial changes as being related to bargaining among parties in government and between the government and the legislature. Diermeier and Merlo (2000), for example, argue that changes in the political and economic environment might make it necessary for the ruling coalition to reshuffle the cabinet in order to preserve the government. This happens because, after the initial cabinet formation, a shift in the status quo might change the incentives of coalition parties and the opposition to support the government. In this view, cabinet posts are transferable benefits that can be allocated both among the members of the government coalition and to parties in the opposition in exchange for political support. In recent years, a similar view of appointments has been used to explain patterns of cabinet stability in Latin America. In this view, cabinet instability should increase when there are more political and economic shocks and when other available political resources (such as the legislative process) are unavailable or costly. In particular, variations in the distribution of policymaking powers should affect the extent to which concessions in the form of cabinet changes are necessary to get policy done; presidents who have majority support in congress or can govern by decree will be less likely to need to use appointments as part of their policymaking strategy (Martínez-Gallardo 2008; Amorim Neto 2006).

Empirically, Martínez-Gallardo (2008) finds evidence that shocks are related to cabinet turnover for a cross-section of 12 Latin American countries; higher rates of inflation and more political conflict are associated with increased turnover, while higher rates of growth and higher approval rates for the president are associated, as expected, with lower rates of turnover (see also Altman 2000 on Uruguay). Martínez-Gallardo (2008) also provides evidence for the view of appointments as a tool in interbranch bargaining, finding that cabinet stability is substantially higher where presidents have a combination of decree powers and reactive authority that permits them to essentially bypass the legislature in making policy.

6. CABINET STABILITY AND POLICYMAKING: SOME PRELIMINARY RESULTS

I have argued that resulting patterns of cabinet stability are important because they shape the interactions between individual ministers and between the cabinet and bureaucratic agencies, and, consequently affect the quality of policymaking. Longer and more stable tenures contribute to ministers' policy expertise and experience and improve the quality of relations between ministers in the cabinet, giving them time to develop means of cooperation and the ability to commit each other to intertemporal trade-offs. For the principals managing bureaucratic agencies, stability helps ministerial credibility, authority, knowledge, and control. In the light of these arguments, cabinet stability ought to contribute to improvements in the making of public policy.

There are many methodological and conceptual issues that complicate the task of linking cabinet stability and policymaking. I surveyed before some of the work that links cabinet stability to policy outcomes, especially in the economic area, including the reciprocal relationship between stability, on the one hand, and inflation, the size of government, and the volatility of markets, on the other. However, this work generally assumes, rather than demonstrating empirically, the causal mechanisms that relate ministerial tenures to the aspects of policymaking, like coordination and learning, that are supposed to lead to better policies. In concluding this chapter I use data developed by Bertelsmann Stiftung that seeks to measure the "performance, capacity and accountability of [a country's] political leadership" to illustrate these links (BTI 2010, 7). I use scores on two indexes: the first index (Market Economy Performance) ranks countries (119 countries in the 2006 edition used in the figures below) in terms of their progress in establishing a market economy and the second index (Management Performance) ranks the management skills of their leadership. The Management Index, in particular, provides data on the features of policymaking that we would expect cabinet stability to affect.

I start by showing the relationship between cabinet stability and the establishment of a market economy in Latin America. Figure 13.4 relates the average length of ministerial tenures in the 1990s and 2000s (measured in months, as a proportion of the presidential term) with the score received by each country in the 2006 edition of the Bertelsmann Market Economy Performance Index, which scores countries on their progress in establishing property rights, establishing a framework for competition, and achieving currency and price stability. The figure shows a clear positive relationship between progress in developing a market economy and cabinet stability. The ability to establish clear rules for competition and implement the types of reforms that lead to price stability seems to be related, at least in part, to the stability of the cabinet. Two countries appear to be clear outliers, however. In 2006 Chile was the highest-ranked country in Latin America in terms of its progress in establishing the institutions of a market economy (and ranked 10th in the world) but ranked third in terms of cabinet stability, behind Mexico and Costa Rica. The second outlier, Paraguay, scored around the mean for cabinet stability but very poorly in terms of its progress in establishing a market economy. As we will see, Chile consistently outperforms countries that have more cabinet stability and Paraguay often scores lower on performance measures than countries with a worse record of cabinet stability.

The value of cabinet stability is further supported by evidence that it seems to improve the policymaking capacity of the government, as the literature reviewed before would suggest. Figure 13.5 again uses data from the 2006 Bertelsmann index to compare the performance of political leaders, including cabinet members and other relevant political actors, with a measure of portfolio stability. As we would

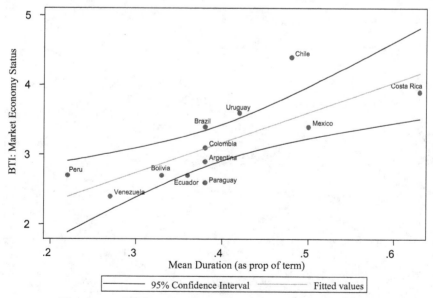

Figure 13.4 Market economy and stability in Latin America.
Market Economy Status Index is from Bertelsmann Stiftung (http://www.bertelsmann-transformation-index.de/en/bti/). Mean duration is the average duration for all ministers in each country as a proportion of the presidential term.

expect, there is a positive relationship between portfolio stability and the manage-rial performance of the government. Chile again has better managerial performance than one would expect from its level of portfolio stability, as do Brazil and Uruguay. Paraguay, instead, has worse management performance than predicted by its level of portfolio stability.

The Management Performance Index scores countries on several aspects of the government's policymaking performance, including the steering capabilities of their leaders, their resource efficiency, and their ability to build consensus and to conduct international negotiations. In the next paragraphs I focus specifically on the first two criteria, steering capability and resource efficiency, which are the aspects of policymaking that we would expect from the literature to be most closely related to cabinet stability. The index defines the government's steering capability as the ability to realize goals even in the face of political resistance (BTI 2006, 18) and determines each country's score by asking how effective the government is in imple-menting reform policy and whether it is flexible enough and has the capability to learn from experience and incorporate this information into policymaking. The resource efficiency of governments is scored based on how efficiently they use avail-able economic and human resources and on their ability to coordinate conflicting objectives into coherent policymaking.

The top two panels in figure 13.6 show the relationship between resource effi-ciency and coordination and portfolio stability. In both cases, countries with longer average ministerial tenures score higher on the efficient use of resources and the ability to coordinate priorities in order to implement coherent policies. The bottom

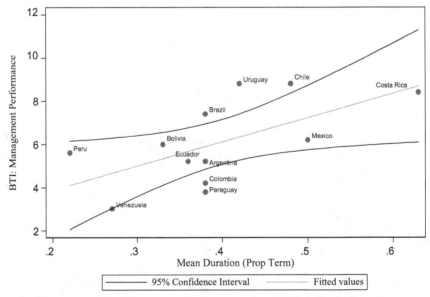

Figure 13.5 Management performance and stability in Latin America.
Management Performance Index is from Bertelsmann Stiftung (http://www.bertelsmann-transformation-index.de/en/bti/). Mean duration is the average duration for all ministers in each country as a proportion of the presidential term.

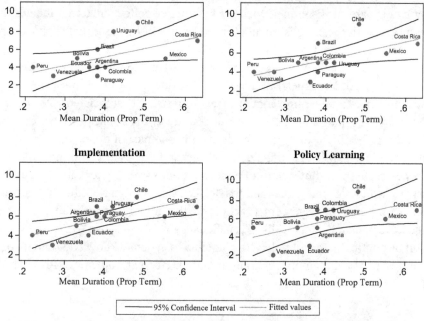

Figure 13.6 Dimensions of management performance and cabinet stability.
Data on the different dimensions of management performance are from Bertelsmann
Stiftung (http://www.bertelsmann-transformation-index.de/en/bti/). Mean duration is the
average duration for all ministers in each country, as a proportion of the presidential term.

two panels also show a positive relationship between implementation and learning
capacity and portfolio stability. While on their own these bivariate relationships are
far from conclusive and do not show causality, the patterns do suggest that stability
does bring some of the benefits that theory would suggest. Less turnover does appear to aid the accumulation of experience and knowledge, help coordination across
different levels of the government, and facilitate the conditions for more efficient
implementation of policies. These general patterns have some exceptions, however.
In every case Chile scores better in the Management Index than would be expected
given its level of portfolio stability. This is true to a lesser degree for Uruguay and
Brazil as well. On the other extreme, Ecuador performs worse on most dimensions
of the index than would be predicted based on its level of portfolio stability. The
same is true of Venezuela on the two dimensions of steering capabilities, policy
learning and implementation, and to a certain extent of Paraguay on resource efficiency and coordination.

These patterns are obviously only suggestive without more detailed and careful
empirical work recognizing the multiple factors that can influence the management
performance of the government and its ability to establish the institutions of a market economy. Nevertheless, they provide prima facie evidence that portfolio stability
affects the capacity of governments for coordinating and combining different goals
into coherent policies, as well as the accumulation of experience and knowledge that

allows for better policies. Measures of cabinet stability based on the length of ministerial tenures are consistently associated with better policy outcomes, including, as shown here, with the establishment of the rules and institutions that support a market economy. Mexico, Costa Rica, and Chile have consistently long tenure lengths and they also score relatively high on the BTI Market Economy Performance Index. By contrast, Peru, Venezuela, Bolivia, and Ecuador score much lower on both dimensions. Ministerial tenure lengths are also consistently associated with measures of policymaking like the efficient use of resources, the capacity for coordinating across the government to achieve goals even in the face of opposition or differing goals, and the ability to accumulate knowledge and integrate it into the policymaking process. On these dimensions of policymaking as well, higher cabinet stability in Mexico, Costa Rica, and Chile (and to a lesser extent Uruguay and Brazil) are associated with better management practices in the government. Cabinet instability, instead, is associated in places like Peru, Ecuador, and Venezuela with worse coordination by political actors of policy, the inability to generate knowledge and incorporate it into policy, and, more generally, a more inefficient implementation of public policy.

NOTES

....

1. See Feng (1997) on the relationship between different types of instability, democracy, and economic growth.

2. Pérez-Liñán (2007) identifies 58 presidential crises in Latin America between 1950 and 2004 in which the president (or executive branch) or congress unilaterally decided to impeach the other, force the resignation of the other branch's main officers, or support a coup against the other.

3. Some examples are Przeworski et al. (2000), Stepan and Skach (1993), and Cheibub (2002). See Samuels and Eaton (2002) for a review of the literature.

4. For studies on incomplete mandates, see Pérez-Liñán (2005, 2007), Weyland (1993, 1998), Carey (2003), Coppedge (1994), Negretto (2006), and Valenzuela (1994).

5. In contrast, Bussière and Mulder (2000) do not find a statistically significant relationship between the economic vulnerability of countries and the incidence of coalition government.

6. In the literature on parliamentary regimes, these cabinets have been found to survive longer (Warwick 1994), which should further contribute to better policymaking. Martínez-Gallardo (2008) tests this relationship for Latin American presidential systems and finds that although the empirical relationship seems to go in the expected direction, the relationship is not robust.

7. Beyond the number of political actors with veto power over policy, the electoral calendar also plays a central role in shaping economic outcomes. On the relationship between fiscal and political cycles in Latin America, see Nieto Parra and Santiso (2008, 2009).

8. Despite the known negative effects of rapid turnover, executives continue to reshuffle their cabinets. Indridason and Kam (2008) argue that prime ministers do so in

order to minimize the problem of moral hazard inherent in ministerial selection. Huber and Martínez-Gallardo (2008) argue that reshuffles allow presidents to deal also with problems of adverse selection in selecting the individuals best suited for cabinet positions.

9. For other examples of work that uses measures of turnover based on a certain number of changes in the composition of the government, see Alt (1975) and Kam and Indridason (2005).

10. The most obvious exception is work on political appointees in the United States (see Chang, Lewis, and McCarty 2001; Gordon, Anderson, and Tomlinson 2001). This work is based on remarkable individual-level data on the careers of political appointees throughout the history of the United States.

11. Data collection would have not been possible had it not been for the excellent research assistance provided by Ines Valdez and Ali Stoyan. Some of the main sources used to construct the data set are *Keesings Record of World Events* (several years), LexisNexis Academic Universe, Internet Securities, Inc. (ISI) Emerging Markets, and other country-specific news sources.

12. I exclude Central American countries from the database because of limitations in the availability of reliable data on the composition of their cabinets.

13. For reference purposes, Chang, Lewis, and McCarty (2001) find that the average tenure of political appointees in the United States is 33 months for all positions (down to assistant secretaries) and 34.7 months (almost three years) for secretaries only (with a presidential term of four years). Their data covers the period 1789–2000. Huber and Martínez-Gallardo (2004) find that ministers in parliamentary democracies stayed in their positions an average of 1,175.5 days, or about 39 months. Their data cover the postwar period to 1999.

14. Martínez-Gallardo and Schleiter (2010) also find that presidents are more likely to name independent ministers (rather than partisans) to the ministry of defense but not finance.

15. These numbers include finance ministers as well as ministers of the economy, budget, and planning.

16. Data on growth are based on gross domestic product growth (annual percentage), from World Development Indicators website, with decade means used. I use years up to, and including, 2006 to calculate average growth in the 2000s.

17. I measure political constraints using the Polconv index of political constraints constructed by Witold Henisz. See Henisz (2000).

18. Average approval rates for Mexican presidents Vicente Fox (2000–2006) and Felipe Calderón (2006 to 2012) have averaged 57 percent. In Bolivia, President Evo Morales has had an average approval of 52 percent. Approval rates are from Carlin, Hartlyn, and Martínez-Gallardo (2009).

REFERENCES

Abuelafia, Emanuel, Sergio Berensztein, Miguel Braun, and Luciano di Grezia. 2009. "Who Decides on Public Expenditures? A Political Economy Analysis of the Budget Process: The Case of Argentina." In *Who Decides the Budget? A Political Economy Analysis of the Budget Process in Latin America*, edited by Mark Hallerberg, Carlos Scartascini, and Ernesto H. Stein, 23–56. Washington, DC: Inter-American Development Bank; Cambridge, MA: David Rockefeller Center for Latin American Studies, Harvard University.

Aisen, Ari, and Francisco José Veiga, 2010. "How Does Political Instability Affect Eco-
    nomic Growth?" NIPE Working Paper No. 5/2010, Núcleo de Investigação em
    Políticas Económicas (NIPE), Universidade do Minho, Minho, Portugal.
Alemán, Eduardo, and George Tsebelis. 2008. "Coalitions in Presidential Democracies:
    How Preferences and Institutions Affect Cabinet Membership." Paper presented at the
    Annual Meeting of the Midwest Political Science Association, Chicago.
Alesina, Alberto, Sule Ozler, Nouriel Roubini, and Phillip Swagel. 1992. *Political Instability
    and Economic Growth*. Cambridge, MA: National Bureau of Economic Research.
Alt, James E. 1975. "Continuity, Turnover and Experience in the British Cabinet, 1968–
    1970." In *Cabinet Studies: A Reader*, edited by Valentine Herman and James E. Alt,
    33–54. London: Macmillan.
Altman, David. 2000. "The Politics of Coalition Formation and Survival in Multi-Party
    Presidential Democracies: The Case of Uruguay, 1989–1999." *Party Politics* 6: 259–83.
Amorim Neto, Octavio. 2006. "The Presidential Calculus: Executive Policy Making
    and Cabinet Formation in the Americas." *Comparative Political Studies* 39(4):
    415–40.
Amorim Neto, Octavio, and Hugo Borsani. 2004. "Presidents and Cabinets: The Political
    Determinants of Fiscal Behavior in Latin America." *Studies in Comparative Interna-
    tional Development* 39(1): 3–27.
Araujo, María Caridad, Andrés Mejía Acosta, Aníbal Pérez-Liñán, and Sebastián Saiegh.
    2004. "Political Institutions, Policymaking Processes, and Policy Outcomes in Ecuador."
    Unpublished manuscript, Latin American Research Network, Inter-American
    Development Bank, Washington, DC.
Axelrod, Robert M. 1970. *Conflict of Interest: A Theory of Divergent Goals with Applications
    to Politics*. Chicago: Markham.
Bawn, Kathleen, and Frances M. Rosenbluth. 2006. "Short versus Long Coalitions:
    Electoral Accountability and the Size of the Public Sector." *American Journal of
    Political Science* 50(2): 251–65.
Bernhard, William, and David Leblang. 2006. *Democratic Processes and Financial Markets:
    Pricing Politics*. New York: Cambridge University Press.
Blondel, Jean. 1985. *Government Ministers in the Contemporary World*. London: SAGE.
BTI (Bertelsmann Transformation Index). 2010. *Manual for Country Assessments*. Munich:
    Center for Applied Policy Research; Gütersloh: Bertelsmann Stiftung.
Bussière, Mathieu, and Christian Mulder. 2000. "Political Instability and Economic
    Vulnerability." *International Journal of Finance and Economics* 5: 309–30.
Carey, John M. 2003. "Presidentialism and Representative Institutions." In *Constructing
    Democratic Governance in Latin America*, edited by Jorge I. Domínguez and Michael
    Shifter, 11–42. Baltimore: Johns Hopkins University Press.
Carlin, Ryan, Jonathan Hartlyn, and Cecilia Martínez-Gallardo. 2009. "The Dynamics of
    Executive Approval under Alternative Democratic Regimes." Unpublished grant
    proposal and data set, University of North Carolina, Chapel Hill.
Chang, Kelly, David Lewis, and Nolan McCarty. 2001. "The Turnover of Political Appoin-
    tees." Paper presented at the 2001 Meeting of the Midwest Political Science Associa-
    tion, April 19–21, Chicago.
Cheibub, José Antonio. 2002. "Minority Governments, Deadlock Situations and the
    Survival of Presidential Democracies." *Comparative Political Studies* 35(3): 284–312.
Cheibub, José Antonio, and Fernando Limongi. 2002. "Democratic Institutions and
    Regime Survival: Parliamentary and Presidential Democracies Reconsidered." *Annual
    Review of Political Science* 5: 151–79.

Cheibub, José Antonio, Adam Przeworski, and S. Saiegh. 2004. "Government Coalitions and Legislative Success under Presidentialism and Parliamentarism." *British Journal of Political Science* 34: 565–87.

Coppedge, Michael. 1994. "Prospects for Democratic Governability in Venezuela." *Journal of Interamerican Studies and World Affairs* 36(2): 39–64.

Corrales, Javier. 1999. *The Politics of Education Reform: Bolstering the Supply and Demand: Overcoming Institutional Blocks.* The Education Reform and Management Series, vol. 2, no. 1. Washington, DC: World Bank.

———. 2004."Multiple Preferences, Variable Strengths: The Politics of Education Reforms in Argentina." In *Crucial Needs, Weak Incentives: Social Sector Reform, Democratization, and Globalization in Latin America*, edited by Robert R. Kaufman and Joan M. Nelson. Baltimore: Johns Hopkins University Press

Cukierman, Alex, Sebastián Edwards, and Guido Tabellini. 1992. "Seignorage and Political Instability." *American Economic Review* 82: 537–55.

De Swann, Abram. 1973. *Coalition Theories and Cabinet Formation.* Amsterdam: Elsevier.

Dewan, Torun, and Keith Dowding. 2005. "The Corrective Effect of Ministerial Resignations on Government Popularity." *American Journal of Political Science* 49: 46–56.

Diermeier, Daniel, and Antonio Merlo. 2000. "Government Turnover in Parliamentary Democracies." *Journal of Economic Theory* 94(1): 46–79.

Edwards, Sebastián, and Guido Tabellini. 1991. "Political Instability, Political Weakness and Inflation: An Empirical Analysis." NBER Working Paper No. W3721, National Bureau of Economic Research, Cambridge, MA.

Escobar-Lemmon, María, and Michelle Taylor-Robinson. 2010. "Coming or Going: How Background Affects Duration in 5 Presidential Systems." Paper presented at the American Political Science Association Annual Meeting, Washington, DC, September 2–5.

Feng, Yi. 1997. "Democracy, Political Stability and Economic Growth." *British Journal of Political Science* 27(3): 391–418.

Gelbach, Scott, and Edmund J. Malesky. 2010. "The Contribution of Veto Players to Economic Reform." *Journal of Politics* 72(4): 957–75.

Gordon, Sanford C., William Anderson, and Andrew Tomlinson. 2001. "Reconsidering Presidential Appointee Tenure." Paper presented at the Annual Meeting of the Midwest Political Science Association April 19–21, Chicago.

Grilli, Vittorio, Donato Masciandaro, and Guido Tabellini. 1991. "Political and Monetary Institutions and Public Financial Policies in the Industrial Countries." *Economic Policy* 6(2): 341–92.

Haggard, Stephen, and Robert Kaufman, eds. 1992. *The Politics of Economic Adjustment: International Constraints, Distributive Conflicts, and the State.* Princeton, NJ: Princeton University Press.

Haggard Stephen, and MD McCubbins, eds. 2001. *Presidents, Parliaments, and Policy.* New York: Cambridge University Press.

Heclo, Hugh. 1988. "The In-and-Outer System: A Critical Assessment." In *Political Science Quarterly* 103(1): 37–56.

Henisz, Witold J. 2000. "The Institutional Environment for Economic Growth." *Economics and Politics* 12(1): 1–31.

Huber, John D. 1998. "How Does Cabinet Instability Affect Political Performance? Portfolio Volatility and Health Care Cost Containment in Parliamentary Democracies." *American Political Science Review* 92(3): 577–91.

Huber, John D., and Cecilia Martínez-Gallardo. 2004. "Cabinet Instability and the Accumulation of Experience by Cabinet Ministers: The French Fourth and Fifth Republics in Comparative Perspective." *British Journal of Political Science* 34(1): 27–48.

———. 2008. "Replacing Cabinet Ministers: Patterns of Ministerial Stability in Parliamentary Democracies." *American Political Science Review* 102(2): 169–80.

Huber, John D., and Charles R. Shipan. 2002. *Deliberate Discretion: The Institutional Foundations of Bureaucratic Autonomy.* Cambridge: Cambridge University Press.

Indridason, Indridi, and Christopher Kam. 2008. "Cabinet Reshuffles and Ministerial Drift." *British Journal of Political Science* 38: 621–56.

Kam, Christopher, and Indridi Indridason. 2005. "The Timing of Cabinet Reshuffles in Five Westminster Parliamentary Systems." *Legislative Studies Quarterly* 30: 327–63.

Kastner, Scott L., and Chad Rector. 2003. "International Regimes, Domestic Veto Players and Capital Controls Policy Stability." *International Studies Quarterly* 47(1): 1–22.

Kellam, Marissa. 2007. "Parties for Hire: The Instability of Presidential Coalitions in Latin America." PhD diss., University of California, Los Angeles.

Laver, Michael, and Kenneth Shepsle. 1996. *Making and Breaking Governments: Cabinets and Legislatures in Parliamentary Democracies.* Cambridge: Cambridge University Press.

Linz, Juan José. 1994. "Presidential or Parliamentary Democracy: Does It Make a Difference?" In *The Failure of Presidential Democracy*, vol. 2, *The Case of Latin America*, edited by Juan José Linz and Arturo Valenzuela, 3–87. Baltimore: Johns Hopkins University Press.

Mackenzie, Galvin C. 1987. *The In-and-Outers: Presidential Appointees and Transient Government in Washington.* Baltimore: Johns Hopkins University Press.

Mainwaring, Scott, and Mathew Soberg Shugart, editors. 1997. *Presidentialism and Democracy in Latin America.* Cambridge: Cambridge University Press.

Martínez-Gallardo, Cecilia. 2008. "Designing Cabinets: Ministerial Instability in Latin America." Unpublished manuscript, University of North Carolina, Chapel Hill.

———. 2009. "Coalition Duration in Presidential Systems." Paper presented at the Annual Meeting of the Latin American Studies Association, Rio de Janeiro, Brazil, July.

Martínez-Gallardo, Cecilia, and Petra Schleiter. 2010. "A Transaction Costs Approach to Ministerial Selection in Latin America." Paper presented at the American Political Science Association Annual Meeting, Washington, DC, September 2–5.

Moore, Will H., and Bumba Mukherjee. 2006. "Government Formation in Parliamentary Democracies and Foreign Exchange Markets: Theory and Evidence from Europe." *International Studies Quarterly* 50(1): 93–118.

Mukherjee, Bumba. 2003. "Political Parties and the Size of Government in Multiparty Legislatures: Examining Cross Country and Panel Data Evidence." *Comparative Political Studies* 36(6): 699–728.

Negretto, G. 2006. "Minority Presidents and Democratic Performance in Latin America." *Latin American Politics and Society* 48(3): 63–92.

Nieto Parra, Sebastián, and Javier Santiso. 2008. "Wall Street and Election in Latin American Emerging Democracies." Working Paper No. 272, OECD Development Center, Paris.

———. 2009. "Revisiting Political Budget Cycles in Latin America." Working Paper No. 281, OECD Development Centre, Paris.

Oszlak, Oscar. 2002. "Redemocratization and the Modernization of the State: The Alfonsín Era in Argentina." In *Transitions from Authoritarianism: The Role of the Bureaucracy*, edited by Randall Baker, 207–27. Westport, CT: Praeger.

Ozler, Sule, and Guido Tabellini. 1991. "External Debt and Political Instability." NBER Working Paper No. 3772, July, National Bureau of Economic Research, Cambridge, MA.

Pérez-Liñán, Aníbal. 2005. "Democratization and Constitutional Crises in Presidential Regimes." *Comparative Political Studies* 38(1): 51–74.

———. 2007. *Presidential Impeachment and the New Political Instability in Latin America.* Cambridge: Cambridge University Press.

Persson, Torsten, and Guido Tabellini. 2000. *Political Economics: Explaining Economic Policy*. Cambridge, MA: MIT Press.

Przeworski, Adam, Michael E. Alvarez, José Antonio Cheibub, and Fernando Limongi. 2000. *Democracy and Development: Political Institutions and Well-Being in the World, 1950–1990*. Cambridge: Cambridge University Press.

Roubini, Nouriel. 1991. "Economic and Political Determinants of Budget Deficits in Developing Countries." *Journal of International Money and Finance* 10, Supplement 1: S49–S72.

Roubini, Nouriel, and Jeffrey Sachs. 1989. "Political and Economic Determinants of Budget Deficits in the Industrial Democracies." *European Economic Review* 33(5):903-933.

Samuels, David, and Kent Eaton. 2002. "Presidentialism, and, or and versus Parliamentarism: The State of the Literature and an Agenda for Future Research." Paper presented at the Conference on Consequences of Political Institutions in Democracy, Duke University, April 5–7, 2002.

Sanders, David. 1981. *Patterns of Political Unstability*. New York: St. Martin's Press.

Simmons, Beth. 1994. *Who Adjusts? Domestic Sources of Foreign Economic Policy during the Interwar Years 1923–1939*. Princeton, NJ: Princeton University Press.

Spiller, Pablo T., Ernesto Stein, and Mariano Tommasi. 2003. "Political Institutions, Policymaking Processes, and Policy Outcomes: An Intertemporal Transactions Framework." Unpublished manuscript, Research Department, Inter-American Development Bank, Washington, DC, March.

Stepan, Alfred, and Cindy Skach. 1993. "Constitutional Frameworks and Democratic Consolidation: Parliamentarism versus Presidentialism." *World Politics* 46(1): 1–22.

Valenzuela, Arturo. 1994. "Party Politics and the Crisis of Presidentialism in Chile: A Proposal for a Parliamentary Form of Government." In *The Failure of Presidential Democracy. The Case of Latin America*, edited by Juan José Linz and Arturo Valenzuela, 91–150, Baltimore: Johns Hopkins University Press.

Warwick, Paul V. 1994. *Government Survival in Parliamentary Democracies*. Cambridge: Cambridge University Press.

Weyland, Kurt. 1993. "The Rise and Fall of President Collor and Its Impact on Brazilian Democracy." *Journal of Interamerican Studies and World Affairs* 35(1): 1–37.

Weyland, Kurt. 1998. "Peasants or Bankers in Venezuela? Presidential Popularity and Economic Reform Approval, 1989–1993." *Political Research Quarterly* 51(2): 341–62.

CHAPTER 14

INTERNATIONAL CAPITAL MARKETS AND THEIR LATIN AMERICAN DISCONTENTS

CHRISTOPHER BALDING

1. INTRODUCTION

In 2002, while leading in the polls, then-candidate and future president Luiz Inácio Lula da Silva called Brazilian agreements with the International Monetary Fund (IMF) mistakes. Already concerned about his labor-organizing past and heated rhetoric about globalization and financial markets, traders sent the Brazilian real and primary stock indexes plummeting leading up to the second round runoff. The weeks surrounding the October 2002 election of Lula witnessed severe swings in the Brazilian stock, currency, and bond markets with historic lows followed by large rebounds. Ten days before the 2002 election, the index of the São Paulo stock exchange, the Bovespa, touched a historic low of 8,225 but by one week after the election, a mere 13 trading days later, had risen by 26 percent. As one article noted, "the consequence of Wall Street's aversion is that leaders who do not share this approved pedigree must find a way to win over the financial markets" (Martínez and Santiso 2003, 388). Four years later during his second presidential campaign in 2006, enjoying strong macroeconomic fundamentals with sound growth, low inflation, and declining debt levels, Lula lamented his inability to prevent financial market gyrations when the Bovespa swung a more moderate 20 percent around the election. The international financial markets appeared to disregard the record of stable macroeconomic management and consider the election a risk despite the history of sound money and stable growth promoted by Lula in his first term. The election itself was a financial risk.

International capital markets are a major source of instability in emerging markets, and Latin America has frequently been at the center of financial crises. In a globalized world with few restrictions on international capital movement, sustained inflows can become outflows destabilizing developing economies. However, even as Latin American economies adopted the Washington Consensus, they became disenchanted with the results of opening up to international capital flows. The volatility from sudden stops and rapid turnarounds concerned those focused on promoting a sound and stable environment for growth. A driving criticism by developing Latin American economies is that even when they embrace the economic orthodoxy of low inflation, well-managed trade and fiscal accounts, and a progrowth regulatory environment, international finance may cause significant instability.[1] One source of potential financial market volatility is political instability. Financial markets are concerned with the stability of financial assets, based on the underlying soundness of the domestic economy. Holding fixed-income assets, international investors are concerned with the creditworthiness of the country, which depends on a small list of economic indicators such as gross domestic product (GDP) growth, fiscal deficit or surplus, outstanding debt as a percentage of GDP, and inflation. However, numerous examples exist of Latin American countries with sound underlying macroeconomic fundamentals that faced financial instability for reasons seemingly unrelated to their economic fundamentals. Specifically, short-term speculators cause destabilizing financial swings while the long-term economic fundamentals remain prudent and sound.

There are many reasons emerging market economies face financial instability. Developing countries with less-established democracies and institutions, political instability, and, specifically, unstable elections can prompt financial market volatility due to a perceived risk increase, irrespective of macroeconomic fundamentals. There has been an increasing interest in the relationship of the political business cycle and international financial markets (Nieto-Parra and Santiso 2008). Investors depend on continued economic growth, the stability of the policy environment, and the commitments of the government to abide by its obligations. Developing countries without a sustained record of political and economic stability may face higher levels of investor fear during periods of potential instability. Elections in countries without a lengthy history of institutionalized democracy and well-managed macroeconomic indicators may prompt investor nervousness over the commitment of a new government to honor past contracts. Developing countries argue that even when the political parties are respected, moderate, and commit to honoring debt obligations either pre- or postelection, the mere existence of an election can cause harmful financial market instability.

A second potential source of instability is contagion. The herding behavior of international investors can bring about sudden stops of capital flows to countries not experiencing political or economic instability, but which are related to other emerging market economies. Known as "contagion," this indirect source of financial instability can harm well-managed countries by causing them to be grouped with other emerging market economies, geographic neighbors, or countries with other shared traits. The direct and indirect impacts of electoral and contagion effects can affect the financial stability of countries.

I present research indicating that financial markets react to elections in Latin America, raising the cost of credit default swaps (CDS), even when controlling for standard sovereign credit risk variables. Even for countries with sound public finances, financial markets can still swing rapidly when concerned by political events. Furthermore, supporting the suspicions of politicians that much of the volatility is driven by short-term investors, a distinct divergence emerges between long- and short-term instruments. While elections have a minimal, short-term, and frequently insignificant impact on the prices of ten-year CDS prices, they have a large, longer lasting, and statistically significant impact on the prices of one-year CDS. In other words, the existence of an election increases the basis point cost of a CDS and the perceived credit risk of that election. The perceived credit risk of Latin American governments is higher at an election, even after controlling for a range of economic and political variables. Finally, contagion effects in Latin America are economically and statistically significant. Elections in one emerging market country increase the price of credit insurance for all emerging market sovereigns. In the chapter's three sections, I study the relationship between electoral politics and CDS pricing and after, detailing the data and methodology used, I discuss the results of and explain nuances and derivative models. The results indicate that investors view elections in emerging markets as an increased risk factor in credit pricing.

2. CAPITAL MARKETS, EMERGING MARKET VOLATILITY, AND ELECTORAL POLITICS

Liberalized financial markets have increased the probability of crises in emerging markets. As one researcher wryly noted, recent history has "shown that if any country in the world sneezes, Latin America catches pneumonia" (Forbes and Rigobon 2001, 1). The instability of Latin American financial markets and debt commitments has been well documented as a lengthy and repeated cycle of defaults and sudden stops in investment (Jorgensen and Sachs 1988). Research indicates that free trade will benefit emerging market economies, but that financial "globalization" may increase the susceptibility of developing economies to sudden stops, with Latin America suffering from repeated crises (Martin and Rey 2006). Even when the crisis has not originated in Latin America, its impact is quickly felt there. Smaller countries and emerging market economies that have liberalized their financial markets have experienced sudden stops in capital flows from investors, with numerous defaults. One study noted that "changes in spreads were dominated by sharp adverse shifts in market sentiment more than by changes in fundamentals" (Eichengreen and Mody 2000, 110). The East Asian and Russian crises in 1997 and 1998, respectively, followed by the Argentinean crisis in 2001 involved a rapid reversal of investment flows to developing countries. In each instance, significant contractions in real output occurred after the financial crisis. Freeing trade and financial markets bring benefits but also risks to emerging market economies dependent on international capital to drive rapid growth.

Instability for developing economies in international financial markets stems from their use of foreign-denominated credit markets. Equity markets in developing countries, while experiencing higher levels of volatility than those in developed economies, do not induce financial crisis like sudden stops in credit access. Numerous specific risks exist for both borrower and lender when they gain access to international credit markets for emerging market economies.[2] First are those related to the macroeconomic fundamentals. These are quantifiable risks, based on the macroeconomic policy and management of the government, that establish the creditworthiness of a country. Research has established that a small group of macroeconomic indicators explain the risk factors of a country's cost of credit (Ciarlone, Piselli, and Trebeschi 2007; Weigel and Gemmill 2006; Rowland 2005; Rowland and Torres 2004; Fiess 2003; Grandes 2002; McGuire and Schrijvers 2003; Min 2003; Beck 2001; Nogues and Grandes 2001; Westphalen 2001; Bussière and Mulder 1999).[3] The primary domestic macroeconomic factors that influence the risk premium on emerging market credit pricing include GDP growth, inflation, public debt, reserves, and exports. These macroeconomic fundamentals demonstrate the creditworthiness of a country by indicating whether it will have the capacity for repaying its debt obligations through sustained economic growth and prudent financial management. The macroeconomic fundamentals umbrella covers inflation and default risk. Both inflation and default risk can be reduced by a sound domestic macroeconomic policy framework. Unfortunately, Latin America does not have a long established history of sound macroeconomic policies. Brazil and Argentina among others have a history of poor macroeconomic management, with rampant inflation and sovereign defaults from excessive debt levels. The low levels of growth and high inflation rates have driven up the cost of gaining access to the international capital markets for Latin American states.

Second, fixed-income investors in emerging markets face exogenous financial risks. Emerging market access to international credit markets incurs exogenous economic risks not present in many developed countries' fixed-income instruments. Research indicates that a large portion of emerging market bond spreads can be explained by monetary and economic fundamentals of the United States and other developed countries (Oztay, Ozmen, and Sahinbeyoglu 2009; Dailami, Masson, and Padou 2008; González-Rosada and Levy Yeyati 2008; Longstaff et al. 2011; Pan and Singleton 2008; Uribe and Yue 2006; Weigel and Gemmill 2006; Ferrucci 2003; Fiess 2003; McGuire and Schrijvers 2003; Min et al. 2003; Arora and Cerisola 2001; Beck 2001).[4] In Latin America, many countries are closely tied to the United States economy and depend on its growth to drive manufacturing and commodity exports. Even more fundamentally, numerous countries have been or are dollarized economies, essentially outsourcing monetary policy to Washington in an effort to reduce inflation and currency risk. The exogenous risk of Latin American countries serves as proxy for their relation to the U.S. economy. One recent study argued that investors in sovereign credit earn returns as compensation for bearing *global risk*; that is, there is little country-specific credit risk premium once global risk factors. . . have been adequately controlled for (Longstaff et al. 2011).

Exogenous economic risk of emerging market sovereign debt also includes currency risk.[5] Developed countries like the United States, Japan, and European Union members issue bonds in local currency, while emerging markets issue bonds in foreign currency, primarily the U.S. dollar. Research indicates that exchange rates affect credit pricing via the relative terms of trade, indicating an improved probability of repayment (Hilscher and Nosbusch 2010; Min 2003). Exchange rates and the terms of trade matter because they are strongly linked to defaults through currency crises, the liquidity of the domestic country, and its ability to service its debt obligations (Ferrucci 2003; Min et al. 2003; Min 2003; Reinhart 2002; and Bussière and Mulder 1999). It has been noted that in Latin American cases, countries with lower levels of foreign-denominated debt and higher export levels have suffered during periods of financial stress, even while avoiding outright defaults (Calvo and Talvi 2005). Volatile currency movements affect the real debt level and the ability of the domestic economy to service foreign currency debt. Latin American economies' access to financial markets and cost of capital is affected by their external financial dependence and rigidities.

Emerging market sovereign debt, however, also prices in noneconomic exogenous risk factors such as contagion and political risk. For the purposes of this study, I define contagion as the "significant increase in cross-market linkages after a shock to an individual country (or group of countries)" (Dornbusch, Park, and Claessens 2000).[6] Research has found high degrees of correlation between financial markets of emerging markets, especially in times of crisis (Oztay, Ozmer, and Sahinbeyoglu 2009; González-Rosada and Levy Yeyati 2008; Cifarelli and Paladino 2007; Boyer, Kumagi, and Yuan 2006; Fiess 2003; Grandes 2002; Kumar and Persaud 2003; Kaminsky and Schmukler 2002; Hernández and Valdés 2001; Dornbusch, Park, and Claessens 2000). Contagion and cross-country correlation, however, may be declining as there is evidence that investors increasingly distinguish between emerging market economies (Oddonat and Rahmouni 2006). Countries receiving a credit rating downgrade will negatively affect their regional neighbors (Gande and Parsley 2005). Contagion risk for emerging market economies implies they must concern themselves with the economic risks presented by other developing countries. Latin American countries have long suffered from contagion effects via the fallout from other emerging market economies and nearby neighbors. The Russian default prompted financial market volatility in Latin America and Brazil suffered from the Argentine default even though its fundamentals and monetary structures differed markedly (Miller, Thampanishvong, and Zhang 2004; Forbes and Rigobon 2001). Even less profound financial events have triggered large market movements in Latin America with a high degree of correlation between markets. If investors do not distinguish between specific policies, then Latin American countries with sound macroeconomic fundamentals may suffer sudden stops in capital when other emerging markets enter a crisis period.

Emerging market sovereign debt prices in other risks, most notably for the purposes of this research, political risk. Though the credit cost indicates the pricing of political and policy risk, little research has studied and quantified it. Previous research on the relationship between the emerging markets' access to the international credit market and domestic politics has tended to focus on the role of credit-rating agencies (Biglaiser and DeRouen 2007; Biglaiser, DeRouen, and Archer 2011; Vaaler, Burhard, and Block 2006; Block and Vaaler 2004). Numerous problems exist with using credit ratings. First, sovereign credit rating is a poor measure to use because of the time inconsistency problem. Credit ratings change infrequently and fail to capture changes in investor sentiment or fundamentals. While economic and political data is updated daily, monthly, and quarterly, credit ratings may change as little as every few years. This prevents any serious study of the impact of new information on investors. Second, the ordinal values of credit ratings fail to allow discrete differentiation between ratings. Pricing data has a discrete and absolute difference between units of measurement, while credit-rating differences, as ordinal values, fail to capture a similar level of detail.

Research on the cost of political risk in developing economy credit markets has been sparse. Research studying the relationship between the cost of credit and emerging market political risk has either been methodologically rudimentary or geographically segmented (see Moser 2007 Block and Vaaler 2004). Other research used corruption indicators to study the change in the cost of external debt financing for developing countries, and found a positive relationship (Ciocchini, Durbin, and Ng 2003). Policy volatility can in fact play a negative role in the pricing of credit risk. One study notes that "countries with historically higher macroeconomic volatility are more prone to default, and particularly so if part of this volatility is policy induced. Reducing policy volatility thus appears to be key to improving a country's credit standing" (Catão and Sutton 2002, 1). Policy volatility may manifest itself in large swings between governments or the renunciation of previous policies by leaders elected again. Due to the history of swings in economic policies and lack of credibility in instituting low-inflation, strong-growth policies, markets price in additional credit risk to Latin American sovereign debt. For instance, even when leaders or parties publicly commit themselves to policies either before or after the election, credibility issues may hinder the market's belief in the stated policy framework. Prior to his election in 2002, Lula made conflicting statements about his views on Brazilian agreements with the International Monetary Fund before publicly supporting them. Since he was the front-runner, this caused large fluctuations in the real and debt markets, as uncertainty over future policy increased with spreads on Brazilian sovereign debt increasing to 2,400 basis points (Federal Reserve 2003). After his first election, Lula, faced with large debt and anxious financial markets, installed an orthodox economic team intent on increasing the primary surplus target, disappointing many supporters (Loureiro et al. 2009; Mollo and Saad-Filho

2006). This pattern of politically induced financial market volatility plays out throughout Latin America with many countries experiencing such swings in sentiment. The IMF even noted that "policy performance" can reduce market-driven fluctuations based on the economic history of a country in fulfilling its obligations and in its macroeconomic management (IMF 2002).[7] The variety of political parties without a clear commitment to prudent macroeconomic management and lack of established economic credibility prevents financial markets from reducing the premium dedicated to political risk. Financial markets may price in an implied political or commitment risk to emerging market cost of credit.

The concern for Latin American economies and other emerging markets stems from volatility even when governments have followed a path of prudent macroeconomic management. During Lula's second election campaign after his administration established a firm commitment to prudent macroeconomic management, Brazil endured volatile financial markets due to an increase in perceived political risk. A year after his second election, the IMF wrote glowingly about Lula's economic policies, noting:

> Today, the Brazilian economy is reaping the benefits of the continued implementation of strong stabilization and social policies, in the context of a favorable external environment. Real GDP growth is projected to rise from 3¾ percent in 2006 to 4½ percent in 2007. The inflation outlook remains benign, with 12-month inflation expected at around 4 percent by year-end. Strong social policies have recently helped place Brazil among the high ranking countries in the UN Human Development Index. (IMF 2007)

This upbeat assessment, while true, ignores numerous swings in financial market sentiment about the risk factor of the Brazilian market. Only one year earlier, the primary Brazilian stock index enjoyed a jump of more than 22 percent in the period surrounding Lula's second election, demonstrating the importance financial markets place on political credibility, placing higher confidence in a reelection because of certainty. As one economist wrote, ". . . calculating the conditions necessary for debt sustainability is not the same as delivering those conditions in the political and financial market place" (Goldstein 2003). By 2006; Lula had established the credibility to sustain the existing debt level and markets rose in support of his expected reelection. Some have argued that this means that when market actors do not have the ability to accurately assess a party's or politician's intent on carrying out their stated policies, they will increase the political risk premium (Mosely and Brooks 2008). The interplay between financial markets and electoral politics is not limited to Brazil but extends throughout Latin America. Mexico, Argentina, and Colombia among others have experienced higher volatility in currency, bond, and equity markets in combination with political uncertainty, resulting in real economic effects (Cermeño, Grier, and Grier 2010; Mendoza and Oviedo 2009; Adelman 1998; Milesi-Ferretti and Razin 1996). As figure 14.1 shows, electoral politics appears to have a strong impact on Latin American equity markets.

Prior to one election in Colombia, for example, equity markets had remained at lower levels, while after the election, equity indexes rose by nearly 40 percent.

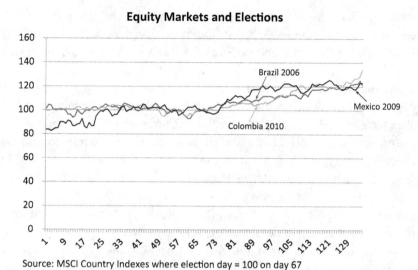

Equity Markets and Elections

Source: MSCI Country Indexes where election day = 100 on day 67

Figure 14.1 Equity markets and elections.

Elections in Latin America and other emerging market economies appear to be a prominent risk factor in investor analysis. Political risk is a primary driver of financial market concern behind economic policy management.

The political business cycle has received increased attention as research demonstrates its importance to investors in prudent risk management, and countries understand that politics matter. The tendency of politicians to increase spending in election years and the uncertainty of an election increases the risk profile of states, especially if its economic fundamentals are not ideal (Phillips 2006). Latin American governments specifically have been urged to avoid preelection spending binges (Nieto-Parra and Santiso 2009a). Political uncertainty can come in a variety of ways, such as public policy pronouncements by a government. During the Tequila Crisis in Mexico from 1994 to 1995; Argentina made credible and firm policy pronouncements designed to reassure financial markets of the ability of its currency board to prevent a contagion-prompted financial crises (Schmukler and Servén 2002; Ganapolsky and Schmukler 1998). Even less drastic events can cause an increase in the perceived risk of a country's sovereign debt. One study found that cabinet reshuffles in Latin American countries were driven by increased bond spreads, rising on average by 40 basis points (Moser 2007). The difference between developed and emerging markets appears not to be accounting for electoral risk but rather the pricing of a political premium (Campello 2009). The high mobility of capital has made it increasingly difficult for governments to implement their planned ideological changes. Elections may provide the impetus for financial crisis because of the increased uncertainty they raise. One author notes that " . . . although democracies are no less likely to experience banking crises . . . their countries suffer far smaller growth collapses" (Keefer 2007, 607). Part of the blame for the financial market volatility, however, appears to fall at the feet of politicians and governments. Research indicates that prior to elections, incumbents increase spending, worsening the fiscal situation and raising political uncertainty about the commitment of future governments to honor debt obligations (Cuadra and Sapriza 2008). This interplay of financial market turbulence and political risk has been particularly acute in Latin America. As early adopters of financial globalization, Latin American states were especially dependent on financial markets for access to credit and vulnerable to sudden stops or outflows prompted by political uncertainty (Frenkel 2003). Some scholars have argued, however, that because of increasing sophistication of countries' economic and political management, as well as improved investor differentiation between states, the link between elections and financial market volatility in Latin America is weakening (Nieto-Parra and Santiso 2009b). While lower volatility around elections in Latin America could help avert panics, history provides less reason for optimism. Nonetheless, the improved economic fundamentals and continued strengthening of democratic and prudent macroeconomic policies have increased the perception that Latin American politicians and governments will abide by their obligations.

Financial markets have evolved rapidly over the past decade. Access to international financial markets has expanded rapidly for emerging market economies assisted by improved macroeconomic management and sustained growth. The evidence, however, that financial globalization has prompted higher structural growth or provided other large benefits to emerging market economies remains elusive (Rodrik and Subramanian 2009). The mainstreaming of emerging market access to capital markets has also prompted a similar evolution of financial development in developed economies. Yet even as the volatility of financial markets in Latin America has prompted a reevaluation of their regulation, recent research compiling a new database of lending and equity issuance originating in Latin America has discovered that cyclical volatility has been lower in recent history than in the boom-and-bust cycles in the nineteenth century and early twentieth century (Kaminsky 2009). A primary source of concern for financial market risk is the increased use of derivatives to hedge risk and for speculative purposes. There remain arguments over how to value derivatives from an accounting perspective, as the risk and market value in many cases remain difficult to ascertain. Derivatives in currency, equity, commodity, and debt instruments amounted to a notional value of nearly US$600 trillion at the end of 2008 with nearly $42 trillion of that in credit default swaps (BIS 2009). A credit default swap is a derivative for which a seller provides a defined amount of money to the purchaser of the CDS in the case of a "credit event" or default.[8] For instance, if investors purchase a bond from country A and want to protect themselves in case the country decides not to repay the bond, they can purchase a CDS, which will repay them the outstanding amount of the bond if country A defaults. CDS have become increasingly used by investors seeking to either hedge their specific risks or hold them as speculative assets (Carr and Wu 2007). The market for emerging market sovereign CDS has grown rapidly the past decade, with daily pricing for many available only back until 2004. It is important to note that a CDS does not protect the investor against other types of risk such as inflation or currency fluctuations.

3. DATA AND METHODOLOGY

The methodology used here is straightforward and the data compiled from standard sources. First, I compiled daily one- and ten-year CDS pricing from Thomson Datastream from 2004 through 2007 for seven emerging market Latin American countries.[9] It is worth noting some of the data limitations and peculiarities with regards to the use of CDS data. Due to the evolving nature of sovereign debt trading and more specifically the growth of the CDS market, not all countries have daily pricing data for the entire period specified. Second, I use general macroeconomic data downloaded from the IMF International Financial Statistics Database. I excluded countries that did not have complete data meeting the time interval requirements needed for the study. As already noted, scholars have found a small number of variables to be important with regard to sovereign debt pricing, and I restrict this study to these variables. For the purpose of thoroughness, I tested a range of related variables simply to study their importance, but utilize the commonly used macroeconomic indicators of sovereign creditworthiness. For instance, while I used quarterly GDP growth in the baseline study, I also tested related variables that might act as a proxy, such as monthly industrial production. I also tested different measures of indebtedness and liquidity to ensure the accuracy and stability of the results. Third, I created election variables from the Adam Carr Election Archive, a range of election-related variables to test the importance of pre- and postelection changes in credit pricing and contagion effects both within a region and around the world.

Although methodologically the study is straightforward, it has a few minor points to note. First, as with other cross-country spread and CDS studies, I used a panel data set and employed standard econometric techniques and robustness tests.[10] These include fixed, random, time, and country effects as well as different robustness tests. Methodologically I rely on widely utilized techniques and do not stray from accepted techniques. Second, integrating inconsistent time data posed a challenge, for instance, daily CDS pricing, monthly debt data, and quarterly GDP growth statistics. I merged the data into the relevant period so that within a given quarter, some variables changed daily, monthly, or not at all. The baseline model presented settled on quarterly data, but I tested a much larger array of data and periods for different variables not presented here, as they do not change the outcomes or add to the discussion.[11] I also created leading and lagging variables to test for time effects, borrower reputation, and economic information. This helps better test the impact of economic fundamentals on changes in implied credit risk. However, it also applies theory on investor decision making. Investors may rely on the past performance, creating a proxy for reputation and the probability of repayment. Investors also look forward, forming expectations about the future, and estimate probable economic performance, adjusting their price of credit risk.

Finally, the importance of the CDS rather than bond spreads as the dependent variable cannot be overstated when pricing political risk. While bond spreads incorporate political risk and price it daily, they are a blunt instrument for a few reasons.

First, bond spreads incorporate many more risk factors into the cost of credit. While default risk is the primary risk of any debt instrument, there are a large number of risks, at varying price levels, associated with debt pricing. For instance, inflation and prepayment risk are excluded from the CDS risk profile. Second, CDS data clearly price time in the differentiation between ten- and one-year CDS. While some measure ten- and one-year spreads, for reasons of security, sales, and yield-curve constructions, the data are less exact than the sale of a ten- or one-year CDS. The daily price is the cost to insure against a credit event for the given period. Third, the use of a CDS limits the channels via which a political event, not an ongoing policy, party, or government, can affect the financial market pricing of credit risk. Bond spreads, by accounting for a larger number of risks, also increase the number of methods by which politics can affect financial risks. CDS limits that risk to a clearly defined credit event.

4. THE BASELINE MODEL

The model is straightforward and designed to cover the primary risk factors associated with a sovereign CDS and previous literature. It uses daily data covering from 2004 to 2007 for seven Latin American countries, creating a large number of observations when presented in panel form, with fixed time and country effects as is now widely done in the literature. The baseline model can be presented as follows:

$$(1)\ \ln(CDS_{it}) = BOP_{it} + EXT_{it} + GDP_{it} + ELEC_{it} + \varepsilon$$

CDS_{it} = the daily price of a credit default swap in basis point for country i at time t

BOP_{it} = the quarterly balance of payments as a percentage of GDP for country i at time t

EXT_{it} = the quarterly external government debt as a percentage of GDP for country i at time t

GDP_{it} = is quarterly GDP year on year growth for country i at time t

$ELEC_{it}$ = is a dummy variable representing an election for all countries coded 1 on the day of the election and 0 if there is no election.[12]

Descriptive statistics of all variables can be found in appendixes 14.1 through 14.3, which provide the countries studied, correlation, and average values.

Balance of payments, external government debt, and GDP growth are the fundamental economic variables that determine sovereign creditworthiness. Election is used around the fundamental determinations of creditworthiness to examine their impact on CDS pricing. I use the basic model for three reasons. First, it accords well with economic logic. BOP indicates both the direction of a country's finances and of existing economic policy. External government debt captures the historical value of previous economic policy and explicitly quantifies the debt that investors are seeking to insure. GDP measures the ability of the sovereign to repay the debt owed to foreign investors. Second, this closely follows the literature of the number of variables that significantly affect the cost of credit. As noted previously, and specifically focusing on the bond spread literature, a small number of variables explain the variance and significantly affect bond spreads. Though there has been very little published academic literature on the determinants of sovereign CDS prices, I adhered closely, formally speaking, to the bond spread literature and its explanatory workings. Third, other economic variables that I tested, but do not present here, are highly correlated with the three economic variables. For instance, other measures of debt, current or capital accounts, and liquidity are strongly related to the three economic variables used. The three primary variables, and others used for robustness tests, demonstrate low levels of correlation, while other variables add nothing to the analysis. Subsequent derivations of the baseline model include additional domestic economic and global risk variables, which, as I show, do not change the economic and statistical significance, and do not add to the analysis or insights.

5. THE BASELINE RESULTS

Table 14.1 shows the baseline results and reveals a number of results consistent with expectation. First, the economic variables are all statistically and economically significant. Statistically, the variables are all significant at the 1 percent level with high t-statistics. For instance, the marginal impact of GDP growth implies that a 1 percent increase in GDP growth lowers the price of a CDS by 3 percent. The largest impact on sovereign CDS pricing comes from external government indebtedness. A 1 percent increase in external government debt as a percentage of GDP increases the one-year CDS price by 76 percent. Second, the results are similar across both methodological specification and time differences between CDS. The differences between the ten and one-year CDS in both methodological specifications is minimal, with only marginal differences in economic variables. Third, the variables all return the expected sign. Balance of payment surpluses and positive economic growth result in lower CDS prices and a negative coefficient. Conversely, higher external government debt is positive because of the higher risk and subsequent higher CDS pricing. The economic variables all return expected levels of statistical and economic significance.

The most interesting result, however, comes from the perceived difference in election risk between the ten and one-year CDS. While the impacts on balance of payments, external government debt, and GDP growth are similar between the ten and one-year CDS, the economic impact of an election on the one-year CDS in the baseline model is more than twice as large. The election coefficient for the ten-year CDS is .09 and statistically insignificant while it is .24 and significant for the one-year CDS. In other words, one-year CDS investors believe that the credit risk from an

Table 14.1. The Baseline Results

Dependent Variable	10-Year CDS	1-Year CDS
Balance of payments	-.003***	-.003***
	(.0002)	(.001)
External government debt	.59***	.76***
	(.03)	(.05)
GDP growth	-.03***	-.04***
	(.002)	(.004)
Election dummy	.09	.24*
	(.07)	(.13)
Observations	6,122	6,122
Countries	7	7
Specification	Fixed effects	Fixed effects
Time effects	Yes	Yes
R-squared within	.74	.41

Standard errors are in parentheses below the coefficient.

*$p < .10$

***$p < .01$

election is much higher than owners of the ten-year CDS. In one way, this result seems oddly counterintuitive. The risk of a credit event stemming from election-related politics seems significantly higher to holders of the ten-year CDS, who will typically witness a minimum of two major national elections if holding to maturity. Longer-term instruments carry higher risk premiums for precisely this reason, because while short-term economic growth and balance of payments are relatively predictable, forecasting over the medium and long term requires more faith. It seems counterintuitive that short-term investors should perceive such a large difference in credit risk in an election.

My theory behind this finding is that of investor self-selection bias between time horizons. In other words, the investors in the ten-year CDS are different than the investors in the one year CDS, creating a self-selection bias between the holders and how they price perceived risk. Specifically, there are three subcategories of risk that help us understand the risk differentiation patterns of investors. First, investors evaluate short- and long-term future economic and political risk differently. For instance, investors may see high risk in the short term but lower long-term risk. Just as yield curves indicate the market's belief in future economic activity, investors may be differentiating between the short- and long-term risks. Second, investors have fundamentally different country risk evaluations. Investors willing to provide long-term credit insurance assume much larger risk but arrive at a fundamentally different country risk profile than short-term investors. Third, different products may attract different investors. In other words, the one-year CDS may be attracting more speculative or rapidly trading investors while the long-term or buy-and-hold investors are represented in the ten-year CDS. Though I cannot say for sure what is driving the difference in the evaluation of political risk between the ten- and one-year CDS, each time horizon values risk differently.

6. CROSS-BORDER RISK

An important issue in emerging market finance concerns the possibility of contagion. Emerging market finance has suffered from sudden stops in the investments in a country, either from its domestic situation, or more frustratingly, from the economic situation of its neighbor. "Contagion" refers to the specific situation where states, through a variety of potential channels, suffer from economic or financial problems due to the issues in another economy similar geographically or economically. A contingent factor is the role of international investors. International investors have tended to group emerging market economies or geographically similar states into their evaluation of a specific country or region. Consequently, if one country in a region suffered, it could easily harm, through international mechanisms of financial transmission, the economy of its neighbor even if that nation did not experience similar problems. To address this issue, I created two different contagion variables capturing election risk. The contagion variables capture the impact of regional and global emerging market elections.

Table 14.2 shows results from the regressions capturing contagion. There are a few interesting results. First, regional contagion is economically and statistically insignificant. There is no regression presented under any model in which the contagion dummy variable was economically or statistically significant.[13] The coefficients are very small, and since the dummy variables are regressed against a natural log, this implies that the economic value of contagion from election is approaching zero and statistically its significance is not even borderline. Second, the model is as expected in all other respects, and continues to confirm my previous findings. The economic variables continue to perform as expected, demonstrating empirical robustness. The interesting paradox here is that while investors seem to differentiate the impact of an election on credit risk between states within a given region, they do not appear to differentiate election risk across time. Third, when accounting for global contagion risk, the contagion coefficient is both economically and statistically significant, at the 1 percent level for the one-year CDS. Global contagion is priced into credit risk across countries, even for political factors. In other words, investors seem to link Brazilian elections with Malaysian elections but not Argentinean ones. This seems somewhat paradoxical. If political risk is priced into a CDS, it would seem to flow first to neighboring countries and not around the world. In other words, while global economic risk pricing is logical, global political risk from isolated elections seems driven more by emotions than by calculated and rational thought.

Table 14.2. Contagion and the CDS

Dependent Variable	10-Year CDS	10-Year CDS	10-Year CDS	1-Year CDS	1-Year CDS	1-Year CDS
Balance of payments	-.003***	-.003***	-.003****	-.003***	-.003***	-.003***
	(.00)	(.00)	(.00)	(.00)	(.00)	(.00)
External government debt	.59***	.59***	.59***	.76***	.77***	.77***
	(.03)	(.03)	(.03)	(.05)	(.05)	(.05)
GDP growth	-.03***	-.03***	-.03***	-.04***	-.04***	-.04***
	(.00)	(.00)	(.00)	(.00)	(.00)	(.00)
Election dummy		.09			.24*	
		(.07)			(.13)	
Global election contagion			.03			.09***
			(.02)			(.04)
Regional election contagion	.02	.02		.005	-.006	
	(.03)	(.03)		(.05)	(.06)	
Comment						
Observations	6,122	6,122	6,122	6,122	6,122	6,122
Countries	7	7	7	7	7	7
Specification	Fixed	Fixed	Fixed	Fixed	Fixed	Fixed
Time effects	Yes	Yes	Yes	Yes	Yes	Yes
R-squared within	.74	.74	.74	.41	.41	.41

Standard errors are in parentheses below the coefficient.
*$p < .10$
***$p < .01$

7. EVENT METHODOLOGY AND A LITTLE MORE POLITICS

Table 14.3 presents the results from regressions testing the impact of different voting methodologies on ten- and one-year CDS pricing. Different countries have different political and election systems, which could affect the perceived market risk.

While researchers have shown that parliamentary and presidential systems affect economic decision making, because of the large number of presidential systems in Latin America, the distinction between those systems is omitted in this study. The biggest finding from table 14.3 is no finding at all. In both the ten- and one-year CDS, none of the political variables yield statistical significance.

The electoral structure appears to have little if any impact on the perceived risk of default in Latin America. This implies that the electoral process by which governments

Table 14.3. Politics

Dependent Variable	10-Year CDS	10-Year CDS	1-Year CDS	1-Year CDS
Balance of payments	-.003***	-.003***	-.003***	-.003***
	(.00)	(.00)	(.00)	(.00)
External government debt	.59***	.59***	.76***	.76***
	(.03)	(.03)	(.05)	(.05)
GDP growth	-.03***	-.03***	-.04***	-.04***
	(.00)	(.00)	(.00)	(.00)
Election dummy		.18		.27
		(.11)		(.21)
Multiround	.03	-.15	.22	-.05
	(.09)	(.15)	(.17)	(.28)
Comment				
Observations	6,122	6,122	6,122	6,122
Countries	7	7	7	7
Specification	Fixed	Fixed	Fixed	Fixed
Time effects	Yes	Yes	Yes	Yes
R-squared within	.74	.74	.41	.41

Standard errors are in parentheses below the coefficient.
*p < .10
***p < .01

are elected does not increase the risk of sovereign debt default, but that only the existence of the election does. Table 14.4 presents a brief analysis using event methodology by changing the time perspective of election by leading key variables. Three basic results stand out in these regressions. First, the economic variables fall within the expected range of both economic and statistical significance based upon previous regressions. Second, the time variations of the election dummy variable are statistically insignificant. In other words, in Latin America there is little evidence of anticipatory run-ups in the cost of credit insurance before an election. Credit markets are more concerned with the economic environment inherited by the government than the existence of an election. Third, in line with the divergent investor risk assessment found in previous regressions, elections do not increase the cost of sovereign credit insurance in the ten-year CDS market but do so in the one-year CDS market. The time horizon of investors treats the risk of an election differently for ten- versus one-year CDS. As, for instance, figure 14.2 shows in the case of Argentina, there was significant divergence between the ten- and one-year CDS in the 2007 election cycle.

There was a distinct narrowing between the ten- and one-year CDS due to divergent risk analysis between the long- and short-term investor. In real terms, the spread between the ten- and one-year Argentinean CDS narrowed during the run-up to the 2007 election by more than half, even though there was only a relatively

Table 14.4. What about Time?

Dependent Variable	10-Year CDS	1-Year CDS	10-Year CDS	10-Year CDS
Balance of payments	-0.003***	-0.003*****	-0.005*	-0.004***
	(.00)	(.00)	(.00)	(.00)
External government debt	0.59***	0.76***	0.54***	0.75***
	(.03)	(.05)	(.03)	(.03)
GDP growth	-0.03***	-0.04***		
	(.00)	(.00)		
60-day leading GDP growth			-.01***	-.03***
			(.00)	(.05)
2-day leading election	0.12	.26*		
	(.07)	(.13)		
60-day leading election			.05	.05
			(.07)	(.12)
Observations	6,108	6,108	5,702	5,702
Countries	7	7	7	7
Specification	Fixed	Fixed	Fixed	Fixed
Time effects	Yes	Yes	Yes	Yes
R-squared within	.74	.41	.76	.47

Standard errors are in parentheses below the coefficient.
$*p < .10$
$***p < .01$

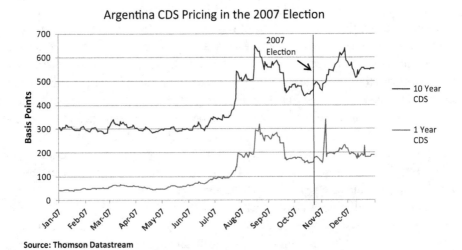

Source: Thomson Datastream

Figure 14.2. Argentina CDS pricing in the 2007 election

small change in the ten-year CDS price. Short- and long-term investors were pricing the risk of default differently.

8. FACTORING GLOBAL RISK

An important risk factor in credit markets in emerging economies is their exposure and relation to larger developed markets. The bond spread literature has found emerging market credit access to be significantly affected by a global risk component. Table 14.5 shows regressions including time variations of U.S. quarterly GDP acting as the global risk component.

The inclusion of a global risk factor provides a number of interesting findings. First, the model, coefficients, and significance levels remain close to previous levels,

Table 14.5. Global Risk

Dependent Variable	10-Year CDS	10-Year CDS	1-Year CDS	1-Year CDS
Balance of payments	-0.003***	-0.005***	-0.003***	-0.004***
	(.00)	(.00)	(.00)	(.00)
External government debt	0.58***	0.53***	0.81***	0.73***
	(.03)	(.03)	(.05)	(.05)
GDP growth	-0.03***		-0.04***	
	(.000)		(.00)	
Leading domestic GDP growth		-0.01***		-0.03***
		(.00)		(.00)
U.S. GDP growth	-.01***		.04***	
	(.00)		(.00)	
Leading U.S. GDP growth		-.05***		-.09***
		(.00)		(.00)
Lagging U.S. GDP growth				
Election	.08	.07	.26*	.20
	(.07)	(.07)	(.13)	(.13)
Observations	6,122	6,122	6,122	5,702
Countries	7	7	7	7
Specification	Fixed	Fixed	Fixed	Fixed
Time effects	Yes	Yes	Yes	Yes
R-squared within	0.74	0.77	0.42	0.51

Standard errors are in parentheses below the coefficient.
*$p < .10$
***$p < .01$

demonstrating continued robustness of the model. The balance of payments, external government debt, local GDP growth, and the election dummy variable all retain expected signs, coefficients, and significance levels. Second, as in previous regressions, I find a significant difference in the impact of an election between ten- and one-year CDS pricing. The one-year CDS election coefficients are statistically significant while the ten-year CDS results are not. Again, investors' risk perceptions differ according to the time horizon of the instrument. Third, when leading domestic and U.S. GDP growth is accounted for, the election variable turns insignificant for the one-year CDS. While elections affect the pricing of credit risk insurance, investors appear more concerned with the economic environment the government is inheriting than with who is doing the inheriting. Fourth, the global risk pricing component is not insignificant. While it is small when not lagged in the ten year CDS results, when leading, the U.S. GDP coefficient is larger than domestic GDP growth, implying it may be used as a proxy by investors to price CDS. Sixth, the overall indebtedness of the country still drives the results. Investors are worried about the overall indebtedness of the country more than shorter-term factors like GDP growth, elections, and balance of payments. Global risk is factored into the overall credit risk factors, but does not drive the fundamental profile analysis of countries.

9. STATIONARITY TESTING

Table 14.6 presents results from testing for the stationarity of the financial asset data and robustness.[14] The findings confirm the methodological techniques. Because of the nature of financial asset data, a reasonable methodological concern will question the stationarity of the CDS dependent variable.

The primary test used here is the Fisher test, which allows me to test the stationarity of data in a panel setting, under which the null hypothesis assumes that all series are nonstationary. Using the results of table 14.6 with up to four lags, I reject the null hypothesis and find that at least one series in the panel is stationary. Tables 14.7 and 14.8 present a variety of stationary tests for individual countries using both ten- and one-year CDS.[15] As the battery of tests conducted on the ten- and one-year CDS shows, numerous countries are stationary, confirming the Fisher test finding that at least one series of the panel is stationary. Consequently, based on the numerous findings of stationarity, I analyze the data as a stationary panel.

10. THOUGHTS, COMMENTS, AND MUSINGS

There are a number of broader points about these results that should be noted. First, if emerging markets fear short-term investors, the results indicate they have good reason to be concerned. Whereas the ten-year CDS price has a lower variance

Table 14.6. Testing for Stationarity

Dependent Variable	10-Year CDS	1-Year CDS
1 lag	23.72*	64.12***
	(.09)	(.00)
2 lags	22.44	60.70***
	(.13)	(.00)
3 lags	20.60	54.26***
	(.00)	(.00)
4 lags	18.67	52.42***
	(.19)	(.00)
Stationary	Enough	Yes
Test	Fisher	Fisher
Chi-square	Yes	Yes

Chi-square probability is in parentheses below the coefficient when testing for stationarity.
Standard errors are in parentheses below the coefficient in other regressions.
*p < .10
***p < .01

within countries than the one-year, it also reacts much less frequently to political risk and when it does the reaction is much smaller. Because I use a derivative in the form of a CDS, these results do not directly test for long-term investors or for speculative, fast-moving "hot money." However, as a U.S. based product with a clearly differentiated time horizon, the daily pricing of the CDS acts as a very good proxy

Table 14.7. Individual Country Stationary Tests for Mexico, Peru, and Chile

Country	Mexico	Peru	Chile
CDS	10-year	10-year	10-year
Total lags	21	6	
Maxlag criterion	Schwert	Newey-West	
Stationary	Yes	Yes	Yes
Test	Dickey-Fuller	Phillips-Perron	Aug. Dickey-Fuller
High tau statistic	-3.60***		
	(20)		
Low tau statistic	-2.52		
	(10)		
Z(rho)		-22.46**	
Z(t)		-3.76**	-3.20***
Control	Trend		Drift
Observations	1,021	962	1,042

Lags are in parentheses below the coefficient.
**p < .05
***p < .01

Table 14.8. Individual Country Stationary Tests for Argentina, Chile, and Brazil

Country	Argentina	Chile	Brazil
CDS	1-year	1-year	1-year
Stationary	Yes	Yes	Yes
Test	Aug. Dickey-Fuller	Aug. Dickey-Fuller	Aug. Dickey-Fuller
$Z(t)$	-3.13*	-5.13***	-3.32***
Control	Trend	Trend	Drift
Obs	673	1,042	955

Lags are in parentheses below the coefficient.
*$p < .10$
***$p < .01$

for differentiating between long- and short-term investors. These results indicate that Latin American countries appear to have valid concerns about the behavior of short-term investors and their impact on financial markets.

Second, short- and long-term investors appear to analyze and value risk very differently. In numerous results presented here, political variables affect CDS pricing very differently for the ten- and one-year CDS. Aggregating the same information, the one-year CDS price is volatile while the ten-year CDS responds with a collective yawn. Though I do not have data to support this assertion, I believe there is a type of selection bias occurring between investors in the ten- and one-year CDS. Ten-year CDS holders assign a lower risk profile to the country while receiving a higher yield. One-year CDS investors assign a higher risk profile to the country and receive a smaller yield for holding a one-year instrument. This results in a smaller margin for error, making them more willing to trade the product and induce higher volatility. Consequently, when reacting to the same information, ten-year CDS investors shrug, while one-year CDS holders panic. In other words, ten-year CDS investors believe there is lower risk in the country than one-year CDS investors.

Third, investors do not appear rational, but rather make decisions based on noise. For instance, the global contagion variable came back positive for elections in one emerging market, making credit risk pricing increase for all emerging markets. Simply the event of an election drives CDS prices up regardless of who wins or by how much. It is difficult to understand how the event of an election, not a change in government or economic policy, would increase credit risk, much less for countries around the world. Fourth, if investors are forward looking on emerging market credit risk, incorporating all known information, they appear to do a poor job. Other than noting the date of an election, they appear to have no specific insight of predictive power about political or policy changes. Fifth, there appear to be pricing inconsistencies between the ten- and one-year CDS that would allow investment opportunities. Whether the further development of the emerging sovereign CDS market will arbitrage out these anomalies remains to be seen; however, these data appear to include exploitable investment data. Sixth, the CDS financial asset stationarity is somewhat puzzling. This might be explained by either the lack of development of the CDS market for emerging sovereigns or by investors treating it as an insurance market and not a financial asset market. If the market simply needs further development, then this condition will veri-fiably change over time. If it does not, then this would seem to present investment opportunities as the CDS would then move in more predictable patterns.

11. CONCLUSION

International financial market volatility can significantly affect and harm emerging market economies. Based on the results of this study, I find that noneconomic political factors play a significant role in the pricing of credit risk by international financial in-vestors within a specific time frame. Though economic factors underpin the analysis, volatility is driven by investor time profile and the existence, not substance, of noneco-nomic factors like elections. Furthermore, the divergent behavior of short- and long-term investors appears to play a significant role in driving some of the volatility. The ten-year CDS enjoys lower volatility and price increases in election cycles than its one-year counterpart. Even more interesting, there is a consistent narrowing of the spread for the long-term instrument indicating that short-term investors are nervous, while the long-term holders share less of this concern. While politicians enjoy railing against the brutish international financier, this study appears to provide some evidence that in the case of Latin American credit insurance, short- and long-term investors behave differently. If small open economies can be subject to volatile financial markets even when pursuing sound and prudent economic policies, there might be, as the IMF has noted, scope to reduce capital flows that have the ability to induce volatility. Though investors may increasingly differentiate between countries within a given region, the risk of contagion for emerging market sovereigns remains large.

APPENDIX 14.1. COUNTRY AND DATA LIST

Country	CDS Pricing	Balance of Payments	External Government Debt	GDP Growth	Industrial Production	Election Date	Observations
Argentina	Daily	Quarterly	Quarterly	Quarterly	Monthly	10/21/05 10/26/07	674
Brazil	Daily	Quarterly	Quarterly	Quarterly	Monthly	09/29/06 10/27/06	956
Chile	Daily	Quarterly	Quarterly	Quarterly	Monthly	12/09/05 01/18/06	1,046
Colombia	Daily	Quarterly	Quarterly	Quarterly	Monthly	5/26/06	935
El Salvador	Daily	Quarterly	Quarterly	Quarterly	Monthly	03/12/06	508
Mexico	Daily	Quarterly	Quarterly	Quarterly	Monthly	06/30/06	1,043
Peru	Daily	Quarterly	Quarterly	Quarterly	Monthly	04/07/06 06/05/06	963

APPENDIX 14.2. VARIABLE CORRELATION TABLE

	10-Year CDS	1-Year CDS	Balance of Payments	External Government Debt	GDP Growth	US GDP Growth	Industrial Production	Inflation
10 Year	1.00							
1 Year	.92	1.00						
BOP	-.05	-.04	1.00					
External Government Debt	.17	.17	.06	1.00				
GDP Growth	.28	.28	.13	.17	1.00			
US GDP Growth	.02	.05	.01	.04	-.06	1.00		
Industrial Production	.00	-.01	.01	.01	.03	.03	1.00	
Inflation	.56	.55	-.04	-.16	.30	-.04	-.01	1.00

APPENDIX 14.3. COUNTRY VARIABLE AVERAGES (PERCENTAGE)

Country	Balance of Payments	External Government Debt	GDP Growth
Argentina	.64	.38	8.84
Brazil	3.40	.34	4.63
Chile	.05	.14	5.22
Colombia	1.69	.68	6.22
El Salvador	4.21	8.75	3.44
Mexico	.14	.07	3.91
Peru	4.49	1.04	7.11
Latin America	2.01	1.36	5.62

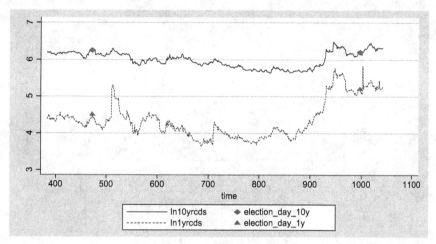

Argentina 10- and 1-year CDS

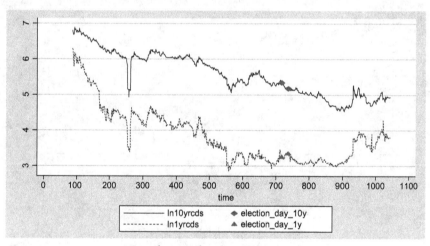

Brazil 10- and 1-year CDS spread

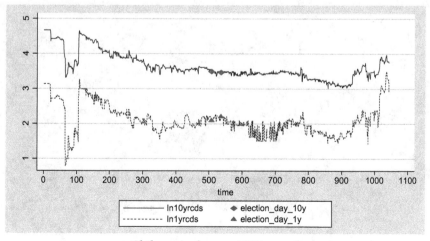

Chile 10- and 1-year CDS spread

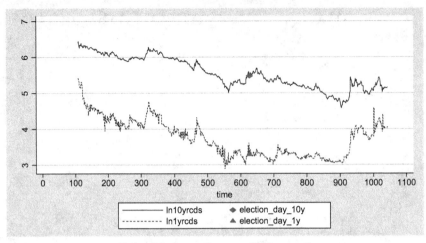

Colombia 10- and 1-year CDS spread

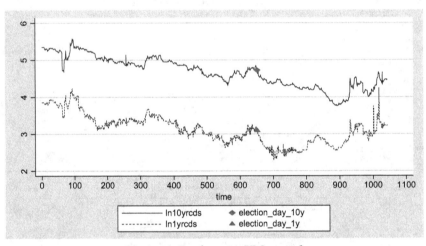

Mexico 10- and 1-year CDS spread

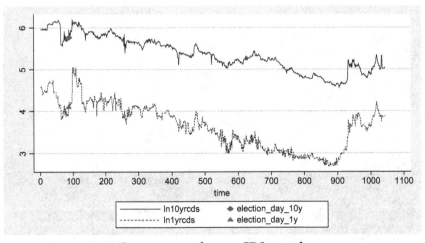

Panama 10- and 1-year CDS spread

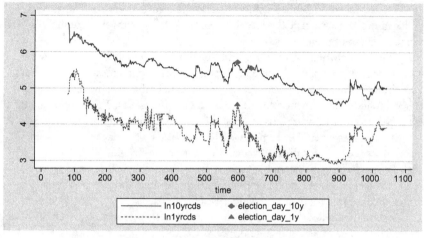

Peru 10- and 1-year CDS spread

NOTES

1. The International Monetary Fund has even begun to rethink its policies on liberalized capital flows, recognizing that they can induce macroeconomic volatility for reasons that have little if anything to do with underlying economic soundness (Blanchard, Dell'Ariccia, and Mauro 2010).

2. The risks presented here are not intended to be an exhaustive list of risks incurred by the lender but only key risks in the sovereign debt market.

3. The research listed specifically describes or calculates the value of basic economic indicators to the spread of emerging market debt. Most other research on the cost of credit to emerging market sovereigns uses a rather focused group of indicators based on this line of study on creditworthiness.

4. This line of research specifically studies the role of either developed country or global economic factors and their impact on the cost of capital to emerging markets.

5. Currency risk is considered an exogenous risk for emerging market sovereign debt investors because unlike the government budget, developing countries cannot unilaterally control it.

6. See Forbes and Rigobon (2001) for a detailed analysis of how to define contagion, the numerous different alternatives, and its application to the case of Latin America. Forbes and Rigobon also use the definition of contagion used in this chapter.

7. In a 2002 press conference for the IMF, Kenneth Rogoff noted that "Mexico has a strong record of policy performance, and I think that's recognized in its investment grade status" (IMF 2002).

8. While different debt instruments and CDS contracts can have different definitions of a "credit event," for purposes of this study, a credit event refers to a default only. In other instances, a credit event may be precipitated by a ratings downgrade, not meeting financial ratios specified in the bond or CDS contract, or bankruptcy. However, in the sovereign debt market, a credit event is defined as a default.

9. See appendix 14.1 for a complete listing of the countries and data frequency included in this study.

10. I tested for multicollinearity and present the results in appendix 14.2. As the appendix shows, the baseline data does not demonstrate any danger of collinearity across the range of variables used.

11. One example of how including additional time differences adds little to the analysis is the inclusion of fixed annual effects as is common in cross-country studies. Because the CDS data was daily and the economic data in the baseline model was quarterly, I tested quarterly, monthly, and daily fixed time effects. This did not change the results either economically or statistically and I decided to present the annual effects.

12. In instances when the election was held on either a holiday or a nonbusiness day, the election was coded 1 for the last trading day before the election.

13. This includes a variety of regressions not presented here.

14. This section on testing for stationarity in panel data draws from Maddala and Wu (1999) but also uses a variety of panel and series methods.

15. It should be noted that results from unit root tests presented here are only a small sampling. Numerous other countries not presented are also stationary. The intent is to show that there are numerous countries that are stationary under numerous unit root tests with different controls. Anyone interested in seeing the full range of country results under all unit root tests is welcome to contact me for data and log files.

REFERENCES

Adelman, Jeremy. 1998. "Tequila Hangover: Latin America's Debt Crisis." *Studies in Political Economy* 55: 5–35.

Arora, Vivek, and Martin Cerisola. 2001. "How Does U.S. Monetary Policy Influence Sovereign Spreads in Emerging Markets?" *IMF Staff Papers* 48(3): 474–98.

Beck, Roland. 2001. "Do Country Fundamentals Explain Emerging Market Bond Spreads?" Working Paper No. 2001/02, Center for Financial Studies, Johann Wolfgang Goethe-Universität, Frankfurt.

Biglaiser, Glen, and Karl DeRouen. 2007. "Sovereign Bond Ratings and Neoliberalism in Latin America." *International Studies Quarterly* 51(1): 121–38.

Biglaiser, Glen, Karl DeRouen, and Candace Archer. 2011. "Lead or Lag? Sovereign Bond Ratings and Credit Markets in the Developing World." *Foreign Policy Analysis* 7: 67–87.

BIS (Bank for International Settlements). 2009. "Semiannual OTC Derivatives Statistics at end-March 2009." Bank for International Settlements, Basel.

Blanchard, Olivier, Giovanni Dell'Ariccia, and Paulo Mauro. 2010. "Rethinking Macroeconomic Policy." *IMF Staff Position Note*, February 12, 2010, International Monetary Fund, Washington, DC.

Block, Steven, and Paul Vaaler. 2004. "The Price of Democracy: Sovereign Risk Ratings, Bond Spreads, and Political Business Cycles in Developing Countries." *Journal of International Money and Finance* 23(6): 917–46.

Boyer, Brian, Tomomi Kumagi, and Kathy Yuan. 2006. "How Do Crises Spread? Evidence from Accessible and Inaccessible Stock Indices." *Journal of Finance* 61(2): 957–1003.

Bussière, Matthieu, and Christian Mulder. 1999. "External Vulnerability in Emerging Market Economies: How High Liquidity Can Offset Weak Fundamentals and the Effects of Contagion." IMF Working Paper No. 99/88, International Monetary Fund, Washington, DC.

Calvo, Guillermo, and Ernesto Talvi. 2005. "Sudden Stop, Financial Factors and Economic Collapse in Latin America: Learning from Argentina and Chile." NBER Working Paper No. 11153, National Bureau of Economic Research, Cambridge, MA, February.

Campello, Daniela. 2009. "Do Markets Vote? A Systematic Analysis of Portfolio Investors' Response to National Election." Unpublished manuscript, Princeton University.

Carr, Peter, and Liuren Wu. 2007. "Theory and Evidence on the Dynamic Interactions between Sovereign Credit Default Swaps and Currency Options." *Journal of Banking and Finance* 31(8): 2383–403

Catão, Luis, and Bennett Sutton. 2002. "Sovereign Defaults: The Role of Volatility." IMF Working Paper No. 02/149, International Monetary Fund, Washington, DC.

Cermeño, Rodolfo, Robin Grier, and Kevin Grier. 2010. "Elections, Exchange Rates, and Reform in Latin America." *Journal of Development Economics* 92(2): 166–74.

Ciarlone, Alessio, Paolo Piselli, and Giorgio Trebeschi. 2007. "Emerging Markets Spreads and Global Financial Conditions." Temi di Discussione del Servizio Studi No. 637, Bank of Italy, Rome.

Cifarelli, Giulio, and Giovanna Paladino. 2007. "An Empirical Analysis of the Co-Movement among Spreads on Emerging Market Debt." Studi e Discussioni No. 127, Dipartimento di Scienzi Economiche, Universita degli Studi di Firenze.

Ciocchini, Francisco, Erik Durbin, and David T.C. Ng. 2003. "Does Corruption Increase Emerging Market Bond Spread?" *Journal of Economics and Business* 55(5): 503–28.

Cuadra, Gabriel, and Horacio Sapriza. 2008. "Sovereign Default, Interest Rates, and Political Uncertainty in Emerging Markets." *Journal of International Economics* 76(1): 78–88.

Dailami, Mansoor, Paul Masson, and Jean Jose Padou. 2008. "Global Conditions versus Country-Specific Factors in the Determination of Emerging Market Debt Spreads." *Journal of International Money and Finance* 27(8): 1325–36.

Dornbusch, Rudiger, Yung Chul Park, and Stijn Claessens. 2000. "Contagion: Understanding How It Spreads." *World Bank Research Observer* 15(2): 177–97.

Eichengreen, Barry, and Ashoka Mody. 2000. "What Explains Changing Spreads on Emerging Market Debt?" In *Capital Flows and the Emerging Economies: Theory, Evidence, and Controversies*, edited by Sebastián Edwards, 107–36. Chicago: University of Chicago Press.

Federal Reserve. 2003. *Monetary Policy Report Submitted to Congress on February 11, 2003 Pursuant to Section 2B of the Federal Reserve Act*. Washington, DC: Government Printing Office.

Ferrucci, Gianluigi. 2003. "Empirical Determinants of Emerging Market Economies' Sovereign Bond Spreads." Working Paper No. 205, Bank of England, London.

Fiess, Norbert. 2003. "Capital Flows, Country Risk, and Contagion." World Bank Policy Research Working Paper No. 2943, World Bank, Washington, DC.

Forbes, Kristin, and Roberto Rigobon. 2001. "Contagion in Latin America: Definitions, Measurement, and Policy Implication." *Economia* 1(2): 1–46

Frenkel, Roberto. 2003. "From the Boom in Capital Inflows to Financial Traps." *Capital Market Liberalization and Development*, May, 101–21.

Ganapolsky, Eduardo, and Sergio Schmukler. 1998. "The Impact of Policy Pronouncements and News on Capital Markets: Crisis Management in Argentina during the Tequila Effect." Policy Research Working Paper Series No. 1951, World Bank, Washington, DC.

Gande, Amar, and David Parsley. 2005. "News Spillovers in the Sovereign Debt Market." *Journal of Financial Economics* 75(3): 691–734.

Goldstein, Morris. 2003. "Debt Sustainability, Brazil, and the IMF." IIE Working Paper Number WP 03–1, Institute for International Economics, Washington, DC, February.

González-Rosada, Martín, and Eduardo Levy Yeyati. 2008. "Global Factors and Emerging Market Spreads." *Economic Journal* 118(533): 1917–36.

Grandes, Martín. 2002. "Convergence and Divergence of Sovereign Bond Spreads: Lessons from Latin America." OECD Development Centre Technical Paper 200, Organisation for Economic Co-operation and Development, Paris.

Hernández, Leonardo, and Rodrigo Valdés. 2001. "What Drives Contagion: Trade, Neighborhood, or Financial Links?" *International Review of Financial Analysis* 10(3): 203–18.

Hilscher, Jens, and Yves Nosbusch. 2010. "Determinants of Sovereign Risk: Macroeconomic Fundamentals and the Pricing of Sovereign Debt." *Review of Finance* 14(2): 235–62.

IMF (International Monetary Fund). 2002. "Transcript of a Press Briefing on the World Economic Outlook." International Monetary Fund, Washington, DC, September 25. Available at http://www.imf.org/external/np/tr/2002/tr020925.htm.

——. 2007. "Brazil: Helping Calm Financial Markets." *The IMF Making a Difference*, November 21, 2007.

Jorgensen, Erika, and Jeffrey Sachs. 1988. "Default and Renegotiation of Latin American Foreign Bonds in the Interwar Period." NBER Working Paper No. 2636, National Bureau of Economic Research, Cambridge, MA, June.

Kaminsky, Graciela Laura. 2009. "Two Hundred Years of Financial Integration: Latin America since Independence." Working paper, George Washington University, Washington, DC.

Kaminsky, Graciela, and Sergio Schmukler. 2002. "Emerging Markets Instability: Do Sovereign Ratings Affect Country Risk and Stock Returns?" *World Bank Economic Review* 16(2): 171–95.

Keefer, Philip. 2007. "Elections, Special Interests, and Financial Crises." *International Organization* 61(3): 607–41.

Kumar, Manmohan, and Avinash Persaud. 2003. "Pure Contagion and Investors' Shifting Risk Appetite: Analytical Issues and Empirical Evidence." *International Finance* 5(3): 401–36.

Longstaff, Francis, Lasse Pedersen, Jun Pan, and Kenneth Singleton. 2011. "How Sovereign Is Sovereign Credit Risk?" *American Economic Journal: Macroeconomics* 3(2): 75–103.

Loureiro, Maria Rita, Fábio Pereira dos Santos, and Alexandre de Ávila Gomide. 2009. "Democracy and Macroeconomic Policymaking in Brazil: The Fiscal Agenda of Lula Administration." Working paper, Fundação Getúlio Vargas, São Paulo.

Maddala, G.S., and Shaowen Wu. 1999. "A Comparative Study of Unit Root Tests with Panel Data and a New Simple Test." *Oxford Bulletin of Economics and Statistics* 61(S1): 631–52.

Martin, Philippe, and Helene Rey. 2006. "Globalization and Emerging Markets: With or without Crash?" *American Economic Review* 96(5): 1631–51.

Martínez, Juan, and Javier Santiso. 2003. "Financial Markets and Politics: The Confidence Game in Latin American Emerging Economies." *International Political Science Review* 24(3): 363–95.

McGuire, Patrick, and Martijn Schrijvers. 2003. "Common Factors in Emerging Market Spreads." *BIS Quarterly Review*, December, 65–78.

Mendoza, Enrique, and P. Marcelo Oviedo. 2009. "Macroeconomic Uncertainty in Latin America: The Cases of Brazil, Colombia, Costa Rica, and Mexico." *Economia Mexicana* 18(2): 133–73.

Milesi-Ferretti, Gian Maria, and Assaf Razin. 1996. "Current Account Sustainability: Selected East Asian and Latin American Experiences." NBER Working Paper No. 5791, National Bureau of Economic Research, Cambridge, MA.

Miller, Marcus, Kannika Thampanishvong, and Lei Zhang. 2004. "Learning to Trust Lula: Contagion and Political Risk in Brazil." Working paper, Department of Economics, University of Warwick.

Min, Hong Ghi. 1998. "Determinants of Emerging Market Bond Spread: Do Economic Fundamentals Matter?" World Bank Policy Research Working Paper No.1899, World Bank, Washington, DC.

Min, Hong-Ghi, Duk-Hee Lee, Changi Nam, Myeong-Cheol Park, and Sang-Ho Nam. 2003. "Determinants of Emerging Market Bond Spreads: Cross Country Evidence." *Global Finance Journal* 14(3): 271–86.

Mollo, Maria de Lourdes Rollemberg, and Alfredo Saad-Filho. 2006. "Neoliberal Economic Policies in Brazil (1994–2005): Cardoso, Lula and the Need for a Democratic Alternative." *New Political Economy* 11(1): 99–123.

Mosely, Layna, and Sarah Brooks. 2008. "Risk Uncertainty and Autonomy: Financial Market Constraints in Developing Nations." Paper presented at the International Studies Association 49th Annual Convention, San Francisco, CA, March 26.

Moser, Christoph. 2007. "The Impact of Political Risk on Sovereign Bond Spreads—Evidence from Latin America," No 24, *Proceedings of the German Development Economics Conference, Göttingen 2007*, Göttingen: Verein für Socialpolitik, Research Committee Development Economics.

Nieto-Parra, Sebastián, and Javier Santiso. 2008. "Wall Street and Elections in Latin America Emerging Democracies." OECD Development Centre Working Paper No. 272, Organisation for Economic Co-operation and Development, Paris.

———. 2009a. "Revisiting Political Budget Cycles in Latin America." OECD Development Centre Working Paper No. 281, Organisation for Economic Co-operation and Development, Paris.

———. 2009b. "Elections and Financial Markets in Emerging Countries: A Latin American Perspective." *Emerging Market Network (EMNet) Brief from the Organisation for Economic Co-operation and Development,* November 24.

Nogues, Julio, and Martín Grandes. 2001. "Country Risk: Economic Policy, Contagion Effect, or Political Noise?" *Journal of Applied Economics* 4(1): 125–62.

Oddonat, Ivan, and Imene Rahmouni. 2006. "Do Emerging Market Economies Still Constitute a Homogeneous Asset Class?" *Banque de France Financial Stability Review*(9): 39–48.

Oztay, Fatih, Erdal Ozmen, and Gulbin Sahinbeyoglu. 2009. "Emerging Market Sovereign Spreads, Global Financial Conditions, and US Macroeconomic News." *Economic Modelling* 26(2): 526–31.

Pan, Jun, and Kenneth Singleton. 2008. "Default and Recovery Implicit in the Term Structure of Sovereign CDS Spreads." *Journal of Finance* 43(4): 2354–84.

Phillips, Lauren. 2006. "Democracy vs. the Financial Markets: How Will Latin America's Busy Electoral Calendar Affect the Performance of Global Financial Markets in 2006?" *ODI Opinions 64*, Overseas Development Institute, London, January.

Reinhart, Carmen. 2002. "Default, Currency Crises, and Sovereign Credit Ratings." *World Bank Economic Review* 16(2): 151–70.

Rodrik, Dani, and Arvind Subramanian. 2009. "Why Did Financial Globalization Disappoint?" *IMF Staff Papers* 56): 112–38.

Rowland, Peter. 2005. "Determinants of Spread, Credit Ratings, and Creditworthiness for Emerging Market Sovereign Debt: A Follow Up Study Using Pooled Data Analysis." Borradores de Economía No. 296, Banco de la República (Central Bank of Colombia), Bogotá.

Rowland, Peter, and José Torres. 2004. "Determinants of Spread and Creditworthiness for Emerging Market Sovereign Debt: A Panel Study." Borradores de Economía No. 295, Banco de la República (Central Bank of Colombia), Bogotá.

Schmukler, Sergio, and Luis Servén. 2002. "Pricing Currency Risk under Currency Boards." *Journal of Development Economics* 69(2): 367–91.

Uribe, Martin, and Vivian Yue. 2006. "Country Spreads and Emerging Countries: Who Drives Whom?" *Journal of International Economics* 69(1): 6–36.

Vaaler, Paul, Schrage Burkhard, and Steven Block. 2006. "Elections, Opportunism, Partisanship and Sovereign Ratings in Developing Countries." *Review of Development Economics* 10(1): 154–70.

Weigel, Dian Diaz, and Gordon Gemmill. 2006. "What Drives Credit Risk in Emerging Markets? The Roles of Country Fundamentals and Market Co-Movements." *Journal of International Money and Finance* 25(3): 476–502.

Westphalen, Michael. 2001. "The Determinants of Sovereign Bond Credit Spread Changes." Working paper, École des Hautes Études Commerciales, Lausanne.

CHAPTER 15

NATURAL RESOURCES AND DEMOCRACY IN LATIN AMERICA: NEITHER CURSE NOR BLESSING

STEPHEN HABER AND VICTOR MENALDO

1. INTRODUCTION

What effect does oil and mineral abundance have on democracy? Broadly speaking, there are three possible answers to this question: oil and minerals are bad for democracy; oil and minerals are good for democracy; and oil and minerals have no effect on democracy one way or the other. A large and influential literature argues for the first answer as a general proposition around the world. A considerably smaller literature argues for the second answer—but only in the case of Latin America; elsewhere in the world, the resource curse holds. A third body of literature argues that democracy and natural resources are unrelated. In this chapter, we review these literatures, as well as present new evidence about the relationship between natural resources and democracy in Latin America. We find that the third hypothesis—that natural resources and democracy are unrelated—best stands the weight of the evidence.

The initial research on the question of the relationship between natural resources and democracy emerged from the field of Middle Eastern studies. Mahdavy (1970, 466–67), on the basis of limited data from a few Middle Eastern cases, hypothesized that because the rents from petroleum can be easily captured, governments in resource-rich countries acquire "an independence from people seldom found in other countries . . . In political terms, the power of the government to bribe pressure groups or to coerce dissidents may be greater than otherwise." That is, governments in resource-reliant countries do not have to exchange representative institutions for tax income from the citizenry. Instead, they can simply extract revenues from an enclave resource sector, which they can then use to repress or buy off the population. Mahdavy's hypothesis soon became a dominant theme in the country case study literature about both the Middle East and Africa (e.g., Skocpol 1982; Anderson 1987; Beblawi 1987; Luciani 1987; Crystal 1989, 1990; Chaudry 1994, 1997; Van de Walle 1994; Khan 1994; Yates 1996; Clark 1997, 1998; Gardinier 2000; Dillman 2000; Hodges 2001; Bellin 2004; Vandewalle 1998, 2006).

These country case studies became so ubiquitous that the view that natural resources and democracy do not mix came to be accepted as a general law. Consider, for example, the unqualified tone in Luciani (1987, 74): "Democracy is not a problem for allocation states. . . . The fact is that there is 'no representation without taxation' and there are no exceptions to this version of the rule." Huntington (1991, 65) makes a similarly general claim: "Oil revenues accrue to the state: they therefore increase the power of the state bureaucracy and, because they reduce or eliminate the need for taxation, they also reduce the need for the government to solicit the acquiescence of the public to taxation. The lower the level of taxation, the less reason for publics to demand representation." This view has since been repeated in policy papers produced by multilateral aid organizations, popular books on world politics and economics, and articles in the mass media that make sweeping claims, such as the existence of a "first law of petropolitics" (Friedman 2006). The view that natural resources and democracy do not go together is often coupled with parallel literatures that find correlations between natural resources and slow economic growth or the onset of civil wars. Taken together, these three literatures have given rise to the stylized fact that there is a "resource curse."

In the late 1990s researchers began to subject the hypothesis that oil and mineral reliance is associated with authoritarianism to tests against large-N data sets (Ross 2001; Wantchekon 2002; Jenson and Wantchekon 2004). Over time, this large-N literature grew increasingly sophisticated: researchers developed better proxies for oil and mineral reliance (Ross 2006); used instrumental variables to address reverse causality (Ramsey 2009); exploited variance at the subnational level (Goldberg, Wibbels, and Myukiyehe 2008); and explored the effects of oil on the durability of authoritarian regimes using survival analysis or dynamic probit regressions (Smith 2004, 2007; Ulfelder 2007; Ross 2009; Papaioannou and Siourounis 2008). While the specific findings vary from study to study, this large-N literature confirmed the association between natural resources and authoritarianism.

In recent years, researchers have begun to explore the possibility that the effect of natural resources on democracy may differ across world regions. Dunning (2008), for example, argues that there is a resource blessing in Latin America. His claim is based on a panel regression with country fixed effects for the Latin American region since 1960. Dunning's explanation for Latin America's exceptionalism is the region's notoriously high levels of income inequality: when a society has a highly unequal distribution of income, natural resource wealth permits democratization because elites do not fear redistribution by the enfranchisement of the poor; conversely, when the distribution of income is more equal, natural resource wealth reinforces authoritarian regimes because leaders do not face demands for redistribution and can therefore deploy the rents from resources to buy off or coerce opponents. Dunning's empirical claim is supported by both Ross (2009) and Treisman (2010), though Ross casts doubt on the validity of the inequality mechanism and suggests other possible explanations for Latin America's resource blessing.

A third literature takes a different approach to the resource curse. This literature focuses on the causal inferences that may reasonably be drawn from the data—both across the world, as well as within particular regions and countries. Herb (2005) points out that any argument about the impact of natural resource rents on regime types requires the specification of a counterfactual: what would a resource-dependent country look like had it not found resources? Herb therefore calculates how much poorer resource-dependent countries would have been had they not developed their natural resource sectors, and then estimates their level of democracy at these counterfactual levels of gross domestic product (GDP). He finds that on average the net negative effect of resource dependence on democracy is negligible. Herb's analysis, however, still leaves open the question of a potential resource blessing in Latin America—an issue that we directly confront in this chapter.

Here we first review the methodological innovations and findings from an ongoing research program that reevaluates the resource curse hypothesis on a global scale using a time-series and counterfactually driven approach to the data (Haber and Menaldo 2010). While we do not find any evidence that increases in natural resource reliance undermine democracy or prevent democratization, some of our results suggest a resource blessing. We then explore why our findings diverge from conventional wisdom, offering both methodological and theoretical reasons why the resource curse theory and its supporting evidence are flawed. We follow with a reevaluation of the evidence for a resource blessing in Latin America along the lines pursued in our general research program. Contradicting extant work on this topic, our findings suggest that natural resources are neither a curse nor a blessing in Latin America.

2. REEVALUATING THE RESOURCE CURSE: IMPROVING CAUSAL INFERENCE

2.1. A Counterfactually Driven, Time-Series Approach

Adjudicating between the three different views about the relationship between natural resources and democracy requires an approach that is both counterfactually driven and sensitive to issues of causal inference. The resource curse is about a dynamic process: the discovery, production, and export of natural resources is hypothesized to distort a country's regime type, putting it on a different path of political development than it would have otherwise followed. The empirical tests that have been used to test the resource curse hypothesis, however, do not tend to employ time-series-centric methods. Nor do they specify counterfactual paths of political development.

In Haber and Menaldo (2010) we employ time-series-centric methods that evaluate the long-run effect of resource reliance on regime types. We carry out this analysis using both a country-by-country time-series approach and a dynamic panel framework with country fixed effects. In order to do this, we construct original data sets whose time-series dimension extends back to 1800 for 168 countries around the world. To ensure that the results are robust to different measures of resource reliance, we construct four different measures based on precedents in the literature: fiscal reliance (the percentage of government revenues from oil, gas, and mineral taxes and royalties); total oil income per capita (oil output multiplied by the real world price of petroleum, divided by population); total fuel income per capita (oil, natural gas, and coal output multiplied by their real world prices, divided by population); and total resource income per capita (oil, natural gas, coal, precious metal, and industrial metal output, multiplied by their real world prices, divided by population).

Our approach also focuses on the specification of the counterfactual: what would have happened to a resource-reliant country had it not found or exploited its natural resources? In order to answer this question we employ a difference-in-differences estimator. We assume that had a resource-reliant country not exploited its natural resources it would have followed the same path of regime change as the non-resource-reliant countries in its geographic region. We then compare that counterfactual path of political development to the country's actual path. Finally, we determine whether any divergence between the actual and counterfactual paths of political development correlates with increases in resource reliance.

To put it concretely, one might argue that Venezuela might have democratized even faster, or more fully, had it not developed an oil-based economy. Producing such a counterfactual requires us to ask a question of the following type: what would Venezuela's political trajectory have looked like had it not been earning oil rents since 1917? This counterfactual version of Venezuela does not, of course, exist. However, we can observe the political trajectory of a set of countries that were broadly similar to Venezuela before it became increasingly reliant on oil—in terms of history, geography, culture, level of economic development, and degree of democratization—but that did not subsequently become major resource producers. That set of countries consists of Latin America's resource-poor countries, and includes cases such as Costa Rica, Nicaragua, Honduras, Uruguay, Paraguay, and Argentina.

To conduct this econometric exercise we employ the most widely used measure of regime type in the political science literature, the polity score, an index of the competitiveness of political participation, the openness and competitiveness of executive recruitment, and the constraints on the chief executive, which is coded for every country in the world since 1800. We make two transformations to the polity score. First, we normalize it to run from 0 to 100. Second, we net out the difference between oil-producing countries and a synthetic, non-resource-reliant country represented by the average polity score of the non-resource-reliant countries in the oil-producing country's geographic and cultural region. For the sake of simplicity, we refer to this variable throughout as net polity. Net polity allows us to see if the yearly differences in the changes in polity between treatment and control groups are a function of changes in the "dose" of oil (after controlling for ongoing civil wars, GDP per capita, the growth rate of GDP per capita, and democratic diffusion effects, both at the regional and global level).

2.2. Findings: Rejecting the Resource Curse Hypothesis

After ruling out the possibility of reverse causality through the use of instrumental variables techniques, we find that the relationship between changes in total oil income per capita and changes in net polity is positive and statistically significant. That is, as oil income increases, countries experience political changes that make them more democratic. Even when we use split-sample techniques to try to detect a resource curse among poor countries, countries with relatively equal distributions of income (as hypothesized by Dunning 2008), and countries that are extremely large oil producers, we continue to produce results that are inconsistent with the resource curse theory: oil income and democracy are positively correlated. We also search for the resource curse on a region-by-region basis and across different time periods with similar results. Of the 15 conditional effects regressions we estimate, only one (a regression on countries in sub-Saharan Africa) produces the predicted negative coefficient—and that result is not statistically significant. Fourteen of the 15 regressions produce coefficients with the wrong (positive) sign, and of these seven are statistically significant at the 1 percent level, while an additional two are significant at 10 percent. In short, to the degree that we detect any statistically significant relationships, they point to a resource blessing: increases in natural resource income are associated with increases in democracy. The weight of the evidence indicates that scholars might want to revisit the idea of a general law known as the resource curse.

3. RECONCILING OUR FINDINGS WITH THE CONSENSUS VIEW

3.1. We Improve Causal Inference

Why do we obtain such different results from the extant literature? The hypothesis that resource wealth fuels authoritarianism implies that the discovery of oil or minerals sent countries down an alternative path of institutional development.

Specifically, the resource curse implies three possible counterfactuals: (1) Autocracy X would have become democratic had it not found oil or minerals, (2) Democracy Y would have remained democratic, instead of lapsing into autocracy, had it not found resources, and (3) Democracy Z would have made the transition from autocracy faster had it not found resources. The methods employed in the literature do not, however, allow researchers to focus on these counterfactuals. Rather, they pool countries together, treating them as identical units, and estimate the relationship between natural resources and regime type centered on the variance between them.

What difference does this make? In a regression setup that exploits variance across countries (rather than within countries over time), major resource producers that are autocracies (e.g., Saudi Arabia) exert a powerful effect on the estimated coefficients. Now consider three facts about countries of this type. First, there are a lot of them. In fact, Haber and Menaldo (2010) show that of the 53 countries whose economies are reliant on natural resources, 19 score at the very bottom of the polity scale. Many of these are also among the biggest oil producers in the world, and include such countries as Saudi Arabia, Kuwait, the United Arab Emirates, and Turkmenistan.

Second, these countries were autocracies *before* they found and exploited their natural resource wealth. In fact, 14 of the 19 are located in areas of the world—the Middle East and North Africa (MENA) and central Asia—that have long histories of tribal social organization, foreign conquest, and authoritarian government. All of the countries in MENA had been kingdoms, sheikdoms, or imamates for centuries before the discovery of oil. The modern-day countries of central Asia were run by political-military strongmen until they were conquered by Russia in the eighteenth and nineteenth centuries. In 1924, Joseph Stalin decreed these tribal areas to be Soviet republics, drawing their boundaries on the basis of the recommendations of Russian ethnographers, and imposing political leadership from Moscow. When the Soviet Union broke apart in 1991, these "republics" became nation-states, but, much like the countries of MENA, they had never in their history had anything remotely resembling democratic political institutions.

Third, the neighbors of these authoritarian "petro states," such as Jordan, Syria, and Uzbekistan, which share the same historical legacies—but importantly not their natural resource wealth—are not democracies either. This suggests that resources were not the decisive factor shaping the political trajectories of the countries that have oil.

We hope that the implication is clear. The pooled or random-effects regressions that are employed in the extant literature treat country-years as isomorphic: the implicit counterfactual to Saudi Arabia without oil in these regressions is Sweden (controlling for the fact that Sweden is poorer and has a smaller Muslim population). But Sweden is not Saudi Arabia without oil; endemic, time-invariant institutions differentiate these countries; and those institutions constrain the possible set of political institutions, and the possible set of economic sectors, that can emerge and be sustained.

In short, the techniques employed in the extant literature—which primarily exploit variance across countries, rather than within countries over time—introduce a mismatch between the theory and empirical strategies used to test it. Moreover, the right comparison for resource-rich authoritarian countries such as Saudi Arabia is their non-resource-rich neighbors who share their long historical legacies. In fact, once researchers take history seriously, the "resource cursed" countries outside of MENA and central Asia start to look more blessed than cursed. Recall that Haber and Menaldo (2010) looked at 53 countries, and that 19 of them were authoritarian before they found oil or minerals. What of the other 34? Simply examining the data reveals that two of them display no easily discernible pattern. Twenty-two of the remaining 32, however, display a pattern consistent with a resource blessing: they remain democracies during a resource boom, or they democratize during a resource boom, or undergo at least a one-standard-deviation increase in their polity score (based on the "within" variation) during a resource boom. Of the 53 cases that Haber and Menaldo look at, a case can be made for a curse in only 10 of them.

3.2. Rethinking the Resource Curse Theory

How can it be that there are countries that become more democratic or that remain democratic when they discover natural resources? Why don't these countries become "rentier states," in which protodemocratic institutions are smothered in their crib by the "fact . . . that there is 'no representation without taxation' and there are no exceptions to this version of the rule" (Luciani 1987, 74)? What this statement implies is that in the absence of natural resources and their associated rents autocratic governments are forced to raise "normal" taxes on their citizens' consumption, income, profits, property, and wealth. Moreover, this "need" to raise taxes then forces them to become more accountable—presumably citizens balk at the idea of paying taxes when they are not politically represented. In other words, the fear of tax revolts induces democratization, and resource-rich countries don't rely on taxes and therefore don't fear tax revolts. Therefore, they do not democratize.

The idea that there is "no representation without taxation" is flawed in three important ways, however. First, there have been scores of autocrats who have taxed both elites and masses at high rates and gotten away with it (e.g., Prussia under Bismarck, Portugal and Italy under fascism, and Taiwan under Chang Kai-shek). Second, the resource curse theory assumes that groups that are taxed have solved their collective action problem to force the government to grant them representation. Third, the theory assumes that what the citizenry desires in exchange for taxation is representation, when in fact this may be one of many means toward different ends such as increased public goods spending.

Indeed, the idea that there is no representation without taxation is also at variance both with recent work in public choice economics and with the actual history of the spread of democracy. It turns out that the diverse paths by which representative governments have historically arisen do not discriminate between resource-reliant and non-resource-reliant countries. One such path is when rivalry between enfranchised and disenfranchised groups induces democratization from below (Conley and Temimi 2001), as occurred in oil-rich Mexico, for example. Another such path is when economic elites are split, and the ruling elite extends suffrage strategically to advance its interest against rival elites (Llavador and Oxoby 2005), as occurred in nitrate-rich Chile in the nineteenth century. A third path is when political elites split, and agree to democratize in order to avoid violence (Bardhan 1993), such as occurred in Colombia. A final path is that democratic institutions develop and thrive when public goods become more highly valued than special interests (Lizzeri and Persico 2004); in the case of Trinidad and Tobago, public goods financed by oil and gas achieved this status and helped sustain democracy. In short, as Herbst (2000) has argued, the idea that democracy develops as a result of rulers trading representation for taxation may only be true about western Europe.[1]

4. REEVALUATING THE RESOURCE CURSE IN LATIN AMERICA

What then are we to make of the claim that there is a resource blessing in Latin America, as argued by Dunning (2008), Ross (2009), and Treisman (2010)? We now turn our attention to this issue. As a first step, in figure 15.1 we graph both the average polity score for the non-resource-reliant countries in Latin America over the long run and the average polity score of the resource-reliant countries over the long run. Figure 15.1 reveals that, since independence in the early nineteenth century, Latin America has had waves of democratization and waves of authoritarianism that have swept across the region. Figure 15.1 also shows that these waves of regime change *have occurred simultaneously in both the resource-reliant and non-resource-reliant countries*. This is most particularly the case since the 1970s, where it is clear that there has been a strong trend toward democracy in both the countries that rely on natural resources and those that do not. The graphed data suggest that resource reliance makes no difference to Latin American countries' political trajectory.

Of course, the patterns revealed in figure 15.1 are simply illustrative; we have not yet detrended the data, controlled for possible (time-varying) confounding factors, or evaluated the marginal effect of changes in resource reliance on countries' regime type. Therefore, in table 15.1 we report the results of a set of autoregressive distributed lag models in first differences for 20 Latin American countries since independence, which include the major, mainland Latin American countries, as well as Cuba, the Dominican Republic, and Haiti. Our econometric models differ from extant empirical approaches in three ways. First, we first differentiate the data to ensure that our series are stationary and to detrend the data. Second, we estimate regressions over the long run, starting at countries' independence. Third, we estimate difference-in-differences models, therefore allowing us to properly specify the

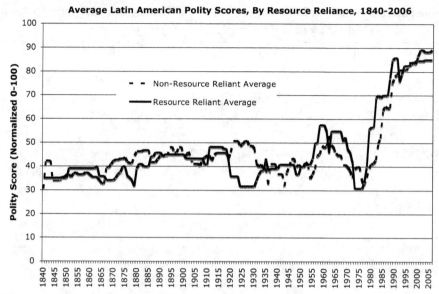

Figure 15.1 Average Latin American Polity Scores, by Resource-Reliance, 1825-2006.

Notes and *Sources:* We code as resource reliant any country that has an average level of Fiscal Reliance on Resources of greater than 5 percent during the period 1972–99, as measured by Herb (2005). For the small number of countries not coded by Herb, we employ the ratio of oil, gas, and mineral exports to GDP and again apply a standard of 5 percent. We code Cuba as not being resource reliant on the basis of the fact that it produces trivial quantities of petroleum (per our data set on Total Oil Income) and on the basis of the fact that in the CIA Factbook, Cuba is not an important producer of minerals.

counterfactual trajectory that countries would have followed in the absence of natural resources and then compare their actual trajectories to these hypothesized trajectories.

While the first two models estimate the relationship between net polity and total oil income per capita, the second set of models estimates the relationship between net polity and total resource income (oil, natural gas, coal, precious metals, and industrial metals). Each model includes the one-year lag of the (differentiated) dependent variable and a lag of the (differentiated) measure of resource reliance, allowing us to calculate the total change made by an increase in resource reliance on net polity. Each model also includes controls for the onset of civil war, the log of GDP per capita, the spread of democracy in the Latin American region, and the spread of democracy around the world. Finally, each model includes country dummies, to control for country-specific trends, and year dummies, to control for shocks that are common across countries.

To contextualize the regressions, note that the average polity score (normalized from 0 to 100) for these countries is 46, with a "between" standard deviation of 14.2 and a "within" standard deviation of 23.3 ($n = 3{,}375$, with an average period of 169 years), indicating that Latin American countries have experienced notable change over time in their degree of democracy. For total oil income per capita, the average

Table 15.1. Difference in Differences Models for the Impact of Resource Reliance on Net Polity in Latin America

	(1)	(2)	(3)	(4)
Sample	*Full*	*1973—2006*	*1900—2006*	*1973—2006*
Measure of resource reliance	*Total Oil Income*	*Total Oil Income*	*Total Resources Income*	*Total Resources Income*
Δ Net polity t-1	-0.005	-0.002	-0.006	-0.002
	[0.17]	[0.14]	[0.18]	[0.14]
ΔResource reliance (immediate impact)	0.153	0.653	0.327	0.72
	[0.21]	[1.34]	[0.58]	[1.48]
ΔResource reliance t-1	0.159	0.319	0.549	0.841
	[0.32]	[0.81]	[0.79]	[1.35]
Total change made by	0.309	0.969	0.871	1.557
Δ resource reliance	[0.30]	[1.37]	[0.86]	[1.68]
Civil war t-1	0.07	-3.163	-0.143	-3.177
	[0.05]	[1.71]	[0.10]	[1.71]
ΔLog(per capita income)	2.51	7.178	3.687	7.075
	[0.57]	[0.50]	[0.70]	[0.50]
ΔRegional democratic diffusion	0.667	1.44	0.667	1.441
	[1.45]	[2.67]**	[1.44]	[2.67]**
ΔGlobal democratic diffusion	-0.26	-2.807	-0.153	-2.805
	[3.08]***	[4.58]***	[3.33]***	[4.59]***
Country fixed effects	YES	YES	YES	YES
Year fixed effects	YES	YES	YES	YES
Observations	1896	663	1667	663
Number of groups	20	20	20	20
R-squared	0.05	0.11	0.05	0.11

$* p < .10; ** p < .05; *** p < .01$

Net polity calculated from polity scores normalized to run from 0 to 100.

Robust t-statistics (calculated with Driscoll Kraay standard errors) in brackets.

Separate country and year intercepts estimated but omitted from table.

Driscoll Kraay standard errors are estimated because they are robust to heteroskedasticity and contemporaneous correlation. Standard errors for the total change made by total oil income estimated using the delta method:((Δtotal oil income t + Δtotal oil income t-1)/(1-(Δpolity t-1)).

Results are robust to using an IV GMM (instrumental variables generalized method of moments) approach where Δ.total oil income is potentially endogenous and is instrumented with proven oil reserves, oil reserves per surface area, and total regional oil reserves (all in levels).

is US$54 (real 2007) dollars, with a "between" standard deviation of $148 and a "within" standard deviation of $236—also indicating considerable variation over time. The maximum value is $5,329, corresponding to Venezuela in 1979. Finally, for total natural resources income per capita, the average is $145 (real 2007) dollars, with a "between" standard deviation of $296 and a "within" standard deviation of $263.

The results reported in Specification 1, run on the full sample, and where total oil income is the measure of resource reliance, do not support the hypothesis that there is a resource blessing in Latin America. The total change distributed over all periods (the long-run effect) is positive, but is far from statistically significant. Even the coefficient on the immediate impact of total oil income (the short-run effect) is far from statistically significant.

Perhaps our regressions are not capturing the fact that increasing oil reliance only began to have a palpable effect on democracy in Latin America during the era in which the developed countries began to rely on these countries' oil imports, circa the first oil crisis? We therefore truncate the data set to 1973–2006, and reestimate the regressions in Specification 2. The coefficients of interest remain positive, but are still not statistically significant.

One might argue that we are underestimating resource income by looking solely at oil. We therefore reestimate t all of the difference-in-differences regressions presented above, but substitute total resource income (oil, natural gas, coal, precious metals, and industrial metals) for total oil income. The results do not overturn our regressions on total oil income. When we estimate the regressions on the 20 Latin American countries since 1900 (which is as far back as we can estimate total resource income) in Specification 3, we find, once again, that the coefficients of interest remain positive, but are far from statistical significance. In a final attempt to produce a result consistent with the notion of a Latin American resource blessing, we truncate the sample once again to the period 1973–2006 (Specification 4). Even when we take this step, the coefficient on the long-run effect still does not achieve statistical significance ($p = .11$), while the coefficient on the short-run impact remains far from significant.

This result is robust to an instrumental variables approach in order to control for possible endogeneities (results not shown). Following Haber and Menaldo (2010), we construct a data set on proven oil reserves on an annual basis from 1943 to 2006, and use it to generate three instruments in levels: total reserves; reserves per surface area; and total reserves in the region. The average oil reserves figure is 1.14 billion barrels of proven reserves, with an overall standard deviation of 6.8 billion barrels, and a maximum of 79.72 billion. When we estimate the models with total oil income as the measure of resource reliance and instrument by these three variables, we obtain a negative coefficient on total oil income on the full sample and a positive coefficient on the 1973–2006 subsample. Neither result is statistically significant (results not shown). In short, natural resources have neither been a curse nor a blessing in Latin America, a (non)finding that holds over both the long run and short run.

5. Conclusion

When a theory is at variance with both logic and evidence, scholars eventually take notice and reject the theory. This was what happened, for example, to structuralism, dependency theory, and bureaucratic authoritarianism—prominent theories that all had their genesis in the study of Latin America and which met with enough inconvenient facts that they were eventually rejected. We would suggest that the resource curse, including its Latin American "crude democracy" variant, is another example of a clever—yet flawed—theory that must now be confronted by a set of inconvenient facts.

NOTE

1. Even the canonical case that resource curse theorists seem to have in mind about rulers conceding representation for taxation—England after the Glorious Revolution—is not, in fact, an example of the phenomenon. The British Crown, as North and Weingast (1989) make clear, did not trade anything in exchange for revenues—it demanded forced loans and confiscated property to fund foreign wars. It was only *after* a protracted civil war that a coalition of nobles and citizens forcibly imposed constraints on the crown to prevent their wealth from being stolen. Higher tax revenues were only an incidental consequence of the strengthened legislature and judiciary—a by-product of more secure property rights—that lagged greater representation (Stasavage 2003).

REFERENCES

Anderson, Lisa. 1987. "The State in the Middle East and North Africa." *Comparative Politics* 20(1): 1–18.
Bardhan, Pranab. 1993. "Symposium on Democracy and Development." *Journal of Economic Perspectives* 7(3): 45–49.
Beblawi, Hazem. 1987. "The Rentier State in the Arab World." In *The Rentier State*, edited by Hazem Beblawi and Giacomo Luciani. 49–62, New York: Croom Helm.
Bellin, Eva. 2004. "The Robustness of Authoritarianism in the Middle East: Exceptionalism in Comparative Perspective." *Comparative Politics* 36(2): 139–57.
Chaudhry, Kiren Aziz. 1994. "Economic Liberalization and the Lineages of the Rentier State." *Comparative Politics* 27: 1–25.
———. 1997. *The Price of Wealth: Economies and Institutions in the Middle East.* Ithaca, NY: Cornell University Press.
Clark, John. 1997. "Petro-Politics in Congo." *Journal of Democracy* 8(3): 62–76.
———. 1998. "The Nature and Evolution of the State in Zaire." *Studies in Comparative International Development* 32(4): 3–24.

Conley, John, and Akram Temini. 2001. "Endogenous Enfranchisement When Groups' Preferences Conflict." *Journal of Political Economy* 109(1): 79–102.

Crystal, Jill. 1989. "Coalitions in Oil Monarchies: Kuwait and Qatar." *Comparative Politics* 21: 427–43.

———. 1990. *Oil and Politics in the Gulf: Rulers and Merchants in Kuwait and Qatar*. New York: Cambridge University Press.

Dillman, Bradford L. 2000. *State and Private Sector in Algeria: The Politics of Rent-Seeking and Failed Development*. Boulder, CO: Westview Press.

Dunning, Thad. 2008. *Crude Democracy: Natural Resource Wealth and Political Regimes*. New York: Cambridge University Press.

Friedman, Thomas. 2006. "The First Law of Petropolitics." *Foreign Policy*, May–June, 28–37.

Gardinier, David E. 2000. "France and Gabon Since 1993: The Reshaping of the Neo-Colonial Relationship." *Journal of Contemporary African Studies* 18: 225–42.

Goldberg, Ellis, Eric Wibbels, and Eric Myukiyehe. 2008. "Lessons from Strange Cases: Democracy, Development, and the Resource Curse in the U.S. States." *Comparative Political Studies* 41: 477–514.

Haber, Stephen, and Victor Menaldo. 2010. "Do Natural Resources Fuel Authoritarianism? A Reappraisal of the Resource Curse." Unpublished manuscript, Stanford University.

Herb, Michael. 2005. "No Representation without Taxation? Rents, Development, and Democracy." *Comparative Politics* 37: 297–317.

Herbst, Jeffrey. 2000. *States and Power in Africa: Comparative Lessons in Authority and Control*. Princeton, NJ: Princeton University Press.

Hodges, Tony. 2001. *Angola: From Afro-Stalinism to Petro-Diamond Capitalism*. Bloomington: Indiana University Press.

Huntington, Samuel. 1991. *The Third Wave: Democratization in the Late Twentieth Century*. Norman: University of Oklahoma Press.

Jensen, Nathan, and Leonard Wantchekon, 2004. "Resource Wealth and Political Regimes in Africa." *Comparative Political Studies* 37: 816–41.

Khan, Sara Ahmad. 1994. *Nigeria: The Political Economy of Oil*. Oxford: Oxford University Press.

Lizzeri, Alessandro, and Nicola Persico. 2004. "Why Did the Elites Extend the Suffrage? Democracy and the Scope of Government with an Application to Britain's 'Age of Reform.'" *Quarterly Journal of Economics* 119(2): 707–65.

Llavador, Humberto, and Robert Oxoby. 2005. "Partisan Competition, Growth, and the Franchise." *Quarterly Journal of Economics* 120(3): 1155–89.

Luciani, Giacomo. 1987. "Allocation versus Production States: A Theoretical Framework." In *The Rentier State*, edited by Hazem Beblawi and Giacomo Luciani, 63–82. New York: Croom Helm.

Mahdavy, Hussein. 1970. "The Patterns and Problems of Economic Development in Rentier States: The Case of Iran." In *Studies in the Economic History of the Middle East*, edited by M. A. Cook, 428–67. London: Oxford University Press.

North, Douglass, and Barry Weingast. 1989. "Constitutions and Commitment: The Evolution of Institutional Governing Public Choice in Seventeenth-Century England." *Journal of Economic History* 49(4): 803–32.

Papaioannou, Elias, and Gregorios Siourounis. 2008. "Economic and Social Factors Driving the Third Wave of Democratization." CEPR Discussion Paper DP6986, Centre for Economic Policy Research, London.

Ramsey, Kristopher. 2009. "Natural Disasters, the Price of Oil, and Democracy." Unpublished manuscript, Princeton University.

Ross, Michael. 2001. "Does Oil Hinder Democracy?" *World Politics* 53: 325–61.

———. 2006. "A Closer Look at Oil, Diamonds, and Civil War." *Annual Review of Political Science* 9: 265–300.

———. 2009. "Oil and Democracy Revisited." Unpublished manuscript, UCLA.

Skocpol, Theda. 1982. "State and Shi'a Islam in the Iranian Revolution." *Theory and Society* 11(3): 265–83.

Smith, Benjamin. 2004. "Oil Wealth and Regime Survival in the Developing World, 1960–1999." *American Journal of Political Science* 48(2): 232–46.

———. 2007. *Hard Times in the Land of Plenty: Oil Politics in Iran and Indonesia.* Ithaca, NY: Cornell University Press.

Stasavage, David. 2003. *Public Debt and the Birth of the Democratic State: France and Great Britain, 1688–1789.* New York: Cambridge University Press.

Treisman, Daniel. 2010. "Is Russia Cursed by Oil?" *Journal of International Affairs* 63(2): 85–102.

Ulfelder, Jay. 2007. "Natural Resource Wealth and the Survival of Autocracies." *Comparative Political Studies* 40(8): 995–1018.

Vandewalle, Dirk. 1998. *Libya since Independence: Oil and State-Building.* Ithaca, NY: Cornell University Press.

———. 2006. *A History of Modern Libya.* New York: Cambridge University Press.

Van de Walle, Nicolas. 1994. "Neopatrimonialism and Democracy in Africa." In *Economic Change and Political Liberalization in Sub-Saharan Africa*, edited by Jennifer Widner, Baltimore: Johns Hopkins University Press.

Wantchekon, Leonard. 2002. "Why do Resource Dependent Countries Have Authoritarian Governments?" *Journal of African Finance and Economic Development* 2: 57–77.

Yates, Douglas A. 1996. *The Rentier State in Africa: Oil Rent Dependency and Neocolonialism in the Republic of Gabon.* Trenton, NJ: Africa World Press.

CHAPTER 16

CONTRASTING CAPITALISMS: LATIN AMERICA IN COMPARATIVE PERSPECTIVE

BEN ROSS SCHNEIDER

1. INTRODUCTION

Many scholars have emphasized special or unique features of capitalism in Latin America and applied a wide range of adjectives like dependent, late, neoliberal, statist, hierarchical, subcapitalist, truncated, peripheral Fordist, associated, comprador, clientelist, rentier, lumpen, corporatist, and the list goes on. Others, though, have emphasized, or assumed, the strong common features of all capitalist systems, including most economies of Latin America: private property, mostly free markets, and profits. My point of departure is to side with the first group and argue that more can be gained analytically by considering capitalism in Latin America (1) as distinct from other regions and (2) with consequential intraregional variations. The major gains come through comparisons of distinctive features in Latin America with capitalist development elsewhere and historically. Thus, comparisons, for example, with more equal and rapid development in Asia help identify sources of higher inequality and lower growth in Latin America, as well as their interaction. Or the truncated industrialization in Latin America and precocious transition (in comparison with Asia and Europe) to a service economy can help highlight differences in the potential of high-skill labor market strategies (Huber 2002a or the significance of the paucity of large manufacturing firms in Latin America (Amsden 2001). And if governments in the region are basing development strategies on sustained commodity booms, then comparison with previous cases of successful commodity-led development (for example, Finland or Australia) can pinpoint factors and policies (such as heavy investment in education) underlying those successes (Palma 2005; Lederman and Maloney 2007; de Ferranti et al. 2002).

The counterview that Latin America belongs to a common, universal class of capitalist economies encouraged some of the mistaken premises and exaggerated, and ultimately frustrated, expectations of market reform in the 1990s. In this view, the underlying economies were fundamentally the same as elsewhere and would become more recognizably so once the artificial restrictions on trade and exchange had been lifted and state intervention reduced to a minimum. On some key macro dimensions of the Washington consensus such as inflation and fiscal and current account balances, as well as financial intermediation, convergence with richer countries has in fact been substantial. However, on deeper structural and institutional dimensions such as dominance of the private sector by huge family-owned business groups, high labor market regulation, and pervasive informality, Latin America looks quite different from both rich countries and other developing regions. What is at stake theoretically is in part the ongoing tension between deductive, universalizing approaches popular in economics and inductive, comparative approaches more common in sociology and political science. What is at stake in practical terms is whether policy-oriented scholars should invest in finding best practices and policies applicable in most cases or invest in understanding individual political economies first in order to tailor policy packages to their peculiarities (Rodrik 2007).

Analyses of contrasts among divergent development trajectories within Latin America have also yielded major theoretical insights. James Mahoney (2010), for a recent example, concludes that more liberal versus more mercantile patterns of incorporation into the Spanish Empire explain long-term differences in economic and social development. Others emphasize the long-term effects of mining enclaves versus diversified agriculture on class structure and prospects for development (Cardoso and Faletto 1979). More recently, patterns of engagement with the latest wave of globalization also set countries on different trajectories, as for example Mexico and other countries of Central America and the Caribbean that integrated deeply through global production networks into the U.S. economy and expanded low-skill employment in manufacturing (Stallings and Peres 2000). Other scholars emphasize the distorting effects of booming gas and oil exports on development (through Dutch disease effects) and on politics (left populism) in countries like Bolivia, Ecuador, and Venezuela (Weyland 2009).[1]

One challenge to any effort to identify a type or types of capitalism in Latin America is the fact that it appears to be a moving target. The typical adjectives "emerging" and "developing" reinforce the impression that Latin American economies are amorphous and in transition. Yet on many core dimensions, capitalism in the region is fairly well institutionalized. Middle-income regions like Latin America may still lag as far behind developed countries as they did decades ago in terms of gross domestic product (GDP) per capita, but on many social, economic, and institutional indicators contemporary middle-income countries are as "modern" as developed countries were by the middle of the twentieth century when varieties of capitalism there became institutionalized and consolidated (Hall 2007). Thus, there are good reasons to think that capitalism in many middle-income countries may have settled into institutional foundations of its own, and therefore requires analysis on its own terms rather than as some form of capitalism in formation.[2]

Many analyses of what is distinctive about development in Latin America start with external factors such as international dependency (resources or investment) or the state (as in developmental states) or with macro policy packages such as import-substituting industrialization (ISI) and later market-oriented reform.[3] These are useful distinctions for many purposes, but they have several shortcomings: especially a tendency to overaggregation and a focus on the macro economy, as well as a related separation from the workings of the real economy. So, for example, many discussions of state intervention, resource dependence, or ISI make little or no references to firms and workers, the actual organizations and agents of the economy. A more micro, grounded view of capitalism in Latin America requires an examination of firms, corporate governance, financial intermediation, labor markets, educational systems, skills, turnover, and informality. Such a focus is similar to that in the "varieties of capitalism" debate that has dominated discussion of comparative capitalisms in developed countries and that section 3 considers in greater depth. The traditional macro view also has a bias toward emphasizing dramatic change—as in shifting development strategies—to the neglect of ongoing continuities in the underlying micro institutions.

Section 2 provides some brief background on successive attempts since the 1960s to identify distinctive features of capitalism in Latin America, especially dependency, statist, and neoliberal approaches. Section 3 then turns to an extended analysis of liberal, coordinated, network, and hierarchical capitalisms and highlights examples of the last in Latin America. This section analyzes core components of hierarchical capitalism—family-owned business groups, multinational corporations (MNCs), low skills, and anomic labor relations—that are common across most countries in Latin America. Section 4 examines how recent trends in globalization, commodity booms, and the revival of state intervention in the economy largely reinforced elements of hierarchical capitalism.

2. Some Brief History of a Long Scholarly Tradition

The distinctiveness of the organization of capitalism in Latin America flourished as a core subject of debate in the emerging social sciences in the 1950s and 1960s among scholars searching for the causes of relative economic backwardness. One group developed a macro, structuralist critique that highlighted the ways in which policy packages (especially ISI) and the process or stages of industrialization in Latin America differed fundamentally from earlier industrializers, as for example in the focus on the production of consumer goods in Latin America versus a concentration on heavy industry and producer goods in later comers in Europe (Hirschman 1971, ch. 3; Ianni 1968).

Another group took a micro approach to examining the personalities, backgrounds, and qualities of entrepreneurs. This research was in the line of Max Weber's *Protestant Ethic* (1958) and asked what individual traits and motivations made the postwar generation of capitalists tick. Some highlighted the immigrant background of early industrialists (Hirschman 1971, 96; Cardoso [1964] 1972). Others used surveys and other research to uncover the sources of insufficiently entrepreneurial behavior (Lauterbach 1965). Much of this analysis, from the North American side especially, was caught up in modernization theory, and maintained a fairly homogeneous view of the region.[4]

The counterattack against modernization theory, much of it initially from Latin America, came from dependency theory in the 1960s and 1970s. There were multiple variants, but most could be roughly classified by whether the crucial vector of dependency was aggregate, sectoral, or firm level. Aggregate, statistical analyses examined relations between high levels of international trade and investment and poor social and economic outcomes (Mahler 1980). Sectoral studies analyzed the mostly negative consequences of dependence on single exports, usually enclaves (Cardoso and Faletto 1979; Shafer 1994). At a firm level, research on MNCs showed how they limited and constrained development options in host countries (Evans 1979). Hirschman argued that foreign direct investment (FDI), at middle levels of development, crowded out domestic entrepreneurs and weakened political support for accelerated development because policymaking is not "invigorated by the influence normally emanating from a strong, confident, and assertive group of industrialists" (Hirschman 1971, 231). In terms of comparative analysis, aggregate studies did not usually differentiate Latin America from the rest of the developing world. In contrast, sectoral and firm-level analyses did start to highlight differences between Latin America and East Asia (Gereffi and Wyman 1990).[5]

The contrasts with East Asia became more prominent with the turn in the 1980s to focus more on state capitalism and developmental states (Evans, Rueschemeyer, and Skocpol 1985; Fajnzylber 1983). This new focus was partly the result of the rapid expansion of state intervention in the 1970s, especially in countries like Peru, Brazil, and Mexico, and the growing criticism of that intervention. The analytic shift also coincided with growing scholarship on state-led development in early industrializers, and an increasingly common analytic division in terms of capitalist models among market-oriented (United Kingdom and United States), statist (Japan and France), and negotiated, managed, or social democratic (Germany and Scandinavia) nations (Johnson 1982).

The contrasts with East Asia were also central to a growing discussion in the 1980s on the superiority of export-oriented development strategies over ISI (Haggard

1990). This debate shifted away from patterns of dependency and qualities of the state to focus on policy packages as the crucial dimension differentiating Latin America from other regions, especially East Asia. However, by the 1990s, the neoliberal critique of the state and the Washington consensus on the virtues of markets projected a homogeneous view of the obstacles and solutions to development in Latin America. Observers acknowledged empirical differences among countries, but mostly in terms of how far they had progressed in implementing a uniform package of reforms (Lora 2007). Whether countries could, and should, converge on a single policy package was less discussed.

This brief overview is not intended to do justice to decades of debate and research on the nature of capitalism in Latin America. The goal was rather to illustrate how scholars of political economy had come at the question from a wide range of different perspectives, in fairly rapid succession, and to highlight the fact that the micro institutions of the economy—corporate governance, skills, labor markets, training practices, and so on—were never central to debates on the particularities of capitalism in the region. Instead, theorists focused on macro structures of the global economy or overall policy packages in national economies. The next section shows how a focus on micro institutions can help illuminate the peculiarities of capitalism in Latin America.

3. Economic Institutions and the Political Economy of Hierarchical Capitalism

For a number of years now, non–Latin Americanist scholars have been asking how many varieties of capitalism exist in contemporary societies. To date the most common answers—based almost exclusively on comparisons among developed countries—are one, two, three, four, five, or many. Hall and Soskice (2001a) divided most developed countries into two varieties: liberal market economies (LMEs) and coordinated market economies (CMEs). Coates (2000, 9–10) distinguishes three "ideal types" of capitalist organization: market-led, state-led, and negotiated or consensual. Schmidt (2002, 112–18) uses a similar three-way typology of market capitalism, managed capitalism, and state capitalism with France and Italy in the last category. Kitschelt et al. (1999) distinguish four main types: uncoordinated liberal market capitalism (same countries as LMEs), national coordinated market economies (labor corporatist) in Scandinavia, sector-coordinated market economies (Rhine capitalism) in much of Europe, and "group-coordinated Pacific Basin market economies" in Japan and Korea. For Boyer (2005, 509), regulation theory "recurrently finds at least four brands of capitalism: market-led, meso-corporatist, social democratic and State-led." Bruno Amable's (2003) distinction among five types of capitalism—market-based, social-democratic, European, Mediterranean, Asian—steps farther south and ventures a bit out of the Organisation for Economic Cooperation and Development (OECD) world (see Crouch [2005] for an extended review of recent typologies).

My more deductive point of departure is that contemporary capitalist systems—defined by the predominance of mostly free markets and private property—accommodate a limited number of alternative mechanisms for allocating resources, especially the gains from investment, production, and exchange. These mechanisms are markets, negotiation, trust, and hierarchy, and correspond in "varieties of capitalism" terms to, respectively, liberal market economies, coordinated market economies, network market economies (NMEs), and hierarchical market economies (HMEs). Markets and coordination, the mechanisms in the original CME-LME dichotomy, do not exhaust all the primary logics or principles of allocation in capitalist economies. In fact, Hall and Soskice (2008a) note two quite different mechanisms for coordination in CMEs, negotiation in Europe and networks in Asia.[6] These three mechanisms seem to parallel Hirschman's (1970) trichotomy of responses to decline—exit (LMEs), voice (CMEs in Europe), and loyalty (NMEs in Asia)—though for Hirschman, loyalty was less a third principle and more a factor mitigating voice and exit. However, loyalty requires trust, which figures centrally in most analyses of Japanese networks, lifetime employment, and group coordination. Lastly, in terms of basic principles, hierarchy is a fourth crucial mechanism for nonmarket allocation. In post-Coasian economics, hierarchy is a feature of all modern firms and a universal response to higher transaction costs (Williamson and Winter 1993). However, transaction costs and hierarchy vary considerably across national institutional contexts, and hierarchy should also be considered a variable option adopted by economic agents instead of market, network, or negotiated alternatives.

The rest of this section analyzes the differences among the four varieties across basic allocative principles and mechanisms, corporate governance, labor relations, and empirical cases. Table 16.1 starts with abstract distinctions underlying each variety. The issue of skills provides a useful illustration of the core principles of allocation. When workers and their employers invest in training, how are the gains from that investment divided? Following the possible mechanisms in table 16.1, both parties can let the market decide the value of the new skills, and employees can sell them to the highest bidder. Or workers and employers can negotiate a plan for sharing the gains from skills in the context of long-term employment relationships. Or workers can invest in skills and trust that they will be compensated in some way in the future, such as seniority-based pay. Or finally, employers can decide unilaterally who gets trained and how the gains are distributed. Of course the power asymmetries between employees and employers are enormous in all types of capitalism, but shared expectations vary on how that power is wielded. Workers may expect employers, variously, to play the market, return regularly for negotiations, keep them on for lifetime employment, or just tell them what to do next.

Table 16.1. Basic Relations in Four Ideal Types of Capitalism

	Liberal (LME)	Coordinated (CME)	Network (NME)	Hierarchical (HME)
Allocative principle	Markets	Negotiation	Trust	Hierarchy
Characteristic interaction among stakeholders	Spot exchange	Institutionalized meeting	Reiterated exchange	Order or directive
Length of relationships	Short	Long	Long	Variable
Representative case	United States	Germany	Japan	Chile

The typical interactions in table 16.1, considered in more detail below, characterize relations among different sets of stakeholders. So, for example, managers in LMEs would expect most relations with shareholders, creditors, suppliers, competing firms, and employees to be short term and market based. Managers in NMEs, in contrast, would expect these relations to be longer term, and each iterated exchange helps build trust for the next round. Managers in CMEs can expect many more meetings with formal, bargained commitments. In HMEs, relations among owners and managers tend to be hierarchical and longer term, while relations with other firms and with workers are shorter term and based on some combination of markets and hierarchy.

Hierarchy and the concept of a hierarchical capitalism were not considered in previous typologies of comparative capitalism. In a Coasian perspective, hierarchy is of course the day-to-day result of firm decisions to "make rather than buy." In hierarchical capitalism, however, hierarchy regulates and orders much more than just internal relations of vertical integration. Hierarchy also informs relations between owners and managers (concentrated ownership) as well as employee relations (unmediated by labor unions) and decisions on investments in skills and training. Hierarchy is also evident in relations among firms both within sectors where large firms dominate economically (oligopoly) and in associations as well as across sectors and borders in that business groups and MNCs buy and control firms that would be independent in other varieties. Thus, hierarchies replace relations that in other varieties would be mediated by markets, networks, or coordination. Empirically, as discussed below, hierarchy is more common in developing countries and especially Latin America, yet conceptually it is a distinctive mechanism of allocation that merits inclusion along with the other three better-known principles.

On the dimension of corporate governance (table 16.2), the first distinction is between dispersed ownership in LMEs like the United States and Great Britain and blockholding (concentrated ownership) in the other three varieties (La Porta, López-de-Silanes, and Shleifer 1999; Gourevitch and Shinn 2005). Concentrated ownership and patient investment facilitate the longer-term relations in negotiated and coordinated capitalisms, as in Germany. While ownership is concentrated in all three blockholding varieties, the type of control varies somewhat. In particular, large firms in NMEs like Japan tend to have more cross-shareholding within business groups (and by financial intermediaries) that crowds out dispersed shareholding and makes it easier to fend off outside takeovers (Dore 2000, 34). In HMEs in many developing countries, ownership tends to be more concentrated, in part because of the relative underdevelopment of stock markets, and mostly held by families (which adds another element of hierarchy) (La Porta, López-de-Silanes, and Shleifer 1999). Hostile takeovers, common in LMEs, are rare or unknown in the other varieties.

Share ownership feeds into different types of corporate structure and authority in the large firms in each variety. Dispersed ownership in LMEs shifts decisional authority to managers, but also subjects them to short-term monitoring and performance pressures. Owners have greater control in the other non-LME varieties, where investors tend to be more "patient." Although business groups are common in non-LME varieties, they tend to be different types, more informally connected in NMEs and more hierarchical in HMEs (see Schneider 2009b; Colpan, Hikino, and Lincoln 2010).[7]

In addition, among the largest firms, MNCs are common in both LMEs and HMEs, but rarer in CMEs and especially NMEs (where they would undermine interfirm coordination in business associations and informal networks). MNCs of course add hierarchy and bureaucracy in HMEs as they absorb subsidiaries into centrally managed corporations (Amsden 2009). The debate on varieties of capitalism pays little attention to MNCs, yet even in developed countries the contrasts are large: the proportion of sales accounted for by MNCs was 21 percent in the United States, 31 percent in the United Kingdom, 11 percent in Germany, and just 2

Table 16.2. Corporate Governance and Interfirm Relations

	Liberal (LME)	Coordinated (CME)	Network (NME)	Hierarchical (HME)
Stock ownership	Dispersed	Blockholding	Blockholding and cross ownership	Family blockholding
Predominant type of large firms	Specialized managerial corporations, MNCs	Bank-controlled firms, business groups	Informal business groups (keiretsu)	Hierarchical business groups, MNCs
Firm relations within sectors	Competitive	Sectoral associations	Associations and informal ties	Oligopolistic
Firm relations across sectors	Few	Encompassing associations	Informal connections	Few (save acquisitions)
Supplier relations	Competitive bidding	Long term, negotiated	Long term, informal	Vertical integration

percent in Japan (Barba Navaretti and Venables 2004, 5). In a different measure, stocks of FDI as a percentage of GDP in 2004, the differences are also large: only a few percent in Japan, close to 15 percent in the United States and Germany, and over 30 percent in the United Kingdom (Cohen 2007, 58, fig. 3–4). The presence of MNCs in most developing countries is even larger, especially in higher-technology manufacturing (such as autos and electronics), with the significant exceptions of Korea and Taiwan (Amsden 2001). In Latin America in 1999, among the largest firms, MNCs accounted for 48 percent of sales in Venezuela, 57 percent in Brazil, and 73 percent in Argentina (as a proportion of the total sales of the 100 largest firms) (Andrade, Barra, and Elstrodt 2001, 83).

Comparisons across three dimensions of interfirm relations—within sectors, across sectors, and with suppliers—reveal differences that are closely related to the guiding principles of each variety. In LMEs, relations are competitive within sectors, largely absent across sectors (encompassing associations are weaker or nonexistent), and competitive among suppliers. At first glance, HMEs seem to resemble LMEs in their shared lack of interfirm coordinating mechanisms. However, firms in HMEs tend to encounter many more hierarchies than market relations. High concentration ratios in many sectors structure markets as oligopolies with a few dominant firms (that are likely to exercise control over industry associations).[8] Moreover, across sectors and across borders, firms in HMEs are more likely to be owned and controlled by either large business groups or MNCs (Khanna and Yafeh 2007). Moreover, relations with suppliers are typically hierarchical, either through direct vertical integration or general dependence of small suppliers on large buyers.

In CMEs, employer and sectoral associations are stronger and more encompassing, and they perform crucial coordinating functions such as bargaining collectively, managing vocational training programs, and negotiating sectoral standards (Hall and Soskice 2001a). Relations with suppliers are based on long-term, negotiated relations that often involve joint efforts at upgrading. Relations with government are also likely to be mediated by strong business associations. In NMEs, crucial coordination also takes place through informal networks of firms, best typified by the *keiretsu* in Japan. Such network-based business groups are multisectoral and provide strong links across sectors. In practice, formal associations in network economies may also be important and help to mediate coordination within sectors, often with government support, as in deliberation councils and publicly supported research and development (R&D) consortia. However, in addition to formal association ties, informal networks also permeate sectoral relations among firms, in "intra-industry loops" (Witt 2006, 11). Relations with suppliers are often long term with formal negotiation, but there are additional network and informal relations (as in the practice of shifting employees from buyer to supplier firms).

On the labor side, there is a greater resemblance between LMEs and HMEs, on the one hand, and between CMEs and NMEs, on the other (table 16.3) (see Schneider and Karcher [2010] for empirical data). In hierarchical and market varieties, employment relations are short term and unmediated by unions, which are generally weak or absent. Workers therefore have few incentives to invest in sector- or

Table 16.3. Labor Relations and Skills

	Liberal (LME)	Coordinated (CME)	Network (NME)	Hierarchical (HME)
Employment relations	Short term, market	Long term, negotiated	Lifetime employment	Short term, market
Industrial relations	Few unions	Strong, encompassing unions	Company unions	Few unions
Labor-management committees	No	Yes	Yes	No
Skills	General	Sector specific	Firm specific	Low

firm-specific skills, and invest, if they do invest, in more general skills. In CMEs and NMEs, in contrast, employment relations are longer term, and employees therefore have stronger incentives to invest in sector- and firm-specific skills (Estevez-Abe, Iversen, and Soskice 2001). Beyond very high turnover (median job tenure is only three years), labor markets in Latin America also differ from other varieties in terms of higher regulation and larger informal sectors (Schneider and Karcher 2010).

In the abstract, unions do not mesh well with the organizing principles in market and hierarchical varieties, and in practice large majorities of workers in purer cases of each do not belong to unions. By one calculation, median union density in the 2000s was 45 percent in CMEs (including Japan), 28 percent in LMEs, and 15 percent in Latin America (Schneider and Karcher 2010, fig. 1.2). Beyond, or alongside, unions, there is a further issue of additional forums for consultation and negotiation over work organization and other shop-floor issues. On this dimension, both theoretical expectations and practice are more black and white: LMEs and HMEs have none while CMEs and NMEs have a range of different forms of ongoing consultation between management and labor, including statutory bodies like work councils (codetermination), representation on company boards, and shop-floor work teams.

Overall, each variety has distinctive strengths and weaknesses (table 16.4). For Hall and Soskice (2001a), the adaptability of LMEs combined with high-level skills in cutting-edge technology and service sectors promotes radical innovation in new products and businesses. CMEs and NMEs, in contrast, manage through longer-term relationships to innovate incrementally, especially in manufacturing, and to make constant improvements in quality and productivity in more established lines of activity. HMEs lack both of these kinds of innovative capacities because of lower skills overall and short-term hierarchical relations that impede collaborative shop-floor relations needed to promote incremental production innovation. Firms in HMEs develop stronger competitive advantages in commodity production, often based on natural resources, in sectors like agroindustry (pulp and paper, vegetable oils, fish and meat packing, and ethanol), minerals and metals (steel, aluminum,

Table 16.4. Comparative Institutional Advantage and Empirical Cases

	Liberal (LME)	Coordinated (CME)	Network (NME)	Hierarchical (HME)
Comparative institutional advantages	Radical innovation, services	Incremental innovation, manufacturing	Incremental innovation, manufacturing	Commodities, global production networks
National cases	United States, Great Britain, Australia, Estonia	Germany, Scandinavia, Slovenia, (Korea?)	Japan, Taiwan	Latin America, South East Asia, Turkey, South Africa

copper, and cement), and more routine industrial commodities (textiles, electronic components, and auto parts), where the design and marketing are located in developed countries and production is subcontracted to firms in developing countries in global production networks (Gereffi, Humphrey, and Sturgeon 2005).

Table 16.4 categorizes some major empirical cases, based primarily on the leading sectors and big firms in each country. The LME, CME, and NME classifications follow the conventional wisdom on OECD countries that most closely approximate each ideal type, and add in some emerging cases of each. Many of the larger, middle-income developing countries approximate the HME variety. The economies of large countries of Latin America and Southeast Asia, as well as countries like Turkey and South Africa, have many hierarchical business groups and MNCs, high labor turnover and lower average skills, and generally weak labor unions that lack capacity to negotiate effectively. Chile, for example, was a leader among developing countries in liberalizing its economy and is also a leader, not coincidentally, in the concentration of corporate control. By one recent measure, the sales of the 63 largest firms in 2006 equaled 87 percent of GDP, so a small number of hierarchies controlled a large proportion of economic activity.[9]

Among the emerging capitalist economies of east Europe and the former Soviet Union, some governments adopted more or less explicit programs of transition to a particular variety. The Baltic countries (Lithuania, Latvia, and Estonia) adopted the most extreme market reforms, pushing them in an LME direction, while Slovenia stands out for the sustained reliance on CME kinds of institutions such as strong business associations, labor unions, and tripartite negotiations (Bohle and Greskovits 2007; Feldmann 2007; Nölke and Vliegenthart 2009). Russia and some of the other former Soviet republics seemed to be moving toward hierarchical capitalism, but several cases have ended up better classified as state or patrimonial capitalism (discussed below).

Among the rising industrial economies of East Asia, Korea and Taiwan seem to hover between CMEs and NMEs, and on some dimensions drift over to HMEs (though they are pretty clearly not LMEs). Taiwan, for example, has extensive business networks but also strong business associations that coordinate, CME-style, standards, R&D, and exports (Cheng 1996; Amsden and Chu 2003). Korea has a form of very hierarchically structured business groups, the *chaebol*. Because of the apparent similarities between keiretsu and chaebol, Japan and Korea are often classified together as group-based CMEs (Kitschelt et al. 1999). However, chaebol and keiretsu rely on quite different coordinating mechanisms: loose, informal networks in keiretsu, and rigid hierarchical control in chaebol (see Whitley 1990). In contrast, Taiwanese groups are less vertically integrated (and hierarchical), are smaller, and rely more on network ties to buyers and suppliers (Chang 2006). To the extent that Korean business associations perform important coordinating functions among chaebol and that Korean labor unions are less company based than in Japan, then Korea starts to look more like a European-style CME. Moreover, in the late 1990s the Korean government mandated that all large firms create internal labor-management committees (Haagh 2004).

The ideal typical distinctions also help identify significant within-case deviations and combinations. In the United States, for example, networks are crucial to Silicon Valley as well as smaller niche sectors like diamonds and fashion designing. Moreover, some privately held firms in the United States (some in commodities like Cargill) resemble hierarchical HME business groups. In the case of the other three varieties, the growing service sector has many LME features: general skills, smaller firms without network or association ties, and shorter-term employment. Last, some world leading manufacturing firms in HMEs (some of the best-known cases are Embraer [aircraft, Brazil] and Techint [steel tubes, Argentina]), have managed to create pockets of lasting investment in skills and well-mediated employment relations and consequently look more like CME firms. For the most part these anomalies are exceptions that prove the rule, and their exceptionalism can often be traced to peculiar and determined efforts not to conform to the prevailing complementarities, as for example was the state's long-term subsidization of skill development in Embraer (Goldstein 2002), or the refusal of family-owned hierarchical groups in the United States to list their firms.

States so overwhelm some developing economies that it is less appropriate to use a market economy suffix to describe them. For the most part, these statist types belong under Weber's umbrella concept of political capitalism where profits depend more on politics than markets. In such cases of state dominance, the nature of the state is more important than the organization of private firms in determining the type of political economy. In instances of state capitalism, the public control of the economy, especially in the largest firms and sectors, exceeds the private sector, either by virtue of public property (as in China through the 1990s) or natural resource rents. In the latter case (rentier or petro states), the state, by virtue of its control of overwhelming natural resource rents, dominates economic activity and forecloses the emergence of a large, independent private sector (Karl 1997). At an extreme level of intervention, developmental states (perhaps in Taiwan and Korea in the 1960s) regulate so much of economic activity that they can be considered cases of political capitalism (Amsden 1989). Last, political leaders may favor particular businesses in what is variously termed crony, cliental, or patrimonial capitalism (see King [2007], for example, on Russia and other former Soviet republics). By the 2000s, political capitalism characterized Venezuela, Bolivia, and Ecuador, rather than hierarchical capitalism (Weyland 2009).

A great deal more empirical work would be required to determine if and how much actual economies approximate the four ideal types analyzed here. The main goal of this section was to develop a framework that would help bring some developing countries into the debate on varieties of capitalism and facilitate microinstitutional comparisons among developing countries and with developed economies.

4. Globalization, Resource Dependence, and the Return of the State

The most recent round of globalization reinforced elements of hierarchical capitalism in Latin America while reviving some aspects of dependency, especially dependence on MNCs and natural resource exports. For example, neoliberal reforms of the 1990s attracted a new wave of MNC investment to Latin America. Privatization in particular attracted large investments, and shifted the composition of the largest firms by reducing the state share and increasing the MNC share (Santiso 2008). This wave did not, though, attract much scholarly or political attention, as it had in earlier decades (for an exception, see Egan 2010). However, the pervasive presence of MNCs continued to distinguish Latin America from many countries of Asia (Japan, Korea, and India, for example) and helped explain the absence of large manufacturing firms among the largest firms in Latin America, which were mostly concentrated in services and raw materials (Schneider 2009a). Moreover, scattered research continued to show that MNCs were footloose (as in the many firms that left Mexico for China [Gallagher and Zarsky 2007]), less likely to invest in R&D (ECLAC 2005), and less responsive to domestic policy initiatives to promote upgrading (Schrank 2011).

By the 2000s, the other major impact of globalization was the boom in commodities and the resulting reorientation of economies in the region. Resource dependence is not new in Latin America, but it did have dramatic effects in the 2000s by generating current account and fiscal surpluses (not seen in decades) and pressuring currencies to overvalue (with consequent Dutch disease effects such as specialization in natural resource exports and deindustrialization). Commodity price surges also boosted revenues, investment, and valuation of dominant, hierarchical business groups in major commodity sectors (groups like Vale, EBX, and Votorantim in Brazil; Agnelli, Luksic, and Matte in Chile; and Cemex and Grupo Mexico in Mexico) that displaced slower-growing manufacturing firms. Buoyed by windfall profits, overvalued domestic currencies, and easy access to local and international credit, these commodity groups went on acquisitions sprees, buying up firms at home and abroad, and led the charge of outward FDI from Latin America (Goldstein 2007; Santiso 2008; Casanova 2009).

Both the influx of MNCs and the renewed resource dependence reinforced features of hierarchical capitalism, though in different ways. Brownfield acquisitions (rather than greenfield investment in new production facilities) accounted for a large share, often more than half, of FDI in the 1990s and of course meant that previously freestanding domestic firms were incorporated into new global hierarchies (Amsden 2009). These new subsidiaries then were also unlikely to be engaged in R&D and new product development (ECLAC 2005). Moreover, domestic commodity firms usually had limited demand for skilled labor; capital-intensive firms (mining, steel) employed skilled workers but not many of them, while labor-intensive firms (sugar, cellulose) employed lots of workers but most of them unskilled (ECLAC 2010; on Brazil, see Schneider 2009a).

Although the historical record of MNCs and commodity firms in generating skilled jobs and innovation is weak, some recent signs suggest that patterns could be different in the twenty-first century. MNCs are outsourcing some R&D functions to Latin America, though less than to Asia and eastern Europe.[10] Commodity production, both raw materials and semiprocessed goods like metals, cement, and cellulose, have typically been considered low- or stable-technology activities. However, several sectors have recently witnessed greater returns to innovation in both process and product. Both Cemex (cement) and JBS (meat processing), for example, innovated in processing bulk commodities through the extensive application of information technology (Schrank 2005; Lessard and Lucea 2009). On the product side, innovation has been extensive in agricultural inputs as well as outputs associated with new green fuels like ethanol and bagasse. However, these examples are still more the exceptions than the rule.

After the wave of market-oriented reform of the 1990s, the pendulum swung back in the 2000s in most countries to greater state intervention. For some, this trend signaled a worrisome revival of state capitalism, but in most instances states did not reverse the major liberalizing reforms of the 1990s but rather devised new policies to promote development in more open economies. True, some governments on the populist left like Venezuela and Bolivia enacted major nationalizations, price controls, trade restrictions, and other interventions reminiscent of twentieth-century ISI, but most other countries promoted more indirect forms of intervention. Chile and Brazil developed significant new programs of what could be called "open-economy industrial policy" (Pagés 2010, ch. 10). Although Chile is renowned as the regional leader in market reforms, government intervention, especially sectoral promotion, was key to the success of sectors such as forestry, salmon, and wine (Kurtz 2001). In the late 2000s, the government enacted a huge program to promote innovation using royalty payments from mining. Since its creation in 2006, the Consejo

Nacional de Innovación para la Competitividad has disbursed hundreds of millions of dollars per year on projects in six sectors linked mostly to natural resource exports that it has identified as priority sectors for innovation (Agosin, Larraín, and Grau 2009).

Within Latin America, Brazil has retained and expanded the most consistently interventionist and developmental state. The interventions range from low-profile, decentralized promotion of biotechnology (Embrapa), pharmaceuticals (Fiocruz), worker training (Senai), and small and medium enterprises (Sebrae), to the massive expansion of Petrobrás and the hyperactive and well-endowed development bank, BNDES.[11] The BNDES merits special attention both because it is ubiquitous in funding the private sector and because the government charged it with new functions in the 2000s ranging from promoting SMEs to protecting the environment to helping Brazilian companies acquire subsidiaries abroad (Almeida 2009; Arbix and Martin 2010).

Governments also became more active in the 2000s with programs to fight poverty, in large measure because hierarchical capitalism, market-oriented reform, and the commodity boom did little to alleviate it. These government programs—especially targeted conditional cash transfer policies in Brazil, Mexico, and Chile—had major successes against extreme poverty, and some in reducing inequality, though high inequality remained a defining feature of capitalism in Latin America. The well-known historical causes of inequality in Latin America are mostly overlapping and mutually reinforcing (Mahoney 2010). Politics in the twentieth century further entrenched inequality. Even when governments implemented welfare policies in the twentieth century, they often did so in highly segmented ways, so that by the beginning of the twenty-first century, state spending had virtually no impact on inequality (Schneider and Soskice 2009; Goñi, López, and Servén 2008).

Patterns of recent insertion into the international economy exacerbated inequality in various ways: reducing industrial employment, promoting skill-biased technological change, increasing returns to education, and fomenting informality. In 1970s East Asia and Latin America had similar proportions in industry, but by 2003 the share of GDP in manufacturing was 15 percent in Latin America versus 30 percent in East Asia (Pagés, Pierre, and Scarpetta 2009, 10). In Latin America, the service sector expanded rapidly and generated almost all the new jobs after market reforms. However, much of this employment in services was low wage, low skill, informal, and low productivity in areas like retail trade, hotels, restaurants, and domestic service (Stallings and Peres 2000; Pagés, Pierre, and Scarpetta 2009). The labor market result was growing inequality in returns to education, with higher returns to tertiary versus secondary and primary education. Moreover, as noted earlier, the commodity boom generated few jobs in capital-intensive sectors and lots of low-wage, low-skill, informal jobs in labor-intensive sectors. In sum, globalized hierarchical capitalism continued to pose major challenges to reformers seeking to promote more equitable, higher-skill development and faster transitions to knowledge economies.

5. CONCLUSIONS

The policy implications of concluding that Latin America has distinctive varieties of capitalism go beyond the no-one-size-fits-all bromide. It puts acquiring deep local knowledge of macro and micro institutions well before devising policy recommendations. Moreover, in increasingly complex economies, policymaking needs to take into account the multiple interactions or complementarities among different areas of the economy. Innovation and competitiveness policies, for example, have been at the center of recent policy debates (Rodríguez, Dahlman, and Salmi 2008; Kuznetsov and Dahlman 2008). Devising effective new policies will be difficult without a prior understanding of the main private actors, especially diversified business groups and MNCs, and the causes of their historically low levels of investment in R&D, or else a consideration of ways to bypass these firms (and if so, an analysis too of the political feasibility of bypassing these firms) (Walton and Levy 2009). Moreover, working innovations into the productive economy requires large investments in training, and these investments need to adjust to, or overcome, previous obstacles to investment in human capital, such as high rates of worker turnover.

This essay has emphasized both the commonalities across the region and different clusters of subtypes. The commonalities stand out in the core features of hierarchical capitalism: diversified business groups, MNCs, anomic labor relations, and low skills. The analysis in this chapter has concentrated primarily on Latin America, but the constellation of micro institutions in hierarchical capitalism is not exclusively Latin American and seems to apply as well, with some adjustments, to countries like Turkey, South Africa, and Thailand. Within Latin America there are outliers on some dimensions such as the relative (possibly temporary) absence of business groups in Argentina, or the higher education and skill profile in Costa Rica. Moreover, there are, on other dimensions, centrifugal forces pulling different clusters of countries away from a common Latin American median. One cluster of countries—Mexico, those in Central America, and those in the Caribbean—became more integrated into production in the United States. Another cluster of petro states (Venezuela, Bolivia, and Ecuador) bet heavily on their energy sectors and used them to deepen state intervention in the rest of the economy. Last, a more politically driven cluster—Brazil, Chile, and Uruguay—forged an increasingly stable and institutionalized form of (late) social democracy (Santiso 2006). These external forces—from either the international economy or domestic politics—have had significant impact on hierarchical capitalism; however, they have yet to transform it into another recognized variety.

Theoretically, the main implications of this essay for the study of Latin American political economy are several. For one, if inter- and intraregional institutional differences in the organization of capitalism are consequential, then seeking out and analyzing these differences should be the standard point of departure. Moreover, if these micro institutions matter, then the theoretical focus should shift down from more macro features of the political economy and away from transitory policy packages. Concomitantly, the analysis should look inside organizations (such as business groups and industrial relations bodies) rather than focusing exclusively on the broader institutional "rules of the game" such as property rights and regulatory regimes (North 1990). The current consensus that institutions matter for development should not foreclose more debate on which institutions matter more, and how and why they do.

NOTES

I am grateful to Peter Hall, Javier Santiso, Vivien Schmidt, David Soskice, Kathleen Thelen, and seminar participants at Oxford University and Harvard University for comments on previous versions.

1. In a broad comparative review, Robert Boyer writes that "it is not surprising to find that developing countries exhibit quite original forms of capitalism. This is especially so within Latin American countries" (2005, 523). He identifies at least four modes of regulation: market-led, clientelist, corporatist, and rentier.

2. Looking at labor markets across the world, for example, Botero et al. (2004, 1364) conclude that "there is no evidence that employment laws or collective relations laws vary with the level of economic development." Hancké, Rhodes, and Thatcher (2007, 4) use the term "emerging market economy" to categorize countries "in transition with only partially formed institutional ecologies." This may apply to particularly fluid postcommunist political economies of eastern and central Europe but less so to other poor countries with longer trajectories of capitalist development.

3. Evelyne Huber, for example, sets the goal of her volume as an attempt "to identify different models of capitalism, understood as *sets of core economic and social policies* in the context of market economies" (Huber 2002a, 2, emphasis mine).

4. Although modernization theory was largely eclipsed by the 1970s, a general cultural critique of capitalism in Latin America lived on along the fringes of social science, largely associating underdevelopment with Catholicism and hierarchy (Harrison 1985).

5. For an extended intellectual history of development studies, see Evans and Stephens (1988).

6. On network capitalism, see Lincoln and Gerlach 2004; Feenstra and Hamilton 2006, especially 44–45; and Granovetter 2005. In more complete NMEs, informal networks can permeate business groups (as in keiretsu), as well as relations with employees, banks, government agencies, and sectoral competitors (Witt 2006).

7. The focus here is on corporate governance in the private sector. In many countries of Latin America the state is also a major shareholder both in controlling shares of large state-owned enterprises as well as indirectly in otherwise private firms (in Brazil the government owns large shares of major private firms through the BNDES, the state development bank, and the pension funds of state enterprises (Lazzarini 2010)). This state ownership adds another visible element of hierarchy.

8. On hierarchical relations among firms in Chile, see Taylor (2006, ch. 6) and in France, see Hancké (1998).

9. *América Economia*, July 9, 2007, p. 67. For more empirical indicators for Latin America, see Schneider 2008, 2009c.

10. So far this shift in R&D to Latin America is more pronounced in Brazil than elsewhere in the region (de Negri et al. 2009).

11. The institutions mentioned are Embrapa (Empresa Brasileira de Pesquisa Agropecuária, Brazilian Enterprise for Agricultural Research); Fiocruz (Fundação Oswaldo Cruz); Senai (Serviço Nacional de Aprendizagem Industrial, National Service for Industrial Apprenticeship); Sebrae (Serviço Brasileiro de Apoio às Micro e Pequenas Empresas, Brazilian Service for Supporting Small and Micro Firms); BNDES (Banco Nacional de Desenvolvimento Econômico e Social, National Bank for Economic and Social Development).

REFERENCES

Agosin, Manuel, Christian Larraín, and Nicolás Grau. 2009. *Industrial Policy in Chile: Paper Prepared for a Project on Productive Development Policies.* Washington, DC: Inter-American Development Bank.

Almeida, Mansueto. 2009. *Desafios da Real Política Industrial Brasileira Do Século XXI.* Brasília: IPEA.

Amable, Bruno. 2003. *The Diversity of Modern Capitalism.* New York: Oxford University Press.

Amsden, Alice. 1989. *Asia's Next Giant: South Korea and Late Industrialization.* New York: Oxford University Press.

———. 2001. *The Rise of "the Rest": Challenges to the West from Late-Industrializing Economies.* Oxford: Oxford University Press.

———. 2009. "Nationality of Ownership in Developing Countries: Who Should 'Crowd Out' Whom in Imperfect Markets?" In *Industrial Policy and Development,* edited by Joseph Stiglitz, Giovani Dosi, and M. Cimoli, 289–309. New York: Oxford University Press.

Amsden, Alice, and Wan-wen Chu. 2003. *Beyond Late Development: Taiwan's Upgrading Policies.* Cambridge, MA: MIT Press.

Andrade, Luis, José Barra, and Heinz-Peter Elstrodt. 2001. "All in the *Familia.*" *McKinsey Quarterly* 4:81–89.

Arbix, Glauco, and Scott Martin. 2010. "Beyond Developmentalism and Market Fundamentalism in Brazil: Inclusionary State Activism without Statism." Paper presented at the Workshop on States, Development, and Global Governance, Global Legal Studies Center and the Center for World Affairs and the Global Economy (WAGE), University of Wisconsin, Madison, March 12–13.

Barba Navaretti, Giorgio, and Anthony Venables. 2004. *Multinational Firms in the World Economy.* Princeton, NJ: Princeton University Press.

Bohle, Dorothee, and Bela Greskovits. 2007. "The State, Internationalization, and Capitalist Diversity in Eastern Europe." *Competition and Change* 11(2): 89–115.

Botero, Juan C., Simeon Djankov, Rafael La Porta, Florencio López-de-Silanes, and Andrei Shleifer. 2004. "The Regulation of Labor." *Quarterly Journal of Economics* 119(4): 1339–82.

Boyer, Robert. 2005. "How and Why Capitalisms Differ." *Economy and Society* 34(4): 509–57.

Cardoso, Fernando Henrique. [1964] 1972. *Empresário Industrial e Desenvolvimento Econômico no Brasil.* São Paulo: Difusão Européia do Livro.

Cardoso, Fernando Henrique, and Enzo Faletto. 1979. *Dependency and Development in Latin America*. Berkeley: University of California Press.

Casanova, Lourdes. 2009. *Global Latinas: Latin America's Emerging Multinationals*. Houndsmills: Palgrave Macmillan.

Chang, Sea-Jin, ed. 2006. *Business Groups in East Asia: Financial Crisis, Restructuring, and New Growth*. New York: Oxford University Press.

Cheng, Lu-Lin. 1996. "Embedded Competitiveness: Taiwan's Shifting Role in International Footwear Sourcing Networks." Phd diss., Duke University.

Coates, David. 2000. *Models of Capitalism: Growth and Stagnation in the Modern Era*. Cambridge: Polity.

Cohen, Stephen. 2007. *Multinational Corporations and Foreign Direct Investment: Avoiding Simplicity, Embracing Complexity*. New York: Oxford University Press.

Colpan, Asli, Takashi Hikino, and James Lincoln, eds. 2010. *Oxford Handbook on Business Groups*. New York: Oxford University Press.

Crouch, Colin. 2005. *Capitalist Diversity and Change: Recombinant Governance and Institutional Entrepreneurs*. Oxford: Oxford University Press.

de Ferranti, David, Guillermo Perry, Daniel Lederman, and William Maloney. 2002. *From Natural Resources to the Knowledge Economy*. Washington, DC: World Bank.

de Negri, João Alberto, Ricardo Ruiz, Mauro Lemos, and Fernanda de Negri. 2009. "Liderança Tecnológica e Liderança de Mercado." Paper presented at the Seminar Promovendo Respostas Estratégicas a Globalização, Institutos Nacionais de Ciência e Tecnologia and Pos-Graduação em Políticas Públicas, Estratégias e Desenvolvimento, Universidade Federal do Rio de Janeiro, Rio de Janeiro, November 3–6.

Dore, Ronald. 2000. *Stock Market Capitalism: Welfare Capitalism. Japan and Germany versus the Anglo-Saxons*. New York: Oxford University Press.

ECLAC (Economic Commission for Latin America and the Caribbean). 2005. *Foreign Investment in Latin America and the Caribbean 2004*. Santiago: United Nations, ECLAC.

———. 2010. *Latin America and the Caribbean in the World Economy*. Santiago: United Nations, ECLAC.

Egan, Patrick. 2010. "Hard Bargains: The Impact of Multinational Corporations on Economic Reform in Latin America." *Latin American Politics and Society* 52(1): 1–32.

Estevez-Abe, Margarita, Torben Iversen, and David Soskice. 2001. "Social Protection and the Formation of Skills: A Reinterpretation of the Welfare State." In Hall and Soskice 2001b, 145–83.

Evans, Peter. 1979. *Dependent Development*. Princeton, NJ: Princeton University Press.

Evans, Peter, Dietrich Rueschemeyer, and Theda Skocpol, eds. 1985. *Bringing the State Back In*. New York: Cambridge University Press.

Evans, Peter, and John Stephens. 1988. "Studying Development since the Sixties: The Emergence of a New Comparative Political Economy." *Theory and Society* 17: 713–45.

Fajnzylber, Fernando. 1983. *La Industrialización Trunca de América Latina*. Mexico City: Nueva Imagen.

Feenstra, Robert, and Gary Hamilton. 2006. *Emergent Economies, Divergent Paths: Economic Organization and International Trade in South Korea and Taiwan*. New York: Cambridge University Press.

Feldmann, Magnus. 2007. "The Origins of Varieties of Capitalism: Lessons from Post-Socialist Transition in Estonia and Slovenia." In *Beyond Varieties of Capitalism*, edited by Bob Hancké, Martin Rhodes, and Mark Thatcher, 145–83. Oxford: Oxford University Press.

Gallagher, Kevin, and Lyuba Zarsky. 2007. *The Enclave Economy: Foreign Investment and Sustainable Development in Mexico's Silicon Valley*. Cambridge, MA: MIT Press.

Gereffi, Gary, and Donald Wyman, eds. 1990. *Manufacturing Miracles*. Princeton, NJ: Princeton University Press.

Gereffi, Gary, John Humphrey, and Timothy Sturgeon. 2005. "The Governance of Global Value Chains." *Review of International Political Economy* 12(1): 78–104.

Goldstein, Andrea. 2002. "Embraer: From National Champion to Global Player." *CEPAL Review* 77: 97–115.

———. 2007. *Multinational Companies from Emerging Economies: Composition, Conceptualization and Direction in the Global Economy*. New York: Palgrave Macmillan.

Goñi, Edwin, J. Humberto López, and Luis Servén. 2008. "Fiscal Redistribution and Income Inequality in Latin America." Policy Research Working Paper No. 4487, Washington, DC, World Bank.

Gourevitch, Peter, and James Shinn. 2005. *Political Power and Corporate Control: The New Global Politics of Corporate Governance*. Princeton, NJ: Princeton University Press.

Granovetter, Mark. 2005. "Business Groups and Social Organization." In *Handbook of Economic Sociology*. 2nd ed., edited by Neil Smelser and Richard Swedberg, 429–50. Princeton, NJ: Princeton University Press.

Haagh, Louise. 2004. "The Labour Market and Korea's 1997 Financial Crisis." In *Brazil and Korea*, edited by Edmund Amann and Ha Joon Chang, 152–200. London: ILAS.

Haggard, Stephan. 1990. *Pathways from the Periphery*. Ithaca, NY: Cornell University Press.

Hall, Peter. 2007. "The Evolution of Varieties of Capitalism in Europe." In *Beyond Varieties of Capitalism*, edited by Bob Hancké, Martin Rhodes, and Mark Thatcher, 39–88. Oxford: Oxford University Press.

Hall, Peter, and David Soskice. 2001a. Introduction to Hall and Soskice 2001b, 1–68.

———, eds. 2001b. *Varieties of Capitalism: The Institutional Foundations of Comparative Advantage*. New York: Oxford University Press.

Hancké, Bob. 1998. "Trust or Hierarchy? Changing Relationships between Large and Small Firms in France." *Small Business Economics* 11(3): 237–52.

Hancké, Bob, Martin Rhodes, and Mark Thatcher. 2007. Introduction to *Beyond Varieties of Capitalism*, edited by Bob Hancké, Martin Rhodes, and Mark Thatcher, 3–38. Oxford: Oxford University Press.

Harrison, Lawrence. 1985. *Underdevelopment Is a State of Mind: The Latin American Case*. Lanham, MD: University Press of America.

Hirschman, Albert. 1970. *Exit, Voice, and Loyalty: Responses to Decline in Firms, Organizations, and States*. Cambridge, MA: Harvard University Press.

———. 1971. *A Bias for Hope: Essays on Development and Latin America*. New Haven, CT: Yale University Press.

Huber, Evelyne. 2002a. "Posing the Question." Introduction to Huber 2002b, 1–22.

———, ed. 2002b. *Models of Capitalism: Lessons for Latin America*. University Park, PA: Pennsylvania State University Press.

Ianni, Octavio. 1968. *O Colapso Do Populismo no Brasil*. Rio de Janeiro: Civilização Brasileira.

Johnson, Chalmers. 1982. *MITI and the Japanese Miracle: The Growth of Industrial Policy, 1925–1975*. Stanford, CA: Stanford University Press.

Karl, Terry. 1997. *The Paradox of Plenty: Oil Booms and Petro-States*. Berkely: University of California Press.

Khanna, Tarun, and Yishay Yafeh. 2007. "Business Groups in Emerging Markets: Paragons or Parasites?" *Journal of Economic Literature* 45: 331–72.

King, Lawrence. 2007. "Central European Capitalism in Comparative Perspective." In *Beyond Varieties of Capitalism*, edited by Bob Hancké, Martin Rhodes, and Mark Thatcher, 307–27. Oxford: Oxford University Press.

Kitschelt, Herbert, Peter Lange, Gary Marks, and John Stephens. 1999. "Convergence and Divergence in Advanced Capitalist Democracies." In *Continuity and Change in Contemporary Capitalism*, edited by Herbert Kitschelt, Peter Lange, Gary Marks, and John Stephens, 427–60. New York: Cambridge University Press.

Kurtz, Marcus. 2001. "State Developmentalism without a Developmental State: The Public Foundations of the 'Free Market Miracle' in Chile." *Latin American Politics and Society* 43(2): 1–26.

Kuznetsov, Yevgeny, and Carl Dahlman. 2008. *Mexico's Transition to a Knowledge-Based Economy: Challenges and Opportunities*. Washington, DC: World Bank.

La Porta, Rafael, Florencio López-de-Silanes, and Andrei Shleifer. 1999. "Corporate Ownership around the World." *Journal of Finance* 54(2): 471–517.

Lauterbach, Albert. 1965. "Government and Development: Managerial Attitudes in Latin America." *Journal of Inter-American Studies* 7(2): 201–25.

Lazzarini, Sergio. 2010. *Capitalismo de Laços: Os Donos do Brasil e suas Conexões*. São Paulo: Elsevier.

Lederman, Daniel, and William Maloney, eds. 2007. *Natural Resources: Neither Curse Nor Destiny*. Washington DC: World Bank.

Lessard, Donald, and Rafel Lucea. 2009. "Mexican Multinationals: Insights from Cemex." In *Emerging Multinationals in Emerging Markets*, edited by Ravi Ramamurti and Jitendra Singh, 280–311. New York: Cambridge University Press.

Lincoln, James, and Michael Gerlach. 2004. *Japan's Network Economy: Structure, Persistence, and Change*. New York: Cambridge University Press.

Lora, Eduardo, ed. 2007. *The State of State Reform in Latin America*. Palo Alto, CA: Stanford University Press; Washington, DC: Inter-American Development Bank and World Bank.

Mahler, Vincent. 1980. *Dependency Approaches to International Political Economy*. New York: Columbia University Press.

Mahoney, James. 2010. *Colonialism and Postcolonial Development: Spanish America in Comparative Perspective*. New York: Cambridge University Press.

Nölke, Andreas, and Arjan Vliegenthart. 2009. "Enlarging the Varieties of Capitalism: The Emergence of Dependent Market Economies in East Central Europe." *World Politics* 61(4): 670–702.

North, Douglass. 1990. *Institutions, Institutional Change and Economic Performance*. New York: Cambridge University Press.

Pagés, Carmen, ed. 2010. *The Age of Productivity: Transforming Economies from the Bottom Up*. Washington, DC: Inter-American Development Bank.

Pagés, Carmen, Gaëlle Pierre, and Stefano Scarpetta. 2009. *Job Creation in Latin America and the Caribbean: Recent Trends and Policy Challenges*. Washington, DC: World Bank.

Palma, Gabriel. 2005. "Four Sources of 'De-Industrialization' and a New Concept of the 'Dutch Disease,'" in *Beyond Reforms: Structural Dynamics and Macroeconomic Vulnerability*, edited by Jose Antonio Ocampo, 71–116. Palo Alto, CA: Stanford University Press; Washington, DC: World Bank and UN Economic Commission for Latin America and the Caribbean.

Rodríguez, Alberto, Carl Dahlman, and Jamil Salmi. 2008. *Knowledge and Innovation for Competitiveness in Brazil*. Washington, DC: World Bank.

Rodrik, Dani. 2007. *One Economics, Many Recipes: Globalization, Institutions, and Economic Growth.* Princeton, NJ: Princeton University Press.

Santiso, Javier. 2006. *Latin America's Political Economy of the Possible: Beyond Good Revolutionaries and Free-Marketeers.* Cambridge, MA: MIT Press.

———. 2008. "The Emergence of Latin Multinationals." *CEPAL Review* 95: 7–29.

Schmidt, Vivien. 2002. *The Futures of European Capitalism.* New York: Oxford University Press.

Schneider, Ben Ross. 2008. "Economic Liberalization and Corporate Governance: The Resilience of Business Groups in Latin America." *Comparative Politics* 40(4): 379–98.

———. 2009a. "Big Business in Brazil: Leveraging Natural Endowments and State Support for International Expansion." In *Brazil as an Emerging Economic Superpower?*, edited by Lael Brainard and Leonardo Martinez-Diaz, 159–86. Washington, DC: Brookings Institution.

———. 2009b. "A Comparative Political Economy of Diversified Business Groups, or How States Organize Capitalism." *Review of International Political Economy* 16(2): 178–201.

———. 2009c. "Hierarchical Market Economies and Varieties of Capitalism in Latin America." *Journal of Latin American Studies* 41: 553–75.

Schneider, Ben Ross, and Sebastian Karcher. 2010. "Complementarities and Continuities in the Political Economy of Labor Markets in Latin America." *Socio-Economic Review* 8(4): 623–51.

Schneider, Ben Ross, and David Soskice. 2009. "Inequality in Developed Countries and Latin America: Coordinated, Liberal, and Hierarchical Systems." *Economy and Society* 38(1): 17–52.

Schrank, Andrew. 2005. "Conquering, Comprador, or Competitive: The National Bourgeoisie in the Developing World." *Research in Rural Sociology and Development* 11: 91–120.

———. 2011 "Co-Producing Workplace Transformation: The Dominican Republic in Comparative Perspective." *Socio-Economic Review* 9(3): 419–45.

Shafer, D. Michael. 1994. *Winners and Losers: How Sectors Shape the Developmental Prospects of States.* Ithaca, NY: Cornell University Press.

Stallings, Barbara, and Wilson Peres. 2000. *Growth, Employment, and Equity: The Impact of the Economic Reforms in Latin America and the Caribbean.* Washington, DC: Brookings Institution Press.

Taylor, Marcus. 2006. *From Pinochet to the 'Third Way': Neoliberalism and Social Transformation in Chile.* London: Pluto.

Walton, Michael, and Santiago Levy, eds. 2009. *No Growth without Equity? Inequality, Interests, and Competition in Mexico.* Washington, DC: World Bank.

Weber, Max. 1958. *The Protestant Ethic and the Spirit of Capitalism.* New York: Charles Scribner's Sons.

Weyland, Kurt. 2009. "The Rise of Latin America's Two Lefts: Insights from Rentier State Theory." *Comparative Politics* 41(2): 145–64.

Whitley, Richard. 1990. "Eastern Asian Enterprise Structures and the Comparative Analysis of Business Organization." *Organization Studies* 11(1): 47–74.

Williamson, Oliver, and Sidney Winter, eds. 1993. *The Nature of the Firm: Orgins, Evolution, and Development.* New York: Oxford University Press.

Witt, Michael. 2006. *Changing Japanese Capitalism: Societal Coordination and Institutional Adjustment.* New York: Cambridge University Press.

....

CHAPTER 17

ULYSSES AND THE SIRENS: POLITICAL AND TECHNICAL RATIONALITY IN LATIN AMERICA

....

JAVIER SANTISO AND LAURENCE WHITEHEAD

THIS chapter focuses on relations between experts and politicians in Latin America. It analyzes cognitive institutions that produce applied economic policy knowledge and the formation of policymaking epistemic communities. By "cognitive" we mean sustained organizations that collect, process, analyze, and deliver the kind of information about a society necessary to monitor and interpret the impact of policy measures and to adjust or reformulate them when they prove ineffective or counterproductive. Mapping the cognitive capacities, strengths, and weaknesses is, however, not sufficient to understand the way the game is interplayed—the way policies are constructed and implemented and the way those who construct and implement them interact.

There are no in-depth studies of the cognitive map of Latin America for applied economic policy know-how that measure the institutional density of production centers and the diffusion of applied knowledge, particularly that related to the economic policymaking process. The term "epistemic community," defined in 1992 by Peter Haas as "a network of professionals with recognized expertise and competence in a particular policy domain, and an authoritative claim to policy-relevant knowledge within that domain or issue area," is an accepted idea in international relations theory as applied to international networks of expertise, but has yet to be used by the social sciences. Economists, in particular, have yet to think of themselves in this more sociological light. However, the term invokes "professional" criteria that are still structured and filtered through national associations and national processes of accreditation. From a comparative politics perspective, there is scope for systematic examination of how these state-to-state variations in practice affect the development, quality, and effectiveness of epistemic communities in each country.

It is obviously necessary to place national practices in a wider international context, and in many crucial areas of economic policymaking it may be that international networks of expertise take precedence over domestic recognition and authorization. But this is something that should be studied empirically, rather than assumed by definition. Legal professions are still much more national than economic ones, for example, not to mention military expertise or journalism. There is a tremendous range of variation across countries and issue domains, and in some cases there is rapid change from one generation to the next.[1] Epistemic community literature has also failed to intersect with the flourishing comparative politics literature on democratization in Latin America, given the divergent agendas: the focus of the first is on authority derived from professional competence, and it is only more recently that democratization literature has moved away from formal procedural issues to focus more on policy outcomes and the quality of governance and democracy, opening up channels of communication and convergence between these two lines of study. This section considers the intersection between epistemic community theory and the issues posed by the politics of expertise in a context of democratization. It examines how the existence of deliberate arenas of interaction between "experts" and "politicians" contributes to the quality of public deliberation—a vital (albeit insufficient) condition for an adequate articulation of technical and political rationality.

Latin America certainly provides the analyst with a comprehensive array of alternative possibilities in this field: there are some highly democratic procedures that are apparently not being informed by even the most minimal levels of technical rationality (the current debates on hydrocarbons in Bolivia or Ecuador, for example); there are other emerging democracies that have inherited highly sophisticated and well-entrenched epistemic communities in certain policy domains, where national traditions persist quite independently from the broader trends of both democratization and globalization (the Itamaraty provides a vivid illustration of this factor as a determinant of Brazilian foreign policy); there are also major countries with great traditions of educational achievement, professional development, and a well-developed middle class that nevertheless seem incapable of maintaining an authoritative and stable epistemic community to guide policymaking in critical areas of contention (Argentina today, but perhaps also since the 1940s); and there are contrasting examples where a dense array of think tanks and professional groupings, structured by the criteria of expertise, cover a large part of the political spectrum and thus encourage competent decision making, not only by the parties in power but also by the opposition (Chile may fit this description, although it should not be portrayed in an uncritically positive light). There are examples as well of well-financed and seriously organized communities of expertise that nevertheless represent only one sector of society, and even one partisan alternative among several in the larger polity (Fundación Salvadoreña para el Desarrollo Económico y Social, in El Salvador, seems to almost monopolize various forms of expertise for the benefit of the private sector and the center-right that has been modernized, leaving all other democratic alternatives bereft of serious *asesoría* [advice], in particular the center-left and left); there are epistemic communities that are pretty explicitly nondemocratic in their policy commitments (like those associated with the security sector in Guatemala); and there are examples of communities of expertise that have been more or less entirely co-opted by international agencies and sponsors, and that have gone along with policy reforms that are now viewed as externally imposed and contrary to the national interest and to local democratic choice (the dollarization of the Ecuadorian sucre may represent an example of this, as do some antinarcotic and counterterrorism initiatives).

This chapter maps cognitive economic policymaking institutions in the region, with illustrations from Peru and Uruguay. The focus is on both national and foreign, public and private institutions alike, and the chapter takes into account the state as a cognitive entity, along with institutions such as the analysis and research units of international organizations (IO), government agencies, private consultants, bank research departments, and academic research centers. These institutions form epistemic communities that share the same economic language as well as similar methods and codes—although not necessarily common ideas or interests—for the production and diffusion of knowledge. Not all are equally relevant, as their influence depends, among other factors, on national context, human and financial resources, and the scope of interaction with other actors, but they are all open epistemic communities: experts can move from one cognitive institution to another, in a trespassing game that allows the diffusion of ideas and facilitates the policymaking process.

To sum up, the focus is on how "technopols" articulate acceptable economic policy proposals that are both adoptable by and adaptable to distinctive democratic polities,[2] and how they function as "institutional masts," counterbalancing the rationality of Weberian "ethics of conviction," that is, ethics dominated by ideas, normative thinking and ideologies, and thereby anchoring technical policy debates in the "ethics of responsibility." In this sense, to use Jon Elster's (1984) metaphor on bounded rationality, technopols are like the masts to which Ulysses was attached. They prevented him from jumping into the water and sinking in pursuit of the Sirens' song. Although the institutional presence of the "technopols" is powerful, it is nonetheless insufficient to ensure that technical and political rationality are articulated in a balanced way. Examples abound where a strong cognitive institutional presence has coexisted with an economic policy, as a result of the predominance of the logic of the "ethics of conviction" and of the destabilizing consequences of failing to adequately address the tensions between these forces. In this sense, the development of a framework for the comparative study of democratic epistemic communities in Latin America is essential for an understanding of how such communities may ease the tensions between sound policymaking and the democratic legitimacy of policy decisions.

Over the past decade, the density (number and speed) of first- and second-generation and macro- and microeconomic reforms has been very significant in Latin America, although such efforts have been incomplete and disappointing, and have been criticized for failing to boost regional macroeconomic growth as expected.[3] Furthermore, many have failed because of their lack of democratic legitimacy. Thus, the capacity of Latin American governments for designing, implementing, and implanting reforms in specific political and social contexts remains uncertain, and their ability to persuade and engage society in their efforts is also in question. One can argue that this articulation of expertise and politics is a key to understanding the success or failure not only of reform processes but also of processes of transition to democracy. The existence of counter-vailing powers and cognitive institutions that provide a "protective umbrella" for democratic counterelites has been a fundamental aspect of smooth democratic transitions such as that of Chile, where think tanks like the Economic Research Corporation for Latin America (CIEPLAN), kept alive by the Ford Foundation and the Christian Democratic Party and nurtured until the restoration of democracy, played a pivotal role in ensuring the survival of technocratic countervailing powers and alternative arenas of debate.[4] This success contrasts with the fate of the Mexican Centro de Investigación y Docencia Económicas (CIDE) in the early 1980s, which depended completely on Mexican state patronage and was identified as a focus of potentially dangerous dissent, whose talented team of anti-neoliberals was dispersed. However, since the late 1980s, CIDE has reconstructed itself as a leading social science and policy research center with strong international links and credibility. Although it may be broadly identified as "center-right" in orientation, this is mainly in contrast to the still relatively ideological anti-neoliberal tone of scholarship in UNAM and some other leading Mexican centers. The CIDE of 2010 is de facto a fairly broad organization, delivering high-quality research, and it has credibility with all three of Mexico's leading political parties. It has no direct ties to any of them, but can be seen as a supportive component of Mexico's democratization process and a strong engine of the upgrading of policy debate in the country.

Such organizations also played a pivotal role at critical junctures such as during the liberalization processes of the 1980s and 1990s.[5] In this sense, technopols function rather like traders or, in Hirschman's words (1998), as trespassers of knowledge in the interstices between technical rationality and political rationality. This aspect is important: many of the reformist impulses that are merely transposed from other national or regional contexts and are not adapted to local conditions fail because there is no such trespassing. Hence Adam Przeworski's (2004a,; see also 2004b) contention that the "cemetery of institutional reforms must be enormous" in Latin America. International, multilateral development institutions should promote governance accountability and provide information about government policy so as to allow citizens to sanction rent-seeking cognitive institutions (see Benhabib and Przeworski 2004). Such institutions must work with policymakers rooted in local political and social contexts if they are to be effective.[6]

The chapter has therefore two aims. First, we aim to contribute to the mapping of the contemporary cognitive institutions that produce applied knowledge around economic policies. Second, we will show that the presence of these cognitive institutions contributes to the democratic governance promoting higher deliberative quality in public space. In this work we omit a historical perspective, in order to keep it short. But we invite those interested to consult an earlier version where we also aimed to situate contemporary trends with regard to the relations between experts and politicians in Latin America in their broader historical and sociogeographic settings.[7] We hope that by sketching out the distinctively Latin American antecedents to the rising power of the latest cohort of experts, we can demythologize some fashionable judgments about the present.

Although not sufficient, cognitive institutions are a necessary condition for an adequate articulation of technical rationality and political rationality. Here the concept of democratic epistemic communities is therefore important to take into account: Technocratic cognitive institutions are important, but the existence of an articulated epistemic community, spaces for deliberation, and arenas of interaction between "experts" and "politicians" are fundamental. If the key institutions for development are those that promote governance accountability and provide information on government actions, authorizing citizens to sanction behavior that limits the capturing of rent, then technopols (or more precisely cognitive institutions, i.e., institutions with technical and policy-oriented capacities embedded in the policymaking process) carry out a central role. But above all they need to be adequately articulated with the world of policymaking and policymakers as well as rooted in the local political and social context in order to produce adequate and efficient economic policies.

1. COGNITIVE INSTITUTIONS AND EPISTEMIC COMMUNITIES: MAPPING LATIN AMERICAN EXPERTISE

The final decade of the twentieth century witnessed the unprecedented rise of technocrats and economists, as globalization has stimulated the incorporation into the policymaking community and process of technicians able to deal with the new issues affecting emerging market economics. In this context, it has been recognized that the articulation of political and technical rationality is central to explaining the success or failure of economic policy in Latin America.[8]

The reinforcement of the base of production and dissemination of existing knowledge in open societies, and knowledge sharing between state and the centers of knowledge, is crucial in raising the level of accountability and transparency, which is, in turn, essential for democratic governance, particularly in emerging democracies. This section examines the institutions that facilitate the spread of expert knowledge and its use in policy elaboration and implementation. The aim is to show how knowledge is incorporated into political and administrative institutions and into the executive, judicial, and legislative process in particular. It further examines how such institutions create epistemic economic policymaking communities, and the challenges they face in the Latin American political-economic context.

The map of relations between expertise and politics has been changing. In this section, we would like to stress the contemporary mapping of the cognitive institutions that emerged over the past decades as pivotal in the economic policymaking processes all over Latin America. The aim here will be to establish the cognitive map of applied knowledge in economic policies in the different countries of the region. Some are national, others foreign; some public, others private. They are not all equally relevant for the economic policymaking process, depending on the national context, their respective human and financial resources, the scope of their interactions, and so on. But they are *open* epistemic communities, which means that one expert can move between cognitive institutions and this trespassing game allows the diffusion and communication of ideas, views, and visions and facilitates the policymaking process.

2. STATE COGNITIVE INSTITUTIONS

The preeminent policymaking cognitive entity is the state. State-related cognitive institutions are key cognitive actors in the policymaking processes. One way to illustrate the varying cognitive capacities of states is to examine the performance of national executives and legislatures. A wide range of institutions like central banks or economic ministries have research departments that process, produce, and disseminate expert economic policy know-how, including institutions like the Superintendence of the Pension Funds (Aministradora de Fondos de Pensiones [AFP]) in Chile, the Brazilian National Development Bank (BNDES) or Institute for Policy and Economic Studies (IPEA) in Brazil,[9] and Departamento Administrativo Nacional de Estadística in Colombia. However, while the technical expertise of economics ministries and central banks is quite consolidated across the board, nearly all Latin American countries lack parliamentary technical capacity, which alters the balance of technical and political rationality and does not auger well for the reinforcement and professionalization of regional legislatures. There have been many experiences and attempts to boost these capacities but some have been short-lived and most of them were excessive in scope.

In fact, legislatures at best have limited resources at their disposal for legislative research offices and libraries. In Uruguay, for example, there are no professional staff members serving the budget committee or related ones, and there are less than 10 for budget committees in countries like Argentina, Bolivia, Mexico, and Chile (the exception being Colombia with more than 10 dedicated to budget issues). In countries like Argentina, Bolivia, Colombia, and Uruguay, there is no specialized budget research organization attached to the legislature that conducts analyses of the budget (Chile has one with less than 10 dedicated professionals and Mexico also has one with more than 25 dedicated specialists). In some countries there were attempts, as in Peru in 2001, at enhancing legislative capacity for independent research and analysis, with the support of the Inter-American Development Bank (IADB) and the U.S. Agency for International Development (USAID), with the establishment of a Parliamentary Research Center. Similarly in Colombia, there was a project in 2002, supported by USAID, to create an office providing general research and advice in order to support the legislature (Oficina de Asistencia Técnica Legislativa). In Mexico, the research and advisory capacities of the legislature for independent budget analysis has also been enhanced with the creation in 1998 of a Center for the Study of Public Finances (Centro de Estudios de Finanzas Públicas) located in the lower house, complementing the technical institutions of the Senate established in 1985. Some experiments have, however, been less stellar, such as the Venezuelan Economic and Financial Advisory Office (Oficina de Asesoría Económica y Financiera de la Asamblea Nacional), created in 1997 within the National Assembly and with the support of the IADB but closed and reopened in 2000, reflecting the pressures and tensions since President Hugo Chávez took office.

One interesting and important exception is Brazil, which successfully developed broad technical capacity within Congress in the 1990s on a level comparable to that of the older democracies of Britain, France, or the United States. The budget committee of the lower house is assisted by a Research Office, consisting of about 35 professionals. Congress has an advisory organ, the Legislative Consultancy, with 245 employees, of whom 190 are specialist consultants in diverse areas. These individuals are full-time employees of Congress, and they are selected through a competitive examination. It is a requirement that they should have a postgraduate qualification and prior executive experience or a record of work for the National Audit Offices. Their tasks range from preparing technical papers to providing support to deputies, and they are organized into teams of consultants covering different areas of expertise. Similarly, the Senate also has its technical support service, with 308 consultants selected through a competitive public examination, 22 of whom are trained economists. The positions are adjudged through public competitive examinations and require strong technical credentials (see fig. 17.1 and table 17.1).

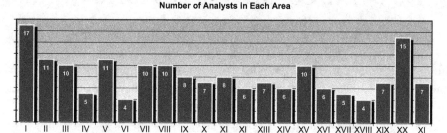

Brazilian Congress - Lower House: Number of Analysts in Each Area

Figure 17.1 State cognitive institutions: the example of the Brazilian Congress.
Source: OECD Development Centre; based on Brazilian Congress, 2006.

Table 17.1. Congress as Cognitive Institutions: Number of Full-time Technical Staff by Areas of Expertise in the Brazilian Congress

Name	Number
Constitutional law, electoral, municipal, administrative, legislative process and judiciary	17
Civil law and procedural law, penal and procedural penal, family, author, successions, private international	11
Tributary law, taxation	10
Public finance	5
Labor law and procedural labor	11
Agrarian law and land policy	4
Financial system, commercial law, economic, consumer rights	10
Public Administration	10
Politics and economic planning, economic development, international economics	8
Agricultural and rural politics	7
Environment and environmental law, territorial organization, urban and regional development	8
Mineral, hydro, and energy resources	6
Urban development, traffic and transportation	7
Social communication, informatics, telecommunications, postal system, science and technology	6
Education, culture, sports, science and technology	10
Public Health, sanitation	6
Security and national defense	5
International public law, international relations	4
Political science, sociological science, history and international relations	7
Writing and parliamentary speech	15
	174

Source: Based on data from Brazilian Congress, 2006.

3. NONSTATE COGNITIVE INSTITUTIONS: THINK TANKS AND BANKS

State organizations in Latin America have traditionally provided the "umbrella" under which various nonstate economic policymaking cognitive institutions operate, compete with one another, and struggle to influence the decision-making process of political authorities. Two key private actors are banks and think tanks.

Think tanks play a vital role in the formulation and dissemination of policy proposals and in supplying key inputs for the policymaking process (see Stone 1996).

However, their power and resources vary greatly from country to country, and are certainly very low when compared with the United States. In some countries like Argentina, the density of this kind of institution tends to be very high; in others, like Venezuela, it is relatively low. However, if we compare their financial resources with those of their U.S. counterparts, the scale is very small, even though they often provide exceptional outputs. The budget for the economic division of the Instituto de Estudios Superiores en Administración or the Centro de Estudios para el Desarrollo (CENDES) in Venezuela, for instance, is barely US$500,000 (compared with the Ministry of Finance research team's $100,000, the $500,000 of the economic research unit of the Planning Ministry, and the $1,000,000 of the economic department of the Central Bank). In all, there are little more than 150 economists (this is a rough estimate, but it does give a general idea of existing technical capacities) (see table 17.2).

If one compares this with the United States, the combined budget of all Venezuela's cognitive institutions mentioned above is barely 50 percent of the annual budget of the Institute for International Economics (IIE) in Washington, which was $7 million in 2004 alone and is not even the largest such institution (the Rand Corporation's budget was $224 million in 2004, and the Brookings Institution's $33 million). The Venezuelan and Latin American situation is even less favorable if one considers the significant endowments of U.S. institutions, which not only contribute to their financial power but also to their intellectual autonomy. In 2004, endowments ranged from $357 million (Rand) to $217 million (Brookings), $159 million (IIE), and $102 million (Heritage) (see table 17.3).

According to a survey of nearly 250 think tanks across Latin America, Asia, and Africa (Braun et al. 2004a), the budget structure of such institutions in developing countries is very similar: about 40 percent have between $100,000 and $500,000 (45 percent in Latin America). Less than 18 percent have budgets of approximately $1,000,000 (13 percent in Latin America). In regard to staff composition, less than 13 percent in Latin America have more than 50 permanent staff members and more than 60 percent employ less than 20. Most importantly, they interact quite intensely with other key policymaking players (74 percent in Latin America meet regularly with policymakers). Generally, however, there is a high number of think tanks in Latin America, and particularly in some countries like Argentina (see table 17.4). The largest in financial terms are not think tanks but consultancies. Tendencias in Brazil, for example, is relatively large in terms of staff (60 people, of whom 85 percent are economists) and budget (the 2004 annual budget was about $3 million). However, Tendencias is completely privately owned, sells its products (unlike U.S. think tanks), and focuses mainly on consulting work for banks or corporations. Its aim is less to influence policymaking than to provide data and analysis to private and public clients.

Among Latin American think tanks, Fedesarrollo deserves a special mention as being one of the largest think tanks in Colombia and one the most prestigious of Latin America.[10] The Foundation for Higher Education and Development, Fedesarrollo, was created in 1970. At that time, neither trustworthy economic information nor systematically produced technical studies were available to help formulate

Table 17.2. State and Nonstate Cognitive Institutions: Comparative Resources in the Case of Venezuela

Research Teams in Economics	Website	Total Staff	Total Economists and Analysts	Total PhD Economists and Analysts	Annual Budget (in US$)
Banco Central de Venezuela	www.bcv.org.ve	40	32	18	1,041,666.67
Instituto de Estudios Económicos y Sociales (IEES)					
Universidad Católica Andrés Bello	www.ucab.edu.ve	20	5	0	208,333.33
Centro de Estudios para el Desarrollo (CENDES)	www.cendes-ucv.edu.ve	45	25	14	468,750.00
Instituto de Estudios Superiores en Administración (IESA)	www.iesa.edu.ve	20	15	10	520,833.33
MetroEconómica (private consulting)	www.metroeconomica.com.ve	8	3	1	83,333.33
VenEconomía (private consulting)	www.veneconomia.com	15	6	0	156,250.00
DataAnálisis (private consulting)	www.datanalisis.com	20	8	0	208,333.33
Ministerio de Finanzas	www.mf.gov.ve	10	7	0	104,166.67
Ministerio de Planificación y Desarrollo	www.mpd.gov.ve	45	37	0	468,750.00
Oficina de Asesoría Económica del Congreso (OAEF)	www.oaef.gov.ve	6	4	0	62,500.00

Source: Based on data compiled by BBVA Venezuela, 2005.

coherent policies or to make decisions in the private sector. The Colombian private sector, keen to create an independent economic research facility, showed interest in underwriting such a cause. A number of talented economists, who stepped forward to staff the organization, created a link among Colombia's top universities, policy-makers, and industrial leaders and helped to develop the institution. Over the nearly four decades of its existence the institution has experienced an important evolution, as its environment also changed and Colombian state capacity improved. However, it has maintained its credibility and autonomy over the years and fostered timely discussions about economic and social themes and maintained its influence on economic policy. It has managed to create an important space for dialogue on topics of

Table 17.3. Nonstate Cognitive Institutions: European- and U.S.-Based Think Tanks' Financial Capacities

	Annual Income	Endowment
Europe		
Real Instituto Elcano	3 million euros	None
CEPR	2.6 million pounds	None
United States		
Rand Corporation	224 million US$	357 million US$
IIE	7 million US$	150 million US$
CEIP (Carnegie)	19 million US$	174 million US$
Brookings Institution	33 million US$	217 million US$
Heritage Foundation	42 million US$	102 million US$
Cato Institute	13 million US$	None

Source: Estimations based on annual reports, 2006.

national interest by periodically organizing debates on social and economic issues (Debates de Coyuntura Económica y Social) and promoting or hosting forums and seminars in which national and foreign economists participate.

In 2005, the number of employees was 44, of whom 26 were economists, seven with PhDs. It regularly publishes the results of its research in a Working Papers Series, publishes two academic journals (*Coyuntura Económica* and *Coyuntura Social*), and disseminates its opinions in the media through statements, seminars, and news conferences. However, as with many other Latin American tanks, its annual budget remains rather small ($1.3 million in 2004; 30 percent coming from the private sector), compared to similar U.S. institutions, even if it manages to maintain a small endowment. Its production is rather impressive and its ability to build intricate links with the official administrations makes Fedesarrollo a unique private institution through its capacity to influence and participate in the policymaking process of the country (most of the top researchers and directors of Fedesarrollo sooner or later trespass to the public sector and vice versa).

Many have participated in the preparation and execution of economic and social policies. For example, many of Fedesarrollo's former executive directors have held offices of enormous influence not only in Colombia but also internationally: Rodrigo Botero has been minister of finance of Colombia; Roberto Junguito rose on several occasions to state positions, becoming minister of finance and agriculture and board member of Colombia's Central Bank (Banco de la República); Miguel Urrutia became a director of national planning and minister of energy and is still involved in policy issues as governor of Banco de la República; José Antonio Ocampo has been a minister of finance, minister of agriculture, director of national planning, and executive director of the Economic Commission for Latin America and the Caribbean (ECLAC) (and currently serves as undersecretary for economic affairs of the United Nations); Guillermo Perry has been a minister of energy and

Table 17.4. Listing of Major Latin American Think Tanks

	Website
Argentina	
FIEL	http://www.fiel.org/
Fundación Mediterránea	http://www.ieral.org/
CIPPIEC	http://www.cippec.org/
CEDI	http://www.fgys.org/
CADAL	http://www.cadal.org/
CEI /Torcuato	http://www.utdt.edu/cei/
IADE	http://www.iade.org.ar/
CENIT	http://www.fund-cenit.org.ar/
CEMA	http://www.cema.edu.ar/
Estudio Broda	http://www.estudiobroda.com.ar/
Fundación Capital	http://www.fcapital.com.ar/
Ecolatina	http://www.ecolatina.com/
Brazil	
CEBRAP	http://www.cebrap.org.br/
AC Pastore	http://www.acpastore.com/
MBAssociados	http://mbassociados.com.br/
Tendencias	http://ww2.tendencias.inf.br/
Fernand Braudel Institute	http://www.braudel.org.br/
FIPE	http://www.fipe.com.br/
IBRE /FGV	http://www.ibre.fgv.br/
Colombia	
Fedesarrollo	http://www.fedesarrollo.org/
CEDE	http://www.uniandes.edu.co/
Chile	
CIEPLAN	http://www.cieplan.cl/
Instituto Libertad y Desarrollo	http://www.lyd.cl/
CEP	http://www.cepchile.cl/
ILADES	http://www.ilades.cl/
Peru	
IPE	http://www.ipeportal.org/
CIUP	http://www.up.edu.pe/ciup/
IEP	http://www.iep.org.pe/
Apoyo	http://www.apoyo.com/
GRADE	http://www.grade.org.pe/
Mexico	
CIDAC	http://www.cidac.org/
CIDE	http://www.cide.edu/

Table 17.4. (*continued*)

	Website
CIE /ITAM	http://cie.itam.mx/
Uruguay	
CERES	http://www.ceres-uy.org/
CLAEH	http://www.claeh.org.uy/

Source: Based on authors' research, 2006.

finance (currently he is the chief economist for Latin America and the Caribbean at the World Bank); Eduardo Lora became senior advisor of the Research Department at the IADB; and Juan José Echavarría trespassed to the Banco de la República, where he became a board member. The immediate past executive director of Fedesarrollo, Mauricio Cárdenas, also held important positions in Colombian administrations, where he served as minister of economic Development (1994), minister of transportation (1998–99), director of national planning (1999–2000), and minister of mines and energy (2011–present).

Academic institutions and scholars also make a key contribution to the Latin American policymaking cognitive capacity by formulating proposals, stimulating debates, and, when academics enter the government arena, promoting implementation. Academics based outside Latin America can be very active in formulating policy and contributing to agenda setting at the national and regional levels. Ricardo Hausmann, for example, released a policy paper in 2005 coauthored with Harvard's Dani Rodrik and the IADB-based economist Andrés Rodríguez-Clare, advocating a growth strategy for Uruguay just after the Tabaré Vázquez government took office in March 2004. Previously on the faculty at Harvard, Hausmann served as the first chief economist of the IADB (1994–2000), whose research department he established. He served as Venezuela's minister of planning (1992–93) and was a member of the board of the country's Central Bank and therefore actively involved in national policymaking. He later remained involved in policy debates with his published writings and by organizing conferences such as that held at the Harvard Business School in 2003 on the challenges posed by the Chávez administration in Venezuela.[11]

Financial institutions and banks in particular are perhaps even more directly involved in the economic policymaking process, given their strong technical and economic competences. They provide data and analysis as well as normative guidelines and advice. Their media presence, their constant interaction with top government officials, and their analyses are woven into the economic policy agenda. Bankers often move into government and vice versa, contributing even more directly to the policymaking process (see J. Santiso 2003, 2004b). In recent years, asset managers like Arminio Fraga or bankers like Henrique Meirelles have been appointed governors of the Brazilian Central Bank. The former chief economist of UNIBANCO, Alex Schwartmann, also joined the Central Bank, and his counterpart at Citibank moved to the BNDES, while, in the reverse direction, former minister Pedro Malan moved to UNIBANCO. Vittorio Corbo, a leading scholar and professor of economics, provides another example of trespassing. He became governor of the Central Bank of Chile in May 2003, having been economic adviser to the Santander Group in Chile (1991–2003) and a member of the Board of Directors of Banco Santander–Chile (1995–2003). There are many such trajectories: the move from banks to government by leading economists such as Guillermo Larraín, the former Chief Economist of Banco Bilbao Vizcaya Argentaria (BBVA) in Chile, who became *superintendente* of the AFP in 2003; Juan Ricardo Ortega, former chief economist of BBVA in Colombia, who became vice minister of finance in 2003, and in 2006 joined the IADB as a senior official; or Luis Carranza, chief economist of BBVA in Peru who was appointed vice minister of finance of Peru in 2004, before being named minister of the economy of Peru in mid-2006.

Typically, major Brazilian banks such as Bradesco, Itaú, and Unibanco have established economic research departments, housing around 15 full-time economists or analysts. In 2005, Itaú, for instance, had 16 employees, of whom nine were economists (four with doctorates and three with previous government or IO experience). The 12-strong team led by Octavio de Barros, chief economist at Bradesco, has had a high media profile and has participated intensively in Brazilian policy debates. Sergio Werlang is another case in point: he is chief economist with Itaú, and was previously deputy governor of the Central Bank of Brazil. All of these banks, however, do not habitually make their publications available to the general public, and papers are only rarely disclosed as a result of internal decisions. Participation in public debate is achieved rather by the presence of bank economists at conferences, and through the media. Chief economists are usually highly qualified individuals with a strong public profile and recognition. Major international banks also participate in local policy debates through the media and through direct contact with top government officials.

One-on-one meetings between these parties are very frequent, and channels of interaction can range from indirect media debate to direct formal and informal exchanges at private meetings or public seminars. The IADB annual meetings or meetings of the International Monetary Fund (IMF) and World Bank provide an important arena for such exchanges, in the parallel sessions organized by bankers to exchange views with top government officials. As an example of this type of interaction, table 17.5 lists the officials who attended a private meeting with investors organized by Citibank, Merrill Lynch, and JP Morgan in Okinawa, Japan, for the 2005 IADB Annual Meeting. The failure or success in articulating the voice (protest), exit (opting out), or loyalty (i.e., continuing to buy bonds) of the market can be crucial in moments of financial tension, leading governments or candidates to try to curb expectations by changing agendas, priorities, or policies.[12]

The resources that banks devote to economic analysis vary, but they are usually significant. If research departments and brokerage arms are taken together, the largest teams in Latin America belong to the two leading Spanish banks, Santander Central Hispano (with close to 70 analysts on Latin America in 2005) and BBVA (with nearly 80 in 2005) (see figs. 17.2 and 17.3).

These are quite significant resources when compared to U.S. investment banks, which generally have about 10 Latin America specialists (economists and fixed-income strategists). Most banks allocate only one (or less) economist per country covered (the

Table 17.5. Meetings between Banks and States' Bank Programs, IADB Annual Meeting 2005

Name	Function	Country or Company	Merrill Lynch Conference	Citigroup Conference
Fan Gang	Director, NERI	China	Yes	No
Guillermo Nielsen	Secretary of finance	Argentina	Yes	No
Alvaro Uribe	President	Colombia	Yes	No
Brian Coulton	Sovereign analyst	Fitch Ratings	Yes	No
John Taylor	Undersecretary, U.S. Treasury	United States	Yes	Yes
Esteban Jadresic	Director, Central Bank	Chile	Yes	No
Lisa Schineller	Senior analyst	S&P	Yes	Yes
Jane Eddy	Head, sovereign funds, Latin America	S&P	Yes	Yes
Henrique Meirelles	President, Central Bank	Brazil	Yes	Yes
Vincent Truglia	Head, sovereign ratings	Moodys	Yes	No
Vicente Bengoa	Secretary of finance	Dominican Republic	Yes	No
Héctor Valdez	Governor, Central Bank	Dominican Republic	Yes	No
Nelson Merentes	Minister of finance	Venezuela	Yes	No
Guillermo Calvo	Chief economist, IADB	IADB	Yes	No
Guillermo Perry	Chief economist	World Bank	Yes	No
Anoop Singh	Director, Western Hemisphere	IMF	Yes	No
Martin Redrado	President, Central Bank	Argentina	Yes	Yes
Ricaurte Vázquez	Minister of economy	Panama	Yes	No
Pedro Pablo Kuczynski	Minister of economy	Peru	Yes	Yes
Danilo Astori	Minister of economy	Uruguay	Yes	No
Mauricio Yepez	Minister of finance	Ecuador	Yes	No
Francisco Gil Díaz	Minister of finance	Mexico	Yes	Yes
Maria Inés Agudelo	Vice minister of finance	Colombia	No	Yes
Sebastián Palla	Undersecretary of finance	Argentina	No	Yes
Robert Devlin	Deputy manager, IADB	IADB	No	Yes
Barbara Stallings	Brown University	Brown University	No	Yes
Joaquim Levy	Secretary of Treasury	Brazil	No	Yes

Sources: Based on authors' research, 2006; Merrill Lynch (2005) and Citibank IADB Conferences, 2005.

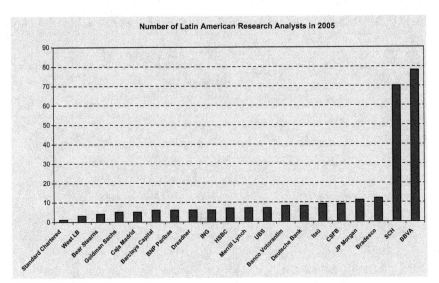

Figure 17.2 Banks as cognitive institutions: number of Latin American research analysts in 2005.

Source: OECD Development Centre, 2006; based on research products and production of BBVA, SCH, Bradesco, JP Morgan, CSFB, Itaú, Deutsche Bank, Banco Votorantim, UBS, Merrill Lynch, HSBC, ING, Dresdner, BNP Paribas, Barclays, Goldman Sachs, WestLB, and Standard Chartered.

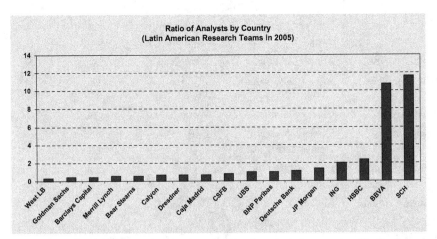

Figure 17.3 Banks as cognitive institutions: ratio of analysts by country (Latin American research teams in 2005).

Source: OECD Development Centre, 2006; based on research products and production of BBVA, SCH, Bradesco, JP Morgan, CSFB, Itaú, Deutsche Bank, Banco Votorantim, UBS, Merrill Lynch, HSBC, ING, Dresdner, BNP Paribas, Barclays, Goldman Sachs, WestLB, and Standard Chartered.

coverage ranges from one to 15 countries). Research and brokerage considered, HSBC and ING have an average of two economists per country, while Santander and BBVA have an average of 10–12 (covering their major markets, usually Brazil and Mexico). In most instances banks tend to focus resources on their preferred countries. This applies not only to Spanish banks but also to Credit Suisse First Boston (CSFB, which has a large team in Brazil), JP Morgan (its chief economist for Latin America is based in Mexico), and others. Although the size of teams varies greatly, CSFB and BBVA have

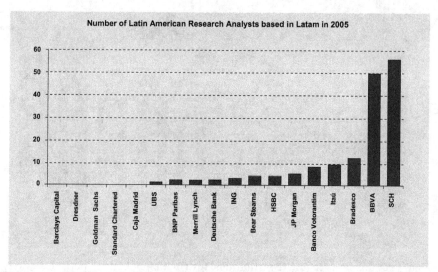

Figure 17.4 Banks as cognitive institutions: distribution of Latin American analysts, number of Latin American research analysts based in Latin America in 2005.
Source: OECD Development Centre, 2006; based on research products and production of BBVA, SCH, Bradesco, JP Morgan, CSFB, Itaú, Deutsche Bank, Banco Votorantim, UBS, Merrill Lynch, HSBC, ING, Dresdner, BNP Paribas, Barclays, Goldman Sachs, WestLB, and Standard Chartered.

65 percent of their analysts based in Latin America. At the opposite end of the spectrum, banks such as Dresdner (Germany) or Bear Stearns (United States) concentrate all their cognitive capacity at their headquarters (see figs. 17. 4 and 17.5).

The contribution of the private sector to building the cognitive capacities of local institutions is therefore incomplete and limited, given that coverage is not evenly distributed and universal. Indeed, only the largest countries benefit from articulated coverage. While the three largest Latin American economies (Brazil, Mexico, and Argentina) are covered by 20 banks included in the sample, only a third cover Uruguay, less than 20 percent cover Costa Rica, and only 5 percent cover the other Central American republics (where in addition, coverage is not regular as it is for the major economies). Only 15 of the region's republics attract attention from the international financial community and only 10 are regularly covered by more than 30 percent of that community. In other words, countries like Bolivia or Nicaragua simply do not exist on Wall Street or in the City (see fig. 17.6). Strengthening economic knowledge of these countries is therefore a pending task.

4. A Specific Mention: Multilateral Institutions as Cognitive Institutions

A last key actor and source of legitimacy and cognitive capacity building is found outside the strictly national ground, in the multilateral arena. Multilateral organizations act as institutional masts for the Latin American community of policymakers

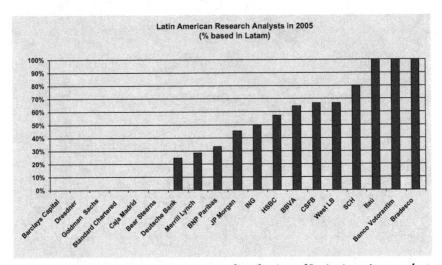

Figure 17.5 Banks as cognitive institutions: distribution of Latin American analysts,
Latin American research analysts in 2005, percentage based in Latin America.
Source: OECD Development Centre, 2006; based on research products and production of BBVA, SCH,
Bradesco, JP Morgan, CSFB, Itaú, Deutsche Bank, Banco Votorantim, UBS, Merrill Lynch, HSBC, ING,
Dresdner, BNP Paribas, Barclays, Goldman Sachs, WestLB, and Standard Chartered.

and experts, having great financial resources and technical capabilities at their disposal. Only multilateral agencies like the ECLAC, IADB, Corporación Andina de
Fomento (CAF), World Bank, and IMF have enough presence in such places to contribute importantly to building the economic policy epistemic community. They
play a key role in the production, communication, and even implementation of policies in various Latin American countries. Some are based in Latin America, such as
ECLAC, CAF, or the Facultad Latino-Americana de Ciencias Sociales, but the most
important are found outside the region: the IMF, the IADB, and the World Bank
(although the latter two have important units in Latin America). Since 2005, the
Organisation for Economic Co-operation and Development (OECD) Development
Centre has also built a strong Latin American team, located in Paris, with 15 members
producing a flagship publication devoted to the region, the *OECD Latin American
Economic Outlook*.

Studies abound on the role of the IMF in defining policy boundaries in Latin
America in the last few decades (see Weyland 2002; Teichman 2001; Thacker 1999;
Vreeland 2003). Its technological and technocratic capacity is highly significant:
more than 100 economists work in the Western Hemisphere unit alone, and this is
only part of the resources dedicated to Latin America, as other divisions provide
expertise on fiscal adjustment, banking, and other areas. Likewise, the World Bank
has more than 100 economists in its Western Hemisphere division, and many other
Latin America experts from other units. The institution has also developed important local units over the last few years (Mexico and Brazil are examples), and the
chief economist for Latin America is based in Colombia. Both institutions have
concentrated a huge critical mass of expertise and act as epistemic communities,

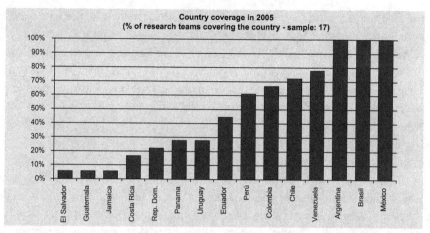

Figure 17.6 Banks as cognitive institutions: an incomplete country coverage, country coverage in 2005 (percentage of research teams covering the country, sample: 17).
Source: Estimations based on research products and production of BBVA, SCH, Bradesco, JP Morgan, CSFB, Itaú, Deutsche Bank, Banco Votorantim, UBS, Merrill Lynch, HSBC, ING, Dresdner, BNP Paribas, Barclays, Goldman Sachs, WestLB, and Standard Chartered, 2005.

vehicles pushing policy ideas from the abstract level to both international organizations and state agendas. Critics of these "econocrats" systems abound, most of them pointing to their (supposed) monolithic thinking (in reality, however, thinking that has changed over the 2000s with more emphasis on diversification) and the common background of their staffs. The IMF in particular has catalyzed all these critics, being perceived as an insular organization lacking in diversity (as pointed out by recent studies, the economist program recruits are dominated by Anglo-American graduates and half of the recruits came from a pool of 20 U.S. universities, the other 45 percent from European ones [see Momani 2005]).

A more interesting institution from the point of view of Latin America is the IADB, an IO that plays a leading and pivotal role in providing sound expertise to the region. The IADB Research Department, for example, as noted, created in the 1990s by Ricardo Hausmann, developed an amount of activity that is, from the point of view of the articulation of technical and political rationality, rather impressive, for a unit of no more than 13 full-time economists, nearly all of them with PhDs from leading universities, and 11 research assistants (it also counts on the support of 12 more administrative staff). The unit, frequently in collaboration with other units of the bank or external scholars and experts, publishes annually the *DIA* (*Development in the Americas, formerly known as the Economic and Social Progress Report*), IADB's flagship publication, which focuses on key issues. It also publishes policy-oriented newsletter three times a year (*Ideas for Development in the Americas*) and a wide range of working papers (approximately 50 technical papers) annually, which circulate in academic and technical milieus, and books, in particular a series cosponsored by the IADB, World Bank, and ECLAC and published by Stanford University Press. The activity of oral dissemination is also intensive, ranging from internal policy seminars to international joint conferences and seminars with other organizations that included in the 2000's

Banco de España, Banco Bilbao Vizcaya Argentaria, the World Bank, the Federal Reserve Bank of Atlanta, Harvard University, and George Washington University.

One important aspect of the IADB Research Department is precisely its contribution to the articulation of scholars, experts, and policymakers on key Latin American issues. This activity is expressed in many ways, from informal interactions between the IADB chief economist, research staff, and policymakers to formal meetings with top Latin American officials and policymakers. The institution, through its Research Department, also contributes to the densification, that is, number of contacts, of this interaction through its networks. The Research Department alone coordinates five networks that not only work as channels of dissemination of its studies but also as tools of promotion of high-level policy discussions between the IADB, national authorities, and the academic community. The Latin American Network of Central Banks and Finance Ministries is, for example, a forum for high-level discussions on macroeconomic policy and financial management, bringing together top officials and leading scholars. The interactions are also extended to financial markets with the Capital Markets Network on Latin American Financial Issues, a forum for Wall Street firms and Washington-based multilateral institutions to exchange views on Latin American macroeconomic and financial issues, and the Latin American Financial Network, which brings together academics, development practitioners, and policymakers in order to discuss current financial policy issues.

Another important dimension related to the IADB is its contribution to deepening locally grounded knowledge in Latin America, that is, to consolidating directly or indirectly cognitive institutions. One means of achieving this is linked with the strategy of the Research Department itself that leverages its internal research capabilities by supporting the in-country research of the Latin American Research Network, which encompasses around 300 public and private institutions in the region. It also contributes to the strengthening of cognitive institutions all around the region with its bank loans and targeted institutional building and governance programs. For example, from 1994 to 2003, the IADB approved seven credit operations in favor of legislative consolidation for a total amount of $45 million (as part of a $60 million program). During the same period it also approved nine projects for more than $50 million in order to strengthen fiscal institutions. In some countries, and for some institutions like the Contraloría General de la República in Nicaragua, these IADB contributions can be quite important, representing 30 percent of the annual budget of the institution (see C. Santiso 2004b).

The ECLAC and CAF are two other particularly interesting regional IOs, as they are locally grounded and illustrate the interaction between technocratic and political rationality in the region. For this reason both deserve a specific mention. Established in 1948, ECLAC is one of the oldest international organizations devoted to Latin America. Headquartered in Santiago, it has six other centers distributed around Latin America and one in Washington. It is therefore also very locally based. In June 1951 the commission established the ECLAC subregional headquarters in Mexico City, which serves the needs of the Central American subregion, and in

December 1966, the ECLAC subregional headquarters for the Caribbean was founded in Port-of-Spain, Trinidad and Tobago. In addition, ECLAC maintains country offices in Buenos Aires, Brasilia, Montevideo, and Bogotá, as well as a liaison office in Washington, DC. In 2005, only half of the nearly 600 staff members were located in the Chilean headquarters (outside Chile, the biggest office is Mexico City, with more than 50 staff members). The annual budget of the institution reaches nearly US$100,000,000. Depending on the definition given to "research," the bulk of this budget (40–70 percent) is committed to the promotion of ideas and policymaking.

Historically, ECLAC has played a pivotal role in promoting policymaking ideas such as import substitution theories, under the leadership of Raúl Prebisch, executive secretary of the organization from 1950 until 1963.[13] Keynesian thought, the historicist school, and the central European institutionalists exerted a decisive influence in the commission's early years and on the development of the "teoría de la dependencia" that had decisive influences on Latin American policymaking during the 1950s, '60s, and part of the '70s. Later the institution, mostly under Gert Rosenthal, José Antonio Ocampo, José Luis Machinea, and now Alicia Bárcena, significantly changed its focus under new pro-market influences (in 2005, for example, the institution organized for the first time a joint conference with the IMF). New theories of international trade and industrial organization have been incorporated into the agenda while theories of the firm, transaction costs and institutional economics emerged as key research agenda. Above all, ECLAC remains one of the most important cognitive institutions in the region with a total of 73 economists, a recognized prestige in Latin America, and important potential in setting the regional agenda.

Another interesting international cognitive institution is the CAF, which has also developed over the past decades an important locally grounded capacity. Based in Caracas, this cognitive institution has around 300 permanently active employees (see table 17.6). To this can be added the external consultants contracted

Table 17.6. International Organizations as Cognitive Institutions Locally Grounded in Latin America: The Example of CAF and ECLAC

Active Staff[a]	Salaried Positions
Directors	36
Professionals	180
Administrative staff	72
Total	288
Hired	20
Temporary	23
Outsourced	20

[a] As of December 31, 2004
Source: Based on CAF, 2005.

for specific works through technical cooperation and strategic programs (like for example those included in the research program). It developed a specific research unit with 14 economists, most of them with PhDs and all based in Latin American countries: 10 in Caracas, one in Bolivia, one in Peru, one in Colombia, and one in Ecuador (for more details, see table 17.7) (see CAF 2003, 2004a, 2004b).[14] The technical and cognitive capacity of this institution is therefore totally grounded in Latin America, contributing more directly to the debates, agenda setting, and spread of policymaking opinions between and within the countries on issues as different as fiscal sustainability in the Andean countries and pension reforms or growth strategies in Latin America. The research program was created to establish a knowledge base that allows the CAF to react to development issues by providing ideas, advice, and policies to governments. The program also has a "brain-gain" dimension as it helps to attract professionals and maintain technocratic capabilities in the region's countries, be it directly through financing technicians in government offices or indirectly through providing research resources to local think tanks or academics. These institutions find greater difficulties in staying updated and above all in attracting new fellows socialized and trained abroad. Finally, the institution plays a pivotal role in the region as an arena of debate and a center of diffusion of policy-oriented knowledge. The CAF always tries to promote interaction between the academy, the private sector, and the public sector on specific policy issues relevant to the policymaking process of the Andean countries through interactive conferences or more focused meetings between the top management of the institution and its board, namely the Andean countries' governments.[15]

The research program of the CAF can be divided into four components: a program of invited researchers, a research contest (i.e., a call for papers), the commission of studies, and finally a program of diffusion. In the first three cases, the program is dedicated to regionally based research fellows working on high-priority issues for the CAF, but which full-time fellows cannot immediately develop because of limited human resources or the priority of a short-term agenda. The fourth component involves the organization of seminars and conferences, as well as publications to propogate ideas among governments. In 2004, the CAF spent US$245,000 to support research studies (see tables 17.8 and 17.9 for more details), providing resources for researchers from institutions such as Torcuato di Tella University in Argentina, Pontificia Universidad Católica del Perú, and Universidad Católica Andrés Bello in Venezuela. This aspect, also important for other institutions such as the IADB, which is also developing a very important Latin American research network,[16] contributes to other cognitive institutions based in Latin American countries (i.e., academia or think tanks), and therefore to the strength and quality of the debates in the local epistemic communities, the quality of agenda setting, and the formulation, diffusion, and, from time to time, implementation of policy recommendations.

Table 17.7. CAF as a Latin America–Based Cognitive Institution: Economic Studies Directorship Team in 2005

Name	Age	Nationality	Position in CAF	Location	Background
Fidel Jaramillo	42	Ecuadorian	Vice president of development strategies and chief economist	Caracas	Economist from Universidad Católica del Ecuador, master's in political economy and PhD in economics from Boston University
L. Miguel Castilla	37	Peruvian	Director of economic studies	Caracas	Economist with honors from McGill University, Montreal, Canada, master's and PhD in economics from Johns Hopkins University
Osmel Manzano	33	Venezuelan	Research Program coordinator	Caracas	Economist from the Universidad Católica Andrés Bello, in Caracas, Venezuela, with PhD in economics from the Massachusetts Institute of Technology
Stefania Scandizzo	36	Italian	Research economist— specialized in integration aspects	Caracas	Economist from the Universita Commerciale "Luigi Bocconi," Milan, Italy, with PhD in economics from the University of Pennsylvania
José Gregorio Pineda	32	Venezuelan	Research Economist— specialized in integration aspects	Caracas	Economist from the Universidad Central de Venezuela, Carcas, with PhD in economics from University of Maryland
Eduardo Antelo	39	Bolivian	Country economist for Bolivia and Chile	La Paz, Bolivia	Economist and PhD in economics from the University of Sao Paulo, Brazil
Cristina Fernández	35	Colombian	Country economist for Colombia and international background	Bogotá, Colombia	Economist and masters in economics from the Universidad de los Andes, master's in economics from New York University
Lenin Parreño	31	Ecuadorian	Country economist for Ecuador and Mexico	Quito, Ecuador	Economist from the Universidad Católica of Quito and master's from the Universidad Católica of Chile

(*continued*)

Table 17.7. (*continued*)

Name	Age	Nationality	Position in CAF	Location	Background
Bartolomé Ríos	35	Peruvian	Country economist for Peru and Argentina	Lima, Peru	Economist from the Universidad del Pacifico (Lima) with master's in public administration from Columbia University
Germán Ríos	39	Venezuelan	Country economist for Venezuela and Brazil	Caracas	Economist from the Universidad Central de Venezuela, Caracas, master's in administration from Instituto de Estudios Superiores en Administración and economics from Johns Hopkins University
Andrea Otero	24	Venezuelan	Research assistant	Caracas	Economist from the Universidad Católica Andrés Bello, Caracas, Venezuela
Federico Ortega	23	Venezuelan	Research assistant	Caracas	Economist from the Universidad Católica Andrés Bello, Carcas, Venezuela
Ricardo Isea	23	Venezuelan	Research assistant	Caracas	Economist from the Universidad Central de Venezuela, Caracas
Mariana Penzini	23	Venezuelan	Research assistant	Caracas	Economist in the Universidad Católica Andrés Bello, Caracas, Venezuela (effective 2006)

Source: Based on CAF data, 2005.

Adopting a country focus rather than making large macrocomparisons helps to confirm the great variability of the density of the cognitive capacity (i.e., the number and quality of knowledge institutions and experts) and of the epistemic communities formed in the economic policymaking arena. By way of illustration of national cognitive maps, what follows is a brief analysis of two different epistemic policymaking communities, Peru and Uruguay, with varying degrees of power and density, and which operate in highly disparate contexts and with greatly divergent results in terms of the quality and legitimacy of policy formulation, implementation, and outcome.

Table 17.8. CAF Research Program Activities in 2004: Cost of Support for Research

Activity	Total US$[a]
Theme selection	0
Researchers' participation	100,000
Invited researchers	25,000
Contest works	25,000
Commissioned works	50,000
Workshops	10,000
Flagship and conference publications	55,000
Knowledge diffusion	75,000
Conference organization	45,000
Book publications	10,000
Contracts of consultants	20,000
Total operation	245,000

[a] Approximate amounts.

Table 17.9. CAF Research Program Activities in 2004: Contracted External Consultants

Name	Nationality	Institution	Studies
Jesús Eduardo Bianco	Venezuelan	Universidad Católica Andrés Bello, Caracas	Evaluation of the works of fiscal sustainability of the country economists of the CAF
David Florian Hoyle	Peruvian	Pontificia Universidad Católica del Perú	Evaluating the impact of the different Latin American processes of integration from a multiregional model of computable general balance
Gabriela Cuadra	Peruvian	Pontificia Universidad Católica del Perú	Evaluating the impact of the different Latin American processes of integration from a multiregional model of computable general balance: implications in the agricultural sector
Devashish Mitra	Indian (U.S. permanent resident)	Maxwell School of Citizenship Public Affairs, Syracuse University	Freeing trade in the Andean Countries: political-economy constraints and the feasibility of alternative approaches
Isidro Morales Moreno	Mexican	Universidad de las Américas, Puebla, Mexico	The goals, scope, and limits of 'open regionalism' in the Americas: Mexico's trade diplomacy since NAFTA and its lessons for Latin American countries within FTAA negotiations

(continued)

Table 17.9. *(continued)*

Name	Nationality	Institution	Studies
Gabriel Ortiz de Zevallos	Peruvian	Instituto APOYO, Lima	The political conditioners of the growth strategy
Carlo Pietrobelli	Italian	Law School of the University of Rome III	Effects of the international insertion on the PYMEs in Latin America
Kamal Saggi	Indian	Department of Economics, Southern Methodist University, Dallas	Increasing Latin America's Trade Presence in the World Economy: effects of FDI: costs and benefits
Pablo J. Sanguinetti	Argentinean	Universidad Torcuato Di Tella, Buenos Aires	The political economy of contingent protection in Latin America, trade liberalization, poverty and income inequality in Latin America, and collaboration in a research program with Apoyo for diverse purposes
Soledad Zignago	Uruguayan	CEPII, Paris	International commercial insertion of Latin America: patterns of commerce and access to markets.

Source: Based on data from CAF, 2005.

5. A Case Study: Peru

Peru presents us with a paradox: it has an epistemic community made up of a dense and powerful set of cognitive institutions, and yet the policymaking ability of the state is weak and fragmented. There are three government institutions that control economic policy decisions in Peru: the Economy and Finance Ministry, the Central Bank, and Congress, of which the ministry is the leading institution. The formulation of policy is formally the responsibility of the Vice Ministry of Economy (with 40 employees, and with the support of the departments responsible for economic and social affairs, international economy, competition and private investment, public revenue policies, and multiannual public sector planning). In practice, however, an informal committee that includes the minister of the economy, the Treasury vice-chancellor, and the Central Bank head of advisory staff and economic studies manager coordinates policy formulation. Once policy is approved it is submitted to Congress or implemented. The Central Bank also participates actively in the design of economic policy (i.e., fiscal policy) through its participation in the aforementioned committee, in which it exerts considerable influence because of its relatively strong institutional development (an "army" of highly qualified technical staff armed with statistics and economic models that the Ministry of Economy and the public sector in general have not adequately developed). A key unit, from the point of view of the formulation of policy proposals, is the Economic Studies Department, which is responsible for the implementation of monetary policy. It has 120 employees, 80 of whom are economists. Its administrative structure, which is shaped by the financial programming schemes of the IMF, is divided into five departments, responsible for global analysis and for external, monetary, fiscal, and real estate matters.

As noted above, the Congress, with 120 members, is not a strong cognitive institution. It participates actively in the policymaking process but without any endogenous technical capacity or permanent technical staff. Legislators participate on various committees that discuss and approve proposals, which they then submit to the General Assembly (Pleno del Congreso) for final approval. Congress has 24 ordinary committees and legislators can participate on as many as three different committees at any given time. The technical capacity of the Congress is extremely low, as its support staff is not sufficiently trained or skilled to help legislators carry out their economic policy duties effectively. In 2002, Congress created the Parliamentary Investigation Center to increase technical support, but it is still incipient, and legislators tend to get backing from private advisors whose services are paid for out of the national budget. On average, each congressman hires two such advisors specializing in different fields (usually law, economics, and finance). However, given the general intellectual capacity of congressmen and the lack of monitoring of the fulfillment of legislative responsibilities, the use of advisors does not necessarily guarantee high-quality policy formulation. Congress employs 2,072 people, of whom 565 are professionals with executive responsibilities who participate on the various committees. The technical capacity of the Congress is very weak: there are four expert analysts in economic areas to serve the whole Congress, and they do not usually give technical advice to deputies.

In the nonstate sector, a key player in policy formulation if not implementation is the think tank. The most influential in Peru are Apoyo Macroconsult, the Analysis Group for Development (GRADE), and the Peruvian Institute of Economics (IPE). Their endowments are small: the largest, Apoyo, is entirely privately owned, employs 65 people, and in 2004 had an annual budget of US$5 million (see table 17.10). Apoyo Consulting is part of the Apoyo Group and was created in 1977 to offer economic, financial, and managerial advice to its clients. It has approximately 150 firms in its portfolio, including the most important national and international firms operating in Peru. With a 250-strong team, it has experienced an average income growth of 25 percent per year since 1977. Its billing reaches $200 per every million dollars of Peruvian gross domestic product. Apoyo shapes economic policy through client advisory services and confidential documents, monthly meetings with clients to discuss key economic and political questions, and member participation in economic debates in various different forums, such as seminars, conferences, or news conferences.[17] IPE, on the other hand, was created in 1995 by 31 national businesses, with initial support from the World Bank Institutional Development Fund (since 1999, funding has come from member contributions and the

Table 17.10. Cognitive Institutions in Peru: Financial and Human Resources of
              Think Tanks in Peru

Name	Website	Total Employees	Total Economists among Employees	Total Economists at PhD Level
IPE	www.ipe.gob.pe	25	10	2
CIUP	www.ciup.gob.pe	70	55	4
GRADE	www.grade.org.pe	47	36	3
Apoyo	www.apoyo.com.pe	65	57	0

Source: Based on data from BBVA Continental, 2005.

sale of research products).[18] IPE is a very active player in policy debates through
conferences, publications, and public debate in the media. Under former president
Alberto Fujimori, most of its members participated directly in the government,
holding different positions in the Ministry of Economy and Finance. Finally, there
is GRADE, a nongovernmental organization established in 1980, which re-
searches public policy design and implementation in economics, education, environment, and social topics. Funds come primarily from international institutions
(90 percent, of which 40 percent is provided by IOs, 40 percent by international
bilateral cooperation agencies from OECD countries, and 14 percent by international foundations; only 10 percent of funding comes from national institutions).
Its work is disseminated through publications, a Web page, and the media, among
other channels. The Associated Assembly, in which most of the principal researchers participate, is the executive organ, which determines the research agenda
and development strategies to guarantee institutional autonomy. GRADE participates in policy debates at the highest technical level and does not normally engage
in public debate.[19]

Also to be considered are the two universities with research centers, which are
also involved in policy formulation: the Research Center at Universidad del Pacífico
(CIUP)[20] and the Center of Sociology, Economics, Politics and Anthropology of the
Catholic University of Lima, which make important contributions to the policy
debate. CIUP was established in 1972 and is funded by the university budget and by
international and multilateral organization contributions. And then there are the
private banks, which also have developed cognitive capacities. There are three key
private banks with economic departments: BBVA Banco Continental, Banco de
Crédito, and Banco Wiese Sudameris. These contribute to economic debate through
sponsored publications, individual articles, media appearances, seminars, conferences, and interviews. The research teams range from three to nine economists,
none with doctorates but most having had previous government experience. It is a
small community with less than 20 economists (30, if one includes those following
the Peruvian economy from U.S. and European institutions). A comparison with
Peru's neighbor, Venezuela, helps put in perspective the cognitive capacities of
banks for both countries, both having about the same number of economists,
around 20 in Peru and less than 25 in Venezuela (see table 17.11).

Table 17.11. Cognitive Institutions in Peru and Venezuela: The Example of Banks

Bank	Website	Total Analysts	Total Analysts at PhD Level	Government
Peru				
Banco de Crédito	www.bcp.com.pe	9	0	Yes
Banco Wiese Sudameris	www.bws.com.pe	7	0	Yes
BBVA	www.bbvabancocontinental.com	3	0	Yes
Venezuela				
Banco Provincial	www.provincial.com	5	2	2
Banco Mercantil	www.bancomercantil.com	7	2	2
Banco Venezuela	www.bancodevenezuela.com	2	0	0
Banco del Caribe	www.bancaribe.com	3	0	0
Banesco	www.banesco.com	2	0	0
Asociación Bancaria	www.asociacionbancaria.com	3	0	0

Source: Peru: Based on data from BBVA Continental, 2005. Venezuela: Based on data from BBVA Provincial, 2005.

Finally, there are the multilateral players. Among multilateral players the most important are the IADB and the CAF.[21] Both institutions bring to the Peruvian—and more generally the Latin American—policy debate and process not only financial resources but also technological and technocratic assets. The IADB focuses mainly on monitoring government financial programs, while the CAF contributes only marginally to the domestic economic policy debate.

6. ANOTHER CASE STUDY: URUGUAY

Uruguay provides an intermediate example. As in Peru, government institutions are at the center of the policymaking process. The Ministry of the Economy and the Central Bank set the agenda and formulate and implement economic policy, although other institutions are involved, such as the Planning and Budget Office, which determines state resource allocation and fiscal policy. The budget is approved by the legislature over a five-year period. Tributary changes are made through law (such as changes in value-added tax rates or the tax basis) and submitted for legislative approval. Uruguay's investment law enables the executive (in this case the minister of the economy in particular) to establish sectoral or general tax exemptions. The economic team comprising the Ministry of the Economy and Finance, the president of the Central Bank, and the Planning and Budget Office formulates policy. In theory, the Central Bank develops monetary policy, but it is effectively subordinated to the Ministry of the Economy and Finance. The ministry teams are organized thematically (macroeconomics and finances with five economists; commercial policy with 10 economists; tax policy with two experts, law with 10 jurists, and a second macroeconomic and finance consultancy with six economists).[22]

As in many other countries, the Central Bank plays a pivotal role. Its function is to formulate, apply, and monitor monetary policy. It has a three-person directory of political appointees, and is governed by the Organic Code of the Central Bank, which does not ensure independence from political authorities. The bank is one of the largest cognitive institutions on applied economic issues, having more than 130 full-time employees, and several units dedicated to policymaking. These are divided into departments, the most important of which are the Economic Policy Unit and the Economic Investigation and Financial Institutions Superintendence (these units house about 35 economists, of whom 12 have doctorates). By contrast, the legislature has very few permanent technical staff members. Policymaking is debated in thematic commissions and each political party has its own army of economic consultants who assist the legislature indirectly. The legislature is composed of a lower House of Representatives (99 members) and a Senate (33 members). In economic matters, legislative committees, composed of legislators, are created for specific subjects and report to the Senate and the House of Representatives. Economic consultations follow a precise structure, involving experts nominated by the political parties.

Think tanks are another player, encompassing a wide range of cognitive institutions such as private consultancies, chambers of commerce, and unions. They influence policy through publications and the specialized media, and many are political consultants and civil servants with much trespassing from think tanks and academia to government and vice versa. The chambers of commerce and unions constitute important lobbies, some of which have economic teams and issue publications. The Uruguayan Chamber of Industries, Ceres, the Economic Investigation Center (CINVE), and Oikos are the most important (see table 17.12).[23] The CIU, a civil association financed by quotas from its member businesses, is sometimes used by the state to deal with issues in which the latter has less competence (the emission of certificates of origin, for instance), and sometimes to work with IOs. It intervenes in policy as a pressure group (Industrialists Lobby), participates through the media and in-house publications, and provides services such as consultancy, training courses, and initiatives to protect the specific interests of industry. Recently, Uruguay's think tanks have had very constructive relations with the Frente Amplio governments. This relationship confirms that epistemic communities can have high international credibility and professional standing without being an obstacle for left-wing governments—rather, they can be a benefit. The question is less about the left-right political divide and more about responsiveness

Table 17.12. The Cognitive Institutions in Uruguay: The Case of Think Tanks

Name	Website	Total Employees	Total Economists and Analysts	Total PhD-Level Economists and Analysts	Budget (% Private)
CINVE	www.cpa.com.uy	15	12	4	100
CERES	www.ceres.com.uy	8	10	2	100
Instituto de Economia	www.ccee.iecon.edu.uy	30	30	7	0
Oikos		5	4	1	100
Cámara de Industrias	www.ciu.com.uy	56	4	1	N.a.
Instituto Cuesta Duarte		7	7	1	N.a.

Source: Data from BBVA Uruguay, 2005.

to independent expert advice and evaluation—something that not all governments of the Left can accept, but some can.

Ceres deserves special mention. It is among the most policy-oriented think tanks, a private nonprofit economic research center that specializes in economic analysis and public policy design. It participates in international, regional, and local debate forums, and influences debate through the media, issuing publications, participating in high-level international seminars, and organizing public conferences. Although it is an independent center, its policy director was recently offered the presidency of the Central Bank, a position he declined. The (CINVE), on the other hand, is associated with the CPA consultancy firm, and specializes in financial forecasts. Its professionals are aligned with the current government, and its current director is in charge of the economic policy design at the Ministry of the Economy. Oikos, a small consultancy firm, also has direct ties with the government, issues monthly publications, and carries out business assessments. All these cognitive institutions participate actively in the policy-making process, be it directly through consultancy or advisory work or through individual moves into government, or indirectly through an active presence in the media.

The most important academic institutions are the Economic Institute, the ORT University, and the University of Montevideo. The Economic Institute is dependent on the University of the Republic and produces economic updates and research on all economic disciplines. Its director was recently appointed president of the Central Bank. The ORT and Montevideo Universities both have economic research departments and publish articles. Altogether, there are around 65 economists devoted to policy-oriented analysis in Uruguay (a rough estimate, but one that gives some idea of the size of this epistemic community), to which one can add another 70 if the Ministry of the Economy and Finance and the Central

Bank are also taken into account, bringing the total to about 150 persons. (Venezuela has an economic policymaking epistemic community of similar size). This figure does not include banks and financial institutions, and the legislature lacks economic professionals. Despite this lack of technical resources, the policymaking process in Uruguay is reasonably sound and stable, as recent decades have shown. Thus, a huge technical community may help, but it is not a solution in itself; rather, what makes the difference is a particular "alchemic" articulation within the epistemic community of experts and politicians. The consensus-driven political culture that has characterized modern Uruguayan politics rather than the size of its epistemic community is central to explaining the quality of the policymaking output.

7. ECONOMIC POLICYMAKING IN EMERGING DEMOCRACIES

Mapping the cognitive capacities, strengths, and weaknesses is therefore not sufficient for understanding the way the game is played—the way policies are constructed and implemented and the interaction of the players. Several strategies can be used to explain the "alchemy" of policymaking.

Once we have basic information on national epistemic communities, one strategy is to construct a multidimensional grid and situate various countries, policy domains, and periods within this comparative framework. One possible approach is to hypothesize that the quality of economic policies depends on the degree to which expert knowledge is institutionalized in the policymaking process. Such institutionalizing depends on two main factors: first, on the existence of a critical mass of knowledge produced by cognitive institutions that can also disseminate expert knowledge; and second, on the effective filtering of such knowledge though interaction between political and technical rationality.

The notions of veto players and policy players prove useful here. The taxonomy of national policymaking environments can be formalized as four combinations of two variables: the number of potential veto players and the number of policy players. We define veto players as actors and institutions whose consent is critical for any change in the *implementation* of reforms and policies (see Tsebelis 1995). We define policy players as actors and institutions that have significant influence over agenda and policy *formulation* and over the actors and institutions involved in the policymaking process. Neither of the two dimensions is dichotomous; rather, they operate along a continuum. There may be only a few, many, or no veto and policy players. When there are none or only a few veto players and policy players, the environment is likely to be insulated and decisive; when the number of veto players expands, the environment is hyperpresidential. The weight of key veto players thus shapes policymaking, and outcomes depend heavily on agreement among them. Another combination is multiple veto and policy players, which produces a resolute and potentially stalemated environment. Finally, when there are only a few or no veto players but various policy players, the likely result is a muddling through (Lindblom 1959), whereby economic policy evolves circuitously, and the environment is replete with "incentives for inter-temporal cooperation" (Spiller, Stein, and Tommasi 2003,). The Brazilian environment typically belongs in this category (see Armijo and 2003; Armijo, Faucher, and Dembinska 2004; Armijo 2004).

Another way is to contrast strongly and weakly institutionalized structures of expertise—ranging from Haiti at one extreme to, say, Chile at the other. Another might be to account for the availability of human and professional resources in the society as a whole, from which these structures might be constructed. This would not necessarily replicate the first dimension, in that some societies may make very good institutional use of quite scarce human resources (like Barbados, perhaps), whereas others may have strong university and professional potentialities that are not so effectively organized (Jamaica, for example). Another dimension could consist of those countries where the coverage of expertise was extremely uneven—either geographically or in terms of policy areas (Brazil, both regionally and as concerns health policy on the positive side, or at the opposite end of the spectrum the issue of restorative justice as an example of gross deficiency)—as opposed to those countries where similar standards of expertise and policy competence were maintained across most regions and issue areas (Uruguay, for example).

Another crosscutting dimension could be to distinguish between cases of longterm progress in a cumulatively positive direction (what Lourdes Sola [1998] has classified as "state-crafting" in Brazil since the early 1990s) and cases of fitful advances, or even of progress followed by worse setbacks, such as Venezuela or most of the Andean republics since the mid-1990s. Obviously there is also a continuum between the more inward-looking and state-centered variants of professional organization and accreditation and those that derive their standards from an external source, or from an international community of like-minded professionals (the Cuban experience would be at one extreme and at the other would be the network of privatization specialists who, in the 1990s at least, rotated between the international financial institutions, international banks, some strongly pro-market sectors of government and academia in the Anglo-Saxon world, and their own countries of origin). In addition, of course, we would need to distinguish between the more democratic (open, pluralist, and accountable) epistemic communities and the more closed, insulated, and unaccountable variants (which might be referred to as technocratic variants of expertise).

We would also need more knowledge on specific reform and policymaking processes and the involvement of technocratic knowledge. A recent working paper by Sebastián Edwards (2005) offers interesting views on the role of foreign advisors in economic stabilization programs. He focuses on Chile's experience with antiinflationary policies during the period 1955–58 when the government implemented a stabilization package with the advice of a U.S.- based consulting firm, Klein-Saks. However, after an initial success, the program failed to achieve durable price stability. The technocratic mission managed to give an initial credibility to the stabilization program launched in 1955, providing a precommitment technology and a type of expertise unavailable in the country but also acting as an umpire and a mediator in a period of acute political polarization. However, the case study also shows that the political system failed to use this foreign technical expertise to create a durable policy. Edwards emphasizes that Congress in particular failed to act decisively on the fiscal front, and this lack of action led to the failure of the program.

One decisive area of policymaking and technocratic involvement in Latin America is that related to budget institutions and fiscal reforms. Legislatures' role in the governance of the budget is pivotal. However, in most emerging countries they tend to lack both the technical ability and the political incentives to assume a responsible role in public finances (for a detailed analysis, see C. Santiso 2005a, 2005b). Internal institutional constraints also abound as a reason for the lack of technical advisory capacity. Budget and public accounts committees, for example, are assigned only a limited number of permanent technical advisers. Chile, Colombia, and Mexico stand out, with over five permanent advisers each, but in all other countries these committees are understaffed. This is not, however, an unusual situation (70 percent of the legislatures surveyed by the OECD and the World Bank do not possess specialized budget offices): policymaking successes or failures are more complex issues, beyond numbers. Existing technical input into the budget review process tends to lack the technical substance required for impartial evaluation because of this absence of tenure-track expertise within most Latin American legislatures. But the difference in budget quality goes beyond this.

A major change in the economic policy landscape in Latin America has been the emergence of a technocratic consensus advocated by a specific epistemic community that is defending greater fiscal prudence and discipline (this is the epistemic community we have been partly focusing on, the neoliberal technocrats), through a process of gradual learning partially influenced by the United States, from Kemmerer "money doctors" to former Chilean president Augusto Pinochet's "Chicago Boys" and later to the CIEPLAN's "Boys." However, this greater influence of economic technocrats has not been uniform across Latin America and has not necessarily been conducive to better economic outcomes. More research is required on this issue. What guarantees that a greater insulation of economic policy would necessarily be invested in improving fiscal outcomes, rather than in capturing rents?

Another issue is related to transparency and asymmetric information. Fiscal knowledge tends to be generated within the government (or in institutions close to it) and, as a result, there insiders hold a certain degree of monopoly over fiscal information. There is a wide information gap between the state (broadly defined) and society, especially as pertains to fiscal information. However, in recent years, the so-called neoliberal technopols and others have tried to make fiscal information more transparent (as transparency is now widely believed to be critical for fiscal discipline and is accepted, one example being the adoption of IMF codes and standards on fiscal transparency). Latin America has innovated in this field since the late 1990s, with the adoption of fiscal transparency legislation, often linked to fiscal discipline legislation (see table 17.13 on the institutionalization of budgetary systems in the region) and including the creation of innovative state agencies tasked with enforcing transparency of and access to public information (beyond the role of ombuds offices), for example the Instituto Federal de Acceso a la Información Pública in Mexico.

Last but not least, we will need to accumulate more knowledge on specific policymaking processes, focusing not only on environments or numbers but also on issues and policies. A good example would be the pension reform process, specifically one of the most successful reform processes "invented" in Latin America, namely in Chile. Pension reforms have not only been among the most important reforms carried out by Latin American countries but also have constituted an innovative policymaking output pioneering an international trend. "Invented" in Chile, in 1981, this reform spread all around Latin America and to many other regions of the world. There is extensive literature evaluating its impact and trends and issues related to pension reforms. The Chilean system is the most commonly recognized as successful. Since implementing the system, the government has improved and adjusted it. The Chilean example is, from this point of view, exemplary (and perhaps unique), in that the privatization of pension funds remained within the framework of regulated, top quality institutional craftsmanship. As noted, uear after year, the government modified and adjusted the system to improve it. Today, the Chilean regulatory body, the Superintendencia, is one of the most credible, technically prestigious, and highly esteemed institutions in the country, making it a strong institutional mast.

This reform, above all, symbolizes the profound change that Chile has undergone over recent decades: the invention of a pragmatic and gradually implemented political economy in contrast to the years of tidal wave (and dizzy) ideologies. Behind this transformation, cognitive masts have helped counterbalance political and technical rationalities. In the 1970s, social and liberal revolutions developed, in both cases trying to implement rigid paradigms invented in other hemispheres. The Good Liberal was nothing more than another side to the Good Revolutionary, both of them coinciding in their search for impossible economic policies. In the 1980s and especially in the '90s, economic pragmatism prevailed. With the return to democracy, there could have been a temptation to create yet another model and break with the previous regime. This was not the case, however, and Chilean democrats decided to carry on with the reforms already under way and tried to combine monetary and fiscal orthodoxy with social reforms and balanced growth. This continuity is clearly reflected in the behavior of assets under management in the pension fund system: after 1989, the year democracy returned, assets shot up and not only were reforms not abandoned but on the contrary, they were intensified, adopted, and adapted.

Table 17.13. Fiscal Policymaking: Legal Framework of Budgetary Transparency and Fiscal Governance

Country	Fiscal Governance: Organic Budget Law, Organic Financial Administration Law[a]	Fiscal Transparency: Access to Public Information Law	Fiscal Responsibility: Habeas Data	Accountability		
				Law on fiscal Transparency	Law on Fiscal Responsibility[a]	Law on Fiscal Control
Argentina	1992, 1997	(2002)[b]	1994	1999	1999, 2001, 2004	LAFCSP Law 24156 (1992)
Bolivia	1990, 1997	2004		2004		SAFCO Law 1178 (1999; 1997)
Brazil	2001		1988	2000	2000	Law 10180 (2001)
Chile	1975					LOAFE Decree 1263 1975
Colombia	2004	1985	1997	2003	2003	Laws 43 (1993) and 2145 (1999)
Costa Rica	2001	2001				LAFPP Law 8131 (2001)
Dominican Republic	1969	2004				LOPSP (1969)
Ecuador	1977	2004	1996	2002	2002	Decree 1429 (1977, 1990)
El Salvador	1995					LOAFE Decree 516 (1995)
Guatemala	1997		1995			LOP Decree 101–97 (1997)
Honduras	1976, 2004	(2003)[b]			2004	LOP Decree 407–76 (1976)
Mexico	1976	2002	2002			LFSF Law (2000)
Nicaragua	1988 (1991)		1995			LOCGRSCAP Decree 625 (1981, 1984, 2000)
Panama	2002	2002	2002	2002	2002	

Country					Budget law
Paraguay	1999	2004	1992	2004	LAFE Law 1535 (1999)
Peru	2004	2002	1993	1999, 2003	1999, 2003	LOSNCCGR Law 27785 (2002)
Uruguay	1999			1999		TOCAF Decree 95 (1991, 1999)
Venezuela	2000, 2003		1999			LOAF SP (2000) and Decrees 2621 and 2268 (2003)[c]

[a] Joint World Bank–IMF Country Budget Law Database, available at http://www1.worldbank.org/publicsector/pe/countrybudgetlaws.cfm, complemented by Web-based research into the websites of the countries' ministries of economy and finance.
[b] Under consideration.
[c] Author compilation, as of December 2004.
Source: C. Santiso (2005).

To put it another way, the great lesson to be learned from Chile is this extraordinary combination of pragmatism and continuity, the emergence of "possibilism," a new style of political economy. This is a combination other countries such as Mexico and Brazil, especially, seek to share (J. Santiso 2005, 2006). In Mexico, pragmatism shone through in the mid-1990s with the signing of a free trade agreement with the United States. For the first time in history, a country from the South signed a free trade accord with a country from the North. Hooking up with an economic powerhouse and the leading democracy was a key undertaking for Mexico. In the same way as Spain did with the European Union, the process allowed the economy to benefit from an anchor of external credibility. In 2000, the country successfully underwent a change of government without an economic crisis; an unheard-of event previously, when the cycle of political change every six years was accompanied by financial turbulence. Throughout the past decade, Mexico has achieved what no other country in the region had managed to do: it broke the tie of the economy to the political cycle.

The country now relies on a wide range of institutional stabilizers or cognitive masts. In the economic area, the independence of the Central Bank of Mexico is reflected not only in orthodox monetary policy but also in the decoupling of the institution from the political cycle: the term of office of the governor does not coincide with that of the president. In the political field, the creation of the Federal Election Institute (IFE) constitutes another institutional innovation that allows the independent supervision of democratic elections in the country. After the achievement of investment-grade status, as well as success in macroeconomic variables, the reduction in foreign debt and inflation, and the attainment of fiscal balance and a flexible exchange rate regime, there are now institutional stanchions in the shape of the Central Bank and the IFE.

Likewise, in Brazil, the latest governments have instigated significant pragmatic changes. The most spectacular without a doubt has been carried out by the current government of President Luiz Inácio Lula da Silva. The financial markets were wary of his arrival in power in 2002. However, he surprised them with his commitment to fiscal discipline and monetary orthodoxy. In 2004, Lula managed to make the country grow, as it did after his reelection in 2006, till the 2009 global financial crisis. The reform drive was vigorous; a number of important tax, pension, and banking reforms survived trial by fire in Congress. As for social programs and the infrastructure investment drive, although these received criticism, they underscored the government's commitment to more equitable growth, which was not only more efficient but also more distributive. The combination of fiscal and monetary orthodoxy alongside social policies drew the attention not only of the financial markets and foreign investors but also of politicians throughout Latin America, particularly left-wing leaders. This could bring about a process of positive political contagion in the whole of the continent: the spread of pragmatic economic policies, continuity, and gradual policies of the possible. On a continent that suffered so many jarring changes on different ideological tacks, this would undoubtedly be great news.

8. Conclusions

Complex policy reforms require both a good measure of economic technical competence and authoritative political endorsement. Sometimes the two may be combined within a single personality (Prebisch's authority as a technical expert was fused with his charisma as a prophet of social transformation, and from the earliest years he combined vision with technical know-how; see Hodara 1987); sometimes they may be harmonized within a strong bureaucratic and technical administration (the Gabinete Económico in Mexico in the 1980s and the 1990s; see López Portillo 1995; or they may be reconciled through an informed process of parliamentary debate and interparty elite negotiation (as in Chile under the Concertación).

But it is not unusual for those with the necessary political authority to lack the appropriate technical competence. There are all sorts of hybrid combinations, and even the experience of the most advanced liberal capitalist democracies provides us with little reason to doubt that this mix will continue to operate in the future. Sometimes the two work well for a while (President Fujimori and his economy minister, Carlos Boloña, in Peru or President Carlos Salinas and his economic dream team led by Pedro Aspe in Mexico); sometimes they break down (President Rafael Caldera and the Venezuelan technocrats); and sometimes the appearance of collaboration proves deceptive (as in the case of President José Sarney and the Cruzado plan in Brazil).

Undoubtedly the secular processes emphasized in modernization theory are genuine and powerful. Overall levels of education are rising fast, and more or less middle-class lifestyles and values are on the increase. Dense and overlapping networks of specialized competence and expertise continue to develop, informing public policy and constraining some forms of misgovernment. But these are merely loose tendency statements, leaving plenty of scope for the perpetuation of inherited authoritarian policy styles. Despite the many structural changes associated with the end of the Cold War, the transition to democracy, the liberalization of the economy, and the increased leverage of the business community, there is really no conclusive evidence that hybrid, potentially unstable, and erratic patterns of policymaking have been eliminated from contemporary Latin America. How can there be any "irreversible" triumph of the technocrats, or even of expertise more broadly understood, as long as many traditional patterns of policymaking continue to persist? The evidence that has accumulated since the collapse of Domingo Cavallo's reckless "convertibility" project in Argentina in 2001 points to the huge backlash that can build up against such pretensions.

To sum up, then, "technocrats" derive their authority from their claimed mastery of certain specialized areas of knowledge that are deemed essential for effective government. If a central problem facing a society is the threat of yellow fever, then those who know best how the disease propagates and how it can be combated may have an irresistible claim to the public resources required for its defeat. If the central problem becomes the threat of hyperinflation, a similar logic may empower those economic experts who alone know how to restore monetary stability. But there are two very striking limitations to the power that can be obtained by such means, even in the most extreme of circumstances. The first is that once the "emergency" has passed, other sources of concern will return to the center of public debate, and there is no reason to suppose that the expert in disease control will also possess the specialized skills required to tackle nonmedical dilemmas. Similarly, there is no good reason to suppose that the expert in monetary stabilization will possess the skills required to combat, say, the reappearance of cholera. Particular types of expert may therefore enjoy brief periods of concentrated power, but if they live up to their promises they will thereby undermine the conditions for their preeminence. Either they may prove false experts and lose power altogether or true experts who, having overcome one policy emergency, retreat from center stage to occupy a no doubt honorable and durable, but also a secondary, role in public life. True expertise becomes professionalized, institutionalized, and even depoliticized as a society moves from national emergency to routine administration. As Kathryn Sikkink (1991) has persuasively argued in relation to the ideology of "developmentalism," unless such ideas acquire institutional embodiment they will lack the staying power and detailed follow-through required to shape public policy over the longer run. Yet if they *do* become institutionalized they also become subject to broader processes of political bargaining and analytical dilution.

This point relates to another limitation. When technical expertise proves scarce, valuable, and a source of empowerment, these rewards will attract an influx of new entrants. Scarce knowledge is therefore likely to become diffused throughout the society, the early technocrats will find themselves held increasingly accountable to a more informed community of peers, and the opportunity to make further breakthroughs on the basis of privileged expertise can be expected to decline. Broader and more "generalist" forms of policy discussion will therefore reassert themselves. Post–Cold War Latin America manifests a range of characteristics that might be expected to reinforce the authority of political generalists and to curb the arrogance of unaccountable experts. Contemporary features favorable to the influence of generalists might include the reassertion of constitutional rule, international détente and regional cooperation, the failure and discrediting of various forms of authoritarian social engineering, and advances in education and science diffused through an increasingly assertive and rising stratum of young professionals. All of this is reinforced by a high degree of media freedom compared to the past. These are surely conditions that ought to favor the emergence of a stratum of political brokers and entrepreneurs capable of assimilating expertise without surrendering to its dictates. Their communication and persuasive skills will be needed to synthesize and popularize the valid insights of the experts. To some extent, the new cohort of technocrats and economic experts have also learned some of the skills of mass communication, and there is often a competition between them and the more traditional intelligentsia over who can dominate the airwaves, but neither has a monopoly and the battle could prove salutary for both. The overall quality of public policymaking may therefore rise as hitherto esoteric forms of expertise become incorporated into the collective understanding of the whole community.

In any real political process we can expect to find dispute over the validity and extent of claims to superior expertise. Inexpert politicians will have to make judgments about whom to believe and therefore how much authority to delegate. Often such judgments may remain contested even with the benefit of hindsight. Here is a further reason why an apparent "triumph of the technocrats" may so often prove ephemeral. Thus, for example, even with all the reinforcement they can now muster from Latin America's reinvigorated business class, today's technicians still seem engaged in an endless campaign against an array of critics who may shift their ground but never seem to disappear. These critics can never be eliminated, in part because insulated technocrats characteristically overreach themselves, but more fundamentally because the viewpoints and interests that the critics represent extend far beyond the reach of any form of bureaucratic rationality. Further, and above all, the critics will persist because the technocrats have failed to produce the results everyone desires—wealth and greater distribution of resources and sustainability of the economic model.

This brings us to our final point, which is the role of judgment (expert and broad-based) in the guidance of policy choices in light of the categories of "technocracy" and "democratic expertise," on the one hand, and rules versus discretion, on the other. *Technocrat* has become something of a term of condemnation in a number of the new democracies in our region. In some cases this language is used to disqualify the advice of professionals and qualified experts more generally. If our project is to be objective, this term will have to be handled with great care. Although there is the growing literature on "technopols" to draw on, it will be essential to reach agreement in advance about the scope and boundaries of these terms. One aspect of our mapping exercise may be to record how usage differs between countries and issue domains, and over time. Here, the doctoral dissertation by Jeffrey Kishor Kulkarni (2005,) may be helpful. He is concerned with only one policy domain—monetary policy in advanced democracies—but his observations about the tension between technocratic expertise and democratic legitimization can probably be generalized:

> Democratic legitimacy does not demand that all groups be represented in the policymaking process; instead, it demands only that representatives retain the capacity to properly evaluate policy *output*. . . . . . . In conventional democratic arrangements, contenders challenge incumbents by contrasting actual performance against counter-factual outcomes, as well as by making (unenforceable) promises about future policymaking. Though this process does not necessarily improve policy quality, it does facilitate the exogenous evaluation of incumbents. [But] this dynamic is absent from central bank independence since the selection of officers is not subject to adversarial competition. Indeed, technocracy is explicitly designed to eliminate such competition so as to improve policy output.

Moreover, at least in the case of central banking, he also argues that technocratic language has the effect of constraining critical discourse and democratic debate about the distributive and other counterfactual alternatives to the "depoliticized" choices of the empowered experts.

This provides the analyst with two empirically observable criteria for determining whether or not to classify an arena of policymaking as technocratic. Do the professionals in question face adversarial competition on assuming public office, and are they subject to effective retrospective evaluation by elected representatives when they have discharged their duties? There is, of course, room for debate about how often their performance should be evaluated, and in what form. There is also a more subjective question, namely whether the democratic monitoring performance permits an informed judgment about possible alternative policy stances. This is where such broader considerations as the availability of independent expertise to assist the elected representatives in their monitoring work (such as congressional research services), the quality of media oversight, and the extent to which expert incumbents of public positions are supervised and held to account by their professional bodies—and in the last instance by the courts—come into play. Clearly, then, there is not a single clear-cut dichotomy between technocrats and democratic experts. But perhaps this discussion helps to identify the objective and comparative yardsticks that can be deployed to place particular cases within our proposed grid.

A second aspect of the tension between expertise and democratic legitimization is that it has become fashionable in public choice theory to view it as at least partially a contrast between the observance of preestablished rules (designed by experts before considering any particular set of circumstances) and political discretion (viewed negatively as subjective, liable to manipulation, and, indeed, as almost inherently arbitrary). But this is not a perspective on most policy choices in democratic Latin America that will generate much discrimination between the contrasting cases in our grid, nor is it a standpoint that will commend itself to the recently enfranchised mass electorates in most of these countries. A supposedly automatic and inaccessible institution such as the European Central Bank may be sustainable in Frankfurt, but there are very few institutions in Latin America or the Caribbean that command this degree of sacralized immunity from political pressure. Citizens who have only recently acquired a democratic outlet for their political preferences after long experience of authoritarian rule are usually loath to accept such claims to put policy "off limits" to political control, especially when the technocratic agents in question lack a convincing track record of effective and disinterested service to the public good. There may be a few scattered exceptions to this generalization—the Controlaría and Superintendencia in Chile or the Chilean Central Bank perhaps, but almost all the institutions and policy domains we might study lie on the other side of the insulated-politicized divide. And the distinctions of greater practical importance in our region are between those somewhat politically answerable institutions that are able to preserve a good degree of coherence, expertise, effectiveness, and democratic legitimacy and the many others that fall short by one or more of these criteria.

Fortunately, we do not need to adopt this stark public choice dichotomy when analyzing the democratic politics of expertise in contemporary Latin America and the Caribbean. At the theoretical level the dichotomy postulates an unbridgeable divide between rules and discretion. At least in our region, however, all rules are provisional and subject to periodic critique and revision (think how frequently Latin America's constitutions are amended, disregarded, or overturned, in contrast to the U.S. constitution, or that of post-1949 Germany). The Latin American experience highlights a truth that is in fact more general, and even applies to the most highly institutionalized of old democracies—although it may be harder to perceive in the latter. Both rules and discretion require judgment: there is no such thing as automatic policymaking according to purely technical criteria. Even the European Central Bank has to address such questions as whether its rule applies to a particular case, the precise meaning of the rule (which Eurozone price index is it the bank must target, for instance). More typically specialized policymaking institutions also have to make judgments about the trade-offs between competing objectives, the limits of their mandates, the time frame within which they must operate, and indeed quite often whether the rules they have set are always internally consistent, and how to respond when standard policy steps precipitate unintended consequences. Equally, decisions that are not rule governed also require a high degree of judgment, and may depend heavily on expert sources of advice.

Most of the policies introduced and implemented by any modern state are highly complex and require a great deal of planning, sophisticated design, and skillful negotiation with a wide range of social partners. As such policies are implemented, governments need to evaluate feedback; monitor compliance; adjust time frames, budgets, and communication strategies; and compensate unexpected losers. In other words, generalized arbitrariness or irrationality is not a frequent characteristic of discretionary policymaking. It would be too costly and self-defeating. Whether operating within tightly prescribed rules or under a more broadly permissive discretionality, most acts of government demand a constant input of informed judgment from the relevant policymakers, and if these are generalists they will need the advice and support of a wide array of professionals and specialized experts. Whether applying rules or discretion, decision makers will normally have to engage in serious and sustained exercises of collective deliberation. Have we taken into account all the relevant evidence? Do models or rules of thumb adequately reflect the realities they engage with? Are we the prisoners of some defunct theory or ideology? If we are making predictive judgments, how much margin of error can we allow before reconsidering?

These are all questions about which categories of professional and expert adviser may have something useful to contribute. But for the most part they are not questions that elected governments can safely delegate to the full and sole discretion of the relevant experts. Just as it would be unwise to invite the military to take full control of decisions concerning war and peace, or the security forces to exercise unfettered discretion over the maintenance of public order, so is the democratic supervision of expertise advisable in almost all policy domains. Of course, that obligation imposes heavy responsibilities on elected governments, and they may well fail to meet such challenges adequately. Experts are likely to believe that they usually know better, and depending on how well or badly the available expertise is used, it is perfectly possible that policy effectiveness could be improved by consulting them more fully. But there should be no blanket presumption that political discretion necessarily leads to worse policy decisions than would be produced by the experts acting alone. Indeed any survey of comparative alternatives should be on the lookout for examples to illustrate the range of possibilities here. Where demonstrably bad policy outcomes were delivered, it will be important to assess which alternative deliberative arrangements would have encouraged sounder judgments.

In any case, democratic policymaking is only partially about arriving at the optimum policy choice. A successful policy must not only rest on sound diagnosis and competent design and implementation. It also requires political and social acceptance. In Latin America, at least, most decisions are made in conditions of fairly high uncertainty, and expert analysis of their consequences is often subject to a high margin of error. Whether or not a given decision pans out as hoped, the public will have to live with the results. The democratic process can be designed to give due weight to the advice of suitably trained experts, embedded in cognitive institutions such as those mentioned in this chapter, but it also needs to be communicated to a broader society, and it needs to be legitimized. Democratic procedures are not just about maximizing policy effectiveness. They are also about winning consent, diffusing responsibility, and keeping open the avenues for feedback from those affected.

Democracy is also an error-correcting mechanism. For all these reasons "good governance" needs to include subjecting experts to political oversight and in the last instance control. Strengthening governability in a currently troubled Latin America will require long-term processes of state crafting and the building of more democratic epistemic communities to support policymaking. One small step in this direction would be to begin mapping the patchy state capacities currently in place, and to start investigating the consequences of these distributions. In due course this might open the way to building a democratic consensus on how to strengthen the role of expertise in policymaking, while simultaneously reinforcing the experts' democratic accountability.

Epistemic communities may be democratic, or at the least they may be structured so that they can operate under democratic constraints. Ideally they may even help, support and guide processes of democratization. But Peter Haas's (1992) definition contains no reference to this possibility. It is equally possible for an authoritarian regime to encourage "professionals with recognised expertise . . . and an authoritative claim to policy-relevant knowledge" in a particular domain or issue area. Some agencies in Brazil's Estado Novo, Pinochet's "Chicago Boys," and some of the policymaking networks of the Partido Revolucionario Institucional of the past could no doubt be classified as successful examples of epistemic communities supported by and supportive of authoritarian rule in their respective Latin American republics. More generally, it has been argued that epistemic networking frequently gives rise to "technocracy," a form of policymaking that may be regarded as inherently antidemocratic. This, at least, is how Frank Fischer (1990, 24) sees it:

> For technocrats, competing interest groups are the *virtual enemy* of rational social organization. The solution is to replace politicians and interest group leaders with technically trained experts who "stand above" the political process [. . .] from this point of view only those above the political fray "can genuinely represent the public interest in the search for solutions. The public interest is said to be safeguarded by the "impartial conscience" and "neutral competence" of the technical expert.

In its extreme form the case for technocracy may assert that it guarantees superior policy performance and this result is in itself sufficient to justify the displacement of democratic authority. Centeno (1993,) referred to this as "legitimation through performance criteria." These questions are not merely of theoretical interest for a region like Latin America. Throughout the twentieth century, its leaders sought the right form of government, and the most appropriate development strategy, to resolve the inherited deficiencies in their societies. In the last decade of the twentieth century, an unusually wide and deep consensus emerged that the best form of government is democracy, and that the most appropriate developmental strategy is outward oriented and pro-market. The idea was that it would help to "depoliticize" economic life and to stimulate a more entrepreneurial society. In view of the still incomplete nature of the reform processes, we can hardly expect to arrive at a definitive and uniform evaluation of its success. We may conclude that at the end of the twentieth century, Latin America finally managed to settle on both a form of government and a strategy for development that could be continued, deepened, and made irreversible for the indefinite future.

If both democracy and the market are to coexist and interact in accordance with the public interest, a considerable degree of mutual adjustment will have to take place. This would mean not merely that a durable liberal democracy must be market friendly, but also that a broadly privatized economy may be subject to extensive political reregulation or reinstitutionalization. These are the challenges facing all market democracies, but they assume a distinctive and acute form in the Latin American regional context. Here, the advocates of liberal reform are likely to rely heavily on external accreditation and protection to validate their purported expertise. Here, a poorly coordinated and easily captured state apparatus may lack the specialized capacities and staying power required to design, implement, and monitor successful transformations of this kind. Here, the lessons of history and the division of interest may generate a reasonable expectation that the public interest rhetoric of the "liberalizing expert" may prove a poor guide to what these experts are really trying to achieve, or how it will turn out in practice. Consequently, in Latin America, more than elsewhere, it may prove difficult to sustain a minimal social consensus around this latest project of modernity. The extremes of social inequality and exclusion that still characterize almost the whole region, despite its embrace of markets and democracy, expose all such projects to potentially destabilizing resistance and even backlash.

In order to avoid such backlash, the region will need macroeconomists who are not only scientists but also engineers, not only architects and designers of policies but implementers.[24] For more cognitive institution building will require, in particular, institutions to be adequately articulated with the world of policymaking and policymakers, as well as rooted in the local political and social context in order to produce adequate and efficient economic policies. Again, it is not only bright economic architects who are scarce in the region (i.e., macroeconomist-scientists with Ivy League pedigrees) but also economic engineers, able to implement sound policies, technically articulated but also politically viable.

Two more final thoughts. Think tanks obviously are not limited to economics or policy-oriented reformers. More research is necessary in this regard to assess the democratic contribution of noneconomic and policy-oriented tanks. In countries such as Mexico and Costa Rica, we can see the important institutional role that epistemic communities not concerned with economic policymaking (e.g., IFE, etc., in Mexico and Estado de la Nación, etc., in Costa Rica) can play in promoting democratic institutionalization and in providing counterweights to the orthodoxy of officialdom. Although these entities do not fall directly within our purview here, they do have an important impact on "the politics of expertise" more generally. Governments that have to contend with reasoned criticism and even censure from other well-regarded noneconomic think tanks are thereby rendered more open to similar feedback from economic experts.

Last but not least: the world economic crisis of 2008 has severely dented the credibility of many economic think tanks all around the world (and economists in general)—and that includes in Latin America. Pluralist challenges to what is now labeled "market fundamentalism" by such authorities as George Soros, or to the observable consequences of trying to apply the so-called Washington consensus in a globalized economy where Washington itself no longer observes its own prescriptions are giving rise to new uncertainties. It is to be hoped that these critical currents of thought (encouraged from the center by such authorities as Paul Krugman, Joseph Stiglitz, and Amartya Sen, from academia, or Olivier Blanchard from core institutions like the IMF) will give rise to further high-quality research and recommendations on the best economic strategies for durable development.

If so, then the democratization of these epistemic communities and the increased breadth and density of these organizational networks can help to stabilize and reinforce the inclusionary policymaking that the region's electorate deserves. But these institutions are still organizationally precarious, and need to avoid engaging in zero-sum confrontations that could dissipate the fragile confidence in academic expertise on which they all depend. Nevertheless, all think tanks deserve much more attention from international donors, something that is lacking: if we want to be serious with giving more "voice" to emerging countries and developing countries, this should go hand in hand with the strengthening of these think tanks.

NOTES

Javier Santiso is professor of economics at ESADE Business School. Previously he was director and chief economist of the OECD Development Centre. His e-mail address is Javier.santiso@esade.edu. Laurence Whitehead is Official Fellow in Politics of Nuffield College, Oxford University. His e-mail address is laurence.whitehead@nuffield.ox.ac.uk.

1. It should however not be assumed that all change is from national to U.S.-led credentialism. In Venezuela, for example, the Hugo Chávez government is now attempting to reverse that trend. And in Cuba one of the awkward problems of any post-Castro transition may be to determine whether nationally trained and promoted economists will have any authority or only U.S.-trained Cubans will be recognized as professionally competent.

2. Technopols can be described as "technically skilled and politically savvy leaders who held key positions. . . . . . . Successful technopols have made economics 'political' and, in doing so, have created their own power and have enabled their politician allies to govern more effectively. Technopols have made economic policies acceptable to the public at large in democratic settings. More important, technopols have fashioned economic policies guided by their political analysis of the circumstances of their respective countries at given historical junctures; economic policies must meet requirements that originate in the political sphere. Thus technopols often act in ways that are unfamiliar to many professional economists. Technopols design economic policies by understanding their nations' politics first. . . . Successful technopols are not mere cooks reproducing the recipes of their foreign instructors, or mere photocopiers of the economic dogmas of other countries. Their discovery of the necessity of politics for the making and selling of sound economic policy in the real contexts of real countries is what makes them pols."

3. For an analysis of this reform process, see Lora and Panizza (2002); Navia and Velasco (2003), Williamson (1994), Lora, Pagés, et al. (2004), Lora, Panizza, and Quispe-Agnoli (2004), Lora and Oliveira (2004a, 2004b), and J. Santiso (2004a).

4. On this topic see Silva (1991), Valdés (1995); Puryear (1994); and Santiso (1995).

5. On Mexico see, for example, Centeno (1994), and for Latin America in general see Dezalay and Garth (2002).

6. On this topic see Sturzenegger and Tommasi (1998); Rodrik and Iyigun (2004); Prichett (2004); and Spiller, Stein, and Tommasi (2003).

7. This version is available from us on request.

8. This point was forcefully made by Fernando Henrique Cardoso (2004).

9. IPEA is probably one of the largest cognitive institutions in Latin America with 600 employees in 2005, half of them economists and analysts. Nearly 70 percent of the 300 economists and analysts hold PhD degrees.

10. On Fedesarrollo, see the case study of Braun et al.

11. See also ksghome.harvard.edu/~rhausma/publication.htm; and ksghome.harvard.edu/~rhausma/publication.htm#seminar.

12. On the Mexican financial crisis of 1994, see, for example, J. Santiso (1999); on the 2002 Brazilian election, see, Santiso and Martínez (2003); J. Santiso (2004a).

13. On the influence of Raúl Prebisch on the organization, see the special issue of the *CEPAL Review* in December 2005.

14. At a conference organized to present an annual economic report on November 29, 2004, top officials from the Peruvian, Colombian, Bolivian, Ecuadorian, and Venezuelan governments, among others, were present.

15. See, for example, the conference around the presentation of the first annual economic report of the CAF (2004b).

16. The Latin American Research Network is one of the most important in terms of support of cognitive institutions. Created in 1991, this network of nearly 300 research institutes has proven to be an effective vehicle for financing quality research to enrich the public policy debate in Latin America and the Caribbean. It has financed more than 40 projects and published 130 working papers.

17. For more information on APOYO, see its website, www.apoyo.com/english/eco_studies/.

18. On IPE, see its website, www.ipeportal.org/.

19. For a detailed analysis of GRADE, see the study directed by Miguel Braun (Braun et al. 2004c).

20. For more on the Research Center, see its website, www.up.edu.pe/ciup/.

21. The Research Department of the IADB in 2005 managed seven networks.

22. There are also technical experts who are not part of any consultancy. There is no exact information on their numbers, so this total of 33 people excludes technical experts. Using available data, we estimate there are between 33 and 43 economists devoted to policy-oriented analysis, formulation, and dissemination in Uruguay.

23. On business involvement in policymaking more generally, see Schneider (2005). There are several other private consultancies that participate in the economic policy debate. Most notable among them are Deloitte and Price Waterhouse Cooper, both with specialized economic analysis departments, providing services to businesses, publishing reports and articles in the press, and broadcasting radio programs. Cuesta Duarte Institute is another cognitive institution, which is in charge of economic studies assessing the Worker's Central Union, unique in this setting. Its director was nominated director of health under the Tabaré government, and it publishes economic updates. Banks and financial institutions lack local experts, with the exception of BBVA. The other private banks, either local or foreign-affiliated ones, have external consultants and produce no reports or studies of the analytic kind mentioned earlier in this note.

24. We use here the distinction elaborated by Gregory Mankiw (2006), who distinguished two types of macroeconomists, those who understand the field as a type of engineering, trying to solve practical problems, and those who are more scientists, developing analytic tools and establishing theoretical principles.

REFERENCES

Armijo, Leslie. 2004. "Modeling Economic Policy Making across History and Political Geography." Paper presented at the Annual Meeting of the International Studies Association, Montreal, Quebec, March 17–20.

Armijo, Leslie E., and Philippe Faucher. 2003. "Currency Crises and Decision-making Frameworks: The Politics of Bouncing Back in Argentina and Brazil." Paper presented at the 24th Congress of Latin American Studies Association, Dallas, Texas, March 27–29.

Armijo, Leslie E., Philippe Faucher, and Magdalena Dembinska. 2004, "Compared to What? Assessing Brazilian Political Institutions." Paper presented at the Annual Meeting of the International Studies Association, Montreal, Quebec, March 17–20.

Benhabib, Jess, and Adam Przeworski. 2004. "Economic Growth under Political Accountability." Unpublished manuscript, New York University, Department of Politics.

Braun, Miguel. 2004a. "A Comparative Study of Think Tanks in Latin America, Asia, and Africa." Unpublished manuscript, CIPPEC, Buenos Aires, prepared for the Global Development Network's Bridging Research and Policy. Available at http://www.cippec.org/ingles/index.html.

———. 2004b. "Fundación para la Eduación Superior y el Desarrollo (Fedesarrollo): Colombia's Case Study." Unpublished manuscript, CIPPEC, Buenos Aires, prepared for the Global Development Network's Bridging Research and Policy, July.

———. 2004c. "Grupo de Análisis para el Desarrollo (GRADE): Peru's Case Study." Unpublished manuscript, CIPPEC, Buenos Aires, July.

CAF (Corporación Andina de Fomento). 2004a. *Sostenibilidad fiscal en la región andina: Políticas e instituciones*. Caracas: CAF.

———. 2004b. *Reflexiones para retomar el crecimiento: Inserción Internacional, Transformación Productiva e Inclusión Social*. Caracas: CAF.

———. 2003. *Perspectivas: Análisis de temas críticos para el desarrollo sostenible*. Vols. 1 and 2. Caracas: CAF.

Cardoso, Fernando Henrique. 2004. "Consideraciones sobre reforma del Estado y gobernanza democrática." Speech delivered at the Annual Meeting of the Board of Governors of the Inter-American Development Bank, Lima, Peru, March 27.

Centeno, Miguel Angel. 1993. "The New Leviathan: The Dynamics and Limits of Technocracy." *Theory and Society* 22(3).

———. 1994. *Democracy within Reason: Technocratic Revolution in Mexico*. University Park: Pennsylvania State University Press.

Dezalay, Yves, and Bryant Garth. 2002. *The Internationalization of Palace Wars: State Restructuring in Latin America between Lawyers and Chicago Boys*. Chicago: University of Chicago Press.

Edwards, Sebastián. 2005. "Establishing Credibility: The Role of Foreign Advisors." NBER Working Paper No. 11429, National Bureau of Economic Research, Cambridge, MA, June.

Elster, Jon. 1984. *Ulysses and the Sirens: Studies in Rationality and Irrationality*, Cambridge: Cambridge University Press.

Fischer, Frank. 1990. *Technocracy and the Politics of Expertise*. London: Sage.

Haas, Peter. 1992. "Introduction: Epistemic Communities and International Policy Coordination." *International Organization* 46(1): 1–35.

Hausmann, Ricardo, Andrés Rodríguez-Clare, and Dani Rodrik. 2005. "Towards a Strategy of Economic Growth in Uruguay." IADB Economic and Social Studies Series, Region 1, Inter-American Development Bank, Washington, DC, February.

Hirschman, Albert. 1998. *Crossing Boundaries*, Zone Books, New York.

Hodara, José. 1987. *Prebisch y la CEPAL*. Mexico City: El Colegio de México.

Kishor Kulkarni, Jeffrey. 2005. "Central Bank Independence as Ideology: Disinflation, Dissimulation, and Labor Market Deregulation." DPhil diss., Oxford University.

Lindblom, Charles. 1959. "The Science of Muddling Through." *Public Administration Review* 19: 79–88.

López Portillo, José Ramón. 1995. "Economic Thought and Economic Policymaking in Contemporary Mexico." DPhil. diss., Oxford University.

Lora, Eduardo, and Mauricio Oliveira. 2004a. "What Makes Reforms Likely: Political Economy Determinants of Reforms in Latin America." *Journal of Applied Economics* 7(1): 99–135.

———. 2004b. "The Electoral Consequences of the Washington Consensus." Unpublished manuscript, Inter-American Development Bank, Research Department, Washington, DC,

Lora, Eduardo, and Ugo Panizza. 2002. "Structural Reforms under Scrutiny." IADBWorking Paper No. 470, Inter-American Development Bank Research Department, Washington, DC.

Lora, Eduardo, Carmen Pagés, Ugo Panizza, and Ernesto Stein. 2004. *A Decade of Development Thinking*. Washington, DC: Inter-American Development Bank, Research Department.

Lora, Eduardo, Ugo Panizza, and Myriam Quispe-Agnoli. 2004. "Reform Fatigue: Symptoms, Reasons, and Implications." *Economic Review (Federal Reserve Bank of Atlanta)* 89(2): 1–28.

Mankiw, Gregory. 2006. "The Macroeconomist as Scientist and Engineer." NBER Working Paper No. 12349, National Bureau of Economic Research, Cambridge, MA.

Merrill Lynch. 2005. "Latam Macro Insights: Chile Portfolio Rotation and Copom Decision." Merrill Lynch, New York, January 14.

Momani, Bessma. 2005. "Recruiting and Diversifying IMF Technocrats." *Global Society* 19(2): 167–87.

Navia, Patricio, and Andrés Velasco. 2003. "The Politics of Second-generation Reforms." In *After the Washington Consensus. Restarting Growth and Reform in Latin America*, edited by Pedro Pablo Kuczynski and John Williamson, 265–303. Washington, DC: Institute for International Economics.

Puryear, Jeffrey. 1994. *Thinking Politics: Intellectuals and Democracy in Chile, 1973–1988*. Baltimore: Johns Hopkins University Press.

Prichett, Lant. 2004. "Reform Is like a Box of Chocolates: Understanding the Growth Disappointments and Surprises." Unpublished manuscript, Kennedy School of Government, Harvard University.

Przeworski, Adam. 2004a. "The Last Instance: Are Institutions a Deeper Cause of Economic Development?" Unpublished manuscript, New York University, Department of Politics.

———. 2004b. "Some Historical, Theoretical, and Methodological Issues Identifying Effects of Political Institutions." Unpublished manuscript, New York University, Department of Politics.

Rodrik, Dani, and Murat Iyigun. 2004. "On the Efficacy of Reforms: Policy Tinkering, Institutional Change and Entrepreneurship." BREAD Working Paper No. 058, March.

Santiso, Carlos. 2004a. "The Contentious Washington Consensus: Reforming the Reforms in Emerging Markets." *Review of International Political Economy* 11(4): 827–43.

———. 2004b. "Los préstamos del BID a las instituciones de control presupuestario." *Revista de la CEPAL* 83: 171–90.

———. 2005a. "Budget Institutions and Fiscal Responsibility: Parliaments and the Political Economy of the Budget Process." Paper presented at the 17th Regional Seminar on Fiscal Policy of the United Nations Economic Commission for Latin America and the Caribbean (ECLAC), Santiago, January 24–27.

———. 2005b. "Legislatures and Budget Oversight in Latin America: Strengthening Public Finance Accountability in Emerging Markets." *OECD Journal on Budgeting*.

Santiso, Javier. 1995. "Elites et démocratisation chilienne: Les centres académiques privés." In *Sociologie des réseaux transnationaux: Communautés, entreprises et individus: lien social et système international*, edited by Ariel Colonomos, 245–75. Paris: L'Harmattan.

———. 1999. "Wall Street and the Mexican Crisis: A Temporal Analysis of Emerging Markets." *International Political Science Review* 20(1): 49–73.

———. 2003. *The Political Economy of Emerging Markets: Actors, Institutions and Financial Crisis in Latin America*, New York: Palgrave.

———. 2004a. "Wall Street and Emerging Democracies: Financial Markets and the Brazilian Presidential Elections." Paper presented at Oxford University Conference on Central Banking and Monetary Policy in New Democracies with Special Reference to Brazil, Centre for Brazilian Studies, Oxford, February 17.

———. 2004b. "Inside the Black Box: A Journey towards Latin American Emerging Markets." CIDOB Latin America Series Working Papers No. 4, Fundación CIDOB.

———. 2005. *Amérique latine: Révolutionnaire, libérale, pragmatique*. Paris: Autrement.

———. 2006. *Latin America and the Political Economy of the Possible: Beyond Good Revolutionaries and Free Marketeers*. Cambridge, MA: MIT Press,

Santiso, Javier, and Juan Martínez. 2003. "Financial Markets and Politics: The Confidence Game in Latin American Emerging Economies." *International Political Science Review* 24(3): 363–97.

Schneider, Ben Ross. 2005. "Business Politics and Policy Making in Contemporary Latin America." Paper presented at the Workshop on State Reform, Public Policies, and Policy Making Processes, Inter-American Development Bank, Washington, DC, February 28–March 2.

Sikkink, Kathryn. 1991. *Ideas and Institutions: Developmentalism in Brazil and Argentina*, Ithaca, NY: Cornell University Press.

Silva, Patricio. 1991. "Technocrats in Politics in Chile: From the Chicago Boys to the CIEPLAN Monks." *Journal of Latin American Studies* 23: 385–410.

Sola, Lourdes. 1998. *Ideas econômicas, decisões políticas: Desenvolvimento e estabilidade na democracia populista*. Sao Paolo: Editora da Universidade de Sao Paolo.

Spiller, Pablo, Ernesto Stein, and Mariano Tommasi. 2003. "Political Institutions, Policymaking Processes and Policy Outcomes: An Inter-temporal Transactions Framework." IADB Design Paper No. 1, Inter-American Development Bank, Washington, DC.

Sturzenegger, Federico, and Mariano Tommasi. 1998. *The Political Economy of Reform*. Cambridge, MA: MIT Press.

Stone, Diane. 1996. *Capturing the Political Imagination: Think-Tanks and Policy Process*. London: Frank Cass.

Teichman, Judith. 2001. *The Politics of Freeing Markets in Latin America: Chile, Argentina, and Mexico*. Chapel Hill: University of North Carolina Press.

Thacker, Strom. 1999. "The High Politics of IMF Lending." *World Politics* 52: 38–75.

Tsebelis, George. 1995. "Decision Making in Political Systems: Veto Players in Presidentialism, Parliamentarism, Multicameralism and Multipartyism." *British Journal of Political Science* 25: 289–325.

Valdés, Juan Gabriel. 1995. *Pinochet's Economists: The Chicago School in Chile*. Cambridge: Cambridge University Press.

Vreeland, James. 2003. *The IMF and Economic Development*. Cambridge: Cambridge University Press.

Weyland, Kurt. 2002. *The Politics of Market Reform in Fragile Democracies: Argentina, Brazil, Peru and Venezuela*. Princeton, NJ: Princeton University Press.

Williamson, John, ed. 1994. *The Political Economy of Economic Policy Reform*. Washington, DC: Institute for International Economics.

PART IV

POLITICAL ECONOMY OF FISCAL AND SOCIAL POLICIES

CHAPTER 18

KILLING ME SOFTLY: LOCAL TERMITES AND FISCAL VIOLENCE IN BRAZIL AND MEXICO

CARLOS ELIZONDO AND JAVIER SANTISO

1. INTRODUCTION

Mexico and Brazil have a lot in common. They are the two largest Latin American countries and their continent's main emerging markets. Their level of development, however, is far below that which might be expected given their population, resources, and expectations at the time of their independence, which seemed so promising. Independence did not allow either of the two countries to grow as expected: setting up effective political institutions after the former conquerors and rulers had departed turned out to be difficult. Mexico was released from paying tribute to the Crown, but was not able to recover growth until the last third of the nineteenth century, when it finally reached political stability.[1] However, this stability was not sustained. It was interrupted by a costly revolution and, then again, by the recession of the 1920s. In Brazil, growth materialized a little later but was also interrupted by the world recession.

Both countries made significant progress in the second half of the twentieth century (fig. 18.1), when they achieved high growth rates thanks to a successful developmental strategy based on import substitution. Both were the economic miracles of their time, but for both this period of growth ended with inflation and serious macroeconomic imbalances. Both countries overcame the debt crisis, but

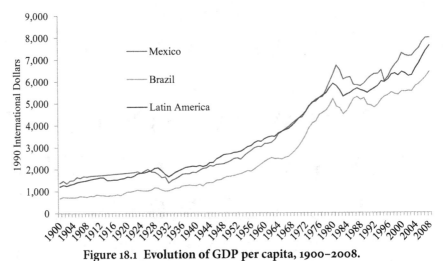

Figure 18.1 **Evolution of GDP per capita, 1900–2008.**
Note: The average for Latin America is for the eight largest economies: Argentina, Brazil, Chile, Colombia, Mexico, Peru, Uruguay, and Venezuela. Source: Based on data from Maddison (2009).

not without hardship and having to face new crises along the way: Mexico in 1994 and Brazil in 1999 and again in 2002.

Both have implemented significant reforms inspired by an economic pragmatism combining fiscal and monetary orthodoxy with social programs (fig. 18.2).[2] It is no small achievement that Mexico closed its 2006 fiscal year with inflation lower than that of its North American neighbor (3.3 percent)[3] and balanced public-sector accounts, while Brazil was also able to reduce its inflation (5.7 percent) and contain its fiscal deficit (3 percent of the gross domestic product [GDP]). These more-or-less intense budgetary efforts (in Latin America, the average fiscal deficit was under 1.5 percent of GDP in 2005) were supported by favorable external circumstances but also by home-grown fiscal-saving achievements, systematic debt reduction, and, most of all, improvements in the fiscal institutions in the region, particularly in Mexico and Brazil.[4] When the financial crisis of 2008 hit, both countries managed without a major fiscal crisis. Nevertheless, both countries suffered in terms of growth, much more Mexico with a recession in which there was a 6.5 percent decrease in GDP compared to only a 0.2 percent decrease in Brazil's GDP in 2009.

Brazil and Mexico have favorable demographic structures that should allow them in the coming decades to each become a developed country; their large populations, manufacturing sectors with a high export capacity, and substantial natural resources give them unquestionable international economic clout. Moreover, although both are budding democracies, they have been able to process significant differences on the basis of plurality and the freedom to select one's rulers. In the case of Brazil, the presidential victory of the left-wing candidate Luiz Inácio Lula da Silva in 2002 confirmed that Brazil´s elites were prepared to accept democracy. The conflicts after the defeat of Andrés Manuel López Obrador in 2006 have left acceptance of democracy an open question in Mexico.

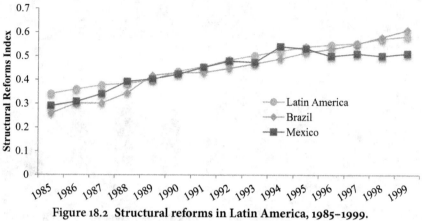

Figure 18.2 Structural reforms in Latin America, 1985–1999.
Source: Based on data from Lora (2001b, appendix 2, 30).

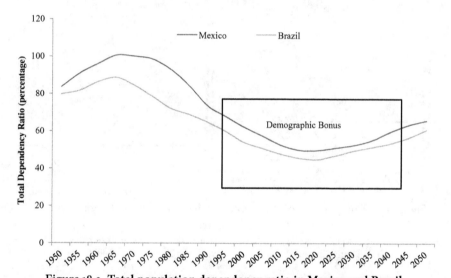

Figure 18.3 Total population dependency ratio in Mexico and Brazil.
Note: The population dependency ratio refers to the percentage of people dependent on the percentage of the population of working age. Source: United Nations, Department of Economic and Social Affairs, Population Division, World Population Prospects: The 2008 Revision (New York, 2009) (advanced Excel tables).

Nevertheless, the two countries are growing at rates that are far below what might be expected, even Brazil, which has entered the "BRIC" economic grouping (Brazil, Russia, India, China). This is clear when compared with the East Asian countries or even with Chile; their potential growth remains under par in relation to countries such as China and India (see fig. 18.4).

Their convergence with the other countries in the Organisation for Economic Co-operation and Development (OECD) has been incomplete in terms of GDP per capita (see fig. 18.5). When compared to the United States, not only are both economies not converging, but the gap is widening. If that were not enough, both

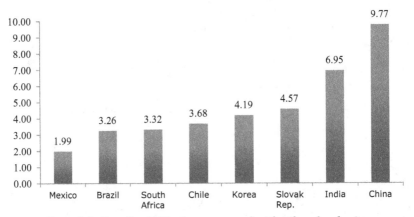

Figure 18.4 Growth in Brazil and Mexico compared with other developing economies (average GDP growth, 2000–2010).
Source: Based on data from International Monetary Fund, International Financial Statistics (Washington, DC: IMF, 2009).

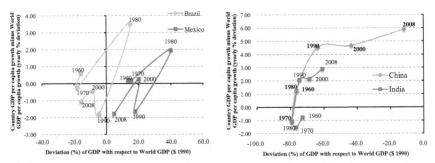

Figure 18.5 Convergence of Brazil and Mexico compared with other emerging economies.
Note: Annual growth (%) calculated as average annual growth rate for the last six decades; deviation (%) at the beginning of each decade. Source: Based on data from Maddison (2009).

countries now have to contend with other emerging economies swiftly catching up, China and India in particular.

Despite these similarities, there is one area in which the two countries are outstandingly different: Mexico collects a little more than 8 percent of its revenue in taxes (this number goes up to 15 percent if nontax revenue, including oil income, is included) and Brazil around 25 percent, a figure that hits a record 40 percent when state and municipal taxes are included (see figs. 18.6 and 18.7). Thus, in terms of tax revenues, Mexico and Brazil stand at the two extremes of the continents' practices. That much difference can be found between no two other Latin American countries. Although their "fiscal spaces" are different,[5] they face the same problem: their shortcomings in terms of generating public goods are analogous (for details on public finances in Brazil and in Mexico, see appendix 18.1).

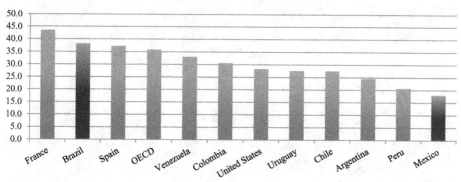

Figure 18.6 Tax revenue in Latin American and in OECD*, percentage of GDP, 2007.
*Selected countries
Source: For OECD countries, OECD, *Source OECD Revenue Statistics of OECD Member Countries Database—Comparative Tables Vol. 2009 release 1* (Paris: OECD, 2009); for Brazil and Latin American countries, Inter-American Development Bank, *Latin America and Caribbean Macro Watch Database* (Washington D.C.: IADB, 2009).

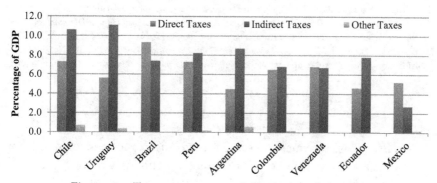

Figure 18.7 Tax revenue sources in Latin America, 2008.
Source: Based on Economic Commission for Latin America and the Caribbean, *Latin America and the Caribbean Statistics* (Santiago: ECLAC, 2009).

Once again, despite their abysmal difference in terms of tax-collection levels, the countries are very similar in terms of their delivery of a number of basic public services and of public goods essential for a modern economy. Brazil, with its high revenues, and Mexico, with its remarkably low ones, provide comparable health and education services. The power wielded by various sectors and interest groups to obtain tax exemptions or benefits, mainly in Mexico, together with the poor quality of their public expenditure, seriously affected by fiscal violence (which we describe later), has limited the state's redistribution capacities.

Generally speaking, both countries continue to experience inequality, geographically and socioeconomically. The poverty levels and the social exclusion of a number of groups are considerable for medium-income countries (see fig. 18.8).

The solution to the problem does not seem to lie in increasing tax revenue, no matter how much Mexico's is seriously deficient, even though the lack has been

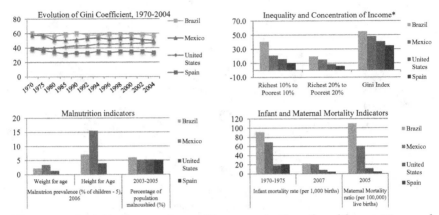

Figure 18.8 Social indicators: inequality, concentration of wealth, nutrition, and mortality indicators.

*Data for Brazil from 2007; data for Mexico from 2008, data for United States from 2000, and data for Spain for 2005.

Sources: Based on United Nations, Department of Economic and Social Affairs, Population Division, *World Population Prospects: The 2008 Revision* (New York, 2009) (advanced Excel tables); United Nations Development Programme (UNDP), *Human Development Report 2009 Overcoming Barriers: Human Mobility and Development* (New York, 2009);UNDP, *Statistical Tables and Human Development Report 2007/2008 Fighting Climate Change: Human Solidarity in a Divided World* (New York, 2007); United Nations Statistics Division, *Millennium Development Goals Database* (New York: United Nations Statistics Division, 2009), July 14, 2009, update; World Bank, *World Development Indicators* (Washington, DC: World Bank, 2009).

partially offset by oil revenues and some tax reforms in 2007 and 2009. A comparison between Brazil and Mexico leads to pondering not only revenue shortage but also spending efficiency.

This is a core theme, not only for these two countries, but for the region as a whole. There are definitely more social needs than resources to attend to them. This is in part a result of the brutal adjustments in social spending imposed to face the debt crisis of the 1980s. The fiscal adjustments of recent years, however, were not implemented at the expense of social expenditure; in fact, social expenditure per capita increased by 50 percent in the course of the 1990s and remained constant in 1998–2002 (Lora and Cárdenas 2006).[6]

Our work aims precisely at understanding the reasons underlying the paradox of two such similar countries with such different revenue structures and highlights a few implications for public policies. The need to increase tax revenue in the region is usually justified by the enormous deficiencies faced by an important part of the population and the lag in physical and institutional infrastructure, which makes more rapid growth difficult. Increasing tax revenues sounds reasonable, but it all depends on how it is spent. Brazil's collecting more than Mexico does has not made a big difference, so where is the problem?

The starting assumption is that the very poor quality of public spending in both countries has made it difficult to use expenditure as a true instrument of

justice and development and, in the case of Mexico, to justify greater tax collection. The core problem is the region's fiscal violence, and Brazil's and Mexico's in
particular.

2. FISCAL VIOLENCE

There are thousands of forms of violence. In Latin America, military violence has
been of particular note. Recently, organized crime violence has become notorious
in Mexico, but it is also present in Brazil. Murders in both countries remain high
compared to countries with similar levels of GDP per capita (fig. 18.9).

There are nonetheless more subtle, but equally devastating forms of violence
from the point of view of the economic and democratic development of a country.
These are completely legal, inherited by the authoritarian governments or voted in
by legislatures, endorsed by the executive, and sanctioned by the judicial bodies. It
is a type of violence unrelated to corruption or even tax evasion, both of which are
also significant in both countries and illegal and reprehensible.

The violence to which we are referring is fully legal: it is fiscal. By *fiscal violence*,
we mean the distortion and alteration of the entire lattice of the tax system, its rules,
processes, and institutions, to favor a particular social sector, the business world or
a well-organized political group. We are speaking of the legal appropriation of tax
resources through wages, pensions, subsidies, exemptions, and redemptions. This is

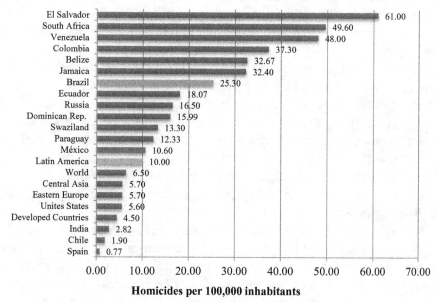

Homicides per 100,000 inhabitants

Figure 18.9 Homicide rates in Latin America, 2006.
Source: Based on G-5 in Centro de Investigación para el Desarrollo, Índice de Incidencia Delictiva y
Violencia 2009 (Mexico City: CIDAC, 2009), 8.

similar to what the economic literature has called "rents," but "fiscal violence" appears to describe the process better and is more specific. As long as there is fiscal violence, delivering public goods for the benefit of the large majority becomes problematic.

Here, it would be appropriate to draw a distinction between "termites," following the economist Vito Tanzi's lead, which take advantage of globalization and devour revenues, and "gluttons," which devour public spending or obtain privileged tax treatment (see Tanzi and Zee 2000 and, in particular, Tanzi 2001). There are many facets to this cannibalistic form of violence. It runs from generous tax exemptions or high salaries, even higher than the averages found in OECD countries, for "top priority" activities, for members of the legislature or leading public officials, to generous pension and retirement systems, also unparalleled in developed countries, allowing, as is the case in Brazil, members of Congress to retire after two terms, whatever their age, and receive a pension for life.

In addition, the poor quality of the services delivered, from education to public security, is, in very good measure, a result of the bureaucracy's and the trade unions' capturing a significant share of available public resources in the sector through high wages and privileged working conditions compared with the rest of the economy. There can be no successful redistributive project unless a solution is found to this fiscal violence. This situation is not specific to the two countries, nor even to Latin America. Nonetheless, the resilience of these fiscal violence enclaves at the core of its political systems contributes to the widespread fiscal delegitimization suffered by Latin American democracies. According to data from Latinobarómetro (2009, 20, table 3), in 2009, only 55 percent of the Brazilian people preferred democracy over another political regime. In Mexico, this number is only 42 percent. It is also significantly lower than the average since 1995, 51 percent.

In many countries, not paying taxes is not perceived as illegitimate. On the contrary, corruption and widespread fiscal violence are seen as legitimate; the lack of public spiritedness is even perceived in some countries as a show of lucidity and intelligence. The poor quality of public spending and the fact that part of it is performed following a cliental rationale have made it impossible to build a social pact behind the welfare state that would enable the acceptance of a greater tax burden in exchange for public spending that clearly benefits the majority of social sectors. For this to occur, as argued by Marcelo Bergman, a minimal measure of equity is essential (Bergman 2009).

Restoring a social pact in Latin America requires restoring the fiscal pact first. This is our main argument here. Making the tax system fair and spending efficiency possible is fundamental to achieving the political dividends of fiscal efforts. An equally pending and urgent task, without which the first is not really possible, is to do away with—or at least to limit—the magnitude of fiscal violence that is undermining any urge for or intention of reform in this area insofar as it erodes every principle of equity.

3. GLOBAL FISCAL TERMITES AND LOCAL DEPREDATORS IN LATIN AMERICA

Mexico and Brazil alike are facing so-called global fiscal termites. The expression denotes one of the negative aspects of globalization, in which international competition translates into a general alignment in favor of low taxing, in particular tax on capital, to the benefit of international capital. In effect, globalization necessarily brings about a fiscal shock resulting not only from expenditure adjustments or some healthy debt reduction but also from obligatory across-the-board reductions in customs duties, as well as in capital and enterprise taxes. All of this allows "global termites" to eat away at the entire fiscal structure and policy of any given country, and emerging-market countries in Latin America are particularly vulnerable in this respect because of their relatively low domestic savings and therefore substantial need for international capital.

This is particularly and strongly reflected in the erosion of customs duties, which before the structural adjustments of the 1990s stood at an average of almost 49 percent for Latin America. By the end of the decade, just two of the 24 countries of the region had maintained their rates at higher than 15 percent (Lora 2001a, 2006). This was a positive trend in terms of economic efficiency, but had a serious fiscal cost in some countries.

At the same time, the termites' relentless appetite progressively reduced the rates of enterprise taxes as well, and these shrank from 43 percent in the mid-1980s to less than 30 percent 20 years later. Although this reduction could reflect an internal tax-collection motivation—lowering rates as an incentive for enterprises to pay their taxes—the competition among countries to attract capital has been an additional force that has eroded governments' tax-collection capacities. European welfare states, which were central to the consolidation of democracy, were built in a world where it was possible, at least for a while, to claim tax rates that were higher than 60 percent.

Today's irreversible international conditions preclude the taxing rates that were typical of the period in which welfare states were developed, which means that the only realistic way out now is to concentrate efforts on the local termites, which are also eroding the tax-collection system. Specialists have partially documented this erosion by showing, for instance, how political processes, with their high transaction costs and their need to settle on trade-offs, have been shaping tax systems or distorting expenditure (see, e.g., Aizenman and Jinarak 2008; Kenney and Winer 2001; Cheibub 1998).

In the regressions reported by Lora and Olivera (2006), they found the collected revenues remarkably sensitive to variables such as political fragmentation and the influence of interest groups. In countries like those of Latin America, where both of these features are prominent, this result certainly draws attention when it comes to explaining not only the low levels of tax collection but also the inefficiencies of the entire system, which is flawed from the formulation of the taxes to the implementation of expenditure.

The 1980s crisis made it mandatory to adjust public spending severely and seek larger revenues. Fiscal adjustments tend to be easier to carry out in systems where institutional veto players capable of thwarting efforts to do away with termites are scarce. The more governments are fragmented, the more difficult it is for them to achieve fiscal stabilization quickly, because termites and gluttons are in a much stronger position when government is broken into fragments (Persson and Tabellini 2003).[7] Conversely, stabilization works better and faster when governments are unified, are not the result of a coalition, and, in particular, when both the executive and the legislative branches are in the hands of the same party (Alesina, Ardagna, and Trebbi 2006).[8] Fiscal adjustments, translated into public expenditure cutbacks and debt-to-GDP reduction, tend to be more frequently made by left-wing governments (Alesina, Ardagna, and Trebbi 2006). It does not seem to matter much whether the system is presidential or parliamentary; only fragmentation is an active factor.

In situations where spending is cut spectacularly within a short period, fiscal discipline and the capacity to make adjustments should not be confused with fiscal violence, which can subsist even during cutback periods. Mexico, for example, made a substantial cut in public expenditure, social spending included, in the 1980s. A substantial part of this effort went to trimming the real wages of public servants through very high inflation. Once inflation was under control, government workers recovered their precrisis wages, or even got higher ones. However, during the crisis wage rounds, when income could not be adjusted to aggregate inflation, a frequent trade-off, especially in government-owned enterprises, was to improve retirement conditions, as pensions did not have to be paid right away. Nearly 30 years after the crisis those generous pensions are pressuring public finances.

In Latin America, tax-collection levels are relatively low in general (18.4 percent in Central America and 27.4 percent for the seven largest economies on the region on average in 2008) and are particularly low for income taxes, especially where personal income tax is not withheld at the source by employers (at least this is the case in Mexico). Although in principle minorities are vulnerable in a democratic system, in practice they can wield a lot of influence (Lora 2006).

Initial inequality is not only income inequality; it is also inequality of human capital, of political sway, and of social expectations. All of these resources are skillfully used to maintain this inequality. Elites in unequal societies even have a strategy available to them, whereby in order to avoid the higher taxes that might result from a democracy where majorities could impose their taxing preferences, they encourage inefficient bureaucracies that will retain a substantial portion of the collected taxes, thus putting part of society on their side and preventing the emergence of a majority that might impose higher taxes. Translated into our terminology, the elites reach an agreement whereby the gluttons allow the termites to fulfill their infinite desire to eat away at government revenues.

This is why it is impossible to read Latin American fiscal systems without using the filters of economic policy. Poor tax collection in countries like Guatemala or multiple tax distortions as in Colombia, for example, can only be examined in the light of these dynamics, which are foreign to the balance of power exercised in models where rational players mysteriously become political eunuchs. Furthermore, as pointed out in some very stimulating work carried out by an Inter-American Development Bank (IADB) research team, the results of fiscal-reform drives cannot be understood exclusively through the economic filter (Cárdenas, Lora, and Mercer-Blackman 2006; IADB 2006).[9] They also need to be analyzed through political filters. Fiscal systems are architectures designed through an intense process of political and economic formulation, a policymaking process (Stein and Tomassi 2005). In this sense, tax collection systems, the combination of tax rates, tax administration, and a legal system that tends to protect, at least in countries like Mexico, constituents with resources to pay a good lawyer, are artifacts resulting from balances and transactions among government, the managerial private sector, and different social groups.

National fiscal termites, however, maneuver differently depending on the country. Weak states and political fragmentation and political polarization play a significantly influential role in their work. Eduardo Lora and Mauricio Olivera's previously mentioned econometric work on 15 Latin American countries since the 1980s provides a first description of this role (Lora and Olivera 2006).

The impact is amplified in countries lacking powerful institutional fiscal anchors that are able to contain the work of the political and socioeconomic termites, check corruption or simply manage the tax system efficiently, from revenue collection to spending, and control the whole process. Tax systems are thus particularly sensitive to these local termites. Tax-collection capacity and efficiency are eroded when the party in power is connected with the business world, including the rural one. Low tax collection in Mexico is paradoxical insofar as in principle, it is heir both to a revolution and a political system in which power is extremely concentrated.

4. MEXICO AND BRAZIL IN A COMPARATIVE PERSPECTIVE

Within their different tax-collection capacities, both Mexico and Brazil have been able to balance their public finances after years of problematic fiscal imbalances that were basically political imbalances, which demonstrates the inability of the respective governments, before democratization, to mediate between expenditure demands and their capacity to generate income sustainably over time.

Brazilian democracy had to implement adjustment at great cost for its first presidents. Conditions were somewhat better for Mexican democracy. Adjustment

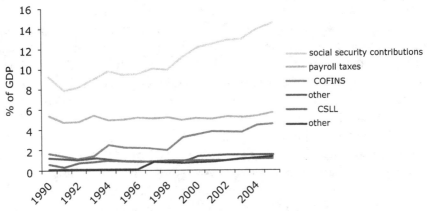

Figure 18.10 Expansion of social security contributions in Brazil, 1990–2005.
Source: Figure 7 in Melo, Pereira, and Souza (2010, 13).

had been implemented previously and it even had the benefit of lower interest rates and high oil prices. Both democracies are now, however, facing the challenge of having to control their termites and gluttons.

In the case of Mexico the new fiscal balance is based, as it has always been throughout its history, on low taxes, hence low and poor investment in the people. It also depends on the oil rent, which is not predicted to last more than 10 years, and it is threatened by pensions in the public sector that have not been properly funded.

In the case of Brazil, a significant part of the fiscal adjustment was made possible by a very important increase in tax revenues since the mid-1980s. The tax burden was already high; nevertheless, it rose around 12 percentage points (from 25 to 37) between 1993 and 2005. This increase was due to the introduction of new taxes and increasing the existing tax rates, as well as the so-called social contributions (fig. 18.10). This permitted the expansion of the social security budget, which rose 84 percent from 1991 to 2005. State taxes also increased significantly, in line with federal taxes and contributions (fig. 18.11), and in 2007 this tandem accounted for 26 percent of the GDP (Melo, Periera, and Souza).

However, this balance based on higher taxes has come at a very high cost to the private sector, which is growing less than it should be since those taxes are then not fully returned as public goods. Moreover, it feeds a bureaucracy that is developing regulations that are often useless. The government seems to need to justify its existence with paperwork that overwhelms would-be entrepreneurs when they wish to start a business (figs. 18.12 and 18.13).

Certain budgetary balances can be politically unsustainable. This was the case for Mexico in the late nineteenth century and early twentieth century, the first moment in the history of independent Mexico when budget and growth balance was achieved.[10] The balance was achieved, however, to a large degree by not spending, as well as not caring that in 1910 70.2 percent of Mexicans were illiterate (Thorp 1998, 374) and a large percentage of the population was excluded from a number of basic services.[11]

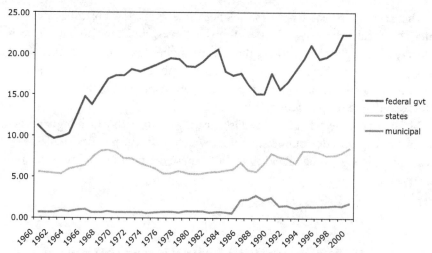

Figure 18.11 Tax revenue by tier of government, 1960–2000 (as % of GDP).
Source: Figure 9 in Melo, Pereira, and Souza (2010, 15).

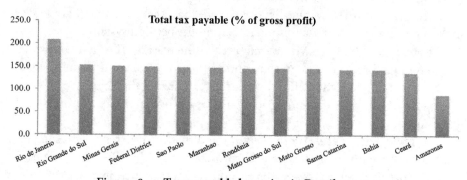

Figure 18.12 Taxes payable by region in Brazil, 2006.
Source: Based on International Bank for Reconstruction and Development, World Bank (2006).

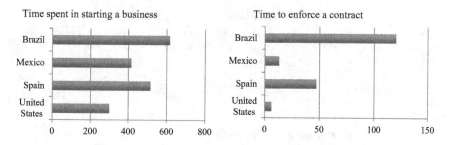

Figure 18.13 Start-up and regulation costs (days).
Source: International Finance Corporation, World Bank, Doing Business 2010
(Washington, DC: World Bank Group). Data available at http://www.doingbusiness.org/.

There are two possible perverse balances: one with a low tax-collection level, in which the fiscal termites win the battle over those who stand to gain from fiscal violence, the big gluttons, and another with a higher tax-collection level, in which the big gluttons are able to press for greater income. This does not mean that in the first kind of perverse balance there are no gluttons, nor that the second is rid of termites; only the proportions are different.

Ideally, of course, what is needed is a healthy balance, in which higher revenues lead to more and better public spending, which, in turn, justifies the larger revenues. The challenge to be taken up by both these countries is to build this type of fiscal pact.

5. Revenues in Mexico and Brazil

Mexican tax revenue is lower than Brazilian revenue and has been consistently low, as fig 18.14 shows. Most of the difference between the two countries is mainly due to consumption taxes, not income taxes. When adding the revenues corresponding to social security, Brazil's revenues increase more than Mexico's, which are low and make it necessary to use fiscal resources to fund the pension systems.

The difference between Mexico and Brazil is increasing. The main difference is due to more indirect taxes, a greater contribution to social security, and a significantly greater tax-collection effort by local states in Brazil than by those in Mexico (table 18.1), these latter depending to a large degree on transfers from the federal government.

It is nonetheless necessary to keep in mind that the difference of resources in the hands of government between the two countries is smaller than the difference in what they collect, given Mexico's oil revenues, which increase the federal

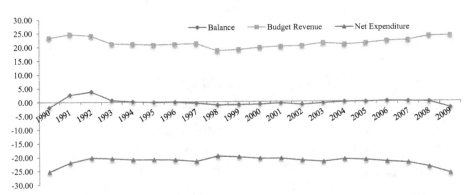

Figure 18.14 Evolution of the public sector situation in Mexico, 1990–2009 (as a percentage of GDP)
Source: Based on Secretaría de Hacienda y Crédito Público, Estadísticas Oportunas de Finanzas Públicas (Mexico City: SHCP).

government's income by an average of about 4 percentage points to 8.7 percent of the GDP in 2008 and somewhat less in 2009, when estimated income was reported at 7.4 percent (table 18.2).[12] This has facilitated the Mexican fiscal pact, but on foundations that are not only unstable over time—the price of oil can fall and the export platform diminish—but that also diminish the relation between taxes and expenditures. This makes citizens and the political class lazy.

Brazil is about to face a major increase in its oil income. It will need to reinforce its spending and revenue institutions to avoid even more wasteful expenditure or an erosion of its tax structure.

As much in Brazil as in Mexico, tax-evasion rates seem to be relatively high, and justified socially by the poor quality of public expenditure. In Mexico, additional reasons for such low tax collection are a costly judicial system that protects the taxpayers who should most contribute and can therefore pay for their defense (Elizondo and Pérez de Acha 2006) and an inefficient tax administration.

Table 18.1. **Distribution of the Fiscal Burden by Jurisdiction in Brazil (Tax Burden as a Percentage of GDP)**

	1988	1994	2000	2002	2003	2004	2006
Federal	16.10	13.40	14.80	17.10	16.40		
State	5.70	7.80	8.35	8.84	8.61		
Municipal	0.60	1.00	0.84	1.11	1.20		
Social security		5.63	7.12	7.45	7.41		
Total	22.40	27.90	31.60	34.90	34.00	35.90	38.00

Source: Baer and Galvao (2008, 348).

Table 18.2. **Evolution of Oil-Based Public Revenue in Mexico, 1990–2009 (% of GDP)**

	1990–99	2000–2009	Difference
Total	21.36	21.42	0.06
Oil-based revenue	5.18	6.95	1.77
PEMEX	2.30	2.47	0.17
Rights to oil	2.79	4.28	1.49
Other oil-based revenue	0.09	0.20	0.11
Total tax revenue	9.61	9.39	-0.22
Gasoline tax[a]	8.56	9.04	0.48
Non-tax- and non-oil-based revenue	1.05	0.35	-0.70
Public enterprises	2.13	1.41	-0.72

[a]As explained in n. 12, this tax is a consumption tax and is not counted as part of the oil revenue.
Source: Based on data from SHCP (2009).

6. Termites in Action

As a result of an effort to increase transparency of the tax and expenditure structure, Mexican law requires the yearly publication of a study on the incidence of spending and taxes and another on the cost of tax expenditure, that is to say, of special preferences in tax treatment. Both studies provide pretty faithful accounts of the termites' and gluttons' work.

Despite the tax expenditures described further below, taxes in Mexico are progressive. Given the inequality in the country, there could hardly be any other option. More than 80 percent of income taxes are collected from the top two income deciles (see table 18.3). The value-added tax (VAT) is also progressive in that 75 percent of its

Table 18.3. Incidence of Income-Tax Collection and Social Security per Decile in Mexico (2008 Mexican Pesos)

Income Decile	Contribution to Income Tax Collection	Tax Incidence	Contribution to Social Security Collection	Social Security Incidence
Households				
1	-1.2	-1.7	1.1	0.2
2	-1.9	-1.6	2.7	0.3
3	-1.3	-0.9	4.0	0.4
4	0.0	-0.2	5.4	0.4
5	0.6	0.3	6.7	0.4
6	2.4	0.9	8.3	0.4
7	5.9	1.8	10.5	0.4
8	11.0	2.7	13.3	0.4
9	20.5	3.7	17.6	0.4
10	64.4	3.3	30.4	0.2
Total or average	100.0	2.4	100.0	0.3
population				
1	-0.9	-1.7	0.8	0.2
2	-1.6	-1.7	1.9	0.3
3	-1.4	-1.1	3.1	0.3
4	-0.9	-0.6	4.4	0.4
5	0.1	0.1	5.6	0.4
6	1.2	0.5	7.1	0.4
7	3.7	1.4	9.5	0.5
8	8.0	2.1	12.3	0.4
9	18.5	3.3	18.2	0.4
10	73.1	3.4	37.2	0.2
Total or average	100.0	2.4	100.0	0.3

collection comes from the top three deciles. The VAT is less progressive than income tax, of course, as it taxes consumption, but the enormous inequality in consumption itself also translates into a concentration of its source of payment. It is a lot lower than it could be, in view of the exemptions that mainly favor the top deciles (see table 18.4).

Tax expenditure in Mexico, that is to say, all the special treatments of the income law that imply loss of revenue, amounts to 3.87 percent of GDP and tends to remain constant, although there has been a reduction in comparison with previous years (tables 18.5–7). Every item is the living image of a termite weakening the tax system.

There is a little of everything. Benefits vary in magnitude, such as the consolidated tax return that benefits all large enterprises, including some that are clearly corporate. These feature among others, agricultural producers, the cost of which to government in terms of noncollected taxes is equivalent to 0.23percent of GDP.

Table 18.4. Composition of Household Spending per Type of VAT Rate, 2008

	General	Zero tax Rate	No VAT Tax
Households			
1	43.8	46.0	10.2
2	45.9	42.2	11.9
3	47.0	40.1	12.8
4	49.6	37.5	12.8
5	51.8	35.3	12.9
6	54.4	32.8	12.8
7	57.6	29.7	12.7
8	61.2	26.4	12.5
9	65.2	22.0	12.8
10	71.0	15.1	13.8
Average	59.3	27.8	12.9
population			
1	43.7	46.2	10.0
2	45.6	42.9	11.5
3	46.3	41.1	12.5
4	48.7	38.3	13.0
5	50.8	36.7	12.6
6	52.2	34.8	13.1
7	55.6	31.5	12.9
8	59.4	28.0	12.6
9	63.5	24.0	12.5
10	70.1	16.2	13.7
Average	59.3	27.8	12.9

Source: SCHP (2010a, 15).

Table 18.5. Tax-Expenditure Budget 2009–10

Concept	% of GDP[a]	2009 Billions of Mexican Pesos	% of total	% of GDP[a]	2010 Billions of Mexican Pesos	% of Total
Total	3.87	496.9147	100.0	3.98	502.5334	100.0
Income tax (ISR)	1.70	203.6668	43.8	1.69	213.0300	42.4
Busines ISR	1.24	148.6919	32.0	1.23	155.1519	30.9
ISR for persons	0.46	54.9749	11.8	0.46	57.8781	11.5
Single rate business tax	0.71	85.5677	18.4	0.66	82.7915	16.5
Value-added tax	1.32	158.5216	34.1	1.32	166.8593	33.2
Special taxes[b]	0.06	7.4817	1.6	0.27	33.5501	6.7
Fiscal incentives	0.08	9.6769	2.1	0.05	6.3025	1.2

Note: Totals may not be exact due to rounding of numbers.
[a] With an estimated GDP of 12.0083 trillion pesos for 2009 and 12.6399 trillion pesos for 2010.
[b] Includes special tax on production and services, new automobiles tax, and possession and use of automobiles tax.
Source: SHCP (2010b, 9).

Table 18.6. Tax-Expenditure Budget 2002–7, Business Income Tax and Personal Income Tax

Concept	% of GDP						Percentage Variation in Real Terms				
	2002	2003	2004	2005	2006	2007	2003	2004	2005	2006	2007
Business income tax	0.83	1.48	1.53	2.56	0.24	0.23	80.68	7.51	72.42	-20.11	-1.79
Contributors from autotransports sector	na	0.08	0.05	0.05	0.05	0.05	na	-27.17	-1.62	6.08	-0.28
Contributors from primary sector	0.19	0.20	0.20	0.24	0.19	0.18	4.86	9.23	22.95	-20.83	2.96
Authorized deductions		0.49	0.67	0.82	1.73	1.13	1.05	38.75	28.70	117.37	-35.13	0.54
Personal income tax	1.84	1.64	1.41	1.46	1.32	1.26	-9.96	-10.12	6.35	-6.33	-1.36
Income tax on salaries	1.08	0.73	0.51	0.70	0.59	0.54	-31.99	-27.48	43.17	na	na
Income exemption due to salaries	0.62	0.68	0.69	0.48	0.51	0.46	10.20	6.03	-28.34	10.45	-6.35
Authorized personal deductions	0.11	0.14	0.14	0.11	0.09	0.08	29.24	-0.29	-16.19	-19.94	-0.28

Source: Based on Chamber of Deputies, Center for Public Finances Studies, CEPF/007/2007, with data from Secretaría de Hacienda y Crédito Público, *Presupuesto de Gastos Fiscales 2002–2007* (Mexico City: SHCP, 2007).

Table 18.7. Fiscal-Expenditure Budget 2009–10, Enterprise Income Tax

	2009		2010	
Concept	% of GDP[a]	Billions of Pesos	% of GDP[a]	Billions of Pesos
Enterprise income tax	1.2382	148.6919	1.2276	155.1519
Special regimes	0.2961	35.5527	0.2961	37.4223
Fiscal consolidation regime[b]	0.1039	12.4780	0.1039	13.1340
Ground transport contributors	0.0170	2.0414	0.0170	2.1488
Immediate deduction of fixed asset investments[b]	0.0153	1.8973	0.0153	1.9339
Intermediate regime investment deductions[c]	0.0017	.2041	0.0017	.2149

[a] With an estimated GDP of 12.0083 billion pesos for 2009 and 12.6399 billion pesos for 2010.
[b] This deduction consists in posponing the payment of the tax; therefore, the reported fiscal expenditure is compensated for in future fiscal years.
[c] When investments are permitted as deductions as a part of the fiscal year, part of the fiscal expenditure corresponds to postponing the tax payment that is compensated for in future years. The payment that is postponed corresponds to the excess deduction to which the deduction tax rates would be immediately applied.
Source: SHCP (2010b, 11–12).

Although it makes sense to support the rural world, where the poorest Mexicans live, this type of subsidy helps only the large producers.

Support of the labor sector can seem progressive, but those who really stand to gain are the trade unions of the large public and private enterprises, which is where this type of benefit is concentrated. Transport is another favored sector with tax privileges amounting to 0.05 percent of GDP for 2006 and 2007.

7. SPENDING QUALITY IN MEXICO AND BRAZIL

As John Scott (2002) argues, there are three income-redistribution instruments: progressive taxes, cash transfers, and transfers in kind through subsidized public goods and services. In countries with considerable inequality like Brazil and Mexico, these instruments can be very powerful in principle, more than in countries with less inequality, provided the resources are substantial or precisely targeted in such a way that resources reach the worst off (Scott 2002, 15). In practice, however, this has not been the case.

Although the available data are not necessarily adequate, the evidence indicates that redistribution capabilities have been poor, due as much to supply as to demand problems (prohibitive opportunity costs for lower-income groups, such as for access to postbasic education). As Scott (2002, 13) clarifies through these calculations, redistributive efficiency tends to be overestimated as it assumes that the private benefits of a service are equal to public costs.

Herein lies one of the core problems. The quality of these services is usually poor. As Scott (2002, 7) argues, one of the reasons for the progressivity of public services in Latin America (i.e., that these services go to the worst off) is that those who can do so pay for a service in the private market and do not use the public service. But it is fake progressivity. Buying the service on the private market usually leads to a higher quality of education or health, and therefore increases the capacity for earning a high wage.

Let us take the case of the Programme for International Student Assessment (PISA), the OECD project to assess knowledge at age 15. It is of particular interest in the Mexican case. The sample was enlarged to enable comparisons at the state level and among the different educational options in which 15-year-old students are found. Added to other assessments by the Mexican national institute for education assessment, this allows us to fine-tune our analysis.

Mexico is a country with much inequality, but not in its educational performance: almost all students are on a low level in this area. There is no significant group of good students. In mathematics, for instance, only 0.6 percent attain the highest proficiency level. Brazil has many more students who do not complete even the minimum levels, but it also has a larger number of outstanding students: 1.1 percent. This figure can be compared to Finland's 16.7 percent of the population found at this level. In Mexico, the coverage rate (i.e., the percentage of children at a particular age who receive an education) at age 15 is only 54 percent, compared to more than 90 percent for the OECD countries. As for Brazil, it has been able to increase this coverage significantly.

Contrary to what some believe, this is not exclusively a public-education problem. In Mexico, 10 percent of 15-year-old students attend a private school, which is a higher percentage than the average for the OECD countries. Student performance in private schools is better on average than that in public schools. The difference is not much, however. The average for private schools is still below that for all schools in Turkey, the OECD country ranked just about Mexico. In addition, when adjusted for the parents' socioeconomic level, the difference becomes very small, and when the advantage derived from the socioeconomic environment of the school is factored in, the difference becomes negative. Private education seems to be more useful as a place for learning English (a very useful instrument) and social networking than as one of pure academic benefit. A household head does not have much objective information on the quality of the school that he or she chooses: there are no figures regarding the acceptance of a school's graduates by the best universities nor national exams that can be used as school-selection criteria for the children.

What is commonly said in Mexico is that the country does not spend enough. The bad news is that Mexico is in fact among the countries that have most increased spending since 2000. Mexico's lag is not fundamentally a problem of money. Although Mexico is one of the OECD countries that spends the least per student, due in part to the fact that it is also the second-to-poorest after Turkey, its spending is comparable to that of the Slovak Republic, where students' achievement in mathematics is more than 100 percent higher than Mexico's. Thus, Mexico, to-gether with the United States, Greece, Portugal, Norway, and Italy, is one of the countries that obtain the least results in terms of the resources invested.

For many years, the only thing that mattered was to increase the coverage. This led to a huge national effort to provide education to a growing society. It was no small effort. Yet Mexico has still not achieved the desired coverage for secondary school. In addition, having a diploma in itself posed problems for efforts to improve the quality of schools. Having a diploma paid off. Its quality did not seem to matter much.

The authorities bear primary responsibility for this poor performance and should engage in a process of analysis and reform. However, it is not easy to deter-mine specific responsibilities. PISA is not an assessment of what the students learned in the previous school year, nor even in all the years of secondary education. It is an indication of the learning that has occurred since birth. The results for a country in the PISA project depend on the quality of the care and the stimuli pro-vided to a child during his or her childhood and in preschool years, as well as on the learning opportunities both at school and at home during the primary- and second-ary-education years (OECD, 2003b). Students the project assessed had spent at least nine years in the educational system (see fig. 18.15).

8. Sketching out the Fiscal-Violence Map

The sectors that do not use the basic services have had the political clout to press for greater social spending, in relative terms, on nonbasic education or special-ized health care even before basic educational and health services have been cov-

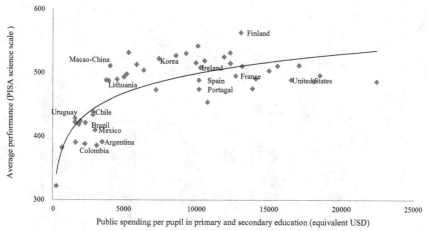

Figure 18.15 Performance in science in terms of expenditure (OECD, PISA, 2006).
Source: OECD Development Centre calculations based on OECD, PISA 2006 Science Competences for Tomorrow's World (Paris: OECD, 2007), and UNESCO, Institute for Statistics Database, in OECD (2008).

ered (Scott 2002, 20). Looking at the distribution of social spending is therefore one way get an approximation of fiscal violence. Distribution that is of relatively more benefit to low-income groups (as in Chile) tends to indicate less fiscal violence in the system. In Latin America, except for Chile, social spending tends, however, to be equally distributed among the different income groups (see figs. 18.16–18).

The data we have for Mexico on the incidence of public spending show a large number of very regressive items. Although total spending in education is mildly

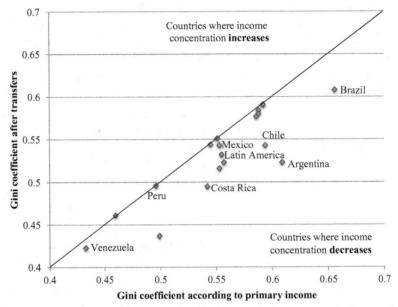

Figure 18.16 Gini coefficient in household income in Latin America before and after transfers, 2006–2008.
Source: Chapter 2 in ECLAC (2009, fig. 2.10).

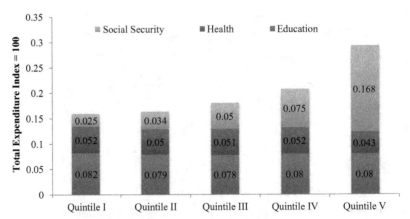

Figure 18.17 Transfer-spending impact in primary income in Latin America.
Source: ECLAC (2005).

progressive, in higher education it is highly regressive (see table 18.8). The highest regressivity in spending, though, can be seen in other items (tables 18.9–10). For instance, in pensions—for which there are problems in their calculation—spending for federal-government workers is highly regressive (CEDI 2006). Although in ag-

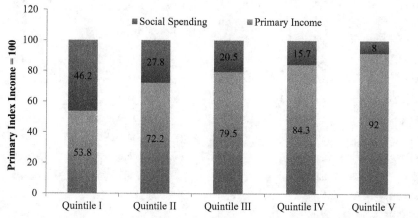

Figure 18.18 Social spending impact distribution on income per quintile in Latin America.

Source: ECLAC (2005, 22).

Table 18.8. Public-Spending Distribution in Education in Mexico, 2008

		Basic			Medium-Higher		
	Total	Preprimary	Primary	Secondary	Bachelor's	Technical	Higher
Decile							
1 (%)	16.4	20.6	19.3	16.3	9.7	4.8	2.6
2 (%)	14.3	15.8	16.2	14.8	10.5	6.5	0.6
3 (%)	12.8	13.2	14.1	12.5	11.7	7.5	0.2
4 (%)	10.9	10.5	11.1	11.2	11.5	9.4	5.0
5 (%)	9.9	11.2	9.5	9.0	11.1	10.6	5.8
6 (%)	9.3	7.5	8.2	9.6	11.3	13.7	11.8
7 (%)	8.2	7.2	6.6	8.6	11.2	12.2	18.0
8 (%)	7.5	5.6	6.6	6.8	9.6	13.1	19.7
9 (%)	6.2	5.4	4.9	6.4	7.5	11.9	20.8
10 (%)	4.6	3.1	3.5	4.8	5.9	10.3	15.5
Urban (%)	74.7	72.1	70.7	73.3	82.0	92.7	98.2
Rural (%)	25.3	28.0	29.3	26.7	18.0	7.3	11.1
Concentration coefficient							
National	-0.20	-0.28	-0.27	-0.20	-0.07	0.13	0.40
Urban	-0.11	-0.20	-0.18	-0.10	-0.01	0.15	0.40
Rural	-0.47	-0.49	-0.50	-0.46	-0.46	-0.12	0.56

Source: National Treasury estimations with data from ENIGH 2008 in SHCP (2010a, 33).

Table 18.9. Public-Spending Distribution in Health Services in Mexico, 2008

	Basic Care	Hospital Care	Pregnancy and Birth	Total
Decile				
1 (%)	7.4	2.1	5.4	6.9
2 (%)	9.0	3.9	7.5	8.3
3 (%)	9.6	7.7	9.4	9.4
4 (%)	9.7	6.3	13.6	9.7
5 (%)	9.7	6.8	14.2	9.8
6 (%)	12.1	7.4	11.8	11.8
7 (%)	11.4	17.1	12.0	11.8
8 (%)	12.1	12.3	14.7	12.3
9 (%)	10.3	19.8	6.6	10.6
10 (%)	8.8	16.6	4.7	9.0
Urban (%)	69.3	87.4	80.1	80.1
Rural (%)	17.8	12.6	19.9	19.9
Concentration coefficient				
National	0.04	0.30	0.01	0.05
Urban	0.12	0.34	0.06	0.13
Rural	-0.26	0.01	-0.23	-0.24

Source: National Treasury estimations with data from ENIGH 2008 in SHCP (2010a, 38).

gregate income spending there is a slight improvement with regard to inequality, it is more modest than one would expect for a country with the inequality of Mexico (CEDI 2006, 43).

Some governments, Brazil's in particular, under President Fernando Cardoso as well as under Lula, tried to check this trend by increasing the most progressive social spending. These changes were made possible thanks to the 1988 Constitution, which expanded the entitlements of social security and social assistance, significantly extending the types and value of social benefit and transfers. These new social benefits have been reflected in more income for the government and higher social spending, which is usually on primary education, health and redistribution, and conditional-transfer programs such as the Bolsa Familia, for instance. The number of families that benefited from the Bolsa Familia program thus increased from 3.6 million in 2003 to more than 12.4 million by March 2010. In addition, the minimum wage increased by 26 percent in real terms during the Lula government. At the same time, there was an attempt to contain the social spending most concentrated on the higher-income brackets, such as on higher education, unemployment compensation, subsidies for electric-power consumption, and pensions.

A first component in measuring fiscal violence would thus be to build a social-spending ratio, aggregating on one side the most progressive (primary education, health services, and transfer programs of the Bolsa Familia type) and on the other

Table 18.10. Public-Spending Distribution in Pensions in Mexico, 2008

	Population Entitled			Pensioners		
	IMSS	Federal ISSSTE	State ISSSTE	IMSS	Federal ISSSTE	State ISSSTE
Decile						
1 (%)	4.4	2.7	1.1	6.4	4.5	1.3
2 (%)	8.7	4.7	5.2	8.9	4.6	8.9
3 (%)	11.3	5.3	8.7	8.6	9.1	4.1
4 (%)	12.6	10.1	8.5	9.7	6.8	20.6
5 (%)	12.3	11.4	15.0	10.4	7.7	17.0
6 (%)	11.6	14.9	13.2	12.5	12.6	3.9
7 (%)	11.3	14.6	12.3	12.0	12.1	4.2
8 (%)	10.6	14.5	12.5	10.8	15.8	13.1
9 (%)	9.5	11.3	15.2	11.1	7.4	18.0
10 (%)	7.7	10.4	8.4	9.7	19.3	9.1
Urban	91.2	90.9	94.9	96.4	97.3	99.6
Rural	8.8	9.1	5.1	3.6	2.7	0.4
Concentration coefficient						
National	0.03	0.18	0.16	0.06	0.21	0.12
Urban	0.05	0.20	0.18	0.08	0.22	0.12
Rural	−0.22	−0.04	−0.05	−0.23	−0.12	

Source: National Treasury estimations with data from ENIGH 2008 in SHCP (2010a, 39).

the most regressive (higher education, unemployment compensation, subsidies for electric-power consumption, and pensions).

In Brazil, under the government of Lula, there was considerable will to deal with the problem of fiscal violence, as demonstrated by the tax reforms and even more by the pension reforms. The latter were of particular importance since spending on pensions will tend to increase in the future, which will lower even further the redistribution capacity of the taxing and spending system. In other words, fiscal violence also has a nonnegligible long-term component. Another way to approach fiscal violence could then consist of getting an "x-ray" of the existing asymmetries in the pension system: general and specific regimes, for public- and private-sector workers, and so on.

In the case of Brazil, this approach is particularly illustrative. The Brazilian social-security system has two basic pillars: one for workers in the private sector and another for civil servants (table 18.11). In addition, there are separate regimes for the federal government, states, and municipalities. It is therefore notable when Brazilian social-security accounts are examined that the deficit, although stabilized, still reached −5.3 of GDP in 2005. Equally notable is the fact that the lion's share of this deficit is explained by the public-sector regime (−3.4 percent of GDP), whereas the private-sector regime barely represents −1.9 percent,

Table 18.11. Public-Spending Distribution on Pensions in Brazil

	1999	2000	2001	2002	2003	2004	2005
Social security balance (% GDP)	-4.4	-4.6	-4.0	-4.2	-4.7	-4.5	-4.3
Private-sector regime	-1.0	-0.9	-1.1	-1.3	-1.7	-1.8	-1.9
Public-sector regime	-3.4	-3.7	-2.9	-3.0	-3.0	-2.7	-2.4
Revenue (% GDP)	5.8	5.7	6.7	6.9	6.6	6.9	7.3
Private-sector regime	5.0	5.1	5.2	5.3	5.2	5.3	5.6
Public-sector regime	0.8	0.7	1.5	1.6	1.4	1.6	1.7
Expenditure (% GDP)	10.2	10.4	10.7	11.2	11.2	11.4	11.6
Private-sector regime	6.0	6.0	6.3	6.5	6.9	7.1	7.5
Public-sector regime	4.2	4.4	4.4	4.6	4.4	4.3	4.1
Beneficiaries (millions)							
Private-sector regime	17.1	17.7	18.1	18.5	19.2	20.1	20.7
Public-sector regime	0.9	0.9	0.9	0.9	1.0	1.0	1.0

Source: Ministério de Seguridade Social, Ministério da Fazenda, Brazil, 2006.

which is almost half as much, although it covers 21 million of the 24.5 million officially registered members.[13] The asymmetry is partially a consequence of the expansion of entitlements that granted the status of civil servants to about 250,000 federal employees in 1988. This, in turn, created pension commitments at a much higher level than before, and it now points to a high level of fiscal violence in the country.

Moreover, an analysis of this violence on the expenditure side reveals that the better part of this spending is concentrated on the public-sector regime: 4.1 percent of GDP in 2005, with 7.5 percent of GDP for the private sector for five times more beneficiaries. In 2005, expenditure per capita on pensions in the public sector was 11.3 times greater than in the private sector. When these figures are compared with spending on transfer programs such as Bolsa Familia (0.4 percent of GDP), the need to make expenditure adjustments appears even more urgent.

In addition, and in spite of the reforms, there are other asymmetries: in the private sector the retirement age is 65 for men, 60 for women, while in the public sector until 2003, the retirement age was 53 for men and 48 for women. The reform undertaken by the Lula government attempted to reduce this asymmetry by raising the retirement age in the public sector for the newly retired, to 60 for men and 55 for women. Despite these efforts, a five-year asymmetry persists, whether for men or for women, among pensioners of the public sector and those of the private sector. This is not to mention the large proportion of the working population that simply has no access to pensions or social public goods, in that it works in the informal sector. The informal-economy sector is in fact somewhat more important in Brazil (37 percent of the total working-age population in 2000) than in countries like Chile.[14]

Other asymmetries can be added to these. For instance, there are special regimes for given categories of public servants, judges, or members of parliament. Teachers and professors can also retire at a younger age and after fewer years of contribution than in the other private sectors.

9. ITEMIZING FISCAL VIOLENCE: A FEW EXAMPLES

Examples of fiscal violence abound in both countries. In Mexico, an obvious instance of fiscal violence is at work at the Instituto Mexicano del Seguro Social (IMSS), the public institution responsible for the social security of workers in the private sector. The labor liabilities of IMSS workers, that is, the pensions of currently active workers plus those of already pensioned retired workers according to the standing collective labor contract, and not counting the meager existing reserves, are greater than the institute's assets. In other words, a set of private agents, the workers, have claims on the institute that amount to more than the worth of all of the latter's buildings and resources. This is revealed in the report that by law the IMSS authorities presented to Congress in March 2006.

The means became the end. IMSS workers, whose justification is to provide a service to the workers insured by the institute, are due a growing part of the institute's budget. Even after a long conflict that led to an agreement and the 2004 reform of their pension regime, on December 31, 2008, the 173,934 pensioned IMSS employees consumed 10 percent of the institute's income. By 2030, the projected 380,352 retirees will take 12.96 percent of this income (IMSS 2008). This is an improvement from the regime's condition before the reform, but still a very poor one, since the reform does not apply to any of the rights of the workers hired before the end of 2004, only to those hired after the law was enacted.

This is the result of years of generosity in which budgetary fantasy was the rule. To avoid problems, every two years, the IMSS authorities accepted better retirement conditions to include in the collective labor contract, much better than the best ones in the rest of the economy, but did not establish the proper reserves to fund them. In this budgetary Disneyland, IMSS female workers can retire after 27 years of service and male ones after 28. There is no minimum retirement age. If workers begin working at the Institute at age 20, they can retire at 48. If they then live to be more than 76, they will have received pension benefits for longer than they received wages for their work. IMSS workers retire on average at 53, and one-third of them retire before they are 50.

Their situation stands in sharp contrast with that of the workers affiliated to the Institute, who can only claim their pension when they are 60 for an old age unemployment pension, or 65 in the event of an old age pension without having paid enough into it to actually finance it. In addition, pensions are 36 percent higher than the average wage and benefits of active workers as a result of a variety of generous moves, such as housing aid to pay rent, seniority bonuses, and aid to buy books, benefits not granted to the rest of the economy. Pensions are adjusted to inflation (IMSS 2008, 210).

Employment is guaranteed. Firing a unionized IMSS worker is practically impossible. The intensity of the work therefore depends mostly on the employee's motivation. Some are excellent and have a sense of duty. This is unfortunately not the case for the majority. Such is human nature. The word "privilege" comes from Latin and refers to private law, the law for a group as opposed to general interest. A restricted group of workers, whose justification is the social security of all affiliates and who are supported by the rest of the workers through their contributions, has privileged conditions. It has the privilege of a special regime although its work is not qualitatively different.

These promises could not be paid by the institution directly but instead of leading to bankruptcy, they were covered by a subsidy because the IMSS is a public institution. Paying into the IMSS is mandatory for all private-sector workers, which means that the latter cannot take their contributions elsewhere, no matter how poor the quality of the IMSS and no matter that the institution has to subsidize the pensions of IMSS employees, thus diverting resources that could be use to provide better medical services. You either have to put up with the bad service, become part of the informal economy, break the law, or pay your contribution and find solutions elsewhere, all for the benefit of the IMSS, which takes money and gives nothing in exchange.

Other public enterprises have similar privileges. These enterprises do not go bankrupt, some have very good income and well-organized workers, they have in the past been strong supporters of the Partido Revolucionario Institucional (PRI) governments, and they have been used for purposes other than those they are assigned, mainly during election periods. For this reason, in the whole of the public sector—in the Instituto de Seguridad y Servicios Sociales de los Trabajadores del Estado (Institute of Social Security and Services for State Workers, or ISSSTE) and other public enterprises—pensions are much better than those in the private sector and not properly funded. If ISSSTE were to reserve funds for its current labor liabilities, that is to say if it were to set aside the necessary resources to be able in the future to pay for today's commitments without using resources from other sources, it would require about 300 billion Mexican pesos. For the oil enterprise, Petróleos Mexicanos (PEMEX), this figure runs close to 318 billion (CEFP 2005b) and for the Comisión Federal de Electricidad (CFE), 173 billion.[15]

The public electricity utility, Luz y Fuerza del Centro (LyFC), was probably the institution where this condition was the most blatant. Its retirement age was so low that it has one pensioner for every two active workers. In 2006, LyFC paid out 8.693 billion Mexican pesos in pensions, 3.69 billion pesos more than what it spent on its physical-investment program (SCHP 2006). Added to this is the rigidity of the collective labor contract. The productivity of a worker at CFE, the other and largest government electricity utility, is up to five times greater than that of a worker at

LyFC. LyFC was liquidated on October 11, 2009, at a great fiscal cost, as severance payments to workers were high by Mexican standards, but a major source of fiscal violence was finally confronted.

Users have to put up with a number of the enterprise's inefficiencies, for instance regarding their payment or their request to be connected to the power grid. They do not, however, directly cover the cost of the enterprise's pensions or operational problems (fig. 18.19). Many consumers are able to take advantage of the situation by being connected to the power grid without paying a cent; others simply do not pay but are not disconnected. The enterprise's problems are not actually paid for by those who cause them. Their cost is instead widely diluted. Luz y Fuerza receives a colossal transfer from the federal government—from everyone's taxes. In 2008, it collected over 40 billion Mexican pesos (CEFP 2005a, 8), enough to finance the entire budgets of UNAM and UAM, the two main public universities in Mexico City. This sum is more than three times larger than the whole of property taxes paid in Mexico City. Residents of the central region of Mexico do not pay low electricity rates. In other parts of the world, such rates allow enterprises to make money and they even pay taxes.

In the federal government's budget for 2005, pension spending was set out to amount to 2.7 percent of GDP, just above total public-investment expenditure (CEFP 2010, 57, table 3). Mexico is covering the past and dismissing the future. A young and lagging country such as Mexico cannot afford this luxury, but the interest groups defending the past are much more powerful that those standing up for the future and the former always prevail, which is not very promising for the future.

Almost all countries are facing the same problem: what can be done about pension systems that were calculated in terms of a life expectancy that was much shorter that it has actually become? Workers with the right to a retirement pension see this income as a sort of personal property and they will defend it to the

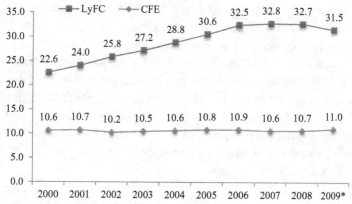

Figure 18.19 Total energy losses, CFE and LyFC (% of total). *Note*: "Energy losses" refers to percentage of energy given to the firm for its distribution that is lost because of technical problems or administrative shortcomings.

Source: Secretaría de Energía, Indicadores de CFE y LyFC (Mexico City: SENER, 2009).

hilt. Any change will be perceived as a form of expropriation. Fortunately for all, people today can live longer than was expected just a few decades ago. Unfortunately for all, the necessary resources to pay for those extra years are not there. There are only two ways out. One is to get taxpayers to cover the new costs and the other is to redesign the pension systems, either by pushing up the retirement age or by claiming the greater amounts needed to cover the right to retire at the current age.

In Brazil and in Mexico, broad and generous rights are concentrated on a relatively small group: public employees. The bulk of citizens have absolutely no access to social security because they work in the informal sector. Others have a limited access to it because they work in the private sector. Moreover, given that public employees are so expensive, it is very costly to expand social services, and they also have multiple labor-protection agreements and cannot easily be laid off for bad performance, delivering quality services is very difficult.

10. A Possible Solution: Fiscal and Civil Institutionality

Mapping fiscal violence is still a pending task in Latin America. This violence is probably greater in states where confiscation of the oil rent, for instance, can be systematic and widespread, favoring a minority,[16] but fiscal violence is practiced in all states. An indicator of this violence remains to be designed and developed. Taking up this challenge is in fact indispensable, as much for economic reasons as for political ones.

This imperative is of particular significance in emerging democracies. In a democracy, charging taxes is always a complicated task. The foundation of democratic legitimacy is fiscal legitimacy. Reaching a fiscal balance, a fiscal pact in keeping with a social pact and vice versa, is especially difficult in contexts where suspicion of corruption, evasion, and inefficiency abounds. Citizens are not always aware of the benefits of public spending in that part of it is diffuse, but they often definitely perceive the cost of paying taxes, especially direct taxes (Downs 1960). Indirect taxes, the VAT in particular, are more obscure, but when they are increased or their base is enlarged, they become very visible politically. If suspicion of evasion, corruption, or inefficiency is added to these asymmetries, democratic and fiscal legitimacy becomes even more difficult to achieve.

To attenuate the sharpness of these tensions, expenditure needs to be supported by appropriate representation mechanisms, clarity and quality. The old "no taxation without representation" motto is not enough. We have to make sure that representation makes transparency and accountability in the use of public resources mandatory. Without such mechanisms, citizens will be even less willing to pay higher taxes and the state's capacity for delivering on social claims will be very limited, with the added risk of being unable to accommodate the social pressures from institutions.

In the case of countries like Brazil and Mexico, a historical opacity—which is changing (see the tables in the appendix)—and some excess in public spending have led to this kind of fiscal violence, which has weakened the core pact of any fiscal policy: taxes are justified by spending on collective benefits. Insofar as these benefits need to be clear and shared, raising government revenue is very difficult when failings are as blatant as they are in these two countries.

A way to contain these failings is to strengthen fiscal institutions. Strengthening the budgetary institutions (which discuss the budget, make decisions on it, and control it), as well as of those in charge of tax collection and those in charge of overseeing expenditure, has been particularly intense in the last decade. National governments and international institutions have in fact combined their efforts in this direction. Pension systems and monetary institutions, which also have an impact on fiscal policy, have also experienced particular strengthening in the past decade.

The two countries have implemented numerical restrictions by means of fiscal-responsibility laws (as in Brazil during Cardoso's second term),[17] stabilization funds (as in Mexico in 1998, although by law the fund is very limited with regard to the magnitude of the country's oil income), single treasury accounts to improve control over fiscal resources and expenditure oversight, fiscal-transparency rules that have established free access to information on fiscal results and its dissemination, and others. Brazil and Mexico have thus introduced multiannual fiscal frameworks and limits on spending and debt (Mexico has also imposed restrictions on the deficit). In both countries, a rule has been imposed according to which the legislature can increase spending only if it identifies a new source to finance it.[18] They have also imposed spending limits on ministries. In both countries, the minister of finances now also has the last word in negotiations with the cabinet. Both now have single accounts (Brazil was in fact the pioneer in Latin America in establishing a single treasury account in 1986). Both have also voted in fiscal-transparency laws. Progress in both countries has been remarkable, as shown by the fiscal balances and substantial public-debt reductions they have achieved.

Notwithstanding, these efforts have not rid them of the termites, nor of the fiscal violence that we have pointed out: this is an especially difficult task, as the various unsuccessful attempts at tax reform and at reforming the public-sector pension system during the six-year term of the Vicente Fox government in Mexico show, as do the difficulties in passing reform in this area during the Lula government in Brazil in recent years.

Maintaining this fiscal-reinforcement effort is therefore crucial. A survey by Filc and Scartascini (2007) shows in fact that fiscal results tend to improve with the quality of the fiscal institutions (fig. 18.20). In countries where the budgetary institutions are rated better, the primary fiscal deficit, before interests are paid, is lower by 2.5 percentage points of GDP than in countries with fiscal institutions of poorer quality. In addition, the countries with the better ratings have fiscal surpluses of an average of 0.8 percent of GDP, whereas the countries with the poorer ratings have

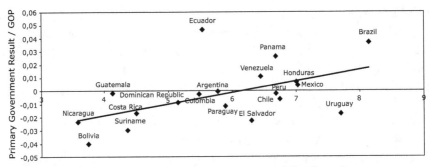

Figure 18.20 Budgetary institutions and fiscal results.
Source: Based on figure 5.2 in Filc and Scartascini (2007).

fiscal deficits of an average of 1.5 percent of GDP. Moving from the group with the poorer institutions to the group with the better institutions carries a fiscal impact of 2 percent of GDP.[19]

Other work has also shown the importance of the quality of procedures in terms of external audit systems. The better they are rated, that is, the higher the quality of the external fiscal audit institutions, the less corruption and greater fiscal transparency exist (C. Santiso 2006; for the rankings, see Lavielle, Pérez, and Hofbauer 2003). This model says little, however, of the work of the termites and of fiscal violence, both of which are legal expressions of the power of certain groups.

Institutional improvement is therefore of the essence, but not enough, as these studies also highlight: a good rating for budgetary institutions does not guarantee success. Policy incentives have a key role to play (institutions that seem to be well designed can also alter over time).[20] Put differently, although institutions can contain the damage by delimiting the termites' feeding area, this neither neutralizes nor destroys the bugs' activity. Political will is critical to ending fiscal violence, and to be able to do so, the latter needs to be clearly documented and shown not to persist in other areas besides budgetary institutions. Even if the technical design of reform is perfectly suitable, its implementation depends on political efforts (for emerging countries, see Kopits 2004). These efforts can be amplified by increasing the transparency of the processes: for their formulation, their approval, their execution, and their oversight. Three possible allies could step up for this: legislatures, the media, and civil society in general.

The first have been for the most part kept away from the fiscal processes. They tend to be short on the technical skills and the political incentives to assume a responsible role in public finances (Alesina and Perotti 1995, 1996). The fiscal indiscipline that has been practiced in the past, especially in Latin America, has had an extreme political cost, which political leaders, and even legislators, are not willing to forget, and they will try to avoid taking that risk again. In fact, tax reforms carried out in the region have largely tried to isolate economic-governance institutions from political influence, whether from central banks, fiscal agencies, or economy and treasury ministries, in order to reduce the probability of fiscal crises of the kind experienced in the past.

Attention now needs to be drawn to the role that legislatures can play in the fiscal processes, especially in the area of an effective control of expenditure (Santiso 2005). This requires strengthening the technical capacities of legislatures so they can perform an independent analysis of budget execution. The majority of legislatures in Latin America have less than five experts serving the committees dealing with budget-related issues (which is comparable to 50 percent of the countries surveyed by the OECD).[21] Mexico and Chile's legislatures both have more than five. The Brazilian Congress also has relatively more resources (there are a total of about 200 experts working for Congress on all issues, which is the largest expertise capacity in a Latin American legislature).

The Mexican Congress has professionals in this area, but there are none in Argentina's, Bolivia's, Colombia's, or Uruguay's. In Brazil, Congress's Joint Committee on Plans, Public Budgets, and Auditing has 35 professionals on staff (OECD 2003a). As for Chile, in 2003 it began to set up a similar entity (with three professionals) as part of a broader reform process intended to amplify legislative powers (OECD 2004). Mexico also established a comparable entity in 1998 (Centro de Estudios en Finanzas Públicas) in the lower chamber, intended to complete the legislative library's existing research and analysis service, the Servicio de Investigación y Análisis, as well as the Senate's legislative research institute, the Instituto de Investigaciones Legislativas del Senado de la República, set up in 1985. Both, however, still lack the institutional strength to provide high-quality and influential information.

Venezuela's attempts to consolidate comparable entities, partly with support from the Inter-American Development Bank,[22] illustrates the key role played by political will in this area (Monaldi et al. 2005). These are all, however, in-house resources processing internal reports and information, generally lacking in media visibility. Once again, the essence here lies much more in political will than in technical design.[23]

All in all, failing greater openness of these procedures to citizen participation, the political authorities can always override the technicians' recommendations. Recent experience in Mexico indicates that when a special-interest group is well organized, its veto power makes it possible to maintain the fiscal violence of the past and, when it is particularly strong, it succeeds in obtaining favorable legal reforms with no previous technical discussion, which has been the case for the media conglomerate Televisa, which drafted a custom-made law for itself and got it approved.

To improve accountability, what is also needed is an electoral system that requires legislators to be more responsible for what they approve. In Mexico, this objective is blocked by the law preventing members of the legislature from seeking reelection for successive terms. This is supported by the political parties' wish to maintain their control over legislators, which comes precisely from the fact that members of lower house will have to look for work in three years and senators in six.

Legislators, along with the media and civil society in general, could also be allies, although this is problematic. To make this happen, fiscal transparency is indispensable, with data and information widely available and also analyzed and debated. This in turn requires being able to rely on knowledge centers that are under official authority, so that the technical approach can be significantly reinforced with the support of think tanks and academic centers (Santiso and Whitehead 2006; also ch. 17 here). Just as important, then, is increasing the information and data available to think tanks so they can accomplish their analytical work. A particularly interesting institution in this sense, which deserves greater attention, is the Mexican federal institute for access to information, the Instituto Federal de Acceso a Información. This experience could serve other countries as an example of a change in transparency, even though, as usually happens in the region, it involves new bureaucracy for a task that in other countries is already dealt with by existing bodies.

All of this, however, requires a much more professional media that would place greater importance on analysis than on sensationalist declarations. As Norbert Lechner found for Chile, people are getting tired of democracy. This dissatisfaction is highly related to the inability of political discourse to give sense and meaning to collective existence. The feeling of living day-to-day with no long-term perspectives, as if everything was a "matter of the moment," is not just the consequence of a democratization process that subjects policy to the rhythm of short-term election cycles (Lechner 2003). It is above all the result of the fact that "the culture disseminated by the media is devoid of historical context because it is focused exclusively on the current time" (Cruz 2002, 20). For the media, in sum, everything happens in an all-embracing present, in which the past that has been and the future that is not yet are boiled down to a single today in which they are blended indistinctly. Thus, "pressed to provide immediate answers, policy is bereft of any medium- or long-term strategy" (Lechner 2003, 63–64). By disregarding long-term content and wanting to offer quick results, by succumbing to the temptation to keep up with the accelerated pace that governs the media, the region's mediatized regimes end up only confusing their citizens.

Democracy does not solve problems. It probably even makes facing them more difficult. It is, however, supposed to give solutions legitimacy. This is why it is especially important that voters, the ultimate voice of any democracy, have a minimum understanding of their context and of the restrictions that define the margin in which their government can act. A society that cannot distinguish the desirable from the possible, that is not willing to accept the costs of what it most desires, is an adolescent society, one permanently dissatisfied with the democratization of its political system, as Brazil's, Mexico's, and so many others in Latin America seem to be.

Such societies, for which what is possible is not enough, which have not been socialized to Adam Michnik's (1997) "Beautiful Grey," engender a steadfast opposition that questions, no longer the immanent validity, but the minimal usefulness of a democratic regime. If by definition whatever rulers do they do poorly, what difference does it make whether citizens can elect them or not?

If there are magic solutions that offer not the possible but the ideal, if there is someone out there who can sweep away poverty, insecurity, and corruption without raising taxes, have stricter public-safety bodies, or apply the law across the board with no exceptions, then why not elect him or her? Sooner or later, voters end up convincing themselves that this can be the solution. The bad news is that those who are elected on a platform of those expectations or who try to meet them and either lead their country to disaster or fail to keep their promises because such promises cannot be kept end up generating even more disenchantment among the citizens. It is not only that reality is "bad," of course: it is that, in addition, citizens' expectations are not reasonable.

Michnik himself has suggested that the problem, at the end of the day, is one of learning, when he explains that during the Cold War everything was clear: friends and foes, good and evil, strikes and police brutality, choosing between angels and demons, between persecuted angels and demons in power. Today, Michnik argues, the angels are in power and we need to live without the demons, but how can we live without the demon of communism? (Michnik 1993, 58–59)

In the young democracies of Latin America, the media have yet to learn how to live without the demon of authoritarianism. This may be the reason that they insist on pursuing their ruthless fight against it, even though they are fighting against a corpse. This would not be a serious problem if in their vehemence they did not sacrifice rigor and by doing so, complicate the "internalization" of the democratic logic (sometimes you win, sometimes you lose; what comes within the possible is not the greatest goods, only the lesser evils) into the minds and habits of citizens.

11. CONCLUSIONS

With their vote and their consumption, societies stimulate certain types of behavior. The work of Eduardo Lora suggests that greater participation in elections requires greater public spending. Since all Latin American societies are highly unequal, average voters have an incentive to get others to pay more taxes to finance spending (Lora 2006), but the quality of the spending and its appropriation by all types of gluttons makes it more difficult to build a coalition that will push for higher taxes and redistributive social spending like the kind that allowed the construction of welfare states in western Europe.

For this reason, voters must now demand quality in spending, which is the only way the fiscal pact can be sustainable. Achieving greater efficiency in tax collection and in spending is indispensable in emerging democracies. Fiscal legitimacy is the key to democratic legitimacy (see in particular OECD 2008). If there is no change in how taxes are spent, collecting more alone will not significantly change the state's capacity for reversing the trends of poverty and inequality and generating the conditions for faster growth. It can even have negative effects by taking away from the private sector resources that it could allocate better and by further weakening government legitimacy in the eyes of citizens who do not see the benefits of their taxes. The challenge is to reach a fiscal balance based on quality spending that will warrant increasing public revenue further in order to progressively address the many gaps that exist in the results of spending.

The problem is particularly complex because, as Lora shows in his work for the seminar on Economic Policies for a New Social Pact in Latin America (CIDOB Foundation, Barcelona, Oct. 6–7, 2006), social expenditure by Latin American governments is greater than that of developed countries when they had a level of development similar to Latin America's today. This spending does not, however, seem to yield what it should, in terms of development or as a social-cohesion mechanism, because it tends to be appropriated by the bureaucracy that spends it and the best-organized groups that receive it (Lora 2006).

Greater social participation with more transparent institutions is a possible solution. Nonetheless, institutional improvement alone is insufficient if there is no political will. From this point of view, solving the problem of fiscal violence is a particularly delicate matter. Fiscal violence undermines democratic legitimacy itself. Exercising checks and balances, in particular in the oversight of the quality of spending, through legislatures, the media, and think tanks, is a possible solution.

This requires, however, being able to afford greater controlling power to legislatures, that is, greater human capital and technical rationality that can produce an independent analysis to enable legislators to exercise this control. It is just as important to endow countries with powerful think tanks, particularly in the area of fiscal policies, for their contribution to a critical analysis that can be used in public debates. In both cases, the media can also become allies by broadly circulating these processes.

There is no doubt that one of the keys is the existence of willful political leaders who can convince society that it is to everyone's benefit to put an end to arrangements that are of benefit to just a few. Citizens must also be able to become better organized and get more involved in the reform processes. Government can provide guidance, but in the end, the force must come from a society to whom the termites' action appears immoral, a society willing to take up the battle to stop being devoured.

All of this implies increasing and consolidating transparency, and in particular facilitating access to public data and information. This means tax administrations must have the necessary resources to be able to produce the data and information. Above all, what is needed are agencies that will generate transparency.

A concrete contribution to these efforts could be to develop a fiscal-violence index. As we noted, fiscal violence has yet to be mapped. What we present here is an outline that needs to be developed and systematized.

Appendix 18.1. Financial Situation of the Federal Public Sectors in Mexico and Brazil Mexico, including State Owned Enterprises, 1990–2009 (as % of GDP)

	1990	1991	1992	1993	1994	1995	1996	1997	1998	1999	2000	2001	2002	2003	2004	2005	2006	2007	2008	2009
A. Total Public Revenue	23.3	24.6	24	21.1	21	20.7	20.9	21.1	18.5	18.9	19.6	20	20.2	21.2	20.7	21.1	21.9	22.2	23.7	23.8
Federal Government	14.7	17.3	17.1	14.2	14.1	13.9	14.2	14.6	12.9	13.4	14.4	14.7	14.4	15	14.8	15.3	15.1	15.3	17	16.9
Tax-revenue	9.8	9.8	10.3	10.4	10.3	8.4	8.1	9	9.6	10.3	9.7	10.3	10.6	10.1	9	8.8	8.6	9	8.2	9.6
ISR-IETU-IDE	4.1	4.2	4.7	5	4.7	3.7	3.5	3.9	4	4.3	4.3	4.5	4.6	4.5	4	4.2	4.3	4.7	5.2	5
IVA	3.3	3.1	2.5	2.4	2.5	2.6	2.6	2.8	2.8	3	3.1	3.3	3.2	3.4	3.3	3.5	3.7	3.7	3.8	3.4
IEPS[a]	1.4	1.2	1.5	1.4	1.8	1.2	1.1	1.3	1.8	2.1	1.4	1.7	2	1.6	1	0.5	-0.1	-0.1	-1.4	0.4
Import taxes	0.8	1	1	0.9	0.8	0.6	0.5	0.5	0.5	0.5	0.5	0.5	0.4	0.4	0.3	0.3	0.3	0.3	0.3	0.4
Tax on Oil surplus	n.s.	na	na	na	na	na	na	na	na	na	na	na	na	na	na	0	0	0	0	0.3
Other taxes	0.3	0.3	0.6	0.6	0.5	0.4	0.4	0.5	0.4	0.4	0.3	0.3	0.4	0.4	0.3	0.3	0.3	0.3	0.3	0.4
Non-tax revenue	4.9	7.5	6.8	3.8	3.8	5.4	6	5.6	3.3	3	4.8	4.5	3.8	4.8	5.8	6.5	6.5	6.3	8.7	7.4
Oil-based revenue	3.2	3	2.8	2.5	2	3.6	4	3.7	2.1	1.9	3.7	3	2.1	3.5	4.6	5.7	5.7	4.9	7.5	4.1
Public enterprises and entities	8.6	7.2	6.8	6.9	6.8	6.9	6.7	6.5	5.6	5.6	5.2	5.2	5.8	6.2	5.9	5.8	6.8	6.9	6.7	6.9
PEMEX	3.2	2.4	2.1	2	2	2.4	2.6	2.4	1.9	2	1.7	1.6	2.2	2.3	2.2	2	3.1	3.4	3	3.2
B. Net Expenditure	25.3	22	20.2	20.5	20.9	20.9	21	21.6	19.7	20	20.6	20.6	21.3	21.8	20.9	21.2	21.8	22.2	23.8	26.1
Planned	14	13.9	13.9	14.7	15.6	14	14.2	14.7	14.1	13.9	14.1	14.5	15.4	16.1	15.4	15.8	16	17	18.3	20.6
Current	10.6	10.5	10.5	11.8	12.3	11.1	10.9	11.6	11.3	11.4	11.7	12.2	12.6	13.5	12.4	12.9	12.9	13.3	13.9	15.5
Personnel Expenditure[1]	4.1	4.3	4.6	5.2	5.5	5.8	5.7	6.2	6.3	6.7	6.5	6.6	6.7	6.7	6	6	5.9	5.8	5.9	6.5

(continued)

Mexico, including State Owned Enterprises, 1990–2009 (as % of GDP) *(continued)*

	1990	1991	1992	1993	1994	1995	1996	1997	1998	1999	2000	2001	2002	2003	2004	2005	2006	2007	2008	2009
Other	5.2	4.5	4.3	4.5	4.4	4.1	4.1	4	3.5	3.2	3.6	3.6	3.8	4.5	4.1	4.5	4.7	5.2	5.3	5.9
Subsidies and transfers	1.2	1.6	1.6	2.2	2.4	1.1	1.2	1.4	1.5	1.6	1.6	1.9	2	2.3	2.3	2.4	2.3	2.3	2.7	3.1
Expenditure in Capital	3.4	3.4	3.4	2.8	3.3	2.9	3.3	3.1	2.8	2.5	2.4	2.4	2.9	2.6	3	3	3.1	3.6	4.4	5.1
Not Planned programable	11.4	8.1	6.4	5.8	5.3	6.9	6.8	6.9	5.6	6	6.4	6.1	5.8	5.7	5.6	5.4	5.8	5.3	5.5	5.5
Financial Costs (interests and commissions)	8.3	4.7	3.3	2.4	2.1	4.2	4	3.7	2.6	3.3	3.3	3	2.6	2.5	2.4	2.3	2.4	2.1	1.9	2.2
Participations	2.6	2.6	2.7	2.7	2.7	2.4	2.6	2.7	2.7	2.8	3	3.1	3.1	3	2.8	3	3.2	3	3.5	3.2
Others	0.5	0.9	0.4	0.7	0.6	0.3	0.2	0.4	0.2	-0	0.1	0	0.1	0.2	0.3	0.1	0.2	0.1	0.1	0.1
C. Budgetary Balance (A - B)	-2	2.6	3.7	0.6	0	-0.2	-0.1	-0.6	-1.1	-1	-1	-0.6	-1.1	-0.6	-0.2	-0.1	0.1	0	-0.1	-2.3

¹ Includes expenditure by public entities under direct budgetary control, as well as transfers to states, municipalities and other public entities for other public entities for personal services.

* Includes IEPS on gasoline.

Note: Partial sums and variations may not coincide due to rounding of numbers.

ns: Insignificant

na: not available

NA: not applicable

Source: Secretaría de Hacienda y Crédito Público, *Estadísticas Oportunas de Finanzas Públicas.*

Brazil, 1997–2009 (as % of GDP)

	1990	1991	1992	1993	1994	1995	1996	1997	1998	1999	2000	2001	2002	2003	2004	2005	2006	2007	2008	2009
A. Total Public Revenue	23.3	24.6	24	21.1	21	20.7	20.9	21.1	18.5	18.9	19.6	20	20.2	21.2	20.7	21.1	21.9	22.2	23.7	23.8
Federal Government	14.7	17.3	17.1	14.2	14.1	13.9	14.2	14.6	12.9	13.4	14.4	14.7	14.4	15	14.8	15.3	15.1	15.3	17	16.9
Tax-revenue	9.8	9.8	10.3	10.4	10.3	8.4	8.1	9	9.6	10.3	9.7	10.3	10.6	10.1	9	8.8	8.6	9	8.2	9.6
ISR-IETU-IDE	4.1	4.2	4.7	5	4.7	3.7	3.5	3.9	4	4.3	4.3	4.5	4.6	4.5	4	4.2	4.3	4.7	5.2	5
IVA	3.3	3.1	2.5	2.4	2.5	2.6	2.6	2.8	2.8	3	3.1	3.3	3.2	3.4	3.3	3.5	3.7	3.7	3.8	3.4
IEPS*	1.4	1.2	1.5	1.4	1.8	1.2	1.1	1.3	1.8	2.1	1.4	1.7	2	1.6	1	0.5	-0.1	-0.1	-1.4	0.4
Import taxes	0.8	1	1	0.9	0.8	0.6	0.5	0.5	0.5	0.5	0.5	0.5	0.4	0.4	0.3	0.3	0.3	0.3	0.3	0.3
Tax on Oil surplus	n.s.	na	na	na	na	na	na	na	na	na	na	na	na	na	na	0	0	0	0	0
Other taxes	0.3	0.3	0.6	0.6	0.5	0.4	0.4	0.5	0.4	0.4	0.3	0.3	0.4	0.4	0.3	0.3	0.3	0.3	0.3	0.4
Non-tax revenue	4.9	7.5	6.8	3.8	3.8	5.4	6	5.6	3.3	3	4.8	4.5	3.8	4.8	5.8	6.5	6.5	6.3	8.7	7.4
Oil-based revenue	3.2	3	2.8	2.5	2	3.6	4	3.7	2.1	1.9	3.7	3	2.1	3.5	4.6	5.7	5.7	4.9	7.5	4.1
Public enterprises and entities	8.6	7.2	6.8	6.9	6.8	6.9	6.7	6.5	5.6	5.6	5.2	5.2	5.8	6.2	5.9	5.8	6.8	6.9	6.7	6.9
PEMEX	3.2	2.4	2.1	2	2	2.4	2.6	2.4	1.9	2	1.7	1.6	2.2	2.3	2.2	2	3.1	3.4	3	3.2
B. Net Expenditure	25.3	22	20.2	20.5	20.9	20.9	21	21.6	19.7	20	20.6	20.6	21.3	21.8	20.9	21.2	21.8	22.2	23.8	26.1
Planned	14	13.9	13.9	14.7	15.6	14	14.2	14.7	14.1	13.9	14.1	14.5	15.4	16.1	15.4	15.8	16	17	18.3	20.6
Current	10.6	10.5	10.5	11.8	12.3	11.1	10.9	11.6	11.3	11.4	11.7	12.2	12.6	13.5	12.4	12.9	12.9	13.3	13.9	15.5
Personnel Expenditure[1]	4.1	4.3	4.6	5.2	5.5	5.8	5.7	6.2	6.3	6.7	6.5	6.6	6.7	6.7	6	6	5.9	5.8	5.9	6.5
Other	5.2	4.5	4.3	4.5	4.4	4.1	4.1	4	3.5	3.2	3.6	3.6	3.8	4.5	4.1	4.5	4.7	5.2	5.3	5.9

(continued)

495

Brazil, 1997–2009 (as % of GDP) (continued)

	1990	1991	1992	1993	1994	1995	1996	1997	1998	1999	2000	2001	2002	2003	2004	2005	2006	2007	2008	2009
Subsidies and transfers	1.2	1.6	1.6	2.2	2.4	1.1	1.2	1.4	1.5	1.6	1.6	1.9	2	2.3	2.3	2.4	2.3	2.3	2.7	3.1
Expenditure in Capital	3.4	3.4	3.4	2.8	3.3	2.9	3.3	3.1	2.8	2.5	2.4	2.4	2.9	2.6	3	3	3.1	3.6	4.4	5.1
Not Planned programable	11.4	8.1	6.4	5.8	5.3	6.9	6.8	6.9	5.6	6	6.4	6.1	5.8	5.7	5.6	5.4	5.8	5.3	5.5	5.5
Financial Costs (interests and commissions)	8.3	4.7	3.3	2.4	2.1	4.2	4	3.7	2.6	3.3	3.3	3	2.6	2.5	2.4	2.3	2.4	2.1	1.9	2.2
Participations	2.6	2.6	2.7	2.7	2.7	2.4	2.6	2.7	2.7	2.8	3	3.1	3.1	3	2.8	3	3.2	3	3.5	3.2
Others	0.5	0.9	0.4	0.7	0.6	0.3	0.2	0.4	0.2	-0	0.1	0	0.1	0.2	0.3	0.1	0.2	0.1	0.1	0.1
C. Budgetary Balance (A - B)	-2	2.6	3.7	0.6	0	-0.2	-0.1	-0.6	-1.1	-1	-1	-0.6	-1.1	-0.6	-0.2	-0.1	0.1	0	-0.1	-2.3

(1) Only Central Government Reveneue, does not indude State or Municpal Revenue

(2) These are also Social Contributions

Source: Ministerio da Fazenda, Tesuoro Nacional,Central Government Primary Result since 1997 (available at http://www.stn.fazenda.gov.br/estatistica/est_resultado.asp).

NOTES

Carlos Elizondo was posted as permanent representative of Mexico to the OECD until Nov. 15, 2006, after which he returned to being professor at the Centro de Investigación y Docencia Económicas in Mexico. His e-mail address is carlos.elizondo@cide.edu. Javier Santiso is professor of economics at ESADE Business School in Madrid. He was previously director and chief economist of the OECD Development Centre. His e-mail address is Javier.santiso@esade.edu. We thank Rolando Avendaño, economist at the OECD Development Centre and PhD student at PSE (DELTA/ENS/EHESS), for his support in this research. We also thank Eduardo Lora, Germán Ríos, Juan Antonio Rodríguez, José Luis Machinea, Carlos Santiso, and John Scott for the documents and data they provided. All opinions, errors, or omissions in this work are the sole responsibility of the authors and do not reflect the opinions of the OECD or the OECD Development Centre.

1. New Spain collected more than it spent. This was due not only to the wealth of its mines but also to the development of a remarkable extractive capacity imposed on New Spain residents by a heavier tributary burden than that for most European countries. See Marichal (1999).

2. On the emergence of economic pragmatism in Latin America, see J. Santiso (2006).

3. Some of the inflation was contained, however, because energy prices were not adjusted to the changes in global prices.

4. For a broader evaluation of the fiscal effort in the region, see Lora and Cárdenas (2006).

5. On the concept of "fiscal space" (i.e., restrictions to public spending that prevent the country from raising productivity and generating future cost effectiveness), see Development Committee (2006).

6. In the 1990s, social spending rose from an average of $303 in 1990 to $458 in 1998 (1990 prices). According to the data from the Economic Commission for Latin America and the Caribbean we used, this level was subsequently maintained for the five following years.

7. For the governments of the OECD countries, see Alesina et al. (1998).

8. The frequency of fiscal crises does not seem to depend on the type of political system. Whether they were presidential or parliamentary, unified or fragmented, they showed similar frequencies. Reaction to the crises does vary, however: it is twice as intense in presidential systems as in parliamentary ones. Reduction of the fiscal deficit is also less important in election years.

9. The IADB's analytic effort is not new, as shown by the work of Ricardo Hausmann, then chief economist, and of economists such as Ernesto Stein, for instance. For an evaluation of this analytic effort, see Filc and Scartascini (2007).

10. From 1896 onward, the policy designed by José Yves Limantour began to generate surplus resources for government. In the fiscal year 1903–4, government revenues amounted to 86.5 million Mexican pesos, while expenditure increased to 83.5 million. It should be pointed out that in Limantour's period, the most important component of total government revenues was foreign-trade taxing, which represented on average 46 percent of the total between 1895 and 1910. See Sánchez (2000, 75–100).

11. As Thorp points out, only 8.2 percent of the U.S. population was illiterate in 1910, a little less than the 10.4 percent that Mexico would achieve by 1994.

12. The government always reports taxes on fuels as oil revenues. This is not correct, as it is simply one more consumption tax. It is calculated by subtracting the sale price of fuels in Mexico from the international one. Domestic prices have hardly changed—they remained below international ones for most of 2005 and 2006—so the tax figure was negative. An additional problem is that a high percentage of the oil income is extracted from PEMEX, which makes its investment program depend to a large degree on indebtedness, which in turn makes the real public deficit larger.

13. Estimates based on OECD (2006).

14. On the challenges of the Brazilian social-security and fiscal systems, see in particular Giambiagi and de Mello (2006). On the tax reforms undertaken, and in particular the fiscal-responsibility law, see also de Mello (2006) and de Mello and Moccero (2006).

15. This was the financial status of the CFE on Sept. 30, 2005.

16. In this sense, a particularly interesting case study in Latin America is that of Venezuela, as shown by Puente et al. (2007).

17. The Fiscal Responsibility Law in Brazil granted constitutional status to several expenditure rules and introduced new ones. Some examples are the restriction that caps personnel expenditures at 50 percent of net revenues for the federal government and 60 percent for subnational governments, the specification of funding for new expenditure commitments, or the prohibition of executives' committing expenditures that exceed one budgetary period after their last year in office. This law also includes contingency provisions and procedural requirements to assure fiscal governance, with the participation of several institutions, and rules to ensure fiscal transparency, like the publication of a monthly list of subnational governments that exceed the expenditure limit or even legal sanctions applicable to individuals, stipulated in the Public Finance Crimes Law of 2000.

18. Notwithstanding, Mexico continues to pass laws that induce costs without increasing tax collection. This gives rise to heated discussions in the legislature as to whether the cost of the new law is entirely covered or not, which disrupts the decision-making process. The latest approach is to set certain kinds of expenditure, such as that for education, as a percentage of GDP.

19. Fiscal-balance situations can also include termites and fiscal violence, but there is less fiscal violence and there is some quality in the public services.

20. Argentina in the 1990s had one of the highest reform rankings, for instance, but the rules changed, in particular, with the crisis of the 2000s. See Gadaño (2003).

21. OECD World Bank Budget Database.

22. On support of institutional bodies, the IADB's and the World Bank's in particular, to strengthen this type of fiscal institutionality, see C. Santiso (2006, 2004).

23. There has been some progress in this area, in particular in Brazil, where the federal bureau of general auditing issues preliminary reports on the fiscal state of the nation featured in the president's annual report to Congress.

REFERENCES

Aizenman, Joshua, and Yothin Jinarak. 2008. "The Collection Efficiency of the Value Added Tax: Theory and International Evidence." *Journal of International Trade & Economic Development* 17: 391–410

Alesina, Alberto, Silvia Aradagna, and Francesco Trebbi. 2006. "Who Adjusts and When? On the Political Economy of Reforms." NBER Working Paper No. 12049. National Bureau of Economic Research, Cambridge MA.

Alesina, Alberto, and Roberto Perotti. 1995. "The Political Economy of Budget Deficits." *IMF Staff Papers* 42:.

——— 1996. "Budget Institutions and Budget Deficits." NBER Working Paper No. 5556, National Bureau of Economic Research, Cambridge MA.

Alesina, Alberto, Roberto Perotti, José Tavares, Maurice Obstfeld, and Barry Eichengreen. 1998. "The Political Economy of Fiscal Adjustments." In *Brookings Papers on Economic Activity*, edited by George L. Perry and William C. Brainard, 197–266. Washington, DC: Brookings Institution.

Baer, Werner, and Antonio Fialho Galvao Jr. 2008. "Tax Burden, Government Expenditures and Income Distribution in Brazil," *Quarterly Review of Economics and Finance* 48: 345–58,

Bergman, Marcelo. 2009. *Tax Evasion and the Rule of Law in Latin America: The Political Culture of Cheating and Compliance in Argentina and Chile.* University Park: Pennsylvania State University Press.

Cárdenas, Mauricio, Eduardo Lora, and Valerie Mercer-Blackman. 2006. "The Policy Making Process of Tax Reform in Latin America." IADB Presentation P-445, Inter-American Development Bank, Washington, DC.

CEDI (Centro de Documentación e Información). 2006. *Distribución del pago de impuestos y recepción del gasto público por deciles de hogares y personas.* Mexico City: Instituto de Investigaciones Económicas, UNAM.

Centro de Estudios de Finanzas Públicas (CEFP). 2005a. *Balances Presupuestales de Empresas Paraestatales de Sector Energético y Seguridad Social 2004–2005.* Mexico City: Palacio Legislativo de San Lázaro.

———. 2005b. *Pasivo de Petróleos Mexicanos al 31 de marzo de 2005.* Mexico City: Palacio Legislativo de San Lázaro.

———. 2010. *Diagnóstico del Sistema Fiscal Mexicano.* Mexico City: CEPF.

Cheibub, José Antonio. 1998. "Political Regimes and the Extractive Capacity of Governments: Taxation in Democracies and Dictatorships." *World Politics* 50: 349–76.

Corporación Latinobarómetro. 2009. *Informe 2009.* Santiago: Corporación Latinobarómetro.

Cruz, Manuel, ed. 2002. *Hacia dónde va el pasado: El porvernir de la memoria en el mundo contemporáneo.* Barcelona: Paidós.

Development Committee (Joint Ministerial Committee of the Boards of Governors of the Bank and the Fund on the Transfer of Real Resources to Developing Countries). 2006. *Políticas fiscales para promover el crecimiento y el desarrollo: Informe provisional.* Washington, DC: International Monetary Fund and World Bank.

Downs, Anthony. 1960 "Why the Government Budget Is Too Small in a Democracy." *World Politics* 12(4): 541–63.

ECLAC (Economic Commission for Latin America and the Caribbean). 2005. *Panorama Social en América Latina 2005.* Santiago: ECLAC.

———. 2009. *Panorama Social en América Latina 2009.* Santiago: ECLAC.

Elizondo, Carlos, and Luis Manuel Pérez de Acha. 2006. "Separación de poderes y garantías individuales: La Suprema Corte y los derechos de los contribuyentes." *Cuestiones Constitucionales* 14: 91–130.

Filc, Gabriel, and Carlos Scartascini. 2007. "Budgetary Institutions." In *The State of the Reforms of the State in Latin America*, edited by Eduardo Lora, 157–84. Washington, DC: Inter-American Development Bank.

Gadaño, Nicolas. 2003. "Rompiendo las reglas: Argentina y la ley de responsabilidad fiscal." *Desarrollo Económico* 43(179): 231–63.

Giambiagi, Fabio, and Luiz de Mello. 2006. "Social Security Reform in Brazil: Remaining Challenges." OECD Economics Department Working Paper No. 534, Paris: Organisation for Economic Co-operation and Development.

IADB (Inter-American Development Bank). 2006. *The Politics of Policies: Economic and Social Progress in Latin America*. Washington, DC: IADB.

IMSS (Instituto Mexicano del Seguro Social). 2008. *Report to the Federal Executive and Congress of the Union on the Financial Situation and the Risks of the Instituto Mexicano del Seguro Social, 2008–2009*. Mexico City: IMSS.

Kenny, Lawrence W., and Stanley Winer. 2001. *Tax Systems in the World: An Empirical Investigation into the Importance of Tax Bases, Collection Costs, and Political Regime*. Gainesville: University of Florida; Ottawa: Carleton University.

Kopits, George, ed. 2004. *Rules-Based Fiscal Policy in Emerging Markets: Background, Analysis and Prospects*. London: Palgrave MacMillan.

Lavielle, Briseida, Mariana Pérez, and Helena Hofbauer. 2003. *Latin America Index of Budget Transparency*, Washington, DC: International Budget Project.

Lechner, Norbert. 2003. "¿Cómo reconstruimos un nosotros?" *Metapolítica* 29: 52–67.

Lora, Eduardo. 2001a. "El futuro de los pactos fiscales en América Latina." Paper presented at seminar on "Políticas Económicas para un Nuevo Pacto Social en América Latina" at the Economic Forum of the Ibero-American Summit, Barcelona, Oct. 6–7.

———. 2001b. "Structural Reforms in Latin America: What Has Been Reformed and How to Measure It." IADB Working Paper No. 466, Research Department, Inter-American Development Bank, Washington, DC.

———, ed. 2006. *El estado de las reformas*. Washington, DC: Inter-American Development Bank.

Lora, Eduardo, and Mauricio Cárdenas. 2006. "La reforma de las instituciones fiscales en América Latina." Working Paper No. 559, Research Department, Inter-American Development Bank, Washington, DC, and Fedesarrollo, Bogota.

Lora, Eduardo, and Mauricio Olivera. 2006. "The Political Determinants of Taxation." Manuscript for the Latin American and Caribbean Economics Association. Inter-American Development Bank, Washington, DC.

Maddison, Angus. 2009. *Historical Statistics of The World Economy: 1–2008 AD*. Groningen, Netherlands: Groningen University.

Marichal, Carlos. 1999. *La bancarrota del virreinato: Nueva España y las finanzas del Imperio español, 1780–810*. Mexico City: Fondo de Cultura Económica.

Melo, Marcus, Carlos Pereira, and Soulo Souza. 2010. "The Political Economy of Fiscal Reform in Brazil: The Rationale for the Suboptimal Equilibrium." IADB Working Paper No. IDB-WP-117, Inter-American Development Bank, Washington, DC.

Mello, Luiz de. 2006. "Fiscal Responsibility Legislation and Fiscal Adjustment: The Case of Brazilian Local Governments." World Bank Policy Research Working Paper No. 3812, World Bank, Washington, DC.

Mello, Luiz de, and Diego Moccero. 2006. "Brazil's Fiscal Stance during 1995–2004: The Effect of Indebtedness on Fiscal Policy over the Business Cycle." OECD Economics Department Working Paper No. 485, Organisation for Economic Co-operation and Development, Paris.

Michnik, Adam. 1993. *La segunda revolución*. Mexico City: Siglo XXI.

————. 1997. "Grey Is Beautiful." *Dissent* 14–20.

Monaldi, Francisco, Rosa Amelia González, Richard Obuchi, and Michael Penfold. 2005. "Political Institutions, Policymaking Process and Policy Outcomes in Venezuela." Latin American Research Network Working Paper No. R-507, Inter-American Development Bank, Washington, DC.

OECD (Organisation for Economic Co-operation and Development). 2003a. *Budgeting in Brazil: OECD Working Party of Senior Budget Officials.* Paris: OECD.

————. 2003b. *PISA Report.* Paris: Programme for International Student Assessment, OECD.

————. 2004. *Budgeting in Chile:* OECD Working Party of Senior Budget Officials. Paris: OECD.

————. 2006. *Economic Survey of Brazil,* Paris, OECD.

————. 2008. *Latin American Economic Outlook 2009.* Paris: OECD.

Paz Sánchez, Fernando. 2000. *La política económica del Porfiriato.* Mexico City: Instituto Nacional de Estudios Históricos de la Revolución Mexicana-Secretaría de Gobernación.

Persson, Torsten, and Guido Tabellini. 2003. *The Economic Effects of Constitutions.* Cambridge, MA: MIT Press.

Puente, José Manuel, Abelardo Daza, Germán Ríos, and Alesia Rodríguez. 2007. "The Political Economy of Budget Process in the Andean Region: The Case of Venezuela." IADB Working Paper No. CS-103, Inter-American Development Bank, Washington, DC, January.

Santiso, Carlos. 2004. "Lending to Credibility: Inter-American Development Bank and Budget Oversight Institutions in Latin America." *ECLAC Review* 83: 171–90.

————. 2005. "Budget Institutions and Fiscal Responsibility: Parliaments and the Political Economy of the Budget Process in Latin America." Working Paper No. 37253, World Bank Institute, World Bank, Washington, DC.

————. 2006. "Banking on Accountability? Strengthening Budget Oversight and Public Auditing in Emerging Economies." *Public Budgeting and Finance* 66: 66–100.

Santiso, Javier. 2006. *Latin America's Political Economy of the Possible: Beyond Good Revolutionaries and Free Marketeers.* Cambridge MA: MIT Press.

Santiso, Javier, and Lawrence Whitehead. 2006. "Ulysses, the Sirens, and the Art of Navigation: Technical and Political Rationality in Latin America." Working Paper No. 256, OECD Development Centre, Paris.

SCHP (Secretaría de Hacieda y Crédito Público). 2006. *Flujo de Efectivo de las Entidades de Control Presupuestario Directo del Presupuesto de Egresos de la Federación 2006.* Mexico City: SHCP.

————. 2009. *Estadísticas Oportunas de Finanzas Públicas.* Mexico: SHCP.

————. 2010a. *Distribución del pago de impuestos y recepción del gasto público por deciles de hogares y personas. Resultados para 2008.* Mexico: SHCP.

————. 2010b. *Presupuesto de Gastos Fiscales 2009.* Mexico: SHCP.

Scott, John. 2002. "Public Spending and Inequality of Opportunities in Mexico: 1970–2000." CIDE Economics Division Working Paper No. 235, Centro de Investigación y Docencia Económicas (CIDE), Mexico City.

Stein, Ernesto, and Mariano Tommasi. 2005. *Democratic Institutions, Policymaking Process, and the Quality of Policies in Latin America.* Washington, DC: IADB.

Tanzi, Vito. 2001. "Globalization, Technological Developments, and the Work of Fiscal Termites." *Brooklyn Journal of International Law* 26(4): 1261–84.

Tanzi, Vito, and Howell H. Zee. 2000. "Tax Policy for Emerging Markets: Developing Countries." IMF Working Paper No. WP/00/35, Fiscal Affairs Department, International Monetary Fund, Washington, DC.
Thorp, Rosemary. 1998. *Progreso, pobreza y exclusión*. Washington, DC: Inter-American Development Bank.
World Bank. 2006. *Doing Business in Brazil*. Washington DC: International Finance Corporation, World Bank.

CHAPTER 19

THE POLITICAL ECONOMY OF PUBLIC SPENDING AND FISCAL DEFICITS: LESSONS FOR LATIN AMERICA

MARCELA ESLAVA

1. INTRODUCTION

Economists have long recognized that the standard textbook explanation for fiscal deficits—that governments run deficits to smooth government consumption over the cycle—cannot fully explain the dynamics of public spending, and the large size and pervasiveness of observed deficits over time (Alesina and Perotti 1995). Latin America has been no exception. Fiscal deficits, for instance, have been much more frequent than surpluses, and not limited to bad times. Figures 19.1–19.3 illustrate this for 1975–2001: central government surpluses in several countries barely touched positive territory over this period.

The natural candidate to explain this failure of standard theory has been politics: fiscal policy is generally not decided by the benevolent planner who implicitly chooses policy in the standard model. Rather, it is designed by authorities subject to political pressures and motivations. Fiscal outcomes are thus likely to reflect, in addition to any consumption smoothing motives, the interplay of political forces. This chapter discusses two leading political economy explanations behind the dynamics of fiscal outcomes: overspending as a result of what we can call the tragedy of the commons, and opportunistic manipulation of fiscal policy during election times. I focus on

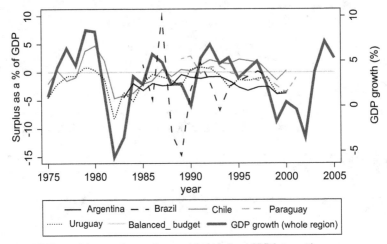

Note: GDP growth is annual percentage growth rate of real GDP for countries
in the sample. GDP is in 2000 US dollars. Source: WDI. Surplus is from Brender &
Drazen (2005).

Figure 19.1 Surplus in Mercosur.

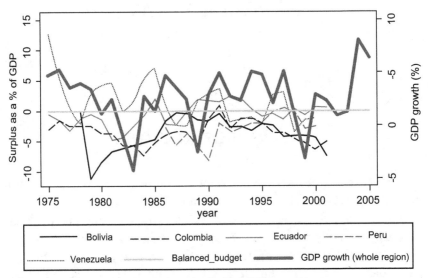

Note: GDP growth is annual percentage growth rate of real GDP for countries
in the sample. GDP is in 2000 US dollars. Source: WDI. Surplus is from Brender &
Drazen (2005).

Figure 19.2 Surplus in Andean countries.

theories and evidence of relevance for Latin America. Not only has the region been
the object of a good part of the literature, but other studies, focusing on countries that
share similarities with those in Latin America, also provide useful insights.[1]

Why is a specific focus on Latin America necessary? Can't we simply learn the lessons we need for the region from the bulk of political economy studies that have focused
on the countries in the Organisation for Economic Co-operation and Development
(OECD), the United States, or European countries? Several peculiarities of Latin

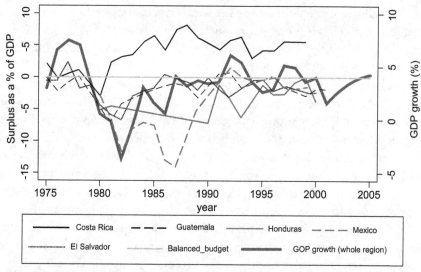

Note: GDP growth is annual percentage growth rate of real GDP for countries
in the sample. GDP is in 2000 US dollars. Source: WDI. Surplus is from Brender &
Drazen (2005).

Figure 19.3 Surplus in Central American countries.

American politics and Latin American policymaking imply the need for analyses that
focus either directly on the region or on counties that share similarities with the region
along specific dimensions. The most obvious of those dimensions, underdevelopment,
is perhaps the least relevant for the phenomena discussed in this chapter. Instead, political history, political institutions, and political practices—more likely determinants of
the influence of politics on fiscal policy than the level of development—all make Latin
America special. Two specific features stand out. First, several countries in the region
went back to democracy in relatively recent times, after episodes of dictatorship. Even
countries that did not go through dictatorship have been moving toward increased
democratization over recent decades. Latin America, in a word, is a region of "new
democracies." Second, in contrast with other regions—including Europe and the OECD
nations—most countries in the region have adopted presidential regimes.

Growing democratization is a determinant for the potential effects on fiscal
outcomes of both the tragedy of the commons and electoral cycles. The former
problem emerges when different interests compete for the distribution of government revenues, leading to excessive spending. The resulting level of overspending
grows with the number of different interests represented in the competition for the
resources. Increasing democratization in the region has given representation to previously disenfranchised interest groups, leading to a more intense fight for the
common pool of government revenues. This phenomenon shows up in different
scenarios relevant to the budget process: party fractionalization has grown, in turn
implying increasing fragmentation in the region's legislatures and cabinets; spending
responsibilities have been transferred from the central government to the regions;
the judiciary has taken on a more active role in the defense of individuals' rights.
Since the undeniable advantages of greater representation come at the potential cost

of fiscal sustainability, understanding the fiscal implications of these processes is of crucial importance. This is one of the objectives of this chapter.

As for the effects of democratization on the use of fiscal policy with electoral purposes, recent literature has pointed that the form that budget cycles during elections, or electoral budget cycles, take differs between new and established democracies. Increases in overall spending and deficits during elections seem to be a phenomenon of relatively young democracies. Scholars have hypothesized that this is a result of voters' inexperience: not being used to electoral manipulation, voters interpret growing spending before elections as a result of the incumbent's effectiveness in delivering public goods. The relatively recent return to democracy in Latin America makes this debate relevant to understanding fiscal policy in the region.

Presidentialism also shapes the way in which political phenomena affect fiscal policies. First, compared to their parliamentary counterparts, presidential democracies tend to have more centralized policymaking processes. Centralization, in turn, may contribute to alleviate the "common pool problem" of fiscal policy. The choice of presidential regimes also affects fiscal policy in more subtle ways. In particular, there are differences with parliamentary regimes in terms of the nature and relevance of the legislative process, as well as negotiations between the executive and legislative powers. As a result, the underlying characteristics of the electoral system and the budget process that matter for fiscal outcomes are particular to the choice of presidential regimes.

The discussion in this chapter focuses on the way in which the aforementioned peculiarities of politics in Latin America affect fiscal policy, as a result of both the common pool problem of public spending and electoral budget cycles. Section 2 discusses the implications of the common pool problem of fiscal policy, including the different dimensions of political fragmentation that lead to overspending, as well as how budget institutions can alleviate their effect. Section 3 presents the recent literature on political budget cycles, with special emphasis on the case of young democracies. Sections 2 and 3 are self-contained: each focuses on a different phenomenon, presenting theory and evidence of relevance for Latin America, as well as reaching conclusions about each of those separate debates. In turn, section 4 focuses on features common to both debates.

2. THE COMMON-POOL PROBLEM OF FISCAL POLICY

The government budget can be thought of as the sum of demands, by different groups in society, that "the budget process" satisfies. A crucial feature is that, while specific groups benefit from specific expenditures, the projects tend to be funded from a common pool of resources: the pool of government revenue. The disconnect between those who benefit from a given government project and those who pay for it leads to excessive demands for expenditure. This is the well-known common pool problem of public spending, one of the leading explanations for pervasive deficits (Weingast, Shepsle, and Johnsen 1981; Velasco 1999, 2000).

A crucial implication of the common pool problem is that the level of spending demanded by the different groups increases with the number of groups involved, an effect termed *fragmentation*. Greater fragmentation implies each group pays for a smaller share of the fiscal burden, worsening the disconnect between the benefits and the costs the group assigns to government projects. One policy lesson, then, is that reducing the level of fragmentation in the budget process should help fiscal discipline. This is so because lower fragmentation implies that the agents involved in choosing the budget internalize a larger fraction of the costs of spending.

But what exactly does one mean by "fragmentation in the budget process"? In other words, who are the relevant agents whose number affects fiscal outcomes? There is no unique answer to this question: different agents represent different interests, at different stages of the budget process, and with varying degrees of influence over the outcome. At the design stage, each of the ministers of the cabinet represents his or her respective sector. A greater number of ministers, or greater "executive fragmentation," should result in a larger budget proposed by the government to the legislature (Perotti and Kontopoulos 2002). The approval stage brings a different set of relevant agents to the process: the legislators and the parties they are affiliated with. To the extent that parties represent constituencies that are more or less homogeneous, the number of parties represented in the legislature—"legislative fragmentation"—should also have a direct relationship with the overall budget approved (Perotti and Kontopoulos 2002).

At a wider level, other sources of political fragmentation, many stemming from institutions with constitutional stature, are expected to lead to larger budgets (Persson and Tabellini 1999, 2003; Milesi-Ferretti, Perotti, and Rostagno 2002). Parliamentary democracies should imply greater spending, given the lower centralization of decisions relative to presidential democracies. A similar case can be made for electoral systems with proportional representation, and other systems with large intra- or interparty fragmentation—in particular those that encourage the personal vote.

I next discuss in greater detail the relationship between different forms of fragmentation and fiscal outcomes, as well as the implications in terms of optimal budget institutions. Section 2.1 discusses the link between fiscal outcomes and executive and legislative fragmentation, as defined above. Section 2.2 discusses the role played by sources of fragmentation stemming from constitutional rules. Section 2.3 discusses the potential of well-designed budgetary institutions for moderating fiscal indiscipline stemming from fragmentation.

2.1. Executive and Legislative Fragmentation

Cross-country evidence on how executive and legislative fragmentation affect fiscal outcomes in Latin America has been scarce. Despite this fact, one of the earliest systematic investigations on the matter focused on the region (Stein, Talvi, and

Grisanti 1999). That work estimates the relationship between fiscal outcomes and fragmentation in 20 Latin American countries. The study uses the effective number of parties in the legislature and the number of legislative seats held by the government's party as proxies for fragmentation. A large degree of legislative power by the government's party is related to both the power the president has over congress and, mechanically, to lower legislative fragmentation; a larger number of seats held by the government thus should imply better fiscal outcomes. The authors find evidence that fragmentation is indeed correlated with worst fiscal outcomes, though their estimates are imprecise: the effects they find are significant only in some of their specifications.

More recently, Amorim-Neto and Borsani (2004) studied the relationship between fiscal outcomes and a series of political phenomena for 10 countries in the region. The number of legislative seats held by the president's party is one of the political determinants of the budget examined. Though the authors do find a positive and significant relationship with fiscal balances, they similarly find a contradictory positive relationship with public spending. They also report having included a direct measure of legislative fragmentation in some of their tests, finding no evidence of a significant relationship. Mejía-Acosta and Coppedge (2001) find no effect of the size of the president's party in congress, though they do find that a composite index summarizing the partisan powers and will of the president to discipline fiscal policy reduces government spending. As far as I know, no work has analyzed the role of executive fragmentation (the number of spending ministers) in explaining fiscal policy in the region as whole.

The message from these studies in terms of the relationship between fragmentation and fiscal policy for the region is, clearly, quite mixed. Estimates are imprecise, and in some cases display counterintuitive signs. This may be explained by a problem that is inherent to this type of work: proper identification requires a sufficiently large sample, especially when the effects of different but interrelated political phenomena are to be disentangled. Satisfying this precondition is made difficult by the small number of countries contained in any single region. For the Latin American case, limited data coverage adds to this problem, both in the cross-sectional and time dimensions—aggravated by the short length of the recent democratic period in many countries of the region.[2] The fact that several years have passed since the existing studies for the region were conducted suggests progress could be made by reexamining the issue taking advantage of more recent data. Figure 19.4 suggests this may be a fruitful avenue. It depicts the (unconditional) relationship between central government spending and the effective number of parties in the legislature, using data on 16 Latin American countries, for a long period between 1975 and 2006, from Eslava and Nupia (2010). Though the graph should only be taken as suggestive, the correlation between the two variables is more precisely identified than in previous work using more limited samples.

On the other hand, much of interest to the region can also be learned from studies that overcome the small sample difficulties by covering larger, albeit more diverse, samples of countries. Much of the existing literature outside Latin America

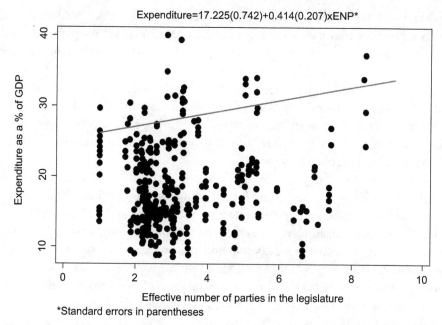

Figure 19.4 Central government expenditure and legislative fragmentation in Latin America.

has focused on OECD countries. However, there are a few comprehensive studies that also cover countries similar to the ones in the region. Woo (2003) finds robust evidence that larger cabinets are associated with lower government surpluses, for a sample of 57 countries from different regions over 1970–90. He finds no significant effect of the number of seats held by the largest party in the legislature, and of the effective number of parties in it. The fiscal balance is the only dependent variable included in this analysis. Meanwhile, Mukherjee (2003) finds that an increase in the effective number of represented parties has a positive effect on public spending in a sample of 110 countries over a 10-year period.[3] Interestingly, he finds the effect of party fragmentation to be significant only for parliamentary democracies. In fact, studies that focus solely on the OECD or European countries, which are samples where presidential democracies are either not included or underrepresented, tend to also find significant positive effects of executive and legislative fragmentation on public spending and deficits. Eslava and Nupia (2010) confirm the finding that legislative fragmentation is directly related to larger spending in parliamentary de-mocracies. In addition, they show that for presidential regimes larger effective numbers of parties in congress also lead to more spending, but only when the degree of polarization between those parties is sufficiently high.

The finding that legislative fragmentation plays different roles in presidential and parliamentary regimes is, clearly, of relevance for Latin America. At the minimum, it implies that the findings of the rich literature that has focused on European countries cannot be directly applied to a region where presidential democracies predominate. It also suggests that future research of interest to the region must either focus direct attention on Latin American countries or concentrate on presidential democracies; the latter strategy may have advantages in light of the small-sample problem within the region discussed above. Heterogeneous effects of party fragmentation between presidential and parliamentary democracies may also signal fundamental differences in fiscal policymaking between the two regimes, of obvious interest to understanding Latin American fiscal policy. What, then, should we make of the different effects of party fragmentation between the two types of democracy? To answer this question, it is worth digging deeper into the relationship between legislative fragmentation and fiscal outcomes at a conceptual level.

What the common pool problem implies is that legislative fragmentation should increase the total demands for spending from legislators. Whether those higher demands end up actually reflected in the approved budget is not evident. To a great extent, the literature has neglected the question; it is as though there was an implicit assumption that legislators amend the proposed budget to incorporate their desired projects. This is not necessarily an unreasonable assumption: legislators are frequently granted the power to amend the budget, in many countries even without restriction (as happens, for instance, in Chile). On the other hand, there are also many examples of countries that impose limits to the changes the legislature can incorporate in the government's proposal, formal or informal, stringent or weak.

In Latin America, in particular, legislative powers over the budget are formally restricted in many countries. For instance, of the seven Latin American countries included in the OECD International Budget Practices and Procedures Database (OECD 2007–8), only one (Argentina) reports that legislators have unlimited powers to amend the budget proposed by the government; as a benchmark, the proportion in the overall sample is 32 of 100 countries surveyed. Restrictions take different forms: banning legislators from including amendments to the project presented by the executive (as is the case in Chile); requiring that proposals to include additional expenditures identify revenue sources to pay for those expenses (e.g., Bolivia); allowing amendments only if the total size of the budget is not changed. Furthermore, the strength of the presidential figure in the region provides a natural limit to legislative powers. Presidents frequently have strong agenda-setting powers, the ability of de facto ruling via decrees, and the ability of overruling congress by limiting the execution of the approved budget. They also control the bureaucracy, which gives them additional power over legislators who frequently exchange legislative support for patronage (e.g., Alston et al. 2009, for the case of Brazil).

Is it the case that, when congressional powers to amend the budget are limited, the demands of legislators don't make it into the budget? If this were the case, legislative fragmentation would be irrelevant to fiscal outcomes. However, the answer, clearly, is no. First, a forward-looking government takes those demands into account from the design stage; the approval of the budget could otherwise be unlikely. Even more important, including legislators' pet projects in the budget is a way of guaranteeing legislative support more generally, so governments pay attention to

the demands of legislators even thinking beyond the approval of the budget proposal. Anecdotal evidence suggests the use of public spending in exchange for legislative support is, in fact, widely extended in Latin America. For instance, Cárdenas,
Mejía, and Olivera (2009) assert that governments in Colombia have traditionally
included regionally targeted spending projects in the budget as a tool to build support from legislators. For Brazil, Alston et al. (2009) point out that the executive
encourages the submission of budget amendments by legislators, as a way of
strengthening the governing coalition.[4]

What this discussion shows is that the government itself can be a vehicle for
transmitting legislators' demands into the budget, trying to build legislative support. As a consequence, the ways in which the government negotiates with the legislature matter for understanding the relationship between legislative fragmentation
and fiscal outcomes. Since executive-legislative relations are fundamentally different in parliamentary and presidential regimes, this may be behind the differential
results found for those types of democracies regarding the effect of legislative fragmentation on public spending and deficits. How? The argument, presented by
Eslava and Nupia (2010), comes in two steps. First, the extent to which coalition-
building efforts are the key factor behind the legislators' success in influencing the
budget is greater in presidential democracies. Second, if coalition building plays a
key role, fragmentation affects fiscal outcomes only when there is high polarization.
Let us look at these two assertions in greater detail.

First, coalition building is fundamentally different in the two types of regimes.
While in a parliamentary democracy each government is supported by a relatively
stable coalition—that is, the coalition is built at the early stages of the government's
period—the need for coalition building in presidential regimes can be more frequent, even project-specific.[5] As a result, the possibility that the demands of legislators for spending are regularly brought into the budget by a government trying to
build or strengthen a coalition may be more relevant for presidential than parliamentary democracies—at least relative to the alternative whereby legislators build
their preferences into the budget by their own means. Second, when public spending
is a primary tool for building coalitions, legislative fragmentation leads to higher
spending only if there is a high degree of political polarization (that is, there is high
tension between the different parties in the legislature). This is so because polarization determines how necessary it is to spend resources on building a new coalition
around the government's projects; in the extreme, if all parties were aligned with the
government, it would be unlikely some of them would block the government's initiatives. Thus, the effect of legislative fragmentation of fiscal policy may depend on
the degree of polarization, and this is more likely for presidential democracies. As I
discussed above, the evidence found by Eslava and Nupia (2010) is consistent with
this argument.

How does Latin America fare in this overall story? The lack of robust evidence
of an unconditional relationship between legislative fragmentation and fiscal outcomes is a first indication that, in the region, the story goes beyond legislators simply writing their preferred projects into the budget. In addition, country accounts

suggest ongoing coalition-building efforts characterize the relationship between the executive and the legislature in the region (e.g., Cárdenas, Mejía, and Olivera 2009 for Colombia, Amorim-Neto 2002 for Brazil). Moreover, as mentioned above, "pork-barrel" spending seems to be a usual currency in those negotiations. It thus seems to be the case that Latin America fits well the idea of budget processes where legislators' demands make it into the budget mainly through the government's efforts to build legislative support.

Summing up, existing empirical work suggests that, while legislative fragmentation matters for fiscal outcomes, the effects differ between presidential and parliamentary democracies. The differences are likely related to the differential ways in which the government negotiates with the legislature in the two regimes. In presidential democracies—like the countries in Latin America—legislative fragmentation is a more likely source of fiscal indiscipline when high polarization makes it more difficult for the government to build support in congress. As for the role of cabinet or executive fragmentation (the number of spending ministers), existing studies find a negative effect on fiscal discipline, even more robust than that found for legislative fragmentation (Perotti and Kontopoulos 2002). No study I know of, however, has looked at the effect of executive fragmentation for Latin America, or specifically for presidential democracies. This is an important gap to be filled, as the cabinet arguably plays a stronger role in presidential democracies than in parliamentary ones.

2.2. Constitutional Rules and Fragmentation

Fragmentation in the policymaking process can be deeply rooted in constitutional and other fundamental rules.[6] Presidential democracies, by making the executive relatively stronger than in parliamentary regimes, centralize decision making. Majoritarian electoral rules have a similar centralizing effect, compared to proportional systems: they provide incentives for politicians to organize in fewer parties, frequently implying that a single party commands the majority (Austin-Smith 2000). Moreover, larger district magnitudes, made possible by proportional representation, imply fragmentation in terms of the interests defended by the representatives of any single district (Milesi-Ferreti et al. 2002). Another relevant dimension of the electoral system is the extent to which it provides incentives for politicians to cultivate the "personal" vote, emphasizing the individual candidate to voters rather than a party-led vote. Greater "personalism" weakens party discipline, implying an additional source of fragmentation (Hallerberg and Marier 2004).

These sources of political fragmentation—proportionality, personalism, and parliamentarism—may imply spending biases. Parliamentary regimes decentralize decision making, potentially aggravating the common pool problem of fiscal policy. As for proportionality and personalism, they create incentives for legislators to target specific interests within districts: another layer is, then, added to the fight for resources that leads to the common pool problem.

Proportionality is empirically associated with larger governments, and in fact with larger deficits as well, but only for large samples of countries and for OECD economies (Persson and Tabellini 2003; Milesi-Ferreti et al. 2003). Cross-country evidence for Latin America, meanwhile, has been less supportive of the importance of choosing proportional electoral systems. Stein et al. (1999) find insignificant co-efficients for district magnitude as determinants of spending and deficits in a sample of 20 Latin American countries, though the estimated coefficients are positive for both dependent variables. They also find that the degree of proportionality is positively correlated with the number of effective parties represented in congress, which in turn is a significant and positive determinant of public spending. One interpretation, thus, is that the main fiscal effect of proportionality comes through its effects on party fractionalization. On the other hand, looking at a sample of countries almost identical to that studied by Stein et al. (1999), Milesi-Ferreti et al. not only fail to find a significant effect of the degree of proportionality—measured slightly differently—on public spending, but actually obtain negative coefficients. These studies argue that weak cross-country evidence for Latin America probably reflects small-sample problems inherent to these studies, together with less precise measurement than in the OECD. A different possibility is that the degree of proportionality (using district magnitude as a proxy in these studies) is less important than other determinants of political fragmentation in the mostly presidential Latin American regimes.[7]

Consistent with this last idea, Hallerberg and Marier (2004) hypothesize that the feature of the electoral system that should matter most for Latin American mainly presidential regimes is the extent of "personalism" in politics, as defined above. They test this hypothesis using data for a sample of Latin American countries similar to that used by the studies mentioned above, but taking advantage of the panel dimension. Their findings strongly support the prediction that fiscal balances should be lower when incentives for emphasizing a personal vote are stronger. Moreover, they continue to find that district magnitude plays no role.

As for the direct effect of adopting a presidential regime, parliamentary democracies have been found to choose higher government spending, though no robust matching negative effect on fiscal balances has been found (Persson and Tabellini 2003). When we bring these findings and those discussed in section 2.1 together, interesting implications emerge about the effects of the prevalent choice of presidential regimes in Latin America. In terms of the direct effect of presidentialism, this choice should be associated with relatively smaller governments, though not necessarily ones with smaller deficits. The choice of a presidential regime also interacts with other dimensions of the political context to determine fiscal choices. First, it implies that overall incentives to cultivate the personal vote matter more than district magnitude in terms of fiscal policy. Second, the logic of executive-legislative negotiations in presidential democracies brings the need for relatively more frequent coalition-building efforts. The potential use of public spending in exchange for legislative support then becomes a main channel to translate legislative fragmentation into greater spending, especially when high polarization makes it harder for the executive to get its projects approved in Congress.

2.3. Budget Institutions

The sources of fragmentation discussed above are rooted in deep institutions and political processes, and it doesn't seem likely, or even desirable, that those fundamental characteristics of a democracy will be changed in an attempt to improve fiscal discipline. Despite this, a nice feature of the literature on the common pool problem of fiscal policy is that it has policy implications of feasible implementation. Lessons derived from this literature shed light on the question of how to design fiscal institutions conducive to fiscal discipline. While fiscal discipline probably should not determine the choice of electoral rules, or the assignment of government duties across levels of government, it should undoubtedly be one of the main objectives of the design of budget institutions—if not the overriding consideration.

The tragedy of the commons is a problem derived from decentralized spending demands. In particular, beneficiaries of spending projects are unable to internalize the costs each of those projects imposes on other individuals. The main lesson from this literature in terms of budget institutions is, therefore, that centralizing the decisions improves the sustainability of public finances. The goal is to bring the resource constraint closer to the choice of spending. The following characteristics of institutions that govern the budget process should thus improve fiscal discipline: (1) greater powers are given to the minister of finance or the president, vis-à-vis spending ministers, during the design stage; (2) during the approval stage, the powers of legislators to amend the budget proposed by the government are limited; (3) congress votes on the total size of the budget before approving its composition, or spending ministers are assigned a total spending amount before deciding what projects to fund (top-down procedures), or both; (4) the government is allowed to cut expenditures during the implementation stage.

Besides procedural budget rules with the aforementioned characteristics, establishing numerical targets for spending, fiscal balances, and debt can also help improve fiscal discipline. If target levels are decided on in a centralized manner, the costs of government projects can be fully internalized. Therefore, numerical targets can alleviate the common pool problem (von Hagen and Harden 1995). This is a particularly interesting option when one geographical unit can even impose the costs of a potential default on others in the same federation (states in a federal country, or countries in the European Monetary Union); a centralized authority can impose debt or deficit limits that fully internalize the costs of this possibility (Jones, Sanguinetti, and Tommasi 2000; Krogstrup and Wyplosz 2010).

One problem with stringent rules aimed at alleviating the effects of the common pool problem is that they hold the seeds of their own destruction: agents whose hands are tied by these rules have incentives to circumvent them through creative accounting (Milesi-Ferretti 2003). Good budget institutions, therefore, should also minimize creative accounting possibilities by encouraging transparency. Rules that limit the space for off-budget expenditures, and those that empower voters and control entities to effectively monitor the budget, play this role.

To assess the effectiveness of budget institutions, several studies create indexes of institutional quality and use them to estimate the impact of institutions on fiscal outcomes. Indexes of budget institutions grade countries on the dimensions mentioned above: powers of the executive vis-à-vis the legislature, and of the minister of finance vis-à-vis spending ministers; top-down procedures; numerical rules; and transparency, as measured by publication procedures, and comprehensiveness of the budget.[8]

For Latin America, studies in this vein have been conducted by Alesina et al. (1999), Stein et al. (1999), and Filc and Scartascini (2005, 2007). They all find that more solid budget institutions reduce spending or increase surpluses, even when electoral institutions and the associated level of political fragmentation are controlled for (Stein et al. 1999). The finding that good budget institutions increase budget discipline is quite robust, despite the fact that these studies concentrate on cross-sections of 20 observations or less. Its validity is also supported by similar findings in a more comprehensive study focusing on 72 low- and middle-income countries (Dabla-Norris et al. 2010). When the indexes of budget institutions are separated into their main components, studies for Latin America tend to find that numerical targets and procedural rules that centralize the process are more effective than rules intended to make the process transparent. These results are likely less robust than those regarding overall institutional quality, because the different dimensions of budget institutions may be highly correlated, making identification more difficult—especially given the small-sample issue that plague these studies. In fact, the analysis in Dabla-Norris et al. (2010), for a much larger sample of developing countries, suggests transparency and comprehensiveness are among the characteristics of the budget process with greatest impact on fiscal performance. I come back to the heterogeneous results across studies regarding the importance of transparency in section 3.

Fortunately, the region has moved decidedly toward the adoption of solid budget institutions. Episodes of fiscal reform were seen in almost all countries in the region during the 1990s and early 2000s (Filc and Scartascini 2007). Reforms included the adoption of numerical targets; fiscal responsibility laws, many covering the subnational level; multiannual planning frameworks; special countercyclical funds; and procedural measures strengthening the centralizing role of the executive in the budget process.

Despite these achievements, recent research on the role of budget institutions for fiscal performance suggests important qualifications to the general finding that solid budget institutions are conducive to better fiscal performance. Perhaps the most important of those qualifications is that, since budget institutions do not live in a political vacuum, their effectiveness depends on how well they adapt to both formal and informal institutions governing the political game (Filc and Scartascini 2007; Hallerberg, Scartascini, and Stein 2009). For instance, in their aforementioned study for 20 countries in Latin America and the Caribbean, Hallerberg and Marier (2004) find that centralization of the budget process in a strong executive improves fiscal performance only when incentives to cultivate the personal vote are sufficiently high to create a severe common pool problem in the legislature.[9] Several country accounts for the region also show how budget institutions that are apparently solid, but incompatible with political practices, are easily circumvented. In Bolivia, for instance, there are provisions banning legislators from adding expenses to the budget, unless sources of financing are properly identified. Congressmen frequently circumvent this rule by modifying revenue projections (Filc and Scartascini 2007). Rules in Colombia used to permit legislators access to "auxilios parlamentarios," unearmarked grants that they used for funding small projects with high personal political benefits. The "auxilios" were subsequently banned by the 1991 Constitution, leading legislators to find less transparent ways of getting public funds to pay for their pet projects (Cárdenas et al. 2009; Echeverry, Fergusson, and Querubin 2004).

Another important lesson from recent research is that creative accounting does indeed inhibit the effectiveness of good budget institutions in Latin America.[10] No systematic cross-country examination of the issue has been conducted for the region, but many country studies point at practices that go around the budget rules to loosen restrictions. Manipulating revenue projections seems a frequent way of circumventing formal restrictions to spending in Latin America (Hallerberg, Scartascini, and Stein 2009). In Argentina and Venezuela, the government underestimates revenues to take advantage of provisions that allow the executive to spend unexpected income at its discretion. Meanwhile, in Bolivia and Brazil revenues are overestimated to increase the space for negotiations with legislators; in Colombia and Ecuador, reduced debt service projections serve the same purpose (IADB 2009).[11] Off-budget spending is also a common vehicle to circumvent formal rules designed to increase fiscal discipline. For instance, while formal procedures to determine the central budget in Argentina follow modern standards, expenditure decentralization implies that a very important fraction of government spending is decided outside the central budget process (Abuelafia et al. 2009).

Budget rigidities, many stemming from the constitutions themselves, are also an important source of fiscal difficulties in Latin America, in spite of modern budget institutions. A high percentage of public spending is earmarked—as high as 80 percent in Brazil and Colombia, over 45 percent in other countries such as Argentina, Guatemala, and Costa Rica—(IMF 2005). Perhaps surprisingly, budget rigidities have had adverse consequences for fiscal discipline in many countries. Two reasons explain this undesirable outcome. First, political negotiations take place even if spending is predetermined to a high degree, and their outcomes build upon those predetermined levels. Second, budget rigidities enable agents to close intertemporal agreements with long-term fiscal consequences. While this allows planning in view of the longer run, it has the undesirable consequence of locking in excessive spending for the future. The outcomes of future political deals thus build upon previous fiscal excesses.

2.4. Discussion

During the last 25 years, there has been growing democratization across Latin America. Several countries went back to democracy in the 1980s, while others have seen important changes in both legislation and political practice, leading to greater inclusion in the political process. This is the case, for instance, in Colombia and Mexico. Political inclusion was the goal of broad constitutional change in 1991 in Colombia—and political fragmentation a well-documented consequence; in Mexico, political competition became a reality in the 1990s, after several decades of single-party command. Such political opening has also been accompanied by growing fiscal decentralization: spending responsibilities have been transferred from the central to the subnational levels of government, in an attempt to bring spending decisions closer to those who benefit from them. In the fiscal arena, these processes have brought undeniable gains in one of the dimensions that must characterize good fiscal policy: representativeness of the different interests in society (Hallerberg, Scartascini, and Stein 2009; IABD 2009). On the other hand, the common-pool problem implies that, in the context of public finances, there is a potential trade-off between representativeness and sustainability. The next subsection discusses two separate aspects of that trade-off generally neglected by the debate around the tragedy of the commons in fiscal policy in the Latin American case: first, the potential fiscal cost of the judiciary's increasing role in enforcing representation, and second, the wider question of how to make representativeness and sustainability compatible.

2.4.1. *Judicial Activism and Fiscal Sustainability*

Not surprisingly, growing democratization in the region has been accompanied by a more active role of the courts (de Sousa 2010). On one hand, individuals increasingly resort to courts to secure their (now more encompassing) rights. On the other, judges are more active in vetoing legislation, establishing the acceptable interpretation of specific laws, and establishing parameters of constitutionality for future legislation. These latter activities make courts into active players in the policymaking process.

Fiscal policy is one of the policy arenas crucially affected by courts' decisions. The reason is twofold. First, in securing the rights of disenfranchised groups, the judiciary acts as an "alternative societal representative" (de Sousa 2010, 81), bringing the interests of additional groups to the budget discussion. The result is likely to be growing spending. Second, courts may block fiscal adjustment. This is because successful fiscal adjustments usually require spending cuts, especially on items such as transfers, social security contributions, and wage payments (Alesina, Perotti, and Tavares 1998; Gupta et al. 2004). The burden of fiscal adjustments thus falls on the specific recipients of those transfers and payments, who have incentives to organize against adjustment. Courts may block fiscal adjustment on the basis of the protection of the rights of those groups, especially because the benefits of fiscal adjustment are so widespread that the recipients do not organize to challenge this type of ruling. These arguments suggest that greater activism by the courts may cause difficulties for fiscal discipline.

Colombia is a case at hand to exemplify these possibilities (e.g., IADB, 2009). Over the last two decades, Colombian courts have been extremely active both in producing rulings that require growing public spending and in blocking fiscal adjustment. For instance, courts have produced rulings—several thousands of them, according to some sources—requiring the social security system to cover health treatments not included in the legal health plan. The basis has been their interpretation that health is a basic right guaranteed by the Constitution. Also, several laws passed by Congress with the purpose of alleviating the growing fiscal deficit have not made it through constitutional revision. The Constitutional Court has ruled that they violate rights acquired by specific groups, and that disparities in the attainment of social rights are unconstitutional. Moreover, the court's rulings have imposed important limitations for future reforms. This was the case, for instance, with two different pension reforms in 2003, intended to make the pension system sustainable.

In Eslava (2006), I present evidence suggesting that this may be an issue of more general importance. I estimate the effect of judicial activism on fiscal deficits for a sample of eight Latin American countries during 1996–2003, using a model that controls for legislative fragmentation, budget institutions, and several economic determinants of deficits. I found judicial activism in fiscal policymaking, as measured in Cárdenas et al. (2009), to be an important determinant of the deficit. In particular, the estimate indicates that increases in the index of judicial activism lead to sizable increases in fiscal deficits. The exercise is only exploratory, but does suggest that neglecting the role of courts may leave out an important part of the story in the literature on institutional determinants of fiscal outcomes.

This discussion suggests that courts play an important role in the determination of fiscal outcomes, more specifically in determining how costly greater representation may be in terms of fiscal discipline. The issue is pressing in many countries of Latin America. Future research should pay attention to it, keeping in mind not only the sustainability of fiscal policies but also the equally important goal of representativeness. I come back to this issue next.

2.4.2. *Representativeness versus Fiscal Discipline: Is There No Way Out?*

Most of the literature on the common pool problem of fiscal policy focuses on its potential negative consequences in terms of fiscal sustainability. As a result, policy recommendations naturally tend to focus on how to limit excessive spending arising from distributive conflict. In practice, this frequently translates into institutions that try to keep government expenditures under control, for a given level of government revenues. This is an excessively narrow approach for addressing the consequences of the tragedy of the commons in fiscal policy.

The size and scope of government is the result of a political process whereby the different groups in society are represented: the result of a "social contract," in practice not always—or even usually—designed with a budget constraint in mind. The extent to which that social contract is satisfied is, of course, constrained by the amount of resources available. However, those resources are also a choice of society. The debate over how to allocate them has much room to improve as far as understanding how endogenous revenues are with respect to political forces, and the related normative issue of to what extent fiscal discipline should be achieved by keeping expenditures under control or further raising revenues to match the level of expenditures implied by wide representation. First, preferences over taxes and tax collection, and the choice of these elements, need further study, both theoretical and empirical. Second, the differences between effects of the common pool problem on spending and its effects on deficits not only have to be identified empirically (something the literature has made progress on) but also explained theoretically.[12]

3. Opportunistic Political Budget Cycles: The 2000s View

The idea that incumbents raise expenditures during elections to get reelected has been around for a long time. This traditional view, based on the expectation that voters reward high spending by voting for the incumbent, has become common wisdom. A recent wave of interest on the issue, however, has resulted in an alternative view about electoral budget cycles (EBC henceforth). Recent theoretical and empirical findings suggest that electorally driven changes in fiscal policy vary considerably across countries and over time, in ways that seem systematically related to specific institutions. Countries within Latin America present wide differences in terms of these institutions, and consequently empirical findings on the occurrence of EBC differ across countries. This section reviews the recent literature on EBC, discussing how the evidence for Latin America fits into that debate.

3.1. Recent Theory

Early models of electoral budget cycles held that voters reward governments when economic activity is vigorous at the end of their terms, reelecting them. As a result, incumbents try to engineer booms when election times are coming close. If expansionary fiscal policy is the tool used to reinvigorate the economy, then fiscal outcomes should deteriorate around election times.

Those early models came under fire, on conceptual grounds, over the last two decades. Many questions appeared. Why should voters, electing authorities for the future, vote on the basis of past outcomes? Why would they fall for the trick of expansionary fiscal policy before elections for more than one electoral cycle? The first event should teach them that it has pure opportunistic roots and is short-lived. Questions also came up about the government's ability to fine-tune the timing of fiscally driven expansions, and about whether those expansions' impact on economic activity was the most pressing reason for voters to care about fiscal policy.

The literature that followed has addressed many of those questions, with empirical implications not fully consistent with conventional wisdom. In the resulting revised view, voters give value to receiving goods and services from the government, even if aggregate economic activity is not affected. Furthermore, Rogoff and Sibert (1988) and Rogoff (1990) gave theoretical support to the plausibility of voters using the incumbent's previous fiscal choices as input for deciding whether to reelect him or her. In particular, informational asymmetries between the incumbent and the electorate may lead voters to use past fiscal outcomes as sources of information about incumbent characteristics relevant to future performance. If these characteristics evolve over time, the incumbent's performance just before the election is the most relevant source of information.

The introduction of informational asymmetries and direct preferences of voters in regard to government spending and taxes showed that it is indeed plausible to expect incumbents to use preelectoral fiscal choices as means to manipulate the election. However, this is not the same as saying that total government spending or deficits should rise prior to elections. Many qualifications have emerged from the body of recent theoretical work. In general, they all point to the fact that the form EBCs take depends on two sets of basic issues: (1) the fiscal preferences of both voters and the incumbent and (2) the source of informational asymmetries and the characterization of information available to voters.

Rogoff's (1990) assumption is that voters are trying to find out the incumbent's "competence" to provide public goods at low cost, based on their observation of the "visible" part of government spending. The result is an incumbent who tries to show his or her competence by increasing visible expenditures while reducing taxes and low-visibility expenses. There is thus no clear implication that overall spending or the deficit should rise. Shi and Svensson (2006) use a very similar model, but assume that the part of fiscal policy (some) voters do not observe is new debt issued by the government. The result is the use of electoral deficits by incumbents trying to show they are highly competent, with the extent of manipulation decreasing with voters' access to information. A different strategy, again with different results, is used by Drazen and Eslava (2006, 2010). They assume both voters and politicians have heterogeneous preferences toward different types of public expenses. Before elections, incumbents try to win support by showing closeness to voters (or important voters) in terms of fiscal preferences. The result is an electoral shift of expenditures toward types of expenses preferred by voters. The EBC can thus occur without affecting either revenues or total expenditures. By contrast with the "competence" approach, Drazen and Eslava's "preference" approach does not require voters to be unable to observe part of the budget to generate EBCs (in the composition of spending).

In summary, recent theory shows that EBC may or may not come in the form of electoral increases of spending or deficits. Electoral alterations of the balance of this sort are likely only when voters are unable to follow fiscal outcomes accurately. On the other hand, when voters have good access to information about fiscal performance, EBCs are more likely to take the form of changes in the composition of spending, toward goods or categories voters focus attention on. This may be either because voters have well-defined preferences about the different types of public spending or because only part of government expenses is visible to them. Taken as a whole, recent empirical evidence seems to conform well to this modern view of the EBC.

3.2. Empirical Evidence

A rich body of empirical research has followed on the footsteps of the recent wave of theory on EBCs. Researchers set out to test a model of "conditional" EBCs. A first version of that line of work focuses on differences between developed and developing countries. Shi and Svensson (2006) examine a large panel of countries, both developed and developing, and find that fiscal balances change unfavorably before elections in developing countries, but not so clearly in the developed world. However, the level of economic development seems to be acting as a proxy for certain institutions in these tests. Brender and Drazen (2005) show, in a large sample of countries, that the finding of EBCs in developing countries is in fact driven by the first few elections in countries that transited to democracy within the sample period. That is, EBCs would be a phenomenon of new democracies rather than one of developing countries more generally understood. In turn, theory would suggest that the role played by democratic infancy reflects media underdevelopment and voters' inexperience in evaluating the government. Shi and Svensson's (2006) article also shows supportive evidence for this view: electoral deficits in their sample are weaker when there is greater access to effective media.[13]

How does Latin America fit into that overall story? Not only is the literature full of messages of evident relevance for the region, but great attention has focused directly on Latin American countries. The general message is that there is evidence of electoral increases in deficits for the region taken as a whole. In one of the few early systematic studies of electoral fiscal cycles across countries, Ames (1987) analyzes a sample of 17 Latin American countries between 1947 and 1982. His findings indicate an increase in public spending before elections. The 2000s have witnessed a wave of renewed interest in cross-country studies about EBCs in the region. Amorim-Neto and Borsani (2004), Mejía-Acosta and Coppedge (2001), and Barberia and Avelino (2011) have all studied the behavior of fiscal outcomes around election times for samples of Latin American countries during the 1980s, 1990s, and the 2000s. They find electoral increases in fiscal imbalances, but are unable to find significant changes in spending. Only Barberia and Avelino look directly at revenue, finding weak evidence of revenue decreases before elections. While they interpret their findings as evidence that electoral deficits are driven by tax cuts, the weakness of their results on revenues could suggest that incumbents use tax cuts and spending increases alternatively, in such a way that no consistent pattern can be found for either.

Latin America fits well into several categories relevant to the theoretical discussion. It is composed of developing countries; several countries in the region transited to democracy in relatively recent times; and the general view is that institutions were relatively weak in the past two or three decades, plausibly implying poor media development and low government accountability. Does the literature shed light about which of these features explains the apparent existence of electoral deficits in the region? The answer is yes.

Barberia and Avelino (2011) divide their sample of Latin American elections according to measures of age and consolidation of the democratic regime. They show that the finding of deficit cycles in their overall sample is driven by countries in the first four elections after democratization. This result closely replicates that by Brender and Drazen (2005) in a larger sample of countries. It also suggests that, if EBCs have been more frequent in Latin America than in other regions over recent decades, this results from the widespread presence of dictatorships followed by episodes of democratization in the region's recent history. Interestingly, Barberia and Avelino also find that countries where democracy is less consolidated (rather than younger) do not show stronger deficit cycles. They use Huntington's (1991) strategy in flagging the consolidation of democracy as the second consecutive democratic turnover (between the government and the opposition parties). It thus seems that what moves the government to manipulate fiscal policies with electoral purposes is facing inexperienced electorates and media, rather than a history of defeats by the opposition that may signal a stable democracy. This seems consistent with the theoretical findings that deficit cycles arise only if voters are sufficiently poorly informed about fiscal policy.

Is fiscal policy unaffected by elections in countries with more experienced electorates? Not necessarily. Consistent with theoretical predictions, several studies find electoral changes in the composition of spending in countries without recent democratic transitions, both in Latin America and other regions. Drazen and Eslava (2010) examine different categories of spending for Colombian municipalities for a 15-year period. They find a shift of public spending from specific categories of current spending, such as transfers, toward public works (specifically housing projects and spending on health services). Khemani (2004) and Kneebone and McKenzie (2001) find similar evidence for India and Canada, respectively. Electoral changes in the composition of spending, interestingly, are not only present in democracies with competitive elections. González (2002) studies federal spending choices in one-party Mexico, finding increases in infrastructure spending and cuts in transfers in the quarters that preceded elections.

This characterization of fiscal policy preceding elections fits well with findings regarding election outcomes. In particular, electoral deficits seem to help incumbents get reelected only in specific contexts that fit the notion of new democracies. In other countries, incumbents seem to rather lose votes if they show fiscal indiscipline. Latin America is no exception to this characterization. Jones, Meloni, and Tommasi (2009) find that Argentinean voters reward incumbent governors for high spending, while Sakurai and Menezes-Filho (2008) find that Brazilian voters do the same with incumbent mayors. In contrast, Drazen and Eslava (2010) found that Colombian mayors who run deficits face a lower probability of reelection. Colombian voters, however, are more likely to reelect incumbents who have incurred higher capital expenditures, controlling for the level of the fiscal deficit (i.e., voters prefer incumbent candidates whose spending is tilted toward capital expenditures independently of their overall level of public spending).[14]

What to make of these apparently mixed results? Notice that Argentina and Brazil lived through a democratic transition in very recent times, while Colombia's only episode of transition took place more than 60 years ago. In fact, empirical studies for the first two cases cover the early years of the transition. One possible assessment of these pieces of evidence is that Colombian voters, more used to exercising their electoral rights than Brazilians and Argentineans, do not fall for electoral spending increases. This story would be consistent with the aforementioned view that electoral cycles in deficits or overall spending are a phenomenon of contexts with less sophisticated voters. In fact, Arvate, Avelino, and Tavares (2009) reexamine the Brazilian case, and show that the effect of fiscal deficits on the incumbent's reelection chances depends on how sophisticated voters are.[15] Running a deficit actually makes the mayor less likely to stay in power in municipalities with high literacy rates.

The aforementioned evidence for Latin America fits well with the more general pattern found by the empirical literature. Brender and Drazen (2008) examine the electoral consequences of fiscal outcomes for a large sample of countries. They find that electoral deficits harm the incumbent's reelection chances in old democracies, but the negative impact disappears for new democracies. Within-country studies for other regions also fit this pattern well. While voters in the United States have been characterized as fiscal conservatives for punishing incumbents running deficits (Peltzman 1992), the post-transition Russian electorate falls on the other end of the spectrum (Akhmedov and Zhuravskaya 2004). In turn, Brender (2003) finds that in Israel deficits hurt incumbents' reelection prospects, but only in a late period characterized by better media and accounting practices.

Recently, Jones et al. (2009) have proposed a different approach to explaining the differential responses of voters to fiscal indiscipline. They note that within-country studies rejecting the view that voters are fiscal conservatives focus on countries where most public spending is decided locally and funded centrally: Argentina, Brazil, and Russia. Since the costs of the excesses by local authorities are not paid for by their constituencies, incumbents are not held accountable. While the argument is appealing, work is still needed to assess its empirical relevance to the argument of naive versus sophisticated voters, and its implications in terms of political budget cycles. If votes depend on past fiscal outcomes because voters are trying to learn about the incumbent's unobserved competence to provide public goods, voters' ability to monitor fiscal outcomes should still play a role.[16] In particular, preelection fiscal performance would have no impact on election results if voters perfectly observed all fiscal choices—at least under the competence approach—even if voters did not have to pay for preelection spending. Fiscal federalism would then interact with voters' degree of sophistication, rather than replacing it as an explanation for voters' willingness to reward fiscal indiscipline. In turn, fiscal federalism should drive politicians to generate electoral deficits only if voters were sufficiently poorly informed to believe that their perceptions of greater spending reflect greater competence by the incumbent.

3.3. Budget Institutions: An Effective Restraint?

If opportunistic deficits are the result of voters' inability to distinguish between competent and wasteful incumbents, improving fiscal transparency should help by empowering voters to punish fiscal profligacy. Unfortunately, even though Latin America has been ground for pioneering studies on the effects of budget institutions, there is no conclusive evidence on the effectiveness of fiscal transparency as a means to reducing political manipulation of the budget in the region. Three influential studies have assessed the effects of budget institutions on fiscal outcomes, and have been unable to identify any significant effect of transparency (Alesina et al. 1999; Stein et al. 1999; Filc and Scartascini 2007). These results stand in contrast to results in studies for other countries of the world, including countries similar to those in Latin America. As mentioned, Dabla-Norris et al. (2010) find the transparency component of their index for budget institutions to have the more robust and stronger positive effect on fiscal balances, for a large sample of low-income countries. In turn, Alt and Lassen (2006) find that more transparent budget institutions in OECD countries ameliorate electoral fiscal cycles, and improve fiscal outcomes in the long run.

Why, then, the lack of evidence on the importance of transparency for fiscal outcomes in Latin America? The answer probably lies in methodological issues. First, the approach to measuring transparency differs across studies. While the focus in Latin American studies is on the possibility that regional governments and public enterprises borrow—creating implicit liabilities for the central government—other studies assess the mechanisms for effectively communicating budget details to the public. Second, indexes of budget transparency typically do not vary over years, so studies have generally focused on cross-sections of countries. This implies very low numbers of observations when attention is focused on specific regions, so much so that the ability of statistical tests to separate the effects of different dimensions of budget institutions (like transparency and procedures) should be called into question. Studies on Latin American budget institutions have focused on cross sections of 20 countries or so. While their finding that budget institutions, as a whole, are crucial determinants of budget outcomes is quite robust, their attempts to identify the precise dimensions that matter most are less compelling in light of the very few observations on which they are based.

Understanding the dimensions of transparency that are effective to limit electoral budget cycles, and improve fiscal outcomes more generally, is crucial for policy purposes in the region. There is still much ground to cover on that front. Fortunately, the vehicles to cover it are becoming increasingly available. Measures of transparency should assess not only how unified government accounts are but also how effectively they are communicated to voters. Recent data collection efforts provide the data to construct these types of measures (e.g., the sources used in Dabla-Norris et al. 2010). In terms of estimation techniques, studies can take advantage of the richness in panel data, even if indexes of budget institutions lack time variability. This is the approach followed by Alt and Lassen (2006), who estimate a panel model of electoral budget cycles, and use their data on budget institutions to judge whether greater transparency dampens cycles.

3.4. Discussion

The evidence for Latin America suggests that, taking the region as a whole, over the last two decades fiscal balances tended to deteriorate in years preceding elections. These electoral deficit cycles in large samples of Latin American countries seem to reflect the specific experiences of some countries in their first few electoral cycles after the return of democracy. Consistent with these findings, case studies for those countries suggest that voters tend to reelect incumbents who undertake fiscal expansions before elections.

Electoral deficit cycles and their electoral rewards, however, are likely to change in the region, as voters in young democracies gain experience regarding incentives and outcomes in a democratic setting. Likely, voters will learn that preelectoral deficits reflect electoral incentives for incumbents, rather than their competence as providers of public goods. Incumbents, in turn, should respond by focusing their preelectoral efforts on shifting resources toward public goods and services most appreciated by voters. This seems to have been the experience of more established democracies, both outside and inside the region.

4. Conclusion

In the discussion of theory and evidence relevant to Latin America on two separate political phenomena affecting fiscal outcomes—the common pool problem of fiscal policy and electoral budget cycles—two overarching issues deserve mention.

First, there is an unexplored likely intersection between some of the implications of the common pool problem and the form electoral budget cycles are likely to take in the future in Latin America. My discussion of the common pool problem should have made clear that the (formal and informal) rules governing the electoral system have implications regarding the way in which legislators target their respective constituencies. In particular, while majoritarian electoral rules create incentives for legislators to target their respective regions, under proportional rules and rules that favor the personal vote, legislators have incentives to target narrower constituencies within their districts. This, in turn, should have implications for the type of spending that renders most electoral gains. For instance, local public goods could be a relatively more effective tool to raise votes in majoritarian systems, while programs that redistribute wealth toward narrower constituencies could be more effective in more proportional systems (e.g., see Persson and Tabellini 2003). These differences are likely to spill over to electoral budget cycles. If we believe that in the future Latin America is likely to transit to electoral changes in the composition of spending, rather than electoral deficit increases, the direction of the composition shifts is likely to be affected by the characteristics of the electoral system. This issue deserves attention in future research.

Second, the two separate issues discussed in this chapter yield lessons that coincide in one dimension: the particular characteristics of Latin American politics do affect the way in which political phenomena affect fiscal outcomes. Two specific features make the region different: relatively young and growing democratization and the predominance of presidential regimes. The literature discussed in this chapter shows that the former may explain why electoral deficit cycles have been more prevalent in Latin America than in other regions. It also suggests that the manipulation of fiscal outcomes with electoral purposes is likely to suffer transformations as democracy takes a stronger hold. Growing democratization has also been shown to imply increasing importance of the common pool problem; how to address the resulting tension between representativeness and fiscal discipline, without excessive sacrifice in terms of democratic representation, is a crucial question facing policymakers in the region. Finally, presidentialism has been shown to affect the way in which legislative fragmentation affects fiscal outcomes. This suggests lessons from the extensive literature focusing on parliamentary democracies should be taken with a grain of salt when applied to the Latin American context.

NOTES

My e-mail address is meslava@uniandes.edu.co. I thank Santiago Ramírez for very helpful research assistance.

   1. While this chapter covers existing evidence for countries less similar to those in Latin America—such as European countries—this is done mainly for comparison purposes. For a more in-depth review of findings for those types of countries, see Eslava (2011).

   2. In fact, only the studies by Amorim-Neto and Borsani (2004) and Mejía-Acosta and Coppedge (2001) take advantage of the time dimension.

   3. The finding of a stronger and more significant effect on government spending than on deficits seems pervasive in the literature (Perotti and Kontopoulos 2002). While the theoretical literature has not made much of these differences, they seem quite important from a policy standpoint. I come back to discussing alternative focuses on spending, revenues, or balances in the conclusions.

   4. "Pork-barrel" spending is widely seen as a main coalition-building tool in Brazil. For instance, Samuels (2002, 315) describes the Brazilian budget process as one where the executive first writes the budget proposal, then "legislators add pork-barrel amendments to proposal, and then pass the budget back to the executive."

   5. Cheibub, Przeworski, and Saiegh (2004) have challenged the view that governments in presidential democracies are less effective because they are less likely to form coalitions. I do not hold that presidential democracies are less likely to feature coalitions around the government, but that coalitions face more frequent transformations under

presidential regimes. Amorim-Neto (2002) holds a similar view for the specific case of Latin America.

6. Persson and Tabellini (2003) present a comprehensive analysis of the fiscal consequences of constitutional rules, including an excellent survey of the literature.

7. In fact, Persson and Tabellini (2003, table 6.7) find only marginal differences in budget surpluses between majoritarian-presidential and proportional-presidential regimes, in a large sample of countries from all regions.

8. Studies have focused on specific regions. Besides the studies I review for Latin America, there are works looking at the European case (or more generally the OECD), including von Hagen (1992); von Hagen and Harden (1995); Hallerberg, Strauch, and von Hagen (2007); de Haan and Sturm (1994); and de Haan, Moessen, and Volkerink (1999). Dabla-Norris et al. (2010) recently conducted the most comprehensive study I know of, looking at 72 low- and middle-income countries. Studies beyond the Latin American case find that budget institutions are effective in improving fiscal outcomes, with qualifications I discuss in the text.

9. In related research, Hallerberg, Strauch, and von Hagen (2007, 2009) find that in Europe highly cohesive governments (coalitions of closely aligned parties in addition to one-party governments) achieve fiscal discipline by delegating budget decisions to the minister of finance, while more dispersed coalitions achieve fiscal discipline through targets.

10. Very convincing evidence of the same phenomenon has been found for the United States and European countries by Canova and Pappa (2006); von Hagen (1991); and von Hagen and Wolff (2006).

11. The outcomes, however, have been quite different in these cases (Hallerberg, Scartascini, and Stein 2009). While in Bolivia and Colombia the resulting excess spending has translated into growing debt, in Brazil the government executes only parts of the pork-barrel projects included in the budget by legislators, keeping fiscal outcomes under control.

12. The common pool problem leads to excessive spending in a well-defined sense, not necessarily implying sustained deficits. In particular, distributive conflict leads to spending that is excessive in the sense of having costs that exceed the benefits. Whether the resulting level of spending is or is not covered by government revenues is an entirely different question. Velasco (1999) presents a model where the common pool problem does result in deficits. However, this result is achieved by assuming that interest groups choose net transfers and have preferences about net transfers (that is, direct preferences about deficits), rather than preferences about spending. But the budget process is generally one where what is being defined is spending, while the tax system is predetermined. It thus seem plausible to consider the possibility of redesigning the tax structure to yield revenues that match the level of spending that the political process is expected to deliver.

13. Unfortunately, they do not show to what extent low economic development reflects limited media access.

14. Similar findings are reported for Israel by Brender (2003).

15. Ferraz and Finan (2008) provide evidence for Brazil on the importance of supplying voters with effective tools to monitor governments. They show that administrations subject to fiscal inspections are strongly punished in the following election if inspectors find evidence of corruption.

16. Voters' access to information plays no explicit role in Jones et al.'s (2009) model because restrospective voting is exogenously imposed.

REFERENCES

Abuelafia, Emanuel, Sergio Berensztein, Miguel Braun, and Luciano di Grezia. 2009. "Who Decides on Public Expenditures? A Political Economy Analysis of the Budget Process: The Case of Argentina." In *Who Decides the Budget? A Political Economy Analysis of the Budget Process in Latin America*, edited by Mark Hallerberg, Carlos Scartascini, and Ernesto H. Stein, 23–56. Washington, DC: Inter-American Development Bank; Cambridge, MA: David Rockefeller Center for Latin American Studies, Harvard University.

Akhmedov, Akhmed, and Ekaterina Zhuravskaya. 2004. "Opportunistic Political Cycles: Test in a Young Democracy Setting." *Quarterly Journal of Economics* 119(4): 1301–38.

Alesina, Alberto, Ricardo Hausmann, Rudolf Hommes, and Ernesto Stein. 1999. "Budget Institutions and Fiscal Performance in Latin America." *Journal of Development Economics* 59(2): 253–73.

Alesina, Alberto, and Roberto Perotti. 1995. "The Political Economy of Budget Deficits." *IMF Staff Papers* 42: 1–31.

Alesina, Alberto, Roberto Perotti, and José Tavares. 1998. "The Political Economy of Fiscal Adjustments." *Brookings Papers on Economic Activity* 1: 197–248.

Alston, Lee, Marcus Melo, Bernardo Mueller, and Carlos Pereira. 2009. "Presidential Powers, Fiscal Responsibility Laws, and the Allocation of Spending: The Case of Brazil." In *Who Decides The Budget? A Political Economy Analysis of the Budget Process in Latin America*, edited by Mark Hallerberg, Carlos Scartascini, and Ernesto Stein, 57–90. Washington, DC: Inter-American Development Bank; Cambridge, MA: David Rockefeller Center for Latin American Studies, Harvard University.

Alt, James E., and David Dryer Lassen. 2006. "Fiscal Transparency, Political Parties, and Debt in OECD Countries." *European Economic Review* 50: 1430–39.

Ames, Barry. 1987. *Political Survival: Politicians and Public Policy in Latin America*. Berkeley: University of California Press.

Amorim-Neto, Octavio. 2002. "Presidential Cabinets, Electoral Cycles, and Coalition Discipline in Brazil." In *Legislative Politics in Latin America*, edited by Scott Morgenstern and Benito Nacif, 48–78. Cambridge: Cambridge University Press.

Amorim-Neto, Octavio, and Hugo Borsani. 2004. "Presidents and Cabinets: The Political Determinants of Fiscal Behavior in Latin America." *Studies in Comparative International Development* 39(1): 3–27.

Arvate, Paulo Roberto, George Avelino, and José Tavares. 2009. "Fiscal Conservatism in a New Democracy: 'Sophisticated' vs. 'Naive' Voters." *Economics Letters* 102: 125–27.

Austin-Smith, David. 2000. "Redistributing Income under Proportional Representation." *Journal of Political Economy* 108(6): 1235–69.

Barberia, Lorena G., and George Avelino. 2011. "Do Political Budget Cycles Differ in Latin American Democracies?" *Economía* 11(2): 101–34.

Brender, Adi. 2003. "The Effect of Fiscal Performance on Local Government Election Results in Israel: 1989–1998." *Journal of Public Economics* 87: 2187–205.

Brender, Adi, and Allan Drazen. 2005. "Political Budget Cycles in New versus Established Democracies." *Journal of Monetary Economics* 52(7): 1271–95.

———. 2008. "How Do Budget Deficits and Economic Growth Affect Reelection Prospects? Evidence from a Large Panel of Countries." *American Economic Review* 98(5): 2203–20.

Canova, Fabio, and Evi Pappa. 2006. "The Elusive Costs and the Immaterial Gains of Fiscal Constraints." *Journal of Public Economics* 90(8–9): 1391–414.

Cárdenas, Mauricio, Carolina Mejía, and Mauricio Olivera. 2009. "Changes in Fiscal Outcomes in Colombia: The Role of the Budget Process." In *Who Decides the Budget?*

A Political Economy Analysis of the Budget Process in Latin America, edited by Mark Hallerberg, Carlos Scartascini, and Ernesto Stein, 91–122. Washington, DC: Inter-American Development Bank; Cambridge, MA: David Rockefeller Center for Latin American Studies, Harvard University.

Cheibub, José Antonio, Adam Przeworski, and Sebastián Saiegh. 2004. "Government Coalitions and Legislative Success under Parliamentarism and Presidentialism." *British Journal of Political Science* 34: 565–87.

Dabla-Norris, Era, Richard Allen, Luis Felipe Zanna, Tej Prakash, Eteri Kvintradze, Victor Lledo, Irene Yackovlev, and Sophia Gollwitzer. 2010. "Budget Institutions and Fiscal Performance in Low-Income Countries." *IMF Working Papers* 10/80: 1–56.

de Haan, Jakob, Wim Moessen, and Bjorn Volkerink. 1999. "Budgetary Procedures, Aspects and Changes: New Evidence for Some European Countries." In *Fiscal Institutions and Fiscal Performance*, edited by James M. Poterba and Jürgen von Hagen, 265–300. Chicago: University of Chicago Press and National Bureau of Economic Research.

de Haan, Jakob, and Jan-Egbert Sturm. 1994. "Political and Institutional Determinants of Fiscal Policy in the European Community." *Public Choice* 80: 157–72.

De Sousa, Mariana Magaldi. 2010. "How Courts Engage in the Policymaking Process in Latin America: The Different Functions of the Judiciary." In eds. *How Democracy Works*, edited by Carlos Scartascini, Ernesto Stein, and Mariano Tommasi, 77–117. Washington, DC: Inter-American Development Bank.

Drazen Allan, and Marcela Eslava. 2006. "Pork Barrel Cycles." NBER Working Paper No. 12190, National Bureau of Economic Research, Cambridge, MA.

———. 2010. "Electoral Manipulation via Expenditure Composition: Theory and Evidence." *Journal of Development Economics* 92(1): 39–52.

Echeverry, Juan Carlos, Leopoldo Fergusson, and Pablo Querubin. 2004. "La Batalla Política Por El Presupuesto De La Nación: Inflexibilidades O Supervivencia Fiscal." Documentos CEDE No. 002944. Bogotá: Centro de Estudios sobre Desarrollo Económico (CEDE), Universidad de Los Andes.

Eslava, Marcela. 2006. "The Political Economy of Fiscal Policy: A Survey." IADB Working Paper No. 683, Inter-American Development Bank, Washington, DC.

———.2011. "The Political Economy of Fiscal Deficits: A Survey." *Journal of Economic Surveys* 25(4): 645–73.

Eslava, Marcela, and Oskar Nupia. 2010. "Fragmentation and Government Spending: Bringing Ideological Polarization into the Picture." Documento CEDE No. 2010-3, Centro de Estudios sobre Desarrollo Económico (CEDE), Universidad de Los Andes, Bogotá.

Ferraz, Claudio, and Frederico Finan. 2008. "Exposing Corrupt Politicians: The Effect of Brazil's Publicly Released Audits on Electoral Outcomes." *Quarterly Journal of Economics* 123(2): 703–45.

Filc, Gabriel, and Carlos Scartascini. 2005. "Budget Institutions and Fiscal Outcomes." *International Journal of Public Budget* 59: 81–138.

———. 2007. "Instituciones presupuestarias." In *El Estado de las Reformas del Estado en América Latina*, edited by Eduardo Lora, 175–208. Washington, DC: Inter-American Development Bank and World Bank; Bogotá: Mayol Editores.

González, María de los Angeles. 2002. "Do Changes in Democracy Affect the Political Budget Cycle? Evidence from Mexico." *Review of Development Economics* 6: 204–24.

Gupta, Sanjeev, Benedict Clements, Emanuele Baldacci, and Carlos Mulas-Granados. 2004. "The Persistence of Fiscal Adjustments in Developing Countries." *Applied Economics Letters* 11(4): 209–12.

Hallerberg, Mark, and Patrick Marier, 2004. "Executive Authority, the Personal Vote, and Budget Discipline in Latin American and Caribbean Countries." *American Journal of Political Science* 48(3): 571–87.

Hallerberg, Mark, Carlos Scartascini, and Ernesto Stein. 2009. "The Budget Process as a Political Arena." In *Who Decides the Budget? A Political Economy Analysis of the Budget Process in Latin America*, edited by Mark Hallerberg, Carlos Scartascini, and Ernesto Stein, 295–302. Washington, DC: Inter-American Development Bank; Cambridge, MA: David Rockefeller Center for Latin American Studies, Harvard University.

Hallerberg, Mark, Rolf Strauch, and Jürgen von Hagen. 2007. "The Design of Fiscal Rules and Forms of Governance in European Union Countries." *European Journal of Political Economy* 23(2): 338–59.

———. 2009. *Fiscal Governance in Europe*. Cambridge: Cambridge University Press.

Huntington, Samuel. 1991. *The Third Wave*. Norman: University of Oklahoma Press.

IADB (Inter-American Development Bank). 2009. *The Politics of the Budget Process*. IDEA No. 20 (Sept.–Dec.). Washington, DC: IADB.

IMF (International Monetary Fund). 2005. "Stabilization and Reform in Latin America: A Macroeconomic Perspective on the Experience since the Early 1990s." Occasional Paper No. 238, IMF, Washington, DC.

Jones, Mark, Osvaldo Meloni, and Mariano Tommasi. 2009. "Voters as Fiscal Liberals: Incentives and Accountability in Federal Systems." Unpublished manuscript, Universidad de San Andrés.

Jones, Mark, Pablo Sanguinetti, and Mariano Tommasi. 2000. "Politics, Institutions, and Fiscal Performance in a Federal System: An Analysis of the Argentine Provinces." *Journal of Development Economics* 61:305–33.

Khemani, Stuti. 2004. "Political Cycles in a Developing Economy." *Journal of Development Economics* 73: 125–54.

Kneebone, Ronald D., and Kenneth J. McKenzie. 2001. "Electoral and Partisan Cycles in Fiscal Policy: An Examination of Canadian Provinces." *International Tax and Public Finance* 8: 753–74.

Krogstrup, Signe, and Charles Wyplosz. 2010. "A Common Pool Theory of Supranational Deficit Ceilings." *European Economic Review* 54(2): 269–78.

Mejía-Acosta, Andrés, and Michael Coppedge. 2001. "Fiscal Policy and Reelection in Brazilian Municipalities." Paper presented at the International Congress of the Latin American Studies Association, Washington, DC, Sept. 5–8, 2001.

Milesi-Ferretti, Gian Maria. 2003. "Good, Bad or Ugly? On the Effects of Fiscal Rules with Creative Accounting." *Journal of Public Economics* 88: 377–94.

Milesi-Ferretti, Gian Maria, Roberto Perotti, and Massimo Rostagno. 2002. "Electoral Systems and Public Spending." *Quarterly Journal of Economics* 117(2): 609–57.

Mukherjee, Bmba. 2003. "Political Parties and the Size of Government in Multiparty Legislatures." *Comparative Political Studies* 26(6): 699–728.

OECD (Organisation for Economic Co-operation and Development). 2007–8. International Database of Budget Practices and Procedures, Paris: Organisation for Economic Co-operation and Development (available at www.oecd.org/gov/budget/database).

Peltzman, Sam. 1992. "Voters as Fiscal Conservatives." *Quarterly Journal of Economics* 107: 327–361.

Perotti, Roberto, and Yianos Kontopoulos. 2002. "Fragmented Fiscal Policy." *Journal of Public Economics* 86: 191–222.

Persson Torsten, and Guido Tabellini. 1999. "The Size and Scope of Government: Comparative Politics with Rational Politicians." *European Economic Review* 43(4–6): 699–735.

———. 2002. "Political Economics and Public Finance?" In *Handbook of Public Economics*, vol. 3, edited by Alan Auerbach and Martin Feldstein, North-Holland.

———. 2003. *The Economic Effects of Constitutions*. Cambridge, MA: MIT Press.

Rogoff, Kenneth. 1990. "Equilibrium Political Budget Cycles." *American Economic Review* 80: 21–36.

Rogoff, Kenneth, and Anne Sibert. 1988. "Elections and Macroeconomic Policy Cycles." *Review of Economic Studies* 55: 1–16.

Sakurai, Sergio Naruhiko, and Naercio Menezes-Filho. 2008. "Fiscal Policy and Reelection in Brazilian Municipalities." *Public Choice* 137: 301–14.

Samuels, D. 2002. "Progressive Ambition, Federalism, and Pork-Barreling in Brazil." In *Legislative Politics in Latin America*, edited by Scott Morgenstern and Benito Nacif, 315–38. Cambridge: Cambridge University Press.

Shi, Min, and Jakob Svensson. 2006. "Political Budget Cycles: Do They Differ across Countries and Why?" *Journal of Public Economics* 90: 1367–89.

Stein, Ernesto, Ernesto Talvi, and Alejandro Grisanti. 1999. "Institutional Arrangements and Fiscal Performance: The Latin American Experience." In *Fiscal Institutions and Fiscal Performance*, edited by James M. Poterba and Jürgen von Hagen, 103–34. Chicago: University of Chicago Press and National Bureau of Economic Research.

Velasco, A. 1999. "A Model of Endogenous Fiscal Deficits and Delayed Fiscal Reforms." In *Fiscal Institutions and Fiscal Performance*, edited by James M. Poterba and Jürgen von Hagen, 37–58. Chicago: University of Chicago Press and National Bureau of Economic Research.

———. 2000. "Debts and Deficits with Fragmented Fiscal Policymaking." *Journal of Public Economics* 76: 105–25.

Von Hagen, Jürgen. 1991. "A Note on the Empirical Effectiveness of Formal Fiscal Restraints." *Journal of Public Economics* 44(2): 199–210.

———. 1992. "Budgeting Procedures and Fiscal Performance in the European Community." EEC Economic Papers No. 96, European Economic Community, Brussels.

Von Hagen, Jürgen, and Ian Harden. 1995. "Budget Processes and Commitment to Fiscal Discipline." *European Economic Review* 39(3–4): 771–79.

Von Hagen, Jürgen, and Guntram B. Wolff. 2006. "What Do Deficits Tell Us about Debt? Empirical Evidence on Creative Accounting with Fiscal Rules in the EU." *Journal of Banking and Finance* 30(12): 3259–79.

Weingast, Barry R., Kenneth A. Shepsle, and Christopher Johnsen. 1981. "The Political Economy of Benefits and Costs: A Neoclassical Approach to Distributive Politics." *Journal of Political Economy* 89: 642–64.

Woo, Jaejoon. 2003. "Economic, Political, and Institutional Determinants of Public Deficits." *Journal of Public Economics* 87: 387–426.

CHAPTER 20

....

TAXATION AND DEMOCRACY IN LATIN AMERICA

....

CHRISTIAN DAUDE AND ÁNGEL MELGUIZO

1. MOTIVATION

....

In the second half of the eighteenth century, the population of the British colonies in North America rallied behind the demand "no taxation without representation!" Citizens in the colonies were taxed by Britain, but had no direct representation in the British Parliament, a state of affairs they considered an illegal denial of their rights as Englishmen. This movement was especially popular in Boston, where protest movements culminated in December 1773. The Boston Tea Party, as it became known, arose when a dispute about whether to accept three shiploads of tea—and pay the British taxes on them—escalated into direct action. A group of colonists boarded the ships and destroyed their cargo by throwing it into the Boston Harbor. Historians point to the incident as the spark that ultimately led to the War of Independence and the establishment of the United States of America, founded on the principles of democracy and fiscal legitimacy. This event highlights how fiscal policy is at the very heart of the social contract between citizens and the state.

Although public finance and democracy do not always go hand-in-hand, democracy is the political regime where social preferences are most likely to be reflected—via fiscal policy—in the allocation of resources, redistribution of income, and stabilization of the economy. Wicksell addressed this relationship more than a century ago in his "voluntary exchange theory of revenue-expenditures," where taxes are voluntary payments by individuals in exchange for public services (see Musgrave 1939 for a critical discussion).

This chapter addresses the relationship between taxation and democratic consolidation in Latin America and the Caribbean. We show that building better institutions, especially by reducing corruption, pays in terms of tax morale, and probably gives more leeway to raise general taxation. In addition, perspectives on upward mobility are generally not an impediment to taxation in the region. Latin Americans who see themselves or their children rising on the social ladder do not justify cheating on taxes (sometimes the opposite, in fact); neither do they consider current taxation too high. Finally, in this process of strengthening the social contract, the middle class may play a key role as the social segment that supports the most fully developed democracy, thanks to its centrist political position.

The relationship between citizens' perceptions regarding the functioning of democracy and their attitudes toward fiscal policy is crucial. Latin America and the Caribbean is a particularly interesting region, characterized by very high levels of income inequality, and relatively low levels of fiscal revenues and redistribution. Figure 20.1 shows that while tax revenues vary considerably within the region, on a general basis they are low (in terms of the gross domestic product [GDP]) compared to the countries in the Organisation for Economic Co-operation and Development (OECD). Only Brazil presents levels of tax collection similar to those in the OECD. Even high-revenue countries like Argentina, where tax revenues are around 27.4 percent of GDP, present a gap with respect to the OECD average of more than 8.4

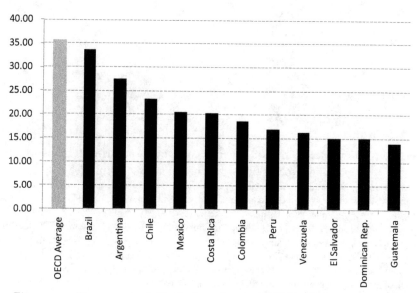

Figure 20.1 Tax revenues in Latin American and OECD economies in 2006
(percentage of GDP).
Source: Based on OECD (2008) and OECD revenue statistics.

percentage points (p.p.) of GDP. Excluding Brazil and Argentina, this difference in tax revenues is on average 18.0 p.p. of GDP for the rest of the region.

In addition, despite recent improvements due to a decline in skill premium and the effect of targeted government transfers, income inequality after the intervention of the public sector remains high by international standards in most countries in the region.

This situation has led some authors to argue that the social contract is broken (or at least extremely weak) in the region. Figure 20.2 shows one key aspect of this discussion, the low levels of tax morale compared to OECD countries.[1] On average, citizens in Latin America are almost three times more likely to justify tax evasion (20 percent in Latin America versus 7 percent in OECD countries), and only 34 percent of respondents in Latin America consider tax evasion always wrong compared to an average of 62 percent in OECD countries.

In the next section we briefly summarize the related theoretical and empirical literature. The third section reports the basic trends in consolidation of democratic regimes in Latin America, the level of support expressed for democracy among different income groups, and some of the main features of taxation (level and composition) in the region. In the fourth section we test empirically whether self-reported income and the perception of future and past mobility matter for support

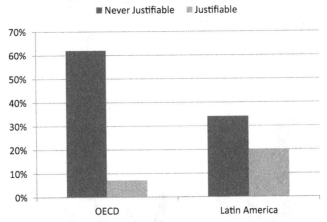

Figure 20.2 Tax morale in Latin America and OECD countries. Responses to the question "Do you think cheating on taxes is justifiable?".

Notes: The average for Latin America includes data from 18 countries: Argentina, Bolivia, Brazil, Chile, Colombia, Costa Rica, Dominican Republic, Ecuador, El Salvador, Guatemala, Honduras, Mexico, Nicaragua, Panama, Paraguay, Peru, Uruguay, and Venezuela for 2008. For the OECD, it includes data from 20 countries: Australia (2005), Canada (2006), Finland (2005), France (2006), Germany (2006), United Kingdom (2006), Italy (2005), Japan (2005), Mexico (2005), Netherlands (2006), New Zealand (2004), Norway (2007), Poland (2005), Slovenia (2005), South Korea (2005), Spain (2007), Sweden (2006), Switzerland (2007), Turkey (2007), United States (2006). The specific question asked is: Please tell me for each of the following statements whether you think it can always be justified, never be justified, or something in between: Cheating on taxes if you have a chance: 1 – Never Justifiable, 2, 3, . . . 10 – Always Justifiable. "Never Justifiable" refers to the percentage of answers that reply 1; "Justifiable" is the percentage of answers between 5 and 10. Source: Based on Latinobarómetro survey 2008 and World Values Survey database.

for and satisfaction with democracy and for political preferences (often associated with the demand for redistribution). Additionally, we ask whether perceptions of social mobility and fairness in the society condition the role of taxation in the social contract. In particular, we study whether people's views about the appropriate levels of taxation and their willingness to pay taxes change when governments use these funds properly or when there are chances of social advancement. Section 5 summarizes the main results, highlighting the main policy implications and lines for further research.

2. A Brief Review of the Literature

The median voter theory (see for instance Downs 1957) suggests that democracy should induce governments to raise revenues and significantly redistribute income if ex ante (i.e., before taxes and government transfers) inequality is high, as it is in Latin America. Simply put, in such a situation the median voter would benefit from progressive income taxation, which will fall more heavily on voters with higher incomes than his or hers, and progressive transfers and spending, which will disproportionately favor the median voter.

However, even in theory, democracy may be a necessary, but not sufficient condition for a larger public sector and more redistribution. As recently surveyed in Alesina and Giuliano (2009), Alt, Preston, and Sibieta (2010), and Robinson (2010), preferences for redistribution stem from numerous sources: from the individual's history (mobility experiences and perceptions might affect political attitudes toward redistribution; Piketty 1995), the political system, the organization of the family, nation- and region-wide cultural and social values (Bénabou and Tirole 2006; Roemer 1998), or even race (Alesina and Glaeser 2004).

In a seminal article, Meltzer and Richards (1981) argue that the demand for redistribution results from a balance between the aspirations of the middle and poor classes and the economy-wide disincentives they expect from a higher level of taxation. In particular, if poor and middle-income voters (potential beneficiaries from redistribution) take into account the effects of taxation on labor-leisure decisions of their fellow rich citizens when voting, this will limit the size of government—tax revenues—and consequently the degree of redistribution.

Alesina and Angeletos (2005b) stress the relevance of social beliefs about the degree of fairness in the society. According to these authors, if a majority of members of a society believe that they live under a "meritocracy" (in which primarily individual effort determines income), and that all have the same rights and opportunities to enjoy the fruits of their effort, they will choose low levels of taxes and redistribution. Consequently, in equilibrium, effort would be high and the role of luck, family background, connections, or corruption limited. In their model there exists also a second and opposite equilibrium. If society believes that luck, birth, connections, or corruption determine wealth, it will levy high taxes, and social beliefs will be self-fulfilling as well.[2]

In fact, as Bénabou and Ok (2001) formalize, even the poor may vote for low levels of redistribution if they think that in the future, they or their offspring could progress (becoming a net payer and not benefiting from higher tax rates and redistribution). Thus, societies with high mobility, or more precisely where people believe that there is high mobility, may therefore opt for low levels of redistribution. This is the so-called prospect of upward mobility (POUM) hypothesis. Conversely, in societies where mobility is perceived to be low, the median voter theorem will rule and the poor will vote for more redistribution. Rodríguez (2004) proposes a reassessment of the POUM effect: in societies where the rich can influence politics to the extent that they do not pay taxes, the median voter will prefer low levels of taxation to reduce the incentives for rent seeking. Additionally, Corneo and Grüner (2000) highlight the role of social incentives. Even if middle-class households may benefit from larger redistribution, the fear of losing social status in favor of the poor may align them with those favoring lower taxes.

Nevertheless, it is important to note that for the POUM to hold, some conditions have to hold. First, policies should be expected to persist.[3] Furthermore, agents should not be very risk averse, as under extreme risk aversion everybody would like to be insured against bad shocks and therefore are likely to vote for a large welfare state. Finally, the distribution of income has to be such that those poorer than the average should expect to become richer than the average (Bénabou and Ok 2001).

All of these factors may be temporary. As illustrated by the "tunnel effect" of Hirschman (1973), poor and middle-class individuals may be willing to accept and support high (or even increasing) levels of inequality during the early stages of development (staying in the slow lane of the traffic jam in the tunnel, according to his evocative metaphor). But they will only do so as long as they keep their hope in progressing (i.e., that their lane starts to advance faster as well). Government credibility, risk aversion, and expectations therefore play a crucial role.

Przeworski (2007) points out that even if those without property constitute a vast majority, they either may not want to or be able to use their political rights to equalize property, incomes, or even opportunities. This might be not just due to the expectation of becoming rich but also to ideological domination, as the media are owned by the elite, or to difficulties of the poor in coordinating political actions when they have heterogeneous preferences about other aspects of life not directly related to the economy. In a related article, Chong and Olivera (2008) show empirically that countries with compulsory voting exhibit less income inequality. Therefore, since poorer countries also have relatively more unequal distributions of income, the authors support the promotion of such voting schemes in developing countries.

However, Przeworski (2007) adds an additional and challenging dimension. Even in situations when governments are elected with the support of the poor to equalize income and then try to do so, they may fail. Modern redistribution policies aim mainly at equalizing human capital by investing in health services and education (in contrast to a focus on redistribution of land or industrial capital as in the past). Such redistribution could not result in an equalization of outcomes anymore, as the same educational system may produce different outcomes depending on the socioeconomic background of pupils.[4] In other words, the equalization of opportunities may not be enough to reduce inequalities. Furthermore, if the people are aware of these weak effects of publicly provided services, they will attach low value to these services and hence have a low willingness to fund them through taxes.

In contrast to this extensive theoretical literature, there are relatively few rigorous empirical studies regarding the topics outlined above. Milanovic (2000), based on household data (which relates decisions on the optimal level of transfers and taxes to inequality before government intervention) for a panel of 24 industrialized countries from the 1970s to the late 1990s, finds that support for redistribution (measured as the variation of inequality pre- and post-tax and also transfers) is positively associated with initial inequality in factor incomes.[5] For a sample of 25 countries, Isaksson and Lindskog (2009) show that self-interest (i.e., the expectation that one will be a net beneficiary or net payer) and meritocracy reduce the demand for redistribution between and within countries, respectively. However, the authors point out that heterogeneity across countries is very high and that in Latin America these effects are among the lowest. Corneo and Grüner (2002), for a sample of 12 countries, both industrialized and from emerging Europe, assert that not only self-interest and meritocracy but also social status play a significant role at the aggregate level.

Among the various explanations of the relationship between growth and inequality, Perotti (1996) analyses the so-called endogenous fiscal policy channel. This author tests whether more equality (measured by the share of income concentrated in the third and fourth quintiles, i.e., the median voter) leads to less demand for redistribution (lower marginal tax rates, lower tax collection from personal income taxes and labor taxes, lower expenditure on social security, health services, housing, or education). The empirical analysis only weakly confirms this view; the signs are the expected ones, but coefficients are not significant once the author controlled for the political regime.

Focusing on tax policy, Profeta and Scabrosetti (2008) suggest that several factors in Latin America may impede development of full democracy by having a significant effect on either the level of taxation or on its progressivity. In particular, they highlight low institutional capacity (especially in the tax administration), low quality of democracy (vulnerable to populisms, "termites" that erode the tax bases, and "devoradores" who capture social expenditure, as Elizondo and Santiso 2012 put it for Mexico and Brazil, respectively), and inefficiencies in the budgetary and tax systems (in the sense that expenditure and tax benefits tend to benefit the high-income population; see Breceda, Rigolini, and Saavedra 2009; OECD 2008). More formally, Profeta and Scabrosetti (2010) test empirically this hypothesis for emerging countries in Europe, Asia, and Latin America, from 1995 to 2004. Standard indicators to characterize political aspects such as democracy and its quality are significantly associated with higher tax revenues (especially among European countries), and with higher direct and indirect taxes. However, both Asia and Latin America show significantly lower levels of tax revenues than European counterparts, even when the authors controlled for differences in political institutions, indicating that other factors are at play.

Finally, there is also a related literature that analyzes perceptions in Latin America. Torgler (2005) highlights the significantly lower "tax morale" (i.e., the values and attitudes regarding tax compliance) in Latin America. He uses the Latinobarómetro survey for 1998 and the World Values Survey for 1981–97 (see note 9). According to the author, the main explanations for this low level of tax morale in Latin America are the perceived tax burden, low levels of honesty within the society and government, and corruption. Taxpayers perceive their relationship with the state not only as a relationship of coercion but also as one of exchange. When they believe they are treated fairly, they are more willing to pay taxes. Gaviria (2007), based on the Latinobarómetro 1996 and 2000 survey rounds, argues that the high demand for redistribution and the weak support for market outcomes in Latin America in the late 1990s and early 2000s stem from pessimistic views on social justice, equality of opportunities, and social mobility. Differences in expressed attitudes between rich and poor are substantial (in fact, larger than in other regions), and the poor are more likely to demand redistributive policies. Finally, Marcel (2008), based on the Chilean ECosociAL Survey for 2007 (carried out by the think tank Corporación de Estudios para Latinoamérica), shows that only a minority of Latin Americans believe that the low- and middle-income population will progress (e.g., gaining access to universities, owning a house, or establishing their own business) with high probability. At the same time, according to the author, Latin American citizens have strong beliefs in the value of effort, in the benefits of education, and in the shared responsibility of the state and the individual, backed by a willingness to pay more taxes to finance social insurance.[6]

3. SOME BASIC FACTS ON DEMOCRACY AND TAXATION IN LATIN AMERICA

As figure 20.1 shows, Latin American countries collect about 18.0 percent of GDP in taxes, on average, while the ratio for OECD countries is 35.8 percent. Certainly, tax revenues have increased in Latin America over the last decade and a half. As extensively analyzed in OECD (2008), between 1990 and 2006 tax revenues grew on average by close to 1.8 percent annually in real terms; and between 2003 and 2006 this rate accelerated to 3.4 percent. Even so, the difference between OECD and Latin American tax revenues remains high. For the period 1990–2005, this "tax gap" was 18.0 p.p. of GDP on average, though this masks a decline over the course of the period from 18.5 to 16.3 p.p., particularly after 2000, when Latin America experienced significant growth in revenues. The interregional gap shrinks further if the comparison is restricted to non-European OECD economies. The tax gap between Latin America and Asia-Pacific and North American OECD economies, while large (10.7 p.p.), is nevertheless lower than the difference with Europe (20.3 p.p.).[7]

How does the structure of taxation differ between Latin American and OECD countries? Figure 20.3 breaks down tax revenues into taxes on goods and services, personal and corporate income taxes, contributions to social security, and other taxes (e.g., property taxes and payroll taxes). Several differences in the structure of taxation between the groups of countries are immediately apparent.

First, compared to the OECD countries, Latin America exhibits a higher relative share of indirect taxation. In particular, countries in the region rely heavily on taxes on goods and services, which make up nearly half of overall tax revenue. As a share of GDP, Latin American taxes on goods and services approach levels observed in OECD countries, and are 2 p.p. higher than in Asia-Pacific and North American OECD countries. This greater reliance on indirect taxes is generally associated with a less progressive impact of taxation.

A comparison of Gini indexes both before and after taxes and transfers demonstrates that fiscal systems in Latin America do much less to reduce inequality. As OECD (2008) shows, the Gini coefficient of inequality in the European OECD countries is on average 47.6 before taxes and transfers, falling to 28.2 afterward. In contrast, for the Latin American economies examined, taxes and transfer affect the Gini index almost imperceptibly, taking it from 51.6 to 49.6. Therefore, much of the high inequality of Latin American countries relative to European countries stems from the relative effectiveness of fiscal systems. Recent analysis in a volume edited by López-Calva and Lustig (2010) points to a significant and widespread advance in the reduction of income inequality in Latin America between 2000 and 2006. In particular, the authors study in depth the cases of Argentina, Brazil, Mexico, and Peru, where inequality has been reduced because of the fall in the earnings gap between

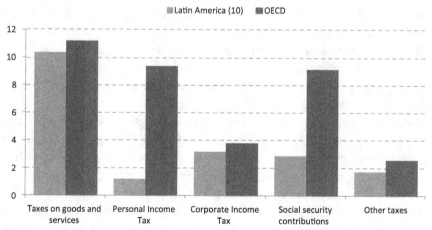

Figure 20.3 Main tax revenues in Latin America and OECD countries (percentage of GDP, 2006).

Note: The average for Latin America includes data from 10 countries: Argentina, Brazil, Chile, Colombia, Costa Rica, El Salvador, Guatemala, Mexico, Peru, and Venezuela. Source: Based on OECD (2008).

skilled and low-skilled workers and the impact of conditional cash transfer programs such as Jefas y Jefes del Hogar in Argentina, Bolsa Escola/Bolsa Familia in Brazil, Progresa/Oportunidades in Mexico, and in-kind transfers in Peru. However, the same authors stress that the reduction in skill premiums is probably temporary, and that a large share of government expenditure remains neutral or even regressive.

A second difference between Latin America and the OECD countries is that personal income taxes and contributions to social security play a secondary role as a source of revenue in the former. In 2005, the tax burden of these categories is a full 14.4 percentage points lower in Latin America than in the OECD. This difference alone explains 88 percent of the revenue gap between the two groups of countries. Income tax revenues amount on average to about 1.2 percent of GDP among Latin American countries, against an average of 9.4 percent in the OECD. Corporate tax revenues are similar in both groups of countries, reaching just under 4 percent of GDP. Thus, the observed tax revenue gap comes mainly from differences in the taxes imposed on individuals.

The small base for direct taxation of individuals is a key characteristic of Latin America tax systems. The main reason for this is that the unequal income distribution implies there are relatively few taxpayers, as income earners are highly concentrated at low income levels. This fact is also very much related to labor informality. Leaving aside the difficulties in measuring or defining it, according to the Economic Commission for Latin America and the Caribbean, informal employment is believed to account for more than 50 percent of total nonagricultural employment in Latin America, with the proportion ranging from around three-quarters in Ecuador and Peru to a little over one-third in Colombia and Chile.

Furthermore, a large proportion of Latin America's workers earn less income than the minimal levels required to pay taxes under the tax code. This has important consequences for the size of the base for income taxes as only a small proportion of individuals will be subject to personal income tax (even in situations where in principle low-income individuals pay income taxes), and they will do so at low marginal rates. This limits the potential role of the public sector not only for redistributing income but also for stabilizing the economy. In particular, Daude, Melguizo, and Neut (2011) estimate that the size of tax automatic stabilizers—the built-in tendency of tax systems to offset economic ups and downs—in the region is on average around half that of the OECD countries.

From the perspective of political economy, a stronger personal income tax may help to legitimize fiscal systems in the region. Only a small fraction of the population in Latin America, and almost nobody within the middle class, is a net payer of this tax, because of a combination of an unequal—and probably underreported—distribution of income and the high tax credits and allowances in the tax codes. OECD (2010) computes the distribution of potential taxpayers using the latest available national household surveys (designed and carried out by national statistical authorities) for Argentina, Chile, Colombia, Costa Rica, Mexico, Peru, and Uruguay, around 2006. The personal income tax in all these Latin American countries is formally progressive, reaching marginal tax rates comparable to those in OECD economies. In other words, formal tax progressivity is similar. But with the exception of Mexico (due to the inter-action of exempted income, individual declarations, and tax credits), labor income earners start paying personal income tax when their income reaches levels ranging from 1.7 times the reported household median labor income in Chile and Costa Rica to 5.5 times in Colombia. These high levels of income exempt from taxation, together with the concentration of households in the lower part of the distribution, imply that only a small number of households with labor income are net personal income tax-payers; to be precise, ranging from around 60 percent in Mexico to less than 10 per-cent in Peru. If we focus on the working middle class, no household in this group (defined as those earning from 0.5 to 1.5 timesthe median national household labor income) is a net taxpayer in the region, with the exception of in Mexico (where the richest half of the middle class does).[8]

Jiménez, Gómez Sabaini, and Podestá (2010) focus on a related, albeit different challenge for fiscal policy in the region: tax evasion. They estimate the degree of tax enforcement for seven Latin American countries (Argentina, Chile, El Salvador, Ecuador, Guatemala, Peru, and Mexico). According to their results, tax evasion for income taxes (both corporate and personal) is very high, ranging from 40 percent to 65 percent, which represents about 4.6 p.p. of GDP each year. According to these authors, evasion rates are similar for the corporate and the personal income tax.

The final outcome of low tax morale and high evasion in the region is visible in figure 20.4. At a cross-country level, countries with low tax morale are countries with low levels of tax revenue as a fraction of GDP. Interestingly, this relationship holds also within Latin American countries, while within OECD economies there is a slightly different trend: countries with a higher tax burden show somewhat lower levels of tax morale. While these simple correlations do not imply causality and could be driven by some common factors, from a cross-country perspective it seems that the tax burden per se could only be a limited explanatory factor for the low levels of tax morale in the region.

As stressed in the literature review, the strength of the link between social mobility and fiscal policy relies on the degree to which citizens can choose freely between alternative political parties or candidates to express their preferences regarding taxation and public expenditures. The region has been steadily moving toward democratic regimes since the mid-1980s, according to the Polity IV ranking of indexes of democratic quality and consolidation (fig. 20.5). Of 23 countries in the region included in the Polity database, 18 countries were ranked as democracies in 2008, with only one country (Cuba) being an autocracy, compared with just seven democracies and eight autocracies in 1980 (Polity IV 2010). At the same time, in contrast to the early 1990s, when the expansion in the number of democracies was accompanied by a decline in the average "quality" of democracy, given the relatively imperfect nature of the new democracies in the region, since the mid-1990s trends have improved. There has been a fairly steady democratic consolidation in the region, although the average index of almost 8.6 for Latin America and the Caribbean in 2008 is still below the average of 9.6 for OECD member countries (maximum score 10). Needless to say that there is also a high degree of variation within the region,

Figure 20.4 Tax collection and tax morale in Latin America and OECD countries.
Source: Based on Latinobarómetro survey 2008, World Values Survey database, OECD (2008), and OECD revenue statistics for 2006.

which includes consolidated democracies like Costa Rica, Chile, and Uruguay (with a Polity score of 10, like most OECD countries), but also countries like Ecuador and Venezuela, where democratic consolidation is considerably weaker, according to this indicator.

What do citizens in Latin America think about their democracies? Does democracy have an intrinsic value for Latin Americans? Is it perceived as a useful tool to solve social conflicts effectively? How do perceptions about social mobility and relative status relate to the perceptions regarding democracy? These are some of the questions we try to tackle using the regional survey Latinobarómetro results for 18 countries of the region.[9]

In figure 20.6, we show that democracy is far from consolidated in popular support and satisfaction across the region. The graph presents two key perception indicators by country: support for democracy as the best system to organize the society and the degree of satisfaction with the way democracy functions in each country. The picture that emerges is one of a preference for democracy in principle, but a very low degree of satisfaction with how democracy is actually working. With the sole exception of Uruguay (where over 70 percent of the population is satisfied), the majority of people in all countries in the region are not satisfied with the current functioning of their democracies. This does not reflect disillusionment with democracy itself, since the support for democracy as a system of organization of their societies is very high in most countries. In Venezuela, the Dominican Republic, Uruguay, Paraguay, and Guatemala, more than 70 percent of the population support democracy. In a second group of countries, while support is lower, democracy nevertheless still enjoys the support of the majority. This group includes Nicaragua, Chile, Honduras, Argentina, and Peru. In the rear, a third group of countries (Bolivia, Colombia, Mexico, Panama,

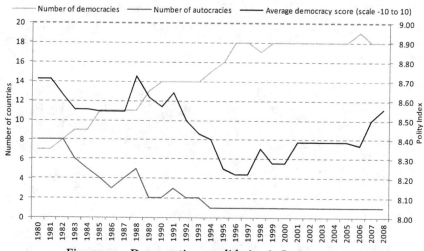

Figure 20.5 Democratic consolidation in Latin America.
Note: Following the criteria of Marshall and Cole (2009) countries are classified as a democracy if the polity score is greater or equal to 6. See http://www.systemicpeace.org/polity/polity4.htm for more details. Source: Based on Polity IV database

Costa Rica, Ecuador, Brazil, and El Salvador) shows relatively low levels of support (just around 50 percent of the population)—a group that contains the largest countries in the region in terms of population (Brazil and Mexico).

The support for democracy and satisfaction with its functioning is unevenly distributed across self-perceived income quintiles in the region (fig. 20.7).[10] Satisfaction with democracy increases monotonically with the perception people have regarding their economic status. For example, a person who puts himself in the highest quintile is almost twice as likely to be satisfied with the way the democratic system works as a person in the lowest quintile (57 versus 31 percent, respectively). Furthermore, the differences between the different quintiles are significant at conventional levels of confidence. With respect to the support of democracy, there seems to be a nonmonotonic relationship with people perceiving themselves as part of the middle quintiles (2 to 4) being significantly more prone to value democracy.

People who perceive themselves as belonging to the middle quintiles (2 to 4) consider themselves more in the center of the political preference distribution and hold less extreme views in general. Figure 20.8 shows the distribution in terms of left-right ideology that people report about themselves in Latin America by the same self-reported income quintile. For example, over 54 percent of these citizens report scores between 4 and 6 (the political center), while for the lowest quintile it descends to 41 percent, and to 28 percent among the uppermost one. In addition, the percentage of the population in these middle quintiles who consider themselves at the extremes (either left or right) is lower than among the poorer or the richer (on both sides of the distribution), which is reflected also by a lower dispersion in political preferences for the middle quintiles vis-à-vis the other groups.

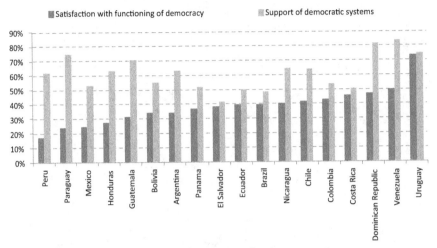

Figure 20.6 Satisfaction and support for democracy by country.

Notes: Satisfaction with the functioning of democracy refers to answers (very and fairly satisfied) to the question: "In general, would you say you are very satisfied, fairly satisfied, not very satisfied or not satisfied at all with the way democracy works in your country?" Support for the democratic system refers to the proportion of persons who agreed with the statement that "Democracy is preferable to any other kind of government." Source: Based on Latinobarómetro survey 2008.

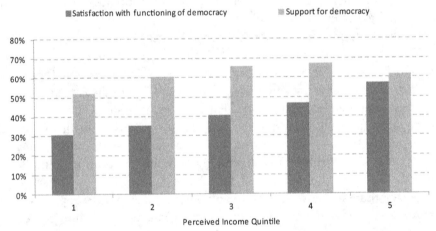

Figure 20.7 Attitudes toward democracy by perceived income quintiles in Latin America.

Source: Based on Latinobarómetro survey 2008.

4. ECONOMETRIC EVIDENCE

In this section, we explore more systematically the links between support for and satisfaction with democracy, political preferences, tax morale, and the perceptions of social mobility and quality of democracy. Thus far, we have focused on aggregate data by country or quintile, but many personal characteristics beyond income have a strong influence on perceptions and social preferences (e.g., see IADB 2009).

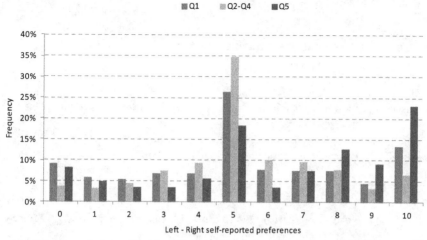

Figure 20.8 Distribution of political preferences by income quintiles.
Source: Based on Latinobarómetro survey 2008

We use two recent rounds of the Latinobarómetro survey (2007 and 2008). We include country dummies in all our regressions to capture the potentially systematic differences in average perceptions that exist across countries. Furthermore, we incorporate several series of controls: age (years), gender (female dummy), a head of household dummy, marital status dummies, occupation dummies, years of education of the respondent, a dummy for households that report economic problems (to be precise, those who are not able to cover needs in a satisfactory manner), ethnicity, and the degree of religiosity.[11]

First, we analyze the support for and satisfaction with democracy, as well as political preferences (the issues shown in figs. 20.4–20.6), focusing on the role of perceptions of social mobility and meritocracy. Table 20.1 reports the main result of estimating a PROBIT model for the dichotomic outcomes (support of democracy, as well as satisfaction with democracy), and ordered PROBIT regressions for the left-right classification.[12]

Our main variables of interest are the dummies for each self-reported income quintile, as well as the perception with respect to future and past mobility (according to whether respondents rank themselves in the same category of income distribution as they think their parents were and children will be).

Column 1 shows that the result of a higher support of democracy within the middle quintiles continues to hold when controlling for individual socioeconomic conditions. However, now the upper quintile also appears as significantly supporting democracy more than the lowest one. This result also holds when we include the perceived social mobility indicators. Interestingly, people who think that they advanced with respect to their parents significantly support democracy more (column 2). With respect to the degree of satisfaction with the functioning of democracy, column 3 shows a positive association between the level of satisfaction and the perceived position in the distribution of income continues to hold (as suggested in fig. 20.7). Furthermore, there is some evidence that people who perceive

Table 20.1 Determinants of attitudes towards democracy in Latin
America (2008)

	(1)	(2)	(3)	(4)	(5)	(6)
Dep. Variable	Support of democracy	Support of democracy	Satisfaction with democracy	Satisfaction with democracy	Left-Right	Left-Right
Estimation Method	PROBIT	PROBIT	PROBIT	PROBIT	Ordered PROBIT	Ordered PROBIT
Female	-0.093	-0.093	-0.062	-0.063	-0.019	-0.021
	(0.030)***	(0.030)***	(0.030)**	(0.030)**	(0.024)	(0.024)
Economic problems	-0.111	-0.11	-0.184	-0.183	-0.012	-0.009
	(0.027)***	(0.027)***	(0.027)***	(0.027)***	(0.022)	(0.022)
Age (years)	0.006	0.006	0.001	0.001	0.004	0.004
	(0.001)***	(0.001)***	(0.001)	(0.001)	(0.001)***	(0.001)***
Head of household	-0.007	-0.007	0.057	0.057	-0.005	-0.006
	(0.033)	(0.033)	(0.034)*	(0.034)*	(0.027)	(0.027)
Years of education	0.031	0.031	-0.015	-0.015	-0.008	-0.008
	(0.003)***	(0.003)***	(0.003)***	(0.003)***	(0.003)***	(0.003)***
Religious	0.093	0.093	0.137	0.137	0.091	0.091
	(0.025)***	(0.025)***	(0.026)***	(0.026)***	(0.022)***	(0.022)***
Quintile 2	0.206	0.201	0.069	0.073	0.083	0.092
	(0.038)***	(0.038)***	(0.040)*	(0.040)*	(0.036)**	(0.036)**
Quintile 3	0.255	0.249	0.179	0.188	0.144	0.166
	(0.038)***	(0.039)***	(0.040)***	(0.041)***	(0.036)***	(0.037)***
Quintile 4	0.209	0.198	0.279	0.295	0.179	0.219
	(0.051)***	(0.053)***	(0.052)***	(0.054)***	(0.046)***	(0.047)***
Quintile 5	0.231	0.224	0.514	0.541	0.246	0.307
	(0.100)**	(0.102)**	(0.100)***	(0.102)***	(0.098)**	(0.100)***
Past perceived mobility		0.018		-0.002		-0.013
		(0.009)*		(0.009)		(0.008)*
Future perceived mobility		0.013		0.015		0.025
		(0.008)		(0.008)*		(0.007)***
Observations	13260	13260	12807	12807	11090	11090
Pseudo-R²:	0.08	0.08	0.07	0.07	0.01	0.01

Notes: Robust standard errors in parenthesis. All regressions include country dummies, employment status
dummies, ethnicity dummies and marital status dummies, not reported because of space considerations.
* $p < .10$; ** $p < .05$; *** $p < .01$.

more prospects of upward mobility in the future also tend to be more satisfied with democracy today in their country of residence (column 4).

Finally, columns 5 and 6 analyze the issue of how people rank themselves in terms of left-right political preferences. The regressions confirm a higher tendency toward the right at higher levels in the (perceived) income distribution. If, as in the literature (Alesina and Giuliano 2009; Gaviria 2007), we interpret these preferences across the political spectrum as corresponding preferences about redistribution (the left taken to be more prone to redistribute than the right), we can highlight two results. First, preferences for redistribution are decreasing with increasing self-perceived income status. This seems rational, given that the richer you are the more likely you are to be a net payer. Second, the results in column 6 imply that people who think that their children will move up tend to support less redistribution, while those who themselves experienced upward mobility in the past tend to support more redistribution. Thus, while the first result clearly is in line with the POUM hypothesis, interpretation of the second is more complicated. Our interpretation is that people who experienced successful upward mobility might believe that their mobility was aided by redistributive public finance, and therefore continue to support redistribution nowadays. Of course, political preferences are much more complex than just attitudes regarding fiscal policy, and therefore the left-right preferences might be an imperfect proxy for preferences about redistribution.

Next, we explore the relationship between satisfaction with democracy, mobility and the perception of the society, and tax morale and tax level preferences, focusing on the main explanatory variables highlighted in the literature. Perception of meritocracy (using the perception that life chances are independent of origin as a proxy) favors tax morale, both increasing the percentage of the population who think that good citizens should pay taxes (table 20.2, columns 5 and 6) and decreasing the percentage of those who justify tax evasion (table 20.3, columns 5–8). Less perception of corruption in the country generates consistently the same results (table 20.2, columns 4 and 6; table 20.3, columns 4 and 6–8).

In contrast, the results from satisfaction with democracy and social mobility are more blurred. The degree of satisfaction with the functioning of democracy increases the share of people who support the position that good citizens should pay taxes (table 20.2, column 2), but its statistical significance is reduced when other variables are included (table 20.2, column 6). Furthermore, satisfaction with democracy seems to increase the proportion of respondents who justify evasion (table 20.3, columns 2 and 6–8). A way to interpret this result is that it mainly reflects the satisfaction of those who profit from the lax tax enforcement.[13]

Finally, the perception of mobility does not affect tax morale results in general, except for the case of past mobility, which reduces the share of population thinking that good citizens should pay taxes (table 20.2, columns 3 and 6). Other socioeconomic variables, such as age, education, and income (both measured by self-assessed income quintiles and by the absence of economic problems), generally increase tax morale.

Table 20.2 Good citizens should pay taxes (PROBIT estimates, 2008)

	(1)	(2)	(3)	(4)	(5)	(6)
Female	-0.043	-0.042	-0.044	-0.047	-0.044	-0.048
	(0.029)	(0.029)	(0.029)	(0.031)	(0.029)	(0.031)
Economic problems	-0.097	-0.094	-0.095	-0.101	-0.096	-0.096
	(0.026)***	(0.026)***	(0.026)***	(0.027)***	(0.026)***	(0.027)***
Age (years)	0.007	0.007	0.007	0.007	0.007	0.007
	(0.001)***	(0.001)***	(0.001)***	(0.001)***	(0.001)***	(0.001)***
Head of household	0.008	0.007	0.007	0.019	0.009	0.018
	(0.032)	(0.032)	(0.032)	(0.034)	(0.032)	(0.034)
Years of education	0.022	0.022	0.021	0.020	0.022	0.020
	(0.003)***	(0.003)***	(0.003)***	(0.003)***	(0.003)***	(0.003)***
Religious	0.035	0.033	0.035	0.010	0.030	0.003
	(0.025)	(0.025)	(0.025)	(0.027)	(0.025)	(0.027)
Quintile 2	0.100	0.099	0.111	0.079	0.100	0.090
	(0.038)***	(0.038)***	(0.039)***	(0.041)*	(0.038)***	(0.041)**
Quintile 3	0.173	0.170	0.194	0.163	0.173	0.181
	(0.038)***	(0.038)***	(0.039)***	(0.041)***	(0.038)***	(0.041)***
Quintile 4	0.169	0.164	0.206	0.175	0.170	0.210
	(0.051)***	(0.051)***	(0.053)***	(0.054)***	(0.051)***	(0.056)***
Quintile 5	0.082	0.073	0.132	0.053	0.083	0.099
	(0.100)	(0.100)	(0.101)	(0.110)	(0.100)	(0.111)
Satisfaction with democracy		0.055				0.040
		(0.026)**				(0.027)
Past perceived mobility			-0.024			-0.023
			(0.009)***			(0.010)**
Future perceived mobility			0.008			0.009
			(0.008)			(0.008)
Corruption				-0.001		-0.001
				(0.000)***		(0.000)**
Life chances are independent of origin					0.055	0.052
					(0.026)**	(0.028)*
Observations	12558	12558	12558	11372	12558	11372
Pseudo-R²:	0.05	0.05	0.05	0.05	0.05	0.05

Notes: Robust standard errors in parenthesis. All regressions are PROBIT estimates that include country dummies, employment status dummies, ethnicity dummies and marital status dummies, not reported because of space considerations.
* $p < .10$; ** $p < .05$; *** $p < .01$.

Table 20.3 Tax evasion is justified (ordered PROBIT estimates, 2008)

	(1)	(2)	(3)	(4)	(5)	(6)	(7)	(8)
Estimation Method	Ordered Probit	Ordered Probit	Ordered Probit	Ordered Probit	Ordered Probit	Ordered Probit	OLS	Probit
Female	0.025	0.027	0.025	0.021	0.026	0.025	0.039	0.051
	(0.027)	(0.027)	(0.027)	(0.027)	(0.027)	(0.027)	(0.061)	(0.033)
Economic problems	0.030	0.035	0.029	0.026	0.027	0.028	0.041	0.070
	(0.024)	(0.024)	(0.024)	(0.024)	(0.024)	(0.024)	(0.056)	(0.029)**
Age (years)	-0.004	-0.004	-0.004	-0.004	-0.004	-0.004	-0.009	-0.006
	(0.001)***	(0.001)***	(0.001)***	(0.001)***	(0.001)***	(0.001)***	(0.002)***	(0.001)***
Head of household	0.078	0.076	0.078	0.078	0.077	0.075	0.172	0.072
	(0.030)***	(0.030)***	(0.030)***	(0.030)***	(0.030)***	(0.030)**	(0.068)**	(0.036)**
Years of education	-0.023	-0.023	-0.023	-0.023	-0.024	-0.023	-0.050	-0.032
	(0.003)***	(0.003)***	(0.003)***	(0.003)***	(0.003)***	(0.003)***	(0.007)***	(0.004)***
Religious	0.059	0.055	0.059	0.063	0.070	0.069	0.192	0.019
	(0.023)**	(0.023)**	(0.023)***	(0.023)***	(0.023)***	(0.023)***	(0.053)***	(0.028)
Quintile 2	0.051	0.049	0.049	0.054	0.051	0.050	0.060	0.193
	(0.038)	(0.038)	(0.039)	(0.038)	(0.038)	(0.039)	(0.091)	(0.044)***
Quintile 3	0.033	0.028	0.029	0.034	0.034	0.025	0.002	0.167
	(0.038)	(0.038)	(0.039)	(0.038)	(0.038)	(0.039)	(0.091)	(0.044)***
Quintile 4	0.181	0.174	0.173	0.184	0.179	0.165	0.328	0.308
	(0.048)***	(0.048)***	(0.051)***	(0.048)***	(0.048)***	(0.051)***	(0.120)***	(0.059)***
Quintile 5	0.281	0.266	0.267	0.282	0.280	0.247	0.529	0.397
	(0.088)***	(0.088)***	(0.091)***	(0.089)***	(0.088)***	(0.091)***	(0.219)**	(0.118)***
Satisfaction with democracy	0.082					0.102	0.222	0.119
	(0.024)***					(0.024)***	(0.056)***	(0.029)***

(continued)

Table 20.3 (continued)

	(1)	(2)	(3)	(4)	(5)	(6)	(7)	(8)
Estimation Method	Ordered Probit	Ordered Probit	Ordered Probit	Ordered Probit	Ordered Probit	Ordered Probit	OLS	Probit
Past perceived mobility			-0.001			-0.001	-0.002	0.003
			(0.009)			(0.009)	(0.019)	(0.010)
Future perceived mobility			-0.010			-0.010	-0.020	-0.016
			(0.008)			(0.008)	(0.018)	(0.009)*
Corruption				0.002		0.002	0.005	0.001
				(0.000)***		(0.000)***	(0.001)***	(0.001)***
Life Chances are independent of origin					-0.110	-0.103	-0.223	-0.125
					(0.023)***	(0.023)***	(0.054)***	(0.029)***
Observations	11023	11023	11023	11023	11023	11023	11023	11023
(Pseudo) R^2	0.01	0.02	0.01	0.02	0.02	0.02	0.06	0.04

Notes: Robust standard errors in parentheses. All regressions are PROBIT estimates that include country dummies, employment status dummies, ethnicity dummies, and marital status dummies, not reported because of space considerations.

* $p < .10$; ** $p < .05$; *** $p < .01$.

Concerning the perception of taxation levels, results consistently refute the POUM hypothesis. Both past and future perceived mobility decrease the likelihood of thinking that taxes are too high (table 20.4, columns 3 and 6). Satisfaction with democracy, trust in the government, and the perception of meritocracy also generate the same result (table 20.4, columns 2 and 4–6).[14]

5. Conclusions

The way taxes are levied and resources allocated is at the heart of the social contract between citizens and the state. For developing countries and for Latin America in particular, frequently characterized by high levels of income inequality and low levels of public revenues, pressing social policy needs, and tenuous democracies, this issue may be even more important than in OECD countries. Fiscal policies to support investments in nutrition, health, education, infrastructure, and unexploited comparative advantages are not only technical challenges; they are also political challenges. Fiscal legitimacy is often low, as citizens in developing countries frequently do not believe that tax revenues are well spent, making them less willing to pay taxes in the first place.

This chapter has analyzed empirically the relationship between fiscal policy, social mobility, and democratic consolidation in Latin America and the Caribbean, both surveying the literature and presenting original research based on the regional Latinobarómetro survey. The results confirm that building better institutions, especially by fighting corruption, pays in terms of tax morale, and probably gives a government leeway to raise general taxation. Besides, the "perspectives of upward mobility" hypothesis is not confirmed, on a general basis. Those that think they have climbed up the social ladder, or expect their children to rise further, do not justify cheating on taxes (sometimes the opposite, in fact) or consider current taxation too high. In this process of strengthening the social contract, the middle class may play a key role as the social segment that supports the most fully developed democracy, thanks to this class's centrist political position.

This is good news. Nevertheless, in several countries in Latin America, low observed levels of tax revenues mean that tax hikes are needed, but low fiscal legitimacy might render the best-designed tax reform unenforceable. So a potentially fruitful way to build confidence in reforms is by increasing the efficiency and transparency of expenditure and by improving conditions of life of important parts of the population at present excluded from the social contract. This would create a broader constituency that supports improvements in public expenditure and would be more willing to finance them.

Many further lines of research seem promising, all of which should address the heterogeneity within Latin American and Caribbean countries. We highlight two of them. First, it would be interesting to analyze more deeply the preferences for

Table 20.4 Taxes are too high (PROBIT estimates, 2007)

	(1)	(2)	(3)	(4)	(5)	(6)
Female	0.028	0.026	0.027	0.023	0.020	0.015
	(0.031)	(0.032)	(0.031)	(0.032)	(0.032)	(0.032)
Economic problems	0.194	0.185	0.189	0.186	0.173	0.163
	(0.028)***	(0.028)***	(0.028)***	(0.028)***	(0.029)***	(0.029)***
Age (years)	0.000	0.000	0.000	0.000	0.001	0.001
	(0.001)	(0.001)	(0.001)	(0.001)	(0.001)	(0.001)
Head of household	-0.067	-0.064	-0.067	-0.066	-0.069	-0.066
	(0.036)*	(0.036)*	(0.036)*	(0.036)*	(0.036)*	(0.036)*
Years of education	-0.009	-0.009	-0.010	-0.010	-0.011	-0.012
	(0.003)***	(0.003)***	(0.003)***	(0.003)***	(0.004)***	(0.004)***
Religious	0.014	0.023	0.015	0.021	0.021	0.028
	(0.028)	(0.028)	(0.028)	(0.028)	(0.028)	(0.028)
Quintile 2	0.020	0.030	0.027	0.020	0.020	0.033
	(0.049)	(0.049)	(0.049)	(0.049)	(0.049)	(0.050)
Quintile 3	-0.071	-0.050	-0.055	-0.065	-0.055	-0.027
	(0.047)	(0.048)	(0.049)	(0.047)	(0.048)	(0.049)
Quintile 4	-0.078	-0.053	-0.055	-0.067	-0.053	-0.013
	(0.059)	(0.059)	(0.061)	(0.059)	(0.059)	(0.062)
Quintile 5	-0.056	-0.039	-0.028	-0.041	-0.031	0.019
	(0.110)	(0.110)	(0.114)	(0.110)	(0.111)	(0.116)
Satisfaction with democracy		-0.146				-0.062
		(0.028)***				(0.030)**
Past perceived mobility			-0.029			-0.025
			(0.008)***			(0.008)***
Future perceived mobility			-0.021			-0.013
			(0.008)***			(0.008)*
Life Chances are independent of origin				-0.166		-0.131
				(0.027)***		(0.027)***
Trust the government					-0.247	-0.203
					(0.028)***	(0.029)***
Observations	13566	13566	13566	13566	13503	13503
Pseudo-R²:	0.08	0.08	0.08	0.08	0.08	0.08

Notes: Robust standard errors in parenthesis. All regressions are PROBIT estimates that include country dummies, employment status dummies, ethnicity dummies and marital status dummies, not reported because of space considerations.

*p < .10; ** p < .05; *** p < .01.

(higher) redistribution, in particular the instruments on expenditure or taxation that citizens prefer. Related to this approach, it may be relevant from a political economy perspective to address explicitly the role of the link between taxation and public expenditure, when evaluating tax morale, and preferences for the level of taxes and the degree of redistribution. Education and health services, the areas of public policies consistently in the social debate, may merit closer attention.

NOTES

The views expressed herein are the sole responsibility of the authors and do not reflect the opinions of the OECD, its Development Centre, or the governments of their member countries.

1. We include Mexico within the OECD average, but not Chile, which joined the OECD in 2010.

2. In a parallel article, Alesina and Angeletos (2005a, 1227) develop a further argument on this second point: "Bigger governments raise the possibilities of corruption; more corruption may in turn raise the support for redistributive policies to intend to correct the inequality and injustice generated by corruption." We are not convinced on the latter point. Alternatively, citizens may start avoiding paying taxes, ending up, again, with a small(er) government and low redistribution. Evidence by Friedman et al. (2000) supports our argument. They show that an informal economy and tax evasion are higher in countries with high levels of corruption. They conclude that only honest governments can sustain high levels of taxation.

3. This condition rules out time-inconsistent fiscal policies and some often observed strategies by politicians (e.g. promising redistributive fiscal policies during campaigns, but not delivering on these promises once they are in office).

4. See Daude (2010) and OECD (2010) for empirical evidence in Latin America on this issue.

5. However, evidence on the median-voter channel is much weaker, probably due to data limitations.

6. For a recent analysis of the determinants of tax morale in Europe, and a survey of the empirical literature for industrialized and emerging regions, see Lago-Peñas and Lago-Peñas (2010).

7. Some caution is needed in this comparison. First, the level of the tax burden in any given country depends in part on the goods and services provided by the state, and the extent of this provision varies systematically across countries. In particular, the reformed pension systems in the region explain part of the OECD-Latin America revenue gap. Second, as mentioned, tax revenue levels tend to be higher in European countries than elsewhere, and these push up OECD tax-to-GDP averages. Third, tax rates have been falling in most OECD countries over the last decade. Finally, the average tax burden—in the OECD or in Latin America—masks important variations among countries.

8. These figures are in line with OECD (2008). Based on labor force survey data, on average only 37.8 percent of employed individuals earn incomes higher than the threshold above which income taxes must be paid. In other words, 62.2 percent of the labor force is not subject to personal income taxes because their incomes are too low. The structure of income distribution in Latin America also limits direct income taxation because many of those who do pay income taxes are not liable to pay much. The share of the labor force in the lowest taxable income bracket reaches 90 percent of working people in Brazil, Chile,

Colombia and Costa Rica (in contrast, Mexico, which has no minimum taxable income, places only 14.5 percent of the labor force in the lowest bracket).

9. The World Values Survey (WVS) is a survey of attitudes and opinions carried out in over 80 countries with at least 5,000 respondents in each country. The WVS has been carried out every five years since 1990 (beginning in 1981 in European countries) by a network of research institutions around the globe, permitting consistent cross-country comparisons of these attitudinal variables (www.worldvaluessurvey.org). Latinobarómetro, used for the original analysis in this chapter, is an annual public opinion survey with data from around 20,000 interviews, covering 18 Latin American countries (Argentina, Bolivia, Brazil, Chile, Colombia, Costa Rica, Dominican Republic, Ecuador, El Salvador, Guatemala, Honduras, Mexico, Nicaragua, Panama, Paraguay, Peru, Uruguay, and Venezuela), i.e., around 1,000—1,200 interviews per country. For most of the analysis, such as the regression analysis performed in the previous section, this limited coverage per country does not allow detailed national-level analysis, so we present results for the region as a whole.

10. Perceived positions in the income distribution differ significantly from the objective positions, with relatively rich individuals self-classifying themselves at lower income quintiles and the poor considering themselves relatively less deprived (see Fajardo and Lora 2010). However, for political views and actions it is precisely the perceived position, rather than the objective one, that matters.

11. For ethnicity, we introduced dummies for each self-reported ethnicity: Asian, black, indigenous, mestizo, mulatto, white, and other race. Marital status dummies include: married or living with partner; single; and separated, divorced, or widowed. Employment status includes: self-employed, salaried employee in a state company, salaried employee in a private company, temporarily out of work, retired or pensioner, nonworker or responsible for shopping and housework, and student.

12. In this classification, people are asked to place themselves on a scale from 1 to 10, 1 being the extreme left and 10 the extreme right.

13. As pointed out before, we do not claim any causality in our analysis, but under the interpretation given in this paragraph, causation would run mainly from low tax morale to satisfaction with democracy.

14. A note of caution may be advisable, though, since the design of the questionnaires does not allow us to determine if respondents are giving their opinion on the general level of taxation or on the one they actually bear.

REFERENCES

Alesina, Alberto, and George-Marios Angeletos. 2005a. "Corruption, Inequality, and Fairness." *Journal of Monetary Economics* 52: 1227–44.
———. 2005b. "Fairness and Redistribution." *American Economic Review* 95(4): 960–80.
Alesina, Alberto, and Paola Giuliano. 2009. "Preferences for Redistribution." NBER Working Paper No. 14825, National Bureau of Economic Research, Cambridge, MA.
Alesina, Alberto, and Edward Glaeser. 2004. *Fighting Poverty in the US and Europe.* Oxford: Oxford University Press.
Alt, James, Ian Preston, and Luke Sibieta. 2010. "The Political Economy of Tax Policy." In *Dimensions of Tax Design,* edited by James A. Mirrlees, 1204–79. Oxford: Oxford University Press.

Bénabou, Roland, and Efe A. Ok. 2001. "Social Mobility and the Demand for Redistribution: The POUM Hypothesis." *Quarterly Journal of Economics* 116: 447–87.

Bénabou, Roland, and Jean Tirole. 2006. "Belief in a Just World and Redistributive Politics." *Quarterly Journal of Economics* 121: 699–746.

Breceda, Karla, Jamele Rigolini, and Jaime Saavedra. 2009. "Latin America and the Social Contract: Patterns of Social Spending and Taxation," *Population and Development Review* 35: 721–48.

Corneo, Giacomo, and Hans Peter Grüner. 2000. "Social Limits to Redistribution." *American Economic Review* 90: 1491–507.

———. 2002. "Individual Preferences for Political Redistribution." *Journal of Public Economics* 83: 83–107.

Chong, Alberto, and Mauricio Olivera. 2008. "Does Compulsory Voting Help Equalize Incomes?" *Economics and Politics* 20: 391–415.

Daude, Christian. 2010. "Ascendance by Descendants? On Intergenerational Mobility in Latin America," OECD Development Centre Working Paper, Organisation for Economic Co-operation and Development, Paris.

Daude, Christian, Ángel Melguizo, and Alejandro Neut. 2011. "Fiscal Policy in Latin America: Countercyclical and Sustainable at Last?" In *Fiscal policy: Lessons from the Crisis*, edited by D. Franco, 49–86. Rome: Banca d'Italia.

Downs, Anthony. 1957. *An Economic Theory of Democracy*. New York: Harper.

Elizondo, Carlos, and Javier Santiso. 2012. "Killing Me Softly: Local Termites and Fiscal Violence in Latin America." Chapter 18 in this Handbook.

Fajardo, Johanna, and Eduardo Lora. 2010. "Understanding the Latin American Middle Classes: Reality and Perception." Unpublished manuscript, Inter-American Development Bank, Washington, DC.

Friedman, Eric, Simon Johnson, Daniel Kaufmann, and Pablo Zoido-Lobatón. 2000. "Dodging the Grabbing Hand: The Determinants of Unofficial Activity in 69 Countries." *Journal of Public Economics* 76(3): 459–93.

Gaviria, Alejandro. 2007. "Social Mobility and Preferences for Redistribution in Latin America." *Economia* 8(1): 55–88.

Hirschman, Albert. 1973. "The Changing Tolerance for Income Inequality in the Course of Economic Development." *Quarterly Journal of Economics* 87: 544–66.

IADB (Inter-American Development Bank). 2009. *Beyond Facts: Understanding Quality of Life*. Washington, DC: IADB.

Isaksson, Anne-Sophie, and Annika Lindskog. 2009. "Preferences for Redistribution—A Country Comparison of Fairness Judgements." *Journal of Economic Behavior and Organization* 72: 884–902.

Jimenez, Juan Pablo, Juan Carlos Gómez Sabaini, and Andrea Podestá. 2010. *Evasión y Equidad en América Latina*. Santiago: Comisión Económica para América Latina y el Caribe.

Lago-Peñas, Ignacio, and Santiago Lago-Peñas. 2010. "The Determinants of Tax Morale in Comparative Perspective: Evidence for European Countries." *European Journal of Political Economy* 26:441–53.

López-Calva, Felipe, and Nora Lustig, eds. 2010. *Declining Inequality in Latin America: A Decade of Progress?* Baltimore: Brookings Institution Press and United Nations Development Programme.

Marcel, Mario. 2008. "Movilidad, Desigualdad y Política Social en América Latina." Unpublished manuscript, Inter-American Development Bank, Washington, DC.

Marshall, M. G., and B. R. Cole. 2009. *Global Report 2009: Conflict, Governance, and State Fragility*. Arlington, VA: Center for Systemic Peace and Center for Global Policy.

Meltzer, Allan H., and Scott F. Richards. 1981. "A Rational Theory of the Size of Government."
    Journal of Political Economy 89: 914–27.

Milanovic, Branko. 2000. "The Median-Voter Hypothesis, Income Inequality, and Income
    Redistribution: An Empirical Test with the Required Data." *European Journal of
    Political Economy* 16: 367–410.

Musgrave, Richard A. 1939. "The Voluntary Exchange Theory of Public Economy."
    Quarterly Journal of Economics 53:213–37.

OECD (Organisation for Economic Co-operation and Development). 2008. *Latin American
    Economic Outlook 2009.* Paris: OECD Development Centre.

———. 2010. *Latin American Economic Outlook 2011: How Middle-Class Is Latin America?*
    Paris: OECD Development Centre.

Perotti, Roberto. 1996. "Growth, Income Distribution, and Democracy: What the Data
    Say." *Journal of Economic Growth* 1: 149–87.

Piketty, Thomas. 1995. "Social Mobility and Redistributive Politics." *Quarterly Journal of
    Economics* 110: 551–84.

Polity IV. 2010. *Polity IV Project: Political Regime Characteristics and Transitions, 1800–2010.*
    Vienna, VA: Political Instability Task Force, Societal-Systems Research, and Center for
    Systemic Peace. Database.

Profeta, Paola, and Simona Scabrosetti. 2008. "Political Economy Issues of Taxation in
    Latin America." In *Tax Systems and Tax Reforms in Latin America*, edited by Luigi Ber-
    nardi, Alberto Barreix, Anna Marenzi, and Paola Profeta, 63–76. Abingdon: Routledge.

———. 2010. *The Political Economy of Taxation: Lessons from Developing Countries.*
    Cheltenham: Edward Elgar.

Przeworski, Adam. 2007. "Democracy, Equality, and Redistribution." In *Political Judgement:
    Essays in Honour of John Dunn*, edited by Raymond Bourke and Richard Geuss,
    281–312. Cambridge: Cambridge University Press.

Robinson, James A. 2010. "The Political Economy of Redistributive Policies." In *Declining
    Inequality in Latin America: A Decade of Progress?*, edited by Luis Felipe López-Calva
    and N. Lustig, 39–71. Baltimore: Brookings Institution Press and United Nations
    Development Programme.

Rodríguez, Francisco. 2004. "Inequality, Redistribution, and Rent-Seeking." *Economics and
    Politics* 16: 287–320.

Roemer, John. 1998. "Why the Poor Do Not Expropriate the Rich: An Old Argument in
    New Garb." *Journal of Public Economics* 70(3): 399–424.

Torgler, Benno. 2005. "Tax Morale in Latin America." *Public Choice* 122(1/2): 133–57.

CHAPTER 21

REVISITING POLITICAL BUDGET CYCLES IN LATIN AMERICA

SEBASTIÁN NIETO-PARRA AND
JAVIER SANTISO

1. INTRODUCTION

Elections matter and can affect economic policies. Specifically, some components of fiscal policy may be expanded around elections in order to attract voters. In that sense, more visible fiscal items or programs would be more manipulated than others in order to ensure election (Alesina, Roubini, and Cohen, 1997).

Political systems permitting reelection of officials can also influence politicians' behavior once they become incumbent candidates. The core idea is that incumbents artificially expand economic activity during election years to improve their chances of reelection. However, empirical evidence shows that expansionary fiscal policy of incumbent candidates around elections does not always "pay off" in terms of a victory in the election (Brender and Drazen 2008).

These observations have implications regarding the efficiency of economic policies around elections. This is particularly evident when there is a risk that expansionary fiscal policy could undermine the effectiveness of monetary policy (i.e., fiscal dominance). Moreover, under some circumstances, monetary policy alone cannot control its main target and fiscal discipline is then a priority. Such was the case of Brazil following the 2002 elections: the most important tool to reduce the inflation rate was a credible fiscal policy and not an increase in interest rates (Blanchard 2004).[1]

In this chapter we revisit the impact of elections on fiscal policy in Latin American countries and we pose the following questions: To what extent do Latin American governments expand fiscal expenditures around elections to attract voters? And especially significantly in the current political context, do different types of electoral systems have different kinds of impact on fiscal policies around elections? Behind these questions, of course, lies a basic issue: fiscal responsibility during elections.

The purpose of this chapter is therefore to answer these questions for Latin American countries. To do this, we first compare the impact of elections on fiscal policy in Latin American economies with that in countries in the Organisation for Economic Co-operation and Development (OECD). More precisely, we analyze the most important components of the expenditure side of the fiscal balance of these economies over the period 1990–2006. Second, in the context of the current debate over the electoral system in some Latin American countries, we study the impact that the reelection system could have on the management of fiscal policy in Latin America, and in particular the role that *immediate* reelections (i.e., when there is the possibility of one or more successive terms for the president elected) could have on the behavior of fiscal components during elections. Third, we compare the electoral cycle of 2005–6 with previous electoral cycles in Latin American countries.

In section 2, we provide a review of the literature on the impact of elections on fiscal policy. Section 3, the core of this chapter, presents the most important facts and analyzes the results of the econometric model gauging the impact of elections on fiscal policy. Finally, section 4 outlines the major policy implications of this research.

2. REVIEW OF THE LITERATURE

The expansionary monetary or fiscal policies adopted during elections could potentially affect economic regimes and then capital markets (Ames 1987; Schuknecht 1996; Alesina et al. 1999; Block and Vaaler 2004). Increases in public expenditure around elections do not necessarily imply a deteriorating fiscal situation.[2] As Drazen and Eslava (2005) point out, in an examination of municipal elections in Colombia, incumbents tend to increase expenditure in ways that maximize the impact on voters without affecting the fiscal deficit. In turn, Eslava (2005) finds that voters indeed reward preelection increases in targeted spending, but punish incumbents who run high deficits prior to an election. For Mexico over the period 1957–97, González (2002) finds that governments make ample use of public spending on infrastructure and current transfers in order to attract voters. More generally, for Latin American countries, Rodríguez (2006) finds that during the period 1990–2004, governments tend to increase public investment one year prior to elections and current transfers during the election year. The findings related to increasing deficits and spending in the year prior to elections has also been corroborated in more recent specific country studies, in particular for Brazil (Sakurai and Menezes-Filho 2008) and Argentina (Jones,

Meloni, and Tommasi 2009). In this last paper, the authors show that Argentine voters reward those governors who provide higher spending, rewarding their capacity to extract more resources from the federal government. The same pattern has also been found under nondemocratic regimes like Mubarak's Egypt (Blaydes 2008).

The results presented above for Latin American countries contrast with those of developed economies. Peltzman (1992) finds that U.S. voters penalize federal and state spending growth, qualifying voters as "fiscal conservatives." Shi and Svensson (2006) analyze elections in 58 developing and 27 developed countries during the period 1975–91, finding that fiscal deficits did not increase during elections in OECD developed countries. Brender and Drazen (2005) find similar results for the period 1960–2001 when differentiating between old and new democracies and using as fiscal variables government balance, total expenditure, and total revenue. Indeed, expansionary fiscal policies around elections are particularly likely in developing countries (see Barberia and Avelino 2011 for an analysis of the link between political budget cycles and new democracies in Latin American economies). In a recent analysis including quarterly data from 1975 to 2000 in 116 countries, Krieckhaus (2005) finds that political business cycles are particularly widespread and influential in Latin America, this phenomenon being more pronounced in this region than in other developing regions like Asia or Africa.[3]

More precisely, the expansion of fiscal policy during elections depends on the capacity of voters for monitoring government policies. The main factors that influence the ability of voters to understand the government's budget balance are often associated with government accounting practices, media transparency, and the education of voters. In particular, the role of informed voters on fiscal outcomes around elections is crucial. Shi and Svensson (2006) find that the negative effect of election periods on the deficit is weaker when voters are better informed.

Empirical evidence for legislative elections in developed countries supports the idea that the probability of being reelected, measured by opinion polls, has no significant effect on the fiscal budget.[4] However, concerning municipal elections in developed countries, no study has produced a systematic result showing that elections do not have an impact on the fiscal actions that could influence voters. For cases in which elections have an impact on government expenditures, see Kneebone and McKenzie (2003) and Veiga and Veiga (2007) for examples in Canada and Portugal respectively.

Finally, depending on the reelection system, the effect of elections on economic policies will tend to be different. Empirical research suggests that incumbent parties facing reelection, particularly incumbents from left-wing parties, face strong incentives to engage in unsustainable expansionary economic policies (Leblang 2002). Voters and incumbent parties are, of course, playing a dynamic game and rational voters who have full information should not be expected to make such a systematic mistake as rewarding incumbents who pursue such policies. However, information asymmetries exist between the two groups regarding the competence of politicians and the conduct of fiscal policy, and rational voters may well prefer incumbent candidates who run fiscal deficits (Rogoff 1990). This view has been recently challenged by Brender and Drazen (2008), who, by using a sample of 74 countries over the period 1960–2003, find no evidence that deficits promote reelection in either developed or developing countries. In this chapter, we analyze the impact of reelections on fiscal policy in Latin American countries by differentiating between two key regimes (nonimmediate reelections and immediate reelections).

The results presented above give important insights concerning the management of fiscal policy around elections as well as the differences that exist across countries and that depend on the type of elections. In line with these analyses, our comparative analysis of Latin American and developed country governments' management of fiscal policy may be a useful contribution to the field. More importantly, we provide useful insights on the impact that different electoral systems could have on the management of fiscal policy.

3. EMPIRICAL EVIDENCE

3.1. Elections and Fiscal Policy: A Comparative Analysis between OECD and Latin American Countries

In this section, we present some empirical evidence on the relation between elections and fiscal policy outcomes over the period 1990–2006. The source of the database used for this study is ILPES, the Public Finance Database for Latin American countries of the Economic Commission for Latin America and the Caribbean (ECLAC), and an OECD database, the General Government Accounts Database for OECD countries.[5] In our study of the period 1990–2006 for 28 OECD countries and 19 Latin American countries,[6], the results suggest that general elections are indeed associated with much greater changes to fiscal policy in Latin America than those in high-income countries.[7] Figure 21.1 summarizes the development of four fiscal variables during election periods: the fiscal deficit before interest payments (primary balance), public expenditure excluding interest payments (primary expenditure), current expenditure, and capital expenditure.

In Latin American countries, the average primary balance declines by an amount close to 0.7 percent of GDP during an election year. Most of this movement is due to the expenditure component and within this it is current (close to 0.8 percent of GDP) rather than capital expenditure that is most affected. There is little change in capital expenditures during election years themselves, but an increase of more than 0.3 percent of GDP is observed in the year prior to the election. By contrast, in OECD countries, observed changes in the primary balance and current expenditures during election years are minimal, less than 0.1 percent of GDP for either measure.

This difference between Latin American and OECD countries is all the more remarkable considering the relatively small size of governments in Latin American

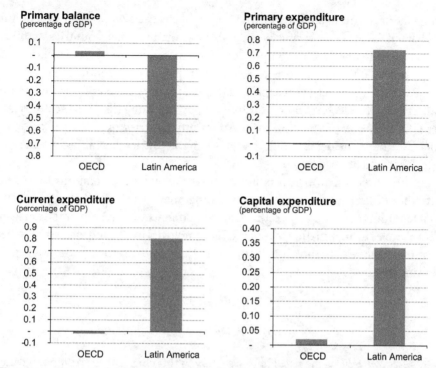

Figure 21.1 Impact of elections on fiscal policy in Latin American and OECD countries (changes in selected fiscal indicators, percentage of GDP).

Notes: We calculate the impact of elections on fiscal policy as the difference between the fiscal variable (as percentage of GDP) during the election year and nonelection years. The exception is capital expenditure, which we assume to lead the election by one year. We use legislative elections for countries with parliamentary political systems and executive elections for countries with presidential systems. Data on fiscal policy refer to central government for Latin American countries and consolidated general government for OECD countries. We use simple averages for the calculation. Source: Based on Secretaria do Tesouro Nacional (for of Brazil), ECLAC ILPES, Public Finance database (for other Latin American countries), and OECD, General Government Accounts (for OECD countries), 2009.

democracies. According to OECD (2008), over the period 1990–2006, primary expenditure accounts for 22 percent of GDP in Latin America, compared with 40 percent in OECD countries.[8] These differences are still evident when upper-middle-income countries are distinguished from lower-middle-income countries in Latin America (24 percent of GDP and 21 percent of GDP respectively). Similar results are found when the ratio of total expenditures to GDP is compared for OECD and Latin American countries (44 percent and 25 percent respectively). Similarly, over the period 1970–95, Gavin and Perotti (1997) report that total expenditures to GDP represent 45 percent for OECD countries and 23 percent for Latin American countries.

Figure 21.1 identifies the importance of primary expenditure among the fiscal variables affected by electoral politics. Figure 21.2 analyzes this across individual

Latin American countries, showing the impact of elections on primary expenditure as a share of GDP, and exposing considerable variation between countries. In Brazil, Bolivia, and Nicaragua, for example, primary expenditure increases by more than 1.5 percent of GDP compared with nonelection periods. By contrast, in Paraguay, Peru, Panama, Venezuela, Guatemala, and Chile primary expenditure is apparently unaffected by the electoral process. Moreover, by analyzing the four fiscal variables over GDP presented above for Latin American countries over the period 1990–2006, we note considerable differences among countries but also for time (see Nieto-Parra and Santiso 2009).

In order to confirm the facts presented above, we use an empirical model to control for other macroeconomic variables that may explain the behavior of fiscal variables around elections. By estimating components of government balance and political cycles using a method similar to that employed by Shi and Svensson (2006), we confirm the results shown in figure 21.1. The empirical specification takes the following form:

$$Fiscal\,variable_{i,t} = \sum_{j=1}^{2} a_j Fiscal\,variable_{i,t-2} + a_k GDPgrowth_{i,t}$$

$$+ \; a_k LogrealGDPcapita_{i,t} + b_0 electiondummy_{i,t} + e_{i,t}$$

where *Fiscal variable* is the fiscal item we study in this chapter (i.e., primary balance, primary expenditure, current expenditure, and capital expenditure). The election dummy variable takes the value of 1 when there is an election and 0 otherwise.[9] The

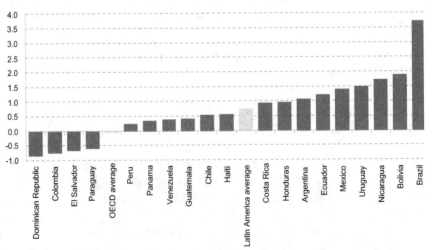

Figure 21.2 Impact of elections on Latin American countries, 1990–2006 (changes in primary expenditure, percentage of GDP).
Notes: We calculate the impact of elections on fiscal policy as the difference between the fiscal variable (as percentage of GDP) during the election year and nonelection years. We use legislative elections for countries with parliamentary political systems and executive elections for countries with presidential systems. Data on fiscal policy refer to central government. Source: Based on Secretaria do Tesouro Nacional (for Brazil), ECLAC ILPES, Public Finance database (for other Latin American countries), and OECD, General Government Accounts (for OECD countries), 2009.

control variables are the logarithm of real GDP per capita, GDP growth rate, and the lagged dependent fiscal variable in periods 1 and 2.

Since ordinary least squares regressions are known to deal inadequately with time series and cross-section heterogeneity, we start the estimation technique with a fixed-effect regression (FE estimators). We then include the lagged dependent variables in FE estimation. We adopt the GMM (generalized method of moments) estimator that Arellano and Bond (1991) developed for dynamic panel data in order to avoid the bias caused by the inclusion of lagged dependent variables. Results obtained in the GMM estimation do not change significantly with respect to the FE model. Table 21.1 presents these results for the case of FE regressions without lagged dependent variables. Table 21.2 reports FE regressions with lagged dependent variables. Table 21.3 presents FE regressions with lagged dependent variables and with time effect, and finally table 21.4 presents GMM estimates with time effect specification.

Table 21.1 Impact of Elections on Fiscal Variables, 1990–2006 (FE Estimation)

	Latin America	OECD	All
Primary balance			
GDP growth	1.490e-01*** [5.60]	3.467e-01*** [6.42]	2.059e-01*** [7.17]
Log GDP per capita	-2.962*** [3.06]	5.401*** [6.21]	3.279*** [4.83]
Election dummy	-6.303e-01*** [0.27]	-6.67E-02 [1.65]	-2.95E-01 [1.74]
Constant	23.026*** [3.09]	-53.539*** [6.28]	-29.554*** [4.87]
Observations	307	445	735
R-squared	0.14	0.18	0.11
Number of countries	19	27	45
Primary expenditure			
GDP growth	-0.0485 [1.58]	-2.919e-01*** [4.19]	-8.260e-02** [2.18]
Log GDP per capita	8.654*** [7.57]	-15.015*** [13.22]	-7.703*** [8.13]
Election dummy	4.526e-01* [1.74]	8.840e-02 [0.29]	3.280e-01 [1.35]
Constant	-51.401*** [5.83]	188.190*** [16.92]	98.618*** [11.70]
Observations	317	414	714
R-squared	0.18	0.35	0.1
Number of countries	19	28	46
Current expenditure			
GDP growth	-9.464e-02*** [3.07]	2.629e-01*** [3.10]	-1.017e-01** [2.28]

(continued)

Table 21.1 (*continued*)

	Latin America	OECD	All
Log GDP per capita	7.010***	-22.481***	-13.164***
	[6.10]	[16.29]	[11.80]
Election dummy	5.226e-01**	1.290e-01	4.310e-01
	[2.00]	[0.34]	[1.51]
Constant	-39.368***	261.947***	147.335***
	[4.44]	[19.39]	[14.84]
Observations	317	414	714
R-squared	0.14	0.43	0.19
Number of countries	19	28	46
Capital expenditure			
GDP growth	0.0096	-0.0135	0.0050
	[0.57]	[0.94]	[0.44]
Log GDP per capita	0.5484	-0.0888	0.1250
	[0.87]	[0.36]	[0.42]
Election dummy	3.067e-01**	1.460e-02	1.440e-01*
	[2.11]	[0.23]	[1.94]
Constant	-1.345	3.841	1.827
	[0.28]	[1.59]	[0.69]
Observations	317	390	690
R-squared	0.02	0	0.01
Number of countries	19	28	46

Notes: This table reports results of FE estimation (country-specific effect). We calculate the impact of elections on fiscal variables from the contemporaneous election year. The exception is capital expenditure, which we assume to lead the election by one year. We use legislative elections for countries with parliamentary political systems and executive elections for countries with presidential systems. Data on fiscal policy refer to central government. Absolute value of t statistics is in brackets.

*$p < .10$; **$p < .05$; ***$p < .01$

Source: Based on Secretaria do Tesouro Nacional (for Brazil), ECLAC ILPES, Public Finance database (for other Latin American countries), and OECD, General Government Accounts (for OECD countries), 2009.

Differentiating between developed and emerging democracies and using as fiscal variables government primary balance, primary expenditure, current expenditure, and capital expenditure, our estimations find the same results. Fiscal variables are not affected during elections for OECD countries. By contrast, for Latin American economies, primary balances decrease during election years because of an increase of the primary expenditure, caused above all by an expansion in current expenditure.

Figure 21.3 summarizes the most important results apparent in table 21.4 (GMM estimation with time effect). The election dummy variable is not significantly different from 0 for OECD countries. This is true for the primary balance as well as for the most important components of the expenditure side. Indeed, for OECD countries, fiscal balances do not deteriorate, and neither do important components of

Table 21.2 Impact of Elections on Fiscal Variables, 1990–2006 (FE Estimation with Lagged Dependent Variables)

	Latin America	OECD	All
Primary balance			
GDP growth	7.797e-02***	3.075e-01***	1.312e-01***
	[3.03]	[7.82]	[5.87]
Log GDP per capita	-0.034	1.690**	1.901***
	[0.03]	[2.48]	[3.22]
Election dummy	-0.475**	-0.147	-0.255*
	[2.35]	[0.90]	[1.90]
Fiscal variable (-1)	5.039e-01***	8.505e-01***	7.590e-01***
	[7.77]	[19.28]	[20.06]
Fiscal variable (-2)	-0.068	-0.205***	-0.163***
	[1.13]	[4.77]	[4.53]
Constant	0.331	-17.250**	-17.241***
	[0.04]	[2.58]	[3.25]
Observations	267	391	643
R-squared	0.3	0.67	0.54
Number of countries	19	27	45
Primary expenditure			
GDP growth	9.99e-03	-3.677e-01*** [8.78]	-7.153e-02*** [3.27]
	[0.43]		
Log GDP per capita	1.438	-2.431***	-2.226***
	[1.29]	[2.82]	[3.38]
Election dummy	0.355*	0.218	0.239*
	[1.85]	[1.31]	[1.75]
Fiscal variable (-1)	5.889e-01*	7.704e-01*** [16.83]	7.576e-01 *** [19.63]
	[9.61]		
Fiscal variable (-2)	0.052	0.013	-0.005
	[0.89]	[0.31]	[0.13]
Constant	-5.425	33.294***	27.294***
	[0.65]	[3.59]	[4.41]
Observations	279	358	622
R-squared	0.49	0.8	0.69
Number of countries	19	28	46
Current expenditure			
GDP growth	-4.383e-02**	-3.999e-01*** [8.97]	-1.231e-01*** [5.85]
	[2.38]		
Log GDP per capita	0.917	-3.142*** [1.06]	-2.351***
	[1.06]	[3.23]	[3.55]
Election dummy	0.565***	0.268	0.379***
	[3.66]	[1.53]	[2.90]
Fiscal variable (-1)	6.729e-01*** [11.81]	8.352e-01*** [18.51]	8.447e-01*** [23.01]

(continued)

Table 21.2 (*continued*)

	Latin America	OECD	All
Fiscal variable (-2)	0.094*	-0.004	-0.016
	[1.73]	[0.09]	[0.46]
Constant	-3.417	38.428***	26.205***
	[0.52]	[3.72]	[4.22]
Observations	279	358	622
R-squared	0.66	0.87	0.82
Number of countries	19	28	46
Capital expenditure			
GDP growth	1.94e-02	-1.57e-02	1.03e-02
	[1.32]	[1.23]	[1.02]
Log GDP per capita	-0.601	0.210	-0.169
	[0.90]	[0.93]	[0.57]
Election dummy	0.230* [1.88]	0.029 [0.54]	0.134** [2.08]
Fiscal variable (-1)	5.809e-01*	4.274e-01*** [7.62]	5.505e-01 *** [13.06]
	[9.51]		
Fiscal variable (-2)	-0.108*	0.175***	-0.052
	[1.83]	[3.24]	[1.28]
Constant	6.166	-0.906	2.936
	[1.20]	[0.40]	[1.11]
Observations	279	334	598
R-squared	0.3	0.33	0.29
Number of countries	19	28	46

Notes: This table reports results of FE estimation (country-specific effect) with lagged dependent variables. We calculate the impact of elections on fiscal variables from the contemporaneous election year. The exception is capital expenditure, which we assume to lead the election by one year. We use legislative elections for countries with parliamentary political systems and executive elections for countries with presidential systems. Data on fiscal policy refer to central government. Absolute value of *t* statistics is in brackets.
*$p < .10$; **$p < .05$; ***$p < .01$
Source: Based on Secretaria do Tesouro Nacional (for Brazil), ECLAC ILPES, Public Finance database (for other Latin American countries), and OECD, General Government Accounts (for OECD countries), 2009.

expenditure increase. In contrast, for Latin American countries, the impact of elections on fiscal policy is high and statistically significant. In particular, practically all the decrease of the primary balance around elections is explained by an increase in primary spending (which rises by close to 0.45 percentage points during election years). In turn, most of the increase in primary spending is due to rises in current expenditure, which, as a share of GDP, increases by over 0.5 percent for the region.[10]

In Latin American countries, a reduction in public investment partially compensates for the increase in current expenditure. Results suggest that in the election year Latin American governments expand components that have a direct impact on voters, such as current expenditures. Indeed, current expenditures have two key characteristics that may serve this purpose: first, they are flexible (i.e., they can be

Table 21.3 Impact of Elections on Fiscal Variables, 1990–2006 (FE Estimation with Lagged Dependent Variables and Time Effect)

	Latin America	OECD	All
Primary balance			
GDP growth	3.09e-02 [1.17]	2.145e-01*** [4.95]	1.034e-01*** [4.42]
Log GDP per capita	-3.692*** [2.71]	0.768 [0.53]	-0.713 [0.74]
Election dummy	-0.488** [2.54]	-0.128 [0.79]	-0.269** [2.04]
Fiscal variable (-1)	4.319e-01*** [6.73]	8.092e-01*** [16.98]	7.454e-01*** [19.32]
Fiscal variable (-2)	-0.053 [0.89]	-0.158*** [3.40]	-0.119*** [3.20]
Constant	28.662*** [2.74]	-8.326 [0.58]	5.942 [0.69]
Observations	267	391	643
R-squared	0.44	0.7	0.58
Number of countries	19	27	45
Primary expenditure			
GDP growth	4.535e-02* [1.84]	-3.005e-01*** [6.60]	-5.074e-02** [2.20]
Log GDP per capita	-0.994 [0.74]	0.992 [0.65]	-1.756* [166]
Election dummy	0.342* [1.80]	0.206 [126]	0.249* [1.82]
Fiscal variable (-1)	5.041e-01*** [7.91]	7.359e-01*** [15.42]	7.634e-01*** [19.56]
Fiscal variable (-2)	-0.0006 [0.01]	0.0625 [1.38]	0.0099 [0.27]
Constant	14.679 [143]	-0.725 [0.05]	22.149** [2.29]
Observations	279	358	622
R-squared	0.55	0.82	0.7
Number of countries	19	28	46
Current expenditure			
GDP growth	-2.44e-02 [1.21]	-3.489e-01*** [7.19]	-1.138e-01*** [5.14]
Log GDP per capita	-1.558 [1.41]	0.905 [0.55]	-1.737* [1.68]
Election dummy	0.539*** [3.46]	0.272 [1.58]	0.391*** [2.98]
Fiscal variable (-1)	5.955e-01*** [9.69]	8.186e-01*** [17.54]	8.515e-01*** [22.93]
Fiscal variable (-2)	0.077 [1.36]	0.015 [0.35]	-0.010 [0.28]

(continued)

Table 21.3 (*continued*)

	Latin America	OECD	All
Constant	16.518*	-0.128	20.045**
	[1.93]	[0.01]	[2.13]
Observations	279	358	622
R-squared	0.7	0.88	0.82
Number of countries	19	28	46
Capital expenditure			
GDP growth	3.730e-02**	-5.25e-03	1.844e-02*
	[2.27]	[0.35]	[1.70]
Log GDP per capita	-1.427	1.452***	-0.207
	[1.58]	[2.69]	[0.44]
Election dummy	0.197	0.032	0.122*
	[1.57]	[0.62]	[1.88]
Fiscal variable (-1)	5.652e-01*** [9.03]	3.874e-01*** [6.61]	5.592e-01*** [13.12]
Fiscal variable (-2)	-0.139** [2.27]	0.168*** [2.96]	-0.054 [1.31]
Constant	12.437* [1.79]	-12.582** [2.38]	3.087 [0.73]
Observations	279	334	598
R-squared	0.35	0.4	0.31
Number of countries	19	28	46

Notes: This table reports results of FE estimation (country-specific effect) with lagged dependent variables and time-specific fixed effects included as regressors. We calculate the impact of elections on fiscal variables from the contemporaneous election year. The exception is capital expenditure, which we assume to lead the election by one year. We use legislative elections for countries with parliamentary political systems and executive elections for countries with presidential systems. Data on fiscal policy refer to central government. Absolute value of t statistics is in brackets.

*$p < .10$; **$p < .05$; ***$p < .01$

Source: Based on Secretaria do Tesouro Nacional (for Brazil), ECLAC ILPES, Public Finance database (for other Latin American countries), and OECD, General Government Accounts (for OECD countries), 2009.

manipulated relatively easily by politicians), and second, voters can rapidly quantify and observe them (e.g., social transfers). Finally, the impact of elections on capital expenditure is observed one year prior to elections. More precisely, particular items observed by voters, such as public investment (infrastructure), increase considerably one year before elections. For all countries of the sample (Latin American and OECD countries), capital expenditures increase 0.11 percent, with yet again a stronger rise for Latin American countries (0.21 percent).

These results confirm earlier studies in the research literature, which found that developed countries are not sensitive to political cycles. This result contrasts with that for Latin American countries, in which current expenditure and public investment as a share of GDP increase during and prior to an election year respectively. Clearly, behind this finding lies the poor governance performance and legitimacy of Latin American economies, in comparison with OECD countries (see Marshall and Cole 2009 for a ranking of state fragility in the world).

Table 21.4 Impact of Elections on Fiscal Variables, 1990–2006 (GMM Estimation with Time Effect)

	Latin America	OECD	All
Primary balance			
GDP growth	5.12e-03 [0.18]	2.060e-01*** [4.08]	9.424e-02*** [3.21]
lLog GDP per capita	-1.896 [1.06]	1.395 [0.54]	-6.123*** [3.06]
Election dummy	-0.512*** [2.72]	-0.120 [0.73]	-0.304** [2.18]
Fiscal variable (-1)	4.290e-01*** [6.54]	8.063e-01*** [16.16]	8.108e-01*** [18.85]
Fiscal variable (-2)	-0.065 [1.11]	-0.138*** [3.03]	-0.073* [1.90]
Constant	15.222 [1.10]	-14.718 [0.59]	53.282*** [3.01]
Observations	247	364	597
Number of countries	19	27	45
Primary expenditure			
GDP growth	9.15e-03 [0.36]	-3.268e-01*** [5.73]	-4.85e-02 [1.64]
Log GDP per capita	1.485	3.476	-0.246
Election dummy	0.441** [2.46]	0.185 [1.04]	0.296** [1.97]
Fiscal variable (-1)	3.836e-01*** [5.17]	7.417e-01*** [13.49]	8.257e-01*** [16.97]
Fiscal variable (-2)	-0.030 [0.51]	0.048 [0.98]	0.005 [0.13]
Constant	-0.734 [0.05]	-23.189 [0.87]	7.085 [0.36]
Observations	260	330	576
Number of countries	19	28	46
Current expenditure			
GDP growth	-2.670e-02 [126]	-3.844e-01*** [6.43]	-1.170e-01*** [4.04]
Log GDP per capita	-1.943 [1.14]	4.209 [1.47]	-0.050 [0.02]
Election dummy	0.469*** [3.16]	0.231 [1.25]	0.370** [2.56]
Fiscal variable (-1)	4.114e-01*** [5.31]	8.178e-01*** [15.63]	9.017e-01*** [19.79]
Fiscal variable (-2)	0.064 [1.17]	0.003 [0.07]	-0.020 [0.51]
Constant	21.949* [1.66]	-32.449 [1.16]	4.001 [0.20]
Observations	260	330	576
Number of countries	19	28	46

(continued)

Table 21.4 (*continued*)

	Latin America	OECD	All
Capital expenditure			
GDP growth	2.61e-02	-1.67e-02	1.77e-03
	[1.47]	[1.01]	[0.14]
Log GDP per capita	1.249	1.243	2.329***
	[1.04]	[1.54]	[2.86]
Election dummy	0.209*	0.032	0.111*
	[1.77]	[0.62]	[1.72]
Fiscal variable (-1)	4.981e-01*** [7.73]	2.817e-01*** [4.29]	4.947e-01*** [9.90]
Fiscal variable (-2)	-0.182**	* 0.094	-0.103**
	[3.13]	[1.61]	[2.44]
Constant	-7.643	-9.987	-18.442***
	[0.84]	[128]	[2.59]
Observations	260	306	552
Number of countries	19	28	46

Notes: This table reports results of GMM estimation with two lags of the dependent variables and time-specific fixed effects included as regressors. We calculate the impact of elections on fiscal variables from the contemporaneous election year. The exception is capital expenditure, which we assume to lead the election by one year. We use legislative elections for countries with parliamentary political systems and executive elections for countries with presidential systems. Data on fiscal policy refer to central government. Absolute value of t statistics is in brackets.

*$p < .10$; **$p < .05$; ***$p < .01$

Source: Based on Secretaria do Tesouro Nacional (for Brazil), ECLAC ILPES, Public Finance database (for other Latin American countries), and OECD, General Government Accounts (for OECD countries), 2009.

Expansionary fiscal policy before elections does not necessarily increase the probability that an incumbent candidate remains in power (see Eslava 2006 for a review of the literature). However, the efficiency of economic policies is affected. Given these factors, an agreement among political parties could avoid fiscal disruptions around elections. Concretely, a consensus among major political parties limiting the menu of options to a range of credible commitments in the fiscal area could reduce the uncertainty traditionally generated by upcoming presidential elections. The 2002 presidential elections in Brazil provide an example of such a multiparty agreement (Chang 2007).

3.2. Reelections and Fiscal Policy in Latin American Countries

The previous section showed that elections have an impact on fiscal policy in Latin American countries. Incumbent politicians can expand fiscal policy before elections in order to increase the probability that they or their political party will be reelected. However, a question remains: does the reelection system in place affect candidates' propensity to use fiscal policy to attract votes? In other words, are

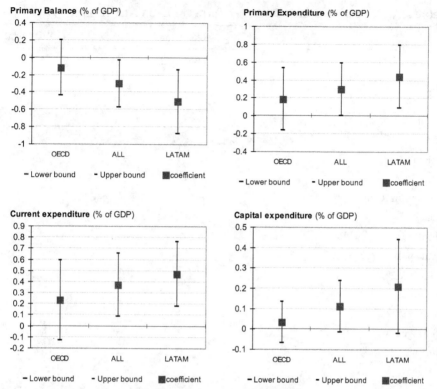

Figure 21.3 Significance of elections in OECD countries, Latin American countries, and the total sample, 1990–2006.

Notes: This figure reports results presented in Table 21.4. More precisely, it estimates the significance of elections on fiscal variables from GMM estimation. Time-specific fixed effects are included as regressors. The significance is at the 5 percent level. We calculate the impact of elections on fiscal variables from the contemporaneous election year. The exception is capital expenditure, which we assume to lead the election by one year. We use legislative elections for countries with parliamentary political systems and executive elections for countries with presidential systems. Data on fiscal policy refer to central government. Source: Based on Secretaria do Tesouro Nacional (for Brazil), ECLAC ILPES, Public Finance database (for other Latin American countries), and OECD, General Government Accounts (for OECD countries), 2009.

incumbent candidates more likely to increase public expenditure before elections when they can be reelected? In order to answer these questions, this section tests the impact that immediate reelections have on fiscal policy in Latin American countries. More precisely, we examine whether or not countries with reelections of incumbent candidates raise fiscal expenditures.

Latin American countries may be classified according to their reelection procedure (Payne et al. 2006). Table 21.5 shows the reelection system and the year terms for the largest Latin American countries. As of 2009, seven countries (Argentina, Brazil, Colombia, Dominican Republic, Ecuador, Haiti, and Venezuela) allow immediate reelection. In eight countries (Bolivia, Chile, Costa Rica, El Salvador, Nicaragua, Panama, Peru, and Uruguay) nonimmediate reelection is allowed, and in four countries (Guatemala, Honduras, Mexico, and Paraguay)

Table 21.5 Reelection System and Year Terms in Latin America (2009)

	Reelection			Year term
	Immediate	No Immediate	Forbidden	No. Years
Argentina	X			4
Bolivia	X			5
Brazil	X			4
Chile		X		4
Colombia	X			4
Costa Rica		X		4
Dominican Republic	X			4
Ecuador	X			4
El Salvador		X		5
Guatemala			X	4
Haiti	X			5
Honduras			X	4
Mexico			X	6
Nicaragua	X			5
Panama		X		5
Paraguay			X	5
Peru		X		5
Uruguay		X		5
Venezuela	X			6

Source: Authors, 2011.

reelection is forbidden. Of 10 presidential elections in 2006, seven took place in countries allowing reelection (immediate or nonimmediate). In six of those seven elections that year, the candidate for reelection was successful (immediate reelection in the case of Brazil, Colombia, and Venezuela and nonimmediate reelection for Costa Rica, Nicaragua, and Peru). Most recently, in 2009 President Rafael Correa was reelected in Ecuador. In Chile, where reelection is allowed but not immediately after a first mandate, former president Eduardo Frei was a candidate for the elections at the end of 2009. More important, the 2009 Honduran coup d'état against President Manuel Zelaya occurred in the context of an ongoing dispute over a new constitution that would allow Zelaya to be reelected, prohibited under the current legislation.

The current trend in election reform in Latin America is a move toward a less restrictive system of reelection. Venezuela (1998), the Dominican Republic (2002), Colombia (2005), Ecuador (2008), Bolivia (2009), and Nicaragua (2009) have adopted immediate reelection in recent years, as it exists in some OECD presidential regimes such as the United States, for example. Some other Latin American countries, like Honduras, are also debating immediate reelection and the 2009 referendum, in Venezuela, abolished term limits for the offices of president, state governors, mayors, and National Assembly deputies. It is clear that the recent trend in a large majority of Latin American countries toward immediate reelection will be a crucial element of upcoming electoral cycles. Immediate reelection can be associated with high incentives for incumbent candidates to increase the components of government expenditure observed by voters, who can then be influenced by these fiscal measures.

To study the impact of immediate reelection on fiscal variables, we use a basic regression of the form:

$$Fiscal\,variable_{i,t} = \sum_{j=1}^{2} a_j Fiscal\,variable_{i,t-2} + a_k GDPgrowth_{i,t} + a_k LogrealGDPcapita_{i,t}$$

$$+ b_0 immediate\_reelection_{i,t} + b_0 nonimmediate\_forbidden_{i,t} + e_{i,t}$$

In particular, instead of using the election dummy variable (as we did in the previous section), we compare immediate reelections (immediate_reelection) with the opposite case (nonimmediate_forbidden): nonimmediate reelections are allowed and reelections are forbidden.

Table 21.6 analyzes the impact of immediate reelections on fiscal policy. The estimation techniques reported are FE and GMM with time effect. Results suggest that immediate reelections have a considerable impact on the expenditure side of the fiscal balance. In particular, immediate reelections increase primary expenditure by more than 1.2 percent of GDP ($p < .01$). This result contrasts with that where immediate reelection is not allowed (less than 0.2 percent of GDP and not significant). Moreover, the impact of immediate reelections on primary expenditure is more than twice the impact for elections as a whole (more than 1.2 percent of GDP for immediate reelections according to table 21.6 versus less than 0.5 percent of GDP for total elections, reported in table 21.4).

Similarly, the expansion of current expenditure during the electoral year (more than 1.0 percent of GDP, $p < .01$) and the increase of capital expenditure one year prior to elections (more than 0.5 percent of GDP, $p < .05$) are considerable in the case of immediate reelections. Again, these results contrast with those when there is no immediate reelection, as well as with those when we analyze elections without differentiating according to electoral system (according to table 21.4, the impact of elections on capital expenditure is close to 0.2 percent of GDP, $p < .10$). Finally, the impact on the primary balance is high. The primary balance is reduced by close to 0.6 percent of GDP during the electoral year, but this is not significant. This last result shows that the impact on the primary balance varies considerably across countries. A possible explanation for this phenomenon is that some Latin American countries that allow immediate reelection expand the expenditure component of the fiscal balance during elections and during a context of high economic growth, which can attenuate (through high revenues) the impact on the primary balance.

The findings presented above suggest that incumbent candidates in Latin American democracies increase considerably the components of government

Table 21.6 Impact of Reelections on Fiscal Variables, 1990–2006 (FE and GMM Estimation with Time Effect)

	FE	GMM
Primary balance		
GDP growth	2.47e-02 [0.89]	3.20e-03 [0.11]
Log GDP per capita	-3.673** [2.41]	-2.174 [1.11]
Immediate reelection	-0.662 [1.49]	-0.659 [1.48]
Nonimmediate and forbidden	-0.452** [2.07]	-0.490** [2.28]
Fiscal variable (-1)	4.298e-01*** [6.54]	4.393e-01*** [6.61]
Fiscal variable (-2)	-0.057 [0.94]	-0.054 [0.91]
Constant	28.925** [2.45]	17.504 [1.16]
Observations	256	238
Number of countries	18	18
R-squared	0.43	
Primary expenditure		
GDP growth	3.05e-02 [1.14]	7.32e-03 [0.27]
Log GDP per capita	-0.727 [0.49]	1.824 [0.86]
Immediate reelection	1.342*** [3.21]	1.237*** [3.11]
Nonimmediate and forbidden	0.079 [0.37]	0.175 [0.86]
Fiscal variable (-1)	5.140e-01*** [7.88]	4.059e-01*** [5.39]
Fiscal variable (-2)	0.002 [0.03]	-0.025 [0.42]
Constant	12.819 [1.10]	-5.025 [0.31]
Observations	264	246
Number of countries	18	18
R-squared	0.57	
Current expenditure		
GDP growth	-5.047e-02** [2.38]	-5.373e-02** [2.46]
Log GDP per capita	-1.091 [0.90]	-2.751 [1.51]

Table 21.6 (continued)

	FE	GMM
Immediate reelection	1.350*** [4.05]	1.046*** [3.27]
Nonimmediate and forbidden	0.326* [1.92]	0.339** [2.13]
Fiscal variable (-1)	6.220e-01*** [10.03]	4.050e-01*** [5.12]
Fiscal variable (-2)	0.062 [1.08]	0.045 [0.82]
Constant	13.217 [1.38]	30.501** [2.07]
Observations	264	246
Number of countries	18	18
R-squared	0.73	
Capital expenditure		
GDP growth	3.363e-02* [1.79]	2.92e-02 [1.48]
Log GDP per capita	-1.385 [130]	1.741 [1.17]
Immediate reelection	0.557* [1.94]	0.553** [1.99]
Nonimmediate and forbidden	0.116 [0.78]	0.154 [1.09]
Fiscal variable (-1)	5.306e-01*** [8.10]	4.746e-01*** [7.00]
Fiscal variable (-2)	-0.140** [2.20]	-0.188*** [3.06]
Constant	12.472 [1.51]	-11.396 [0.99]
Observations	246	228
Number of countries	18	18
R-squared	0.32	

Notes: This table reports results of FE and GMM estimation with two lags of the dependent variables and time-specific fixed effects included as regressors. "Nonimmediate and forbidden" refers to all elections in which there is no immediate reelection (i.e., reelection is forbidden, reelection is not immediate). We calculate the impact of reelections on fiscal variables from the contemporaneous election year. The exception is capital expenditure, which we assume to lead the election by one year. Absolute value of t statistics is in brackets.

*$p < .10$; **$p < .05$; ***$p < .01$

Source: Based on Secretaria do Tesouro Nacional (for Brazil), ECLAC ILPES, Public Finance database (for other Latin American countries), 2009.

expenditure observed by voters. Where there is nonimmediate reelection and when reelection is forbidden, the opposite is true.

3.3. Is Latin American Fiscal Policy Maturing?

The empirical study presented above analyzes Latin America during the period 1990–2006. Results suggest that during this period the region expanded fiscal policy around elections (in contrast to OECD countries). As we stressed in previous work (Nieto-Parra and Santiso 2008), such critical electoral junctures tend to have significant impact on banks' recommendations and financial variables, which are negatively affected by the uncertainty surrounding elections. All major financial crises during the period studied coincided with elections. For 1994, a year in which no less than eight presidential elections took place, a major financial crisis known as the "tequilazo," which originated in Mexico some months after the presidential election of mid-1993, occurred. Since 1994, all of the major financial crises that affected the region coincided with presidential election years in which fiscal deteriorations were already occurring.

However, a question remains: is Latin American democracy maturing in the context of fiscal policy around elections? It is particularly notable that in 2006, a record year of presidential elections in Latin America (more than in 1994, with 10 presidential runoffs and over 80 percent of the region's population heading to the polls), no major financial disruption took place (fig. 21.4). In addition, despite the many elections, financial markets in the region did not experience major disruptions. This was a marked contrast to previous cycles and we are led to wonder whether this was a one-time event or perhaps evidence of a permanent change in the historic jitteriness of financial markets toward the democratic cycle in Latin America.

Perceiving a changed attitude on the part of the markets would certainly have some justification if we look only at the primary balance in Latin American countries. Figure 21.5 compares the effect of elections in 2006 on the primary surplus and on primary expenditure. Strikingly, primary surpluses tended to grow rather than shrink in countries for which 2006 was an election year.

There is no doubt that part of this fiscal discipline can be ascribed to the more forgiving conditions of high real GDP growth. Certainly, as the second panel of figure 21.6 shows, spending restraint was not driving low deficits. Many of those same countries witnessed some increases in primary expenditure as a share of GDP. This is the case for Venezuela, Brazil, and Mexico, in which primary spending booms stimulated fiscal deficits, and is in sharp contrast to Chile, Costa Rica, or Peru. That said, with the exception of Venezuela, which experienced a considerable jump in primary expenditure during its election year, in cases such as Mexico or Colombia the increase was moderate. As we pointed out, fiscal policies have been improving in Latin America over the 2000s and particularly since the mid-2000s (OECD 2008). Structural revenues have improved as a share of GDP, and structural primary balances are currently in surplus in many Latin American

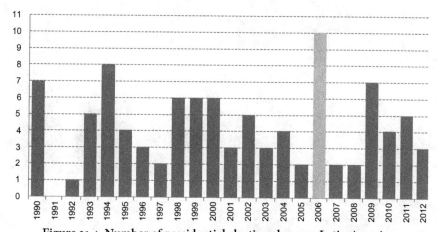

Figure 21.4 Number of presidential elections by year, Latin America.
Notes: The Latin American countries covered are Argentina, Bolivia, Brazil, Chile, Colombia, Costa Rica, the Dominican Republic, Ecuador, El Salvador, Guatemala, Haiti, Honduras, Mexico, Nicaragua, Panama, Paraguay, Peru, Uruguay, and Venezuela. For elections with a second (runoff) round, we use the date of the final round. Source: Based on www.electionguide.org, 2009.

countries (see Vladkova and Zettelmeyer 2008), the case of Chile being particularly impressive, with fiscal surpluses that increased significantly in 2006 and again in 2007–8.

It is clear that Latin America's governments have taken enormous strides to put their fiscal houses in order. The OECD's *Latin American Economic Outlook 2009* shows that, since the end of the debt crisis of the 1980s, governments have assiduously tightened their belts. Fiscal deficits have fallen from 11 percent of public revenues in the 1970s and 1980s to 8 percent since 2000. The year-to-year volatility of taxes, spending, and deficits—long a feature of fiscal policymaking in the region, with harmful effects for economic performance—has likewise fallen: an index of deficit volatility calculated for the *Latin American Economic Outlook 2009* shows a fall of a third from 1990–94 to 2000–6, with Latin America standing just 6 percent above the volatility levels in OECD countries in the latter period.

A closer look at the statistically significant fiscal variables studied in the previous sections shows a relative change in the pattern between fiscal policy and elections. Prior to 2005, primary expenditures were increasing significantly, while for 2005–6 the rise is on average much more moderate for the region (fig. 21.6). Similarly, primary fiscal balances tend to be negative prior to 2005 and positive in 2005–6 (fig. 21.7).[11] Finally, current expenditure increases were cut by nearly half in 2005–6 compared to before 2005 (fig. 21.8). However, even today we note that Latin American countries still increase public expenditure during elections, a result that still contrasts with OECD countries (fig. 21.1), showing that fiscal discipline around elections remains an issue for the region.[12]

Of course there are some caveats and selection bias problems with the stylized facts presented above for the comparison between the electoral cycle of 2005–6

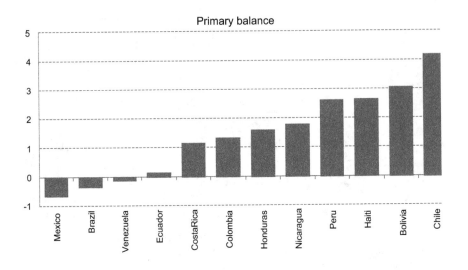

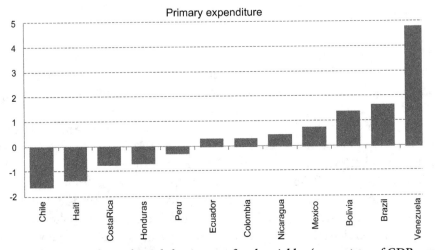

Figure 21.5 Impact of presidential elections on fiscal variables (percentage of GDP, 2005 and 2006 presidential elections compared with prior nonelection years).
Note: We calculate the impact of 2005 and 2006 elections on fiscal policy as the difference between the fiscal variable (as a proportion of GDP) during the election year and prior nonelection years. Source: Based on Secretaria do Tesouro Nacional (for Brazil) and ECLAC ILPES, Public Finance database (for other Latin American countries), 2009.

and prior electoral cycles. First, the size of the sample is much smaller in 2005–6, with a limited number of countries voting. Second, the number of elections between these two periods differs considerably (12 for 2005–6 versus 59 prior to 2005). These last stylized facts are not tested, however. Indeed, one may also justify the result presented above with the boom of commodity prices and argue that the positive shock to the terms of trade has also been a key driver influencing these results.

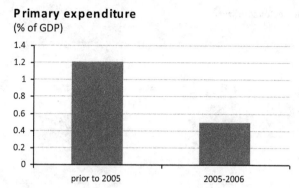

Figure 21.6 Changes in primary expenditure prior to 2005 and for 2005–6 (percentage of GDP).
Note: We calculate the impact of 2005 and 2006 elections on fiscal policy as the difference between the primary expenditure (as a proportion of GDP) during the election year and prior nonelection years. We calculate the impact of elections prior to 2005 on fiscal policy as the difference between the average of the primary expenditure during elections and the average of the primary expenditure for nonelection years. Source: Based on Secretaria do Tesouro Nacional (for Brazil) and ECLAC ILPES, Public Finance database (for other Latin American countries), 2009.

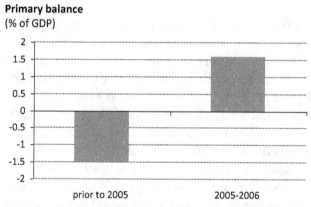

Figure 21.7 Primary balance prior to 2005 and for 2005–6 (percentage of GDP).
Note: We calculate the impact of 2005 and 2006 elections on fiscal policy as the difference between the primary balance (as a proportion of GDP) during the election year and prior nonelection years. We calculate the impact of elections prior to 2005 on fiscal policy as the difference between the average of the primary balance during elections and the average of the primary balance for nonelection years. Source: Based on Secretaria do Tesouro Nacional (for Brazil) and ECLAC ILPES, Public Finance database (for other Latin American countries), 2009.

4. Conclusions

In comparing the impact that elections could have on the deterioration of fiscal positions, particularly the public expenditure components in Latin American countries with respect to OECD countries, our study of 28 OECD countries and 19 Latin

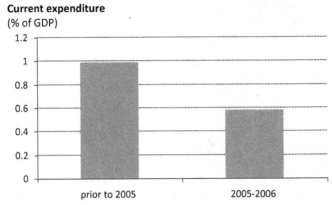

Figure 21.8 Current expenditure prior to 2005 and for 2005–2006 (percentage of GDP).
Note: We calculate the impact of 2005 and 2006 elections on fiscal policy as the difference between the current expenditure (as a proportion of GDP) during the election year and prior nonelection years. We calculate the impact of elections prior to 2005 on fiscal policy as the difference between the average of the current expenditure during elections and the average of the current expenditure for nonelection years. Source: Based on Secretaria do Tesouro Nacional (for Brazil) and ECLAC ILPES, Public Finance database (for other Latin American countries), 2009.

American countries during the period 1990–2006 suggests that general elections are indeed associated with much greater changes to the major components of fiscal policy in Latin America than in high-income countries. In particular, we find that in Latin American countries, the average primary balance declines by an amount close to 0.7 percent of GDP during an election year, confirming the hypothesis of fiscal deteriorations during the election cycle. Most of this movement is due to the expenditure component and within this it is current (close to 0.8 percent of GDP) rather than capital expenditure that is most affected. Our analysis also suggests that immediate reelections in Latin America have a considerable impact on the expenditure side of the fiscal balance. Finally, by comparing the 2005–6 electoral cycle to prior electoral cycles, we note a slight improvement in fiscal management around elections.

Our findings imply several policy recommendations. First, in order to avoid fiscal deterioration, fiscal rules focusing on the stability of the major components of fiscal balance may be an appropriate policy measure for Latin American countries. Moreover, around elections, higher transparency and disclosure of the major components of fiscal balance could be valuable for the region. Second, in the current debate on electoral systems in some Latin American countries, immediate reelection systems perhaps should be avoided in order to minimize the risks of fiscal deterioration ahead of and during election years. Alternatively, ministries of finance can establish special bodies to focus on a long-term perspective on fiscal policy. This recommendation is associated with the independence of fiscal policy from short-term incentives of politicians, a crucial aspect for Latin American countries studied in previous research (Eichengreen, Hausmann, and von Hagen 1999). A final policy implication has to do with the strategy of risk mitigation during political electoral cycles. Following the example of Lula in 2002, presidential candidates, could, for example, signal responsible and credible commitments ahead of elections. A consensus among major political parties aiming to reduce the menu of options to a range of credible commitments in the fiscal area could be a way to reduce the uncertainty traditionally generated by upcoming presidential elections, as Brazil in 2002 exemplified (Chang 2007).

This research contributes to ongoing debates on the influence of politics on economic policy in Latin America. The policy options put forward may serve to mitigate potential fiscal disruptions ahead of elections, which are, after all, regular and normal events in democracies.

NOTES

We wish to thank participants of the OECD Experts Meeting on Fiscal Policy: Towards the Latin American Economic Outlook 2009 held in May 2008 in Paris, for helpful comments and suggestions, as well as Rolando Avendaño, Daniela Campello, Bárbara Castelletti, Roberto Chang, Hye Jee Cho, Teresa Curristine, Jeff Dayton-Johnson, Thomas Dickinson, Jeff Frieden, Kiichiro Fukasaku, Alicia García-Herrero, David Leblang, Angel Melguizo, Elizabeth Nash, Pablo Pinto, Helmut Reisen, Juan Antonio Rodríguez, and Paul Vaaler for the comments, documents, and insights shared with us. All errors are obviously ours.

1. The political cycle is also crucial to capital markets, which have in the past been acutely sensitive to political developments in Latin American democracies, be they cabinet reshuffles or elections. Bankers and financial markets react to elections (Jensen and Schmith 2005; Whitehead 2006; Chang 2007; Nieto-Parra and Santiso 2008), reallocate money after democratic transitions (Rodríguez and Santiso 2008), or react to political announcements and events (Santiso 2003; Hays, Freeman, and Nesseth 2003; Frieden, Leblang, and Valev 2010). While this phenomenon is not specific to emerging economies, it remains especially strong in them (Campello 2007).

2. For a review of the literature regarding voters and fiscal policy around elections, see Eslava (2006).

3. A recent example of expansionary fiscal policy around an election in a developing country is Ghana, in which macroeconomic conditions deteriorated substantially during 2008, in the run-up to the election.

4. Additionally, there is no evidence that more conservative governments spend more on defense and more liberal governments spend more on social security and welfare (Lambertini 2003).

5. The exception is Brazil, for which we use as a source of information the Secretaria do Tesouro Nacional.

6. The OECD countries are Australia, Austria, Belgium, Canada, the Czech Republic, Denmark, Finland, France, Germany, Hungary, Iceland, Ireland, Italy, Japan, Korea, Luxembourg, Mexico, the Netherlands, New Zealand, Norway. Poland, Portugal, the Slovak Republic, Spain, Sweden, Switzerland, the United Kingdom, and the United States. The Latin American countries are Argentina, Bolivia, Brazil, Chile, Colombia, Costa Rica, the Dominican Republic, Ecuador, El Salvador, Guatemala, Haiti, Honduras, Mexico,

Nicaragua, Panama, Paraguay, Peru, Uruguay, and Venezuela. Mexico is the only country belonging to these two groups of countries.

7. Legislative elections are used for countries with parliamentary political systems and executive elections for countries with presidential systems. OECD countries, other than Mexico, Poland, and the United States, have been treated as parliamentary systems (see Keefer 2007).

8. OECD data refer to the consolidated general government sector. In Latin America coverage corresponds to the nonfinancial public sector (OECD 2008).

9. We calculate the impact of elections on fiscal variables from the contemporaneous election year. The exception is capital expenditure, which we assume leads the election by one year.

10. When all (Latin American and OECD) countries are analyzed, fiscal policy tends to be expansionary. Our estimation suggests that, for the full sample, primary expenditure over GDP is close to 0.3 percentage points higher during an electoral year, and current expenditure as a share of GDP increases 0.4 percent.

11. Moreover, by analyzing FE and GMM regressions with time effects (tables 21.3 and 21.4), we note that for Latin American countries, the 2006 time dummy variable is positive and statistically significant for the model that uses as the dependent variable the primary balance.

12. In analyzing FE and GMM regressions with time effect (tables 21.3 and 21.4), we observe that for Latin American countries the 2006 time dummy variable is positive and statistically significant for the model that uses current expenditure as the dependent variable. When we analyze the model with primary expenditure as the dependent variable, results are also positive and significant in the FE specification.

REFERENCES

Alesina, Alberto, Ricardo Hausmann, Rudolf Hommes, and Ernesto Stein. 1999. "Fiscal Institutions and Budget Deficits in Latin America." *Journal of Development Economics* 59: 233–55.

Alesina, Alberto, Nouriel Roubini, and Gerald Cohen. 1997. *Political Cycles and the Macroeconomy.* Cambridge, MA: MIT Press.

Ames, Barry.1987. *Political Survival: Politicians and Public Policy in Latin America.* Berkeley: University of California Press.

Arellano, Manuel, and Stephen Bond. 1991. "Some Specification Tests for Panel Data: Monte Carlo Evidence and an Application to Employment Equations." *Review of Economic Studies* 58: 277–98.

Barberia, Lorena, and George Avelino. 2011. "Do Political Budget Cycles Differ in Latin American Democracies?" *Economía* 11(2): 101–34.

Blaydes, Lisa. 2008. "Electoral Budget Cycles under Authoritarianism: Economic Opportunism under Mubarak's Egypt." Unpublished manuscript, Department of Political Science, Stanford University). Available at www.stanford.edu/~blaydes/Budget.pdf.

Blanchard, Olivier. 2004. "Fiscal Dominance and Election Targeting: Lessons from Brazil." NBER Working Paper No. 10389, National Bureau of Economic Research, Cambridge, MA.

Block, Steven, and Paul Vaaler. 2004. "The Price of Democracy: Sovereign Risk Ratings, Bond Spreads and Political Business Cycles in Developing Countries." *Journal of International Money and Finance* 23(6): 917–46.

Brender, Adi, and Allan Drazen. 2005. "Political Budget Cycles in New versus Established Democracies." *Journal of Monetary Economics* 52(7): 1271–95.

———. 2008. "How Do Budget Deficits and Economic Growth Affect Reelection Prospects? Evidence from a Large Panel of Countries." *American Economic Review* 98: 2203–50.

Campello, Daniela. 2007. "Do Markets Vote? A Systematic Analysis of Portfolio Investors' Response to National Elections." Unpublished manuscript, Department of Political Science, University of California, Los Angeles. Available at http://danicamp.bol.ucla. edu/Danicamp%20files/Do%20Markets%20Vote.pdf.

Chang, Roberto. 2007. "Financial Crises and Political Crises." *Journal of Monetary Economics* 54(8): 2409–20.

Drazen, Allan, and Marcela Eslava. 2005. "Electoral Manipulation via Expenditure Composition: Theory and Evidence." NBER Working Paper No. 11085, National Bureau of Economic Research, Cambridge, MA.

Eichengreen, Barry, Ricardo Hausmann, and Juergen Von Hagen. 1999."Reforming Budgetary Institutions in Latin America: The Case for a National Fiscal Council." *Open Economies Review* 10: 415–42.

Eslava, Marcela. 2005. "Political Budget Cycles or Voters as Fiscal Conservatives? Evidence from Colombia." *Documento CEDE* 22.

———. 2006. "The Political Economy of Fiscal Policy: A Survey." IADB Working Paper No. 683, Inter-American Development Bank, Washington, DC.

Frieden, Jeffry, David Leblang, and Neven Valev. 2010. "The Political Economy of Exchange Rate Regimes in Transition Economies." *The Review of International Organizations* 5(1): 1–25.

Gavin, Michael, and Roberto Perotti. 1997. "Fiscal Policy in Latin America." *NBER Macroeconomics Annual* 12. Cambridge, MA: National Bureau of Economic Research. 11–61.

González, María de los Angeles 2002. "Do Changes in Democracy Affect the Political Budget Cycle? Evidence from Mexico." *Review of Development Economics* 6(2): 204–24.

Hays, Jude, John Freeman, and Hans Nesseth. 2003. "Democratization and Globalization in Emerging Market Countries: An Econometric Study." *International Studies Quarterly* 47(2): 203–28.

Jensen, Nathan, and Scott Schmith. 2005."Market Responses to Politics: The Rise of Lula and the Decline of the Brazilian Stock Market." *Comparative Political Studies* 38(10): 1245–70.

Jones, Mark, Osvaldo Meloni, and Mariano Tommasi. 2009. "Voters as Fiscal Liberals: Incentives and Accountability in Federal Systems." Unpublished manuscript, Universidad de San Andrés. Available at http://faculty.udesa.edu.ar/tommasi/papers/wp/ JMT0108.pdf.

Keefer, Philip. 2007. *Database of Political Institutions: Changes and Variables Definitions*. Washington, DC: Development Research Group, World Bank.

Kneebone, Ronald, and Kenneth McKenzie. 2003. "Removing the Shackles: Some Modest, and Some Immodest, Proposals for Financing Cities." In *Paying for Cities*, edited by Paul Boothe, Institute for Public Economics, University of Alberta, Edmonton.

Krieckhaus, Jonathan. 2005."A Cross-National Comparison of Political Business Cycles: Are They More Prevalent in Developing Countries than in Developed Countries?" Paper presented at the annual meeting of the Americas Political Science Association, Washington, DC, Sept. 1, 2005.

Lambertini, Luisa. 2003. "Are Budget Deficits Used Strategically?" Boston College Working Papers in Economics No. 578, Boston College, Department of Economics.

Leblang, David. 2002. "The Political Economy of Speculative Attacks in the Developing World." *International Studies Quarterly* 46(1): 69–91.

Marshall, Monty, and Benjamin Cole. 2009. *Global Report 2009, Conflict, Governance, and State Fragility*. Fairfax, VA: Center for Global Policy, School of Public Policy, George Mason University. Available at http://www.systemicpeace.org/Global%20Report%20 2009.pdf.

Nieto-Parra, Sebastián, and Javier Santiso. 2008. "Wall Street and Elections in Latin American Emerging Democracies." OECD Development Centre Working Paper No. 272, Organisation for Economic Co-operation and Development, Paris.

———. 2009. "Revisiting Political Budget Cycles in Latin America." OECD Development Centre Working Paper No. 281, Organisation for Economic Co-operation and Development, Paris.

OECD (Organisation for Economic Co-operation and Development). 2008. *Latin American Economic Outlook 2009*. Paris: OECD Development Centre.

Payne, J.Mark, Daniel Zovatto G., Mercedes Mateo Díaz, Andrés Allamand Zavala, Fernando Carrillo-Flórez, Koldo Echebarría, Flavia Freidemberg, and Edmundo Jarquín. 2006. *La Política Importa: Democracia y Desarrollo en América Latina*. Rev. ed. New York: IDEA.

Peltzman, Sam. 1992. "Voters as Fiscal Conservatives." *Quarterly Journal of Economics* 107 (2): 325–45.

Rodríguez, Juan Antonio. 2006. "¿Responden el gasto e inversión públicas a los ciclos económicos y políticos?" *BBVA Latinwatch*, Grupo BBVA, Madrid.

Rodríguez, Javier, and Javier Santiso. 2008. "Banking on Democracy: The Political Economy of International Private Bank Lending in Emerging Democracies." *International Political Science Review* 29(2): 213–44.

Rogoff, Kenneth. 1990. "Equilibrium Political Budget Cycles." *American Economic Review* 80: 21–36.

Sakurai, Sergio, and Naercio Menezes-Filho. 2008. "Fiscal Policy and Re-election in Brazilian Municipalities." *Public Choice* 137: 301–14.

Santiso, Javier. 2003. *The Political Economy of Emerging Markets: Actors, Institutions and Financial Crises in Latin America*. New York: Palgrave Macmillan.

Schuknecht, Ludger. 1996. "Political Business Cycles and Fiscal Policies in Developing Countries." *Kyklos* 49(2): 155–70.

Shi, Min, and Jakob Svensson. 2006. "Political Budget Cycles: Do They Differ Across Countries and Why?" *Journal of Public Economics* 90(8–9): 1367–89.

Veiga, Francisco, and Linda Veiga. 2007. "Political Business Cycles at the Municipal Level." *Public Choice* 131(1): 45–64.

Vladkova-Hollar, Ivanna, and Jeromin Zettelmeyer. 2008. "Fiscal Positions in Latin America: Have They Really Improved?" IMF Working Paper No. 08/137, International Monetary Fund, Washington, DC.

Whitehead, Lawrence. 2006. "The Political Dynamics of Financial Crisis in Emerging Market Democracies." In *State Crafting Monetary Authority: Democracy and Financial Order in Brazil*, edited by Lawrence Whitehead and L. Sola, 13–36. Oxford: Oxford Centre for Brazilian Studies.

CHAPTER 22

LABOR MARKETS IN LATIN AMERICA AND THE CARIBBEAN: THE MISSING REFORM

PABLO EGAÑA AND ALEJANDRO MICCO

1. INTRODUCTION

After the "Lost Decade" of the 1980s, Latin America and the Caribbean (LAC) initiated a complex reform process. Democracies returned to the continent and many countries moved away from the import-substitution model (see table 22.1). The so-called Washington Consensus spread through Latin America and established three main ideas in economic policy: macroeconomic discipline, a market economy, and openness to the world, at least in respect of trade and foreign direct investment. These ideas, already a cornerstone in countries of the Organisation for Economic Co-operation and Development (OECD) at that time, were contrary to previous Latin American economic thinking. That earlier paradigm claimed, first, that developing countries may benefit from inflation as a tax to boost investment; second, that there is a leading role for the state in initiating industrialization; and third, that import substitution was fundamental to getting rid of dependence on raw materials. The new paradigm refuted all these ideas but surprisingly did not emphasize, or even mention as an important element, labor markets (Williamson 1990; Kuczynski and Williamson 2003; Fischer 2003).

Table 22.1. Return to Democracy and Economic Reform in Latin America

Country	Timing of Democratic Transition	Initiation of Economic Reform
Argentina	1983	1989
Bolivia	1982	1985,1990s
Brazil	1985	1994
Chile	1990	1976, 1980, 1990
Colombia	—	1990
Ecuador	1980	1990
Mexico	2000	1985, 1990s
Paraguay	1989	1991
Peru	1980	1992
Uruguay	1985	1991
Venezuela	—	1989

Source: Based on Cook (2007).

Because of the Washington Consensus, fiscal discipline, tax reforms, trade and capital-flow liberalization, privatization of most state-owned enterprises, and deregulation of financial and goods market were at the forefront of policy debates after the first half of the 1980s. As we show below, most countries were able to pass pro-market reforms in most areas with the exception of labor markets. Even though this issue was not directly addressed, reformers expected the shift to a more competitive environment to reduce inefficiencies, increase productivity, and spur growth, thus increasing labor demand and employment in Latin America. In particular higher productivity would increase the marginal product of labor and therefore would imply higher wages (see, e.g., Saavedra 2003).

To put this idea in perspective, we compare Latin America with other groups of countries, using the classification provided by Schneider (2008) (see appendix 22.1). This classification emphasizes the political economy structure of countries. In particular, Latin America is classified as "hierarchical market economies" (HME), including almost all countries in the region. Other classifications are "liberal market economies" (LME), including the United States, United Kingdom, and its former colonies; "coordinated market economies" (CME), including most of the countries of northern Europe and Japan; "Mediterranean market economies" (MME), including France, Italy, Spain, Portugal, and Greece; and southeastern economies (SEA), including all the countries located in southeast Asia. In this chapter, we use HME or LAC interchangeably since they have minor differences in the countries considered.

After the debt crises in the 1980s many countries made extensive pro-market reforms in HME, although reforms were few and timid in the labor market. Even though gross domestic product (GDP) per capita growth was extremely low in Latin America during the 1980s, an average annual rate of -0.9 percent, whereas in the CME and LME countries it was around 2 percent, employment grew by a healthy 29 percent during this period in HME (see table 22.2). The high level of inflation and the substantial presence of an informal economy seemed to drive labor markets, and therefore limitations in these markets did not seem to be an obstacle to reaping the benefits of other structural reforms, like trade liberalization. At the time spending scarce political capital on labor market reforms did not seem necessary.

Once sound macroeconomic policies were in place and most countries opened their economies, labor market issues did eventually raise obstacles to future growth: low human capital, almost no training, lack of flexibility in formal labor markets, dual labor markets, and others (see, e.g., World Bank 2009, 2010). But the momentum for pro-market reforms had waned. Lack of transparency in some reforms, in particular as regards privatization and poor performance in labor markets, reduced public support for pro-market reforms. The Washington Consensus became a bad word in Latin American politics (Williamson (2004). The lack of public support and the opposition of unions, which mainly represented public sector workers and employees from large and regulated firms, blocked any attempt to extend reforms to labor markets (Madrid 2003).

As Cook (2007) pointed out, most labor legislation was originally crafted to reflect government-employer-worker relationships embedded in more protected national economies. After the Washington Consensus, fiscal discipline and trade openness, together with overregulated labor markets, forced LAC economies to find alternative solutions to deal with problems under this new reality. The number of people working in the informal sector increased throughout the region in the 1990s (de Luca 1999). This economic informality reduced pressure on labor market reforms, but increased other chronic Latin American problems. The region entered a vicious circle: highly regulated labor markets leading to informality and then to more regulation, the latter driven by the formal workforce. In addition, the region seemed to get used to high levels of unemployment and low labor market participation (World Bank 2009).

During this century, favorable external conditions for the region, in particular high commodities prices, imply high GDP and employment growth reducing the pressure for labor market reforms. The global financial crises had only transitory effects on unemployment in LAC. Strong and rapid recovery in the whole region has generated a current unemployment rate of only 8.1 percent (IMF 2010).

Section 2 of this chapter shows the evolution of output and labor markets during the last decades in Latin America. Section 3, the core of this study, presents labor market reforms during this period. It provides some evidence that informality and inflation drove labor markets in the 1980s, reducing the urgency to reform them. In particular it shows how inflation, unions, and privatization worked to slow down the process of executing labor market reforms in LAC. The section then presents evidence of how labor markets reacted to Washington Consensus reforms: mainly an increase of informality in the economy. An important point in this section is to establish that the above conclusion was made based on the "insider and outsider" theory. Section 4 describes the vicious circle generated by highly regulated labor markets and informality.

2. OUTPUT AND LABOR MARKET PERFORMANCE DURING RECENT DECADES

For Latin America the 1970s was a transition from the booming '60s, when GDP per capita grew at 2.5 percent per year (World Bank 2009), and the '80s, known as the "Lost Decade." As table 22.2 shows, during the '80s growth per capita was negative, unemployment rose, and inflation was remarkably stubborn. During the '90s, economic performance improved for the region as a whole. This upward trend continued during the first decade of the twenty-first century, which has been one of the best decades for the region in over half a century. Surprisingly, as we show in this section, employment did not follow in tandem with output performance during the 1990s.

As table 22.2 shows, in relation to CME, LME, MME, and SEA, HME had an average performance in the 1970s in terms of GDP per capita growth. For HME countries, output per capita grew on average at 2.4 percent per year, a rate of growth lower than the one presented by CME, MME, and in particular SEA countries, which grew at 4.8 percent per year. Employment, however, does not reflect this average outcome in output. During this period, LAC had the fastest growth in employment, on average growing at a rate of 3.3 percent per year, even more than in SEA.

Liquidity generated by petro dollars overflowed the region. Most countries ran huge fiscal and current account deficits at the beginning of the 1980s. These deficits were financed by foreign banks, increasing the external debt of the region. As table 22.3 shows, the average public deficit in the region was -4.4 percent during the beginning of the 1980s. On the other hand, the current account deficit was almost -4.7 percent. By 1982 the external debt, which was mainly denominated in U.S. dollars, became a problem for some countries in the regions.

Table 22.2. Average Annual Growth of Employment, 1970s–2000s (Percentage)

Group of Countries	Average Annual Growth of Employment Rate in the 1970s	Average Annual Growth of GDP Per Capita in the 1970s	Average Annual Growth of Employment Rate in the 1980s	Average Annual Growth of GDP Per Capita in the 1980s	Average Annual Growth of Employment Rate in the 1990s	Average Annual Growth of GDP Per Capita in the 1990s	Average Annual Growth of Employment Rate in the 2000s[a]	Average Annual Growth of GDP Per Capita in the 2000s[a]
HME	3.3	2.4	2.9	-0.9	2.0	1.6	2.7	2.7
CME	0.5	3.0	0.8	2.2	0.4	1.8	0.9	1.7
LME	1.6	2.1	1.0	2.0	1.4	2.5	1.8	1.9
MME	0.7	3.8	0.7	2.0	0.8	1.8	1.5	1.7
SEA	2.7	4.9	2.8	1.7	2.6	3.4	2.8	4.2

[a]2000s includes until 2008.

Note: See text for definition of country group abbreviations.

Source: World Bank (2009) and Heston, Summers, and Aten (2010)

When Mexico announced in 1982 that it could not pay its foreign debt, capital flows into Latin America and the Caribbean came to an abrupt end, forcing every country in the region to go through severe macroeconomic adjustment processes. When the Federal Reserve Bank increased the interest rate to control inflation in the United States, Latin America's external debt became unsustainable, and capital flows to LAC vanished. Current account balances went from 6.3 percent during 1982 to -3.5 percent in 1983. This huge change in the current account balances was made possible by a collapse of output and drastic cuts in fiscal expenditure in the region. Between 1982 and 1984, HME contracted the fiscal deficit by around 2 percentage points; thus the fiscal crisis induced a procyclical fiscal policy.

During the Lost Decade GDP per capita in LAC fell by 0.9 percent while in southeast Asian countries GDP per capita growth was above 1.7 percent. It is important to note that even though GDP growth in the '80s was negative in LAC, employment growth was relatively high, and similar to that in SEA. On average employment grew at 2.9 percent per year, although huge differences can be observed. In Chile employment figures dropped sharply and unemployment rose to over 30 percent, but in Brazil employment growth was 30 percent in the decade and unemployment was on average 5.3 percent (Ramos 2003). For most countries, labor markets adjusted to the "debt crisis" through real wages. On average in the region real wages fell by 28 percent during the 1980s.[1] Employment did not seem to be a problem during this period; labor markets cleared (reached low, or a natural, rate of unemployment) in most HME countries. High inflation allowed countries to cut real wages.[2]

From the mid-1980s to the mid-1990s Latin America experienced a profound economic revolution as import restrictions were drastically reduced, financial markets liberalized, and numerous state enterprises privatized. The economic effects of these structural reforms show up in Latin American performance during the 1990s. GDP per capita in the region grew on average 1.6 percent per year, 2.5 percentage points faster than during the previous decade (-0.9 percent). This large reversal in

Table 22.3. Current Account Balance and Fiscal Deficits, Various Regions (Percentage)

Group of Countries	1980		1982		1983	
	CA Balance	Fiscal Deficit	CA Balance	Fiscal Deficit	CA Balance	Fiscal Deficit
HME	-4.7	-4.4	-6.3	-9.4	-3.5	-8.3
CME	-2.1	-2.6	-0.1	-4.5	0.9	-4.2
LME	-3.0	-4.3	-2.6	-5.4	-2.3	-6.1
MME	-2.7	-3.5	-2.7	-6.8	-1.5	-6.8
EEE	-5.9	-1.9	-3.1	-2.5	-4.3	-0.9
SEA	3.0	-5.2	-6.6	-9.0	-7.7	-6.9

Note: See text for definition of country group abbreviations.
Source: IMF (2010) and Easterly, Rodriguez, and Schmidt-Hebbel (1994)

output did not show up in terms of employment. On average, employment rates grew by only 2.0 percent per year during the 1990s, one percentage point lower than employment growth rate during the '80s, when it was 2.9 percent per year. This recovery without employment has been one of the reasons behind the increasing opposition to pro-market reforms in HME.

Finally, HME experienced a good economic performance during this new century. High terms of trade and effective financial regulation—as evidenced during the last global financial crises—resulted in an average per-capita growth of 2.7 percent, below only SEA countries.[3] If we focus on the period 2002–8, the region grew 5.4 percent on average, and unemployment fell to 7.5 percent in 2008.

3. The Reform Process in LAC during the 1980s and 1990s

Structural reforms became widespread in the region during the 1990s. After the Lost Decade in LAC, when almost all the countries had run large deficits that led to balance-of-payments crises and high inflation, fiscal discipline became one of the main goals of governments in the region. Table 22.4 compares fiscal deficits during 1975–84 and 1984–95. For LAC the simple average of fiscal deficits during the first half of the 1980s was -6.5 percent of GDP, extremely high compared to European countries, where the average fiscal deficit was only -3.8 percent of GDP. Liberal market economies also presented lower fiscal deficits, shifting from an average of -4.4 in the period 1975–84 to an average of -2.8 in the period 1985–94. In the '90s, countries in LAC reordered their public expenditure priorities, switching expenditure in a way favoring the poor, from things like indiscriminate subsidies to spending on basic health and education.

Furthermore, fiscal discipline came with tax reforms during this period in LAC. The goal was to increase the tax base and to reduce marginal tax rates. Table 22.5 shows how the maximum business tax rate fell for most LAC countries between 1986 and 2001. Tax reform in addition to fiscal rationalization led to important changes in aggregate labor demand in most countries in LAC.

During this reform period domestic markets were liberalized. Countries started to cut tariff and trade barriers. As table 22.4 shows, the average tariff fell from 38.5 percent in 1986 to 10.4 percent in 1999. This process continued during the new century. The main aim of trade liberalization was to increase productivity and competition in the region.

Reallocation is at the heart of productivity gains from openness as factor deployment becomes more efficient, in particular for labor. Inefficient firms in import-competing industries exposed to tariff reductions experience lower profitability of some projects and thus reduce the level of employment, and in some cases they are forced to shut down all production facilities. At the same time, the increased openness

Table 22.4. Fiscal Deficits and Trade Tariffs in Various Regions

Country	Average Fiscal Défit (% GDP)		Average Trade Tariff		Privatization Effort Index	
	1975–84	1985–94	1986	1999	1988	1999
Argentina	-10.78	-5.90	39.50	11.00	0.00	0.39
Bolivia	-14.40	-5.77	21.90	9.00	0.00	0.90
Brazil	-4.60	-4.45	74.10	13.30	0.00	0.50
Chile	0.21	0.46	20.20	10.00	0.03	0.16
Colombia	-4.52	-1.98	46.40	11.80	0.00	0.23
Ecuador	-3.95	-4.48	41.40	12.90	0.00	0.03
Mexico	-7.65	-2.88	27.80	10.10	0.05	0.27
Peru	-6.18	-6.38	63.00	13.00	0.00	0.60
El Salvador			23.00	5.70	0.00	0.36
Uruguay			35.70	4.60	0.00	0.00
Venezuela, Bolivarian Republic			30.60	12.60	0.00	0.27
LAC	**-6.48**	**-3.92**	**38.51**	**10.36**	**0.01**	**0.34**
Austria	-2.73	-2.90	9.09	3.15		
Belgium	-8.60	-7.35				
Denmark	-3.50	0.55	8.24			
Finland	1.22	1.05		4.53		
France	-1.71	-1.98	8.44			
Germany	-3.07	-1.15		4.53		
Italy	-10.57	-11.10	8.24			
Netherlands	-4.34	-5.42	8.54	4.45		
Spain	-3.00	-3.92	8.24			
Sweden	-1.85	2.05		4.31		
Europe	**-3.82**	**-3.02**	**8.47**	**4.19**		
Canada	-3.55	-4.28		4.61		
United States	-1.92	-2.40	4.28	8.14		
HME	-6.57	-4.02			0.01	0.34
CME	-2.58	-0.85				
LME	-4.39	-2.85				
MME	-5.13	-7.93				
SEA	-6.46	-3.93				

Sources: World Bank (2009), Lora (2001), UNIDO (from Nicita and Olarreaga 2007). Consolidated public deficits as percentage of GDP come from Easterly et al. (1994). The privatization effort index comes from Lora (2001). Note: Blank cells indicate data not available.

creates new export opportunities for other producers, leading to expansion of both better-positioned incumbents and start-ups. Competition is also likely to increase the elasticity of employment in response to changes in relative prices, including those generated by real exchange rate fluctuations. All of these effects taken together suggest the greater requirement of factor reallocation in response to trade liberalization: in sum, more flexible labor markets (see appendix 22.2).

As in trade, the region underwent a huge transformation in terms of publicly owned enterprises. The need to raise the efficiency of the production system in the context of an increasingly competitive international market, combined with the financial difficulties of the state and the public demand for better social services, creates relentless pressure for change in the way the state's functions are performed and public utilities provided. Privatization not only involved public utilities but also other sectors like mining in Brazil, manufacturing in Mexico, and oil and gas production in Bolivia. Table 22.4 gives the privatization effort measured as the cumulative value of the sales and transfers of companies (starting in 1986) as a proportion of GDP for the year in

Table 22.5. Tax Rates in LAC, 1986–2001

	PIT 1986 (%)	PIT 2001 (%)	EIT 1986 (%)	EIT 2001 (%)	VAT Introduction (%)	VAT 2001 (%)
Argentina	45	35	33	35	16	21
Bolivia	30	13	30	25	10	14.92
Brazil	60	27.5	35	15	15	20.5
Chile	57	45	37	15	20	18
Colombia	49	35	40	35	10	16
Costa Rica	50	25	50	30	6	12
Dominican Republic	73	25	46	25	4	12
Ecuador	40	15	40	25	10	13
El Salvador	60	30	30	25	7	12
Guatemala	48	31	42	31	3	12
Honduras	40	25	40	35	10	15
Mexico	55	40	42	35	6	15
Nicaragua	50	25	45	25	5	5
Panama	56	30	50	30	12	10
Peru	49	20	40	30	15	18
Uruguay	0	6	30	30	14	23
Venezuela	45	34	67.7	34	10	14.5
Average	**49.20**	**27.70**	**41.00**	**28.30**	**10.20**	**14.70**
OECD	**52.80**	**41.20**	**42.80**	**31.80**		

Notes: Personal income tax (PIT) rates are the top marginal rate. Enterprise (EIT) rates are also the top rate. Value-added tax (VAT) rate is the "standard" rate. Uruguay has no PIT except on income from agriculture and commissions. Years shown are approximate in some cases.
Source: Stotsky and WoldeMariam (2002).

question (Lora 2001). These privatization processes implied reallocation of workers. In some cases, the employment level in privatized firms fell by more than 25 percent (de Luca 1999).

Countries also liberalized interest rates ending the financial repression that characterized financial markets during the 1970s and 1980s. Restrictions to inward foreign investment were also abolished in many cases, and countries aimed at competitive exchange rate. Summing up, Latin America underwent a significant economic transformation during this period.

As Rodrik (1996) observed, a number of countries in Latin America adopted more trade and financial liberalization policies and more privatization in a short period than the east Asian countries did in three decades. Even in the tax area, he pointed out noteworthy reforms. In contrast with the four previous reform areas, during the same period, in the labor market the changes have been few and smaller in scope (see fig. 22.1). Various authors also comment that the region did not embrace significant labor market reforms during this period (e.g., Krueger 2004; Saavedra 2003; Lora 2001; Rodrik 2001, 2006: Kuczynski and Williamson 2003; World Bank 2005). Heckman and Pagés (2004) find that, in general, there is no clear sequencing pattern between trade reforms and labor market reforms. The same authors do find, however, that many labor market reforms tended to take place during periods of negative economic growth, and that many reforms that strengthened workers' rights took place in the period following the return to democracy.

To quantify the magnitude of the whole reform process after the Lost Decade, we presents Lora 2001´s reforms index for the region (fig. 22.1). This index summarizes the advance of structural reform in taxation, privatization, trade, the financial market, and the labor market. It goes from 0 (none) to 1 (full advance). Figure 22.1 shows how the region went into an extensive reform process during the second half of the 1980s and the 1990s. Until 1990, the region had utilized almost 10 percent of the available "margin of reform."[4] By 1999, this figure was almost 40 percent. The

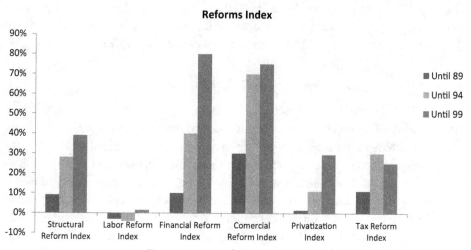

Figure 22.1 Lora's Reforms Index.

greatest reform process was in trade, where the margin utilized was almost 80 percent in 1999. As we mentioned, LAC drastically cut tariff and nontariff barriers. Lora´s indexes show that LAC countries embraced significant reforms toward more market-oriented economies in all areas but labor, where the changes were minor.

Some countries implemented labor reforms, but legislative changes differed drastically in extent and even in direction. In many countries we do not observe changes and in others we observe reforms that made labor market regulation even more stringent. Lora (2001) pointed out that only six countries made substantial labor reforms between the mid-1980s and 1999: Chile (1979 and 1991) Argentina (1991), Colombia (1991), Guatemala (1990), Panama (1995), Peru (1991), and Venezuela (1998), although some of those reforms have subsequently been reversed during this century. This is the case with Argentina. While President Carlos Menem in the 1990s pursued flexibility in the labor market, President Nestor Kirchner in the beginning years of the 2000s aimed to reverse these changes.

3.1 Why the Labor Market Was Not a Political/Policy Worry during the 1980s and Beginning of the 1990s

We argue there are four main reasons for this "lack of interest" in labor reform during this period. These are employment performance in the 1980s, inflation and informality in the economy, lack of bargaining power of employees, and compensation packages initiated during privatization.

3.1.1 Employment Performance during the Lost Decade

First, as we noted, despite the fact that GDP per capita growth in Latin America was extremely low during the 1980s (an annual average rate of -0.9 percent), employment grew by a healthy average annual rate of 2.9 percent during the same period. Labor markets were not the problem behind the Lost Decade; they accommodated the output collapse that followed the debt crises. At the time it did not seem necessary to spend scarce political capital on labor reforms. Fiscal discipline, trade openness, and more competition seemed more important reforms.

3.1.2 Inflation and Informality as Substitute for De Jure Labor Flexibility

Second, high inflation and informality in HME allowed labor markets to adjust through wages and not employment in most countries during the Lost Decade. These same characteristics plus compensation packages in most unionized sectors seemed to be sufficient to take advantage of structural reforms proposed under the Washington Consensus, like trade openness and privatization. High inflation would allow relative wages to adjust after relative prices change due to reforms, and informality would allow labor to move from contracting sectors to industries with increasing demand.

Fiscal deficits in the HME, financed in part with inflation, allowed most countries to maintain their labor market. Inflation not only allows countries to adjust real wages but, as shown by Loboguerrero and Panizza (2006), also reduces the sensitivity of employment to changes in output in countries with highly regulated labor markets (i.e., employment protection laws). In addition to inflation, the higher level of informality and lack of rule of law in many countries made labor markets in LAC, de facto, flexible.[5]

Table 22.6 shows that informality at the beginning of the 1980s was as high as 28.8 percent in LAC, and it increased after the debt crisis and the first stage of trade

Table 22.6. The Informal Economy in Various Regions

Country	% of Self-employed in Nonagricultural Employment				
	1970s	1980s	1990s	2000s	Latest
Argentina	23.7		29.3	25.3	25.3
Bolivia	42.9		59.0	53.6	53.6
Brazil	20.8	20.9	30.8	35.7	35.7
Chile	20.3	19.7	29.1	32.0	32.0
Colombia			48.7	49.3	49.3
Cuba	1.3	1.0			1.0
Ecuador	36.4	39.9	49.3		49.3
Mexico	28.2	41.8	33.9	29.9	29.9
Peru	35.4	31.3			31.3
Uruguay	22.5	22.0		19.5	19.5
Venezuela	24.5	26.8	39.5	40.3	40.3
HME	28.0	28.8	41.8	33.7	33.4
Austria	10.4	7.3	8.0	9.5	9.5
Belgium	15.2	13.8		13.9	13.9
Denmark	13.8	7.9			7.9
Finland	8.8	5.9	8.9	10.9	10.9
France	11.2	10.4	11.3	8.6	8.6
Germany	10.4	8.4	9.8	11.3	11.3
Italy	19.7	19.7	25.8	25.1	25.1
Netherlands	10.4	9.3	8.8	11.3	11.3
Spain	16.2	21.1	18.5	19.3	19.3
Sweden	5.5	2.9	9.2		9.2
CME, MME[a]	12.2	10.7	12.5	13.7	12.7
USA	6.0	5.6	7.4	7.5	7.5
Canada	5.1	4.6	6.9	15.6	15.6
LME[a]	5.6	5.1	7.2	11.6	11.6
SEA	33.6	33.9	33.2	34.2	

Note: Blank cells indicate data not available.
[a] Selected countries
Source: OECD 2009.

openness (see also table 22.7). High levels of informality allowed wages to adjust and, more important, workers to move from one firm or sector to another. This de facto labor flexibility helped labor markets to adjust during the Lost Decade and the structural reform period, although it put most of the adjustment burden on workers.[6] Related to high informality in LAC countries is the fact that HME has the lowest level of rule of law for employment of all the regions (see table 22.8).

3.1.3 Lack of Worker Bargaining Power and De Facto Lack of Labor Protection

Third, as Schneider (2009) observed, most workers in HME are unlikely to have plant-level union representation, both because union density is low and because even where unions do exist, they often do not have much of a formal presence on the shop floor. In addition, in privatized sectors with high levels of formal employment and unions, like utilities, companies often implemented special retirement and compensation plans for workers. These plans did not require changes in national labor legislation.

Labor relations in Latin America are fragmented and workers are often alienated because most workers have short-term links to companies and weak or no horizontal linkages to other workers through unions.[7] Among other things, turnover among workers is high and Latin American economies are characterized by a large number of micro and small enterprises (IADB 2010). Few countries in the region have special

Table 22.7. Characteristics of Labor in Latin America

Country	Union Members as % of Nonagricultural Labor Force, 1980s	Union Members as % of Nonagricultural Labor Force, 1990s	Union Members as % of Formal Sector Wage Earners	Dominant Union Structure	Number of Peak Confederations	Political-Strategic Orientation of Largest Peak Organization	Strength of Organized Labor
Argentina	48.7	25.4	65.6	Industry	Dominant	Conciliatory/militant (split)	High
Brazil		32.1	66	Local	Multiple	Militant	High
Mexico	54.1	31	72.9	Industry/local	Multiple	Conciliatory	Medium
Bolivia		16.4	59.7	Firm	Single	Militant	Medium
Chile	11.6	15.9	33	Firm	Single	Conciliatory	Low
Peru		7.5	18.3	Firm	Multiple	Militant	Low

Sources: O'Connell (1999) and Cook (2007). Union density data are from de Luca (1999), table 1.2. Data for Argentina are from 1995; Brazil, 1991; Mexico, 1991; Bolivia, 1994; Chile, 1993; and Peru, 1991. Dominant union structure information is from McGuire (1997).

institutions for microcoordination within companies, and "organized labor is extremely weak" (Schneider 2009, 561). As a result, labor relations and employment are conducted on an individual level. Turnover and the dominance of small firms are major contributing factors to this dilution of labor relations. Finally, as tables 22.6 and 22.7 show, many people work in the informal sector without unions or legal protection.

These points apply mainly to medium and small enterprises. Large firms in regulated sectors have much higher levels of formal employment and unionization. Unions force more favorable contracts for workers that protect them against inflation and introduce high adjustment costs.[8] As noted, this condition in larger firms contrasts with the situation of the majority of workers in HME. This disparity is evidence of the existence of "insiders" and "outsiders" in the labor market.[9] Moreover, despite the size of workforces of both types, the political influence of the insider group is clearly more important, particularly in state-owned firms. In these sectors—electricity, telecom, water, and similar entities—countries embraced a drastic process of privatization. As we discuss in the next section, to achieve this privatization, the processes adopted included generous compensation packages to insider workers (Chong and López-de-Silanes 2004).

3.1.4 Privatization and Compensation Packages

Fourth, as mentioned in the previous subsection, workers of privatized firms, which include mainly utilities with high degrees of unionization, received large compensation packages during the privatization process. These compensation packages provided the required flexibility to improve productivity through employment reallocation.[10]

As de Luca (1999) pointed out, utilities had a high union density among employees in HME countries. Unions resisted privatization movements at first. In many countries in the region, governments countered this resistance with three basic strategies: offers of generous compensation for workers accepting voluntary retirement, a promise to reemploy large numbers of workers in the new operating company, and the earmarking of shares in the new company for workers from the former operator. This strategy allowed governments to gain workers' support in these privatization processes, without changes in labor market regulation.

For example, in the electricity sector of Argentina, the government facilitated acceptance of the reform by granting employees a 10 percent stake in most of the privatized enterprises. Because of these compensation payments, the sector achieved a sharp reduction in worker numbers. Also, before being privatized, Electrical Services of Greater Buenos Aires experienced a decrease in the number of employees of 22 percent, in which 66 percent of the employees who left were dismissed or retired, while the rest were offered a special retirement package. Those laid off received an average allocation of 10 percent above the statutory limit, as much as US$9,912 each. The total amount paid by Electrical Services for this package was US$55.5 million, of which new private owners provided US$52 million. One of the new private distribution companies compensated its employees with US$30,000. After privatization, worker numbers were reduced by another 28 percent (de Luca 1999).

To summarize, in the 1980s labor markets looked de facto flexible and therefore they did not seem to require reform in the short and medium term. Trade, fiscal, and financial reforms required a lot of political capital to be implemented, therefore there was neither political power nor the necessity of implementing labor reforms that could create unrest among organized workers (Loboguerrero and Panizza 2006). Thereafter, in the 1990s, when the economic necessity of implementing labor market reforms arose, as we show in the next subsection, the initial pro-market momentum was by then extinguished.

3.2 Why, after Privatization, Trade Openness and Financial Liberalization Do We Not Observe Important Labor Reforms in LAC?

By the end of the 1990s, fiscal discipline and trade openness was the norm in the region. The average inflation rate was 7.8 percent per year and the average trade tariff had fallen from around 50 percent in 1985 to almost 10 percent (IMF 2010).

Trade liberalization implies large reallocation effects given the substantial increase in the exposure to international competition. One important aspect of the reallocation process generated by the removal of barriers to trade relates to the impact on job flow. As Haltiwanger et al. (2004) assert, the increased competition associated with international trade yields increases in the pace of job reallocation within sectors across Latin American countries (see also Levinsohn 1999). Firms faced a more volatile environment without high inflation to drive labor markets, and therefore required more flexible labor market regulation. But as table 22.8 shows, labor markets continued to be highly regulated, reflecting government-employer-worker relationships embedded in more protected national economies (see Cook 2007), and no important reforms were introduced during the period.

We argue there are three main reasons for this lack of labor reform in the period after the Washington Consensus.

3.2.1 Increasing Opposition to Pro-Market Reforms

During the 1990s, inflation could not drive labor markets. At that time, when labor market restrictions became binding in some countries the Washington Consensus paradigm became unpopular. Pro-market reform in general, and in particular labor market reforms, did not have the needed political support any more.

Pro-market reforms are accused of being one of the causes of recovery without increases in employment in the 1990s,[12] and the attitude of Latin Americans toward pro-market reforms became increasingly critical (see Lora, Panizza, and Quispe-Agnoli 2004). In 1998 only 50 percent of Latin Americans thought that privatization was beneficial for their country. This percentage dropped to 31 percent in 2001 and to 25 percent in 2003. By 1995, citizens preferred an economy

Table 22.8. Labor Characteristics and Labor Protection Laws, Various Regions

Group	HME	CME	LME	MME	EEE
Mean wage in industry (in US$000s)	5.65	32.09	26.17	17.92	2.26
Rule of law index	3.08	5.92	5.80	5.24	5.02
Unofficial economy (%)	42.22	15.75	13.60	23.22	32.27
Union density	0.21	0.56	0.31	0.26	0.49
Labor union power index	0.47	0.55	0.17	0.59	0.57
Severance payment (weeks)	8.13	5.00	1.33	5.50	13.00
Maternity benefits (weeks)	12.65	19.56	30.75	17.40	22.86
Employment laws index	0.46	0.58	0.27	0.69	0.60
Collective relations laws index	0.50	0.48	0.29	0.60	0.51
Social security laws index	0.62	0.74	0.72	0.76	0.75
Civil rights index	0.72	0.62	0.64	0.74	0.80

Sources: Mean wage industry (average late 1990s and beginning of 2000s) from Nicita and Olarreaga (2007); rule of law index (1997) from Johnson et al. (1998); unofficial economy (mid-1990s), labor union power index (2004), severance payments (2004), employment laws index (2004), collective relations laws index (2004), social security laws index (2004), and civil rights index (2004) from Botero et al. (2004); maternity benefits (2009) from ILO (2009).

driven by a mixed structure, in which the workers directly—or indirectly through the government—participate in ownership of firms. Only 13.5 percent of the population preferred private enterprises without government intervention. In 1998, 77 percent of Latin Americans thought that a market economy was good for the country; by 2003, this percentage had dropped to 18 percent.[13] Moreover, as table 22.9 shows, the majority in HME prefers involvement of the state in solving problems and creating a country's wealth (as Latinobarometer annual surveys show).

As Lora et al. (2004) point out, this lack of public support induced political leaders to blame pro-market, neoliberal policies for "poor" economic growth and unemployment in the region. In Argentina, Nestor Kirchner won the presidency in 2003 campaigning against the neoliberal model imposed by the International Monetary Fund (IMF), and in favor of a greater role for the state in the economy. In

Bolivia, Evo Morales described his electoral campaign as representing "the victims of neoliberalism." In Venezuela and Ecuador, populist presidents Hugo Chávez and Lucio Gutiérrez campaigned on how neoliberal policies had brought "disaster" to their countries. Once in power, some of these leaders reversed previous, timid reforms encouraging flexible labor markets, as occurred in Argentina under the government of Nestor Kirchner.

Positions against pro-market policies started to change by 2005 with the victory of President Luiz Inácio Lula da Silva in Brazil, who took an eclectic economic position. Brazil, under the "Partido dos Trabalhadores," followed the course of Chile, maintaining fiscal discipline and pro-market policies while strongly emphasizing social protection policies. Other elections in the continent confirm this change: President Alan García in Peru (2006), Álvaro Uribe (2002) and Juan Manuel Santos in Colombia (2010), Felipe Calderón in Mexico (2006), and others.

3.2.2 The Shadow Economy and the Political Economy of Labor Reform

As mentioned for the Washington Consensus period, informality may have played an important role providing flexibility to the labor market during the 1990s. Table 22.6 shows that informality in the region increased during this decade. This may be the reaction of Latin American economies to the increasing volatility in an environment of low inflation and high labor market regulation. Once high regulation became more binding and governments enacted no reforms, firms reacted to this new environment by increasing informal contracts.

3.2.3 Economic Boom during the 2000s

Most commodity-exporting countries of South America have faced highly favorable conditions during the 2000s. This includes countries such as Argentina, Chile,

Table 22.9. Attitudes toward State Involvement in Economy (%)

HME	To Solve Problems 2001	To Create Wealth 2006
State and market involved	28	16
2	9	7
3	10	9
4	9	11
5	21	32
6	8	7
7	5	5
8	4	5
9	2	2
Market alone involved	4	5
Total	100	100

Source: Latinobarometer annual surveys.

Peru, Ecuador, Colombia, Paraguay, Venezuela, and Brazil. From2002 the region evidenced an average annual growth rate of 5.4 percent until the financial crisis; during 2009 LAC's GDP fell on average by 1 percent, which compares favorably to developed countries (decline of 2.5 percent) (IMF 2010). Favorable terms of trade allowed the region to have a fast recovery during 2010 (+4.7 percent). This is particularly true for those countries with stronger fundamentals, who have easier access to external financing and stand to benefit the most from low global interest rates. The environment is least favorable for those countries with linkages to the United States (like some Central American countries).

Moreover, as figure 22.2 shows, fast economic growth increased labor demand and reduced unemployment in the region. The unweighted average annual unemployment rate fell from 10.5 percent in 2002 to 7.5 percent in 2008. During the international crisis, unemployment increased but it started to decline the following year with the economic recovery of the region (8 percent) (IMF 2010).

Better economic performance during the 2000s reduced pressure to reform labor markets and informality (see tables 22.2 and 22.6).

4. Insider-Outsider Workers, Job Benefits, Unions, and Informality: A Vicious Circle

Most economists agree that highly regulated labor markets promote informality (see Schneider 2009; Loayza, Oviedo, and Servén 2005; Johnson et al. 1998; IADB 2004). As labor regulations increase, the opportunity costs of formal employment rise. In a context of weak enforcement of labor regulations, the costs for firms to remain completely or partially informal may be much lower than the costs of formal compliance. In addition, enforcement is not applied equally to all firms. As Loayza

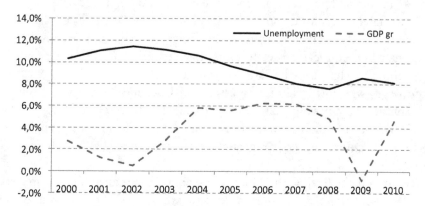

Figure 22.2 Unemployment and GDP growth.
Note: Unweighted average for Argentina, Brazil, Chile, Colombia, Costa Rica, Ecuador, El Salvador, Jamaica, México, Nicaragua, Panama, Paraguay, Peru, and Venezuela.
Source: IMF.

et al. (2005) point out, strict regulations are more likely to be enforced in large firms, particularly in large foreign corporations.

In practice this equilibrium implies an inefficient allocation of resources and less protection for workers. Firms with a lower probability of being inspected or that use bribes to avoid regulations have lower costs, not because they are more efficient but because they have a "privilege." In the end, few workers benefit from the "protection" provided by stringent regulations.

As Schneider and Karcher (2010) observe, labor markets' characteristics in HME reinforce this equilibrium. First, firms' ability to use flexible, informal employment reduces business opposition to high levels of regulation. Although businessmen favor more flexible employment protection laws, the presence of informal employment within firms and through subcontractors reduces the costs of employment protection laws and the incentive to push for reform. Along the same lines, given that enforcement is more likely for foreign firms, local businesses that takes illegal advantage of informality have a regulatory competitive advantage.

Second, government policymakers, knowing that the regulatory burden is too heavy and therefore reduces activity and employment, do not have huge incentives to enforce regulations. Third, as Senén González and Palomino (2006) argue, the informal economy grew during the first half of the 1990s because institutions of labor law enforcement were dismantled to relieve pressure on firms. Evasion of value-added taxes during economic downturns might be evidence of the same activity (Brondolo 2009).

Fourth, there are few organized workers and they have little power to define labor relationships. Unions are small, they are mainly in large firms, they lack plant level representation, and unions´ confederations are politicized (see Schneider and Karcher 2010). This is not surprising because in Latin America workers in the public sector have disproportionally high unionization rates and the sector's labor relations are usually more politicized and influenced by legal developments since the employer is the state (Freeman 1986; Maceira and Murillo 2001). Large informal sectors reinforce the small size of unions and encourage them to focus on the narrow "insider" interests of workers in the formal and public sectors.

These characteristics highlight the insider-outsider issues of unions. Lacking leverage in direct negotiations with employers, unions have invested heavily in ties to the state and political parties to promote extensive protective labor codes and wage-setting mechanisms that favor them but apply to all workers.[14] High minimum wages with low level of enforcement in LAC and high levels of severance payments are examples of results (see table 22.8) (IADB 2004).

Finally, lack of unions in most workplaces reduces the pressure to increase inspections and enforcement of strict employment protection laws, thereby increasing informality.

To sum up, the likelihood of forming a coalition to reform the informal sector and labor regulation is low. Informal workers are not organized, unions are small and mainly in the public sector, businessman may avoid regulation through informality, and moreover for those who abuse informality, strict labor regulation becomes a competitive advantage.

APPENDIX 22.1 GROUPS OF COUNTRIES

Defining Groups of Countries

This appendix classifies the countries into different types of "varieties of capitalism" to improve the comparison between them. This clarifies the results obtained when comparing Latin America and other countries of interest.

Our general framework is based on the "varieties capitalism" approach develop by Hall and Soskice (2001). They distinguish between "liberal market economies" (LME) and "coordinated market economies" (CME). Following Schneider (2009), Amable (2003), and Lane and Myant (2007), we consider the Mediterranean market economies (MME) and southeastern economies (SEA).

In relation to Latin America, we use the definitions used by Schneider and Karcher (2009) and Schneider (2009). The extensive debate on "varieties of capitalism" offers some conceptual and theoretical innovations that can be fruitfully employed to analyze the distinctive institutional foundations of capitalism in this region. Following the authors we might call LAC "hierarchical market economies" (HME). This perspective allows us to identify four key characteristics of HME in Latin America, taking into account business structure with access to essential inputs like capital, technology, and labor. These key characteristics are diversified business groups, multinational enterprises, unskilled labor, and atomistic labor relations. Overall nonmarket, the hierarchical relationships of business groups and multinational corporations are central to the organization of capital and technology in Latin America, and are also pervasive in labor market regulation, union representation, and labor relations. As Schneider (2009) notes, these four characteristics of HME have in common dependence on hierarchy and a particular sort of interactions, creating a new variety of capitalism, different from those identified in the developed and other developing regions. In particular, our objective here is not to establish a variety of Latin American capitalism.

All the groups (CME, LME, MME, SEA, and HME) have strengths and distinctive weaknesses derived from different organization of capital markets, labor markets, education and skills, business-to-business relationships and labor relations, and complementarity between these fundamental institutions of capitalism.

APPENDIX 22.2 TRADE LIBERALIZATION AND LABOR PRODUCTIVITY

In this appendix we mainly follow different chapters of IADB (2004). The core of trade liberalization was the lowering of barriers to imports that formerly sought to protect domestic production, especially in manufacturing. Between the mid-1980s and the beginning of the 1990s, countries in Latin America began trade liberalization programs, with reductions of at least 15 percentage points in the average tariff rate, which fell from an average of 49 percent in the prereform years to 11 percent in 1999. The dispersion of tariffs was also significantly reduced, although in most countries tariffs remain higher for consumer goods than for intermediate and capital goods, and are higher for agricultural goods than for industrial goods.

By the end of the 1990s, only two countries (of 24 for which information is available) had an average tariff of more than 15 percent. Nontariff trade restrictions, which were applied to 37.6 percent of imports in the prereform period, affected only 6.3 percent of imports by the mid-1990s (IADB 2004). Lower tariff and nontariff restrictions enabled imports to rise as a percentage of GDP in most countries. For the Latin American and Caribbean region as a whole, imports increased from 23 percent in 1983-85 to 36 percent in 1998–2000. It should be noted that during this period, export-to-GDP ratios also increased, albeit by much less, from 23 to 30 percent (IADB 2004). The aim of liberalization was to reallocate resources from previously protected sectors toward more efficient sectors, especially export sectors. In almost all countries in the region, exports actually did perform much better in the 1990s than during the previous decade. Nevertheless, the prevailing opinion is that the export sector did not manage to make up for the destruction of employment in the previously protected sectors and that the jobs created have been inferior in terms of pay, stability, and other labor conditions.

Also, it is relevant to examine the impact of market-oriented reforms on plant survival. While trade liberalization increases plant exit, financial and other reforms reduce the probability of exit. In addition, trade liberalization increases the likelihood of exit for plants facing low demand and relatively high input prices. By contrast, financial and other reforms increase the role of efficiency and reduce the role of demand and input prices in determining plant survival. Trade liberalization squeezes out of operation plants with low profit margins. At the same time, improved factor market flexibility (capital and labor market deregulation) and private sector incentives (lower tax burdens and privatization) make plant physical efficiency relatively more important in accounting for plant survival relative to demand and input prices. This is probably due to more productive plants being able to expand at the expense of less productive ones (IADB 2004).

NOTES

We thank Andres Gómez-Lobo. We also acknowledge the funding provided by the Millennium Scientific Initiative "Microdata Center" Project P07S-023-F. Alejandro Micco can be contacted at amicco@fen.uchile.cl.

1. The source for this statistic is the Economic Commission for Latin America and the Caribbean, on the basis of official figures. It is cited in USAID (1996).

2. For example in Chile, where most contracts and wages are indexed to past inflation, real wages did not fall as much as in other countries. In Chile most of the adjustment was made through higher unemployment.

3. For the 2000s we considered the period 2000–2008.

4. Lora (2001) defines "margin of reform" as the difference between the maximum possible value of the index (which is 1) and the current value.

5. Caballero, Cowan, et al. (2004) show that employment protection laws reduce job reallocation, although this effect is statistically and economically significant only in countries with extensive legislation protecting labor rights. Micco and Pagés (2006), using a completely different approach, find similar results.

6. In the 1980s LAC had almost no employment protection systems (see Vodopivec 2004).

7. In Chile, unions cover only 13 percent of workers. For large firms this number is 23 percent and for small firms 11 percent. By industries, mining has the highest percentage (40 percent), followed by utilities with 19 percent ("Encuesta de Protección Social" 2006).

8. Caballero, Cowan, et al. (2004) and Caballero, Engel, and Micco (2004) show that job security increases labor adjustment costs mainly in large firms in countries with more extensive employment protection laws.

9. For details about "insider and outsider" theory see Lindbeck and Snower (2002).

10. Chong and López-de-Silanes (2004) show that in Latin America direct employment by median state-owned firms falls between 5 and 57 percent after privatization, depending on the country.

11. Considering LAC without Bolivia (94 percent) and Ecuador (52 percent).

12. IADB (2010) argues that the 1990s was a "growthless" decade.

13. These results come from the Latinobarometer annual surveys, which cover 17 Latin American countries.

14. Murillo and Schrank (2005) and Cook (2007) argue that this political focus has often been effective in maintaining extensive labor regulations.

REFERENCES

Amable, Bruno. 2003. *The Diversity of Modern Capitalism*. Oxford: Oxford University Press.

Botero, Juan, S. Djankov, Rafael Porta, and Florencio C. López-De-Silanes. 2004. "The Regulation of Labor." *Quarterly Journal of Economics* 119(4): 1339–82.

Brondolo, John. 2009. "Collecting Taxes during an Economic Crisis: Challenges and Polic Options." IMF Staff Position Note SPN/09/17, International Monetary Fund, Washington, DC.

Caballero, Ricardo, Kevin Cowan, Eduardo Engel, and Alejandro Micco. 2004. "Microeconomic Inflexibility and Labor Regulation: International Evidence." NBER Working Paper No. 10744, National Bureau of Economic Research, Cambridge, MA.

Caballero, Ricardo, Eduardo Engel, and Alejandro Micco A. 2004. "Microeconomic Flexibility in Latin America." *Journal Economía Chilena (The Chilean Economy)* 7(2): 5–26.

Chong, Alberto, and Florencio López-de-Silanes. 2004. "Privatization in Latin America: What Does the Evidence Say?" *Economía* 4(2): 37–111.

Cook, María Lorena. 2007. *The Politics of Labor Reform in Latin America*. University Park: Pennsylvania State University Press.

de Luca, Loretta, ed. 1999. *Labour and Social Dimensions of Privatization and Restructuring— Public Utilities Water, Gas, Electricity*. Part 2, *Europe/Latin-America*. Geneva: Interdepartmental Action Programme on Privatization, Restructuring and Economic Democracy, International Labour Organization.

Easterly, William, Carlos Alfredo Rodriguez, and Klaus Schmidt-Hebbel, eds. 1994. *Macroeconomic Effects of Public Sector Deficits*. Oxford: Oxford University Press.

"Encuesta de Protección Social 2006." 2006. Ministerio del Trabajo, Chile, Santiago. Available at www.microdatos.cl.

Fischer, Stanley. 2003. "Globalization and Its Challenges." *American Economic Review* 93(2): 1–30 (spec. issue: *Papers and Proceedings of the One Hundred Fifteenth Annual Meeting of the American Economic Association, Washington DC, January 3–5, 2003*).

Freeman, Richard B. 1986. "Unionism Comes to the Public Sector." *Journal of Economic Literature* 24(1): 41–86.

Hall, Peter, and David Soskice. 2001. *Varieties of Capitalism: The Institutional Foundations of Comparative Advantage.* New York: Oxford University Press.

Haltiwanger, John, Adriana Kugler, Mauricio Kugler, Alejandro Micco, and Carmen Pagés. 2004. "Effects of Tariffs and Real Exchange Rates on Job Reallocation: Evidence from Latin America." *Journal of Policy Reform* 7(4): 191–208.

Heckman, James J., and Carmen Pagés. 2004. *Law and Employment: Lessons from Latin America and the Caribbean.* Chicago: University of Chicago Press.

Heston, Alan, Robert Summers, and Bettina Aten. 2010. "Penn World Tables 6.3." Center for International Comparisons of Production, Income and Prices, University of Pennsylvania.

IADB (Inter-American Development Bank). 2004. "Good Jobs Wanted." IPES, Economic and Social Progress Report, IADB, Washington, DC.

———. 2010. "The Age of Productivity: Transforming Economies from the Bottom Up." In *Inter-American Development*, edited by Carmen Pagés, Washington, DC: IADB.

ILO (International Labour Organization). 2009. "Conditions of Work and Employment Programme (TRAVAIL) Database." ILO, Geneva, Available at http://www.ilo.org/travail.

IMF (International Monetary Fund). 2010. "World Economic Outlook (WEO) Database." IMF, Washington, DC.

Johnson, Simon, Daniel Kaufmann, Pablo Zoido-Lobatón. 1998. "Regulatory Discretion and the Unofficial Economy." *American Economic Review* 88(2): 387–92 (spec. issue: *Papers and Proceedings of the Hundred and Tenth Annual Meeting of the American Economic Association, May 1998*).

Krueger, Anne O. 2004. "Meant Well, Tried Little, Failed Much: Policy Reforms in Emerging Market Economies." Paper presented at the Roundtable Lecture at the Economic Honors Society, New York University, New York, March 23,

Kuczynski, Pedro-Pablo, and John Williamson, eds. 2003. *After the Washington Consensus: Restarting Growth and Reform in Latin America.* Washington, DC: Institute for International Economics.

Lane, David, and Martin Myant, eds. 2007. *Varieties of Capitalism in Post-Communist Countries.* New York: Palgrave Macmillan.

Levinsohn, J. 1999. "Employment Responses to International Liberalization in Chile." *Journal of International Economics* 47(2): 321–56.

Lindbeck, A. and D. Snower. 2002. "The Insider-Outsider Theory: A Survey." IZA Discussion Paper No. 534, Institute for the Study of Labor (IZA), Bonn.

Loayza, Norman, Ana María Oviedo and Luis Servén. 2005. "The Impact of Regulation of Growth and Informality. Cross-Country Evidence." World Bank Development Policy Working Paper No. WPS3623, World Bank, Washington, DC.

Loboguerrero, Ana María, and Ugo Panizza. 2006. "Inflation and Labor Market Flexibility: The Squeaky Wheel Gets the Grease." POLIS Working Paper No. 63, Department of Public Policy and Public Choice—POLIS, Alessandria, Italy.

Lora, Eduardo. 2001. "Structural Reforms in Latin America: What Has Been Reformed and How to Measure It." IADB Working Paper No. 466, Inter-American Development Bank, Washington, DC.

Lora, Eduardo, Ugo Panizza, and Myriam Quispe-Agnoli. 2004. "Reform Fatigue: Symptoms, Reasons, and Implications." *Economic Review* 89(2): 1–28.

Madrid, Raúl. 2003. "Labouring against Neoliberalism: Unions and Patterns of Reform in Latin America." *Journal of Latin American Studies* 35: 53–88.

Maceira, Daniela, and María Victoria Murillo. 2001. "Social Sector Reform in Latin America and the Role of Unions." IADB Working Paper No. 456, Inter-American Development Bank Research Department, Washington, DC.

McGuire, James. 1997. *Peronism without Perón: Unions, Parties, and Democracy in Argentina*. Stanford: Stanford University Press.

Micco, Alejandro, and Carmen Pagés. 2006. "The Economic Effects of Employment Protection: Evidence from International Industry-Level Data." IZA Discussion Paper No. 2433, Institute for the Study of Labor (IZA), Bonn.

Murillo, María Victoria, and Andrew Schrank. 2005. "With a Little Help from My Friends: Partisan Politics, Transnational Alliances, and Labor Rights in Latin America." *Comparative Political Studies* 38(8): 971–99.

Nicita, Alessandro, and Marcelo Olarreaga. 2007. "Trade, Production and Protection 1976–2004." *World Bank Economic Review* 21(1):.

O'Connell, Lesley D. 1999 "Collective Bargaining Systems in 6 Latin American Countries: Degrees of Autonomy and Decentralization." Working Paper No. 399, Inter-American Development Bank, Washington, DC.

OECD (Organisation for Economic Co-operation and Development). 2009. *Is Informal Normal? Towards More and Better Jobs in Developing Countries*. OECD, Paris.

Ramos, Carlos Alberto. 2003. "Las Politicas de Empleo en Brasil." Manuscript, Universidade de Brasília, commissioned by ILO-Argentina.

Rodrik, Dani. 1996. "Understanding Economic Policy Reform." *Journal of Economic Literature* 34(1): 9–41.

———. 2001. *The Global Governance of Trade as if Development Really Mattered*. New York: United Nations Development Programme.

———. 2006. "Goodbye Washington Consensus, Hello Washington Confusion?" *Journal of Economic Literature* 44: 969–83.

Saavedra, Jaime (2003). "Labor Markets during the 1990s." In Kuczynszi and Williamson 2003, 213–63.

Schneider, Ben Ross. 2008. "Comparing Capitalisms: Liberal, Coordinated, Network, and Hierarchical Varieties." Unpublished manuscript, MIT.

———. 2009. "Hierarchical Market Economies and Varieties of Capitalism in Latin America." *Journal of Latin American Studies* 41: 553–75.

Schneider, Ben Ross, and Sebastian Karcher. 2010. "Complementarities and Continuities in the Political Economy of Labor Markets in Latin America." *Socio-Economic Review* 8(4): 623–51.

Senén González, Cecilia, and Héctor Palomino. 2006. "Diseño Legal y Desempeño Real: Argentina." In *Diseño Legal y Desempeño Real: Instituciones Laborales en América Latina*, edited by Graciela Bensusan, 95–165.

Stotsky Janet G., and Asegedech WoldeMariam. 2002. "Central American Tax Reform: Trends and Possibilities," IMF Working Paper No. WP/02/227, International Monetary Fund, Washington, DC, December.

USAID (U.S. Agency for International Development). 1996. Washington, DC: GPO.

Vodopivec, Milan. 2004. *Income Support for the Unemployed: Issues and Options*. World Bank Regional and Sectoral Studies Series. Washington, DC: World Bank.

Williamson, John. 1990. "What Washington Means by Policy Reform." In *Latin American Adjustment: How Much Has Happened?*, edited by John Williamson, Washington, DC: Peterson Institute for International Economics.

————. 2004. "A Short History of the Washington Consensus." Paper commissioned by Fundacion CIDOB presented at the "From the Washington Consensus towards a New Global Governance" conference, Barcelona, September 24.

World Bank. 2005. *Economic Growth in the 1990s: Learning from a Decade of Reform.* Washington, DC: World Bank.

————. 2009. "World Development Indicators (WDI)." World Bank, Washington, DC.

————. 2010. "Doing Business Database." World Bank, Washington, DC. Available at http://www.doingbusiness.org/.

Index